THE DUCHESS
OF MALFI

SEVEN MASTERPIECES OF
JACOBEAN DRAMA

THE DUCHESS
OF MALFI

SEVEN MASTERPIECES OF
JACOBEAN DRAMA

*Edited and with an Introduction
by Frank Kermode*

THE MODERN LIBRARY

NEW YORK

2005 Modern Library Paperback Edition

Introduction and editorial commentary copyright © 2005 by Frank Kermode
Compilation copyright © 2005 by Random House, Inc.

Published in the United States by Modern Library, an imprint of
The Random House Publishing Group, a division of Random House, Inc., New York.

MODERN LIBRARY and the TORCHBEARER Design are registered trademarks of
Random House, Inc.

CIP information available upon request.

ISBN 0-679-64243-9

Modern Library website address: www.modernlibrary.com

Printed in the United States of America

2   4   6   8   9   7   5   3

CONTENTS

INTRODUCTION

Frank Kermode

All the plays in this collection were written and first performed during the reign of King James I of England and VI of Scotland. Queen Elizabeth died in 1603, and in that year James arrived in London to claim the throne. One of his earliest acts was to change the name of Shakespeare's company from the Lord Chamberlain's Men, as they had been called in the later years of Elizabeth, to The King's Men, a gesture that enhanced the status of the theaters and the players.

Shakespeare's company, performing at The Globe but frequently also at court, staged within the first decade of the reign an extraordinary series of masterpieces by Shakespeare himself, including *Measure for Measure, Othello, King Lear, Macbeth,* and *Coriolanus.* But Shakespeare, despite what the playwright Webster called his "copious industry," could not provide all the material that was needed. Of the plays in this anthology, the following were produced by his company at The Globe or, after 1609, in the indoor Blackfriars Theatre: *The Revenger's Tragedy, Volpone, The Maid's Tragedy,* and *The Duchess of Malfi.* The third and fourth of these may also have been performed at The Blackfriars, a very successful investment by The King's Men. It proved so profitable that in the future, no more open-air theaters were built. Among rival indoor playhouses, the most celebrated was The Phoenix; one play in this collection, *A Chaste Maid in Cheapside,* was performed there.

Older open-air theaters nevertheless continued to exist—one of them, The Rose, close to The Globe, was the venue of *A Woman Killed with Kindness*. The older, larger playhouses provided cheaper and generally cruder entertainment than The Globe and The Blackfriars, but still made a substantial contribution to the various and lively Jacobean theatrical scene. More plays have been lost than survive, but the evidence is still conclusive: The reign of James I was the great age of English drama. Patrons of The Globe in the early years of the reign could have seen, in repertory at various times, *King Lear, Macbeth, Volpone, The Revenger's Tragedy,* and *Antony and Cleopatra*, as well as many plays by other authors.

The plays included in this anthology represent, as far as seven plays can, the variety and quality of the non-Shakespearean works presented during this period. With great regret I have had to omit plays by such important dramatists as John Marston, George Chapman, Philip Massinger, John Ford, and others. Thomas Middleton has claimed what might seem a disproportionate share of my space, the reason being that he excelled in city comedy as well as in tragedy.

———

It used to be argued that there was a catastrophic change in the national mood about this time—a shift from Elizabethan to Jacobean, from a merry to a more melancholy, disillusioned England, from a society that had not yet quite lost touch with the religion and the customs so violently assailed by the reformers during the reigns of Henry VIII and Edward VI to one in which doubts and anxieties—economic, political, even metaphysical—took firmer hold. In fact, the last years of Queen Elizabeth were not very serene. She was aging and increasingly difficult; she had to suffer the treasonable conduct of her favorite Essex; there were bad harvests, inflation, severe visitations of the plague, and continuing foreign threats. The world was changing fast as the queen's health failed. The question as to who should succeed her was made harder by her refusal to discuss it.

The arrival of James was a relief, but only until his own troubles imposed themselves. James prided himself on being a king by divine right, an absolutist claim that was to prove fatal to his son Charles I. James, with some justice, regarded himself a man of peace, though his relationship with his parliaments was anything but peaceful. Those who had welcomed him became disillusioned in their turn; there were manifold reasons for discontent, as there are under most governments. There were certainly grounds for it under so complex a monarch, with his pretensions to absolute power, his favorites, his passions for hunting and theology, and his unpopular way of encouraging the immigration into England of yet more alien Scotsmen.

When James changed the name of Shakespeare's company to The King's Men, the poet and his fellows became royal servants and had thereafter a valuable, though relatively humble, connection with the court, where they performed more than all the other companies put together. They had most of the best actors, and the best theaters. They kept on good terms with the Master of the Revels, the official in the Lord Chamberlain's office who was responsible for licensing plays.

In the early days of the Elizabethan theater, many plays were thrown together by several writers, piecework done for the likes of the impresario Philip Henslowe. The days when actors were strolling players in the tradition of medieval entertainers, and liable to be treated as vagabonds, were still not so far away, but the case was different with independent, well-established companies, of which The King's Men was the most powerful. The actors were now professionals, men of talent and experience. The "sharers" who held stock in the company and its theater, Shakespeare among them, grew rich. Shakespeare sued successfully for a grant of arms to his father, thus making himself a gentleman in an age when you could tell a gentleman from a yeoman or tradesman by the way he dressed. To support this social promotion, Shakespeare acquired a good deal of property, mostly in the Stratford area. But there were dramatists, contemporaries of Shakespeare, who did not prosper as he did, and they continued to collaborate in many hastily written plays to satisfy what seems to have been the virtually insatiable appetite of the playgoing public.

———

THOMAS HEYWOOD (1574?–1641) was an actor and the author of a well-known and informative book about his trade called *An Apology for Actors* (1612), in which he claimed to have had a hand in 220 plays, of which only a handful survive. He wrote many other books, including a long poem called *Troia Britannica* about Troy and its fabled connection with English history, and a curious work of mystical theology called *The Hierarchy of the Blessed Angels*. Readers of *A Woman Killed with*

Kindness may detect in it a pious strain consistent with his religious interests.

Heywood had a contract with the entrepreneur Philip Henslowe, who owned The Rose. He may have served both as actor and dramatist for this playhouse, which was smaller and less grand than The Globe, its younger Bankside neighbor. Yielding to the competition, Henslowe abandoned The Rose and the Bankside in 1600, and built a larger theater, The Fortune, in another part of the town. Henslowe often employed more than one playwright on a single play, and The Rose, like another popular playhouse, The Red Bull, catered primarily to a citizen audience, lacking the stronger middle- and upper-class connections of The Globe. Nevertheless, at least in the open-air theaters, there would still be a good mixture of social classes, citizens, apprentices, law students from the Inns of Court, gentlemen, and, somewhat to the surprise of foreign visitors, women.

It was for what might be called a bourgeois audience, united for the moment by their common interests and ethical assumptions, that Heywood wrote *A Woman Killed with Kindness,* by far the best known of his plays. It contains the lines of his that are most often quoted, namely Frankford's lament:

> O God! O God! That it were possible
> To undo things done; to call back yesterday;
> That Time could turn up his swift sandy glass,
> To untell the days, and to redeem these hours!

Doubtless the note of genuine grief in these lines lifts the play above its more usual level of moralistic sentiment. A modern reader may find some cause for ridicule in the conduct of the story. Mistress Anne Frankford, a model of domestic virtue, needs only a few impassioned speeches by Wendoll to persuade her to disastrous adultery. And Acton suddenly and implausibly abandons a position of venomous retaliation and becomes a generous benefactor.

We are accustomed to rapid changes of attitude in the drama of the period. Time, in Elizabethan and Jacobean plays, does not simulate real time. The action of Heywood's play stretches over several years, from the heroine's wedding to her death, by which time she is the mother of two children. Events far apart can be crowded onto one another—think, for instance, of the speed with which Othello capitulates to Iago. Here it may seem merely a matter of substituting one pose for another, but we are expected to understand that the lapse of time between events and attitudes is for us to take into account. The time between the desire to retaliate and the readiness to forgive may seem too brief only if the audience does not supply that understanding.

We must also, of course, allow for the very different social conventions of the time—the upper-class insistence on personal and family honor, which demands the unconditional obedience of wives and endorses the notion that children are besmirched by the dishonorable acts of their mothers. It hardly needs adding that there was a general interest in questions relating to marriage and adultery—handbooks on marriage were numerous at the time. Divorce was unavailable to anybody who was not a grandee. Meanwhile, the honor of a woman was simply her chastity, and her husband's honor also depended on that quality. It might have been thought by some auditors that it was by sparing his wife the proper punishment for her crime that Frankford could be said to have killed her with kindness.

The main points of both the main plot and the Mountford subplot are those at which the affected character gives way to lamentation and self-reproach:

> My God, what have I done? What have I done?
> My rage hath plunged me into a sea of blood,
> In which my soul lies drowned. . . .

Frankford is dangerously certain of his happiness (2.1) and later equally sure of his misery. Wendoll is "melancholy" and full of self-condemnation before he seduces Anne. He blames his guilt on his passion, just as Mountford blames his rage, not himself, for committing murder, and can still feel, despite that crime, that he will inherit "Th' immortal birthright which my Saviour keeps" (2.2). Anne's deathbed scene is sentimental in the highest degree, and although moral warnings are frequently issued, the principals seem more conscious of their unhappiness than of their ruinous faults.

The subplot ends in improbable happiness: The heroine beautifully starves herself to death and is reconciled at the last moment with her wronged husband. The play is hardly a domestic tragedy; it is domestic but hardly tragic, for all except the false friends and usurers achieve the ending they desire; so it departs from Shakespeare's concept of tragedy and by an even greater degree from the classically oriented doctrine of Ben Jonson. Yet it has a vitality absent from much later domestic drama, and that is in large part due to the liveliness of the minor characters and their sprightly allusions to falconry and card games.

These, which must have fascinated the original audience, are likely to be obscure to modern readers, who may need to imagine how they would enjoy a serious play that contained arcane references to football or baseball, pleasantly recognizable to them but obscure to strangers. The account of the falconry wager and quarrel contains many technical terms that would have been familiar to the first audiences, and a knowledge of several card games now obsolete would have afforded them the different kind of pleasure to be had from a series of sexual double meanings. Most of the technical terms, whether relating to falconry or cards, can be provided with learned explanations, but the labor of following them distracts attention from the play. It is enough for the modern reader to have a general understanding of what is going on, without going deeply into all the details.

With its mixture of sentimental propriety and adultery, its background of county sports, dances, and cards, *A Woman Killed with Kindness* has deserved its success in the minor league of Jacobean drama. In the years immediately following its production, London was to see plays much darker, more complex—as one might say, more modern.

———

The achievement of BEN JONSON (1572–1637) is of quite another order, for he was a major poet, master of all the genres of contemporary verse except epic. A Londoner, he attended Westminster School, where he acquired his mastery of the classical languages. His career was adventurous; when fighting in Flanders he killed an enemy in single combat, and later he killed another actor in a duel, for which he was branded a felon. His contribution to the lost play *The Isle of Dogs,* deemed seditious, also won him a spell in prison. *Eastward Ho!,* another play to which he contributed, got him into trouble about the time he wrote *Volpone,* and he was again in prison. In 1618–19 he walked from London to Scotland, where William Drummond of Hawthornden kept a fascinating record of the great man's conversation.

In 1597 he had begun to work for Henslowe, but his first play of importance, *Everyman in His Humor*, was written for Shakespeare's company and performed in 1597 with Shakespeare in the cast. Jonson, as he himself remarked, was a follower of the ancients, but he treated them as "guides, not commanders," and his comedies illustrate an independence and willingness to experiment that bears out that claim. They differ greatly from Shakespeare's comedies, and may nowadays seem at times to be overloaded with learned allusions, but Jonson was also a master of the complex, fast-moving plot. Coleridge rated his play *The Alchemist* (1610) as one of the three best plots in the world, the others being Sophocles' *Oedipus Rex* and Fielding's *Tom Jones*. Among Jonson's other admired comedies are *Epicene, or the Silent Woman* (1609) and the long, splendid *Bartholemew Fair* (1614) with its vivid scenes of London life in its carnival phase.

He was less successful in his tragedies, partly because a pedantic fidelity to their Latin sources makes them heavy and dull, especially when compared with the brilliance of Shakespeare's less scholarly Roman plays. For the Jacobean court he wrote learned, ingenious masques, adorned with scenery and costumes by the great architect Inigo Jones. Their sophistication brought what had been a relatively simple ceremonious form to such a remarkable degree of refinement that it is only in recent years that scholars have come close to explaining their detail.

As a writer of lyrics and epigrams, Jonson became the model for a generation of excellent minor poets. He also wrote strong, effective prose. He was virtually the first poet laureate, and was awarded a pension by King James. He was teased for his presumption in publishing his collected *Works* in 1616, being the first dramatist to do so, and he saw the book through the press himself. Seven years later the First Folio of Shakespeare's collected works, published posthumously by the poet's friends and colleagues, followed Jonson's example. Jonson admired Shakespeare "this side idolatry"—"There was ever more in him to be praised than to be pardoned." He spoke deprecatingly of his friend's "small Latin and less Greek," but the verses he contributed to the Folio of 1623 reflect the genuine character of his admiration. The reputations of the two friends and rivals were long subject to comparison, Jonson escaping censure by critics who shared a revived interest in the rules of classical dramaturgy, Shakespeare proving more attractive to poets.

According to Jonson himself, *Volpone* was written in five weeks, and certainly it belongs to the period when he was close to the height of his powers. In giving the dramatis personae allegorical names—Fox, Fly, Vulture, Crow, Raven—he establishes the moralistic character of his fable while at the same time seizing on possibilities of caricature.

The ingenuity of the structure of the play makes up for the two-dimensional nature of characters involved in what G. K. Hunter, in modern terminology, calls the series of "scams" that make up the plot. Jonson accepted the classical requirement that poetry should instruct while it delighted. He was by nature a satirist in an age when satire was so popular, and thought so dangerous, that in 1598 it was banned, whereupon it was, for a time, to be found only on the stage, and principally in Jonson's plays.

His later works—which Dryden unkindly called his "dotages"—were mostly failures, partly because his blend of caricature and didacticism no longer pleased. It succeeds in *Volpone* because of the richness of the language and the skillful presentation of the metropolitan setting. *The Alchemist* and *Bartholomew Fair* are celebrated because of the density of allusion to London life, especially low life—the thieves, pimps, and prostitutes, the con men, the bustle of the fair and the streets of the city. *Volpone,* though set in Venice, has its share of such detail, and Jonson is careful, as Shakespeare never would be, to sketch the topography of this city, probably to English audiences the most famous outside their own country, and to give realistic attention to its canals and gondolas, its hospitals and magistrates and policemen, as well as to such gullible tourists as Sir Politick Would-be and his lady.

The structure of the piece is classical, with the proper opening, development, catastrophe, and conclusion. Despite its affinity with popular speech, the language of the play is often classically derived. In the opening scene Volpone's speech about his love of gold draws on an ode of the Greek poet Pindar, but it can be perfectly well understood without that information; an overwrought speech in praise of gold was exactly what the moment required, and Pindar offered a perfect precedent. One of the skills of a poet, according to Jonson, is "Invention"—finding and if possible overgoing the best models. Perhaps grandeur of theme calls for a lofty style; perhaps a passage might, on the other hand, call for a low style. We need "height as well as humbleness," said Jonson, and he could provide both. For the most part the mood of *Volpone* is close to that of the Latin satirists, especially Juvenal and Martial, who commented on the corruptions of Rome.

"Language most shows a man: speak, that I may see thee." So Jonson, advising poets. He set great store by language and the importance of saving it from corruption, for he held the view that language reflects the condition of the social order: "it imitates the public riot." Where men are corrupt, so will their language be.

He thought a person's speech reflected the speaker's spirit—"speak, that I may see thee"—an excellent credo for a dramatist. We know what we need to know about Volpone by the false grandeur of his opening lines and the splendor of his talk when he attempts to seduce Celia, but also by the "humbleness" of his conversation with Mosca and his unnatural family of entertainers. Lady Politick is a joke, but her part is so written that we sympathize with the suffering of Volpone under the barrage of her conversation. Her scene in court is delightful because even the judges cannot shut her up. Sir Politick is a caricature of a type Jonson found especially ridiculous: the projector, peddling his absurd ideas, obsessed with secrets of state. Even the judges themselves are at once grave and corrupt—witness their attentiveness to Mosca when they believe him to have become rich, even a possible husband for one of their daughters. The fate of the criminals is harsh, but the depiction of vice and its consequences for the vicious is a proper part of the dramatist's job, as Jonson explains at length in the prefatory letter to "The Two Famous Universities." The writing of that epistle, to those addressees, is further evidence of Jonson's confidence in his own powers, and in the correctness of his practice. We may also reflect that this play was performed at The Globe, on the south bank of the Thames, where it stood among the inns, brothels, and bear pits, as well as at the universities. The popular theater could handle learned comedy, at least as long as it had a lively plot, energetic language, and some good jokes.

———

The Revenger's Tragedy was published as a cheap quarto in 1607–08. Its authorship has been the subject of protracted scholarly argument: Cyril Tourneur (1575–1626) or Thomas Middleton? The argument is best conducted in terms of what is known of the metrical and lexical habits of each writer, and the prevailing opinion of the learned seems to favor Middleton. It is true that in the early years of the century he was mostly occupied with comedies, often in collaboration with other playwrights, but he is celebrated for his versatility and productiveness, and there is no external evidence against his authorship. On the other hand, there is no such evidence in favor of it. Tourneur, a much more obscure figure, is known as the author of one other play, *The Atheist's Tragedy,* and *The Revenger's Tragedy* was ascribed to him only in 1656, forty years after his death. My own sense of the matter is that Middleton did not write the play. Its language and syntax are more bizarre than Middleton's, and its treatment of aristocratic corruption even more gloatingly comical.

As an admittedly subjective test, consider the two most famous passages in *The Revenger's Tragedy* and *The Changeling,* both of which were made famous by T. S. Eliot. This, from the former:

> Does the silkworm expend her yellow labors
> For thee? For thee does she undo herself?
> Are lordships sold to maintain ladyships,
> For the poor benefit of a bewitching minute?
> Why does yon fellow falsify highways,
> And put his life between the judge's lips,
> To refine such a thing—keeps horse and men
> To beat their valors for her?

This from the latter:

> O, come not near me, sir, I shall defile you!
> I am that of your blood was taken from you
> For your better health; look no more upon't,
> But cast it to the ground regardlessly,
> Let the common sewer take it from distinction....

In Tourneur's lines we notice first a contraction of focus: Rich clothes are reduced to the silk laboriously produced by the silkworm from its yellow cocoon. From the idea of the silkworm undoing itself, we move to that of great men undoing themselves by squandering their estates ("lordships") on women in return for what in the end is a "poor benefit," the pleasure of sex ("a bewitching minute"—not, as Eliot thought, "a bewildering minute," though that may be thought even finer). The rest is a development of the idea, showing that the same folly besets men lower in the social scale: The highwayman risks his life for the same moment of pleasure, and the horses and men, in their version of the labors of the silkworm, "beat their valors" for *her* (there is a move from the sexual act to the woman who provides it). Now there is great strength and activity in these lines. It is astonishing to the modern ear that such complex verse can play a part in a drama; it not only expresses Vendice's contempt for riches and for women, part of his character, but also forces the auditor to make an intellectual effort that mimics the labors of lord, highwayman, and silkworm. Yet there are oddities in the diction that strike me as pointing to a difference in tone and manner from Middleton. "Falsify" is a strange word in the context; the commentators are not able to find a comparable use of the word elsewhere. "To beat their valors" is equally strange. These expressions seem to be well over the margin of normal Jacobean English, though they do enhance the speech and increase its already great distance from the commonplace.

Middleton's lines, on the other hand, follow out, with great ingenuity, the metaphor with which Beatrice-Joanna begins. Her family is her "blood." She presents herself as blood let by a surgeon to help cure a disease for which she is responsible. Her departure by bloodletting purifies the family's body, and, since her blood is base, it should be disposed of basely: "Let the common sewer take it from distinction." The discarded blood flows into the common sewer and away from—"distinction." This word is strange and surprising but absolutely just; its abstractness allows it first to mean "the distinguished blood of my family," but it then associates that idea with a much larger notion of distinction, of civility and honor, of a purity that is distinct from anything to be called "common."

It would be wrong, I think, to say that one of these famous passages excels the other. Both are fine, both show us the strange world of Jacobean revenge tragedy at its most splendid, yet they seem to come not from one but from two different talents working in the same tradition.

Whoever wrote it, the peculiar greatness of *The Revenger's Tragedy* has been widely acknowledged since the late Victorians put it into circulation and T. S. Eliot, who undertook but never finished a book on the drama of the period, gave it canonical sanction in an early essay on Thomas Middleton. The celebrity of this, and other, bloody Italianate tragedies has never waned, though they are sometimes subjected to ridicule and parody, of which hilarious examples occur in Thomas Pynchon's novel *The Crying of Lot 49* (1965) and Nigel Dennis's *Cards of Identity* (1955). As John Kerrigan remarks in his book *Revenge Tragedy,* there is a natural affinity between revenge tragedy and the ridiculous. But we may think of these parodies as tributes as well as satires.

Tourneur's play, like Middleton's *The Changeling,* is a sophisticated development of a well-established genre, the revenge play. The vogue began with Kyd's *The Spanish Tragedy* and the lost *Hamlet* of the 1580s. Later examples include plays by Shakespeare, Marston, and Chapman. A favorite way to bring the drama to its climax was to stage a play or a masque or a banquet in the course of which the wicked are ingeniously slaughtered and the revengers themselves punished, as they are in Tourneur's play and as they were in *The Spanish Tragedy* and *Hamlet.*

Tourneur gives his characters allegorical names—Vendice, the Revenger; Lussurioso, the libertine lecher; Spurio, the Bastard; Ambitioso; and so on. Vendice's motives arise from the total corruption of the court. Though himself a malcontent, he has ethical standards, no doubt perverted; he enjoys all the "quaint" tricks by which he brings the royal family to grief, and is in any case a murderer himself. Readers of this play, and those of Middleton and others of the period, cannot help being struck by the omnipresence of the word "honor" and its derivatives. Everybody has it, seeks it, must hold on to it and, if possible, augment it. It is not a simple ideal. Women's honor may seem simple, since it calls only for virginity and marital fidelity, but it is intricately entangled with men's honor (brothers must, in the cause of honor, avenge dishonored sisters) because their blood is the blood of the family, and the loss of female honor affects all the kin. Honor has only the most tenuous connection with virtuous behavior. One is reminded of the Sicilian Mafia, "men of honor" whose compliance with the standards of conduct required of them has nothing whatever to do with virtue, and insists on the same immediate recourse to violence that we find in the Jacobean plays. *Omertà* is virtuous only among "men of honor."

What may strike the modern reader as most extraordinary about *The Revenger's Tragedy* is its obvious relish for the horrible, for gutwrenching surprises. Such moments are part of the popular heritage of the Elizabethan theater—witness the amputations, murders, and cannibalism of Shakespeare's early *Titus Andronicus* and, later, the dead man's hand in Webster's *Duchess of Malfi*. Yet Tourneur contrives to be more shocking than any of the others. Moreover, the hatred expressed by some of the characters for women, as the targets of lust and themselves lustful, probably exceeds what is to be found elsewhere. The reader, or auditor, has a growing sense that this is a fantasy world, where murder plots and seductions have a far more striking place in the life of courts than might be expected, even by audiences accustomed to thinking of courts as sinks of corruption rather than the sources of just rule, as the French court is said to be in the opening lines of *The Duchess of Malfi*. The function of those lines is to provide a contrast with the wickedness of rulers in the rest of the play. The fantasy world, with its refined cruelties, poisons, and tortures, was identified primarily with Italy, though it might be Spain or even ancient Rome. Certainly the fantasy was exotic. Not that Elizabeth's court was without its moral monsters, but it lacked most of those exciting refinements.

JOHN FLETCHER (1579–1625) was Shakespeare's successor as chief playwright for The King's Men. His background was very different from Shakespeare's, for his father was a bishop (the poets Giles and Phineas Fletcher were his cousins) and he was educated at Cambridge. He was fifteen years younger than Shakespeare, and although they collaborated on *Henry VIII*, *The Two Noble Kinsmen*, and the lost play *Cardenio*, they had little in common as playwrights and poets.

Fletcher's first known collaborator was FRANCIS BEAUMONT (1584–1616). Both had done some work for the theater before establishing themselves as co-authors. Fifteen or sixteen plays are attributed to them jointly, though they were produced in a short span of time, and other hands might also have been involved. Beaumont and Fletcher were highly valued, and only they, apart from Jonson and Shakespeare, were honored with a Folio edition, which appeared in 1647, long after their deaths and five years after Parliament closed the theaters.

Fletcher was a highly skilled dramatist, and evidently had a strong rapport with the Blackfriars audience. He had a distinctive blank-verse style, and most people feel that they can distinguish between his hand and Shakespeare's in their collaborations, though arguments about their respective contributions still go on. Fletcher worked not only with Beaumont and Shakespeare but also with other dramatists, and it is not really possible to list definitively the plays he wrote alone. In this respect his career was more characteristic of the theater of the period than Shakespeare's, though even he, with his steady employment as playwright for the premier company, may have had more collaborators than we normally choose to think.

The Maid's Tragedy is often listed as a "Beaumont and Fletcher" play, one of the products of the relatively brief period during which the two writers shared a house as well as an occupation, yet it may be Fletcher's alone. The two young men were alike of good family and entered the theatrical profession after studies at Oxford and Cambridge. Beaumont abandoned the theater in 1613, but Fletcher continued in it until his death of the plague in 1625, the year also of King James's death. Their works are associated with the private rather than the public playhouse, but are nevertheless remarkably varied, including the lively and sometimes farcical comedy *The Knight of the Burning Pestle* (1607) and tragicomedies such as *Philaster* (1609) and *A King and No King* (1611): "A tragicomedy," wrote Fletcher "is not so called in respect of mirth and killing, but in respect it wants deaths, which is enough to make it no tragedy, yet brings some near it, which is enough to make it no comedy. . . ."

Fletcher and his collaborators could claim proficiency in all three departments—comedy, tragicomedy, tragedy. As its title suggests, the play here included belongs to the third category, but it still has something in common with tragicomedy, and it stands apart from the plays Shakespeare wrote around the same time. The last of his tragedies, *Coriolanus*, is usually dated 1608, and *The Winter's Tale* a year or two later, so they were virtually contemporaneous with *The Maid's Tragedy*, which bears little or no resemblance to either. *The Winter's Tale* can be thought of as a tragicomedy, though not in accordance with Fletcher's definition, since the king's son Mamilius dies; and in any case it is quite unlike Fletcher's writing in that genre.

The principal differences from Shakespeare should be sought in the tone of the verse and the social mood of the play. Shakespeare has no character resembling Evadne, the king's cynical mistress, who mocks and torments her titular husband, Amintor, before being driven to repentance and death. It is noteworthy that the most famous lines in the play are spoken by Evadne when her newly married husband arrives in the bridal chamber and mentions her maidenhead: "A maidenhead, Amintor, / At my years!" she replies, and goes on to say that she will never lie with him: " 'tis not for a night / Or two that I forbear thy bed, but ever."

It is typical of Fletcher that this scene makes the most of the salacious possibilities of the situation. They echo, in another key, all the jokes about bridal nights, marriage beds, and maidenheads made by the other characters, including Evadne's female attendants. Evadne, having forfeited her woman's honor, can be called a whore. Amintor's situation is such that he has been tricked into forfeiting his male honor and is a cuckold. Melantius needs to exact vengeance for the loss of his soldier's honor, besmirched by the whoredom of his sister. Callanax, incapable of honor, becomes the butt of Melantius and a traitor to his king; he is described in the dramatis personae as "an old humorous lord," humorous in the contemporary sense, being comically the victim of his own temperament. He therefore acts as a foil to the attitudinizing of the principal characters, and is involved also as the father of Aspatia, the maid whose tragedy we are witnessing. Aspatia is sometimes thought to have more time than she should have been granted to express her woes, and there is certainly an artificial air about her speeches; but this raises a difficult political issue.

Several times in the play we are reminded that it is sacrilege to kill a king, even when an offense like his, if committed by a less godlike person, would require reprisal. The idea of the divine right of kings, with the obvious corollary that one must not, on any account, kill them, was not new; it is obvious, for example, that Shakespeare's Richard II subscribed to it, and on the other side of the argument there were those who believed and wrote in defense of the view that if kings became tyrants one had the right to be rid of them. However, the Stuarts embraced the doctrine with a new fervency, and one may guess that much of the interest of this play, for the kind of audience it probably had at The Blackfriars, would lie in the conflict between honor—male, female, soldierly, whatever—and the prohibition, whether political or divine, of revenge against the man who had caused all the trouble. In the end it is Evadne, the fallen woman restored to virtue, who overcomes her scruple about regicide. "I am any thing / That knows not pity," she remarks, having tied the monarch to the bed as the first of the vengeful "love-tricks" she then plays upon him.

That scene (5.1) demonstrates, as well as any, Fletcher's strengths. Brooding over the sleeping king, Evadne decides to wake him up before killing him, in a speech reminiscent of Hamlet's over King Claudius at prayer. At first he tries to take her threats as sexual solicitations, but of this misapprehension she lengthily disabuses him. As a woman Evadne is liable to all the charges Fletcher, in the mood of his times, would bring against her sex. Nor can she escape male coarseness: When, after Evadne's departure, the king's attendants enter, they are joking about her as "a fine wench." "We'll have a snap at her one of these nights, as she goes from him." As attendants of the bedchamber they know her status and joke about her as if she were a whore indeed. A poignant little dialogue, and a trick probably learned from Shakespeare, who liked to give such characters as murderers their right to comment on the great events they were employed to bring about; they may have little to say, but their words are enriching and memorable, as when Banquo's remark "It will be rain tonight" is followed by a murderer's "Let it come down," which richly completes the blank-verse line.

Fletcher was fashionable. At the time he was writing, the Jacobean court staged many sophisticated masques, in some of which The King's Men participated, and it was modish to include one, or part of one, in plays, as, for instance, in Shakespeare's *The Tempest*. When Fletcher writes a quite elaborate masque for the marriage of Amintor and Evadne at the beginning of his play, he means to please his audience with an upper-class entertainment, but not at the expense of the play's construction, for the masque is quite relevant to the business of the plot and serves to emphasize the cruelty of the deception practiced on Amintor, revealed only when the supposed lovers meet in the bridal chamber.

The remainder of the play is the work of a similarly practiced hand, and one sees why Fletcher (and his collaborators) were successful, and even why The King's Men picked him to take over from Shakespeare as their principal dramatist. His reputation continued to flourish, and in the judgment of later-seventeenth-century commentators his name stood with those of Jonson and Shakespeare. The Folio of his works of 1647 was followed by a second Folio in 1679, containing fifty-two plays in all. No doubt his work had made that of older contemporaries seem old-fashioned, but to the modern eye it suffers by the comparison, which exposes its rhetorical habit—a relative thinness of language, inferior rhetorical resource, and a consequent artificiality of characterization. The critic Clifford Leech argues that his comedies and tragicomedies "far from being mere pieces of entertainment, are at their best capable of disturbing us and of setting our intelligences working. The main trouble, perhaps, is that he has written no masterpiece." This seems a just appraisal.

———

THOMAS MIDDLETON (1580–1627) left Oxford without a degree and even before he was twenty was trying to earn a living as a writer, but—failing in that attempt—he took what we now see was the usual solution: He was, by 1602, on the payroll of Philip Henslowe. A number of plays in which he then had a hand are lost. Later, with Thomas Dekker, he wrote satirical comedies for the boys' companies of St. Paul's and The Blackfriars, where they played before The King's Men were able to move in. His first important city comedy, *A Mad World, My Masters,* was written, c. 1604, for boys, but their companies collapsed in 1607 and *A Chaste Maid in Cheapside,* perhaps the most remarkable of all such comedies, was performed by an adult company at the Swan Theater on Bankside.

Comedies involving the London citizenry were not a novelty; for example, Dekker's *The Shoemaker's Holiday* (1599), though set in fifteenth-century London, is remembered for the way it chronicles the rise of Simon Eyre from shoemaker to Lord Mayor, offering a distinctly modern commentary on the life of the artisan class and on contemporary economic conditions. Middleton had written several other citizen comedies, played by boys' companies, before producing this masterpiece of the genre. G. K. Hunter plausibly suggests that it was this change from boy to adult actors that was "responsible for the increased complexity of the characters."

Middleton's conception lacks the slightly fairy-tale aspect of Dekker's play and is unrelentingly though coolly satirical. The characters range from licentious knights to immoral goldsmiths, from men of disastrous sexual potency to men who forgo sex and prostitute their willing wives in order to live in comfort. The cast includes a great variety of figures—a stupid Cambridge student, a Welsh whore, "promoters," and so on. All are more or less involved in a complex intrigue about sex and money. In the opening scene a mother, Mistress Yellowhammer, is cross with her daughter for omitting to acquire the graces that will attract a husband from the class above her, and they await the return of Mistress Yellowhammer's son from Cambridge so that they can marry him to the Welsh woman wrongly supposed to be Sir Walter Whorehound's "landed niece," not his whore. The scene is remarkable for the diligence with which Middleton establishes the themes of money and of sex as convertible to money, and his rendering of the intercourse between social classes. It ends with the business of the ring ordered from Yellowhammer by Touchwood junior, who is in love with the goldsmith's daughter, a passage punctuated by risky and risqué innuendos. Perhaps the most remarkable speech of the first act is the soliloquy in which Allwit (= wittol, a complaisant cuckold) congratulates himself on the arrangement whereby Sir Walter enjoys the favors of Allwit's wife in return for bearing all his domestic expenses and sparing him the troubles of housekeeping:

> I thank him, has maintained my house this ten years,
> Not only keeps my wife, but 'a keeps me
> And all my family: I'm at his table:
> He gets me all my children, and pays the nurse
> Monthly or weekly; puts me to nothing, rent,
> Nor church-duties, not so much as the scavenger:
> The happiest state that ever man was born to! . . .

And so on, for forty-odd lines, demonstrating the reversal of values by which money perverts normal human relationships in a paradox neatly summed up in the very idea of the willing cuckold. Allwit even addresses his sons as "whoresons," which, of course, they are.

In a comic variation on the sexual theme, the impossibly fertile Touchwood senior, as a desperate measure of birth control, has to leave the loving wife with whom he produces "every year a child, and some years two," in addition to those he begets on "country wenches." For contrast, Sir Oliver Kix and his wife quarrel because he cannot make her conceive, though a very costly "water" will remedy the situation, while possibly ruining Sir Oliver's fortune. The interplay of money and flesh continues; christenings, betrothals, partings are all animated by it. The vivacity of the plotting, the lively dialogue, the satirical characterization—for instance, of the Puritans and "promoters"—and the complex denouement make this probably the greatest of city comedies. It ends conventionally enough with marriages and feasting, but all is colored by Middleton's calm but grim understanding of life in a city dominated by money. This understanding never relaxes its hold on the play, however fantastic and funny it may be on the surface. And, unlike most comedies of the period, it is firmly set in the city where the playhouse stands, and is intensely topical: For example, the "promoters" and their tricks were a much-hated aspect of life during the fasting time of Lent, when citizens who sought to augment their diet with black-market meat were stopped and searched and reported to the authorities, the promoter having his share of the fine. The satire on the Puritan women is equally pointed and topical.

———

JOHN WEBSTER was born about 1578 and died about 1634. He may have studied law, but by 1602 he was working, as actor and writer, for the impresario Henslowe. His first major play, *The White Devil*, was performed at The Red Bull playhouse in 1612, but, as he remarked in a preface to the published version, it was "acted in so dull a time of winter, presented in so open and black a theater," that, lacking "a full and understanding auditory," it failed.

The Duchess of Malfi, which has a rather similar theme, had better luck, having been presented by Shakespeare's company, The King's Men, at both of their theaters, the open-air Globe and the private indoor Blackfriars. It seems to have done rather better than its predecessor, and was published in 1623, with a dedication to a nobleman and commendatory verses by fellow playwrights Thomas Middleton, William Rowley, and John Ford, with all of whom he had worked on collaborative dramatic ventures. Another play, *The Devil's Law-Case* (1619), is usually included in editions of Webster, but his fame depends on the two Italianate tragedies, *The White Devil* and *The Duchess of Malfi*. Of the two, the latter seems to me the greater achievement.

Webster was a strong poet, with a taste for the sexual macabre that especially pleased the critics of the late nineteenth century, but there is much more to him than praise of that kind suggests. He probably wrote more memorable lines than any of the other dramatists except Shakespeare. As a rough guide, the *Oxford Dictionary of Quotations* lists twenty-five quotations for Webster and eleven for Middleton, five of which are, in my view, by Tourneur. (Shakespeare has more than eighteen hundred, about twenty per play.)

Italy was still remote, and tales of Italian wickedness from a country of fabulously cruel, rich, and ostentatious princes and prelates, of pistols and subtle poisons, of great women, courtesans, malcontents, and adulterers, were fascinating to readers and playgoers. Webster's interest is obvious but also distinctive. Twice he chose to write about eminent women, each belonging to the historical record, and each suffering from the cruelty of men. Yet his most remarkable creation is the penniless, educated hanger-on, who has served a sentence in the galleys and makes himself wicked while knowing what it would be to be virtuous. Comparable characters in Shakespeare are relatively straightforward. Aaron in *Titus Andronicus* makes no secret of his evil nature, Iago in *Othello* is a devotee of wickedness and lies, Iachimo in *Cymbeline* is conscienceless in his desire to cheat Posthumus. Yet none has the ambiguous fascination of Bosola. We are told that he was educated at the great university in Padua and is described as "a fantastical scholar," sourly witty and ironical. Connected as he is with the main characters—Ferdinand, the Cardinal, the Duchess and her husband—it is largely by his comments that the tone of the play is established. He himself acts with cruelty yet without wholly sacrificing his conscience; he is a malcontent but can judge the corruption of the court (demonstrated at the beginning of the play by the contrast with the good government of the French). He has nothing of the mad fury of the two brothers, Ferdinand and the Cardinal; nothing of the naïveté and nothing of the magnanimity of the Duchess, who, despite the certainty that her marriage, once made known, would be condemned, is too confident of her natural dignity to escape forever the vengeful strategies of her brothers. Bosola acts as their "intelligencer" or spy, and finally as her executioner.

We first meet him soliciting an appointment of the Cardinal, then achieving, via Ferdinand, a post in the Duchess's household. In dealing with these great men he goes beyond candor into contempt, which is taken to be part of his character, his "humor." It is his trick with the apricots that reveals to him the pregnancy of the Duchess, and it is he who finds the child's horoscope. Still supposing that Antonio, the father, is merely a bawd or go-between, he sees through the Duchess's scheme to dismiss Antonio and send him away for his safety, and, by praising her husband, induces the Duchess to confess her marriage to him. There follows his act of betrayal, and it is he who arrests her, taking a hand in her torments and finally in her death.

These passages—the dead man's hand, the dancing lunatics, the horrible waxworks, and the execution—are the high point of Webster's achievement. Everybody remembers Bosola's reply to the Duchess when she says she could curse the stars: "Look you, the stars shine still." Her suffering will not affect the universe. The raving of the madmen is followed by Bosola's characterization, in deadly prose, of the doomed Duchess, when she asks him, "Am I not thy duchess?":

> Thou art some great woman, sure, for riot begins to sit on thy forehead (clad in grey hairs) twenty years sooner than on a merry milk-maid's . . . a little infant that breeds its teeth, should it lie with thee, would cry out, as if thou wert the more unquiet bedfellow.

His calm but cruel view of the world cannot include a true understanding of this great lady. When he expects her to be terrified by the executioner's cord, she memorably replies:

> What would it pleasure me to have my throat cut
> With diamonds? or to be smothered
> With cassia? or to be shot to death with pearls?
> I know death hath ten thousand several doors
> For men to take their exits; and 'tis found
> They go on such strange geometric hinges,
> You may open them both ways. . . .

Observations of this kind reflect an acceptance of the educated amorality of Webster's world. They are not confined to two characters. Ferdinand—brutal, jealous, mad for revenge—is given the most famous line of all: "Cover her face; mine eyes dazzle; she died young."

Scholars remark, rightly, on the descent of this dark Jacobean tragedy from earlier dramas of revenge, some of which, like Kyd's *The Spanish Tragedy*, were still being revived almost a generation after they were written. But Webster's characters have an inwardness, a complexity, almost a modernity, quite lacking in the old plays. He knew his Shakespeare and acknowledged a debt; yet the tone of his great tragedies, written when the older poet was at the end of his career, is quite different. Jacobean tragedy, though it might be played along with Shakespeare's at The Globe and The Blackfriars, is a new, subtler, darker world.

———

In the pages above I have treated the plays of Heywood, Jonson, Tourneur, Fletcher/Beaumont, Middleton, and Webster in chronological order, an arrangement that involved splitting Middleton's comedy from his tragedy. After *A Chaste Maid*, Middleton indeed wrote several more comedies, but in the second decade of the century he turned to tragicomedy, and then to tragedy. *Women Beware Women* and *The Changeling* (in which he had William Rowley as his collaborator) were produced about 1621 and 1622, and together may represent the finest dramatic works of the later Jacobean period.

Nathaniel Richards, in commendatory verses written for an edition of 1647, says that Middleton, "knew the rage, / Madness of women cross'd" and their "hell-bred malice"—which is not an exactly adequate account of Middleton's treatment of his subject.

———

Like Middleton's earlier tragedy *Women Beware Women, The Changeling* has a double plot, but the two elements are apparently less well integrated, a discrepancy often explained by the supposition that Rowley wrote the subplot and Middleton the main plot. The relationship between the two plots is defended in a famous chapter of William Empson's book *Some Versions of Pastoral* (1935). Empson argues that we now fail to understand the Elizabethan view of lunatics as funny, though possibly also possessed by evil spirits; the madhouse scenes in the play can be shown to be far from irrelevant, and the connection between plot and subplot is not merely that the fake madmen as absentees from the court belong to the main plot, indeed become murder suspects. Despite the differences of tone, the two plots are similar, having as heroines women forced into unwelcome marriages and liable to take revenge by being, in their different ways, unfaithful to their husbands. To give another example, there is a parallel between De Flores and the keeper Lollio, who demands his sexual "share" from Isabella as De Flores does from Beatrice-Joanna. Empson traces other subtle links, and, though brief, these pages in his essay on double plots are probably the most interesting of critical comments on the play.

Despite this validation of the double plot, the focus of our interest is bound to be the relationship of Beatrice-Joanna and De Flores. Its perverse pathology seizes the attention: The woman remains unaware of the immorality of her decision to have her betrothed murdered until its cost is violently represented to her by the man she thought to use without cost. The ugly De Flores is an inferior she has no obvious need to fear; yet she does fear him, though her loathing disguises her fear. She hates him as if his deformity were something that threatened her own beauty—"As much as youth and beauty hates a sepulcher." The violence of her reaction to him as he stalks her conceals a sexual and mortal terror. A comparable overreaction prompts De Flores to haunt her and suffer her insults as if they were tokens of affection. The play was written for a private, indoor theater, and in the scenes between these two it has a quiet, sick intensity that suits well with that more intimate setting.

The scene (2.2) in which Beatrice pretends to change her attitude and flatters De Flores in order to have him kill her betrothed, Alonzo de Piracquo, is particularly fine, especially when she speaks of the reward he shall have, and he ambiguously says what it must be:

BEATRICE: ... Thy reward shall be precious.
DE FLORES: That I've thought on;
             I have assured myself of that beforehand,
             And know it will be precious; the thought ravishes!

He is already rejoicing in the prospect of a reward of which Beatrice has no conscious notion. In 3.4 he reports the murder, and again the conversation turns on his reward. It must surely be higher than the value of the ring from Alonzo's finger; so far they agree. She proposes "three thousand golden florins" and doubles it when he indignantly rejects the offer. Finally he has to explain to Beatrice, who has behaved like a moral idiot, that she is as guilty as he is and that a financial reward, a quietus made possible by her wealth, is not relevant to their situation. When he tries to kiss her, she tells him to "take heed ... of forgetfulness." He replies that it is she who has grown forgetful. We may recall a line from *Women Beware Women:* "Lust and forgetfulness have been amongst us." Here Beatrice means De Flores's forgetfulness of security—his forward conduct will give away their secret—or perhaps his forgetfulness is of his inferior social position. But in his reply

De Flores means the moral forgetfulness that causes individuals to sin without thought of the cost, as Beatrice sins to be rid of an unwanted husband by murder. Base as he is, De Flores here has all the best lines: "Justice," he says rather magnificently, "invites your blood to understand me." He insists on his price, which is her honor, her virginity. Beatrice is still trapped in the illusion that she has lost nothing by her deed, certainly not her honor, to the security of which she cannot regard a mere murder as a plausible threat, though De Flores is about to teach her otherwise:

> BEATRICE: Why, 'tis impossible thou canst be so wicked,
> Or shelter such a cunning cruelty,
> To make his death the murderer of my honor!
> Thy language is so bold and vicious,
> I cannot see which way I can forgive it
> With any modesty.
> DE FLORES: Pish! you forget yourself;
> A woman dipped in blood, and talk of modesty!

And, memorably, he tells her she is not now what she originally was but what the act has made her; she is henceforth "the deed's creature." If she will not yield to him he will confess all and ruin her along with himself. "Can you weep Fate from its determined purpose? / So soon may you weep me." This finely executed dialogue is worth all the praise that has been lavished on it.

The use of a substituted bride, Diaphanta, to prevent Alsemero from finding out Beatrice is not a virgin is almost farcical, especially when the substitute enjoys herself so much that she won't leave Alsemero's bed. De Flores saves the day by arranging a fire, and now Beatrice loves him as much as she had despised him: "The east is not more beauteous than his service" ... "Here's a man worth loving" ... "A wondrous necessary man."

In the end, having recognized her crimes, she makes her last great speech. There is much talk of blood in the final scene: the power of blood and beauty combined to deform their possessor; the "bridge of blood" Beatrice should have gone "a thousand leagues about" to avoid; the blood on De Flores's clothes; Tomazo's revenge, "urgent in ... blood"; and Beatrice's climactic figure:

> I am that of your blood was taken from you . . .
> Let the common sewer take it from distinction. . . .

where the blood of kinship becomes the blood let by the doctor as a cure, and drained away as mere sewage. De Flores is triumphant in death:

> I loved this woman in spite of her heart. . . .
> . . . her honor's prize
> Was my reward; I thank life for nothing
> But that pleasure; it was so sweet to me,
> That I have drunk up all, left none behind
> For any man to pledge me.

Here, as the complex plot—murder, madness, adultery, perverted love—is unraveled, Middleton writes poetry of a high order. To do so in situations that may strike us as close to farcical—fit for parody—was his great achievement, and others—Tourneur, Webster—came near, on occasion, to writing at the same level. Indeed it is here that we see the ultimate irrelevance of those parodies of Nigel Dennis and Thomas Pynchon. The plots are close to the sensationalism of Grand Guignol; to endow them with high poetry was a feat never to be matched in the tragedies of four succeeding centuries.

A Woman Killed
with Kindness

Thomas Heywood

DRAMATIS PERSONAE

MASTER FRANKFORD
MISTRESS ANNE FRANKFORD, *his wife*
SIR FRANCIS ACTON, *her brother*
SIR CHARLES MOUNTFORD
MASTER MALBY
MASTER WENDOLL, *befriended by Frankford*
MASTER CRANWELL, *an old gentleman*

NICHOLAS
JENKIN
SPIGOT, *Butler*   *Household servants to*
CICELY MILKPAIL   *Frankford*
Other serving-men and women

JACK SLIME
ROGER BRICKBAT   *Country Fellows*

JOAN MINIVER
JANE TRUBKIN   *Country Wenches*
ISBELL MOTLEY

Musicians
FALCONER *and Huntsmen*
SUSAN, *sister to Sir Charles Mountford*
SHERIFF, *Officers,* KEEPER, SHAFTON

OLD MOUNTFORD, *uncle*
SANDY, *former friend*
RODER, *former tenant*   *to Sir Charles*
TIDY, *cousin*

Serving-woman and ANNE'S *two little children*
Carters, *Coachman*

PROLOGUE

I come but like a harbinger,[1] being sent
To tell you what these preparations mean.
Look for no glorious state; our Muse is bent
Upon a barren subject, a bare scene.
We could afford this twig a timber-tree,
Whose strength might boldly on your favors build;
Our russet, tissue; drone, a honey-bee;
Our barren plot, a large and spacious field;
Our coarse fare, banquets; our thin water, wine;
Our brook, a sea; our bat's eyes, eagle's sight;
Our poet's dull and earthly Muse, divine;
Our ravens, doves; our crow's black feathers, white.
    But gentle thoughts, when they may give the foil,
    Save them that yield, and spare where they may spoil

1. The officer who goes ahead of the court to arrange for its entertainment.

A Woman Killed
with Kindness

Act I, Scene I

Enter Master John Frankford, Mistress Anne [Frankford,]
Sir Francis Acton, Sir Charles Mountford, Master Malby,
Master Wendoll, and Master Cranwell

SIR F. Some music, there! None lead the bride a dance?
SIR C. Yes, would she dance *The Shaking of the Sheets;*
    But that's the dance her husband means to lead her.
WEN. That's not the dance that every man must dance,
    According to the ballad.
SIR F. Music, ho!
    By your leave, sister,—by your husband's leave,
    I should have said,—the hand that but this day
    Was given you in the church I'll borrow.—Sound!
    This marriage music hoists me from the ground.
FRANK. Ay, you may caper; you are light and free!
    Marriage hath yoked my heels; pray, then, pardon me.
SIR F. I'll have you dance too, brother!
SIR C. Master Frankford
    Y'are a happy man, sir, and much joy
    Succeed your marriage mirth: you have a wife
    So qualified, and with such ornaments
    Both of the mind and body. First, her birth
    Is noble, and her education such
    As might become the daughter of a prince;
    Her own tongue speaks all tongues, and her own hand
    Can teach all strings to speak in their best grace,
    From the shrill'st treble to the hoarsest bass.

To end her many praises in one word,
She's Beauty and Perfection's eldest daughter,
Only found by yours, though many a heart hath sought her.
FRANK. But that I know your virtues and chaste thoughts,
I should be jealous of your praise, Sir Charles.
CRAN. He speaks no more than you approve.
MAL. Nor flatters he that gives to her her due.
ANNE. I would your praise could find a fitter theme
Than my imperfect beauties to speak on!
Such as they be, if they my husband please
They súffice me now I am marrièd.
This sweet content is like a flattering glass,
To make my face seem fairer to mine eye;
But the least wrinkle from his stormy brow
Will blast the roses in my cheeks that grow.
SIR F. A perfect wife already, meek and patient!
How strangely the word husband fits your mouth,
Not married three hours since! Sister, 'tis good;
You that begin betimes thus must needs prove
Pliant and duteous in your husband's love.—
Gramercies, brother! Wrought her to't already,—
"Sweet husband," and a curtsey, the first day?
Mark this, mark this, you that are bachelors,
And never took the grace of honest man;
Mark this, against[1] you marry, this one phrase:
In a good time that man both wins and woos
That takes his wife down in her wedding shoes.
FRANK. Your sister takes not after you, Sir Francis:
All his wild blood your father spent on you;
He got her in his age, when he grew civil.
All his mad tricks were to his land entailed,
And you are heir to all; your sister, she
Hath to her dower her mother's modesty.
SIR C. Lord, sir, in what a happy state live you!
This morning, which to many seems a burden,
Too heavy to bear, is unto you a pleasure.

---

1. In case.

This lady is no clog, as many are;
She doth become you like a well-made suit,
In which the tailor hath used all his art;
Not like a thick coat of unseasoned frieze,[1]
Forced on your back in summer. She's no chain
To tie your neck, and curb ye to the yoke;
But she's a chain of gold to adorn your neck.
You both adorn each other, and your hands,
Methinks, are matches. There's equality
In this fair combination; y'are both
Scholars, both young, both being descended nobly.
There's music in this sympathy; it carries
Consort and expectation of much joy,
Which God bestow on you from this first day
Until your dissolution,—that's for aye!

SIR F. We keep you here too long, good brother Frankford.
Into the hall; away! Go cheer your guests.
What! Bride and bridegroom both withdrawn at once?
If you be missed, the guests will doubt their welcome,
And charge you with unkindness.

FRANK. To prevent it,
I'll leave you here, to see the dance within.

ANNE. And so will I.

Exeunt Frankford and Mistress Frankford

SIR F. To part you it were sin.—
Now, gallants, while the town musicians
Finger their frets[2] within, and the mad lads
And country lasses, every mother's child,
With nosegays and bride-laces[3] in their hats,
Dance all their country measures, rounds and jigs,
What shall we do? Hark! They're all on the hoigh;[4]
They toil like mill-horses, and turn as round,—
Marry, not on the toe! Ay, and they caper,

---

1. Coarse cloth.
2. The points at which the strings are stopped on the lute.
3. Favors.
4. Excited.

Not without cutting; you shall see, to-morrow,
The hall-floor pecked and dinted like a mill-stone,
Made with their high shoes. Though their skill be small,
Yet they tread heavy where their hobnails fall.

SIR C. Well, leave them to their sports!—Sir Francis Acton,
I'll make a match with you! Meet to-morrow
At Chevy Chase; I'll fly my hawk with yours.

SIR F. For what? for what?

SIR C. Why, for a hundred pound.

SIR F. Pawn me some gold of that!

SIR C. Here are ten angels;[1]
I'll make them good a hundred pound to-morrow
Upon my hawk's wing.

SIR F. 'Tis a match; 'tis done.
Another hundred pound upon your dogs;—
Dare ye, Sir Charles?

SIR C. I dare; were I sure to lose,
I durst do more than that; here's my hand.
The first course for a hundred pound!

SIR F. A match.

WEN. Ten angels on Sir Francis Acton's hawk;
As much upon his dogs!

CRAN. I am for Sir Charles Mountford: I have seen
His hawk and dog both tried. What! Clap ye hands,
Or is't no bargain?

WEN. Yes, and stake them down.
Were they five hundred, they were all my own.

SIR F. Be stirring early with the lark to-morrow;
I'll rise into my saddle ere the sun
Rise from his bed.

SIR C. If there you miss me, say
I am no gentleman! I'll hold my day.

SIR F. It holds on all sides.—Come, to-night let's dance;
Early to-morrow let's prepare to ride:
We had need be three hours up before the bride.

Exeunt

---

1. Gold coins.

SCENE II

Enter Nick and Jenkin, Jack Slime, Roger Brickbat, [Cicely,]
with Country Wenches, and two or three Musicians

JEN. Come, Nick, take you Joan Miniver, to trace withal, Jack Slime, traverse you with Cicely Milkpail; I will take Jane Trubkin, and Roger Brickbat shall have Isbell Motley. And now that they are busy in the parlor, come, strike up; we'll have a crash[1] here in the yard.

NICK. My humor is not compendious: dancing I possess not, though I can foot it; yet, since I am fallen into the hands of Cicely Milkpail, I consent.

SLIME. Truly, Nick, though we were never brought up like serving courtiers, yet we have been brought up with serving creatures,—ay, and God's creatures, too; for we have been brought up to serve sheep, oxen, horses, bogs, and such like; and, though we be but country fellows, it may be in the way of dancing we can do the horse-trick as well as the serving-men.

BRICK. Ay, and the cross-point[2] too.

JEN. O Slime! O Brickbat! Do not you know that comparisons are odious? Now we are odious ourselves, too; therefore there are no comparisons to be made betwixt us.

NICK. I am sudden, and not superfluous;
I am quarrelsome, and not seditious;
I am peaceable, and not contentious;
I am brief, and not compendious.

SLIME. Foot it quickly! If the music overcome not my melancholy, I shall quarrel; and if they suddenly do not strike up, I shall presently strike thee down.

JEN. No quarreling, for God's sake! Truly, if you do, I shall set a knave between ye.

SLIME. I come to dance, not to quarrel. Come, what shall it be? *Rogero?*[3]

JEN. *Rogero?* No; we will dance *The Beginning of the World.*

CIC. I love no dance so well as *John come kiss me now.*

1. Frolic.
2. Dance steps.
3. Name of dance tune.

NICK. I that have ere now deserved a cushion, call for the *Cushion-dance.*

BRICK. For my part, I like nothing so well as *Tom Tyler.*

JEN. No; we'll have *The Hunting of the Fox.*

SLIME. *The Hay, The Hay!* There's nothing like *The Hay.*[1]

NICK. I have said, do say, and will say again—

JEN. Every man agree to have it as Nick says!

ALL. Content.

NICK. It hath been, it now is, and it shall be—

CIC. What, Master Nicholas? What?

NICK. *Put on your Smock a' Monday.*

JEN. So the dance will come cleanly off! Come, for God's sake, agree of something: if you like not that, put it to the musicians; or let me speak for all, and we'll have *Sellenger's Round.*

ALL. That, that, that!

NICK. No, I am resolved thus it shall be: First take hands, then take ye to your heels!

JEN. Why, would you have us run away?

NICK. No; but I would have ye shake your heels.—Music, strike up!

[*They dance; Nick dancing, speaks stately and scurvily,*[2]
the rest, after the country fashion]

JEN. Hey! Lively, my lasses! Here's a turn for thee!

Exeunt

SCENE III

Wind horns. Enter Sir Charles [*Mountford,*] *Sir Francis* [*Acton,*]
Malby, Cranwell, Wendoll, Falconer, and Huntsmen

SIR C. So; well cast off! Aloft, aloft! Well flown!
O, now she takes her at the souse,[3] and strikes her
Down to th' earth, like a swift thunder-clap.

WEN. She hath struck ten angels out of my way.

SIR F. A hundred pound from me.

SIR C. What, falconer!

1. A lively dance.
2. Ridiculously.
3. Swoop.

FALC. At hand, sir!

SIR C. Now she hath seized the fowl and 'gins to plume her,[1]
 Rebeck[2] her not; rather stand still and check her!
 So, seize her gets,[3] her jesses,[4] and her bells! Away!

SIR F. My hawk killed, too.

SIR C. Ay, but 'twas at the querre
 Not at the mount, like mine.

SIR F. Judgment, my masters!

CRAN. Yours missed her at the ferre.[5]

WEN. Ay, but our merlin first had plumed the fowl,
 And twice renewed[6] her from the river too.
 Her bells, Sir Francis, had not both one weight,
 Nor was one semi-tune above the other.
 Methinks, these Milan bells do sound too full,
 And spoil the mounting of your hawk.

SIR C. 'Tis lost.

SIR F. I grant it not. Mine likewise seized a fowl
 Within her talons, and you saw her paws
 Full of the feathers; both her petty singles[7]
 And her long singles griped her more than other;
 The terrials[8] of her legs were stained with blood,
 Not of the fowl only, she did discomfit
 Some of her feathers; but she brake away.
 Come, come; your hawk is but a rifler.[9]

SIR C. How!

SIR F. Ay, and your dogs are trindle-tails[10] and curs.

SIR C. You stir my blood.
 You keep not one good hound in all your kennel,
 Nor one good hawk upon your perch.

---

1. Scatter feathers.
2. Call back.
3. Part of the hawk's harness.
4. Leg-straps.
5. On the same side of the river as the falconer.
6. Renewed the attack.
7. Toes.
8. Talons.
9. Bungler.
10. Curly-tailed.

SIR F. How, knight!

SIR C. So, knight. You will not swagger, sir?

SIR F. Why, say I did?

SIR C. Why, sir,
I say you would gain as much by swaggering
As you have got by wagers on your dogs.
You will come short in all things.

SIR F. Not in this!
Now I'll strike home.

> [*Strikes Sir Charles*]

SIR C. Thou shalt to thy long home,
Or I will want my will.

SIR F. All they that love Sir Francis, follow me!

SIR C. All that affect Sir Charles, draw on my part!

CRAN. On this side heaves my hand.

WEN. Here goes my heart.

> [*They divide themselves. Sir Charles Mountford, Cranwell,
> Falconer, and Huntsman, fight against Sir Francis Acton,
> Wendoll, his Falconer and Huntsman; and Sir Charles hath the
> better, and beats them away, killing both of Sir Francis's men.*]
>
> *Exeunt all but Sir Charles Mountford*

SIR C. My God, what have I done? What have I done?
My rage hath plunged me into a sea of blood,
In which my soul lies drowned. Poor innocents,
For whom we are to answer! Well, 'tis done,
And I remain the victor. A great conquest,
When I would give this right hand, nay, this head,
To breathe in them new life whom I have slain!—
Forgive me, God! 'Twas in the heat of blood,
And anger quite removes me from myself.
It was not I, but rage, did this vile murder;
Yet I, and not my rage, must answer it.
Sir Francis Acton, he is fled the field;
With him all those that did partake his quarrel;
And I am left alone with sorrow dumb,
And in my height of conquest overcome.

> *Enter Susan*

SUSAN. O God! My brother wounded 'mong the dead!
  Unhappy jests, that in such earnest ends!
  The rumor of this fear stretched to my ears,
  And I am come to know if you be wounded.
SIR C. O, sister, sister! Wounded at the heart.
SUSAN. My God forbid!
SIR C. In doing that thing which he forbad.
  I am wounded, sister.
SUSAN. I hope, not at the heart.
SIR C. Yes, at the heart.
SUSAN. O God! A surgeon, there.
SIR C. Call me a surgeon, sister, for my soul!
  The sin of murder, it hath pierced my heart
  And made a wide wound there; but for these scratches,
  They are nothing, nothing.
SUSAN. Charles, what have you done?
  Sir Francis hath great friends, and will pursue you
  Unto the utmost danger[1] of the law.
SIR C. My conscience hath become mine enemy,
  And will pursue me more than Acton can.
SUSAN. O! Fly, sweet brother!
SIR C. Shall I fly from thee?
  Why, Sue, art weary of my company?
SUSAN. Fly from your foe!
SIR C. You, sister, are my friend,
  And flying you, I shall pursue my end.
SUSAN. Your company is as my eyeball dear;
  Being far from you, no comfort can be near.
  Yet fly to save your life! What would I care
  To spend my future age in black despair,
  So you were safe? And yet to live one week
  Without my brother Charles, through every cheek
  My streaming tears would downwards run so rank,[2]
  Till they could set on either side a bank,

1. Limit.
2. Excessively.

And in the midst a channel; so my face
For two salt-water brooks shall still find place.
SIR C. Thou shalt not weep so much; for I will stay,
In spite of danger's teeth. I'll live with thee,
Or I'll not live at all. I will not sell
My country and my father's patrimony,
Nor thy sweet sight, for a vain hope of life.

Enter Sheriff, with Officers

SHER. Sir Charles, I am made the unwilling instrument
Of your attach and apprehension.
I'm sorry that the blood of innocent men
Should be of you exacted. It was told me
That you were guarded with a troop of friends,
And therefore I come thus armed.
SIR C. O Master Sheriff!
I came into the field with many friends,
But see, they all have left me; only one
Clings to my sad misfortune, my dear sister.
I know you for an honest gentleman;
I yield my weapons, and submit to you.
Convey me where you please!
SHER. To prison, then,
To answer for the lives of these dead men.
SUSAN. O God! O God!
SIR C. Sweet sister, every strain
Of sorrow from your heart augments my pain;
Your grief abounds, and hits against my breast.
SHER. Sir, will you go?
SIR C. Even where it likes you best.

Exeunt

ACT II, SCENE I

Enter Frankford in a study

FRANK. How happy am I amongst other men,
That in my mean estate embrace content!
I am a gentleman, and by my birth

Companion with a king; a king's no more.
I am possessed of many fair revénues,
Sufficient to maintain a gentleman;
Touching my mind, I am studied in all arts;
The riches of my thoughts and of my time
Have been a good proficient;[1] but, the chief
Of all the sweet felicities on earth,
I have a fair, a chaste, and loving wife,
Perfection all, all truth, all ornament.
If man on earth may truly happy be,
Of these at once possessed, sure, I am he.

Enter Nicholas

NICK. Sir, there's a gentleman attends without
    To speak with you.
FRANK. On horseback?
NICK. Yes, on horseback.
FRANK. Entreat him to alight, and I'll attend him.
    Know'st thou him, Nick?
NICK. Know him? Yes; his name's Wendoll.
    It seems, he comes in haste: his horse is booted
    Up to the flank in mire, himself all spotted
    And stained with plashing. Sure, he rid in fear,
    Or for a wager. Horse and man both sweat;
    I ne'er saw two in such a smoking heat.
FRANK. Entreat him in: about it instantly!

Exit Nicholas

This Wendoll I have noted, and his carriage
Hath pleased me much; by observation
I have noted many good deserts in him.
He's affable, and seen[2] in many things;
Discourses well; a good companion;
And though of small means, yet a gentleman
Of a good house, somewhat pressed by want.
I have preferred him to a second place
In my opinion and my best regard.

1. Advanced student.
2. Proficient.

Enter Wendoll, Mistress Frankford, and Nicholas

ANNE. O, Master Frankford! Master Wendoll here
    Brings you the strangest news that e'er you heard.
FRANK. What news, sweet wife? What news, good Master Wendoll?
WEN. You knew the match made 'twixt Sir Francis Acton
    And Sir Charles Mountford?
FRANK. True; with their hounds and hawks?
WEN. The matches were both played.
FRANK. Ha? And which won?
WEN. Sir Francis, your wife's brother, had the worst,
    And lost the wager.
FRANK. Why, the worse his chance;
    Perhaps the fortune of some other day
    Will change his luck.
ANNE. O, but you hear not all.
    Sir Francis lost, and yet was loath to yield.
    At length the two knights grew to difference,
    From words to blows, and so to banding[1] sides;
    Where valorous Sir Charles slew, in his spleen,
    Two of your brother's men,—his falconer,
    And his good huntsman, whom he loved so well.
    More men were wounded, no more slain outright.
FRANK. Now, trust me, I am sorry for the knight
    But is my brother safe?
WEN. All whole and sound.
    His body not being blemished with one wound.
    But poor Sir Charles is to the prison led,
    To answer at th' assize for them that's dead.
FRANK. I thank your pains, sir. Had the news been better,
    Your will was to have brought it, Master Wendoll.
    Sir Charles will find hard friends; his case is heinous.
    And will be most severely censured on.
    I'm sorry for him. Sir, a word with you!
    I know you, sir, to be a gentleman

---

1. Taking.

In all things; your possibility but mean;
Please you to use my table and my purse;
They're yours.

WEN. O Lord, sir! I shall ne'er deserve it.

FRANK. O sir, disparage not your worth too much:
You are full of quality¹ and fair desert.
Choose of my men which shall attend you, sir,
And he is yours. I will allow you, sir,
Your man, your gelding, and your table, all
At my own charge; be my companion!

WEN. Master Frankford, I have oft been bound to you
By many favors; this exceeds them all,
That I shall never merit your least favor;
But when your last remembrance I forget,
Heaven at my soul exact that weighty debt!

FRANK. There needs no protestation; for I know you
Virtuous, and therefore grateful.—Prithee, Nan,
Use him with all thy loving'st courtesy!

ANNE. As far as modesty may well extend,
It is my duty to receive your friend.

FRANK. To dinner! Come, sir, from this present day,
Welcome to me for ever! Come, away!

          Exeunt Frankford, Mistress Frankford, and Wendoll

NICK. I do not like this fellow by no means:
I never see him but my heart still yearns.²
Zounds! I could fight with him, yet know not why;
The devil and he are all one in mine eye.

Enter Jenkin

JEN. O Nick! What gentleman is that, that comes to lie³ at our house?
My master allows him one to wait on him, and I believe it will fall
to thy lot.

---

1. Accomplishment.
2. Grieves.
3. Stay.

NICK. I love my master; by these hilts[1] I do;
   But rather than I'll ever come to serve him,
   I'll turn away my master.

Enter Cicely

CIC. Nich'las! where are you, Nich'las? You must come in, Nich'las,
   and help the gentleman off with his boots.
NICK. If I pluck off his boots, I'll eat the spurs,
   And they shall stick fast in my throat like burrs.
CIC. Then, Jenkin, come you!
JEN. Nay, 'tis no boot[2] for me to deny it. My master hath given me a
   coat here, but he takes pains himself to brush it once or twice a day
   with a hollywand.[3]
CIC. Come, come, make haste, that you may wash your hands again,
   and help to serve in dinner!
JEN. You may see, my masters, though it be afternoon with you, 'tis
   but early days with us, for we have not dined yet. Stay but a little;
   I'll but go in and help to bear up the first course, and come to you
   again presently.

Exeunt

SCENE II

Enter Malby and Cranwell

MAL. This is the sessions-day; pray can you tell me
   How young Sir Charles hath sped? Is he acquit,
   Or must he try the law's strict penalty?
CRAN. He's cleared of all, spite of his enemies,
   Whose earnest labor was to take his life.
   But in this suit of pardon he hath spent
   All the revenues that his father left him;
   And he is now turned a plain countryman,
   Reformed in all things. See, sir, here he comes.

---

1. Swords.
2. Use.
3. Switch of holly.

Enter Sir Charles and his Keeper

KEEP. Discharge your fees, and you are then at freedom.
SIR C. Here, Master Keeper, take the poor remainder
 Of all the wealth I have! My heavy foes
 Have made my purse light; but, alas! to me
 'Tis wealth enough that you have set me free.
MAL. God give you joy of your delivery!
 I am glad to see you abroad, Sir Charles.
SIR C. The poorest knight in England, Master Malby;
 My life has cost me all my patrimony
 My father left his son. Well, God forgive them
 That are the authors of my penury!

Enter Shafton

SHAFT. Sir Charles! A hand, a hand! At liberty?
 Now, by the faith I owe, I am glad to see it.
 What want you? Wherein may I pleasure you?
SIR C. O me! O, most unhappy gentleman!
 I am not worthy to have friends stirred up,
 Whose hands may help me in this plunge of want.
 I would I were in heaven, to inherit there
 Th' immortal birthright which my Saviour keeps,
 And by no unthrift can be bought and sold;
 For here on earth what pleasures should we trust?
SHAFT. To rid you from these contemplations,
 Three hundred pounds you shall receive of me;
 Nay, five for fail. Come, sir, the sight of gold
 Is the most sweet receipt for melancholy,
 And will revive your spirits. You shall hold law
 With your proud adversaries. Tush! let Frank Acton
 Wage, with his knighthood, like expense with me,
 And he will sink, he will.—Nay, good Sir Charles,
 Applaud your fortune and your fair escape
 From all these perils.
SIR C. O sir! they have undone me.
 Two thousand and five hundred pound a year
 My father at his death possessed me of;

All which the envious Acton made me spend;
And, notwithstanding all this large expense,
I had much ado to gain my liberty;
And I have only now a house of pleasure
With some five hundred pounds reserved,
Both to maintain me and my loving sister.

SHAFT. [*Aside*] That must I have, it lies convenient for me.
If I can fasten but one finger on him,
With my full hand I'll gripe him to the heart.
'Tis not for love I proffered him this coin,
But for my gain and pleasure.—Come, Sir Charles,
I know you have need of money; take my offer.

SIR C. Sir, I accept it, and remain indebted
Even to the best of my unable[1] power.
Come, gentlemen, and see it tendered down!

Exeunt

SCENE III

Enter Wendoll, melancholy

WEN. I am a villain, if I apprehend
But such a thought! Then, to attempt the deed,
Slave, thou art damned without redemption.—
I'll drive away this passion with a song.
A song! Ha, ha! A song! As if, fond[2] man,
Thy eyes could swim in laughter, when thy soul
Lies drenched and drownèd in red tears of blood!
I'll pray, and see if God within my heart
Plant better thoughts. Why, prayers are meditations,
And when I meditate (O, God forgive me!)
It is on her divine perfections.
I will forget her; I will arm myself
Not t' entertain a thought of love to her;
And, when I come by chance into her presence,

1. Feeble.
2. Foolish.

I'll hale¹ these balls until my eye-strings crack,
From being pulled and drawn to look that way.

Enter, over the Stage, Frankford, his Wife, and Nicholas

O God, O God! With what a violence
I'm hurried to mine own destruction!
There goest thou, the most perfect'st man
That ever England bred a gentleman,
And shall I wrong his bed?—Thou God of thunder!
Stay, in thy thoughts of vengeance and of wrath,
Thy great, almighty, and all-judging hand
From speedy execution on a villain,
A villain, and a traitor to his friend.

Enter Jenkin

JEN. Did your worship call?
WEN. He doth maintain me; he allows me largely
    Money to spend.
JEN. By my faith, so do not you me: I cannot get a cross² of you.
WEN. My gelding, and my man.
JEN. That's Sorrel and I.
WEN. This kindness grows of no alliance 'twixt us.
JEN. Nor is my service of any great acquaintance.
WEN. I never bound him to me by desert.
    Of a mere stranger, a poor gentleman,
    A man by whom in no kind he could gain,
    And he hath placed me in his highest thoughts,
    Made me companion with the best and chiefest
    In Yorkshire. He cannot eat without me,
    Nor laugh without me; I am to his body
    As necessary as his digestion,
    And equally do make him whole or sick.
    And shall I wrong this man? Base man! Ingrate!
    Hast thou the power, straight with thy gory hands
    To rip thy image from his bleeding heart,

1. Drag.
2. A piece of money.

To scratch thy name from out the holy book
Of his remembrance, and to wound his name
That holds thy name so dear? or rend his heart
To whom thy heart was knit and joined together?—
And yet I must. Then Wendoll, be content!
Thus villains, when they would, cannot repent.

JEN. What a strange humor is my new master in! Pray God he be not
mad; if he should be so, I should never have any mind to serve
him in Bedlam. It may be he's mad for missing of me.

WEN. [*Seeing Jenkin*] What, Jenkin! Where's your mistress?

JEN. Is your worship married?

WEN. Why dost thou ask?

JEN. Because you are my master; and if I have a mistress, I would be
glad, like a good servant, to do my duty to her.

WEN. I mean Mistress Frankford.

JEN. Marry, sir, her husband is riding out of town, and she went very
lovingly to bring him on his way to horse. Do you see, sir? Here
she comes, and here I go.

WEN. Vanish!

Exit Jenkin

Enter Mistress Frankford

ANNE. Y'are well met, sir; now, in troth, my husband,
Before he took horse, had a great desire
To speak with you; we sought about the house,
Hallooed into the fields, sent every way,
But could not meet you. Therefore, he enjoined me
To do unto you his most kind commends;
Nay, more: he wills you, as you prize his love,
Or hold in estimation his kind friendship,
To make bold in his absence, and command
Even as himself were present in the house;
For you must keep his table, use his servants,
And be a present Frankford in his absence.

WEN. I thank him for his love.—
[*Aside*] Give me a name, you, whose infectious tongues
Are tipped with gall and poison: as you would
Think on a man that had your father slain,

    Murdered your children, made your wives base strumpets,
    So call me, call me so; print in my face
    The most stigmatic title of a villain,
    For hatching treason to so true a friend!
ANNE. Sir, you are most beholding to my husband;
    You are a man most dear in his regard.
WEN. I am bound unto your husband, and you too.
    [*Aside*] I will not speak to wrong a gentleman
    Of that good estimation, my kind friend.
    I will not; zounds! I will not. I may choose,
    And I will choose. Shall I be so misled,
    Or shall I purchase[1] to my father's crest
    The motto of a villain? If I say
    I will not do it, what thing can enforce me?
    What can compel me? What sad destiny
    Hath such command upon my yielding thoughts?
    I will not;—ha! Some fury pricks me on;
    The swift fates drag me at their chariot wheel,
    And hurry me to mischief. Speak I must:
    Injure myself, wrong her, deceive his trust!
ANNE. Are you not well, sir, that ye seem thus troubled?
    There is sedition in your countenance.
WEN. And in my heart, fair angel, chaste and wise.
    I love you! Start not, speak not, answer not;
    I love you,—nay, let me speak the rest;
    Bid me to swear, and I will call to record
    The host of heaven.
ANNE. The host of heaven forbid
    Wendoll should hatch such a disloyal thought!
WEN. Such is my fate; to this suit was I born,
    To wear rich pleasure's crown, or fortune's scorn.
ANNE. My husband loves you.
WEN. I know it.
ANNE. He esteems you,
    Even as his brain, his eye-ball, or his heart.

---

1. Acquire.

WEN. I have tried[1] it.

ANNE. His purse is your exchequer, and his table
Doth freely serve you.

WEN. So I have found it.

ANNE. O! With what face of brass, what brow of steel,
Can you, unblushing, speak this to the face
Of the espous'd wife of so dear a friend?
It is my husband that maintains your state;
Will you dishonor him? I am his wife,
That in your power hath left his whole affairs.
It is to me you speak.

WEN. O speak no more;
For more than this I know, and have recorded
Within the red-leaved table[2] of my heart.
Fair, and of all beloved, I was not fearful
Bluntly to give my life into your hand,
And at one hazard all my earthly means.
Go, tell your husband; he will turn me off,
And I am then undone. I care not, I;
'Twas for your sake. Perchance, in rage he'll kill me;
I care not, 'twas for you. Say I incur
The general name of villain through the world,
Of traitor to my friend; I care not, I.
Beggary, shame, death, scandal, and reproach,
For you I'll hazard all. Why, what care I?
For you I'll love, and in your love I'll die.

ANNE. You move me, sir, to passion and to pity.
The love I bear my husband is as precious
As my soul's health.

WEN. I love your husband too,
And for his love I will engage my life.
Mistake me not; the augmentation
Of my sincere affection borne to you
Doth no whit lessen my regard of him.
I will be secret, lady, close as night;

---

1. Tested.
2. Notebook.

And not the light of one small glorious star
Shall shine here in my forehead, to bewray
That act of night.

ANNE. What shall I say?
My soul is wandering, and hath lost her way.
O, Master Wendoll! O!

WEN. Sigh not, sweet saint;
For every sigh you breathe draws from my heart
A drop of blood.

ANNE. I ne'er offended yet:
My fault, I fear, will in my brow be writ.
Women that fall, not quite bereft of grace,
Have their offences noted in their face.
I blush, and am ashamed. O, Master Wendoll,
Pray God I be not born to curse your tongue,
That hath enchanted me! This maze I am in
I fear will prove the labyrinth of sin.

Enter Nicholas, [behind]

WEN. The path of pleasure, and the gate to bliss,
Which on your lips I knock at with a kiss!

NICK. I'll kill the rogue.

WEN. Your husband is from home, your bed's no blab.
Nay, look not down and blush!

Exeunt Wendoll and Mistress Frankford

NICK. Zounds! I'll stab.
Ay, Nick, was it thy chance to come just in the nick?
I love my master, and I hate that slave;
I love my mistress; but these tricks I like not.
My master shall not pocket up this wrong;
I'll eat my fingers first. What say'st thou, metal?[1]
Does not that rascal Wendoll go on legs
That thou must cut off? Hath he not ham-strings
That thou must hough?[2] Nay, mettle, thou shalt stand
To all I say. I'll henceforth turn a spy,

1. Man of mettle, spirit.
2. Hew.

And watch them in their close conveyances.[1]
I never looked for better of that rascal,
Since he came miching[2] first into our house.
It is that Satan hath corrupted her;
For she was fair and chaste. I'll have an eye
In all their gestures. Thus I think of them:
If they proceed as they have done before,
Wendoll's a knave, my mistress is a—

Exit

Act III, Scene I

Enter [Sir] Charles and Susan

SIR C. Sister, you see we are driven to hard shift,
　　To keep this poor house we have left unsold.
　　I am now enforced to follow husbandry,
　　And you to milk; and do we not live well?
　　Well, I thank God.
SUSAN. O, brother! here's a change,
　　Since old Sir Charles died, in our father's house.
SIR C. All things on earth thus change, some up, some down;
　　Content's a kingdom, and I wear that crown.

Enter Shafton, with a Sergeant

SHAFT. Good morrow, morrow, Sir Charles! What! With your sister,
　　Plying your husbandry?—Sergeant, stand off!—
　　You have a pretty house here, and a garden,
　　And goodly ground about it. Since it lies
　　So near a lordship that I lately bought,
　　I would fain buy it of you. I will give you—
SIR C. O, pardon me; this house successively
　　Hath longed to me and my progenitors
　　Three hundred years. My great-great-grandfather,
　　He in whom first our gentle style[3] began,

1. Secret doings.
2. Snooping.
3. Title.

Dwelt here, and in this ground increased this mole-hill
Unto that mountain which my father left me.
Where he the first of all our house began,
I now the last will end, and keep this house,
This virgin title, never yet deflowered
By any unthrift of the Mountfords' line.
In brief, I will not sell it for more gold
Than you could hide or pave the ground withal.
SHAFT. Ha, ha! a proud mind and a beggar's purse!
Where's my three hundred pounds, besides the use?[1]
I have brought it to execution
By course of law. What! Is my monies ready?
SIR C. An execution, sir, and never tell me
You put my bond in suit? You deal extremely.
SHAFT. Sell me the land, and I'll acquit you straight.
SIR C. Alas, alas! 'Tis all trouble hath left me,
To cherish me and my poor sister's life.
If this were sold, our names should then be quite
Razed from the bead-roll[2] of gentility.
You see what hard shift we have made to keep it
Allied still to our own name. This palm you see,
Labor hath glowed within; her silver brow,
That never tasted a rough winter's blast
Without a mask or fan, doth with a grace
Defy cold winter, and his storms outface.
SUSAN. Sir, we feed sparing, and we labor hard;
We lie uneasy, to reserve to us
And our succession this small spot of ground.
SIR C. I have so bent my thoughts to husbandry,
That I protest I scarcely can remember
What a new fashion is; how silk or satin
Feels in my hand. Why, pride is grown to us
A mere, mere stranger. I have quite forgot
The names of all that ever waited on me.
I cannot name ye any of my hounds,

1. Interest.
2. List.

Once from whose echoing mouths I heard all music
That e'er my heart desired. What should I say?
To keep this place, I have changed myself away.

SHAFT. [*To the Sergeant*] Arrest him at my suit!—Actions and actions
Shall keep thee in continual bondage fast;
Nay, more, I'll sue thee by a late appeal,
And call thy former life in question.
The keeper is my friend; thou shalt have irons,
And usage such as I'll deny to dogs.—
Away with him!

SIR C. Ye are too timorous.
But trouble is my master,
And I will serve him truly.—My kind sister,
Thy tears are of no use to mollify
This flinty man. Go to my father's brother,
My kinsmen, and allies; entreat them for me,
To ransom me from this injurious man
That seeks my ruin.

SHAFT. Come, irons, irons! Come, away;
I'll see thee lodged far from the sight of day.

Exeunt [except Susan]

SUSAN. My heart's so hardened with the frost of grief,
Death cannot pierce it through.—Tyrant too fell!
So lead the fiends condemnèd souls to hell.

Enter [Sir Francis] Acton and Malby

SIR F. Again to prison! Malby, hast thou seen
A poor slave better tortured? Shall we hear
The music of his voice cry from the grate,[1]
Meat, for the Lord's sake? No, no; yet I am not
Throughly revenged. They say, he hath a pretty wench
To his sister; shall I, in mercy-sake
To him and to his kindred, bribe the fool
To shame herself by lewd, dishonest lust?
I'll proffer largely; but, the deed being done,
I'll smile to see her base confusion.

---

1. Of the debtors' prison.

MAL. Methinks, Sir Francis, you are full revenged
    For greater wrongs than he can proffer you.
    See where the poor sad gentlewoman stands!
SIR F. Ha, ha! Now will I flout her poverty,
    Deride her fortunes, scoff her base estate;
    My very soul the name of Mountford hate.
    But stay, my heart! O, what a look did fly
    To strike my soul through with thy piercing eye!
    I am enchanted; all my spirits are fled,
    And with one glance my envious spleen struck dead.
SUSAN. Acton! That seeks our blood!

                               Runs away

SIR F. O chaste and fair!
MAL. Sir Francis! Why, Sir Francis! in a trance?
    Sir Francis! What cheer, man? Come, come, how is't?
SIR F. Was she not fair? Or else this judging eye
    Cannot distinguish beauty.
MAL. She was fair.
SIR F. She was an angel in a mortal's shape,
    And ne'er descended from old Mountford's line.
    But soft, soft, let me call my wits together!
    A poor, poor wench, to my great adversary
    Sister, whose very souls denounce stern war
    Each against other! How now, Frank, turned fool
    Or madman, whether? But no! Master of
    My perfect senses and directest wits.
    Then why should I be in this violent humor
    Of passion and of love? And with a person
    So different every way, and so opposed
    In all contractions[1] and still-warring actions?
    Fie, fie! How I dispute against my soul!
    Come, come; I'll gain her, or in her fair quest
    Purchase my soul free and immortal rest.

                               Exeunt

---

1. Legal transactions.

SCENE II

Enter three or four Serving-men, one with a voider[1] and a wooden knife, to take away; another [with] the salt and bread; another [with] the table-cloth and napkins; another [with] the carpet;[2] Jenkin with two lights after them

JEN. So; march in order, and retire in battle array! My master and the guests have supped already; all's taken away. Here, now spread for the serving-men in the hall!—Butler, it belongs to your office.

BUT. I know it, Jenkin. What d'ye call the gentleman that supped there to-night?

JEN. Who? My master?

BUT. No, no; Master Wendoll, he's a daily guest. I mean the gentleman that came but this afternoon.

JEN. His name's Master Cranwell. God's light! Hark, within there; my master calls to lay more billets[3] upon the fire. Come, come! Lord, how we that are in office[4] here in the house are troubled! One spread the carpet in the parlor, and stand ready to snuff the lights; the rest be ready to prepare their stomachs![5] More lights in the hall, there! Come, Nicholas.

Exeunt [all but Nicholas]

NICK. I cannot eat; but had I Wendoll's heart, I would eat that. The rogue grows impudent. O! I have seen such vild,[6] notorious tricks, ready to make my eyes dart from my head. I'll tell my master; by this air, I will; fall what may fall, I'll tell him. Here he comes.

Enter Master Frankford, as it were brushing the crumbs from his clothes with a napkin, as newly risen from supper

FRANK. Nicholas, what make you here? Why are not you
At supper in the hall, among your fellows?

NICK. Master, I stayed your rising from the board,
To speak with you.

1. Basket.
2. Tablecloth.
3. Logs.
4. Service.
5. Appetites.
6. Vile.

FRANK. Be brief then, gentle Nicholas;
    My wife and guests attend me in the parlor.
    Why dost thou pause? Now, Nicholas, you want money,
    And, unthrift-like, would eat into your wages
    Ere you had earned it. Here, sir, 's half-a-crown;
    Play the good husband,[1]—and away to supper!
NICK. By this hand, an honorable gentleman! I will not see him
    wronged.
    Sir, I have served you long; you entertained me
    Seven years before your beard; you knew me, sir,
    Before you knew my mistress.
FRANK. What of this, good Nicholas?
NICK. I never was a make-bate[2] or a knave;
    I have no fault but one—I'm given to quarrel,
    But not with women. I will tell you, master,
    That which will make your heart leap from your breast,
    Your hair to startle from your head, your ears to tingle.
FRANK. What preparation's this to dismal news?
NICK. 'Sblood! sir, I love you better than your wife.
    I'll make it good.
FRANK. Y' are a knave, and I have much ado
    With wonted patience to contain my rage,
    And not to break thy pate. Th' art a knave.
    I'll turn you, with your base comparisons,
    Out of my doors.
NICK. Do, do.
    There is not room for Wendoll and me too,
    Both in one house. O master, master,
    That Wendoll is a villain!
FRANK. Ay, Saucy?
NICK. Strike, strike, do strike; yet hear me! I am no fool;
    I know a villain, when I see him act
    Deeds of a villain. Master, master, that base slave
    Enjoys my mistress, and dishonors you.

1. Husbandman.
2. Maker of quarrels.

FRANK. Thou hast killed me with a weapon, whose sharp point
    Hath pricked quite through and through my shivering heart.
    Drops of cold sweat sit dangling on my hairs,
    Like morning's dew upon the golden flowers,
    And I am plunged into strange agonies.
    What did'st thou say? If any word that touched
    His credit, or her reputation,
    It is as hard to enter my belief,
    As Dives[1] into heaven.

NICK. I can gain nothing:
    They are two that never wronged me. I knew before
    'Twas but a thankless office, and perhaps
    As much as is my service, or my life
    Is worth. All this I know; but this, and more,
    More by a thousand dangers, could not hire me
    To smother such a heinous wrong from you.
    I saw, and I have said.

FRANK. [*Aside*] 'Tis probable. Though blunt, yet he is honest.
    Though I durst pawn my life, and on their faith
    Hazard the dear salvation of my soul,
    Yet in my trust I may be too secure.[2]
    May this be true? O, may it? Can it be?
    Is it by any wonder possible?
    Man, woman, what thing mortal can we trust,
    When friends and bosom wives prove so unjust?—
    What instance hast thou of this strange report?

NICK. Eyes, master, eyes.

FRANK. Thy eyes may be deceived, I tell thee;
    For should an angel from the heavens drop down,
    And preach this to me that thyself hast told,
    He should have much ado to win belief;
    In both their loves I am so confident.

NICK. Shall I discourse the same by circumstance?

FRANK. No more! To supper, and command your fellows

---

1. Luke, chapter 16.
2. Careless.

To attend us and the strangers! Not a word,
I charge thee, on thy life! Be secret, then;
For I know nothing.

NICK. I am dumb; and, now that I have eased my stomach,[1]
I will go fill my stomach.

Exit

FRANK. Away! Begone!
She is well born, descendèd nobly;
Virtuous her education; her repute
Is in the general voice of all the country
Honest and fair; her carriage, her demeanor,
In all her actions that concern the love
To me her husband, modest, chaste, and godly.
Is all this seeming gold plain copper?
But he, that Judas that hath borne my purse,
And sold me for a sin! O God! O God!
Shall I put up these wrongs? No! Shall I trust
The bare report of this suspicious groom,
Before the double-gilt, the well-hatch[ed][2] ore
Of their two hearts? No, I will lose these thoughts;
Distraction I will banish from my brow,
And from my looks exile sad discontent.
Their wonted favors in my tongue shall flow;
Till I know all, I'll nothing seem to know.—
Lights and a table there! Wife, M[aster] Wendoll,
And gentle Master Cranwell!

*Enter Mistress Frankford, Master Wendoll, Master Cranwell,
Nicholas, and Jenkin with cards, carpets,[3] and other necessaries*

FRANK. O! Master Cranwell, you are a stranger here,
And often baulk[4] my house; faith y' are a churl!—
Now we have supped, a table and to cards!

1. Resentment.
2. Nobly wrought.
3. Tablecloths.
4. Avoid.

JEN. A pair[1] of cards, Nicholas, and a carpet to cover the table! Where's
   Cicely, with her counters and her box! Candles and candlesticks,
   there! Fie! We have such a household of serving-creatures! Unless it
   be Nick and I, there's not one amongst them all that can say bo to a
   goose. —Well said, Nick!

   [*They spread a carpet; set down lights and cards*]

ANNE. Come, Mr. Frankford, who shall take my part?

FRANK. Marry, that will I, sweet wife.

WEN. No, by my faith, when you are together, I sit out.
   It must be Mistress Frankford and I, or else it is no match.

FRANK. I do not like that match.

NICK. [*Aside*] You have no reason, marry, knowing all.

FRANK. 'Tis no great matter, neither.—Come, Master Cranwell,
   shall you and I take them up?

CRAN. At your pleasure, sir.

FRANK. I must look to you, Master Wendoll; for you'll be playing false.
   Nay, so will my wife, too.

NICK. [*Aside*] I will be sworn she will.

ANNE. Let them that are taken false, forfeit the set!

FRANK. Content; it shall go hard but I'll take you.

CRAN. Gentlemen, what shall our game be?

WEN. Master Frankford, you play best at noddy.[2]

FRANK. You shall not find it so; indeed, you shall not.

ANNE. I can play at nothing so well as double-ruff.

FRANK. If Master Wendoll and my wife be together, there's no playing against them at double-hand.

NICK. I can tell you, sir, the game that Master Wendoll is best at.

FRANK. What game is that, Nick?

NICK. Marry, sir, knave out of doors.

WEN. She and I will take you at lodam.

ANNE. Husband, shall we play at saint?

FRANK. [*Aside*] My saint's turned devil.—No, we'll none of saint:
   You are best at new-cut, wife, you'll play at that.

WEN. If you play at new-cut, I'm soonest hitter of any here, for a wager.

---

1. Deck.

2. Noddy, double-ruff, knave out of doors, lodam, saint (cent), new-cut are all games at
cards. The double meaning attached to most of these terms is clear.

FRANK. [*Aside*] 'Tis me they play on.—Well, you may draw out;
For all your cunning, 'twill be to your shame;
I'll teach you, at your new-cut, a new game.
Come, come!

CRAN. If you cannot agree upon the game, to post and pair![1]

WEN. We shall be soonest pairs; and my good host,
When he comes late home, he must kiss the post.[2]

FRANK. Whoever wins, it shall be to thy cost.

CRAN. Faith, let it be vide-ruff,[3] and let's make honors!

FRANK. If you make honors, one thing let me crave:
Honor the king and queen, except the knave.

WEN. Well, as you please for that.—Lift,[4] who shall deal?

ANNE. The least in sight. What are you, Master Wendoll?

WEN. I am a knave.

NICK. [*Aside*] I'll swear it.

ANNE. I am queen.

FRANK. [*Aside*] A quean, thou should'st say.—Well, the cards are mine:
They are the grossest pair that e'er I felt.

ANNE. Shuffle, I'll cut: would I had never dealt!

FRANK. I have lost my dealing.

WEN. Sir, the fault's in me;
This queen I have more than mine own, you see.
Give me the stock![5]

FRANK. My mind's not on my game.
Many a deal I've lost; the more's your shame.
You have served me a bad trick, Master Wendoll.

WEN. Sir, you must take your lot. To end this strife,
I know I have dealt better with your wife.

FRANK. Thou hast dealt falsely, then.

ANNE. What's trumps?

WEN. Hearts. Partner, I rub.[6]

---

1. A popular gambling game.
2. Be shut out.
3. A betting game.
4. Cut.
5. Deck.
6. Take all the cards of a suit.

FRANK. [*Aside*] Thou robb'st me of my soul, of her chaste love;
 In thy false dealing thou hast robbed my heart.
 Booty you play;[1] I like a loser stand,
 Having no heart or here, or in my hand.
 I will give o'er the set, I am not well.
 Come, who will hold my cards?
ANNE. Not well, sweet Master Frankford?
 Alas, what ails you? 'Tis some sudden qualm.
WEN. How long have you been so, Master Frankford?
FRANK. Sir, I was lusty, and I had my health,
 But I grew ill when you began to deal.—
 Take hence this table!—Gentle Master Cranwell,
 Y'are welcome; see your chamber at your pleasure!
 I am sorry that this megrim takes me so,
 I cannot sit and bear you company.
 Jenkin, some lights, and show him to his chamber!
ANNE. A nightgown[2] for my husband; quickly, there!
 It is some rheum or cold.
WEN. Now, in good faith,
 This illness you have got by sitting late
 Without your gown.
FRANK. I know it, Master Wendoll.
 Go, go to bed, lest you complain like me!—
 Wife, pr'ythee, wife, into my bed-chamber!
 The night is raw and cold, and rhéumatic.
 Leave me my gown and light; I'll walk away my fit.
WEN. Sweet sir, good night!
FRANK. Myself, good night!

           Exit Wendoll

ANNE. Shall I attend you, husband?
FRANK. No, gentle wife, thou'lt catch cold in thy head.
 Pr'ythee, begone, sweet; I'll make haste to bed.
ANNE. No sleep will fasten on mine eyes, you know,
 Until you come.
FRANK. Sweet Nan, I pr'ythee, go!—

---

1. You join in confederacy to plot against another player.
2. Robe.

Exit Anne

I have bethought me; get me by degrees
The keys of all my doors, which I will mould
In wax, and take their fair impression,
To have by them new keys. This being compassed,
At a set hour a letter shall be brought me,
And when they think they may securely play,
They nearest are to danger.—Nick, I must rely
Upon thy trust and faithful secrecy.
NICK. Build on my faith!
FRANK. To bed, then, not to rest!
Care lodges in my brain, grief in my breast.

Exeunt

SCENE III

Enter Sir Charles' Sister, Old Mountford, Sandy, Roder and Tidy

OLD MOUNT. You say my nephew is in great distress;
Who brought it to him, but his own lewd life?
I cannot spare a cross.[1] I must confess,
He was my brother's son; why, niece, what then?
This is no world in which to pity men.
SUSAN. I was not born a beggar, though his extremes
Enforce this language from me. I protest
No fortunes of mine own could lead my tongue
To this base key. I do beseech you, uncle,
For the name's sake, for Christianity,—
Nay, for God's sake, to pity his distress.
He is denied the freedom of the prison,
And in the hole is laid with men condemned;
Plenty he hath of nothing but of irons,
And it remains in you to free him thence.
OLD MOUNT. Money I cannot spare; men should take heed.
He lost my kindred when he fell to need.

Exit

---

1. Piece of money.

SUSAN. Gold is but earth; thou earth enough shalt have,
　　When thou hast once took measure of thy grave.
　　You know me, Master Sandy, and my suit.
SANDY. I knew you, lady, when the old man lived;
　　I knew you ere your brother sold his land.
　　Then you were Mistress Sue, tricked up in jewels;
　　Then you sang well, played sweetly on the lute;
　　But now I neither know you nor your suit.

Exit

SUSAN. You, Master Roder, was my brother's tenant;
　　Rent-free he placed you in that wealthy farm,
　　Of which you are possessed.
RODER. True, he did;
　　And have I not there dwelt still for his sake?
　　I have some business now; but, without doubt,
　　They that have hurled him in, will help him out.

Exit

SUSAN. Cold comfort still. What say you, cousin Tidy?
TIDY. I say this comes of roysting, swaggering.
　　Call me not cousin; each man for himself!
　　Some men are born to mirth, and some to sorrow:
　　I am no cousin unto them that borrow.

Exit

SUSAN. O Charity, why art thou fled to heaven,
　　And left all things [up]on this earth uneven?
　　Their scoffing answers I will ne'er return,
　　But to myself his grief in silence mourn.

Enter Sir Francis and Malby

SIR F. She is poor, I'll therefore tempt her with this gold.
　　Go, Malby, in my name deliver it,
　　And I will stay thy answer.
MAL. Fair mistress, as I understand your grief
　　Doth grow from want, so I have here in store
　　A means to furnish you, a bag of gold,
　　Which to your hands I freely tender you.
SUSAN. I thank you, heavens! I thank you, gentle sir:
　　God make me able to requite this favor!

MAL. This gold Sir Francis Acton sends by me,
  And prays you—

SUSAN. Acton? O God! That name I'm born to curse.
  Hence, bawd; hence, broker! See, I spurn his gold.
  My honor never shall for gain be sold.

SIR F. Stay, lady, stay!

SUSAN. From you I'll posting hie,
  Even as the doves from feathered eagles fly.

Exit

SIR F. She hates my name, my face; how should I woo?
  I am disgraced in every thing I do.
  The more she hates me, and disdains my love,
  The more I am rapt in admiration
  Of her divine and chaste perfections.
  Woo her with gifts I cannot, for all gifts
  Sent in my name she spurns; with looks I cannot,
  For she abhors my sight; nor yet with letters,
  For none she will receive. How then? how then?
  Well, I will fasten such a kindness on her,
  As shall o'ercome her hate and conquer it.
  Sir Charles, her brother, lies in execution
  For a great sum of money; and, besides,
  The appeal is sued still for my huntsmen's death,
  Which only I have power to reverse.
  In her I'll bury all my hate of him.—
  Go seek the Keeper, Malby, bring him to me!
  To save his body, I his debts will pay;
  To save his life, I his appeal will stay.

Exeunt

ACT IV, SCENE I

Enter Sir Charles [Mountford,] in prison, with irons, his feet bare,
his garments all ragged and torn

SIR C. Of all on the earth's face most miserable,
  Breathe in this hellish dungeon thy laments!
  Thus like a slave ragg'd, like a felon gyved,—[1]

1. Fettered.

That hurls thee headlong to this base estate.
O, unkind uncle! O, my friends ingrate!
Unthankful kinsmen! Mountford's all too base,
To let thy name be fettered in disgrace.
A thousand deaths here in this grave I die;
Fear, hunger, sorrow, cold, all threat my death,
And join together to deprive my breath.
But that which most torments me, my dear sister
Hath left to visit me, and from my friends
Hath brought no hopeful answer; therefore, I
Divine they will not help my misery.
If it be so, shame, scandal, and contempt
Attend their covetous thoughts; need make their graves!
Usurers they live, and may they die like slaves!

Enter Keeper

KEEP. Knight, be of comfort, for I bring thee freedom
   From all thy troubles.
SIR C. Then, I am doomed to die:
   Death is the end of all calamity.
KEEP. Live! Your appeal is stayed; the execution
   Of all your debts discharged; your creditors
   Even to the utmost penny satisfied.
   In sign whereof your shackles I knock off.
   You are not left so much indebted to us
   As for your fees; all is discharged; all paid.
   Go freely to your house, or where you please;
   After long miseries, embrace your ease.
SIR C. Thou grumblest out the sweetest music to me
   That ever organ played.—Is this a dream?
   Or do my waking senses apprehend
   The pleasing taste of these applausive news?
   Slave that I was, to wrong such honest friends,
   My loving kinsman, and my near allies!
   Tongue, I will bite thee for the scandal breath
   Against such faithful kinsmen; they are all
   Composed of pity and compassion,

Of melting charity and of moving ruth.
That which I spake before was in my rage;
They are my friends, the mirrors[1] of this age;
Bounteous and free. The noble Mountford's race
Ne'er bred a covetous thought, or humor base.

Enter Susan

SUSAN. I can no longer stay from visiting
 My woful brother. While I could, I kept
 My hapless tidings from his hopeful ear.
SIR C. Sister, how much am I indebted to thee
 And to thy travail!
SUSAN. What, at liberty?
SIR C. Thou seest I am, thanks to thy industry.
 O! Unto which of all my courteous friends
 Am I thus bound? My uncle Mountford, he
 Even of an infant loved me; was it he?
 So did my cousin Tidy; was it he?
 So Master Roder, Master Sandy, too.
 Which of all these did this high kindness do?
SUSAN. Charles, can you mock me in your poverty,
 Knowing your friends deride your misery?
 Now, I protest I stand so much amazed,
 To see your bonds free, and your irons knocked off,
 That I am rapt into a maze of wonder;
 The rather for I know not by what means
 This happiness hath chanced.
SIR C. Why, by my uncle,
 My cousins and my friends; who else, I pray,
 Would take upon them all my debts to pay?
SUSAN. O, brother! they are men [made] all of flint,
 Pictures of marble, and as void of pity
 As chasèd bears. I begged, I sued, I kneeled,
 Laid open all your griefs and miseries,

1. Models.

Which they derided; more than that, denied us
A part in their alliance; but, in pride
Said that our kindred with our plenty died.

SIR C. Drudges too much![1] What! did they? O, known evil!
Rich fly the poor, as good men shun the devil.
Whence should my freedom come? Of whom alive,
Saving of those, have I deserved so well?
Guess, sister, call to mind, remember me!
These I have raised, they follow the world's guise,
Whom rich in honor, they in woe despise.

SUSAN. My wits have lost themselves; let's ask the keeper!

SIR C. Gaoler!

KEEP. At hand, sir.

SIR C. Of courtesy resolve me one demand!
What was he took the burden of my debts
From off my back, stayed my appeal to death,
Discharged my fees, and brought me liberty?

KEEP. A courteous knight, and called Sir Francis Acton.

SIR C. Ha! Acton! O, me! More distressed in this
Than all my troubles! Hale me back,
Double my irons, and my sparing meals
Put into halves, and lodge me in a dungeon
More deep, more dark, more cold, more comfortless!
By Acton freed! Not all thy manacles
Could fetter so my heels, as this one word
Hath thralled my heart; and it must now lie bound
In more strict prison than thy stony gaol.
I am not free, I go but under bail.

KEEP. My charge is done, sir, now I have my fees;
As we get little, we will nothing leese.[2]

SIR C. By Acton freed, my dangerous opposite![3]
Why, to what end, on what occasion? Ha!
Let me forget the name of enemy,

---

1. Too base in their conduct.
2. Lose.
3. Enemy.

And with indifference balance this high favor!
Ha!

SUSAN. [*Aside*] His love to me, upon my soul, 'tis so!
That is the root from whence these strange things grow.

SIR C. Had this proceeded from my father, he
That by the law of nature is most bound
In offices of love, it had deserved
My best employment to requite that grace.
Had it proceeded from my friends or his,
From them this action had deserved my life,
And from a stranger more, because from such
There is less execution[1] of good deeds.
But he, nor father, nor ally, nor friend,
More than a stranger, both remote in blood,
And in his heart opposed my enemy,
That this high bounty should proceed from him!
O! there I lose myself. What should I say,
What think, what do, his bounty to repay?

SUSAN. You wonder, I am sure, whence this strange kindness
Proceeds in Acton; I will tell you, brother.
He dotes on me, and oft hath sent me gifts,
Letters, and tokens; I refused them all.

SIR C. I have enough, though poor: my heart is set,
In one rich gift to pay back all my debt.

Exeunt

SCENE II

Enter Frankford and Nick with keys, and a letter in his hand

FRANK. This is the night that I must play my part,
To try two seeming angels.—Where's my keys?

NICK. They are made, according to your mould, in wax.
I bade the smith be secret, gave him money
And here they are. The letter, sir!

---

1. The stranger will do such deeds less often.

FRANK. True, take it, there it is;
   And when thou seest me in my pleasant'st vein,
   Ready to sit to supper, bring it me!
NICK. I'll do't; make no more question, but I'll do't!

Exit

Enter Mistress Frankford, Cranwell, Wendoll, and Jenkin

ANNE. Sirrah, 'tis six o'clock already struck;
   Go bid them spread the cloth, and serve in supper!
JEN. It shall be done, forsooth, mistress. Where's
   Spigot, the butler, to give us our salt and trenchers?

Exit

WEN. We that have been hunting all the day
   Come with preparèd stomachs.—Master Frankford,
   We wish'd you at our sport.
FRANK. My heart was with you, and my mind was on you.—
   Fie, Master Cranwell! You are still thus sad.—
   A stool, a stool! Where's Jenkin, and where's Nick?
   'Tis supper time at least an hour ago.
   What's the best news abroad?
WEN. I know none good.
FRANK. [*Aside*] But I know too much bad.

*Enter Butler and Jenkin, with a tablecloth, bread, trenchers, and salt;
[then exeunt]*

CRAN. Methinks, sir, you might have that interest
   In your wife's brother, to be more remiss
   In his hard dealing against poor Sir Charles,
   Who, as I hear, lies in York Castle, needy
   And in great want.
FRANK. Did not more weighty business of mine own
   Hold me away, I would have labored peace
   Betwixt them with all care; indeed I would, sir.
ANNE. I'll write unto my brother earnestly
   In that behalf.
WEN. A charitable deed,
   And will beget the good opinion
   Of all your friends that love you, Mistress Frankford.

FRANK. That's you, for one; I know you love Sir Charles—
  [*Aside*] And my wife too, well.
WEN. He deserves the love
  Of all true gentlemen; be yourselves judge!
FRANK. But supper, ho!—Now, as thou lov'st me, Wendoll,
  Which I am sure thou dost, be merry, pleasant,
  And frolic it to-night!—Sweet Mr. Cranwell,
  Do you the like!—Wife, I protest, my heart
  Was ne'er more bent on sweet alacrity.[1]
  Where be those lazy knaves to serve in supper?

Enter Nick

NICK. Here's a letter, sir.
FRANK. Whence comes it, and who brought it?
NICK. A stripling that below attends your answer,
  And, as he tells me, it is sent from York.
FRANK. Have him into the cellar, let him taste
  A cup of our March beer; go, make him drink!
NICK. I'll make him drunk, if he be a Trojan.
FRANK. [*After reading the letter*] My boots and spurs!
  Where's Jenkin? God forgive me,
  How I neglect my business!—Wife, look here!
  I have a matter to be tried to-morrow
  By eight o'clock; and my attorney writes me,
  I must be there betimes with evidence,
  Or it will go against me. Where's my boots?

Enter Jenkin, with boots and spurs

ANNE. I hope your business craves no such despatch,
  That you must ride to-night?
WEN. [*Aside*] I hope it doth.
FRANK. God's me! No such despatch?
  Jenkin, my boots! Where's Nick? Saddle my roan,
  And the grey dapple for himself!—Content me,
  It much concerns me.—Gentle Master Cranwell,

1. Liveliness.

And Master Wendoll, in my absence use
The very ripest pleasures of my house!

WEN. Lord! Master Frankford, will you ride to-night?
The ways are dangerous.

FRANK. Therefore will I ride
Appointed[1] well; and so shall Nick, my man.

ANNE. I'll call you up by five o'clock to-morrow.

FRANK. No, by my faith, wife, I'll not trust to that:
'Tis not such easy rising in a morning
From one I love so dearly. No, by my faith,
I shall not leave so sweet a bedfellow,
But with much pain. You have made me a sluggard
Since I first knew you.

ANNE. Then, if you needs will go
This dangerous evening, Master Wendoll,
Let me entreat you bear him company.

WEN. With all my heart, sweet mistress.—My boots, there!

FRANK. Fie, fie, that for my private business
I should disease[2] my friend, and be a trouble
To the whole house!—Nick!

NICK. Anon, sir!

Exit

FRANK. Bring forth my gelding!—As you love me, sir,
Use no more words: a hand, good Master Cranwell!

CRAN. Sir, God be your speed!

FRANK. Good night, sweet Nan; nay, nay, a kiss, and part!
[*Aside*] Dissembling lips, you suit not with my heart.

Exeunt Frankford and Nicholas

WEN. [*Aside*] How business, time, and hours, all gracious prove,
And are the furtherers to my new born love!
I am husband now in Master Frankford's place,
And must command the house.—My pleasure is
We will not sup abroad so publicly,
But in your private chamber, Mistress Frankford.

1. Armed.
2. Discomfort.

ANNE. [*Aside*] O, sir! you are too public in your love,
   And Master Frankford's wife—
CRAN. Might I crave favor,
   I would entreat you I might see my chamber.
   I am on the sudden grown exceeding ill,
   And would be spared from supper.
WEN. Light there, ho!—
   See you want nothing, sir, for if you do,
   You injure that good man, and wrong me too.
CRAN. I will make bold; good night!

Exit

WEN. How all conspire
   To make our bosom[1] sweet, and full entire!
   Come, Nan, I pr'ythee, let us sup within!
ANNE. O! what a clog unto the soul is sin!
   We pale offenders are still full of fear;
   Every suspicious eye brings danger near;
   When they, whose clear heart from offence are free,
   Despite report, base scandals do outface,
   And stand at mere defiance with disgrace.
WEN. Fie, fie! You talk too like a puritan.
ANNE. You have tempted me to mischief, M[aster] Wendoll:
   I have done I know not what. Well, you plead custom;
   That which for want of wit I granted erst,
   I now must yield through fear. Come, come, let's in;
   Once o'er shoes, we are straight o'er head in sin.
WEN. My jocund soul is joyful above measure;
   I'll be profuse in Frankford's richest treasure.

Exeunt

SCENE III

Enter Cicely, Jenkin, and Butler

JEN. My mistress and Master Wendoll, my master, sup in her chamber
   to-night. Cicely, you are preferred, from being the cook, to be

---

1. Intimacy.

chambermaid. Of all the loves betwixt thee and me, tell me what thou think'st of this?

CIC. Mum; there's an old proverb,—when the cat's away, the mouse may play.

JEN. Now you talk of a cat, Cicely, I smell a rat.

CIC. Good words, Jenkin, lest you be called to answer them!

JEN. Why, God make my mistress an honest woman! Are not these good words? Pray God my new master play not the knave with my old master! Is there any hurt in this? God send no villainy intended; and if they do sup together, pray God they do not lie together! God make my mistress chaste, and make us all his servants! What harm is there in all this? Nay, more; here is my hand, thou shalt never have my heart, unless thou say, amen.

CIC. Amen; I pray God, I say.

Enter Serving-man

SERVING-MAN. My mistress sends that you should make less noise, lock up the doors, and see the household all got to bed. You, Jenkin, for this night are made the porter, to see the gates shut in.

JEN. Thus by little and little I creep into office. Come, to kennel, my masters, to kennel; 'tis eleven o'clock already.

SERVING-MAN. When you have locked the gates in, you must send up the keys to my mistress.

CIC. Quickly, for God's sake, Jenkin; for I must carry them. I am neither pillow nor bolster, but I know more than both.

JEN. To bed, good Spigot; to bed, good honest serving-creatures; and let us sleep as snug as pigs in pease-straw!

Exeunt

SCENE IV

Enter Frankford and Nicholas

FRANK. Soft, soft! We've tied our geldings to a tree,
Two flight-shot[1] off, lest by their thundering hoofs
They blab our coming. Hear'st thou no noise?

NICK. I hear nothing but the owl and you.

---

1. Bow-shot.

FRANK. So; now my watch's hand points upon twelve,
    And it is just midnight. Where are my keys?
NICK. Here, sir.
FRANK. This is the key that opes my outward gate;
    This, the hall-door; this, the withdrawing-chamber;
    But this, that door that's bawd unto my shame,
    Fountain and spring of all my bleeding thoughts,
    Where the most hallowed order and true knot
    Of nuptial sanctity hath been profaned.
    It leads to my polluted bed-chamber,
    Once my terrestrial heaven, now my earth's hell,
    The place where sins in all their ripeness dwell.—
    But I forget myself; now to my gate!
NICK. I must ope with far less noise than Cripplegate, or your plot's
    dashed.
FRANK. So; reach me my dark lantern to the rest!
    Tread softly, softly!
NICK. I will walk on eggs this pace.
FRANK. A general silence hath surprised the house,
    And this is the last door. Astonishment,
    Fear, and amazement, beat upon my heart,
    Even as a madman beats upon a drum.
    O, keep my eyes, you heavens, before I enter,
    From any sight that may transfix my soul;
    Or, if there be so black a spectacle,
    O, strike mine eyes stark blind, or if not so,
    Lend me such patience to digest my grief,
    That I may keep this white and virgin hand
    From any violent outrage, or red murder!—
    And with that prayer I enter.

Exeunt

SCENE V

Enter Nicholas

NICK. Here's a circumstance!
    A man may be made a cuckold in the time
    That he's about it. An the case were mine,

As 'tis my master's ('sblood! that he makes me swear!),
I would have placed his action,[1] entered there;
I would, I would!

Enter Frankford

FRANK. O! O!

NICK. Master! 'Sblood! Master, master!

FRANK. O me unhappy! I have found them lying
　　Close in each other's arms, and fast asleep.
　　But that I would not damn two precious souls,
　　Bought with my Saviour's blood, and send them, laden
　　With all their scarlet sins upon their backs,
　　Unto a fearful judgment, their two lives
　　Had met upon my rapier.

NICK. Master, what, have ye left them sleeping still?
　　Let me go wake 'em!

FRANK. Stay, let me pause awhile!—
　　O God! O God! That it were possible
　　To undo things done; to call back yesterday;
　　That Time could turn up his swift sandy glass,
　　To untell the days, and to redeem these hours!
　　Or that the sun
　　Could, rising from the west, draw his coach backward;
　　Take from th' account of time so many minutes,
　　Till he had all these seasons called[2] again,
　　Those minutes, and those actions done in them,
　　Even from her first offence; that I might take her
　　As spotless as an angel in my arms!
　　But, O! I talk of things impossible,
　　And cast beyond the moon. God give me patience;
　　For I will in, and wake them.

　　　　　　　　　　　　　　　　　　　　　　　　　　Exit

NICK. Here's patience perforce!
　　He needs must trot afoot that tires his horse.

1. Made his move.
2. Called back.

Enter Wendoll, running over the stage in a nightgown, [*Frankford*] *after him with a sword drawn; the maid in her smock stays his hand, and clasps hold on him. He pauses for awhile*

FRANK. I thank thee, maid; thou, like an angel's hand,
   Hast stayed me from a bloody sacrifice.[1]

                                                Exit Maid

   Go, villain; and my wrongs sit on thy soul
   As heavy as this grief doth upon mine!
   When thou record'st my many courtesies,
   And shalt compare them with thy treacherous heart,
   Lay them together, weigh them equally,—
   'Twill be revenge enough. Go, to thy friend
   A Judas; pray, pray, lest I live to see
   Thee, Judas-like, hang'd on an elder-tree!

Enter Mistress Frankford in her smock, nightgown, and night-attire

ANNE. O, by what word, what title, or what name,
   Shall I entreat your pardon? Pardon! O!
   I am as far from hoping such sweet grace,
   As Lucifer from heaven. To call you husband,—
   (O me, most wretched!) I have lost that name;
   I am no more your wife.
NICK. 'Sblood, sir, she swoons.
FRANK. Spare thou thy tears, for I will weep for thee;
   And keep thy countenance, for I'll blush for thee.
   Now, I protest, I think 'tis I am tainted,
   For I am most ashamed; and 'tis more hard
   For me to look upon thy guilty face
   Than on the sun's clear brow. What! Would'st thou speak?
ANNE. I would I had no tongue, no ears, no eyes,
   No apprehension, no capacity.
   When do you spurn me like a dog? When tread me
   Under feet? When drag me by the hair?
   Though I deserve a thousand, thousand-fold,

1. *Gen.* xxii, 10, 11.

More than you can inflict—yet, once my husband.
For womanhood, to which I am a shame,
Though once an ornament—even for his sake,
That hath redeemed our souls, mark not my face,
Nor hack me with your sword; but let me go
Perfect and undeformèd to my tomb!
I am not worthy that I should prevail
In the least suit; no, not to speak to you,
Nor look on you, nor to be in your presence;
Yet, as an abject, this one suit I crave;—
This granted, I am ready for my grave.

FRANK. My God, with patience arm me!—Rise, nay, rise.
And I'll debate with thee. Was it for want
Thou play'dst the strumpet? Wast thou not supplied
With every pleasure, fashion, and new toy,—
Nay, even beyond my calling?

ANNE. I was.

FRANK. Was it, then, disability in me;
Or in thine eye seemed he a properer man?

ANNE. O, no!

FRANK. Did not I lodge thee in my bosom?
Wear thee here in my heart?

ANNE. You did.

FRANK. I did, indeed; witness my tears, I did.—
Go, bring my infants hither!

Enter Serving-woman with two little children

O Nan! O Nan!
If neither fear of shame, regard of honor,
The blemish of my house, nor my dear love,
Could have withheld thee from so lewd a fact:[1]
Yet for these infants, these young, harmless souls
On whose white brows thy shame is charactered,
And grows in greatness as they wax in years,—
Look but on them, and melt away in tears!—
Away with them; lest, as her spotted body

1. Act.

Hath stained their names with stripe of bastardy,
So her adulterous breath may blast their spirits
With her infectious thoughts! Away with them!

Exit Serving-woman with children

ANNE. In this one life, I die ten thousand deaths.
FRANK. Stand up, stand up! I will do nothing rashly.
I will retire awhile into my study,
And thou shalt hear thy sentence presently.

Exit

ANNE. 'Tis welcome, be it death. O me, base strumpet,
That, having such a husband, such sweet children,
Must enjoy neither! O, to redeem mine honor,
I would have this hand cut off, these my breasts seared;
Be racked, strappadoed, put to any torment:
Nay, to whip but this scandal out, I would hazard
The rich and dear redemption of my soul!
He cannot be so base as to forgive me,
Nor I so shameless to accept his pardon.
O women, women, you that yet have kept
Your holy matrimonial vow unstained,
Make me your instance; when you tread awry,
Your sins, like mine, will on your conscience lie.

Enter Cicely, Spigot, all the Serving-men, and Jenkin,
as newly come out of bed

ALL. O, mistress, mistress! What have you done, mistress?
NICK. What a caterwauling keep you here!
JEN. O Lord, mistress, how comes this to pass? My master is run away
in his shirt, and never so much as called me to bring his clothes after
him.
ANNE. See what guilt is! Here stand I in this place,
Ashamed to look my servants in the face.

Enter Frankford and Cranwell; whom seeing, she falls
on her knees

FRANK. My words are registered in heaven already.
With patience hear me! I'll not martyr thee,
Nor mark thee for a strumpet; but with usage

Of more humility torment thy soul,
And kill thee even with kindness.

CRAN. Master Frankford—

FRANK. Good Master Cranwell!—Woman, hear thy judgment!
Go make thee ready in thy best attire;
Take with thee all thy gowns, all thy apparel;
Leave nothing that did ever call thee mistress,
Or by whose sight, being left here in the house,
I may remember such a woman by.
Choose thee a bed and hangings for thy chamber;
Take with thee every thing which hath thy mark,
And get thee to my manor seven mile off,
Where live; 'tis thine, I freely give it thee.
My tenants by shall furnish thee with wains
To carry all thy stuff within two hours;
No longer will I limit[1] thee my sight.
Choose which of all my servants thou lik'st best,
And they are thine to attend thee.

ANNE. A mild sentence.

FRANK. But, as thou hop'st for heaven, as thou believ'st
Thy name's recorded in the book of life,
I charge thee never after this sad day
To see me, or to meet me, or to send,
By word or writing, gift or otherwise,
To move me, by thyself, or by thy friends;
Nor challenge any part in my two children.
So farewell, Nan; for we will henceforth be
As we had never seen, ne'er more shall see.

ANNE. How full my heart is, in mine eyes appears;
What wants in words, I will supply in tears.

FRANK. Come, take your coach, your stuff; all must along.
Servants and all make ready; all begone!
It was thy hand cut two hearts out of one.

Exeunt

---

1. Allow.

ACT V, SCENE I

Enter Sir Charles [Mountford,] gentleman-like and his Sister,
gentlewoman-like

SUSAN. Brother, why have you tricked me like a bride,
    Bought me this gay attire, these ornaments?
    Forget you our estate, our poverty?
SIR C. Call me not brother, but imagine me
    Some barbarous outlaw, or uncivil kern;[1]
    For if thou shutt'st thy eye, and only hear'st
    The words that I shall utter, thou shalt judge me
    Some staring ruffian, not thy brother Charles,
    O, sister!—
SUSAN. O, brother! what doth this strange language mean?
SIR C. Dost love me, sister? Wouldst thou see me live
    A bankrupt beggar in the world's disgrace,
    And die indebted to mine enemies?
    Wouldst thou behold me stand like a huge beam
    In the world's eye, a bye-word and a scorn?
    It lies in thee of these to acquit me free,
    And all my debt I may outstrip by thee.
SUSAN. By me? Why, I have nothing, nothing left;
    I owe even for the clothes upon my back;
    I am not worth—
SIR C. O sister, say not so!
    It lies in you my downcast state to raise;
    To make me stand on even points with the world.
    Come, sister, you are rich; indeed you are,
    And in your power you have, without delay
    Acton's five hundred pound back to repay.
SUSAN. Till now I had thought y' had loved me. By my honor
    (Which I have kept as spotless as the moon),
    I ne'er was mistress of that single doit[2]
    Which I reserved not to supply your wants;
    And d'ye think that I would hoard from you?

1. Rough Irish soldier.
2. Farthing

Now, by my hopes in heaven, knew I the means
To buy you from the slavery of your debts
(Especially from Acton, whom I hate),
I would redeem it with my life or blood!

SIR C. I challenge it, and, kindred set apart,
Thus, ruffian-like, I lay siege to thy heart.
What do I owe to Acton?

SUSAN. Why, some five hundred pounds towards which, I swear,
In all the world I have not one denier.[1]

SIR C. It will not prove so. Sister, now resolve me:
What do you think (and speak your conscience)
Would Acton give, might he enjoy your bed?

SUSAN. He would not shrink to spend a thousand pound,
To give the Mountfords' name so deep a wound.

SIR C. A thousand pound! I but five hundred owe:
Grant him your bed, he's paid with interest so.

SUSAN. O, brother!

SIR C. O, sister! only this one way,
With that rich jewel you my debts may pay.
In speaking this my cold heart shakes with shame;
Nor do I woo you in a brother's name,
But in a stranger's. Shall I die in debt
To Acton, my grand foe, and you still wear
The precious jewel that he holds so dear?

SUSAN. My honor I esteem as dear and precious
As my redemption.

SIR C. I esteem you, sister.
As dear, for so dear prizing it.

SUSAN. Will Charles
Have me cut off my hands, and send them to Acton?
Rip up my breast, and with my bleeding heart
Present him as a token?

SIR C. Neither, sister;
But hear me in my strange assertion!
Thy honor and my soul are equal in my regard;
Nor will thy brother Charles survive thy shame.

---

1. Penny.

His kindness, like a burden, hath surcharged me,
And under his good deeds I stooping go,
Not with an upright soul. Had I remained
In prison still, there doubtless I had died.
Then, unto him that freed me from that prison,
Still do I owe this life. What moved my foe
To enfranchise me? 'Twas, sister, for your love;
And shall he not enjoy it? Shall the weight
Of all this heavy burden lean on me,
And will not you bear part? You did partake
The joy of my release; will you not stand
In joint-bond bound to satisfy the debt?
Shall I be only charged?

SUSAN.   But that I know
These arguments come from an honored mind,
As in your most extremity of need
Scorning to stand in debt to one you hate,—
Nay, rather would engage your unstained honor,
Than to be held ingrate,—I should condemn you.
I see your resolution, and assent;
So Charles will have me, and I am content.

SIR C.   For this I tricked you up.

SUSAN.   But here's a knife,
To save mine honor, shall slice out my life.

SIR C.   I know thou pleasest me a thousand times
More in thy resolution than thy grant.
Observe her love; to soothe it to my suit,
Her honor she will hazard, though not lose;
To bring me out of debt, her rigorous hand
Will pierce her heart,—O wonder!—that will choose,
Rather than stain her blood, her life to lose.
Come, you sad sister to a woful brother,
This is the gate. I'll bear him such a present,
Such an acquittance for the knight to seal,
As will amaze his senses, and surprise
With admiration all his fantasies.

Enter [Sir Francis] Acton and Malby

SUSAN. Before his unchaste thoughts shall seize on me,
  'Tis here shall my imprisoned soul set free.
SIR F. How! Mountford with his sister, hand in hand!
  What miracle's afoot?
MAL. It is a sight
  Begets in me much admiration.
SIR C. Stand not amazed to see me thus attended!
  Acton, I owe thee money, and, being unable
  To bring thee the full sum in ready coin,
  Lo! for thy more assurance, here's a pawn,—
  My sister, my dear sister, whose chaste honor
  I prize above a million. Here! Nay, take her;
  She's worth your money, man; do not forsake her.
SIR F. I would he were in earnest!
SUSAN. Impute it not to my immodesty.
  My brother, being rich in nothing else
  But in his interest that he hath in me,
  According to his poverty hath brought you
  Me, all his store; whom, howsoe'er you prize,
  As forfeit to your hand, he values highly,
  And would not sell, but to acquit your debt,
  For any emperor's ransom.
SIR F. [*Aside*] Stern heart, relent,
  Thy former cruelty at length repent!
  Was ever known, in any former age,
  Such honorable, wrested[1] courtesy?
  Lands, honors, life, and all the world forego,
  Rather than stand engaged to such a foe!
SIR C. Acton, she is too poor to be thy bride,
  And I too much opposed to be thy brother.
  There, take her to thee; if thou hast the heart
  To seize her as a rape, or lustful prey;
  To blur our house, that never yet was stained;
  To murder her that never meant thee harm;
  To kill me now, whom once thou sav'dst from death:—

---

1. Enforced.

Do them at once; on her all these rely,
And perish with her spotless chastity.

SIR F. You overcome me in your love, Sir Charles.
I cannot be so cruel to a lady
I love so dearly. Since you have not spared
To engage your reputation to the world,
Your sister's honor, which you prize so dear,
Nay, all the comfort which you hold on earth,
To grow out of my debt, being your foe,—
Your honored thoughts, lo! thus I recompense.
Your metamorphosed foe receives your gift
In satisfaction of all former wrongs.
This jewel I will wear here in my heart;
And where before I thought her, for her wants,
Too base to be my bride, to end all strife,
I seal you my dear brother, her my wife.

SUSAN. You still exceed us. I will yield to fate,
And learn to love, where I till now did hate.

SIR C. With that enchantment you have charmed my soul,
And made me rich even in those very words!
I pay no debt, but am indebted more;
Rich in your love, I never can be poor.

SIR F. All's mine is yours; we are alike in state;
Let's knit in love what was opposed in hate!
Come, for our nuptials we will straight provide,
Blest only in our brother and fair bride.

Exeunt

SCENE II

Enter Cranwell, Frankford, and Nick

CRAN. Why do you search each room about your house,
Now that you have despatched your wife away?

FRANK. O, sir! To see that nothing may be left
That ever was my wife's. I loved her dearly;
And when I do but think of her unkindness,
My thoughts are all in hell; to avoid which torment,
I would not have a bodkin or a cuff,

    A bracelet, necklace, or rebato wire,[1]
    Nor any thing that ever was called hers,
    Left me, by which I might remember her.—
    See round about.
NICK. 'Sblood! master, here's her lute flung in a corner.
FRANK. Her lute! O, God! Upon this instrument
    Her fingers have ran quick division,[2]
    Sweeter than that which now divides our hearts.
    These frets have made me pleasant, that have now
    Frets of my heart-strings made. O, Master Cranwell,
    Oft hath she made this melancholy wood
    (Now mute and dumb for her disastrous chance)
    Speak sweetly many a note, sound many a strain
    To her own ravishing voice; which being well strung,
    What pleasant strange airs have they jointly rung!—
    Post with it after her!—Now nothing's left;
    Of her and hers I am at once bereft.
NICK. I'll ride and overtake her; do my message,
    And come back again.

                                       Exit

CRAN. Meantime, sir, if you please,
    I'll to Sir Francis Acton, and inform him
    Of what hath passed betwixt you and his sister.
FRANK. Do as you please.—How ill am I bested,[3]
    To be a widower ere my wife be dead!

                                   Exeunt

SCENE III

*Enter Mistress Frankford, with Jenkin, her maid Cicely,
her Coachman, and three Carters*

ANNE. Bid my coach stay! Why should I ride in state,
    Being hurled so low down by the hand of fate?

---

1. To sustain the ruff.
2. Variation.
3. Placed.

A seat like to my fortunes let me have,
Earth for my chair, and for my bed a grave!

JEN. Comfort, good mistress; you have watered your coach with tears already. You have but two miles now to go to your manor. A man cannot say by my old master Frankford as he may say by me, that he wants manors; for he hath three or four, of which this is one that we are going to now.

CIC. Good mistress, be of good cheer! Sorrow, you see, hurts you, but helps you not; we all mourn to see you so sad.

CARTER. Mistress, I see some of my landlord's men
Come riding post: 'tis like be brings some news.

ANNE. Comes he from Master Frankford, he is welcome;
So is his news, because they come from him.

Enter Nicholas

NICK. There!

ANNE. I know the lute. Oft have I sung to thee;
We both are out of tune, both out of time.

NICK. Would that had been the worst instrument that e'er you played on! My master commends him unto ye; there's all he can find was ever yours; he hath nothing left that ever you could lay claim to but his own heart,—and he could afford you that! All that I have to deliver you is this: he prays you to forget him; and so he bids you farewell.

ANNE. I thank him; he is kind, and ever was.
All you that have true feeling of my grief,
That know my loss, and have relenting hearts,
Gird me about, and help me with your tears
To wash my spotted sins! My lute shall groan;
It cannot weep, but shall lament my moan.

Enter Wendoll [behind][1]

WEN. Pursued with horror of a guilty soul,
And with the sharp scourge of repentance lashed,
I fly from mine own shadow. O my stars!

---

1. Wendoll remains unseen during most of this scene.

What have my parents in their lives deserved,
That you should lay this penance on their son?
When I but think of Master Frankford's love,
And lay it to my treason, or compare
My murdering him for his relieving me,
It strikes a terror like a lightning's flash,
To scorch my blood up. Thus I, like the owl,
Ashamed of day, live in these shadowy woods,
Afraid of every leaf or murm'ring blast,
Yet longing to receive some perfect knowledge
How he hath dealt with her.

[Seeing Mistress Frankford]

O my sad fate!
Here, and so far from home, and thus attended!
O, God! I have divorced the truest turtles
That ever lived together, and being divided,
In several places make their several moan;
She in the fields laments, and he at home.
So poets write that Orpheus made the trees
And stones to dance to his melodious harp,
Meaning the rustic and the barbarous hinds,
That had no understanding part in them.
So she from these rude carters tears extracts,
Making their flinty hearts with grief to rise,
And draw down rivers from their rocky eyes.

ANNE. *[To Nicholas]* If you return unto your master, say
(Though not from me, for I am all unworthy
To blast his name so with a strumpet's tongue)
That you have seen me weep, wish myself dead!
Nay, you may say, too (for my vow is past),[1]
Last night you saw me eat and drink my last.
This to your master you may say and swear;
For it is writ in heaven, and decreèd here.

NICK. I'll say you wept; I'll swear you made me sad.
Why, how now, eyes? What now? What's here to do?
I'm gone, or I shall straight turn baby too.

---

1. Made.

WEN. I cannot weep, my heart is all on fire.
　Curs'd be the fruits of my unchaste desire!
ANNE. Go, break this lute upon my coach's wheel,
　As the last music that I e'er shall make,—
　Not as my husband's gift, but my farewell
　To all earth's joy; and so your master tell!
NICK. If I can for crying.
WEN. Grief, have done,
　Or, like a madman, I shall frantic run.
ANNE. You have beheld the wofull'st wretch on earth,—
　A woman made of tears; would you had words
　To express but what you see! My inward grief
　No tongue can utter; yet unto your power
　You may describe my sorrow, and disclose
　To thy sad master my abundant woes.
NICK. I'll do your commendations.
ANNE. O, no!
　I dare not so presume; nor to my children!
　I am disclaimed in both; alas! I am.
　O, never teach them, when they come to speak,
　To name the name of mother: chide their tongue,
　If they by chance light on that hated word;
　Tell them 'tis naught;[1] for when that word they name,
　Poor, pretty souls! they harp on their own shame.
WEN. To recompense her wrongs, what canst thou do?
　Thou hast made her husbandless, and childless too.
ANNE. I have no more to say.—Speak not for me;
　Yet you may tell your master what you see.
NICK. I'll do't.

Exit

WEN. I'll speak to her, and comfort her in grief.
　O, but her wound cannot be cured with words!
　No matter, though; I'll do my best good will
　To work a cure on her whom I did kill.
ANNE. So, now unto my coach, then to my home,
　So to my death-bed; for from this sad hour,

---

1. Wicked.

I never will nor eat, nor drink, nor taste
Of any cates[1] that may preserve my life.
I never will nor smile, nor sleep, nor rest;
But when my tears have washed my black soul white,
Sweet Saviour, to thy hands I yield my sprite.

WEN. [*Coming forward*] O, Mistress Frankford!

ANNE. O, for God's sake, fly!
The devil doth come to tempt me, ere I die.
My coach!—This sin, that with an angel's face
Conjured mine honor, till be sought my wrack,[2]
In my repentant eye seems ugly black.

    Exeunt all [except Wendoll and Jenkin;] the Carters whistling

JEN. What, my young master, that fled in his shirt! How come you by
your clothes again? You have made our house in a sweet pickle, ha'
ye not, think you? What, shall I serve you still, or cleave to the
house?

WEN. Hence, slave! Away, with thy unseasoned mirth!
Unless thou canst shed tears, and sigh, and howl,
Curse thy sad fortunes, and exclaim on fate,
Thou art not for my turn.

JEN. Marry, an you will not, another will! farewell, and be hanged!
Would you had never come to have kept this coil[3] within our doors!
We shall ha' you run away like a sprite again.

    Exit

WEN. She's gone to death; I live to want and woe,
Her life, her sins, and all upon my head.
And I must now go wander, like a Cain,
In foreign countries and remoted climes,
Where the report of my ingratitude
Cannot be heard. I'll over first to France,
And so to Germany and Italy;
Where, when I have recovered, and by travel
Gotten those perfect tongues, and that these rumors
May in their height abate, I will return:

1. Food.
2. Ruin.
3. Trouble.

And I divine (however now dejected),
My worth and parts being by some great man praised,
At my return I may in court be raised.

Exit

SCENE IV

Enter Sir Francis Acton, Sir Charles Mountford, Cranwell,
[Malby,] and Susan

SIR F. Brother, and now my wife, I think these troubles
 Fall on my head by justice of the heavens,
 For being so strict to you in your extremities;
 But we are now atoned.[1] I would my sister
 Could with like happiness o'ercome her griefs
 As we have ours.
SUSAN. You tell us, Master Cranwell, wondrous things
 Touching the patience of that gentleman,
 With what strange virtue he demeans his grief.
CRAN. I told you what I was witness of;
 It was my fortune to lodge there that night.
SIR F. O, that same villain, Wendoll! 'Twas his tongue
 That did corrupt her; she was of herself
 Chaste, and devoted well.—Is this the house?
CRAN. Yes, sir; I take it, here your sister lies.[2]
SIR F. My brother Frankford showed too mild a spirit
 In the revenge of such a loathèd crime.
 Less than he did, no man of spirit could do.
 I am so far from blaming his revenge,
 That I commend it. Had it been my case,
 Their souls at once had from their breasts been freed;
 Death to such deeds of shame is the due meed.

Enter Jenkin and Cicely

JEN. O, my mistress, mistress! my poor mistress!

1. Reconciled.
2. Lodges.

CIC. Alas! that ever I was born; what shall I do for my poor mistress?

SIR C. Why, what of her?

JEN. O, Lord, sir! she no sooner heard that her brother and her friends
were come to see how she did, but she, for very shame of her guilty
conscience, fell into such a swoon, that we had much ado to get life
in her.

SUSAN. Alas, that she should bear so hard a fate!
Pity it is repentance comes too late.

SIR F. Is she so weak in body?

JEN. O, sir! I can assure you there's no hope of life in her; for she will
take no sustenance: she hath plainly starved herself, and now she's
as lean as a lath. She ever looks for the good hour. Many gentlemen
and gentlewomen of the country are come to comfort her.

SCENE V

*Enter Sir Charles Mountford, Sir Francis Acton, Malby,
Cranwell, and Susan*

MAL. How fare you, Mistress Frankford?

ANNE. Sick, sick, O, sick! Give me some air. I pray you!
Tell me, O, tell me, where's Master Frankford?
Will not [he] deign to see me ere I die?

MAL. Yes, Mistress Frankford; divers gentlemen,
Your loving neighbors, with that just request
Have moved, and told him of your weak estate:
Who, though with much ado to get belief,
Examining of the general circumstance,
Seeing your sorrow and your penitence,
And hearing therewithal the great desire
You have to see him, ere you left the world,
He gave to us his faith to follow us,
And sure he will be here immediately.

ANNE. You have half revived me with the pleasing news.
Raise me a little higher in my bed.—
Blush I not, brother Acton? Blush I not, Sir Charles?
Can you not read my fault writ in my cheek?
Is not my crime there? Tell me, gentlemen.

SIR C. Alas, good mistress, sickness hath not left you
  Blood in your face enough to make you blush.
ANNE. Then, sickness, like a friend, my fault would hide.—
  Is my husband come? My soul but tarries his arrive;
  Then I am fit for heaven.
SIR F. I came to chide you, but my words of hate
  Are turned to pity and compassionate grief.
  I came to rate you, but my brawls,[1] you see,
  Melt into tears, and I must weep by thee.—
  Here's M[aster] Frankford now.

Enter Frankford

FRANK. Good morrow, brother; morrow, gentlemen!
  God, that hath laid this cross upon our heads,
  Might (had he pleased) have made our cause of meeting
  On a more fair and more contented ground;
  But he that made us, made us to this woe.
ANNE. And is he come? Methinks, that voice I know.
FRANK. How do you, woman?
ANNE. Well, Master Frankford, well; but shall be better,
  I hope, within this hour. Will you vouchsafe,
  Out of your grace and your humanity,
  To take a spotted strumpet by the hand?
FRANK. This hand once held my heart in faster bonds
  Than now 'tis gripped by me. God pardon them
  That made us first break hold!
ANNE. Amen, amen!
  Out of my zeal to heaven, whither I'm now bound,
  I was so impudent to wish you here;
  And once more beg your pardon. O, good man,
  And father to my children, pardon me.
  Pardon, O, pardon me: my fault so heinous is,
  That if you in this world forgive it not,
  Heaven will not clear it in the world to come.
  Faintness hath so usurped upon my knees,
  That kneel I cannot; but on my heart's knees

---

1. Reproaches.

My prostrate soul lies thrown down at your feet,
To beg your gracious pardon. Pardon, O, pardon me!

FRANK. As freely, from the low depth of my soul,
As my Redeemer hath forgiven his death,
I pardon thee. I will shed tears with thee;
Pray with thee; and, in mere pity of thy weak estate,
I'll wish to die with thee.

ALL. So do we all.

NICK. So will not I;
I'll sigh and sob, but, by my faith, not die.

SIR F. O, Master Frankford, all the near alliance
I lose by her, shall be supplied in thee.
You are my brother by the nearest way;
Her kindred hath fall'n off, but yours doth stay.

FRANK. Even as I hope for pardon, at that day
When the Great Judge of heaven in scarlet sits,
So be thou pardoned! Though thy rash offence
Divorced our bodies, thy repentant tears
Unite our souls.

SIR C. Then comfort, Mistress Frankford!
You see your husband hath forgiven your fall;
Then, rouse your spirits, and cheer your fainting soul!

SUSAN. How is it with you?

SIR F. How d'ye feel yourself?

ANNE. Not of this world.

FRANK. I see you are not, and I weep to see it.
My wife, the mother to my pretty babes!
Both those lost names I do restore thee back,
And with this kiss I wed thee once again.
Though thou art wounded in thy honored name,
And with that grief upon thy death-bed liest,
Honest in heart, upon my soul, thou diest.

ANNE. Pardoned on earth, soul, thou in heaven art free;
Once more: [*Kisses him*] thy wife dies thus embracing thee.

Dies

FRANK. New-married, and new-widowed.—O! she's dead,
And a cold grave must be her nuptial bed.

SIR C. Sir, be of good comfort, and your heavy sorrow

Part equally amongst us; storms divided
Abate their force, and with less rage are guided.

CRAN. Do, Master Frankford; he that hath least part,
Will find enough to drown one troubled heart.

SIR F. Peace with thee, Nan!—Brothers and gentlemen,
All we that can plead interest in her grief,
Bestow upon her body funeral tears!
Brother, had you with threats and usage bad
Punished her sin, the grief of her offence
Had not with such true sorrow touched her heart.

FRANK. I see it had not; therefore, on her grave
Will I bestow this funeral epitaph,
Which on her marble tomb shall be engraved.
In golden letters shall these words be filled:
Here lies she whom her husband's kindness killed.

EPILOGUE

An honest crew, disposèd to be merry,
    Came to a tavern by, and called for wine.
The drawer brought it, smiling like a cherry,
    And told them it was pleasant, neat and fine.
"Taste it," quoth one. He did so. "Fie!" (quoth he).
"This wine was good; now't runs too near the lee."

Another sipped, to give the wine his due,
    And said unto the rest, it drank too flat;
The third said, it was old; the fourth, too new;
    Nay, quoth the fifth, the sharpness likes me not.
Thus, gentlemen, you see how, in one hour,
The wine was new, old, flat, sharp, sweet, and sour.

Unto this wine we do allude our play,
    Which some will judge too trivial, some too grave:
You as our guests we entertain this day,
    And bid you welcome to the best we have.
Excuse us, then; good wine may be disgraced,
When every several mouth hath sundry taste.

VOLPONE,

OR

THE FOX

BEN JONSON

VOLPONE, OR THE FOX

To the most noble and most equal sisters,
The Two Famous Universities
for their love and acceptance shewn to his poem in
the presentation,
BEN JONSON
the grateful acknowledger,
DEDICATES BOTH IT AND HIMSELF.

Never, most equal Sisters, had any man a wit so presently excellent, as that it could raise itself; but there must come both matter, occasion, commenders, and favourers to it. If this be true, and that the fortune of all writers doth daily prove it, it behoves the careful to provide well towards these accidents; and, having acquired them, to preserve that part of reputation most tenderly, wherein the benefit of a friend is also defended. Hence is it, that I now render myself grateful, and am studious to justify the bounty of your act; to which, though your mere authority were satisfying, yet it being an age wherein poetry and the professors of it hear so ill on all sides, there will a reason be looked for in the subject. It is certain, nor can it with any forehead be opposed, that the too much license of poetasters in this time, hath much deformed their mistress; that, every day, their manifold and manifest ignorance doth stick unnatural reproaches upon her: but for their petulancy, it were an act of the greatest injustice, either to let the learned suffer, or so divine a skill (which indeed should not be attempted with unclean hands) to fall under the least contempt. For, if men will impartially, and not asquint, look toward the offices and function of a poet, they will easily conclude to themselves the impossibility of any man's being the good poet, without first being a good man. He that is said to be able to inform young men to all good disciplines, inflame grown men to all great virtues, keep old men in their best and supreme state, or, as they decline to childhood, recover them to their first strength; that comes forth the interpreter and arbiter of nature, a teacher of things divine no less than human, a master in manners; and can alone, or with a few, effect the business of mankind: this, I take him, is no subject for pride and ignorance to exercise their railing rhetoric upon. But it will here be hastily answered, that the writers of these days are other things; that not only their manners, but their natures, are inverted, and nothing remaining with them of the dignity of poet, but the abused name, which every scribe usurps; that now, especially in dramatic, or, as they term it, stage-poetry, nothing but ribaldry, profanation, blasphemy, all license of offence to God and man is practised. I dare not deny a great part of this, and am sorry I dare not, because in some men's abortive features (and would they had never boasted the light) it is over-true; but that all are embarked in this bold adventure for hell, is a most uncharitable thought, and, uttered, a more malicious slander. For my particular, I can, and from a most clear conscience, affirm, that I have ever trembled to think toward the least profaneness; have loathed the use of such foul and unwashed bawdry, as is now made the food of the scene: and, howsoever I cannot escape from some, the imputation of sharpness, but that they will say, I have taken a pride, or lust, to be bitter, and not my youngest infant but hath come into the world with all his teeth; I would ask of these supercilious politics, what nation, society, or general order or state, I have provoked? What public person? Whether I have not in all these preserved their dignity, as mine own person, safe? My works are read, allowed, (I speak of those that are intirely mine,) look into them, what broad reproofs have I used? where have I been particular? where personal? except to a mimic, cheater, bawd, or buffoon, creatures, for their insolencies, worthy to be taxed? yet to which of these so pointingly, as he might not either ingenuously have confest, or wisely dissembled his disease? But it is not rumour can make men guilty, much less entitle me to other men's crimes. I know, that nothing can be so innocently writ or carried, but may be made obnoxious to construction; marry, whilst I bear mine innocence about me, I fear it not. Application is now grown a trade with many; and there are that profess to have a key for the decyphering of every thing: but let wise and noble persons take heed how they be too credulous, or give leave to these invading interpreters to be overfamiliar with their fames, who cunningly, and often, utter their own virulent malice, under other men's simplest meanings. As for those that will (by faults which charity hath raked up, or common honesty concealed) make themselves a name with the multitude, or, to draw their rude and beastly claps, care not whose living faces they intrench with their petulant styles, may they do it without a rival, for me! I choose rather to live graved in obscurity, than share with them in so preposterous a fame. Nor can I blame the wishes of those severe and wise patriots, who providing the hurts these licentious spirits may do in a state, desire rather to see fools and devils, and those antique relics of barbarism retrieved, with all other ridiculous and exploded follies, than behold the wounds of private men, of princes and nations: for, as Horace makes Trebatius speak among these,

"Sibi quisque timet, quanquam est intactus, et odit."[1]

And men may justly impute such rages, if continued, to the writer, as his sports. The increase of which lust in liberty, together with the present trade of the stage, in all their miscelline interludes, what learned or liberal soul doth not already abhor? where nothing but the filth of the time is uttered, and with such impropriety of phrase, such plenty of solecisms, such dearth of sense, so bold prolepses, so racked metaphors, with brothelry, able to violate the ear of a pagan, and blasphemy, to turn the blood of a Christian to water. I cannot but be serious in a cause of this nature, wherein my fame, and the reputation of divers honest and learned are the question; when a name so full of authority, antiquity, and all great mark, is, through their insolence, become the lowest scorn of the age; and those men subject to the petulancy of every vernaculous orator, that were wont to be the care of kings and happiest monarchs. This it is that hath not only rapt me to present indignation, but made me studious heretofore, and by all my actions, to stand off from them; which may most appear in this my latest work, which you, most learned Arbitresses, have seen, judged, and to my crown, approved; wherein I have laboured for their instruction and amendment, to reduce not only the ancient forms, but manners of the scene, the easiness, the propriety, the innocence, and last, the doctrine, which is the principal end of poesie, to inform men in the best reason of living. And though my catastrophe may, in the strict rigour of comic law, meet with censure, as turning back to my promise; I desire the learned and charitable critic, to have so much faith in me, to think it was done of industry: for, with what ease I could have varied it nearer his scale (but that I fear to boast my own faculty) I could here insert. But my special aim being to put the snaffle in their mouths, that cry out, We never punish vice in our interludes, etc., I took the more liberty; though not without some lines of example, drawn even in the ancients themselves, the goings out of whose comedies are not always joyful, but oft times the bawds, the servants, the

---

1. Everyone fears for himself, even though untouched, and hates [you].

rivals, yea, and the masters are mulcted; and fitly, it being the office of a comic poet to imitate justice, and instruct to life, as well as purity of language, or stir up gentle affections; to which I shall take the occasion elsewhere to speak.

For the present, most reverenced Sisters, as I have cared to be thankful for your affections past, and here made the understanding acquainted with some ground of your favours; let me not despair their continuance, to the maturing of some worthier fruits; wherein, if my muses be true to me, I shall raise the despised head of poetry again, and stripping her out of those rotten and base rags wherewith the times have adulterated her form, restore her to her primitive habit, feature, and majesty, and render her worthy to be embraced and kist of all the great and master spirits of our world. As for the vile and slothful, who never affected an act worthy of celebration, or are so inward with their own vicious natures, as they worthily fear her, and think it an high point of policy to keep her in contempt, with their declamatory and windy invectives; she shall out of just rage incite her servants (who are *genus irritabile*[1]) to spout ink in their faces, that shall eat farther than their marrow into their fames; and not Cinnamus the barber, with his art, shall be able to take out the brands; but they shall live, and be read, till the wretches die, as things worst deserving of themselves in chief, and then of all mankind.

From my House in the Black-Friars,
this 11th day of February, 1607.

1. Irritable race (poets).

DRAMATIS PERSONAE

VOLPONE, *a Magnifico*
MOSCA, *his Parasite*
VOLTORE, *an Advocate*
CORBACCIO, *an old Gentleman*
CORVINO, *a Merchant*
BONARIO, *son to Corbaccio*
SIR POLITICK WOULD-BE, *a Knight*
PEREGRINE, *a Gentleman Traveller*
NANO, *a Dwarf*
CASTRONE, *an Eunuch*
ANDROGYNO, *an Hermaphrodite*

GREGE[1]

Commandadori, *Officers of Justice*
Mercatori, *three Merchants*
Avocatori, *four Magistrates*
Notario, *the Register*
LADY WOULD-BE, *Sir Politick's Wife*
CELIA, *Corvino's Wife*
Servitori, Servants, *two* Waiting-women, *etc.*

1. The crowd.

THE SCENE,—VENICE

THE ARGUMENT

*V*olpone, childless, rich, feigns sick, despairs,
*O*ffers his state to hopes of several heirs,
*L*ies languishing: his parasite receives
*P*resents of all, assures, deludes; then weaves
*O*ther cross plots, which ope themselves, are told.
*N*ew tricks for safety are sought; they thrive; when bold,
*E*ach tempts the other again, and all are sold.
Now, luck yet send us, and a little wit
    Will serve to make our play hit;
(According to the palates of the season)
    Here is rhime, not empty of reason.
This we were bid to credit from our poet,
    Whose true scope, if you would know it,
In all his poems still hath been this measure,
    To mix profit with your pleasure;
And not as some, whose throats their envy failing,
    Cry hoarsely, All he writes is railing:
And when his plays come forth, think they can flout them,
    With saying, he was a year about them.
To this there needs no lie, but this his creature,
    Which was two months since no feature;
And though he dares give them five lives to mend it,
    'Tis known, five weeks fully penned it,
From his own hand, without a co-adjutor,
    Novice, journey-man, or tutor.
Yet thus much I can give you as a token
    Of his play's worth, no eggs are broken,
Nor quaking custards with fierce teeth affrighted,
    Wherewith your rout are so delighted;

Nor hales he in a gull old ends reciting,
  To stop gaps in his loose writing;
With such a deal of monstrous and forced action,
  As might make Bethlem[1] a faction:
Nor made he his play for jests stolen from each table,
  But makes jests to fit his fable;
And so presents quick comedy refined,
  As best critics have designed;
The laws of time, place, persons he observeth,
  From no needful rule he swerveth.
All gall and copperas from his ink he draineth,
  Only a little salt remaineth,
Wherewith he'll rub your cheeks, till red, with laughter,
  They shall took fresh a week after.

1. Bedlam, hospital for the insane.

ACT I, SCENE I

Enter Volpone and Mosca

VOLP. Good morning to the day; and next, my gold!—
  Open the shrine, that I may see my saint.
    [*Mosca withdraws the curtain, and reveals piles of gold, plate,
                                              jewels, etc.*]
  Hail the world's soul, and mine! more glad than is
  The teeming earth to see the long'd-for sun
  Peep through the horns of the celestial Ram,
  Am I, to view thy splendour darkening his;
  That lying here, amongst my other hoards,
  Show'st like a flame by night, or like the day
  Struck out of chaos, when all darkness fled
  Unto the center.[1] O thou son of Sol,
  But brighter than thy father, let me kiss,
  With adoration, thee, and every relic
  Of sacred treasure in this blessed room.
  Well did wise poets, by thy glorious name,
  Title that age which they would have the best;
  Thou being the best of things, and far transcending
  All style of joy, in children, parents, friends,
  Or any other waking dream on earth:
  Thy looks when they to Venus did ascribe,
  They should have given her twenty thousand Cupids;
  Such are thy beauties and our loves! Dear saint,
  Riches, the dumb god, that giv'st all men tongues,
  Thou canst do nought, and yet mak'st men do all things;
  The price of souls; even hell, with thee to boot,
  Is made worth heaven. Thou art virtue, fame,

---

1. Of the earth (and so of the universe).

Honor, and all things else. Who can get thee,
He shall be noble valiant, honest, wise—
MOS. And what he will, sir. Riches are in fortune
A greater good than wisdom is in nature.
VOLP. True, my beloved Mosca. Yet I glory
More in the cunning purchase of my wealth,
Than in the glad possession, since I gain
No common way; I use no trade, no venture;
I wound no earth with plough-shares, fat no beasts,
To feed the shambles; have no mills for iron,
Oil, corn, or men, to grind them into powder:
I blow no subtle glass, expose no ships
To threat'nings of the furrow-facèd sea;
I turn no monies in the public bank,
Nor usure private.
MOS. No, sir, nor devour
Soft prodigals. You shall have some will swallow
A melting heir as glibly as your Dutch
Will pills of butter, and ne'er purge for it;
Tear forth the fathers of poor families
Out of their beds, and coffin them alive
In some kind clasping prison, where their bones
May be forth-coming, when the flesh is rotten:
But your sweet nature doth abhor these courses;
You loathe the widow's or the orphan's tears
Should wash your pavements, or their piteous cries
Ring in your roofs, and beat the air for vengeance.
VOLP. Right, Mosca; I do loathe it.
MOS. And besides, sir,
You are not like the thresher that doth stand
With a huge flail, watching a heap of corn,
And, hungry, dares not taste the smallest grain,
But feeds on mallows, and such bitter herbs;
Nor like the merchant, who hath fill'd his vaults
With Romagnia, and rich Candian wines,[1]

---

1. Greek wines.

Yet drinks the lees of Lombard's vinegar:[1]
You will lie not in straw, whilst moths and worms
Feed on your sumptuous hangings and soft beds;
You know the use of riches, and dare give now
From that bright heap, to me, your poor observer,
Or to your dwarf, or your hermaphrodite,
Your eunuch, or what other household trifle
Your pleasure allows maintenance—
VOLP. Hold thee, Mosca,

> [*Gives him money*]

Take of my hand; thou strik'st on truth in all,
And they are envious term thee parasite.
Call forth my dwarf, my eunuch, and my fool,
And let them make me sport. [*Exit Mosca*] What should I do,
But cocker up my genius, and live free
To all delights my fortune calls me to?
I have no wife, no parent, child, ally,
To give my substance to; but whom I make
Must be my heir: and this makes men observe me:
To give my substance to; but whom I make
Women and men of every sex and age,
That bring me presents, send me plate, coin, jewels,
With hope that when I die (which they expect
Each greedy minute) it shall then return
Ten-fold upon them; whilst some, covetous
Above the rest, seek to engross me whole,
And counter-work the one unto the other,
Contend in gifts, as they would seem in love:
All which I suffer, playing with their hopes,
And am content to coin them into profit,
And look upon their kindness, and take more,
And look on that; still bearing them in hand,
Letting the cherry knock against their lips,
And draw it by their mouths, and back again.—
How now!

> *Enter Mosca with Nano, Androgyno, and Castrone*

---

1. Italian wine.

NAN. Now, room for fresh gamesters, who do will you to know,
    They do bring you neither play nor university show;
And therefore do entreat you, that whatsoever they rehearse,
    May not fare a whit the worse, for the false pace of the verse.
If you wonder at this, you will wonder more ere we pass,
    For know, here is inclosed the soul of Pythagoras,
That juggler divine, as hereafter shall follow;
    Which soul, fast and loose, sir, came first from Apollo,
And was breath'd into Æthalides, Mercurius his son,
    Where it had the gift to remember all that ever was done.
From thence it fled forth, and made quick transmigration
    To goldly-locked Euphorbus, who was killed in good fashion,
At the siege of old Troy, by the cuckold of Sparta.[1]
    Hermotimus was next (I find it in my charta)
To whom it did pass, where no sooner it was missing
    But with one Pyrrhus of Delos it learn'd to go a fishing;
And thence did it enter the sophist of Greece.
    From Pythagore, she went into a beautiful piece,
Hight Aspasia, the meretrix; and the next toss of her
    Was again of a whore, she became a philosopher,
Crates the cynick, as it self doth relate it:
    Since kings, knights, and beggars, knaves, lords, and fools gat it,
Besides ox and ass, camel, mule, goat, and brock,[2]
    In all which it hath spoke, as in the cobbler's cock.
But I come not here to discourse of that matter,
    Or his one, two, or three, or his great oath, *By quater!*[3]
His musics, his trigon, his golden thigh,
    Or his telling how elements shift, but I
Would ask, how of late thou hast suffered translation
    And shifted thy coat in these days of reformation.
AND. Like one of the reformed, a fool, as you see,
    Counting all old doctrine heresie.
NAN. But not on thine own forbid meats hast thou ventured?
AND. On fish, when first a Carthusian I entered.
NAN. Why, then thy dogmatical silence hath left thee?

1. Menelaus.
2. Badger.
3. Equilateral triangle (trigon).

AND. Of that an obstreperous lawyer bereft me.

NAN. O wonderful change, when sir lawyer forsook thee!
    For Pythagore's sake, what body then took thee?

AND. A good dull mule.

NAN. And how! by that means
    Thou wert brought to allow of the eating of beans?

AND. Yes.

NAN. But from the mule into whom didst thou pass?

AND. Into a very strange beast, by some writers called an ass;
    By others, a precise,¹ pure, illuminate brother,
        Of those devour flesh, and sometimes one another;
    And will drop you forth a libel, or a sanctified lie,
        Betwixt every spoonful of a nativity-pie.

NAN. Now quit thee, for heaven, of that profane nation,
    And gently report thy next transmigration.

AND. To the same that I am.

NAN. A creature of delight,
        And, what is more than a fool, an hermaphrodite!
    Now, prithee, sweet soul, in all thy variation,
        Which body would'st thou choose, to keep up thy station?

AND. Troth, this I am in: even here would I tarry.

NAN. 'Cause here the delight of each sex thou canst vary?

AND. Alas, those pleasures be stale and forsaken;
        No, 'tis your fool wherewith I am so taken,
    The only one creature that I can call blessed;
        For all other forms I have proved most distressed.

NAN. Spoke true, as thou wert in Pythagoras still.
        This learned opinion we celebrate will,
    Fellow eunuch, as behoves us, with all our wit and art,
        To dignify that whereof ourselves are so great and special a part.

VOLP. Now, very pretty! Mosca, this
    Was thy invention?

MOS. If it please my patron,
    Not else.

VOLP. It doth, good Mosca.

MOS. Then it was, sir.

---

1. Puritan.

Nano and Castrone sing

Fools, they are the only nation
Worth men's envy or admiration:
Free from care or sorrow-taking,
Selves and others merry making:
All they speak or do is sterling.
Your fool he is your great man's darling,
And your ladies' sport and pleasure;
Tongue and bauble are his treasure.
E'en his face begetteth laughter,
And he speaks truth free from slaughter;
He's the grace of every feast,
And sometimes the chiefest guest;
Hath his trencher and his stool,
When wit waits upon the fool.
    O, who would not be
    He, he, he?

[One knocks without]

VOLP. Who's that? Away!

Exeunt Nano and Castrone

Look, Mosca. Fool, begone!

Exit Androgyno

MOS. 'Tis signior Voltore, the advocate;
   I know him by his knock.
VOLP. Fetch me my gown,
   My furs and night-caps; say, my couch is changing,
   And let him entertain himself awhile
   Without i' the gallery. *[Exit Mosca]* Now, now, my clients
   Begin their visitation! Vulture, kite,
   Raven, and gorcrow,[1] all my birds of prey,
   That think me turning carcase, now they come;
   I am not for them yet—

Re-enter Mosca, with the gown, etc.

Now now! the news?
MOS. A piece of plate, sir.
VOLP. Of what bigness?

1. Carrion crow.

Mos. Huge,
    Massy, and antique, with your name inscribed,
    And arms engraven.
Volp. Good! and not a fox
    Stretched on the earth, with fine delusive sleights,
    Mocking a gaping crow? ha, Mosca!
Mos. Sharp, sir.
Volp. Give me my furs. [*Puts on his sick dress*] Why dost thou
    laugh so, man?
Mos. I cannot choose, sir, when I apprehend
    What thoughts he has without now, as he walks:
    That this might be the last gift he should give;
    That this would fetch you; if you died to-day,
    And gave him all, what he should be to-morrow;
    What large return would come of all his ventures;
    How he should worshipped be, and reverenced;
    Ride with his furs, and foot-cloths;[1] waited on
    By herds of fools, and clients; have clear way
    Made for his mule, as lettered as himself;
    Be call'd the great and learned advocate:
    And then concludes, there's nought impossible.
Volp. Yes, to be learned, Mosca.
Mos. O, no: rich
    Implies it. Hood an ass with reverend purple,
    So you can hide his two ambitious ears,
    And he shall pass for a cathedral doctor.
Volp. My caps, my caps, good Mosca. Fetch him in.
Mos. Stay, sir; your ointment for your eyes.
Volp. That's true;
    Dispatch, dispatch: I long to have possession
    Of my new present.
Mos. That, and thousands more,
    I hope to see you lord of.
Volp. Thanks, kind Mosca.
Mos. And that, when I am lost in blended dust,
    And hundred such as I am, in succession—

1. Ornamental cloth placed on the back of a horse.

VOLP. Nay, that were too much, Mosca.

MOS. You shall live,
   Still, to delude these harpies.

VOLP. Loving Mosca!
   'Tis well: my pillow now, and let him enter.

                                                  Exit Mosca

   Now, my feign'd cough, my phthisic, and my gout,
   My apoplexy, palsy, and catarrhs,
   Help, with your forced functions, this my posture,
   Wherein, this three year, I have milked their hopes.
   He comes; I hear him—Uh! [*coughing*] uh! uh! uh! O—

      Enter Mosca, with Voltore, carrying a piece of Plate

MOS. You still are what you were, sir. Only you,
   Of all the rest, are he commands his love,
   And you do wisely to preserve it thus,
   With early visitation, and kind notes
   Of your good meaning to him, which, I know,
   Cannot but come most grateful! Patron! sir!
   Here's signior Voltore is come—

VOLP. [*Faintly*] What say you?

MOS. Sir, signior Voltore is come this morning
   To visit you.

VOLP. I thank him.

MOS. And hath brought
   A piece of antique plate, bought of St. Mark,[1]
   With which he here presents you.

VOLP. He is welcome.
   Pray him to come more often.

MOS. Yes.

VOLT. What says he?

MOS. He thanks you, and desires you see him often.

VOLP. Mosca.

MOS. My patron!

VOLP. Bring him near, where is he?
   I long to feel his hand.

----

1. i.e., In Venice.

Mos. The plate is here, sir.

Volt. How fare you, sir?

Volp. I thank you, signior Voltore;
Where is the plate? mine eyes are bad.

Volt. [*Putting it into his hands*] I'm sorry,
To see you still thus weak.

Mos. [*Aside*] That he's not weaker.

Volp. You are too munificent.

Volt. No, sir; would to heaven,
I could as well give health to you, as that plate!

Volp. You give, sir, what you can: I thank you. Your love
Hath taste in this, and shall not be unanswered:
I pray you see me often.

Volt. Yes, I shall, sir.

Volp. Be not far from me.

Mos. Do you observe that, sir?

Volp. Hearken unto me still; it will concern you.

Mos. You are a happy man, sir; know your good.

Volp. I cannot now last long—

Mos. You are his heir, sir.

Volt. Am I?

Volp. I feel me going; Uh! uh! uh! uh!
I'm sailing to my port, Uh! uh! uh! uh!
And I am glad I am so near my haven.

Mos. Alas, kind gentleman! Well, we must all go—

Volt. But, Mosca—

Mos. Age will conquer.

Volt. 'Pray thee, hear me:
Am I inscribed his heir for certain?

Mos. Are you!
I do beseech you, sir, you will vouchsafe
To write me in your family. All my hopes
Depend upon your worship: I am lost,
Except the rising sun do shine on me.

Volt. It shall both shine, and warm thee, Mosca.

Mos. Sir, I am a man, that hath not done your love
All the worst offices: here I wear your keys,
See all your coffers and your caskets locked,

Keep the poor inventory of your jewels,
Your plate and monies; am your steward, sir,
Husband your goods here.

VOLT. But am I sole heir?

MOS. Without a partner, sir; confirmed this morning:
The wax is warm yet, and the ink scarce dry
Upon the parchment.

VOLT. Happy, happy, me!
By what good chance, sweet Mosca?

MOS. Your desert, sir;
I know no second cause.

VOLT. Thy modesty
Is not to know it; well, we shall requite it.

MOS. He ever liked your course, sir; that first took him.
I oft have heard him say, how he admired
Men of your large profession, that could speak
To every cause, and things mere contraries,
Till they were hoarse again, yet all be law;
That, with most quick agility, could turn,
And return; make knots, and undo them;
Give forkèd counsel; take provoking gold
On either hand, and put it up: these men,
He knew, would thrive with their humility.
And, for his part, he thought he should be blessed
To have his heir of such a suffering spirit,
So wise, so grave, of so perplexed a tongue,
And loud withal, that would not wag, nor scarce
Lie still, without a fee; when every word
Your worship but lets fall, is a chequin!'—[*Knocking without*]
Who's that? one knocks; I would not have you seen, sir.
And yet—pretend you came, and went in haste:
I'll fashion an excuse—and, gentle sir,
When you do come to swim in golden lard,
Up to the arms in honey, that your chin
Is borne up stiff, with fatness of the flood,
Think on your vassal; but remember me:

---

1. Gold coin.

I have not been your worst of clients.

VOLT. Mosca!—

MOS. When will you have your inventory brought, sir?
  Or see a copy of the will?—Anon!—
  I'll bring them to you, sir. Away, be gone,
  Put business in your face.

Exit Voltore

VOLP. [*Springing up*] Excellent Mosca!
  Come hither, let me kiss thee.

MOS. Keep you still, sir.
  Here is Corbaccio.

VOLP. Set the plate away:
  The vulture's gone, and the old raven's come!

MOS. Betake you to your silence, and your sleep.
  Stand there and multiply. [*Putting the plate to the rest*]
    Now, shall we see
  A wretch who is indeed more impotent
  Than this can feign to be; yet hopes to hop
  Over his grave—

Enter Corbaccio

  Signior Corbaccio!
  You're very welcome, sir.

CORB. How does your patron?

MOS. Troth, as he did, sir; no amends.

CORB. What! mends he?

MOS. No, sir: he's rather worse.

CORB. That's well. Where is he?

MOS. Upon his couch, sir, newly fallen asleep.

CORB. Does he sleep well?

MOS. No wink, sir, all this night.
  Nor yesterday; but slumbers.[1]

CORB. Good! he should take
  Some counsel of physicians: I have brought him
  An opiate here, from mine own doctor.

MOS. He will not hear of drugs.

---

1. Naps.

CORB. Why? I myself
    Stood by while it was made, saw all the ingredients:
    And know, it cannot but most gently work:
    My life for his, 'tis but to make him sleep.
VOLP. [*Aside*] Ay, his last sleep, if he would take it.
MOS. Sir,
    He has no faith in physic.
CORB. Say you, say you?
MOS. He has no faith in physic: he does think
    Most of your doctors are the greater danger,
    And worse disease, to escape. I often have
    Heard him protest, that your physician
    Should never be his heir.
CORB. Not I his heir?
MOS. Not your physician, sir.
CORB. O, no, no, no,
    I do not mean it.
MOS. No, sir, nor their fees
    He cannot brook: he says, they flay a man,
    Before they kill him.
CORB. Right, I do conceive you.
MOS. And then they do it by experiment;
    For which the law not only doth absolve them,
    But gives them great reward: and he is loath
    To hire his death, so.
CORB. It is true, they kill
    With as much license as a judge.
MOS. Nay, more;
    For he but kills, sir, where the law condemns,
    And these can kill him too.
CORB. Ay, or me;
    Or any man. How does his apoplex?
    Is that strong on him still?
MOS. Most violent.
    His speech is broken, and his eyes are set,
    His face drawn longer than 'twas wont—
CORB. How! how!
    Stronger than he was wont?

MOS. No, sir: his face
　Drawn longer than 'twas wont.
CORB. O, good!
MOS. His mouth
　Is ever gaping, and his eyelids hang.
CORB. Good.
MOS. A freezing numbness stiffens all his joints,
　And makes the color of his flesh like lead.
CORB. 'Tis good.
MOS. His pulse beats slow, and dull.
CORB. Good symptoms still.
MOS. And from his brain—
CORB. I conceive you; good.
MOS. Flows a cold sweat, with a continual rheum,
　Forth the resolved corners of his eyes.
CORB. Is't possible? Yet I am better, ha!
　How does he, with the swimming of his head?
MOS. O, sir, 'tis past the scotomy;[1] he now
　Hath lost his feeling, and hath left to snort:
　You hardly can perceive him, that he breathes.
CORB. Excellent, excellent! sure I shall outlast him!
　This makes me young again, a score of years.
MOS. I was a coming for you, sir.
CORB. Has he made his will?
　What has he given me?
MOS. No, sir.
CORB. Nothing! ha?
MOS. He has not made his will, sir.
CORB. Oh, oh, oh!
　What then did Voltore, the lawyer, here?
MOS. He smelt a carcase, sir, when he but heard
　My master was about his testament;
　As I did urge him to it for your good—
CORB. He came unto him, did he? I thought so.
MOS. Yes, and presented him this piece of plate.
CORB. To be his heir?

---

1. Dizziness.

Mos. I do not know, sir.

Corb. True:

    I know it too.

Mos. [*Aside*] By your own scale, sir.

Corb. Well,

    I shall prevent¹ him, yet. See, Mosca, look,

    Here, I have brought a bag of bright sequins,

    Will quite weigh down his plate.

Mos. [*Taking the bag*] Yea, marry, sir.

    This is true physic, this your sacred medicine;

    No talk of opiates, to this great elixir!

Corb. 'Tis aurum palpabile, if not potabile.²

Mos. It shall be minister'd to him, in his bowl.

Corb. Ay, do, do, do.

Mos. Most blessed cordial!

    This will recover him.

Corb. Yes, do, do, do.

Mos. I think it were not best, sir.

Corb. What?

Mos. To recover him.

Corb. O, no, no, no; by no means.

Mos. Why, sir, this

    Will work some strange effect, if he but feel it.

Corb. 'Tis true, therefore forbear; I'll take my venture:

    Give me it again.

Mos. At no hand; pardon me:

    You shall not do yourself that wrong, sir. I

    Will so advise you, you shall have it all.

Corb. How?

Mos. All, sir; 'tis your right, your own: no man

    Can claim a part: 'tis yours, without a rival,

    Decreed by destiny.

Corb. How, how, good Mosca?

Mos. I'll tell you, sir. This fit he shall recover.

Corb. I do conceive you.

---

1. Get ahead of.
2. Touchable, if not drinkable.

MOS. And, on first advantage
   Of his gained sense, will I re-importune him
   Unto the making of his testament:
   And show him this.

CORB. Good, good.

MOS. 'Tis better yet,
   If you will hear, sir.

CORB. Yes, with all my heart.

MOS. Now, would I counsel you, make home with speed:
   There, frame a will; whereto, you shall inscribe
   My master your sole heir.

CORB. And disinherit
   My son!

MOS. O, sir, the better: for that color
   Shall make it much more taking.

CORB. O, but color?

MOS. This will, sir, you shall send it unto me.
   Now, when I come to inforce, as I will do,
   Your cares, your watchings, and your many prayers,
   Your more than many gifts, your this day's present,
   And last, produce your will; where, without thought,
   Or least regard, unto your proper issue,
   A son so brave, and highly meriting,
   The stream of your diverted love hath thrown you
   Upon my master, and made him your heir:
   He cannot be so stupid, or stone-dead,
   But out of conscience, and mere gratitude—

CORB. He must pronounce me his?

MOS. 'Tis true.

CORB. This plot
   Did I think on before.

MOS. I do believe it.

CORB. Do you not believe it?

MOS. Yes, sir.

CORB. Mine own project.

MOS. Which, when he hath done, sir—

CORB. Published me his heir?

MOS. And you so certain to survive him—

CORB. Ay.

MOS. Being so lusty a man—

CORB. 'Tis true.

MOS. Yes, sir—

CORB. I thought on that too. See, how he should be
　　The very organ to express my thoughts!

MOS. You have not only done yourself a good—

CORB. But multiplied it on my son.

MOS. 'Tis right, sir.

CORB. Still, my invention.

MOS. 'Las, sir! heaven knows,
　　It hath been all my study, all my care,
　　(I e'en grow gray withal,) how to work things—

CORB. I do conceive, sweet Mosca.

MOS. You are he,
　　For whom I labor here.

CORB. Ay, do, do, do:
I'll straight about it.

　　　　　　　　　　　　　　　　　　　　　　[Going]

MOS. Rook go with you, raven!

CORB. I know thee honest.

MOS. *[Aside]* You do lie, sir!

CORB. And—

MOS. Your knowledge is no better than your ears, sir.

CORB. I do not doubt, to be a father to thee.

MOS. Nor I to gull my brother of his blessing.

CORB. I may have my youth restored to me, why not?

MOS. Your worship is a precious ass!

CORB. What say'st thou?

MOS. I do desire your worship to make haste, sir.

CORB. 'Tis done, 'tis done; I go.

　　　　　　　　　　　　　　　　　　　　　　Exit

VOLP. *[Leaping from his couch]* O, I shall burst!
　　Let out my sides, let out my sides—

MOS. Contain
　　Your flux of laughter, sir: you know this hope
　　Is such a bait, it covers any hook.

VOLP. O, but thy working, and thy placing it!

I cannot hold; good rascal, let me kiss thee:
I never knew thee in so rare a humor.
Mos. Alas, sir, I but do as I am taught;
    Follow your grave instructions; give them words;
    Pour oil into their ears, and send them hence.
Volp. 'Tis true, 'tis true. What a rare punishment
    Is avarice to itself!
Mos. Ay, with our help, sir.
Volp. So many cares, so many maladies,
    So many fears attending on old age,
    Yea, death so often call'd on, as no wish
    Can be more frequent with them, their limbs faint,
    Their senses dull, their seeing, hearing, going,
    All dead before them; yea, their very teeth,
    Their instruments of eating, failing them:
    Yet this is reckoned life! nay, here was one,
    Is now gone home, that wishes to live longer!
    Feels not his gout, nor palsy; feigns himself
    Younger by scores of years, flatters his age
    With confident belying it, hopes be may,
    With charms, like Æson,[1] have his youth restored:
    And with these thoughts so battens, as if fate
    Would be as easily cheated on, as he,
    And all turns air! [*Knocking within*] Who's that there, now? a third!
Mos. Close, to your couch again; I hear his voice:
    It is Corvino, our spruce merchant.
Volp. [*Lies down as before*] Dead.
Mos. Another bout, sir, with your eyes. [*Anointing them*]
    —Who's there?

Enter Corvino

    Signior Corvino! come most wished for! O,
    How happy were you, if you knew it, now!
Corv. Why? what? wherein?
Mos. The tardy hour is come, sir.
Corv. He is not dead?

---

1. Restored to youthful health by the witch Medea.

Mos. Not dead, sir, but as good;
    He knows no man.
Corv. How shall I do then?
Mos. Why, sir?
Corv. I have brought him here a pearl.
Mos. Perhaps he has
    So much remembrance left, as to know you, sir:
    He still calls on you; nothing but your name
    Is in his mouth. Is your pearl orient, sir?
Corv. Venice was never owner of the like.
Volp. [*Faintly*] Signior Corvino!
Mos. Hark.
Volp. Signior Corvino!
Mos. He calls you; step and give it to him.—He's here, sir,
    And he has brought you a rich pearl.
Corv. How do you, sir?
    Tell him, it doubles the twelfth caract.[1]
Mos. Sir,
    He cannot understand, his hearing's gone;
    And yet it comforts him to see you—
Corv. Say,
    I have a diamond for him, too.
Mos. Best show it, sir;
    Put it into his hand; 'tis only there
    He apprehends: he has his feeling, yet.
    See how he grasps it!
Corv. 'Las, good gentleman!
    How pitiful the sight is!
Mos. Tut! forget, sir.
    The weeping of an heir should still be laughter
    Under a visor.
Corv. Why, am I his heir?
Mos. Sir, I am sworn, I may not show the will
    Till he be dead; but here has been Corbaccio,
    Here has been Voltore, here were others too,
    I cannot number 'em, they were so many;

---

1. Twenty-four carats.

All gaping here for legacies: but I,
Taking the vantage of his naming you,
Signior Corvino, Signior Corvino, took
Paper, and pen, and ink, and there I asked him,
Whom he would have his heir? *Corvino.* Who
Should be executor? *Corvino.* And,
To any question he was silent to,
I still interpreted the nods he made,
Through weakness, for consent: and sent home th' others,
Nothing bequeathed them, but to cry and curse.

CORV.   O, my dear Mosca! [*They embrace*] Does he not perceive us?

MOS.   No more than a blind harper. He knows no man,
No face of friend, nor name of any servant,
Who 'twas that fed him last, or gave him drink:
Not those he hath begotten, or brought up,
Can he remember.

CORV.   Has he children?

MOS.   Bastards,
Some dozen, or more, that he begot on beggars,
Gypsies, and Jews, and black-moors, when he was drunk.
Knew you not that, sir? 'tis the common fable.
The dwarf, the fool, the eunuch, are all his;
He's the true father of his family.
In all, save me:——but he has given them nothing.

CORV.   That's well, that's well! Art sure he does not hear us?

MOS.   Sure, sir! why, look you, credit your own sense.

[*Shouts in Volpone's ear*]
The pox approach, and add to your diseases,
If it would send you hence the sooner, sir,
For your incontinence, it hath deserved it
Thoroughly, and thoroughly, and the plague to boot!——
You may come near, sir.——Would you would once close
Those filthy eyes of yours, that flow with slime,
Like two frog-pits; and those same hanging cheeks,
Cover'd with hide instead of skin—Nay, help, sir—
That look like frozen dish-clouts set on end!

CORV.   [*Aloud*] Or like an old smoked wall, on which the rain
Ran down in streaks!

Mos. Excellent, sir! speak out:
  You may be louder yet; a culverin[1]
  Discharged in his ear would hardly bore it.
Corv. His nose is like a common sewer, still running.
Mos. 'Tis good! And what his mouth?
Corv. A very draught.[2]
Mos. O, stop it up—
Corv. By no means.
Mos. 'Pray you, let me:
  Faith I could stifle him rarely with a pillow,
  As well as any woman that should keep him.
Corv. Do as you will; but I'll begone.
Mos. Be so:
  It is your presence makes him last so long.
Corv. I pray you, use no violence.
Mos. No, sir! why?
  Why should you be thus scrupulous, pray you, sir?
Corv. Nay, at your discretion.
Mos. Well, good sir, begone.
Corv. I will not trouble him now, to take my pearl.
Mos. Puh! nor your diamond. What a needless care
  Is this afflicts you? Is not all here yours?
  Am not I here, whom you have made your creature?
  That owe my being to you?
Corv. Grateful Mosca!
  Thou art my friend, my fellow, my companion,
  My partner, and shalt share in all my fortunes.
Mos. Excepting one.
Corv. What's that?
Mos. Your gallant wife, sir,—

                                        Exit Corvino

  Now is he gone: we had no other means
  To shoot him hence, but this.
Volp. My divine Mosca!
  Thou hast to-day outgone thyself. [*Knocking within*]—Who's there?
  I will be troubled with no more. Prepare

1. Cannon.
2. Cesspool.

Me music, dances, banquets, all delights;
The Turk is not more sensual in his pleasures,
Than will Volpone. [*Exit Mosca*] Let me see; a pearl!
A diamond! plate! sequins! Good morning's purchase
Why, this is better than rob churches, yet,
Or fat, by eating, once a month, a man—

Enter Mosca

Who is't?
MOS. The beauteous lady Would-be, sir,
 Wife to the English knight, sir Politick Would-be,
 (This is the style,¹ sir, is directed me,)
 Hath sent to know how you have slept to-night,
 And if you would be visited?
VOLP. Not now:
 Some three hours hence—
MOS. I told the squire so much.
VOLP. When I am high with mirth and wine; then, then:
 'Fore heaven, I wonder at the desperate valour
 Of the bold English, that they dare let loose
 Their wives to all encounters!
MOS. Sir, this knight
 Had not his name for nothing, he is *politick*.²
 And knows, howe'er his wife affect strange airs,
 She hath not yet the face to be dishonest:
 But had she signior Corvino's wife's face—
VOLP. Has she so rare a face?
MOS. O, sir, the wonder,
 The blazing star of Italy! a wench
 Of the first year! a beauty ripe as harvest!
 Whose skin is whiter than a swan all over,
 Than silver, snow, or lilies! a soft lip,
 Would tempt you to eternity of kissing!
 And flesh that melteth in the touch to blood!
 Bright as your gold, and lovely as your gold!

1. Title.
2. Devious, cunning.

VOLP. Why had not I known this before?
MOS. Alas, sir,
    Myself but yesterday discover'd it.
VOLP. How might I see her?
MOS. O, not possible;
    She's kept as warily as is your gold;
    Never does come abroad, never takes air,
    But at a window. All her looks are sweet,
    As the first grapes or cherries, and are watched
    As near as they are.
VOLP. I must see her.
MOS. Sir,
    There is a guard of spies ten thick upon her,
    All his whole household; each of which is set
    Upon his fellow, and have all their charge,
    When he goes out, when he comes in, examined.
VOLP. I will go see her, though but at her window.
MOS. In some disguise, then.
VOLP. That is true; I must
    Maintain mine own shape still the same: we'll think.

Exeunt

ACT II, SCENE I

Enter Sir Politick Would-be, and Peregrine

SIR P. Sir, to a wise man, all the world's his soil:
    It is not Italy, nor France, nor Europe,
    That must bound me, if my fates call me forth.
    Yet, I protest, it is no salt[1] desire
    Of seeing countries, shifting a religion,
    Nor any disaffection to the state
    Where I was bred, and unto which I owe
    My dearest plots, hath brought me out; much less,
    That idle, antique, stale, gray-headed project
    Of knowing men's minds and manners, with Ulysses!
    But a peculiar humour of my wife's

1. Wanton.

Laid for this height[1] of Venice, to observe,
To quote, to learn the language, and so forth—
I hope you travel, sir, with license?
PER. Yes.
SIR P. I dare the safelier converse—How long, sir,
Since you left England?
PER. Seven weeks.
SIR P. So lately!
You have not been with my lord ambassador?
PER. Not yet, sir.
SIR P. Pray you, what news, sir, vents our climate?
I heard last night a most strange thing reported
By some of my lord's followers, and I long
To hear how 'twill be seconded.
PER. What was't, sir?
SIR P. Marry, sir, of a raven that should build
In a ship royal of the king's.
PER. This fellow,
Does he gull me, trow? or is gulled? [*Aside*] Your name, sir.
SIR P. My name is Politick Would-be.
PER. [*Aside*] O, that speaks him.—
A knight, sir?
SIR P. A poor knight, sir.
PER. Your lady
Lies here in Venice, for intelligence
Of tires, and fashions, and behaviour,
Among the courtezans? the fine lady Would-be?
SIR P. Yes, sir; the spider and the bee, ofttimes,
Suck from one flower.
PER. Good sir Politick,
I cry you mercy; I have heard much of you:
'Tis true, sir, of your raven.
SIR P. On your knowledge?
PER. Yes, and your lion's whelping in the Tower.
SIR P. Another whelp!
PER. Another, sir.

1. Latitude.

SIR P. Now heaven!
　　What prodigies be these? The fires at Berwick!
　　And the new star! these things concurring, strange,
　　And full of omen! Saw you those meteors?
PER. I did, sir.
SIR P. Fearful! Pray you, sir, confirm me,
　　Were there three porpoises seen above the bridge,
　　As they give out?
PER. Six, and a sturgeon, sir.
SIR P. I am astonish'd.
PER. Nay, sir, be not so;
　　I'll tell you a greater prodigy than these.
SIR P. What should these things portend?
PER. The very day
　　(Let me be sure) that I put forth from London,
　　There was a whale discovered in the river,
　　As high as Woolwich, that had waited there,
　　Few know how many months, for the subversion
　　Of the Stode[1] fleet.
SIR P. Is't possible? believe it,
　　'Twas either sent from Spain, or the archdukes:
　　Spinola's whale, upon my life, my credit!
　　Will they not leave these projects? Worthy sir,
　　Some other news.
PER. Faith, Stone the fool is dead,
　　And they do lack a tavern fool extremely.
SIR P. Is Mass Stone dead?
PER. He's dead, sir; why, I hope
　　You thought him not immortal?—[*Aside*] O, this knight,
　　Were he well known, would be a precious thing
　　To fit our English stage: he that should write
　　But such a fellow, should be thought to feign
　　Extremely, if not maliciously.
SIR P. Stone dead!
PER. Dead.—Lord! how deeply, sir, you apprehend it?
　　He was no kinsman to you?

1. Merchant adventurers based in a German port.

SIR P. That I know of.

    Well! the same fellow was an unknown[1] fool.

PER. And yet you knew him, it seems?

SIR P. I did so. Sir,

    I knew him one of the most dangerous heads

    Living within the state, and so I held him.

PER. Indeed, sir?

SIR P. While he lived, in action.

    He has received weekly intelligence,

    Upon my knowledge, out of the Low Countries,

    For all parts of the world, in cabbages;

    And those dispensed again to ambassadors,

    In oranges, musk-melons, apricocks,

    Lemons, pome-citrons, and such-like; sometimes

    In Colchester oysters, and your Selsey cockles.

PER. You make me wonder.

SIR P. Sir, upon my knowledge.

    Nay, I've observed him, at your public ordinary,[2]

    Take his advertisement[3] from a traveller,

    A concealed statesman, in a trencher of meat;

    And instantly before the meal was done,

    Convey an answer in a tooth-pick.

PER. Strange!

    How could this be, sir?

SIR P. Why, the meat was cut

    So like his character, and so laid, as he

    Must easily read the cipher.

PER. I have heard,

    He could not read, sir.

SIR P. So 'twas given out,

    In policy, by those that did employ him:

    But he could read, and had your languages,

    And to't, as sound a noddle—

PER. I have heard, sir,

    That your baboons were spies, and that they were

1. Unequaled.

2. Inn.

3. Message.

    A kind of subtle nation near to China.

SIR P. Ay, ay, your Mamaluchi.¹ Faith, they had
    Their hand in a French plot or two; but they
    Were so extremely given to women, as
    They made discovery of all: yet I
    Had my advices here, on Wednesday last.
    From one of their own coat, they were returned,
    Made their relations, as the fashion is,
    And now stand fair for fresh employment.

PER. [*Aside*] 'Heart!
    This sir Pol will be ignorant of nothing.
    It seems, sir, you know all.

SIR P. Not all, sir, but
    I have some general notions. I do love
    To note and to observe: though I live out,
    Free from the active torrent, yet I'd mark
    The currents and the passages of things,
    For mine own private use; and know the ebbs
    And flows of state.

PER. Believe it, sir, I hold
    Myself in no small tie unto my fortunes,
    For casting me thus luckily upon you,
    Whose knowledge, if your bounty equal it,
    May do me great assistance, in instruction
    For my behaviour, and my bearing, which
    Is yet so rude and raw.

SIR P. Why, came you forth
    Empty of rules for travel?

PER. Faith, I had
    Some common ones, from out that vulgar grammar,
    Which he that cried Italian to me, taught me.

SIR P. Why this it is that spoils all our brave bloods,
    Trusting our hopeful gentry unto pedants,
    Fellows of outside, and mere bark. You seem
    To be a gentleman, of ingenuous² race:—

---

1. Slaves who seized power in thirteenth-century Egypt.
2. Noble.

I not profess it, but my fate hath been
To be, where I have been consulted with,
In this high kind, touching some great men's sons,
Persons of blood and honor.—

Enter Mosca and Nano disguised, followed by persons with materials for erecting a Stage

PER. Who be these, sir?

MOS. Under that window, there 't must be. The same.

SIR P. Fellows, to mount a bank.[1] Did your instructor
In the dear tongues, never discourse to you
Of the Italian mountebanks?

PER. Yes, sir.

SIR P. Why,
Here you shall see one.

PER. They are quacksalvers:
Fellows, that live by venting oils and rugs.

SIR P. Was that the character he gave you of them?

PER. As I remember.

SIR P. Pity his ignorance.
They are the only knowing men of Europe!
Great general scholars, excellent physicians,
Most admired statesmen, professed favourites,
And cabinet counsellors to the greatest princes;
The only languaged men of all the world!

PER. And, I have heard, they are most lewd impostors;
Made all of terms and shreds; no less beliers
Of great men's favors, than their own vile med'cines;
Which they will utter upon monstrous oaths,
Selling that drug for two-pence, ere they part,
Which they have valued at twelve crowns before.

SIR P. Sir, calumnies are answered best with silence.
Yourself shall judge.—Who is it mounts, my friends?

MOS. Scoto of Mantua, sir.

SIR P. Is't he? Nay, then
I'll proudly promise, sir, you shall behold

---

1. The word *mountebank* derives from the Italian meaning "to mount a bank."

Another man than has been phant'sied to you.
I wonder yet, that he should mount his bank,
Here in this nook, that has been wont t'appear
In face of the Piazza!—Here he comes.

*Enter Volpone, disguised as a mountebank Doctor, and followed
by a crowd*

VOLP. Mount, zany. [*To Nano*]
MOB. Follow, follow, follow, follow!
SIR P. See how the people follow him! he's a man
May write ten thousand crowns in bank here. Note,
[*Volpone mounts the Stage*]
Mark but his gesture:—I do use to observe
The state he keeps in getting up.
PER. 'Tis worth it, sir.
VOLP. Most noble gentlemen, and my worthy patrons! It may seem
strange, that I, your Scoto Mantuano, who was ever wont to fix my
bank in face of the public Piazza, near the shelter of the Portico to
the Procuratia, should now, after eight months' absence from this illustrious city of Venice, humbly retire myself into an obscure nook
of the Piazza.
SIR P. Did not I now object the same?
PER. Peace, sir.
VOLP. Let me tell you: I am not, as your Lombard proverb saith, cold
on my feet; or content to part with my commodities at a cheaper
rate, than I accustomed: look not for it. Nor that the calumnious reports of that impudent detractor, and shame to our profession, (Ales-
sandro Buttone, I mean,) who gave out, in public, I was condemned
a sforzato[1] to the galleys, for poisoning the cardinal Bembo's—cook,
hath at all attached, much less dejected me. No, no, worthy gentlemen; to tell you true, I cannot endure to see the rabble of these
ground ciarlitani,[2] that spread their cloaks on the pavement, as if
they meant to do feats of activity, and then come in lamely, with
their mouldy tales out of Boccacio, like stale Tabarine, the fabulist:
some of them discoursing their travels, and of their tedious captiv-
ity in the Turks' gallies, when, indeed, were the truth known, they

1. Prisoner.
2. Low charlatans.

were the Christians' galleys where very temperately they eat bread, and drunk water, as a wholesome penance, enjoined them by their confessors, for base pilferies.

SIR P. Note but his bearing, and contempt of these.

VOLP. These turdy-facy-nasty-paty-lousy-fartical rogues, with one poor groat's-worth of unprepared antimony, finely wrapt up in several scartoccios, are able, very well, to kill their twenty a week, and play; yet, these meagre, starved spirits, who have half stopt the organs of their minds with earthy oppilations,[1] want not their favorers among your shrivelled sallad-eating artizans, who are overjoyed that they may have their ha'perth of physic; though it purge them into another world, it makes no matter.

SIR P. Excellent! have you heard better language, sir?

VOLP. Well, let them go. And, gentlemen, honourable gentlemen, know, that for this time, our bank, being thus removed from the clamours of the canaglia,[2] shall be the scene of pleasure and delight; for I have nothing to sell, little or nothing to sell.

SIR P. I told you, sir, his end.

PER. You did so, sir.

VOLP. I protest, I, and my six servants, are not able to make of this precious liquor, so fast as it is fetched away from my lodging by gentlemen of your city; strangers of the Terrafirma,[3] worshipful merchants; ay, and senators too: who, ever since my arrival, have detained me to their uses, by their splendidous liberalities. And worthily; for, what avails your rich man to have his magazines stuffed with moscadelli, or of the purest grape, when his physicians prescribe him, on pain of death, to drink nothing but water cocted with aniseeds? O, health! health! the blessing of the rich! the riches of the poor! who can buy thee at too dear a rate, since there is no enjoying this world without thee? Be not then so sparing of your purses, honorable gentlemen, as to abridge the natural course of life—

PER. You see his end.

SIR P. Ay, is't not good?

VOLP. For, when a humid flux, or catarrh, by the mutability of air, falls from your head into an arm or shoulder, or any other part; take you

1. Obstructions.
2. Mob.
3. Venice, beyond the lagoon.

a ducket, or your sequin of gold, and apply to the place affected: see
what good effect it can work. No, no, 'tis this blessed unguento,[1] this
rare extraction, that hath only power to disperse all malignant humors, that proceed either of hot, cold, moist, or windy causes—

PER. I would he had put in dry too.

SIR P. 'Pray you, observe.

VOLP. To fortify the most indigest and crude stomach, ay, were it of
one that, through extreme weakness, vomited blood, applying only
a warm napkin to the place, after the unction and fricace;[2]—for the
vertigine in the head, putting but a drop into your nostrils, likewise
behind the ears; a most sovereign and approved remedy: the mal ca-
duco,[3] cramps, convulsions, paralysies, epilepsies, tremor-cordia,
retired nerves, ill vapours of the spleen, stopping of the liver, the
stone, the strangury, hernia ventosa, iliaca passio; stops a dysenteria
immediately; easeth the torsion of the small guts; and cures melan-
cholia hypondriaca, being taken and applied according to my
printed receipt. [*Pointing to his bill and his vial*] For, this is the
physician, this the medicine; this counsels, this cures; this gives the
direction, this works the effect; and, in sum, both together may be
termed an abstract of the theorick and practick in the Æsculapian
art. 'Twill cost you eight crowns. And,—Zan Fritada, prithee sing a
verse extempore in honor of it.

SIR P. How do you like him, sir?

PER. Most strangely, I!

SIR P. Is not his language rare?

PER. But alchemy,
    I never heard the like; or Broughton's books.[4]

Nano sings

> Had old Hippocrates, or Galen,
> That to their books put med'cines all in,
> But known this secret, they had never
> (Of which they will be guilty ever)
> Been murderers of so much paper,

---

1. Ointment.
2. Massage.
3. Epilepsy.
4. Hugh Broughton, a Puritan divine despised by Jonson.

> Or wasted many a hurtless taper;
> No Indian drug had e'er been famed,
> Tobacco, sassafras not named;
> Ne yet, of guacum one small stick, sir,
> Nor Raymund Lully's[1] great elixir.
> Ne had been known the Danish Gonswart,
> Or Paracelsus, with his long sword.

PER. All this, yet, will not do; eight crowns is high.

VOLP. No more.—Gentlemen, if I had but time to discourse to you the miraculous effects of this my oil, surnamed Oglio del Scoto; with the countless catalogue of those I have cured of the aforesaid, and many more diseases; the patents and privileges of all the princes and commonwealths of Christendom; or but the depositions of those that appeared on my part, before the signiory of the Sanita and most learned College of Physicians; where I was authorised, upon notice taken of the admirable virtues of my medicaments, and mine own excellency in matter of rare and unknown secrets, not only to disperse them publicly in this famous city, but in all the territories, that happily joy under the government of the most pious and magnificent states of Italy. But may some other gallant fellow say, O, there be divers that make professions to have as good, and as experimented[2] receipts as yours: indeed, very many have assayed, like apes, in imitation of that, which is really and essentially in me, to make of this oil; bestowed great cost in furnaces, stills, alembecks, continual fires, and preparation of the ingredients, (as indeed there goes to it six hundred several simples,[3] besides some quantity of human fat, for the conglutination, which we buy of the anatomists,) but, when these practitioners come to the last decoction, blow, blow, puff, puff, and all flies in fumo: ha, ha, ha! Poor wretches! I rather pity their folly and indiscretion, than their loss of time and money; for these may be recovered by industry: but to be a fool born, is a disease incurable.

For myself, I always from my youth have endeavoured to get the rarest secrets, and book them, either in exchange, or for money: I

---

1. Lull, medieval alchemist.
2. Tried by experience.
3. Herbs.

spared nor cost nor labour, where any thing was worthy to be learned. And, gentlemen, honorable gentlemen, I will undertake, by virtue of chemical art, out of the honourable hat that covers your head, to extract the four elements; that is to say, the fire, air, water, and earth, and return you your felt without burn or stain. For, whilst others have been at the Balloo,[1] I have been at my book; and am now past the craggy paths of study, and come to the flowery plains of honour and reputation.

SIR P. I do assure you, sir, that is his aim.

VOLP. But to our price—

PER. And that withal, sir Pol.

VOLP. You all know, honorable gentlemen, I never valued this ampulla, or vial, at less than eight crowns; but for this time, I am content to be deprived of it for six: six crowns is the price, and less in courtesy I know you cannot offer me; take it or leave it, howsoever, both it and I am at your service. I ask you not as the value of the thing, for then I should demand of you a thousand crowns, so the cardinals Montalto, Fernese, the great Duke of Tuscany, my gossip,[2] with divers other princes, have given me; but I despise money. Only to shew my affection to you, honourable gentlemen, and your illustrious State here, I have neglected the messages of these princes, mine own offices, framed my journey hither, only to present you with the fruits of my travels.—Tune your voices once more to the touch of your instruments, and give the honorable assembly some delightful recreation.

PER. What monstrous and most painful circumstance
Is here, to get some three or four gazettes,[3]
Some three-pence in the whole! for that 'twill come to.

Nano sings

> You that would last long, list to my song,
> Make no more coil, but buy of this oil.
> Would you be ever fair and young?
> Stout of teeth, and strong of tongue?
> Tart of palate? quick of ear?

1. Ball games.
2. Good friend.
3. Smallest Venetian coins.

> Sharp of sight? of nostril clear?
> Moist of hand? and light of foot?
> Or, I will come nearer to't,
> Would you live free from all diseases?
> Do the act your mistress pleases,
> Yet fright all aches from your bones?
> Here's a medicine for the nones.

VOLP. Well, I am in a humor at this time to make a present of the small quantity my coffer contains; to the rich in courtesy, and to the poor for God's sake. Wherefore now mark: I asked you six crowns; and six crowns, at other times, you have paid me; you shall not give me six crowns, nor five, not four, nor three, nor two, nor one; nor half a ducat; no, nor a moccinigo.[1] Sixpence it will cost you, or six hundred pound—expect no lower price, for, by the banner of my front, I will not bate a bagatine,[2]—that I will have, only, a pledge of your loves, to carry something from amongst you, to shew I am not contemned by you. Therefore, now, toss your handkerchiefs, cheerfully, cheerfully; and be advertised, that the first heroic spirit that deigns to grace me with a handkerchief, I will give it a little remembrance of something, beside, shall please it better, than if I had presented it with a double pistolet.[3]

PER. Will you be that heroic spark, sir Pol?

> [*Celia at a window above, throws down her handkerchief*]

O, see! the window has prevented[4] you.

VOLP. Lady, I kiss your bounty; and for this timely grace you have done your poor Scoto of Mantua, I will return you, over and above my oil, a secret of that high and inestimable nature, shall make you for ever enamored on that minute, wherein your eye first descended on so mean, yet not altogether to be despised, an object. Here is a powder concealed in this paper, of which, if I should speak to the worth, nine thousand volumes were but as one page, that page as a line, that line as a word; so short is this pilgrimage of man (which some call life) to the expressing of it. Would I reflect on the price?

---

1. Small Venetian coin.
2. Small coin.
3. Large Spanish coin.
4. Got in before you.

why, the whole world is but as an empire, that empire as a province, that province as a bank, that bank as a private purse to the purchase of it. I will only tell you; it is the powder that made Venus a goddess (given her by Apollo,) that kept her perpetually young, cleared her wrinkles, firmed her gums, fill'd her skin, colored her hair; from her derived to Helen, and at the sack of Troy unfortunately lost: till now, in this our age, it was as happily recovered, by a studious antiquary, out of some ruins of Asia, who sent a moiety of it to the court of France, (but much sophisticated,)[1] wherewith the ladies there, now, color their hair. The rest, of this present, remains with me; extracted to a quintessence: so that, wherever it but touches, in youth it perpetually preserves, in age restores the complexion; seats your teeth, did they dance like virginal jacks,[2] firm as a wall; makes them white as ivory, that were black as—

Enter Corvino

CORV. Spite o' the devil, and my shame! come down here;
Come down;—No house but mine to make your scene?
Signior Flaminio, will you down, sir? down?
What, is my wife your Franciscina,[3] sir?
No windows on the whole Piazza, here,
To make your properties, but mine? but mine?
                              [*Beats away Volpone, Nano, etc.*]
Heart! ere to-morrow I shall be new-christened,
And call'd the Pantalone di Besogniosi,[4]
About the town.
PER. What should this mean, sir Pol?
SIR P. Some trick of state, believe it; I will home.
PER. It may be some design on you.
SIR P. I know not,
I'll stand upon my guard.
PER. It is your best, sir.

---

1. Adulterated.
2. They pluck the strings of a harpsichord (or "virginals").
3. Stock character in *commedia dell'arte*.
4. Old man in the *commedia*.

SIR P. This three weeks, all my advices, all my letters,
    They have been intercepted.
PER. Indeed, sir!
    Best have a care.
SIR P. Nay, so I will.
PER. This knight,
    I may not lose him, for my mirth, till night.

Exeunt

SCENE II

Enter Volpone and Mosca

VOLP. O, I am wounded!
MOS. Where, sir?
VOLP. Not without;
    Those blows were nothing: I could bear them ever.
    But angry Cupid, bolting from her eyes,
    Hath shot himself into me like a flame;
    Where, now, he flings about his burning heat,
    As in a furnace an ambitious fire,
    Whose vent is stopt. The fight is all within me.
    I cannot live, except thou help me, Mosca;
    My liver melts, and I, without the hope
    Of some soft air, from her refreshing breath,
    Am but a heap of cinders.
MOS. 'Las, good sir,
    Would you had never seen her!
VOLP. Nay, would thou
    Had'st never told me of her!
MOS. Sir, 'tis true;
    I do confess I was unfortunate,
    And you unhappy: but I'm bound in conscience,
    No less than duty, to effect my best
    To your release of torment, and I will, sir.
VOLP. Dear Mosca, shall I hope?
MOS. Sir, more than dear,

I will not bid you to despair of aught
Within a human compass.

VOLP. O, there spoke
My better angel. Mosca, take my keys,
Gold, plate, and jewels, all's at thy devotion;
Employ them how thou wilt; nay, coin me too:
So thou, in this, but crown my longings, Mosca.

MOS. Use but your patience.

VOLP. So I have.

MOS. I doubt not
To bring success to your desires.

VOLP. Nay, then,
I not repent me of my late disguise.

MOS. If you can horn[1] him, sir, you need not.

VOLP. True:
Besides, I never meant him for my heir.—
Is not the color of my beard and eyebrows
To make me known?

MOS. No jot.

VOLP. I did it well.

MOS. So well, would I could follow you in mine,
With half the happiness!—[*Aside*] and yet I would
Escape your epilogue.

VOLP. But were they gulled
With a belief that I was Scoto?

MOS. Sir,
Scoto himself could hardly have distinguished!
I have not time to flatter you now; we'll part;
And as I prosper, so applaud my art.

Exeunt

SCENE III

Enter Corvino, with his sword in his hand, dragging in Celia

CORV. Death of mine honor, with the city's fool!
A juggling, tooth-drawing, prating mountebank!

---

1. Cuckold.

And at a public window! where, whilst he,
With his strained action, and his dole of faces,
To his drug-lecture draws your itching ears,
A crew of old, unmarried, noted letchers,
Stood leering up like satyrs; and you smile
Most graciously, and fan your favours forth,
To give your hot spectators satisfaction!
What, was your mountebank their call? their whistle?
Or were you enamored on his copper rings,
His saffron jewel, with the toad-stone in't,
Or his embroidered suit, with the cope-stitch,
Made, of a hearse cloth? or his old tilt-feather?
Or his starched beard? Well, you shall have him, yes!
He shall come home, and minister unto you
The fricace for the mother.[1] Or, let me see,
I think you'd rather mount; would you not mount?
Why, if you'll mount, you may; yes, truly, you may:
And so you may be seen, down to the foot.
Get you a cittern,[2] lady Vanity,
And be a dealer with the virtuous man;
Make one: I'll but protest myself a cuckold,
And save your dowry. I'm a Dutchman, I!
For, if you thought me an Italian,
You would be damned, ere you did this, you whore!
Thou'dst tremble, to imagine, that the murder
Of father, mother, brother, all thy race,
Should follow, as the subject of my justice.

CEL. Good sir, have patience.

CORV. What couldst thou propose
  Less to thyself, than in this heat of wrath.
  And stung with my dishonor, I should strike
  This steel into thee, with as many stabs,
  As thou wert gazed upon with goatish eyes?

1. Massage for hysteria.
2. Guitar.

CEL. Alas, sir, be appeased! I could not think
    My being at the window should more now
    Move your impatience, than at other times.
CORV. No! not to seek and entertain a parley
    With a known knave, before a multitude!
    You were an actor with your handkerchief,
    Which he most sweetly kist in the receipt,
    And might, no doubt, return it with a letter,
    And point the place where you might meet; your sister's,
    Your mother's, or your aunt's might serve the turn.
CEL. Why, dear sir, when do I make these excuses,
    Or ever stir abroad, but to the church?
    And that so seldom—
CORV. Well, it shall be less;
    And thy restraint before was liberty,
    To what I now decree: and therefore mark me.
    First, I will have this bawdy light dammed up;
    And till't be done, some two or three yards off,
    I'll chalk a line: o'er which if thou but chance
    To set thy desperate foot, more hell, more horror,
    More wild remorseless rage shall seize on thee,
    Than on a conjuror, that had needless left
    His circle's safety ere his devil was laid.
    Then here's a lock which I will hang upon thee,
    And, now I think on't, I will keep thee backwards;
    Thy lodging shall be backwards; thy walks backwards;
    Thy prospect, all be backwards; and no pleasure,
    That thou shalt know but backwards: nay, since you force
    My honest nature, know, it is your own,
    Being too open, makes me use you thus:
    Since you will not contain your subtle nostrils
    In a sweet room, but they must snuff the air
    Of rank and sweaty passengers. [*Knocking within*]—One knocks.
    Away, and be not seen, pain of thy life;
    Nor look toward the window: if thou dost—
    Nay, stay, hear this—let me not prosper, whore,
    But I will make thee an anatomy,
    Dissect thee mine own self, and read a lecture

Upon thee to the city, and in public.
Away!—

Exit Celia

Enter Servant

Who's there?

SERV. 'Tis signior Mosca, sir.

CORV. Let him come in. His master's dead: there's yet
    Some good to help the bad.

Enter Mosca

My Mosca, welcome!
    I guess your news.

MOS. I fear you cannot, sir.

CORV. Is't not his death?

MOS. Rather the contrary.

CORV. Not his recovery?

MOS. Yes, sir.

CORV. I am cursed,
    I am bewitched, my crosses meet to vex me.
    How? how? how? how?

MOS. Why, sir, with Scoto's oil;
    Corbaccio and Voltore brought of it,
    Whilst I was busy in an inner room—

CORV. Death! that damned mountebank; but for the law
    Now, I could kill the rascal: it cannot be,
    His oil should have that virtue. Have not I
    Known him a common rogue, come fiddling in
    To the osteria,[1] with a tumbling whore,
    And, when he has done all his forced tricks, been glad
    Of a poor spoonful of dead wine, with flies in't?
    It cannot be. All his ingredients
    Are a sheep's gall, a roasted bitch's marrow,
    Some few sod[2] earwigs, pounded caterpillars,

1. Tavern.
2. Stewed.

    A little capon's grease, and fasting spittle:
    I know them to a dram.
MOS. I know not, sir;
    But some on't, there, they poured into his ears,
    Some in his nostrils, and recovered him;
    Applying but the fricace.
CORV. Pox o' that fricace!
MOS. And since, to seem the more officious
    And flatt'ring of his health, there, they have had,
    At extreme fees, the college of physicians
    Consulting on him, how they might restore him;
    Where one would have a cataplasm of spices,
    Another a flayed ape clapped to his breast,
    A third would have it a dog, a fourth an oil,
    With wild cats' skins: at last, they all resolved
    That, to preserve him, was no other means,
    But some young woman must be straight sought out,
    Lusty, and full of juice, to sleep by him;
    And to this service, most unhappily,
    And most unwillingly, am I now employed,
    Which here I thought to pre-acquaint you with,
    For your advice, since it concerns you most;
    Because, I would not do that thing might cross
    Your ends, on whom I have my whole dependence, sir:
    Yet, if I do it not, they may delate
    My slackness to my patron, work me out
    Of his opinion; and there all your hopes,
    Ventures, or whatsoever, are all frustrate!
    I do but tell you, sir. Besides, they are all
    Now striving, who shall first present him; therefore—
    I could entreat you, briefly conclude somewhat;
    Prevent[1] them if you can.
CORV. Death to my hopes,
    This is my villainous fortune! Best to hire
    Some common courtezan.

1. Anticipate.

MOS. Ay, I thought on that, sir;
    But they are all so subtle, full of art—
    And age again doting and flexible,
    So as—I cannot tell—we may, perchance,
    Light on a quean[1] may cheat us all.
CORV. 'Tis true.
MOS. No, no: it must be one that has no tricks, sir,
    Some simple thing, a creature made unto it;
    Some wench you may command. Have you no kinswoman?
    Odso—Think, think, think, think, think, think, think, sir.
    One o' the doctors offered there his daughter.
CORV. How!
MOS. Yes, signior Lupo, the physician.
CORV. His daughter!
MOS. And a virgin, sir. Why, alas,
    He knows the state of 's body, what it is;
    That nought can warm his blood, sir, but a fever;
    Nor any incantation raise his spirit:
    A long forgetfulness hath seized that part.
    Besides sir, who shall know it? some one or two—
CORV. I pray thee give me leave. If any man
    But I had had this luck—The thing in't self,
    I know, is nothing—Wherefore should not I
    As well command my blood and my affections,
    As this dull doctor? In the point of honor,
    The cases are all one of wife and daughter.
MOS. [*Aside*] I hear him coming.
CORV. She shall do't: 'tis done.
    Slight! if this doctor, who is not engaged,
    Unless 't be for his counsel, which is nothing,
    Offer his daughter, what should I, that am
    So deeply in? I will prevent him: Wretch!
    Covetous wretch!—Mosca, I have determined.
MOS. How, sir?
CORV. We'll make all sure. The party you wot of
    Shall be mine own wife, Mosca.

1. Loose girl.

MOS. Sir, the thing,
    But that I would not seem to counsel you,
    I should have motioned to you, at the first:
    And make your count, you have cut all their throats.
    Why, 'tis directly taking a possession!
    And in his next fit, we may let him go.
    'Tis but to pull the pillow from his head,
    And he is throttled: it had been done before,
    But for your scrupulous doubts.
CORV. Ay, a plague on't,
    My conscience fools my wit! Well, I'll be brief,
    And so be thou, lest they should be before us:
    Go home, prepare him, tell him with what zeal
    And willingness I do it; swear it was
    On the first hearing, as thou may'st do, truly,
    Mine own free motion.
MOS. Sir, I warrant you,
    I'll so possess him with it, that the rest
    Of his starved clients shall be banished all;
    And only you received. But come not, sir,
    Until I send, for I have something else
    To ripen for your good, you must not know't.
CORV. But do not you forget to send now.
MOS. Fear not.

Exit

CORV. Where are you, wife? my Celia! wife!

Re-enter Celia

    —What, blubbering?
    Come, dry those tears. I think thou thought'st me in earnest;
    Ha! by this light I talked so but to try thee:
    Methinks the lightness of the occasion
    Should have confirmed thee. Come, I am not jealous.
CEL. No!
CORV. Faith I am not, I, nor never was;
    It is a poor unprofitable humor
    Do not I know, if women have a will,
    They'll do 'gainst all the watches of the world,

And that the fiercest spies are tamed with gold?
Tut, I am confident in thee, thou shalt see't:
And see I'll give thee cause too, to believe it.
Come kiss me. Go, and make thee ready, straight,
In all thy best attire, thy choicest jewels,
Put them all on, and, with them, thy best looks:
We are invited to a solemn feast,
At old Volpone's, where it shall appear
How far I am free from jealousy or fear.

Exeunt

ACT III, SCENE I

Enter Mosca

MOS. I fear, I shall begin to grow in love
With my dear self, and my most properous parts,
They do so spring and burgeon; I can feel
A whimsy in my blood: I know not how,
Success hath made me wanton. I could skip
Out of my skin, now, like a subtle snake,
I am so limber, O! your parasite
Is a most precious thing, dropt from above,
Not bred 'mongst clods and clodpoles, here on earth.
I muse, the mystery[1] was not made a science,
It is so liberally professed! almost
All the wise world is little else, in nature,
But parasites or sub-parasites.—And yet,
I mean not those that have your bare town-art,
To know who's fit to feed them; have no house,
No family, no care, and therefore mould
Tales for men's ears, to bait that sense; or get
Kitchen-invention, and some stale receipts
To please the belly, and the groin; nor those,
With their court dog-tricks, that can fawn and fleer,
Make their revenue[2] out of legs and faces,

1. Trade, craft.
2. Revenue.

Echo my lord, and lick away a moth:
But your fine elegant rascal, that can rise,
And stoop, almost together, like an arrow;
Shoot through the air as nimbly as a star;
Turn short as doth a swallow; and be here,
And there, and here, and yonder, all at once;
Present to any humor, all occasion;
And change a visor, swifter than a thought!
This is the creature had the art born with him;
Toils not to learn it, but doth practise it
Out of most excellent nature: and such sparks
Are the true parasites, others but their zanies.

Enter Bonario

Who's this? Bonario, old Corbaccio's son?
The person I was bound to seek.—Fair sir,
You are happily met.
BON. That cannot be by thee.
MOS. Why, sir?
BON. Nay, pray thee, know thy way, and leave me
I would be loath to interchange discourse
With such a mate[1] as thou art.
MOS. Courteous sir,
Scorn not my poverty.
BON. Not I, by heaven;
But thou shalt give me leave to hate thy baseness.
MOS. Baseness!
BON. Ay; answer me, is not thy sloth
Sufficient argument? thy flattery?
Thy means of feeding?
MOS. Heaven be good to me!
These imputations are too common, sir,
And easily stuck on virtue when she's poor.
You are unequal to me, and however
Your sentence may be righteous, yet you are not,

---

1. Contemptible fellow.

That, ere you know me, thus proceed in censure:
St. Mark bear witness 'gainst you, 'tis inhuman.

[*Weeps*]

BON. [*Aside*] What! does he weep? the sign is soft and good:
  I do repent me that I was so harsh.
MOS. 'Tis true, that, swayed by strong necessity,
  I am enforced to eat my careful bread
  With too much obsequy;[1] 'tis true, beside,
  That I am fain to spin mine own poor raiment
  Out of my mere observance,[2] being not born
  To a free fortune: but that I have done
  Base offices, in rending friends asunder,
  Dividing families, betraying counsels,
  Whispering false lies, or mining men with praises,
  Trained their credulity with perjuries,
  Corrupted chastity, or am in love
  With mine own tender ease, but would not rather
  Prove the most rugged, and laborious course,
  That might redeem my present estimation,
  Let me here perish, in all hope of goodness.
BON. [*Aside*] This cannot be a personated passion.—
  I was to blame, so to mistake thy nature;
  Prithee, forgive me: and speak out thy business.
MOS. Sir, it concerns you; and though I may seem,
  At first to make a main offence in manners,
  And in my gratitude unto my master;
  Yet, for the pure love, which I bear all right,
  And hatred of the wrong, I must reveal it.
  This very hour your father is in purpose
  To disinherit you—
BON. How!
MOS. And thrust you forth,
  As a mere stranger to his blood; 'tis true, sir,
  The work no way engageth me, but, as
  I claim an interest in the general state
  Of goodness and true virtue, which I hear

1. Servility.
2. Service.

To abound in you: and, for which mere respect,
Without a second aim, sir, I have done it.
BON. This tale hath lost thee much of the late trust
Thou hadst with me; it is impossible:
I know not how to lend it any thought,
My father should be so unnatural.
MOS. It is a confidence that well becomes,
Your piety; and formed, no doubt, it is
From your own simple innocence: which makes
Your wrong more monstrous and abhorred. But, sir,
I now will tell you more. This very minute,
It is, or will be doing; and, if you
Shall be but pleased to go with me, I'll bring you,
I dare not say where you shall see, but where
Your ear shall be a witness of the deed;
Hear yourself written bastard, and professed
The common issue of the earth.[1]
BON. I am amazed!
MOS. Sir, if I do it not, draw your just sword,
And score your vengeance on my front and face:
Mark me your villain: you have too much wrong,
And I do suffer for you, sir. My heart
Weeps blood in anguish—
BON. Lead; I follow thee.

Exeunt

SCENE II

Enter Volpone

VOLP. Mosca stays long, methinks.—Bring forth your sports,
And help to make the wretched time more sweet.

Enter Nano, Androgyno, and Castrone

NAN. Dwarf, fool, and eunuch, well met here we be.
A question it were now, whether[2] of us three,

1. *Filius Terrae*—a Roman term for a child with no known father.
2. Which.

Being all the known delicates of a rich man,
In pleasing him, claim the precedency can?

CAS. I claim for myself.

AND. And so doth the fool.

NAN. 'Tis foolish indeed: let me set you both to school.
First for your dwarf, he's little and witty,
And every thing, as it is little, is pretty;
Else why do men say to a creature of my shape,
So soon as they see him, It's a pretty little ape?
And why a pretty ape, but for pleasing imitation
Of greater men's actions, in a ridiculous fashion?
Beside, this feat body of mine doth not crave
Half the meat, drink, and cloth, one of your bulks will have.
Admit your fool's face be the mother of laughter,
Yet, for his brain, it must always come after:
And though that do feed him, it's a pitiful case,
His body is beholding to such a bad face.

[Knocking within]

VOLP. Who's there? my couch; away! look! Nano, see:

Exeunt Androgyno and Castrone

Give me my caps, first—go, enquire. [*Exit Nano*]—Now, Cupid
Send it be Mosca, and with fair return!

NAN. [*Within*] It is the beauteous madam—

VOLP. Would-be—is it?

NAN. The same.

VOLP. Now torment on me! Squire her in;
For she will enter, or dwell here for ever:
Nay, quickly. [*Retires to his couch*]—That my fit were past! I fear
A second hell too, that my loathing this
Will quite expel my appetite to the other:[1]
Would she were taking now her tedious leave.
Lord, how it threats me what I am to suffer!

Enter Nano, with Lady Politick Would-be

LADY P. I thank you, good sir. 'Pray you signify
Unto your patron, I am here.—This band

---

1. i.e., Celia.

Shews not my neck enough.—I trouble you, sir;
Let me request you, bid one of my women
Come hither to me.—In good faith, I am dressed
Most favorably to-day! It is no matter:
'Tis well enough.—

Enter 1st Waiting-woman

Look, see, these petulant things,
How they have done this!
VOLP. [*Aside*] I do feel the fever
Entering in at mine ears; O, for a charm,
To fright it hence!
LADY P. Come nearer: is this curl
In his right place, or this? Why is this higher
Than all the rest? You have not washed your eyes, yet!
Or do they not stand even in your head?
Where is your fellow? call her.

Exit 1st Woman

NAN. Now, St. Mark
Deliver us! anon, she'll beat her women,
Because her nose is red.

Re-enter 1st with 2nd Woman

LADY P. I pray you, view
This tire, forsooth: are all things apt, or no?
1 WOM. One hair a little, here, sticks out, forsooth.
LADY P. Does't so, forsooth! and where was your dear sight,
When it did so, forsooth! What now! bird-eyed?
And you, too? 'Pray you, both approach and mend it.
Now, by that light, I muse you are not ashamed!
I, that have preached these things so oft unto you,
Read you the principles, argued all the grounds,
Disputed every fitness, every grace,
Called you to counsel of so frequent dressings—
NAN. [*Aside*] More carefully than of your fame or honor.
LADY P. Made you acquainted, what an ample dowry
The knowledge of these things would be unto you,
Able, alone, to get you noble husbands

At your return: and you thus to neglect it!
Besides you seeing what a curious nation
The Italians are, what will they say of me?
The English lady cannot dress herself.
Here's a fine imputation to our country!
Well, go your ways, and stay in the next room.
This fucus[1] was too coarse too; it's no matter.—
Good sir, you'll give them entertainment?

Exeunt Nano and Waiting-women

VOLP. The storm comes toward me.

LADY P. [*Goes to the couch*] How does my Volpone?

VOLP. Troubled with noise, I cannot sleep; I dreamt
That a strange fury entered, now, my house,
And, with the dreadful tempest of her breath,
Did cleave my roof asunder.

LADY P. Believe me, and I
Had the most fearful dream, could I remember't—

VOLP. [*Aside*] Out of my fate! I have given her the occasion
How to torment me: she will tell me hers.

LADY P. Me thought, the golden mediocrity,[2]
Polite and delicate—

VOLP. O, if you do love me,
No more: I sweat, and suffer, at the mention
Of any dream; feel how I tremble yet.

LADY P. Alas, good soul! the passion of the heart.[3]
Seed-pearl were good now, boiled with syrup of apples,
Tincture of gold, and coral, citron-pills,
Your elicampane root, myrobalanes—

VOLP. [*Aside*] Ah me, I have ta'en a grass-hopper by the wing!

LADY P. Burnt silk, and amber: You have muscadel
Good in the house—

VOLP. You will not drink, and part?

LADY P. No, fear not that. I doubt, we shall not get
Some English saffron, half a dram would serve;

---

1. Makeup.
2. Golden mean.
3. Heartburn.

Your sixteen cloves, a little musk, dried mints,
Bugloss, and barley-meal—
VOLP. [*Aside*] She's in again!
Before I feigned diseases, now I have one.
LADY P. And these applied with a right scarlet cloth.
VOLP. [*Aside*] Another flood of words! a very torrent!
LADY P. Shall I, sir, make you a poultice?
VOLP. No, no, no,
I'm very well, you need prescribe no more.
LADY P. I have a little studied physic; but now,
I'm all for music, save, in the forenoons,
An hour or two for painting. I would have
A lady, indeed, to have all, letters and arts,
Be able to discourse, to write, to paint,
But principal, as Plato holds, your music,
And so does wise Pythagoras, I take it,
Is your true rapture: when there is concent[1]
In face, in voice, and clothes: and is, indeed,
Our sex's chiefest ornament.
VOLP. The poet
As old in time as Plato, and as knowing,[2]
Says, that your highest female grace is silence.
LADY P. Which of your poets? Petrarch, or Tasso, or Dante?
Guarini? Ariosto? Aretine?
Cieco di Hadria? I have read them all.
VOLP. [*Aside*] Is every thing a cause to my destruction?
LADY P. I think I have two or three of them about me.
VOLP. [*Aside*] The sun, the sea, will sooner both stand still
Than her eternal tongue! nothing can 'scape it.
LADY P. Here's Pastor Fido—[3]
VOLP. [*Aside*] Profess obstinate silence;
That's now my safest.
LADY P. All our English writers,
I mean such as are happy in the Italian,

1. Harmony.
2. Sophocles.
3. Pastoral play by G. B. Guarini.

Will deign to steal out of this author, mainly:
Almost as much as from Montagnié:
He has so modern and facile a vein,
Fitting the time, and catching the court-ear!
Your Petrarch is more passionate, yet he,
In days of sonnetting, trusted them with much:
Dante is hard, and few can understand him.
But, for a desperate wit, there's Aretine;[1]
Only, his pictures are a little obscene—
You mark me not.

VOLP. Alas, my mind's perturbed.

LADY P. Why, in such cases, we must cure ourselves,
Make use of our philosophy—

VOLP. Oh me!

LADY P. And as we find our passions do rebel,
Encounter them with reason, or divert them,
By giving scope unto some other humor
Of lesser danger: as, in politic bodies,
There's nothing more doth overwhelm the judgment,
And cloud the understanding, than too much
Settling and fixing, and, as 'twere, subsiding
Upon one object. For the incorporating
Of these same outward things, into that part,
Which we call mental, leaves some certain fæces
That stop the organs, and as Plato says,
Assassinate our knowledge.

VOLP. [*Aside*] Now, the spirit
Of patience help me!

LADY P. Come, in faith, I must
Visit you more a days; and make you well;
Laugh and be lusty.

VOLP. [*Aside*] My good angel save me!

LADY P. There was but one sole man in all the world,
With whom I e'er could sympathise; and he
Would lie you, often, three, four hours together
To hear me speak; and be sometimes so rapt,

1. His pornographic poems were famous.

As he would answer me quite from the purpose,
Like you, and you are like him, just. I'll discourse,
An't be but only, sir, to bring you asleep,
How we did spend our time and loves together,
For some six years.

VOLP. Oh, oh, oh, oh, oh, oh!

LADY P. For we were coætanei,[1] and brought up—

VOLP. Some power, some fate, some fortunes rescue me!

Enter Mosca

MOS. God save you, madam!

LADY P. Good sir.

VOLP. Mosca! welcome,
Welcome to my redemption.

MOS. Why, sir?

VOLP. Oh,
Rid me of this my torture, quickly, there;
My madam, with the everlasting voice:
The bells, in time of pestilence, ne'er made
Like noise, or were in that perpetual motion!
The cock-pit comes not near it. All my house,
But now, steamed like a bath with her thick breath,
A lawyer could not have been heard; nor scarce
Another woman, such a hail of words
She has let fall. For hell's sake, rid her hence.

MOS. Has she presented?

VOLP. O, I do not care;
I'll take her absence, upon any price,
With any loss.

MOS. Madam—

LADY P. I have brought your patron
A toy, a cap here, of mine own work.

MOS. 'Tis well.
I had forgot to tell you, I saw your knight.
Where you would little think it.—

---

1. Of the same age.

LADY P. Where?

MOS. Marry,
Where yet, if you make haste, you may apprehend
Rowing upon the water in a gondole
With the most cunning courtezan of Venice.

LADY P. Is't true?

MOS. Pursue them, and believe your eyes:
Leave me, to make your gift. [*Exit Lady P. hastily*]—I knew
'twould take:
For, lightly, they that use themselves most license,
Are still most jealous.

VOLP. Mosca, hearty thanks,
For thy quick fiction, and delivery of me.
Now to my hopes, what say'st thou?

Re-enter Lady Politick Would-be

LADY P. But do you hear, sir?—

VOLP. Again! I fear a paroxysm.

LADY P. Which way
Rowed they together?

MOS. Toward the Rialto.

LADY P. I pray you lend me your dwarf.

MOS. I pray you take him.—

Exit Lady P.

Your hopes, sir, are like happy blossoms, fair,
And promise timely fruit, if you will stay
But the maturing; keep you at your couch,
Corbaccio will arrive straight, with the will;
When he is gone, I'll tell you more.

Exit

VOLP. My blood,
My spirits are returned; I am alive:
And like your wanton gamester at primero,[1]
Whose thought had whispered to him, not go less,
Methinks I lie, and draw—for an encounter.[2]

1. Card game.
2. Winning card.

Scene III

Enter Mosca and Bonario

Mos. Sir, here concealed, [*shows him a closet*] you may hear all. But,
    pray you,
    Have patience, sir; [*Knocking within*]—the same's your father knocks:
    I am compelled to leave you.

Exit

Bon. Do so.—Yet
    Cannot my thought imagine this a truth

Goes into the closet

Scene IV

Enter Mosca and Corvino, Celia following

Mos. Death on me! you are come too soon, what meant you?
    Did not I say, I would send?
Corv. Yes, but I feared
    You might forget it, and then they prevent us.
Mos. [*Aside*] Prevent! did e'er man haste so, for his horns?
    A courtier would not ply it so, for a place.
    Well, now there is no helping it, stay here;
    I'll presently return.

Exit

Corv. Where are you, Celia?
    You know not wherefore I have brought you hither?
Cel. Not well, except you told me.
Corv. Now, I will:
    Hark hither.

Exeunt

Scene V

Enter Mosca and Bonario

Mos. Sir, your father hath sent word,
    It will be half an hour ere he come;
    And therefore, if you please to walk the while

Into that gallery—at the upper end,
There are some books to entertain the time:
And I'll take care no man shall come unto you, sir.
BON. Yes, I will stay there.—[*Aside*] I do doubt this fellow.

Exit

MOS. There; he is far enough; he can hear nothing:
And, for his father, I can keep him off.

Exit

SCENE VI

Enter Corvino, forcing in Celia

CORV. Nay, now, there is no starting back, and therefore,
Resolve upon it: I have so decreed.
It must be done. Nor would I move't afore,
Because I would avoid all shifts and tricks,
That might deny me.
CEL. Sir, let me beseech you,
Affect not these strange trials; if you doubt
My chastity, why, lock me up for ever;
Make me the heir of darkness. Let me live,
Where I may please your fears, if not your trust.
CORV. Believe it, I have no such humor,
All that I speak I mean; yet I 'm not mad;
Nor horn-mad, see you? Go to, show yourself
Obedient, and a wife.
CEL. O heaven!
CORV. I say it,
Do so.
CEL. Was this the train?[1]
CORV. I've told you reasons;
What the physicians have set down: how much
It may concern me; what my engagements are;
My means; and the necessity of those means,
For my recovery: wherefore, if you be
Loyal, and mine, be won, respect my venture.

1. Your scheme.

CEL. Before your honor?

CORV. Honor! tut, a breath:
  There's no such thing in nature: a mere term
  Invented to awe fools. What is my gold
  The worse for touching, clothes for being looked on?
  Why, this is no more. An old decrepit wretch,
  That has no sense, no sinew; takes his meat
  With others' fingers; only knows to gape,
  When you do scald his gums; a voice, a shadow;
  And, what can this man hurt you?

CEL. [*Aside*] Lord! what spirit
  Is this hath entered him?

CORV. And for your fame,[1]
  That's such a jig,[2] as if I would go tell it,
  Cry it on the Piazza! who shall know it,
  But he that cannot speak it, and this fellow,
  Whose lips are in my pocket? save yourself,
  (If you'll proclaim't, you may,) I know no other
  Shall come to know it.

CEL. Are heaven and saints then nothing?
  Will they be blind or stupid?

CORV. How!

CEL. Good sir,
  Be jealous still, emulate them; and think
  What hate they burn with toward every sin.

CORV. I grant you: if I thought it were a sin,
  I would not urge you. Should I offer this
  To some young Frenchman, or hot Tuscan blood
  That had read Aretine, conned all his prints,[3]
  Knew every quirk within lust's labyrinth,
  And were professed critic in lechery;
  And I would look upon him, and applaud him,
  This were a sin: but here, 'tis contrary,
  A pious work, mere charity for physic,
  And honest polity, to assure mine own.

1. Reputation.
2. Joke.
3. Pornographic illustrations.

CEL. O heaven! canst thou suffer such a change?

VOLP. Thou art mine honor, Mosca, and my pride,
My joy, my tickling, my delight! Go bring them.

MOS. [*Advancing*] Please you draw near, sir.

CORV. Come on, what—
You will not be rebellious? by that light—

MOS. Sir,
Signior Corvino, here, is come to see you.

VOLP. Oh!

MOS. And hearing of the consultation had,
So lately, for your health, is come to offer,
Or rather, sir, to prostitute—

CORV. Thanks, sweet Mosca.

MOS. Freely, unasked, or unintreated—

CORV. Well.

MOS. As the true fervent instance of his love,
His own most fair and proper wife; the beauty,
Only of price in Venice—

CORV. 'Tis well urged.

MOS. To be your comfortress, and to preserve you.

VOLP. Alas, I am past, already! Pray you, thank him
For his good care and promptness; but for that,
'Tis a vain labor e'en to fight 'gainst heaven;
Applying fire to stone—uh, uh, uh, uh! [*Coughing*]
Making a dead leaf grow again. I take
His wishes gently, though; and you may tell him,
What I have done for him: marry, my state is hopeless.
Will him to pray for me; and to use his fortune
With reverence, when he comes to't.

MOS. Do you hear, sir?
Go to him with your wife.

CORV. Heart of my father!
Wilt thou persist thus? come, I pray thee, come.
Thou seest 'tis nothing, Celia. By this hand,
I shall grow violent. Come, do't, I say.

CEL. Sir, kill me, rather: I will take down poison,
Eat burning coals, do any thing.—

CORV. Be damned!

Heart, I will drag thee hence, home, by the hair;
Cry thee a strumpet through the streets; rip up
Thy mouth unto thine ears; and slit thy nose,
Like a raw rochet!¹—Do not tempt me; come,
Yield, I am loath—Death! I will buy some slave
Whom I will kill, and bind thee to him, alive;
And at my window hang you forth, devising
Some monstrous crime, which I, in capital letters,
Will eat into thy flesh with aquafortis,
And burning corsives, on this stubborn breast.
Now, by the blood thou hast incensed, I'll do it!

CEL. Sir, what you please, you may, I am your martyr.

CORV. Be not thus obstinate, I have not deserved it:
Think who it is intreats you. 'Prithee, sweet;—
Good faith, thou shalt have jewels, gowns, attires,
What thou wilt think, and ask. Do but go kiss him.
Or touch him, but. For my sake.—At my suit.—
This once.—No! not! I shall remember this.
Will you disgrace me thus? Do you thirst my undoing?

MOS. Nay, gentle lady, be advised.

CORV. No, no.
She has watched her time. Ods precious, this is scurvy,
'Tis very scurvy; and you are—

MOS. Nay, good sir.

CORV. An arrant locust, by heaven, a locust!
Whore, crocodile, that hast thy tears prepared,
Expecting how thou'lt bid them flow—

MOS. Nay, pray you, sir!
She will consider.

CEL. Would my life would serve
To satisfy—

CORV. S'death! if she would but speak to him,
And save my reputation, it were somewhat;
But spitefully to affect my utter ruin!

MOS. Ay, now you have put your fortune in her hands.
Why i'faith, it is her modesty, I must quit¹ her.

---

1. A fish.

    If you were absent, she would be more cunning;
    I know it: and dare undertake for her.
    What woman can before her husband? 'pray you,
    Let us depart, and leave her here.
CORV. Sweet Celia,
    Thou may'st redeem all, yet; I'll say no more:
    If not, esteem yourself as lost. Nay, stay there.
                     Shuts the door, and exits with Mosca
CEL. O God, and his good angels! whither, whither,
    Is shame fled human breasts? that with such ease,
    Men dare put off your honors, and their own?
    Is that, which ever was a cause of life,
    Now placed beneath the basest circumstance,
    And modesty an exile made, for money?
VOLP. Ay, in Corvino, and such earth-fed minds,
                     [*Leaping from his couch*]
    That never tasted the true heaven of love.
    Assure thee, Celia, he that would sell thee,
    Only for hope of gain, and that uncertain,
    He would have sold his part of Paradise
    For ready money, had he met a cope-man.[2]
    Why art thou mazed to see me thus revived?
    Rather applaud thy beauty's miracle;
    'Tis thy great work: that hath, not now alone,
    But sundry times raised me, in several shapes,
    And, but this morning, like a mountebank,
    To see thee at thy window: ay, before
    I would have left my practice, for thy love,
    In varying figures, I would have contended
    With the blue Proteus, or the hornèd flood.
    Now art thou welcome.
CEL. Sir!
VOLP. Nay, fly me not.
    Nor let thy false imagination
    That I was bed-rid, make thee think I am so:

1. Acquit.
2. Buyer.

Thou shalt not find it. I am, now, as fresh,
As hot, as high, and in as jovial plight,
As when, in that so celebrated scene,
At recitation of our comedy,
For entertainment of the great Valois,[1]
I acted young Antinous;[2] and attracted
The eyes and ears of all the ladies present,
To admire each graceful gesture, note, and footing.

[*Sings*]

Come, my Celia, let us prove,
While we can, the sports of love,
Time will not be ours for ever,
He, at length, our good will sever;
Spend not then his gifts in vain;
Suns, that set, may rise again;
But if once we lose this light,
'Tis with us perpetual night.
Why should we defer our joys?
Fame and rumor are but toys.
Cannot we delude the eyes
Of a few poor household spies?
Or his easier ears beguile,
Thus removèd by our wile?—
'Tis no sin love's fruits to steal:
But the sweet thefts to reveal;
To be taken, to be seen,
These have crimes accounted been.

CEL. Some serene[3] blast me, or dire lightning strike
    This my offending face!
VOLP. Why droops my Celia?
    Thou hast, in place of a base husband, found
    A worthy lover: use thy fortune well,
    With secrecy and pleasure. See, behold,

1. Henri III of France.
2. The favorite of the emperor Hadrian.
3. Mist.

What thou art queen of; not in expectation,
As I feed others: but possessed and crowned.
See, here, a rope of pearl; and each, more orient
Than that the brave Ægyptian queen[1] caroused:
Dissolve and drink them. See, a carbuncle,[2]
May put out both the eyes of our St. Mark;
A diamond, would have bought Lollia Paulina,[3]
When she came in like star-light, hid with jewels,
That were the spoils of provinces; take these,
And wear, and lose them: yet remains an ear-ring
To purchase them again, and this whole state.
A gem but worth a private patrimony,
Is nothing: we will eat such at a meal.
The heads of parrots, tongues of nightingales,
The brains of peacocks, and of ostriches,
Shall be our food: and, could we get the phœnix,
Though nature lost her kind, she were our dish.

CEL. Good sir, these things might move a mind affected
With such delights; but I, whose innocence
Is all I can think wealthy, or worth th' enjoying,
And which, once lost, I have nought to lose beyond it,
Cannot be taken with these sensual baits:
If you have conscience—

VOLP. 'Tis the beggar's virtue;
If thou hast wisdom, hear me, Celia.
Thy baths shall be the juice of July-flowers,
Spirit of roses, and of violets,
The milk of unicorns, and panthers' breath
Gathered in bags, and mixt with Cretan wines.
Our drink shall be prepared gold and amber;
Which we will take, until my roof whirl round
With the vertigo: and my dwarf shall dance,
My eunuch sing, my fool make up the antic,

1. Cleopatra.
2. Jewel, usually a ruby.
3. Wife of a Roman governor, who had many jewels.

Whilst we, in changed shapes, act Ovid's tales,
Thou, like Europa now, and I like Jove,
Then I like Mars, and thou like Erycine.[1]
So, of the rest, till we have quite run through,
And wearied all the fables of the gods.
Then will I have thee in more modern forms,
Attired like some sprightly dame of France,
Brave Tuscan lady, or proud Spanish beauty;
Sometimes, unto the Persian sophy's[2] wife;
Or the grand signior's[3] mistress; and, for change,
To one of our most artful courtezans,
Or some quick Negro, or cold Russian;
And I will meet thee in as many shapes:
Where we may so transfuse our wandering souls
Out at our lips, and score up sums of pleasures,

                                                              [*Sings*]

        That the curious shall not know
        How to tell[4] them as they flow;
        And the envious, when they find
        What their number is, be pined.[5]

CEL. If you have ears that will be pierced—or eyes
That can be opened—a heart that may be touched—
Or any part that yet sounds man about you—
If you have touch of holy saints—or heaven—
Do me the grace to let me 'scape—if not,
Be bountiful and kill me. You do know,
I am a creature, hither ill betrayed,
By one, whose shame I would forget it were:
If you will deign me neither of these graces,
Yet feed your wrath, sir, rather than your lust,
(It is a vice comes nearer manliness,)
And punish that unhappy crime of nature,
Which you miscall my beauty: flay my face,

1. Venus.
2. Shah's.
3. Sultan of Turkey's.
4. Count.
5. Depressed, envious.

Or poison it with ointments, for seducing
Your blood to this rebellion. Rub these hands,
With what may cause an eating leprosy,
E'en to my bones and marrow: any thing,
That may disfavor me, save in my honor—
And I will kneel to you, pray for you, pay down
A thousand hourly vows, sir, for your health;
Report, and think you virtuous—

VOLP. Think me cold,
Frozen and impotent, and so report me?
That I had Nestor's hernia[1] thou wouldst think.
I do degenerate, and abuse my nation,
To play with opportunity thus long;
I should have done the act, and then have parleyed.
Yield, or I'll force thee.

[Seizes her]

CEL. O! just God!
VOLP. In vain—
BON. [*Rushing in*] Forbear, foul ravisher, libidinous swine!
Free the forced lady, or thou diest, impostor.
But that I'm loath to snatch thy punishment
Out of the hand of justice, thou shouldst, yet,
Be made the timely sacrifice of vengeance,
Before this altar, and this dross, thy idol.—
Lady, let's quit the place, it is the den
Of villainy; fear nought, you have a guard:
And he, ere long, shall meet his just reward.

Exeunt Bonario and Celia

VOLP. Fall on me, roof, and bury me in ruin!
Become my grave, that wert my shelter! O!
I am unmask'd, unspirited, undone,
Betrayed to beggary, to infamy—

Enter Mosca, bleeding

MOS. Where shall I run, most wretched shame of men,
To beat out my unlucky brains?

---

1. Nestor was the oldest of the Greeks at Troy.

VOLP. Here, here.
 What! dost thou bleed?
MOS. O that his well-driv'n sword
 Had been so courteous to have cleft me down
 Unto the navel, ere I lived to see
 My life, my hopes, my spirits, my patron, all
 Thus desperately engaged, by my error!
VOLP. Woe on thy fortune!
MOS. And my follies, sir.
VOLP. Thou hast made me miserable.
MOS. And myself, sir.
 Who would have thought he would have hearkened so?
VOLP. What shall we do?
MOS. I know not; if my heart
 Could expiate the mischance, I'd pluck it out.
 Will you be pleased to hang me, or cut my throat?
 And I'll requite you, sir. Let's die like Romans,
 Since we have lived like Grecians.

            [*Knocking without*]

VOLP. Hark! who's there?
 I hear some footing; officers, the saffi,[1]
 Come to apprehend us! I do feel the brand
 Hissing already at my forehead; now,
 Mine ears are boring.
MOS. To your couch, sir, you,
 Make that place good, however.

             [*Volpone lies down*]

 Guilty men
 Suspect what they deserve still.

       Enter Corbaccio

 Signior Corbaccio!
CORB. Why, how now, Mosca?
MOS. O, undone, amazed, sir.
 Your son, I know not by what accident,

---

1. Police.

Acquainted with your purpose to my patron,
Touching your will, and making him your heir,
Entered our house with violence, his sword drawn
Sought for you, called you wretch, unnatural,
Vowed he would kill you.

CORB. Me!

MOS. Yes, and my patron.

CORB. This act shall disinherit him indeed;
Here is the will.

MOS. 'Tis well, sir.

CORB. Right and well:
Be you as careful now for me.

Enter Voltore, behind

MOS. My life, sir,
Is not more tendered; I am only yours.

CORB. How does he? will he die shortly, think'st thou?

MOS. I fear
He'll outlast May.

CORB. To-day?

MOS. No, last out May, sir.

CORB. Could'st thou not give him a dram?

MOS. O, by no means, sir.

CORB. Nay, I'll not bid you.

VOLT. [*Coming forward*] This is a knave, I see.

MOS. [*Seeing Voltore. Aside*] How, signior Voltore! did he hear me?

VOLT. Parasite!

MOS. Who's that?—O, sir, most timely welcome—

VOLT. Scarce,
To the discovery of your tricks, I fear.
You are his, *only*? and mine also, are you not?

MOS. Who? I, sir?

VOLT. You, sir. What device is this
About a will?

MOS. A plot for you, sir.

VOLT. Come,
Put not your foists upon me; I shall scent them.

MOS. Did you not hear it?

VOLT. Yes, I hear Corbaccio
    Hath made your patron there his heir.
MOS. 'Tis true,
    By my device, drawn to it by my plot,
    With hope—
VOLT. Your patron should reciprocate?
    And you have promised?
MOS. For your good, I did, sir.
    Nay, more, I told his son, brought, hid him here,
    Where he might hear his father pass the deed:
    Being persuaded to it by this thought, sir,
    That the unnaturalness, first, of the act,
    And then his father's oft disclaiming in him,
    (Which I did mean t'help on,) would sure enrage him
    To do some violence upon his parent,
    On which the law should take sufficient hold,
    And you be stated in a double hope:
    Truth be my comfort, and my conscience,
    My only aim was to dig you a fortune
    Out of these two old rotten sepulchres—
VOLT. I cry thee mercy, Mosca.
MOS. Worth your patience,
    And your great merit, sir. And see the change!
VOLT. Why, what success?
MOS. Most hapless! you must help, sir.
    Whilst we expected the old raven, in comes
    Corvino's wife, sent hither by her husband—
VOLT. What, with a present?
MOS. No, sir, on visitation;
    (I'll tell you how anon;) and staying long,
    The youth he grows impatient, rushes forth,
    Seizeth the lady, wounds me, makes her swear
    (Or he would murder her, that was his vow)
    To affirm my patron to have done her rape:
    Which how unlike it is, you see! and hence,
    With that pretext he's gone, to accuse his father,
    Defame my patron, defeat you—

VOLT. Where is her husband?
  Let him be sent for straight.
MOS. Sir, I'll go fetch him.
VOLT. Bring him to the Scrutineo.[1]
MOS. Sir, I will.
VOLT. This must be stopped.
MOS. O you do nobly, sir.
  Alas, 'twas labored all, sir, for your good;
  Nor was there want of counsel in the plot:
  But fortune can, at any time, o'erthrow
  The projects of a hundred learned clerks, sir.
CORB. [*Listening*] What's that?
VOLT. Will't please you, sir, to go along?

> *Exit Corbaccio, followed by Voltore*

MOS. Patron, go in, and pray for our success.
VOLP. [*Rising from his couch*] Need makes devotion: heaven your
  labor bless!

> *Exeunt*

ACT IV, SCENE I

Enter Sir Politick Would-be and Peregrine

SIR P. I told you, sir, it was a plot; you see
  What observation is! You mentioned me
  For some instructions: I will tell you, sir,
  (Since we are met here in the height of Venice,)
  Some few particulars I have set down,
  Only for this meridian, fit to be known
  Of your crude[2] traveller; and they are these.
  I will not touch, sir, at your phrase, or clothes,
  For they are old.
PER. Sir, I have better.
SIR P. Pardon,
  I meant, as they are themes.

---

1. Law court.
2. Raw.

PER. O, sir, proceed:
    I'll slander you no more of wit, good sir.
SIR P. First, for your garb, it must be grave and serious,
    Very reserved and locked; not tell a secret
    On any terms, not to your father; scarce
    A fable, but with caution: made sure choice
    Both of your company, and discourse; beware
    You never speak a truth—
PER. How!
SIR P. Not to strangers,
    For those be they you must converse with most;
    Others I would not know, sir, but at distance,
    So as I still might be a saver in them:[1]
    You shall have tricks else past upon you hourly.
    And then, for your religion, profess none,
    But wonder at the diversity, of all:
    And, for your part, protest, were there no other
    But simply the laws o' the land, you could content you,
    Nic. Machiavel, and Monsieur Bodin,[2] both
    Were of this mind. Then must you learn the use
    And handling of your silver fork[3] at meals,
    The metal of your glass; (these are main matters
    With your Italian;) and to know the hour
    When you must eat your melons, and your figs.
PER. Is that a point of state too?
SIR P. Here it is:
    For your Venetian, if he see a man
    Preposterous in the least, he has him straight;
    He has; he strips him. I'll acquaint you, sir,
    I now have lived here, 'tis some fourteen months
    Within the first week of my landing here,
    All took me for a citizen of Venice,
    I knew the forms so well—
PER. [*Aside*] And nothing else.

---

1. Not be obliged to lend them money.
2. French philosopher.
3. Still not used in England.

SIR P. I had read Contarene,[1] took me a house,
    Dealt with my Jews to furnish it with moveables—
    Well, if I could but find one man, one man
    To mine own heart, whom I durst trust, I would—
PER. What, what, sir?
SIR P. Make him rich; make him a fortune:
    He should not think again. I would command it.
PER. As how?
SIR P. With certain projects that I have;
    Which I may not discover.
PER. [*Aside*] If I had
    But one to wager with, I would lay odds now,
    He tells me instantly.
SIR P. One is, and that
    I care not greatly who knows, to serve the state
    Of Venice with red herrings for three years,
    And at a certain rate, from Rotterdam,
    Where I have correspondence. There's a letter,
    Sent me from one o' the states, and to that purpose:
    He cannot write his name, but that's his mark.
PER. He is a chandler?
SIR P. No, a cheesemonger.
    There are some others too with whom I treat
    About the same negotiation;
    And I will undertake it: for, 'tis thus.
    I'll do't with ease, I have cast it all: Your hoy[2]
    Carries but three men in her, and a boy;
    And she shall make me three returns a year:
    So, if there come but one of three, I save;
    If two, I can defalk:[3]—but this is now,
    If my main project fail.
PER. Then you have others?
SIR P. I should be loath to draw the subtle air
    Of such a place, without my thousand aims.
    I'll not dissemble, sir: where'er I come,

1. Writer on Venetian government.
2. Small boat.
3. Lower the price.

I love to be considerative; and 'tis true,
I have at my free hours thought upon
Some certain goods unto the state of Venice,
Which I do call *my Cautions;* and, sir, which
I mean, in hope of pension, to propound
To the Great Council, then unto the Forty,
So to the Ten.[1] My means are made already—

PER. By whom?

SIR P. Sir, one that, though his place be obscure,
Yet he can sway, and they will hear him. He's
A commandador.

PER. What! a common serjeant?

SIR P. Sir, such as they are, put it in their mouths,
What they should say, sometimes as well as greater:
I think I have my notes to show you— [*Searching his pockets*]

PER. Good sir.

SIR P. But you shall swear unto me, on your gentry,
Not to anticipate—

PER. I, sir!

SIR P. Nor reveal
A circumstance—My paper is not with me.

PER. O, but you can remember, sir.

SIR P. My first is
Concerning tinder-boxes. You must know,
No family is here without its box.
Now, sir, it being so portable a thing,
Put case, that you or I were ill affected
Unto the state, sir; with it in our pockets,
Might not I go into the Arsenal,[2]
Or you, come out again, and none the wiser?

PER. Except yourself, sir.

SIR P. Go to, then. I therefore
Advertise to the state, how fit it were,
That none but such as were known patriots,
Sound lovers of their country, should be suffered

1. Grades in Venetian government.
2. Armament store.

  To enjoy them in their houses; and even those
  Sealed at some office, and at such a bigness
  As might not lurk in pockets.

PER. Admirable!

SIR P. My next is, how to enquire, and be resolved,
  By present demonstration, whether a ship,
  Newly arrived from Syria, or from
  Any suspected part of all the Levant,
  Be guilty of the plague: and where they use
  To lie out forty, fifty days, sometimes,
  About the Lazaretto, for their trial,[1]
  I'll save that charge and loss unto the merchant,
  And in an hour clear the doubt.

PER. Indeed, sir!

SIR P. Or—I will lose my labor.

PER. 'My faith, that's much.

SIR P. Nay, sir, conceive me. It will cost me in onions,[2]
  Some thirty livres—

PER. Which is one pound sterling.

SIR P. Beside my water-works: for this I do, sir.
  First, I bring in your ship 'twixt two brick walls;
  But those the state shall venture: On the one
  I strain me a fair tarpaulin, and in that
  I stick my onions, cut in halves: the other
  Is full of loop-holes, out at which I thrust
  The noses of my bellows; and those bellows
  I keep, with water-works, in perpetual motion,
  Which is the easiest matter of a hundred.
  Now, sir, your onion, which doth naturally
  Attract the infection, and your bellows blowing
  The air upon him, will show, instantly,
  By his changed color, if there be contagion;
  Or else remain as fair as at the first.
  —Now it is known, 'tis nothing.

PER. You are right, sir.

---

1. Quarantine.
2. Thought to be effective against plague.

SIR P. I would I had my note.

PER. 'Faith, so would I:
But you have done well for once, sir.

SIR P. Were I false,
Or would be made so, I could show you reasons
How I could sell this state now to the Turk,
Spite of their galleys or their—

[*Examining his papers*]

PER. Pray you, sir Pol.

SIR P. I have them not about me.

PER. That I feared:
They are there, sir.

SIR P. No, this is my diary,
Wherein I note my actions of the day.

PER. Pray you, let's see, sir. What is here? [*Reads*]
Notandum,
A rat had gnawn my spur-leathers; notwithstanding,
I put on new, and did go forth: but first
I threw three beans over the threshold. Item,
I went and bought two tooth-picks, whereof one
I burst immediately, in a discourse
With a Dutch merchant, 'bout ragion del stato.[1]
From him I went and paid a moccinigo
For piecing my silk stockings; by the way
I cheapened[2] sprats; and at St. Mark's I urined.
'Faith these are politic notes!

SIR P. Sir, I do slip
No action of my life, but thus I quote it.

PER. Believe me, it is wise!

SIR P. Nay, sir, read forth.

*Enter, at a distance, Lady Politick Would-be, Nano, and two
Waiting-women.*

LADY P. Where should this loose knight be, trow? sure he's housed.

NAN. Why, then he's fast.

1. Reason of state.
2. Bargained for.

LADY P. Ay, he plays both with me.
 I pray you stay. This heat will do more harm
 To my complexion, than his heart is worth.
 (I do not care to hinder, but to take him.)
 How it comes off!

                                              [*Rubbing her cheeks*]

1 WOM. My master's yonder.
LADY P. Where?
2 WOM. With a young gentleman.
LADY P. That same's the party;
 In man's apparel! 'Pray you, sir, jog my knight:
 I will be tender to his reputation,
 However he demerit.
SIR P. [*Seeing her*] My lady!
PER. Where?
SIR P. 'Tis she indeed, sir; you shall know her. She is,
 Were she not mine, a lady of that merit,
 For fashion and behavior; and for beauty
 I durst compare—
PER. It seems you are not jealous,
 That dare commend her.
SIR P. Nay, and for discourse—
PER. Being your wife, she cannot miss that.
SIR P. [*Introducing Peregrine*] Madam,
 Here is a gentleman, pray you, use him fairly;
 He seems a youth, but he is—
LADY P. None.
SIR P. Yes, one
 Has put his face as soon into the world—
LADY P. You mean, as early? but to-day?
SIR P. How's this?
LADY P. Why, in this habit, sir; you apprehend me:—
 Well, master Would-be, this doth not become you;
 I had thought the odor, sir, of your good name
 Had been more precious to you; that you would not
 Have done this dire massacre on your honor;
 One of your gravity and rank besides!

But knights, I see, care little for the oath
They make to ladies; chiefly, their own ladies.
SIR P. Now, by my spurs, the symbol of my knighthood,—
PER. [*Aside*] Lord, how his brain is humbled for an oath!
SIR P. I reach you not.
LADY P. Right, sir, your policy
    May bear it through thus.—Sir, a word with you.

[To Peregrine]

I would be loath to contest publicly
With any gentlewoman, or to seem
Forward, or violent, as the courtier says;
It comes too near rusticity in a lady,
Which I would shun by all means: and however
I may deserve from master Would-be, yet
T'have one fair gentlewoman thus be made
The unkind instrument to wrong another,
And one she knows not, ay, and to perséver;
In my poor judgment, is not warranted
From being a solecism in our sex,
If not in manners.
PER. How is this!
SIR P. Sweet madam,
    Come nearer to your aim.
LADY P. Marry, and will, sir.
    Since you provoke me with your impudence,
And laughter of your light land-siren here,
Your Sporus,[1] your hermaphrodite—
PER. What's here?
    Poetic fury, and historic storms!
SIR P. The gentleman, believe it, is of worth,
    And of our nation.
LADY P. Ay, Your White-friars[2] nation.
    Come, I blush for you, master Would-be, I;
And am ashamed you should have no more forehead,[3]

---

1. Lover of Nero's.
2. Red-light district.
3. Shame.

Than thus to be the patron, or St. George,
To a lewd harlot, a base fricatrice,[1]
A female devil, in a male outside.

SIR P. Nay,
An you be such a one, I must bid adieu
To your delights. The case appears too liquid.

Exit

LADY P. Ay, you may carry't clear, with your state-face!—
But for your carnival concupiscence,
Who here is fled for liberty of conscience,
From furious persecution of the marshal,
Her will I dis'ple.[2]

PER. This is fine, i'faith!
And do you use this often? Is this part
Of your wit's exercise, 'gainst you have occasion?
Madam—

LADY P. Go to, sir.

PER. Do you hear me, lady?
Why, if your knight have set you to beg shirts,
Or to invite me home, you might have done it
A nearer way, by far.

LADY P. This cannot work you
Out of my snare.

PER. Why, am I in it, then?
Indeed your husband told me you were fair.
And so you are; only your nose inclines,
That side that's next the sun, to the queen-apple.

LADY P. This cannot be endured by any patience.

Enter Mosca

MOS. What is the matter, madam?

LADY P. If the senate
Right not my quest in this, I will protest them
To all the world, no aristocracy.

MOS. What is the injury, lady?

---

1. Whore.
2. Discipline with a whip.

LADY P. Why, the callet
    You told me of, here I have ta'en disguised.
MOS. Who? this! what means your ladyship? the creature
    I mentioned to you is apprehended now,
    Before the senate; you shall see her—
LADY P. Where?
MOS. I'll bring you to her. This young gentleman,
    I saw him land this morning at the port.
LADY P. Is't possible! how has my judgment wandered?
    Sir, I must, blushing, say to you, I have erred;
    And plead your pardon.
PER. What, more changes yet!
LADY P. I hope you have not the malice to remember
    A gentlewoman's passion. If you stay
    In Venice here, please you to use me, sir—
MOS. Will you go, madam?
LADY P. 'Pray you, sir, use me; in faith,
    The more you see me, the more I shall conceive
    You have forgot our quarrel.
              Exeunt Lady Would-be, Mosca, Nano, and Waiting-women
PER. This is rare!
    Sir Politick Would-be? no; sir Politick Bawd,
    To bring me thus acquainted with his wife!
    Well, wise sir Pol, since you have practised thus
    Upon my freshman-ship, I'll try your salt-head,
    What proof it is against a counter-plot.

                        Exit

SCENE II

Enter Voltore, Corbaccio, Corvino, and Mosca

VOLT. Well, now you know the carriage of the business,
    Your constancy is all that is required
    Unto the safety of it.
MOS. Is the lie
    Safely conveyed amongst us? is that sure?
    Knows every man his burden?
CORV. Yes.

MOS. Then shrink not.

CORV. But knows the advocate the truth?

MOS. O, sir,
    By no means; I devised a formal tale,
    That salved your reputation. But be valiant, sir.

CORV. I fear no one but him, that this his pleading
    Should make him stand for a co-heir—

MOS. Co-halter!
    Hang him; we will but use his tongue, his noise,
    As we do Croaker's[1] here.

CORV. Ay, what shall he do?

MOS. When we have done, you mean?

CORV. Yes.

MOS. Why, we'll think:
    Sell him for mummia; he's half dust already.
    Do you not smile, [*to Voltore*] to see this buffalo,
    How he doth sport it with his head?—I should,
    If all were well and past. [*Aside*]—Sir, [*to Corbaccio*] only you
    Are he that shall enjoy the crop of all,
    And these not know for whom they toil.

CORB. Ay, peace.

MOS. [*Turning to Corvino*] But you shall eat it. Much!
    [*Aside*]—Worshipful sir, [*to Voltore*]
    Mercury sit upon your thundering tongue,
    Or the French Hercules, and make your language
    As conquering as his club, to beat along,
    As with a tempest, flat, our adversaries;
    But much more yours, sir.

VOLT. Here they come, have done.

MOS. I have another witness, if you need, sir,
    I can produce.

VOLT. Who is it?

MOS. Sir, I have her.

Enter Avocatori and take their seats, Bonario, Celia, Notario,
Commandadori, Saffi, and other Officers of justice

---

1. i.e., Voltore's.

1 AVOC. The like of this the senate never heard of.

2 AVOC. 'Twill come most strange to them when we report it.

4 AVOC. The gentlewoman has been ever held
    Of unreproved name.

3 AVOC. So has the youth.

4 AVOC. The more unnatural part that of his father.

2 AVOC. More of the husband.

1 AVOC. I not know to give
    His act a name, it is so monstrous!

4 AVOC. But the impostor, he's a thing created
    To exceed example!

1 AVOC. And all after-times!

2 AVOC. I never heard a true voluptuary
    Described, but him.

3 AVOC. Appear yet those were cited?

NOT. All but the old magnifico, Volpone.

1 AVOC. Why is not he here?

MOS. Please your fatherhoods
    Here is his advocate: himself's so weak,
    So feeble—

4 AVOC. What are you?

BON. His parasite,
    His knave, his pandar: I beseech the court,
    He may be forced to come, that your grave eyes
    May bear strong witness of his strange impostures.

VOLT. Upon my faith and credit with your virtues,
    He is not able to endure the air.

2 AVOC. Bring him, however.

3 AVOC. We will see him.

4 AVOC. Fetch him.

VOLT. Your fatherhoods' fit pleasures be obeyed;

                                   Exeunt Officers

    But sure, the sight will rather move your pities,
    Than indignation. May it please the court,
    In the mean time, he may be heard in me;
    I know this place most void of prejudice,
    And therefore crave it, since we have no reason
    To fear our truth should hurt our cause.

3 AVOC. Speak free.

VOLT. Then know, most honored fathers, I must now
    Discover to your strangely abused ears,
    The most prodigious and most frontless[1] piece
    Of solid impudence, and treachery,
    That ever vicious nature yet brought forth
    To shame the state of Venice. This lewd woman,
    That wants no artificial looks or tears
    To help the vizor she has now put on,
    Hath long been known a close adulteress
    To that lascivious youth there; not suspected,
    I say, but known, and taken in the act
    With him; and by this man, the easy husband,
    Pardoned; whose timeless bounty makes him now
    Stand here, the most unhappy, innocent person,
    That ever man's own goodness made accused.
    For these not knowing how to owe a gift
    Of that dear grace, but with their shame; being placed
    So above all powers of their gratitude,
    Began to hate the benefit; and, in place
    Of thanks, devise to extirpe the memory
    Of such an act: wherein I pray your fatherhoods
    To observe the malice, yea, the rage of creatures
    Discovered in their evils; and what heart
    Such take, even from their crimes:—but that anon
    Will more appear.—This gentleman, the father,
    Hearing of this foul fact, with many others,
    Which daily struck at his too tender ears,
    And grieved in nothing more than that he could not
    Preserve himself a parent, (his son's ills
    Growing to that strange flood,) at last decreed
    To disinherit him.

1 AVOC. These be strange turns!

2 AVOC. The young man's fame was ever fair and honest.

VOLT. So much more full of danger is his vice,
    That can beguile so under shade of virtue.

1. Shameless.

But, as I said, my honored sires, his father
Having this settled purpose, by what means
To him betrayed, we know not, and this day
Appointed for the deed; that parricide,
I cannot style him better, by confederacy
Preparing this his paramour to be there,
Entered Volpone's house, (who was the man,
Your fatherhoods must understand, designed
For the inheritance,) there sought his father:—
But with what purpose sought he him, my lords?
I tremble to pronounce it, that a son
Unto a father, and to such a father,
Should have so foul, felonious intent!
It was to murder him: when being prevented
By his more happy absence, what then did he?
Not check his wicked thoughts; no, now new deeds,
(Mischief doth never end where it begins)
An act of horror, fathers! he dragged forth
The agèd gentleman that had there lain bed-rid
Three years and more, out of his innocent couch,
Naked upon the floor, there left him; wounded
His servant in the face: and, with this strumpet
The stale[1] to his forged practice, who was glad
To be so active,—(I shall here desire
Your fatherhoods to note but my collections,[2]
As most remarkable,—) thought at once to stop
His father's ends, discredit his free choice
In the old gentleman, redeem themselves,
By laying infamy upon this man,
To whom, with blushing, they should owe their lives.

1 AVOC. What proofs have you of this?

BON. Most honored fathers,
     I humbly crave there be no credit given
     To this man's mercenary tongue.

2 AVOC. Forbear.

BON. His soul moves in his fee.

1. Decoy.
2. Deductions.

3 AVOC. O sir.

BON. This fellow,
For six sols more, would plead against his Maker.

1 AVOC. You do forget yourself.

VOLT. Nay, nay, grave fathers,
Let him have scope: can any man imagine
That he will spare his accuser, that would not
Have spared his parent?

1 AVOC. Well, produce your proofs.

CEL. I would I could forget I were a creature.

VOLT. Signior Corbaccio!

[*Corbaccio comes forward*]

4 AVOC. What is he?

VOLT. The father.

2 AVOC. Has he had an oath?

NOT. Yes.

CORB. What must I do now?

NOT. Your testimony's craved.

CORB. Speak to the knave?
I'll have my mouth first stopped with earth; my heart
Abhors his knowledge: I disclaim in him.

1 AVOC. But for what cause?

CORB. The mere portent of nature!
He is an utter stranger to my loins.

BON. Have they made you to this?

CORB. I will not hear thee,
Monster of men, swine, goat, wolf, parricide!
Speak not, thou viper.

BON. Sir, I will sit down,
And rather wish my innocence should suffer,
Than I resist the authority of a father.

VOLT. Signior Corvino!

[*Corvino comes forward*]

2 AVOC. This is strange.

1 AVOC. Who's this?

NOT. The husband.

4 AVOC. Is he sworn?

NOT. He is.

3 AVOC. Speak, then.

CORV. This woman, please your fatherhoods, is a whore,
  Of most hot exercise, more than a partridge,
  Upon record—

1 AVOC. No more.

CORV. Neighs like a jennet.[1]

NOT. Preserve the honor of the court.

CORV. I shall,
  And modesty of your most reverend ears.
  And yet I hope that I may say, these eyes
  Have seen her glued unto that piece of cedar,
  That fine well-timbered gallant; and that here[2]
  The letters may be read, thorough the horn,[3]
  That makes the story perfect.

MOS. Excellent! sir.

CORV. [*Aside to Mosca*] There is no shame in this now, is there?

MOS. None.

CORV. Or if I said, I hoped that she were onward
  To her damnation, if there be a hell
  Greater than whore and woman; a good Catholic
  May make the doubt.

3 AVOC. His grief hath made him frantic.

1 AVOC. Remove him hence.

2 AVOC. Look to the woman.

                                        [*Celia swoons*]

CORV. Rare!
  Prettily feigned, again!

4 AVOC. Stand from about her.

1 AVOC. Give her the air.

3 AVOC. [*To Mosca*] What can you say?

MOS. My wound,
  May it please your wisdoms, speaks for me, received
  In aid of my good patron, when he missed
  His sought-for father, when that well-taught dame
  Had her cue given her, to cry out, A rape!

1. Mare.
2. He points to his cuckold's horns.
3. Horn was the transparent cover of children's first readers.

BON. O most laid impudence! Fathers—

3 AVOC. Sir, be silent;
 You had your hearing free, so must they theirs.

2 AVOC. I do begin to doubt the imposture here.

4 AVOC. This woman has too many moods.

VOLT. Grave fathers,
 She is a creature of a most professed
 And prostituted lewdness.

CORV. Most impetuous,
 Unsatisfied, grave fathers!

VOLT. May her feignings
 Not take your wisdoms: but this day she baited
 A stranger, a grave knight, with her loose eyes,
 And more lascivious kisses. This man saw them
 Together on the water, in a gondola.

MOS. Here is the lady herself, that saw them too;
 Without; who then had in the open streets
 Pursued them, but for saving her knight's honor.

1 AVOC. Produce that lady.

2 AVOC. Let her come.

             Exit Mosca

4 AVOC. These things,
 They strike with wonder.

3 AVOC. I am turned a stone.

    Enter Mosca with Lady Would-be

MOS. Be resolute, madam.

LADY P. Ay, this same is she.

           [*Pointing to Celia*]

 Out, thou chameleon harlot! now thine eyes
 Vie tears with the hyæna. Darest thou look
 Upon my wrongèd face?—I cry your pardons,
 I fear I have forgettingly transgressed
 Against the dignity of the court—

2 AVOC. No, madam.

LADY P. And been exorbitant—

2 AVOC. You have not, lady.

4 AVOC. These proofs are strong.

LADY P. Surely, I had no purpose
    To scandalise your honors, or my sex's.
3 AVOC. We do believe it.
LADY P. Surely, you may believe it.
2 AVOC. Madam, we do.
LADY P. Indeed you may; my breeding
    Is not so coarse—
4 AVOC. We know it.
LADY P. To offend
    With pertinacy—
3 AVOC. Lady—
LADY P. Such a presence!
    No surely.
1 AVOC. We well think it.
LADY P. You may think it.
1 AVOC. Let her o'ercome. What witnesses have you
    To make good your report?
BON. Our consciences.
CEL. And heaven, that never fails the innocent.
4 AVOC. These are no testimonies.
BON. Not in your courts,
    Where multitude, and clamor overcomes.
1 AVOC. Nay, then you do wax insolent.

      Re-enter Officers, bearing Volpone on a couch

VOLT. Here, here,
    The testimony comes, that will convince,
    And put to utter dumbness their bold tongues:
    See here, grave fathers, here's the ravisher,
    The rider on men's wives, the great impostor,
    The grand voluptuary! Do you not think
    These limbs should affect venery? or these eyes
    Covet a concubine? pray you mark these hands;
    Are they not fit to stroke a lady's breasts?—
    Perhaps he doth dissemble!
BON. So he does.
VOLT. Would you have him tortured?
BON. I would have him proved.

VOLT. Best try him then with goads, or burning irons;
　　Put him to the strappado: I have heard
　　The rack hath cured the gout; 'faith, give it him,
　　And help him of a malady; be courteous.
　　I'll undertake, before these honored fathers,
　　He shall have yet as many left diseases,
　　As she has known adulterers, or thou strumpets.—
　　O my most equal hearers, if these deeds,
　　Acts of this bold and most exorbitant strain,
　　May pass with sufferance, what one citizen
　　But owes the forfeit of his life, yea, fame,
　　To him that dares traduce him? which of you
　　Are safe, my honored fathers? I would ask,
　　With leave of your grave fatherhoods, if their plot
　　Have any face or color like to truth?
　　Or if, unto the dullest nostril here,
　　It smell not rank, and most abhorred slander?
　　I crave your care of this good gentleman,
　　Whose life is much endangered by their fable;
　　And as for them, I will conclude with this,
　　That vicious persons, when they're hot and fleshed
　　In impious acts, their constancy abounds:
　　Damned deeds are done with greatest confidence.
1 AVOC. Take them to custody, and sever them.
2 AVOC. 'Tis pity two such prodigies should live.
1 AVOC. Let the old gentleman be returned with care.
　　　　　　　　　　　　　Exeunt Officers with Volpone
　　I'm sorry your credulity hath wronged him.
4 AVOC. These are two creatures!
3 AVOC. I've an earthquake in me.
2 AVOC. Their shame, even in their cradles, fled their faces.
4 AVOC. [*To Voltore*] You have done a worthy service to the state, sir,
　　In their discovery.
1 AVOC. You shall hear, ere night,
　　What punishment the court decrees upon them.
　　　　　Exeunt Avocatori, Notario, and Officers with Bonario and Celia
VOLT. We thank your fatherhoods.—How like you it?
MOS. Rare.

I'd have your tongue, sir, tipped with gold for this;
I'd have you be the heir to the whole city;
The earth I'd have want men, ere you want living:
They're bound to erect your statue in St. Mark's.
Signior Corvino, I would have you go
And show yourself, that you have conquered.

CORV. Yes.

MOS. It was much better that you should profess
Yourself a cuckold thus, than that the other
Should have been proved.

CORV. Nay, I considered that:
Now it is her fault.

MOS. Then it had been yours.

CORV. True; I do doubt this advocate still.

MOS. I'faith
You need not, I dare ease you of that care.

CORV. I trust thee, Mosca.

Exit

MOS. As your own soul, sir.

CORB. Mosca!

MOS. Now for your business, sir.

CORB. How! have you business?

MOS. Yes, yours, sir.

CORB. O, none else?

MOS. None else, not I.

CORB. Be careful, then.

MOS. Rest you with both your eyes, sir.

CORB. Dispatch it.

MOS. Instantly.

CORB. And look that all,
Whatever, be put in, jewels, plate, moneys,
Household stuff, bedding, curtains.

MOS. Curtain-rings, sir:
Only the advocate's fee must be deducted.

CORB. I'll pay him now; you'll be too prodigal.

MOS. Sir, I must tender it.

CORB. Two sequins is well.

MOS. No, six, sir.

CORB. 'Tis too much.

MOS. He talked a great while;
   You must consider that, sir.

CORB. Well, there's three—

MOS. I'll give it him.

CORB. Do so, and there's for thee.

                                              Exit

MOS. Bountiful bones! What horrid strange offence
   Did he commit 'gainst nature, in his youth,
   Worthy this age? [*Aside*]—You see, sir, [*to Voltore*] how I work
   Unto your ends: take you no notice.

VOLT. No,
   I'll leave you.

                                              Exit

MOS. All is yours, the devil and all:
   Good advocate!—Madam, I'll bring you home.

LADY P. No, I'll go see your patron.

MOS. That you shall not:
   I'll tell you why. My purpose is to urge
   My patron to reform his will; and for
   The zeal you have shown to-day, whereas before
   You were but third or fourth, you shall be now
   Put in the first: which would appear as begged,
   If you were present. Therefore—

LADY P. You shall sway me.

                                           Exeunt

ACT V, SCENE I

Enter Volpone

VOLP. Well, I am here, and all this brunt is past.
   I ne'er was in dislike with my disguise
   'Till this fled moment: here 'twas good, in private;
   But in your public,—*cave*[1] whilst I breathe.
   'Fore God, my left leg 'gan to have the cramp,

---

1. Beware.

And I apprehended straight some power had struck me
With a dead palsy: Well! I must be merry,
And shake it off. A many of these fears
Would put me into some villainous disease,
Should they come thick upon me: I'll prevent 'em.
Give me a bowl of lusty wine, to fright
This humor from my heart. [*Drinks*]—Hum, hum, hum!
'Tis almost gone already; I shall conquer.
Any device, now, of rare ingenious knavery,
That would possess me with a violent laughter,
Would make me up again. [*Drinks again*]—So, so, so, so!
This heat is life; 'tis blood by this time:—Mosca!

Enter Mosca

MOS. How now, sir? does the day look clear again?
Are we recovered, and wrought out of error,
Into our way, to see our path before us?
Is our trade free once more?
VOLP. Exquisite Mosca!
MOS. Was it not carried learnedly?
VOLP. And stoutly:
Good wits are greatest in extremities.
MOS. It were a folly beyond thought, to trust
Any grand act unto a cowardly spirit:
You are not taken with it enough, methinks.
VOLP. O, more than if I had enjoyed the wench:
The pleasure of all woman-kind's not like it.
MOS. Why now you speak, sir. We must here be fixed;
Here we must rest; this is our masterpiece;
We cannot think to go beyond this.
VOLP. True,
Thou hast played thy prize, my precious Mosca.
MOS. Nay, sir,
To gull the court—
VOLP. And quite divert the torrent
Upon the innocent.
MOS. Yes, and to make
So rare a music out of discords—

VOLP. Right.
> That yet to me's the strangest, how thou hast borne it!
> That these, being so divided 'mongst themselves,
> Should not scent somewhat, or in me or thee,
> Or doubt their own side.

MOS. True, they will not see't.
> Too much light blinds them, I think. Each of them
> Is so possessed and stuffed with his own hopes,
> That any thing unto the contrary,
> Never so true, or never so apparent,
> Never so palpable, they will resist it—

VOLP. Like a temptation of the devil.

MOS. Right, sir.
> Merchants may talk of trade, and your great signiors
> Of land that yields well; but if Italy
> Have any glebe more fruitful than these fellows,
> I am deceived. Did not your advocate rare?

VOLP. O—*My most honored fathers, my grave fathers,*
> *Under correction of your fatherhoods,*
> *What face of truth is here? If these strange deeds*
> *May pass, most honored fathers*—I had much ado
> To forbear laughing.

MOS. It seemed to me, you sweat, sir.

VOLP. In troth, I did a little.

MOS. But confess, sir,
> Were you not daunted?

VOLP. In good faith, I was
> A little in a mist, but not dejected;
> Never, but still my self.

MOS. I think it, sir.
> Now, so truth help me, I must needs say this, sir,
> And out of conscience for your advocate,
> He has taken pains, in faith, sir, and deserved,
> In my poor judgment, I speak it under favor,
> Not to contrary you, sir, very richly—
> Well—to be cozened.

VOLP. Troth, and I think so too,
> By that I heard him, in the latter end.

MOS. O, but before, sir: had you heard him first
  Draw it to certain heads, then aggravate,
  Then use his vehement figures[1]—I looked still
  When he would shift a shirt:[2] and, doing this
  Out of pure love, no hope of gain—
VOLP. 'Tis right.
  I cannot answer him, Mosca, as I would,
  Not yet; but for thy sake, at thy entreaty,
  I will begin, even now—to vex them all,
  This very instant.
MOS. Good sir.
VOLP. Call the dwarf
  And eunuch forth.
MOS. Castrone, Nano!

Enter Castrone and Nano

NANO. Here.
VOLP. Shall we have a jig[3] now?
MOS. What you please, sir.
VOLP. Go.
  Straight give out about the streets, you two,
  That I am dead; do it with constancy,
  Sadly, do you hear? impute it to the grief
  Of this late slander.

Exeunt Castrone and Nano

MOS. What do you mean, sir?
VOLP. O,
  I shall have instantly my Vulture, Crow,
  Raven, come flying hither, on the news,
  To peck for carrion, my she-wolf, and all,
  Greedy, and full of expectation—
MOS. And then to have it ravished from their mouths!
VOLP. 'Tis true. I will have thee put on a gown,
  And take upon thee, as thou wert mine heir:
  Show them a will: Open that chest, and reach

1. Of rhetoric.
2. I was expecting him to have to change his shirt.
3. Hoax.

Forth one of those that has the blanks; I'll straight
Put in thy name.

MOS. It will be rare, sir.

[*Gives him a paper*]

VOLP. Ay,
When they ev'n gape, and find themselves deluded—

MOS. Yes.

VOLP. And thou use them scurvily!
Dispatch, get on thy gown.

MOS. [*Putting on a gown*] But what, sir, if they ask
After the body?

VOLP. Say, it was corrupted.

MOS. I'll say, it stunk, sir; and was fain to have it
Coffined up instantly, and sent away.

VOLP. Any thing; what thou wilt. Hold, here's my will.
Get thee a cap, a count-book, pen and ink,
Papers afore thee; sit as thou wert taking
An inventory of parcels: I'll get up
Behind the curtain, on a stool, and hearken;
Sometime peep over, see how they do look,
With what degrees their blood doth leave their faces,
O, 'twill afford me a rare meal of laughter!

MOS. Your advocate will turn stark dull upon it.

VOLP. It will take off his oratory's edge.

MOS. But your clarissimo, old round-back, he
Will crump you[1] like a hog-louse,[2] with the touch.

VOLP. And what Corvino?

MOS. O, sir, look for him,
To-morrow morning, with a rope and dagger,
To visit all the streets; he must run mad.
My lady too, that came into the court,
To bear false witness for your worship—

VOLP. Yes,
And kissed me 'fore the fathers, when my face
Flowed all with oils.

1. Curl up on you.
2. Wood louse.

MOS. And sweat, sir. Why, your gold
   Is such another med'cine, it dries up
   All those offensive savors: it transforms
   The most deformèd, and restores them lovely,
   As 'twere the strange poetical girdle.[1] Jove
   Could not invent t' himself a shroud more subtle
   To pass Acrisius' guards.[2] It is the thing
   Makes all the world her grace, her youth, her beauty.
VOLP. I think she loves me.
MOS. Who? the lady, sir?
   She's jealous of you.
VOLP. Dost thou say so?

[Knocking within]

MOS. Hark,
   There's some already.
VOLP. Look.
MOS. It is the Vulture;
   He has the quickest scent.
VOLP. I'll to my place,
   Thou to thy posture.

[Goes behind the curtain]

MOS. I am set.
VOLP. But, Mosca,
   Play the artificer[3] now, torture them rarely.

Enter Voltore

VOLT. How now, my Mosca?
MOS. [*Writing*] Turkey carpets, nine—
VOLT. Taking an inventory! that is well.
MOS. Two suits of bedding, tissue—
VOLT. Where's the will?
   Let me read that the while.

Enter Servants, with Corbaccio in a chair

---

1. Of Venus.
2. He locked up his daughter, but Jove reached her.
3. Skilled worker, artist.

CORB. So, set me down,
  And get you home.

                                        Exeunt Servants

VOLT. Is he come now, to trouble us!
MOS. Of cloth of gold, two more—
CORB. Is it done, Mosca?
MOS. Of several velvets eight—
VOLT. I like his care.
CORB. Dost thou not hear?

                    Enter Corvino

CORB. Ha! is the hour come, Mosca?
VOLP. [*Peeping over the curtain*] Ay, now they muster.
CORV. What does the advocate here,
  Or this Corbaccio?
CORB. What do these here?

                Enter Lady Politick Would-be

LADY P. Mosca!
  Is his thread spun?
MOS. Eight chests of linen—
VOLP. O,
  My fine dame Would-be, too!
CORV. Mosca, the will,
  That I may show it these, and rid them hence.
MOS. Six chests of diaper,¹ four of damask.—There.
            [*Gives them the will carelessly, over his shoulder*]
CORB. Is that the will?
MOS. Down-beds and bolsters—
VOLP. Rare!
  Be busy still. Now they begin to flutter:
  They never think of me. Look, see, see, see!
  How their swift eyes run over the long deed,
  Unto the name, and to the legacies,
  What is bequeathed them there—
MOS. Ten suits of hangings—

---

1. Linen.

VOLP. Ay, in their garters, Mosca. Now their hopes
    Are at the gasp.
VOLT. Mosca the heir!
CORB. What's that?
VOLP. My advocate is dumb; look to my merchant,
    He has heard of some strange storm, a ship is lost,
    He faints; my lady will swoon. Old glazen eyes,
    He hath not reached his despair yet.
CORB. All these
    Are out of hope; I am, sure, the man.
CORV. But, Mosca—
MOS. Two cabinets.
CORV. Is this in earnest?
MOS. One
    Of ebony—
CORV. Or do you but delude me?
MOS. The other, mother of pearl—I am very busy.
    Good faith, it is a fortune thrown upon me—
    Item, one salt[1] of agate—not my seeking.
LADY P. Do you hear, sir?
MOS. A perfumed box—'Pray you forbear,
    You see I'm troubled—made of an onyx—
LADY P. How!
MOS. To-morrow or next day, I shall be at leisure
    To talk with you all.
CORV. Is this my large hope's issue?
LADY P. Sir, I must have a fairer answer.
MOS. Madam!
    Marry, and shall: 'pray you, fairly quit my house.
    Nay, raise no tempest with your looks; but hark you,
    Remember what your ladyship offered me
    To put you in an heir; go to, think on it:
    And what you said e'en your best madams did
    For maintenance; and why not you? Enough.
    Go home, and use the poor sir Pol, your knight, well,
    For fear I tell some riddles; go, be melancholy.

---

1. Salt cellar.

Exit Lady Would-be

VOLP. O, my fine devil!

CORV. Mosca, pray you a word.

MOS. Lord! will you not take your dispatch hence yet?
    Methinks, of all, you should have been the example.
    Why should you stay here? with what thoughts, what promise?
    Hear you; do you not know, I know you an ass,
    And that you would most fain have been a wittol,[1]
    If fortune would have let you? that you are
    A declared cuckold, on good terms? This pearl,
    You'll say, was yours? right: this diamond?
    I'll not deny't, but thank you. Much here else?
    It may be so. Why, think that these good works
    May help to hide your bad. I'll not betray you;
    Although you be but extraordinary,[2]
    And have it only in title, it sufficeth:
    Go home, be melancholy too, or mad.

Exit Corvino

VOLP. Rare Mosca! how his villainy becomes him!

VOLT. Certain he doth delude all these for me.

CORB. Mosca the heir!

VOLP. O, his four eyes have found it.

CORB. I am cozened, cheated, by a parasite slave;
    Harlot,[3] thou hast gulled me.

MOS. Yes, sir. Stop your mouth,
    Or I shall draw the only tooth is left.
    Are not you he, that filthy covetous wretch,
    With the three legs,[4] that here, in hope of prey,
    Have, any time this three years, snuffed about,
    With your most grovelling nose, and would have hired
    Me to the poisoning of my patron, sir?
    Are not you he that have to-day in court
    Professed the disinheriting of your son?

1. A willing cuckold.
2. Supernumerary.
3. Scoundrel.
4. Counting his cane.

Perjured yourself? Go home, and die, and stink.
If you but croak a syllable, all comes out:
Away, and call your porters! [*Exit Corbaccio*] Go, go, stink.
VOLP. Excellent varlet!
VOLT. Now, my faithful Mosca,
I find thy constancy.
MOS. Sir!
VOLT. Sincere.
MOS. A table
Of porphyry—I marle[1] you'll be thus troublesome.
VOLT. Nay, leave off now, they are gone.
MOS. Why, who are you?
What! who did send for you? O, cry you mercy,
Reverend sir! Good faith, I am grieved for you,
That any chance of mine should thus defeat
Your (I must needs say) most deserving travails:
But I protest, sir, it was cast upon me,
And I could almost wish to be without it,
But that the will o' the dead must be observed.
Marry, my joy is that you need it not;
You have a gift, sir, (thank your education,)
Will never let you want, while there are men,
And malice, to breed causes. Would I had
But half the like, for all my fortune, sir!
If I have any suits, as I do hope,
Things being so easy and direct, I shall not,
I will make bold with your obstreperous aid,
Conceive me,—for your fee, sir. In mean time,
You that have so much law, I know have the conscience
Not to be covetous of what is mine.
Good sir, I thank you for my plate; 'twill help
To set up a young man. Good faith, you look
As you were costive;[2] best go home and purge, sir.

                                                    Exit Voltore

VOLP. [*Comes from behind the curtain*] Bid him eat lettuce well. My
    witty mischief,

1. Marvel.
2. Constipated.

Let me embrace thee. O that I could now
Transform thee to a Venus!—Mosca, go,
Straight take my habit of clarissimo,[1]
And walk the streets; be seen, torment them more:
We must pursue, as well as plot. Who would
Have lost this feast?

MOS. I doubt it will lose them.

VOLP. O, my recovery shall recover all.
That I could now but think on some disguise
To meet them in, and ask them questions:
How I would vex them still at every turn!

MOS. Sir, I can fit you.

VOLP. Canst thou?

MOS. Yes, I know
One o' the commandadori, sir, so like you;
Him will I straight make drunk, and bring you his habit.

VOLP. A rare disguise, and answering thy brain!
O, I will be a sharp disease unto them.

MOS. Sir, you must look for curses—

VOLP. Till they burst;
The Fox fares ever best when he is curst.[2]

Exeunt

SCENE II

Enter Peregrine disguised, and three Merchants

PER. Am I enough disguised?

1 MER. I warrant you.

PER. All my ambition is to fright him only.

2 MER. If you could ship him away, 'twere excellent.

3 MER. To Zant,[3] or to Aleppo?

PER. Yes, and have his
Adventures put i' the Book of Voyages,
And his gulled story registered for truth.

---

1. Aristocrat.
2. Cursed, bad-tempered.
3. Zákynthos (Greek island).

Well, gentlemen, when I am in a while,
And that you think us warm in our discourse,
Know your approaches.
1 MER. Trust it to our care.

Exeunt Merchants

Enter Waiting-woman

PER. Save you, fair lady! Is sir Pol within?
WOM. I do not know, sir.
PER. Pray you say unto him,
Here is a merchant, upon earnest business,
Desires to speak with him.
WOM. I will see, sir.

Exit

PER. I pray you.—
I see the family is all female here.

Re-enter Waiting-woman

WOM. He says, sir, he has weighty affairs of state,
That now require him whole; some other time
You may possess him.
PER. Pray you say again,
If those require him whole, these will exact[1] him,
Whereof I bring him tidings. [*Exit Woman*]—What might be
His grave affair of state now; how to make
Bolognian sausages here in Venice, sparing
One o' the ingredients?

Re-enter Waiting-woman

WOM. Sir, he says, he knows
By your word *tidings*, that you are no statesman,
And therefore wills you stay.
PER. Sweet, pray you return him;
I have not read so many proclamations,
And studied them for words, as he has done—
But—here he deigns to come.

Exit Woman

1. Demand.

Enter Sir Politick

SIR P. Sir, I must crave
    Your courteous pardon. There hath chanced to-day,
    Unkind disaster 'twixt my lady and me;
    And I was penning my apology,
    To give her satisfaction, as you came now.
PER. Sir, I am grieved I bring you worse disaster:
    The gentleman you met at the port to-day,
    That told you, he was newly arrived—
SIR P. Ay, was
    A fugitive punk!¹
PER. No, sir, a spy set on you;
    And he has made relation to the senate,
    That you professed to him to have a plot
    To sell the State of Venice to the Turk.
SIR P. O me!
PER. For which, warrants are signed by this time,
    To apprehend you, and to search your study
    For papers—
SIR P. Alas, sir, I have none, but notes
    Drawn out of play-books—
PER. All the better, sir.
SIR P. And some essays. What shall I do?
PER. Sir, best
    Convey yourself into a sugar-chest;
    Or, if you could lie round, a frail² were rare,
    And I could send you aboard.
SIR P. Sir, I but talked so,
    For discourse sake merely.

                             [Knocking within]

PER. Hark! they are there.
SIR P. I am a wretch, a wretch!
PER. What will you do, sir?

---

1. Whore.
2. Fruit basket.

Have you ne'er a currant-butt to leap into?
They'll put you to the rack; you must be sudden.
SIR P. Sir, I have an engine—
3 MER. [*Within*] Sir Politick Would-be!
2 MER. [*Within*] Where is he?
SIR P. That I have thought upon before time.
PER. What is it?
SIR P. I shall ne'er endure the torture.
    Marry, it is, sir, of a tortoise-shell,
    Fitted for these extremities: pray you, sir, help me.
    Here I've a place, sir, to put back my legs,
    Please you to lay it on, sir [*lies down while Peregrine places the*
       shell upon him]—with this cap,
    And my black gloves. I'll lie, sir, like a tortoise,
    'Till they are gone.
PER. And call you this an engine?
SIR P. Mine own device—Good sir, bid my wife's women
    To burn my papers.

                               Exit Peregrine

          The three Merchants rush in

1 MER. Where is he hid?
3 MER. We must,
    And will sure find him.
2 MER. Which is his study?

            Re-enter Peregrine

1 MER. What
    Are you, sir?
PER. I am a merchant, that came here
    To look upon this tortoise.
3 MER. How!
1 MER. St. Mark!
    What beast is this!
PER. It is a fish.
2 MER. Come out here!
PER. Nay, you may strike him, sir, and tread upon him;
    He'll bear a cart.

1 MER. What, to run over him?

PER. Yes, sir.

3 MER. Let's jump upon him.

2 MER. Can he not go?

PER. He creeps, sir.

1 MER. Let's see him creep.

PER. No, good sir, you will hurt him.

2 MER. Heart, I will see him creep, or prick his guts.

3 MER. Come out here!

PER. [*Aside to Sir Politick*] Pray you, sir!—Creep a little.

1 MER. Forth.

2 MER. Yet farther.

PER. Good sir!—Creep.

2 MER. We'll see his legs.

> [*They pull off the shell and discover him*]

3 MER. Ods so, he has garters!

1 MER. Ay, and gloves!

2 MER. Is this
     Your fearful tortoise?

PER. [*Discovering himself*] Now, sir Pol, we are even;
     For your next project I shall be prepared:
     I am sorry for the funeral of your notes, sir.

1 MER. 'Twere a rare motion[1] to be seen in Fleet-street.

2 MER. Ay, in the Term.

1 MER. Or Smithfield, in the fair.

3 MER. Methinks 'tis but a melancholy sight.

PER. Farewell, most politic tortoise!

> *Exeunt Peregrine and Merchants*

> *Re-enter Waiting-woman*

SIR P. Where's my lady?
     Knows she of this?

WOM. I know not, sir.

---

1. Puppet show.

SIR P. Enquire.—

    O, I shall be the fable of all feasts,
    The freight of the gazetti,¹ ship-boy's tale;
    And, which is worst, even talk for ordinaries.²

WOM. My lady's come most melancholy home,
    And says, sir, she will straight to sea for physic.

SIR P. And I to shun this place and clime for ever,
    Creeping with house on back, and think it well
    To shrink my poor head in my politic shell.

Exeunt

SCENE III

*Enter Mosca in the habit of a Clarissimo, and Volpone in that
of a Commandadore*

VOLP. Am I then like him?

MOS. O, sir, you are he:
    No man can sever you.

VOLP. Good.

MOS. But what am I?

VOLP. 'Fore heaven, a brave clarissimo; thou becom'st it!
    Pity thou wert not born one.

MOS. *[Aside]* If I hold
    My made one, 'twill be well.

VOLP. I'll go and see
    What news first at the court.

Exit

MOS. Do so. My Fox
    Is out of his hole, and ere he shall re-enter,
    I'll make him languish in his borrowed case,³
    Except he come to composition with me.—
    Androgyno, Castrone, Nano!

Enter Androgyno, Castrone, and Nano

1. Newsletters.
2. Inns.
3. Clothes.

ALL. Here.

MOS. Go, recreate yourselves abroad; go sport.—

Exeunt

So, now I have the keys, and am possessed.
Since he will needs be dead afore his time,
I'll bury him, or gain by him: I am his heir,
And so will keep me, till he share at least.
To cozen him of all, were but a cheat
Well placed; no man would construe it a sin:
Let his sport pay for't. This is called the Fox-trap.

Exit

SCENE IV

Enter Corbaccio and Corvino

CORB. They say, the court is set.

CORV. We must maintain
Our first tale good, for both our reputations.

CORB. Why, mine's no tale: my son would there have killed me.

CORV. That's true, I had forgot:—[*Aside*] mine is, I'm sure.
But for your will, sir.

CORB. Ay, I'll come upon him
For that hereafter, now his patron's dead.

Enter Volpone

VOLP. Signior Corvino! and Corbaccio! sir,
Much joy unto you.

CORV. Of what?

VOLP. The sudden good
Dropt down upon you—

CORB. Where?

VOLP. And none knows how,
From old Volpone, sir.

CORB. Out, arrant knave!

VOLP. Let not your too much wealth, sir, make you furious.

CORB. Away, thou varlet!

VOLP. Why, sir?

CORB. Dost thou mock me?

VOLP. You mock the world, sir; did you not change[1] wills?
CORB. Out, harlot!
VOLP. O! belike you are the man,
    Signior Corvino? 'faith, you carry it well;
    You grow not mad withal; I love your spirit:
    You are not over-leavened with your fortune.
    You should have some would swell now, like a wine-vat,
    With such an autumn—Did he give you all, sir?
CORV. Avoid, you rascal!
VOLP. Troth, your wife has shown
    Herself a very woman; but you are well,
    You need not care, you have a good estate,
    To bear it out, sir, better by this chance:
    Except Corbaccio have a share.
CORB. Hence, varlet.
VOLP. You will not be acknown, sir; why, 'tis wise.
    Thus do all gamesters, at all games, dissemble:
    No man will seem to win.

                         Exeunt Corvino and Corbaccio

    —Here comes my vulture,
    Heaving his beak up in the air, and snuffing.

              Enter Voltore

VOLT. Outstript thus, by a parasite! a slave,
    Would run on errands, and make legs[2] for crumbs!
    Well, what I'll do—
VOLP. The court stays for your worship.
    I e'en rejoice, sir, at your worship's happiness,
    And that it fell into so learned hands,
    That understand the fingering—
VOLT. What do you mean?
VOLP. I mean to be a suitor to your worship,
    For the small tenement, out of reparations,[3]
    That, to the end of your long row of houses,

---

1. Exchange.
2. Bow.
3. Repair.

By the Piscaria:[1] it was, in Volpone's time,
Your predecessor, ere he grew diseased,
A handsome, pretty, customed bawdy-house
As any was in Venice, none dispraised;
But fell with him: his body and that house
Decayed together.

VOLT. Come, sir, leave your prating.

VOLP. Why, if your worship give me but your hand,
That I may have the refusal, I have done.
'Tis a mere toy to you, sir; candle-rents;
As your learned worship knows—

VOLT. What do I know?

VOLP. Marry, no end of your wealth. sir: God decrease it!

VOLT. Mistaking knave! what, mock'st thou my misfortune?

Exit

VOLP. His blessing on your heart, sir; would 'twere more!—
Now to my first again, at the next corner.

Exit

SCENE V

Enter Corbaccio and Corvino;—Mosca passes before them

CORB. See, in our habit! see the impudent varlet!

CORV. That I could shoot mine eyes at him like gunstones!

Enter Volpone

VOLP. But is this true, sir, of the parasite?

CORB. Again, to afflict us! monster!

VOLP. In good faith, sir,
I'm heartily grieved, a beard of your grave length
Should be so over-reached. I never brooked
That parasite's hair; methought his nose should cozen:
There still was somewhat in his look, did promise
The bane of a clarissimo.

CORB. Knave—

---

1. Fish market.

VOLP. Methinks
Yet you, that are so traded in the world,
A witty merchant, the fine bird, Corvino,
That have such moral emblems on your name,
Should not have sung your shame, and dropped your cheese,
To let the Fox laugh at your emptiness.

CORV. Sirrah, you think the privilege of the place,
And your red saucy cap, that seems to me
Nailed to your jolt-head with those two sequins,
Can warrant your abuses; come you hither:
You shall perceive, sir, I dare beat you; approach.

VOLP. No haste, sir, I do know your valor well,
Since you durst publish what you are, sir.

CORV. Tarry,
I'd speak with you.

VOLP. Sir, sir, another time—

CORV. Nay, now.

VOLP. O lord, sir! I were a wise man,
Would stand the fury of a distracted cuckold.

Enter Mosca

CORB. What, come again!

VOLP. Upon 'em, Mosca; save me.

CORB. The air's infected where he breathes.

CORV. Let's fly him.

Exeunt Corvino and Corbaccio

VOLP. Excellent basilisk![1] turn upon the vulture.

Enter Voltore

VOLT. Well, flesh-fly, it is summer with you now;
Your winter will come on.

MOS. Good advocate,
Prithee not rail, nor threaten out of place thus;
Thou'lt make a solecism, as madam says.
Get you a biggin[2] more, your brain breaks loose.

Exit

1. Which kills with a glance.
2. Skullcap.

VOLT. Well, sir.

VOLP. Would you have me beat the insolent slave,
  Throw dirt upon his first good clothes?

VOLT. This same
  Is doubtless some familiar.

VOLP. Sir, the court,
  In troth, stays for you. I am mad, a mule
  That never read Justinian,[1] should get up,
  And ride an advocate. Had you no quirk
  To avoid gullage, sir, by such a creature?
  I hope you do but jest; he has not done it.
  'Tis but confederacy, to blind the rest.
  You are the heir.

VOLT. A strange, officious,
  Troublesome knave! thou dost torment me.

VOLP. I know—
  It cannot be, sir, that you should be cozened;
  'Tis not within with the wit of man to do it;
  You are so wise, so prudent; and 'tis fit
  That wealth and wisdom still should go together.

Exeunt

Scene VI

*Enter Avocatori, Notario, Bonario, Celia, Corbaccio, Corvino,
Commandadori, Saffi, etc.*

1 AVOC. Are all the parties here?

NOT. All but the advocate.

2 AVOC. And here he comes.

Enter Voltore and Volpone

1 AVOC. Then bring them forth to sentence.

VOLT. O, my most honored fathers, let your mercy
  Once win upon your justice, to forgive—
  I am distracted—

VOLP. [*Aside*] What will he do now?

---

1. Set up the legal codes of the Empire.

VOLT. O,
    I know not which to address myself to first;
    Whether your fatherhoods, or these innocents—
CORV. [*Aside*] Will he betray himself?
VOLT. Whom equally
    I have abused, out of most covetous ends—
CORV. The man is mad!
CORB. What's that?
CORV. He is possessed.
VOLT. For which, now struck in conscience, here, I prostrate
    Myself at your offended feet, for pardon.
1, 2 AVOC. Arise.
CEL. O heaven, how just thou art!
VOLP. [*Aside*] I am caught
    In mine own noose—
CORV. [*To Corbaccio*] Be constant, sir: nought now
    Can help, but impudence.
1 AVOC. Speak forward.
COM. Silence!
VOLT. It is not passion in me, reverend fathers,
    But only conscience, conscience, my good sires,
    That makes me now tell truth. That parasite,
    That knave, hath been the instrument of all.
1 AVOC. Where is that knave? fetch him.
VOLP. I go.

                                                        Exit

CORV. Grave fathers,
    This man's distracted; he confessed it now:
    For, hoping to be old Volpone's heir,
    Who now is dead—
3 AVOC. How!
2 AVOC. Is Volpone dead?
CORV. Dead since, grave fathers.
BON. O sure vengeance!
1 AVOC. Stay,
    Then he was no deceiver.
VOLT. O no, none:
    The parasite, grave fathers.

CORV. He does speak
    Out of mere envy, 'cause the servant's made
    The thing he gaped for: please your fatherhoods,
    This is the truth, though I'll not justify
    The other, but he may be some-deal faulty.
VOLT. Ay, to your hopes, as well as mine, Corvino:
    But I'll use modesty. Pleaseth your wisdoms,
    To view these certain notes, and but confer them;
    As I hope favor, they shall speak clear truth.
CORV. The devil has entered him!
BON. Or bides in you.
4 AVOC. We have done ill, by a public officer
    To send for him, if he be heir.
2 AVOC. For whom?
4 AVOC. Him that they call the parasite.
3 AVOC. 'Tis true,
    He is a man of great estate, now left.
4 AVOC. Go you, and learn his name, and say, the court
    Entreats his presence here, but to the clearing
    Of some few doubts.

                               Exit Notary

2 AVOC. This same's a labyrinth!
1 AVOC. Stand you unto your first report?
CORV. My state,
    My life, my fame—
BON. Where is it?
CORV. Are at the stake.
1 AVOC. Is yours so too?
CORB. The advocate's a knave,
    And has a forked tongue—
2 AVOC. Speak to the point.
CORB. So is the parasite too.
1 AVOC. This is confusion.
VOLT. I do beseech your fatherhoods, read but those—

                        [Giving them papers]

CORV. And credit nothing the false spirit hath writ:
    It cannot be, but he's possessed, grave fathers.

                           The scene closes

Scene VII

Enter Volpone

VOLP. To make a snare for mine own neck! and run
My head into it, wilfully! with laughter!
When I had newly 'scaped, was free, and clear,
Out of mere wantonness! O, the dull devil
Was in this brain of mine, when I devised it,
And Mosca gave it second; he must now
Help to sear up this vein, or we bleed dead.—

Enter Nano, Androgyno, and Castrone

How now! who let you loose? whither go you now?
What, to buy gingerbread, or to drown kitlings?
NAN. Sir, master Mosca called us out of doors,
And bid us all go play, and took the keys.
NAN. Yes.
VOLP. Did master Mosca take the keys? why so!
I'm farther in. These are my fine conceits!
I must be merry, with a mischief to me!
What a vile wretch was I, that could not bear
My fortune soberly? I must have my crotchets,
And my conundrums! Well, go you, and seek him:
His meaning may be truer than my fear.
Bid him, he straight come to me to the court;
Thither will I, and, if 't be possible,
Unscrew my advocate, upon new hopes:
When I provoked him, then I lost myself.

Exeunt

Scene VIII

*Avocatori, Bonario, Celia, Corbaccio, Corvino, Commandadori,
Saffi, etc., as before*

1 AVOC. These things can ne'er be reconciled. He, here,
                              [*Showing the papers*]
Professeth, that the gentleman was wronged,
And that the gentlewoman was brought thither,

Forced by her husband, and there left.

VOLT. Most true.

CEL. How ready is heaven to those that pray!

1 AVOC. But that
Volpone would have ravished her, he holds
Utterly false, knowing his impotence.

CORV. Grave fathers, he's possessed; again, I say,
Possessed: nay, if there be possession, and
Obsession, he has both.

3 AVOC. Here comes our officer.

Enter Volpone

VOLP. The parasite will straight be here, grave fathers.

4 AVOC. You might invent some other name, sir varlet.

3 AVOC. Did not the notary meet him?

VOLP. Not that I know.

4 AVOC. His coming will clear all.

2 AVOC. Yet, it is misty.

VOLT. May't please your fatherhoods—

VOLP. [*Whispers to Voltore*] Sir, the parasite
Willed me to tell you, that his master lives;
That you are still the man; your hopes the same;
And this was only a jest—

VOLT. How?

VOLP. Sir, to try
If you were firm, and how you stood affected.

VOLT. Art sure he lives?

VOLP. Do I live, sir?

VOLT. O me!
I was too violent.

VOLP. Sir, you may redeem it.
They said, you were possessed; fall down, and seem so:
I'll help to make it good. [*Voltore falls*]—God bless the man!—
Stop your wind hard, and swell—See, see, see, see!
He vomits crooked pins! his eyes are set,
Like a dead hare's hung in a poulter's shop!
His mouth's running away! Do you see, signior?
Now it is in his belly.

CORV. Ay, the devil!

VOLP. Now in his throat.

CORV. Ay, I perceive it plain.

VOLP. 'Twill out, 'twill out! stand clear. See where it flies,
In shape of a blue toad, with a bat's wings!
Do you not see it, sir?

CORB. What? I think I do.

CORV. 'Tis too manifest.

VOLP. Look! he comes to himself!

VOLT. Where am I?

VOLP. Take good heart, the worst is past, sir.
You are dispossessed.

1 AVOC. What accident is this!

2 AVOC. Sudden, and full of wonder!

3 AVOC. If he were
Possessed, as it appears, all this is nothing.

CORV. He has been often subject to these fits.

1 AVOC. Show him that writing:—do you know it, sir?

VOLP. [*Whispers to Voltore*] Deny it, sir, forswear it; know it not.

VOLT. Yes, I do know it well, it is my hand;
But all that it contains is false.

BON. O practice![1]

2 AVOC. What maze is this!

1 AVOC. Is he not guilty then,
Whom you there name the parasite?

VOLT. Grave fathers,
No more than his good patron, old Volpone.

4 AVOC. Why, he is dead.

VOLT. O no, my honored fathers,
He lives—

1 AVOC. How! lives?

VOLT. Lives.

2 AVOC. This is subtler yet!

3 AVOC. You said he was dead.

VOLT. Never.

3 AVOC. You said so.

1. Deceit.

CORV. I heard so.

4 AVOC. Here comes the gentleman; make him way.

Enter Mosca

3 AVOC. A stool.

4 AVOC. [*Aside*] A proper man; and, were Volpone dead,
    A fit match for my daughter.

3 AVOC. Give him way.

VOLP. [*Aside to Mosca*] Mosca, I was almost lost; the advocate
    Had betrayed all; but now it is recovered;
    All's on the hinge again—Say, I am living.

MOS. What busy knave is this!—Most reverend fathers,
    I sooner had attended your grave pleasures,
    But that my order for the funeral
    Of my dear patron, did require me—

VOLP. [*Aside*] Mosca!

MOS. Whom I intend to bury like a gentleman.

VOLP. [*Aside*] Ay, quick,[1] and cozen me of all.

2 AVOC. Still stranger!
    More intricate!

1 AVOC. And come about again!

4 AVOC. [*Aside*] It is a match, my daughter is bestowed.

MOS. [*Aside to Volpone*] Will you give me half?

VOLP. First, I'll be hanged.

MOS. I know
    Your voice is good, cry not so loud.

1 AVOC. Demand
    The advocate.—Sir, did you not affirm
    Volpone was alive?

VOLP. Yes, and he is;
    This gentleman told me so. [*Aside to Mosca*]—Thou shalt have
      half.—

MOS. Whose drunkard is this same? speak, some that know him:
    I never saw his face. [*Aside to Volpone*]—I cannot now
    Afford it you so cheap.

VOLP. No!

1. Alive.

1 Avoc. What say you?

Volt. The officer told me.

Volp. I did, grave fathers,
 And will maintain he lives, with mine own life,
 And that this creature [*points to Mosca*] told me. [*Aside*]—I was
  born
 With all good stars my enemies.

Mos. Most grave fathers,
 If such an insolence as this must pass
 Upon me, I am silent: 'twas not this
 For which you sent, I hope.

2 Avoc. Take him away.

Volp. Mosca!

3 Avoc. Let him be whipped.

Volp. Wilt thou betray me?
 Cozen me?

3 Avoc. And taught to bear himself
 Toward a person of his rank.

4 Avoc. Away.

          [*The Officers seize Volpone*]

Mos. I humbly thank your fatherhoods.

Volp. [*Aside*] Soft, soft: Whipped!
 And lose all that I have! If I confess,
 It cannot be much more.

4 Avoc. Sir, are you married?

Volp. They'll be allied anon; I must be resolute:
 The Fox shall here uncase.

          [*Puts off his disguise*]

Mos. Patron!

Volp. Nay, now
 My ruins shall not come alone: your match
 I'll hinder sure: my substance shall not glue you,
 Nor screw you into a family.

Mos. Why, patron!

Volp. I am Volpone, and this is my knave;

          [*Pointing to Mosca*]

 This, [*to Voltore*] his own knave; this, [*to Corbaccio*] avarice's fool;
 This, [*to Corvino*] a chimera of wittol, fool, and knave:

And, reverend fathers, since we all can hope
Nought but a sentence, let's not now despair it.
You hear me brief.

CORV. May it please your fatherhoods—

COM. Silence!

1 AVOC. The knot is now undone by miracle.

2 AVOC. Nothing can be more clear.

3 AVOC. Or can more prove
These innocent.

1 AVOC. Give them their liberty.

BON. Heaven could not long let such gross crimes be hid.

2 AVOC. If this be held the high-way to get riches,
May I be poor!

3 AVOC. This is not the gain, but torment.

1 AVOC. These possess wealth, as sick men possess fevers,
Which trulier may be said to possess them.

2 AVOC. Disrobe that parasite.

CORV. AND MOS. Most honored fathers!—

1 AVOC. Can you plead aught to stay the course of justice?
If you can, speak.

CORV. AND VOLT. We beg favor.

CEL. And mercy.

1 AVOC. You hurt your innocence, suing for the guilty.
Stand forth; and first the parasite: You appear
T'have been the chiefest minister, if not plotter,
In all these lewd impostures; and now, lastly,
Have with your impudence abused the court,
And habit of a gentleman of Venice,
Being a fellow of no birth or blood:
For which our sentence is, first, thou be whipped;
Then live perpetual prisoner in our galleys.

VOLP. I thank you for him.

MOS. Bane to thy wolvish nature!

1 AVOC. Deliver him to the saffi.

Mosca is carried out

—Thou, Volpone,
By blood and rank a gentleman, canst not fall
Under like censure; but our judgment on thee

Is, that thy substance all be straight confiscate
To the hospital of the Incurabili:
And, since the most was gotten by imposture,
By feigning lame, gout, palsy, and such diseases,
Thou art to lie in prison, cramped with irons,
Till thou be'st sick and lame indeed.—Remove him.

[He is taken from the Bar.]

VOLP. This is called mortifying of a Fox.

1 AVOC. Thou, Voltore, to take away the scandal
    Thou hast given all worthy men of thy profession,
    Art banished from their fellowship, and our state.
    Corbaccio!—bring him near—We here possess
    Thy son of all thy state, and confine thee
    To the monastery of San Spirito;
    Where, since thou knewest not how to live well here,
    Thou shalt be learned to die well.

CORB. Ah! what said he?

COM. You shall know anon, sir.

1 AVOC. Thou, Corvino, shalt
    Be straight embarked from thine own house, and rowed
    Round about Venice, through the Grand Canal
    Wearing a cap, with fair long ass's ears,
    Instead of horns; and so to mount, a paper
    Pinned on thy breast, to the Berlina[1]—

CORV. Yes,
    And have mine eyes beat out with stinking fish,
    Bruised fruit, and rotten eggs—'Tis well. I am glad
    I shall not see my shame yet.

1 AVOC. And to expiate
    Thy wrongs done to thy wife, thou art to send her
    Home to her father, with her dowry trebled:
    And these are all your judgments.

ALL. Honored fathers.—

1 AVOC. Which may not be revoked. Now you begin,
    When crimes are done, and past, and to be punished,

---

1. Pillory.

To think what your crimes are: away with them.
Let all that see these vices thus rewarded,
Take heart and love to study 'em! Mischiefs feed
Like beasts, till they be fat, and then they bleed.

Exeunt

Enter Volpone

The seasoning of a play, is the applause.
Now, though the Fox be punished by the laws,
He yet doth hope, there is no suffering due,
For any fact[1] which he hath done 'gainst you;
If there be, censure him; here he doubtful stands:
If not, fare jovially, and clap your hands.

Exit

1. Act.

THE REVENGER'S
TRAGEDY

CYRIL TOURNEUR

DRAMATIS PERSONAE

THE DUKE
LUSSURIOSO, *the Duke's son*
SPURIO, *a bastard*
AMBITIOSO, *the Duchess' eldest son*
SUPERVACUO, *the Duchess' second son*
The Duchess' Youngest Son

VENDICE, *disguised as* PIATO
HIPPOLITO, *also called* CARLO } *brothers of* CASTIZA

ANTONIO
PIERO } *nobles*

DONDOLO
Judges, Nobles, Gentlemen, Officers, Keeper, Servants, Lords
THE DUCHESS
CASTIZA
GRATIANA, *Mother of* CASTIZA

THE REVENGER'S TRAGEDY

ACT I, SCENE I

Enter Vendice.[1] *The Duke, Duchess, Lussurioso, Spurio, with a train,
pass over the stage with torchlight*

VEN. Duke! royal lecher! go, grey-haired adultery!
 And thou his son, as impious steeped as he:
 And thou his bastard, true begot with devil, in evil:
 And thou his duchess, that will do[2] with devil!
 Four excellent characters! O, that marrowless age
 Should stuff the hollow bones with damned desires!
 And, 'stead of heat, kindle infernal fires
 Within the spendthrift veins of a dry duke,
 A parched and juiceless luxur.[3] O God! one,
 That has scarce blood enough to live upon;
 And he to riot it, like a son and heir!
 O, the thought of that
 Turns my abusèd heart-strings into fret.
 Thou sallow picture of my poisoned love,
                              [*Views the skull in his hand*]
 My study's ornament, thou shell of death,
 Once the bright face of my betrothèd lady,
 When life and beauty naturally filled out
 These ragged imperfections;
 When two heaven-pointed diamonds were set

---

1. With a skull in his hand.
2. Copulate.
3. One given to sexual excess.

In those unsightly rings—then 'twas a face
So far beyond the artificial shine
Of any woman's bought complexion,
That the uprightest man (if such there be,
That sin but seven times a day) broke custom,
And made up eight with looking after her.
O, she was able to ha' made a usurer's son
Melt all his patrimony in a kiss;
And what his father fifty years told,[1]
To have consumed, and yet his suit been cold.
But, O accursèd palace!
Thee, when thou wert apparelled in thy flesh,
The old duke poisoned,
Because thy purer part would not consent
Unto his palsied lust; for old men lustful
Do show like young men angry, eager, violent,
Outbidden like their limited performance.
O, 'ware an old man hot and vicious!
"Age, as in gold, in lust is covetous."
Vengeance, thou murder's quit-rent,[2] and whereby
Thou show'st thyself tenant to tragedy;
O keep thy day, hour, minute, I beseech,
For those thou hast determined. Hum! who e'er knew
Murder unpaid? faith, give Revenge her due,
She has kept touch hitherto: be merry, merry,
Advance thee, O thou terror to fat folks,
To have their costly three-piled flesh worn off
As bare as this; for banquets, ease, and laughter
Can make great men, as greatness goes by clay;
But wise men little are more than they.

Enter Hippolito

Hip. Still sighing o'er death's vizard?
Ven. Brother, welcome!
    What comfort bring'st thou? how go things at court?

---

1. Counted, accumulated.
2. Rent paid in lieu of service.

HIP. In silk and silver, brother: never braver.
VEN. Pooh!
    Thou play'st upon my meaning. Prythee, say,
    Has that bald madam, Opportunity,[1]
    Yet thought upon's? speak, are we happy yet?
    Thy wrongs and mine are for one scabbard fit.
HIP. It may prove happiness.
VEN. What is't may prove?
    Give me to taste.
HIP. Give me your hearing, then.
    You know my place at court?
VEN. Ay, the duke's chamber!
    But 'tis a marvel thou'rt not turned out yet!
HIP. Faith, I've been shoved at; but 'twas still my hap
    To hold by the duchess' skirt: you guess at that:
    Whom such a coat keeps up, can ne'er fall flat.
    But to the purpose—
    Last evening, predecessor unto this,
    The duke's son warily inquired for me,
    Whose pleasure I attended: he began
    By policy to open and unhusk me
    About the time and common rumor:
    But I had so much wit to keep my thoughts
    Up in their built houses; yet afforded him
    An idle satisfaction without danger.
    But the whole aim and scope of his intent
    Ended in this: conjuring me in private
    To seek some strange-digested fellow forth,
    Of ill-contented nature; either disgraced
    In former times, or by new grooms displaced,
    Since his step-mother's nutpials; such a blood,
    A man that were for evil only good—
    To give you the true word, some base-coined pander.
VEN. I reach you; for I know his heat is such,
    Were there as many concubines as ladies,

---

1. Represented as bald, with a forelock one must grasp.

He would not be contained; he must fly out.
I wonder how ill-featured, vile-proportioned,
That one should be, if she were made for woman,
Whom, at the insurrection of his lust,
He would refuse for once. Heart! I think none.
Next to a skull, though more unsound than one,
Each face he meets he strongly dotes upon.

HIP. Brother, y' have truly spoke him.
He knows not you, but I will swear you know him.

VEN. And therefore I'll put on that knave for once,
And be a right man then, a man o' the time;
For to be honest is not to be i' the world.
Brother, I'll be that strange-composèd fellow.

HIP. And I'll prefer you, brother.

VEN. Go to, then:
The smallest advantage fattens wrongèd men:
It may point out occasion; if I meet her,
I'll hold her by the foretop fast enough;
Or, like the French mole,[1] heave up hair and all.
I have a habit[2] that will fit it quaintly.
Here comes our mother.

HIP. And sister.

VEN. We must quoyne:[3]
Women are apt, you know, to take false money;
But I dare stake my soul for these two creatures;
Only excuse excepted, that they'll swallow,
Because their sex is easy in belief.

Enter Gratiana and Castiza

GRA. What news from court, son Carlo?

HIP. Faith, mother,
'Tis whispered there the duchess' youngest son
Has played a rape on Lord Antonio's wife.

---

1. The hair falls out as a result of syphilis.
2. Costume.
3. Counterfeit (coin).

GRA. On that religious lady!

CAS. Royal blood monster! he deserves to die,
   If Italy had no more hopes but he.

VEN. Sister, y' have sentenced most direct and true,
   The law's a woman, and would she were you.
   Mother, I must take leave of you.

GRA. Leave for what?

VEN. I intend speedy travel.

HIP. That he does, madam.

GRA. Speedy indeed!

VEN. For since my worthy father's funeral,
   My life's unnaturally to me, e'en compelled;
   As if I lived now, when I should be dead.

GRA. Indeed, he was a worthy gentleman,
   Had his estate been fellow to his mind.

VEN. The duke did much deject him.

GRA. Much?

VEN. Too much:
   And though disgrace oft smothered in his spirit,
   When it would mount, surely I think he died
   Of discontent, the noble man's consumption.

GRA. Most sure he did.

VEN. Did he, 'lack? you know all:—
   You were his midnight secretary.[1]

GRA. No,
   He was too wise to trust me with his thoughts.

VEN. I'faith, then, father, thou wast wise indeed;
   "Wives are but made to go to bed and feed."
   Come, mother, sister: you'll bring me onward, brother?

HIP. I will.

VEN. I'll quickly turn into another.

Exeunt

---

1. Confidante.

SCENE II

*Enter the Old Duke; Lussurioso, his son; the Duchess; Spurio, the
bastard; the Duchess's two sons, Ambitioso and Supervacuo, the third,
her youngest, brought in with Officers for the rape; two Judges*

DUKE. Duchess, it is your youngest son, we're sorry
　　His violent act has e'en drawn blood of honor,
　　And stained our honors;
　　Thrown ink upon the forehead of our state;
　　Which envious spirits will dip their pens into
　　After our death; and blot us in our tombs:
　　For that which would seem treason in our lives
　　Is laughter, when we're dead. Who dares now whisper,
　　That dares not then speak out, and e'en proclaim
　　With loud words and broad pens our closest[1] shame?
1ST JUDGE. Your grace hath spoke like to your silver years,
　　Full of confirmed gravity; for what is it to have
　　A flattering false insculption on a tomb,
　　And in men's hearts reproach? the bowelled[2] corpse
　　May be cered in,[3] but (with free tongue I speak)
　　The faults of great men through their cere-cloths break.
DUKE. They do; we're sorry for't: it is our fate
　　To live in fear, and die to live in hate.
　　I leave him to your sentence; doom him, lords—
　　The fact is great—whilst I sit by and sigh.
DUCH. My gracious lord, I pray be merciful:
　　Although his trespass far exceed his years,
　　Think him to be your own, as I am yours;
　　Call him not son-in-law;[4] the law, I fear,
　　Will fall too soon upon his name and him:
　　Temper his fault with pity.
LUS. Good my lord,
　　Then 'twill not taste so bitter and unpleasant

---

1. Most secret.
2. Disemboweled.
3. Wrapped in a winding-sheet.
4. Stepson.

Upon the judges' palate; for offences,
Gilt o'er with mercy, show like fairest women,
Good only for their beauties, which wash off,
No sin is uglier.

AMB. I beseech your grace,
Be soft and mild; let not relentless law
Look with an iron forehead on our brother.

SPU. [*Aside*] He yields small comfort yet; hope he shall die;
And if a bastard's wish might stand in force,
Would all the court were turned into a corse!

DUCH. No pity yet? must I rise fruitless then?
A wonder in a woman! are my knees
Of such low metal, that without respect—

1ST JUDGE. Let the offender stand forth:
'Tis the duke's pleasure that impartial doom
Shall take fast hold of his unclean attempt.
A rape! why 'tis the very core of lust—
Double adultery.

Y. SON. So, sir.

2ND JUDGE. And which was worse,
Committed on the Lord Antonio's wife,
That general-honest lady. Confess, my lord,
What moved you to't?

Y. SON. Why, flesh and blood, my lord;
What should move men unto a woman else?

LUS. O, do not jest thy doom! trust not an axe
Or sword too far: the law is a wise serpent,
And quickly can beguile thee of thy life.
Though marriage only has made thee my brother,
I love thee so far: play not with thy death.

Y. SON. I thank you, troth; good admonitions, faith,
If I'd the grace now to make use of them.

1ST JUDGE. That lady's name has spread such a fair wing
Over all Italy, that if our tongues
Were sparing toward the fact,[1] judgment itself
Would be condemned, and suffer in men's thoughts.

---

1. Deed.

Y. SON. Well then, 'tis done; and it would please me well,
Were it to do again: sure, she's a goddess,
For I'd no power to see her, and to live.
It falls out true in this, for I must die;
Her beauty was ordained to be my scaffold.
And yet, methinks, I might be easier 'sessed:
My fault being sport, let me but die in jest.
1ST JUDGE. This be the sentence—
DUCH. O, keep't upon your tongue; let it not slip;
Death too soon steals out of a lawyer's lip.
Be not so cruel-wise!
1ST JUDGE. Your grace must pardon us;
'Tis but the justice of the law.
DUCH. The law
Is grown more subtle than a woman should be.
SPU. [*Aside*] Now, now he dies! rid 'em away.
DUCH. [*Aside*] O, what it is to have an old cool duke,
To be as slack in tongue as in performance![1]
1ST JUDGE. Confirmed, this be the doom irrevocable.
DUCH. O!
1ST JUDGE. To-morrow early—
DUCH. Pray be abed, my lord.
1ST JUDGE. Your grace much wrongs yourself.
AMB. No, 'tis that tongue:
Your too much right does do us too much wrong.
1ST JUDGE. Let that offender—
DUCH. Live, and be in health.
1ST JUDGE. Be on a scaffold—
DUCH. Hold, hold, my lord!
SPU. [*Aside*] Pox on't,
What makes my dad speak now?
DUKE. We will defer the judgment till next sitting:
In the meantime, let him be kept close prisoner.
Guard, bear him hence.

1. Sexual performance.

AMB. [*Aside*] Brother, this makes for thee;
    Fear not, we'll have a trick to set thee free.
Y. SON. [*Aside*] Brother, I will expect it from you both;
    And in that hope I rest.
SUP. Farewell, be merry.

Exit with a Guard

SPU. Delayed! deferred! nay then, if judgment have cold blood,
    Flattery and bribes will kill it.
DUKE. About it, then, my lords, with your best powers:
    More serious business calls upon our hours.

Exeunt, excepting the Duchess

DUCH. Was't ever known step-duchess was so mild
    And calm as I? some now would plot his death
    With easy doctors, those loose-living men,
    And make his withered grace fall to his grave,
    And keep church better.
    Some second wife would do this, and despatch
    Her double-loathèd lord at meat or sleep.
    Indeed, 'tis true, an old man's twice a child;
    Mine cannot speak; one of his single words
    Would quite have freed my youngest dearest son
    From death or durance, and have made him walk
    With a bold foot upon the thorny law,
    Whose prickles should bow under him; but 'tis not,
    And therefore wedlock-faith shall be forgot:
    I'll kill him in his forehead;[1] hate, there feed;
    That wound is deepest, though it never bleed.
    And here comes he whom my heart points unto,
    His bastard son, but my love's true-begot;
    Many a wealthy letter have I sent him,
    Swelled up with jewels, and the timorous man
    Is yet but coldly kind.
    That jewel's mine that quivers in his ear,
    Mocking his master's chillness and vain fear.
    He has spied me now!

1. i.e., By cuckolding him.

Enter Spurio

SPU. Madam, your grace so private?
My duty on your hand.
DUCH. Upon my hand, sir! troth, I think you'd fear
To kiss my hand too, if my lip stood there.
SPU. Witness I would not, madam.

[Kisses her]

DUCH. 'Tis a wonder;
For ceremony has made many fools!
It is as easy way unto a duchess,
As to a hatted dame,[1] if her love answer:
But that by timorous honors, pale respects,
Idle degrees of fear, men make their ways
Hard of themselves. What, have you thought of me?
SPU. Madam, I ever think of you in duty,
Regard, and—
DUCH. Pooh! upon my love, I mean.
SPU. I would 'twere love; but 'tis a fouler name
Than lust: you are my father's wife—your grace may guess now
What I could call it.
DUCH. Why, th' art his son but falsely;
'Tis a hard question whether he begot thee.
SPU. I'faith, 'tis true: I'm an uncertain man
Of more uncertain woman. Maybe, his groom
O' the stable begot me; you know I know not!
He could ride a horse well, a shrewd suspicion, marry!—
He was wondrous tall: he had his length, i'faith.
For peeping over half-shut holyday windows,
Men would desire him light.[2] When he was afoot
He made a goodly show under a pent-house;
And when he rid, his hat would check[3] the signs,
And clatter barbers' basons.

1. Only lower-class women wore hats.
2. Ask him to dismount.
3. Knock against.

DUCH. Nay, set you a-horseback once,
  You'll ne'er light off.[1]

SPU. Indeed, I am a beggar.

DUCH. That's the more sign thou'rt great.—
  But to our love:
  Let it stand firm both in thy thought and mind,
  That the duke was thy father, as no doubt then
  He bid fair for't—thy injury is the more;
  For had he cut thee a right diamond,
  Thou had'st been next set in the dukedom's ring,
  When his worn self, like age's easy slave,
  Had dropped out of the collet[2] into th' grave.
  What wrong can equal this? canst thou be tame,
  And think upon't?

SPU. No, mad, and think upon't.

DUCH. Who would not be revenged of such a father,
  E'en in the worst way? I would thank that sin,
  That could most injure him, and be in league with it.
  O, what a grief 'tis that a man should live
  But once i' the world, and then to live a bastard—
  The curse o' the womb, the thief of nature,
  Begot against the seventh commandment,
  Half-damned in the conception by the justice
  Of that unbribèd everlasting law.

SPU. O, I'd a hot-backed devil to my father.

DUCH. Would not this mad e'en patience, make blood rough?
  Who but an eunuch would not sin? his bed, wrapped in!
  By one false minute disinherited.

SPU. Ay, there's the vengeance that my birth was
  I'll be revenged for all: now, hate, begin;
  I'll call foul incest but a venial sin.

DUCH. Cold still! in vain then must a duchess woo?

SPU. Madam, I blush to say what I will do.

DUCH. Thence flew sweet comfort. Earnest,[3] and farewell.

  [Kisses him]

---

1. Set a beggar on horseback, and he'll ride a gallop.
2. Socket.
3. Foretaste, promise.

Spu. O, one incestuous kiss picks open hell.

Duch. Faith, now, old duke, my vengeance shall reach high,
I'll arm thy brow with woman's heraldry.[1]

Exit

Spu. Duke, thou didst do me wrong; and, by thy act
Adultery is my nature.
Faith, if the truth were known, I was begot
After some gluttonous dinner; some stirring dish
Was my first father, when deep healths went round,
And ladies' cheeks were painted red with wine,
Their tongues, as short and nimble as their heels,
Uttering words sweet and thick; and when they rose,
Were merrily disposed to fall again.
In such a whispering and withdrawing hour,
When base male-bawds kept sentinel at stair-head,
Was I stol'n softly. O damnation meet!
The sin of feasts, drunken adultery!
I feel it swell me; my revenge is just!
I was begot in impudent wine and lust.
Step-mother, I consent to thy desires;
I love thy mischief well; but I hate thee
And those three cubs thy sons, wishing confusion,
Death and disgrace may be their epitaphs.
As for my brother, the duke's only son,[2]
Whose birth is more beholding to report
Than mine, and yet perhaps as falsely sown
(Women must not be trusted with their own),
I'll loose my days upon him, hate all I;
Duke, on thy brow I'll draw my bastardy:
For indeed a bastard by nature should make cuckolds,
Because he is the son of a cuckold-maker.

Exit

1. Cuckold's horns.
2. Lussurioso.

SCENE III

Enter Vendice in disguise and Hippolito

VEN. What, brother, am I far enough from myself?
HIP. As if another man had been sent whole
    Into the world, and none wist how he came.
VEN. It will confirm me bold—the child o' the court;
    Let blushes dwell i' the country. Impudence!
    Thou goddess of the palace, mistress of mistresses.
    To whom the costly perfumed people pray,
    Strike thou my forehead into dauntless marble,
    Mine eyes to steady sapphires, Turn my visage;
    And, if I must needs glow, let me blush inward,
    That this immodest season may not spy
    That scholar in my cheeks, fool bashfulness;
    That maid in the old time, whose flush of grace
    Would never suffer her to get good clothes.
    Our maids are wiser, and are less ashamed;
    Save Grace the bawd, I seldom hear grace named!
HIP. Nay, brother, you reach out o' the verge now—
    'Sfoot, the duke's son! settle your looks.
VEN. Pray, let me not be doubted.
HIP. My lord—

Enter Lussurioso

LUS. Hippolito—be absent, leave us!
HIP. My lord, after long search, wary inquiries,
    And politic siftings, I made choice of yon fellow,
    Whom I guess rare for many deep employments:
    This our age swims within him; and if Time
    Had so much hair, I should take him for Time,
    He is so near kin to this present minute.
LUS. 'Tis enough;
    We thank thee: yet words are but great men's blanks;[1]
    Gold, though it be dumb, does utter the best thanks.

                              [*Gives him money*]

---

1. Unsigned promissory notes.

HIP. Your plenteous honor! an excellent fellow, my lord.

LUS. So, give us leave. [*Exit Hippolito*] Welcome, be not far off; we
    must be better acquainted: pish, be bold with us—thy hand.

VEN. With all my heart, i'faith: how dost, sweet musk-cat?
    When shall we lie together?

LUS. Wondrous knave,
    Gather him into boldness! 'sfoot, the slave's
    Already as familiar as an ague,
    And shakes me at his pleasure. Friend, I can
    Forget myself in private; but elsewhere
    I pray do you remember me.[1]

VEN. O, very well, sir—I consider[2] myself saucy.

LUS. What hast been?
    Of what profession?

VEN. A bone-setter.

LUS. A bone-setter!

VEN. A bawd, my lord—
    One that sets bones together.

LUS. Notable bluntness!
    Fit, fit for me; e'en trained up to my hand:
    Thou hast been scrivener to much knavery, then?

VEN. 'Sfoot, to abundance, sir: I have been witness
    To the surrenders of a thousand virgins:
    And not so little;
    I have seen patrimonies washed a-pieces,
    Fruit-fields turned into bastards,
    And in a world of acres
    Not so much dust due to the heir 'twas left to
    As would well gravel[3] a petition.

LUS. [*Aside*] Fine villain! troth, I like him wondrously:
    He's e'en shaped for my purpose.
    Then thou know'st
    I' th' world strange lust?

---

1. Respect my rank.
2. Construe.
3. Dry the ink on.

VEN. O Dutch lust! fulsome lust!
    Drunken procreation! which begets so many drunkards
    Some fathers dread not (gone to bed in wine) to slide from the
        mother,
    And cling[1] the daughter-in-law;
    Some uncles are adulterous with their nieces:
    Brothers with brothers' wives. O hour of incest!
    Any kin now, next to the rim[2] o' th' sister,
    Is men's meat in these days; and in the morning,
    When they are up and dressed, and their mask on,
    Who can perceive this, save that eternal eye,
    That sees through flesh and all? Well, if anything be damned,
    It will be twelve o'clock at night; that twelve
    Will never 'scape;
    It is the Judas of the hours, wherein
    Honest salvation is betrayed to sin.
LUS. In troth, it is true; but let this talk glide.
    It is our blood to err, though hell gape wide.
    Ladies know Lucifer fell, yet still are proud.
    Now, sir, wert thou as secret as thou'rt subtle,
    And deeply fathomed into all estates,[3]
    I would embrace thee for a near employment;
    And thou shouldst swell in money, and be able
    To make lame beggars crouch to thee.
VEN. My lord,
    Secret! I ne'er had that disease o' the mother,[4]
    I praise my father: why are men made close,
    But to keep thoughts in best? I grant you this,
    Tell but some women a secret over night,
    Your doctor may find it in the urinal i' the morning.
    But, my lord—
LUS. So thou'rt confirmed in me,
    And thus I enter thee.

                     [Gives him money]

1. Embrace.
2. Womb.
3. Classes.
4. Hysteria.

VEN. This Indian devil[1]
    Will quickly enter any man but a usurer;
    He prevents that by entering the devil first.
LUS. Attend me. I am past my depth in lust,
    And I must swim or drown. All my desires
    Are levelled at a virgin not far from court,
    To whom I have conveyed by messenger
    Many waxed lines, full of my neatest spirit,
    And jewels that were able to ravish her
    Without the help of man; all which and more
    She (foolish chaste) sent back, the messengers
    Receiving frowns for answers.
VEN. Possible!
    'Tis a rare Phœnix, whoe'er she be.
    If your desires be such, she so repugnant,[2]
    In troth, my lord, I'd be revenged and marry her.
LUS. Pish! the dowry of her blood and of her fortunes
    Are both too mean—good enough to be bad withal.
    I'm one of that number can defend
    Marriage is good; yet rather keep a friend.[3]
    Give me my bed by stealth—there's true delight;
    What breeds a loathing in't, but night by night!
VEN. A very fine religion!
LUS. Therefore thus
    I'll trust thee in the business of my heart;
    Because I see thee well-experienced
    In this luxurious[4] day wherein we breathe.
    Go thou, and with a smooth enchanting tongue
    Bewitch her ears, and cosen her of all grace:
    Enter upon the portion of her soul—
    Her honor, which she calls her chastity,
    And bring it into expense; for honesty
    Is like a stock of money laid to sleep
    Which, ne'er so little broke, does never keep.

1. Gold.
2. Resistant.
3. Lover.
4. Lustful.

VEN. You have gi'en't the tang,[1] i'faith, my lord:
   Make known the lady to me, and my brain
   Shall swell with strange invention: I will move it,
   Till I expire with speaking, and drop down
   Without a word to save me—but I'll work—

LUS. We thank thee, and will raise thee.—
   Receive her name; it is the only daughter to Madam Gratiana, the
   late widow.

VEN. [*Aside*] O my sister, my sister!

LUS. Why dost walk aside?

VEN. My lord, I was thinking how I might begin:
   As thus, O lady—or twenty hundred devices—
   Her very bodkin will put a man in.

LUS. Ay, or the wagging of her hair.

VEN. No, that shall put you in, my lord.

LUS. Shall't? why, content. Dost know the daughter then?

VEN. O, excellent well by sight.

LUS. That was her brother,
   That did prefer thee to us.

VEN. My lord, I think so;
   I knew I had seen him somewhere—

LUS. And therefore, prythee, let thy heart to him
   Be as a virgin close.

VEN. O my good lord.

LUS. We may laugh at that simple age within him.

VEN. Ha, ha, ha!

LUS. Himself being made the subtle instrument,
   To wind up a good fellow.[2]

VEN. That's I, my lord.

LUS. That's thou,
   To entice and work his sister.

VEN. A pure novice!

LUS. 'Twas finely managed.

VEN. Galliantly carried!
   A pretty perfumed villain!

---

1. Got it right.
2. Advance.

LUS. I've bethought me,
  If she prove chaste still and immovable,
  Venture upon the mother; and with gifts,
  As I will furnish thee, begin with her.
VEN. O, fie, fie! that's the wrong end my lord.
  'Tis mere impossible that a mother, by any gifts, should become a
    bawd to her own daughter!
LUS. Nay, then, I see thou'rt but a puisne[1]
  In the subtle mystery of a woman.
  Why, 'tis held now no dainty dish: the name
  Is so in league with the age, that nowadays
  It does eclipse three quarters of a mother.
VEN. Does it so, my lord?
  Let me alone, then, to eclipse the fourth.
LUS. Why, well-said—come, I'll furnish thee, but first
  Swear to be true in all.
VEN. True!
LUS. Nay, but swear.
VEN. Swear?—I hope your honor little doubts my faith.
LUS. Yet, for my humor's sake, 'cause I love swearing—
VEN. 'Cause you love swearing,—'slud,[2] I will.
LUS. Why, enough!
  Ere long look to be made of better stuff.
VEN. That will do well indeed, my lord.
LUS. Attend me.

                                  Exit

VEN. O!
  Now let me burst. I've eaten noble poison;
  We are made strange fellows, brother, innocent villains!
  Wilt not be angry, when thou hear'st on't, think'st thou?
  I'faith, thou shalt: swear me to foul my sister!
  Sword, I durst make a promise of him to thee;
  Thou shalt dis-heir him; it shall be thine honor.
  And yet, now angry froth is down in me,
  It would not prove the meanest policy,

1. Novice.
2. By God's blood.

In this disguise, to try the faith of both.
Another might have had the selfsame office;
Some slave that would have wrought effectually,
Ay, and perhaps o'erwrought 'em; therefore I,
Being thought travelled, will apply myself
Unto the selfsame form, forget my nature,
As if no part about me were kin to 'em,
So touch[1] 'em;—though I durst almost for good
Venture my lands in Heaven upon their blood.

Exit

SCENE IV

*Enter Antonio, whose Wife the Duchess' Youngest Son ravished,
discovering her dead body to Hippolito, Piero, and Lords*

ANT. Draw nearer, lords, and be sad witnesses
    Of a fair comely building newly fallen,
    Being falsely undermined. Violent rape
    Has played a glorious act: behold, my lords,
    A sight that strikes man out of me.
PIERO. That virtuous lady!
ANT. Precedent[2] for wives!
HIP. The blush of many women, whose chaste presence
    Would e'en call shame up to their cheeks, and make
    Pale wanton sinners have good colors—
ANT. Dead!
    Her honor first drank poison, and her life,
    Being fellows in one house, did pledge her honor.
PIERO. O, grief of many!
ANT. I marked not this before—
    A prayer-book, the pillow to her cheek:
    This was her rich confection;[3] and another
    Placed in her right hand, with a leaf tucked up,
    Pointing to these words—

1. Test.
2. Model.
3. Preservative.

Melius virtute mori, quam per dedecus vivere:[1]
True and effectual it is indeed.

HIP. My lord, since you invite us to your sorrows,
Let's truly taste 'em, that with equal comfort,
As to ourselves, we may relieve your wrongs:
We have grief too, that yet walks without tongue;
Curæ leves loquuntur, majores stupent.[2]

ANT. You deal with truth, my lord;
Lend me but your attentions, and I'll cut
Long grief into short words. Last revelling night,
When torch-light made an artificial noon
About the court, some courtiers in the masque,
Putting on better faces than their own,
Being full of fraud and flattery—amongst whom
The duchess' youngest son (that moth to honor)
Filled up a room, and with long lust to eat
Into my wearing,[3] amongst all the ladies
Singled out that dear form, who ever lived
As cold in lust as she is now in death
(Which that step-duchess' monster knew too well),
And therefore in the height of all the revels,
When music was heard loudest, courtiers busiest,
And ladies great with laughter—O vicious minute!
Unfit but for relation to be spoke of:
Then with a face more impudent than his vizard,
He harried her amidst a throng of panders,
That live upon damnation of both kinds,
And fed the ravenous vulture of his lust.
O death to think on't! She, her honor forced,
Deemed it a nobler dowry for her name
To die with poison than to live with shame.

HIP. A wondrous lady! of rare fire compact;
She has made her name an empress by that act.

PIERO. My lord, what judgment follows the offender?

---

1. It is better to die in virtue than to live dishonored.
2. Small woes are eloquent, great ones are dumb.
3. Following the description of the rapist as a moth.

ANT. Faith, none, my lord; it cools, and is deferred.

PIERO. Delay the doom for rape!

ANT. O, you must note who 'tis should die,
  The duchess' son! she'll look to be a saver:
  "Judgment, in this age, is near kin to favor."

HIP. Nay, then, step forth, thou bribeless officer:

  [*Draws sword*]

  I'll bind you all in steel, to bind you surely;
  Here let your oaths meet, to be kept and paid,
  Which else will stick like rust, and shame the blade;
  Strengthen my vow that if, at the next sitting,
  Judgment speak all in gold, and spare the blood
  Of such a serpent, e'en before their seats
  To let his soul out, which long since was found
  Guilty in Heaven—

ALL. We swear it, and will act it.

ANT. Kind gentlemen, I thank you in mine ire.

HIP. 'Twere pity
  The ruins of so fair a monument
  Should not be dipped in the defacer's blood.

PIERO. Her funeral shall be wealthy; for her name
  Merits a tomb of pearl. My Lord Antonio,
  For this time wipe your lady from your eyes;
  No doubt our grief and yours may one day court it,
  When we are more familiar with revenge.

ANT. That is my comfort, gentlemen, and I joy
  In this one happiness above the rest,
  Which will be called a miracle at last;
  That, being an old man, I'd a wife so chaste.

  Exeunt

ACT II, SCENE I

Enter Castiza

CAS. How hardly shall that maiden be beset,
  Whose only fortunes are her constant thoughts!
  That has no other child's part but her honor,

That keeps her low and empty in estate;
Maids and their honors are like poor beginners;
Were not sin rich, there would be fewer sinners;
Why had not virtue a revénue?[1] Well,
I know the cause, 'twould have impoverished hell.

Enter Dondolo

How now, Dondolo?

DON. Madonna, there is one as they say, a thing of flesh and blood—
a man, I take him by his beard, that would very desirously mouth to
mouth with you.

CAS. What's that?

DON. Show his teeth in your company.

CAS. I understand thee not.

DON. Why, speak with you, madonna.

CAS. Why, say so, madman, and cut off a great deal of dirty way;[2] had
it not been better spoke in ordinary words, that one would speak
with me?

DON. Ha, ha! that's as ordinary as two shillings. I would strive a little
to show myself in my place; a gentleman-usher scorns to use the
phrase and fancy of a serving-man.

CAS. Yours be your own, sir; go, direct him hither;

Exit Dondolo

I hope some happy tidings from my brother,
That lately travelled, whom my soul affects.[3]
Here he comes.

Enter Vendice, disguised

VEN. Lady, the best of wishes to your sex—
Fair skins and new gowns.

CAS. O, they shall thank you, sir.
Whence this?

VEN. O, from a dear and worthy mighty friend.

CAS. From whom?

---

1. Inheritance.
2. Road.
3. Loves.

VEN. The duke's son!
CAS. Receive that.

[Boxes his ear]

I swore I would put anger in my hand,
And pass the virgin limits of my sex,
To him that next appeared in that base office,
To be his sin's attorney. Bear to him
That figure of my hate upon thy cheek,
Whilst 'tis yet hot, and I'll reward thee for't;
Tell him my honor shall have a rich name,
When several harlots shall share his with shame.
Farewell; commend me to him in my hate.

Exit

VEN. It is the sweetest box that e'er my nose came nigh;
The finest drawn-work cuff that e'er was worn;
I'll love this blow for ever, and this cheek
Shall still henceforward take the wall[1] of this.
O, I'm above my tongue,[2] most constant sister,
In this thou hast right honorable shown;
Many are called by their honor, that have none;
Thou art approved for ever in my thoughts.
It is not in the power of words to taint thee.
And yet for the salvation of my oath,
As my resolve in that point, I will lay
Hard siege unto my mother, though I know
A siren's tongue could not bewitch her so.
Mass, fitly here she comes! thanks, my disguise—
Madam, good afternoon.

Enter Gratiana

GRA. Y'are welcome, sir.
VEN. The next[3] of Italy commends him to you,
Our mighty expectation, the duke's son.

---

1. Have precedence.
2. Unable to express my delight.
3. Next in succession.

GRA. I think myself much honored that he pleases
    To rank me in his thoughts.
VEN. So may you, lady:
    One that is like to be our sudden duke;
    The crown gapes for him every tide, and then
    Commander o'er us all; do but think on him,
    How blessed were they, now that could pleasure him—
    E'en with anything almost!
GRA. Ay, save their honor.
VEN. Tut, one would let a little of that go too,
    And ne'er be seen in't—ne'er be seen in't, mark you;
    I'd wink,[1] and let it go.
GRA. Marry, but I would not.
VEN. Marry but I would, I hope; I know you would too,
    If you'd that blood now, which you gave your daughter.
    To her indeed 'tis this wheel[2] comes about;
    That man that must be all this, perhaps ere morning
    (For his white father does but mould away),
    Has long desired your daughter.
GRA. Desired?
VEN. Nay, but hear me;
    He desires now, that will command hereafter:
    Therefore be wise. I speak as more a friend
    To you than him: madam, I know you're poor,
    And, 'lack the day!
    There are too many poor ladies already;
    Why should you wax the number? 'Tis despised.
    Live wealthy, rightly understand the world,
    And chide away that foolish country girl
    Keeps company with your daughter—Chastity.
GRA. O fie, fie! the riches of the world cannot hire
    A mother to such a most unnatural task.
VEN. No, but a thousand angels[3] can.
    Men have no power, angels must work you to't:

---

1. Close my eyes.
2. Of fortune.
3. Gold coins.

The world descends into such baseborn evils,
That forty angels can make fourscore devils.
There will be fools still, I perceive—still fools.
Would I be poor, dejected, scorned of greatness,
Swept from the palace, and see others' daughters
Spring with the dew o' the court, having mine own
So much desired and loved by the duke's son?
No, I would raise my state upon her breast;
And call her eyes my tenants; I would count
My yearly maintenance upon her cheeks;
Take coach upon her lip; and all her parts
Should keep men after men, and I would ride
In pleasure upon pleasure.
You took great pains for her, once when it was;
Let her requite it now, though it be but some.[1]
You brought her forth: she may well bring you home.

GRA. O Heavens! this o'ercomes me!

VEN. [*Aside*] Not, I hope, already?

GRA. [*Aside*] It is too strong for me; men know that know us,
We are so weak their words can overthrow us;
He touched me nearly, made my virtues bate,[2]
When his tongue struck upon my poor estate.

VEN. [*Aside*] I e'en quake to proceed, my spirit turns edge.
I fear me she's unmothered; yet I'll venture.
"That woman is all male, whom none can enter."
What think you now, lady? Speak, are you wiser?
What said advancement to you? Thus it said:
The daughter's fall lifts up the mother's head.
Did it not, madam? But I'll swear it does
In many places: tut, this age fears no man.
" 'Tis no shame to be bad, because 'tis common."

GRA. Ay, that's the comfort on't.

VEN. The comfort on't!
I keep the best for last—can these persuade you
To forget Heaven—and—

[*Gives her money*]

1. Partial.
2. Weaken.

GRA. Ay, these are they—
VEN. O!
GRA. That enchant our sex. These are
  The means that govern our affections—that woman
  Will not be troubled with the mother[1] long,
  That sees the comfortable shine of you:
  I blush to think what for your sakes I'll do.
VEN. [*Aside*] O suffering Heaven, with thy invisible finger,
  E'en at this instant turn the precious side
  Of both mine eyeballs inward, not to see myself.
GRA. Look you, sir.
VEN. Hollo.
GRA. Let this thank your pains.
VEN. O, you're kind, madam.
GRA. I'll see how I can move.
VEN. Your words will sting.
GRA. If she be still chaste, I'll ne'er call her mine.
VEN. Spoke truer than you meant it.
GRA. Daughter Castiza.

Re-enter Castiza

CAS. Madam.
VEN. O, she's yonder;
  Meet her: troops of celestial soldiers guard her heart.
  Yon dam has devils enough to take her part.
CAS. Madam, what makes yon evil-officed man
  In presence of you?
GRA. Why?
CAS. He lately brought
  Immodest writing sent from the duke's son,
  To tempt me to dishonorable act.
GRA. Dishonorable act!—good honorable fool,
  That wouldst be honest, 'cause thou wouldst be so,
  Producing no one reason but thy will.
  And't has a good report, prettily commended,
  But pray, by whom? Poor people, ignorant people;

---

1. Hysteria.

The better sort, I'm sure, cannot abide it.
And by what rule should we square out our lives,
But by our betters' actions? O, if thou knew'st
What 'twere to lose it, thou would never keep it!
But there's a cold curse laid upon all maids,
Whilst others clip[1] the sun, they clasp the shades.
Virginity is paradise locked up.
You cannot come by yourselves without fee;[2]
And 'twas decreed that man should keep the key!
Deny advancement! treasure! the duke's son!

CAS. I cry you mercy! lady, I mistook you!
Pray did you see my mother? which way went you?
Pray God, I have not lost her.

VEN. [*Aside*] Prettily put by!

GRA. Are you as proud to me, as coy to him?
Do you not know me now?

CAS. Why, are you she?
The world's so changed one shape into another,
It is a wise child now that knows her mother.

VEN. [*Aside*] Most right i'faith.

GRA. I owe your cheek my hand
For that presumption now; but I'll forget it.
Come, you shall leave those childish 'haviors,
And understand your time. Fortunes flow to you;
What, will you be a girl?
If all feared drowning that spy waves ashore,
Gold would grow rich, and all the merchants poor.

CAS. It is a pretty saying of a wicked one;
But methinks now it does not show so well
Out of your mouth—better in his!

VEN. [*Aside*] Faith, bad enough in both,
Were I in earnest, as I'll seem no less.
I wonder, lady, your own mother's words
Cannot be taken, nor stand in full force.
'Tis honesty you urge; what's honesty?

1. Embrace.
2. i.e., To the jailer.

'Tis but Heaven's beggar; and what woman is
So foolish to keep honesty,
And be not able to keep herself? No,
Times are grown wiser, and will keep less charge.[1]
A maid that has small portion now intends[2]
To break up house, and live upon her friends;
How blessed are you! you have happiness alone;
Others must fall to thousands, you to one,
Sufficient in himself to make your forehead
Dazzle the world with jewels, and petitionary people
Start at your presence.

GRA. O, if I were young; I should be ravished.

CAS. Ay, to lose your honor!

VEN. 'Slid, how can you lose your honor
To deal with my lord's grace?
He'll add more honor to it by his title;
Your mother will tell you how.

GRA. That I will.

VEN. O, think upon the pleasure of the palace!
Secured ease and state! the stirring[3] meats,
Ready to move out of the dishes, that e'en now
Quicken when they are eaten!
Banquets abroad by torchlight! music! sports!
Bareheaded vassals, that had ne'er the fortune
To keep on their own hats, but let horns wear 'em!
Nine coaches waiting—hurry, hurry, hurry—

CAS. Ay, to the devil.

VEN. [*Aside*] Ay, to the devil! To the duke, by my faith.

GRA. Ay, to the duke: daughter, you'd scorn to think o' the devil, an[4]
you were there once.

VEN. [*Aside*] True, for most there are as proud as he for his heart,[5]
i'faith.

---

1. Take less care (of virtue).
2. Decides.
3. Stimulating.
4. If.
5. Proud in the extreme.

Who'd sit at home in a neglected room,
Dealing her short-lived beauty to the pictures,
That are as useless as old men, when those
Poorer in face and fortune than herself
Walk with a hundred acres on their backs,
Fair meadows cut into green foreparts? O,
It was the greatest blessing ever happened to woman
When farmers' sons agreed and met again,
To wash their hands, and come up gentlemen!
The commonwealth has flourished ever since:
Lands that were mete[1] by the rod, that labor's spared:
Tailors ride down, and measure 'em by the yard.
Fair trees, those comely foretops of the field,
Are cut to maintain head-tires—much untold.
All thrives but chastity; she lies a-cold.
Nay, shall I come nearer to you? mark but this:
Why are there so few honest women, but because 'tis the poorer
    profession? that's accounted best that's best followed; least in
    trade, least in fashion; and that's not honesty, believe it; and do
    but note the low and dejected price of it—
Lose but a pearl, we search, and cannot brook it:
But that[2] once gone, who is so mad to look[3] it?
GRA. Troth, he says true.
CAS. False! I defy you both:
I have endured you with an ear of fire;
Your tongues have struck hot irons on my face.
Mother, come from that poisonous woman there.
GRA. Where?
CAS. Do you not see her? she's too inward, then!
Slave, perish in thy office! you Heavens, please
Henceforth to make the mother a disease,
Which first begins with me: yet I've outgone you.

Exit

1. Measured.
2. Honor.
3. Look for.

VEN. [*Aside*] O angels, clap your wings upon the skies,
    And give this virgin crystal plaudites!
GRA. Peevish, coy, foolish!—but return this answer,
    My lord shall be most welcome, when his pleasure
    Conducts him this way. I will sway mine own.
    Women with women can work best alone.

                                                           Exit

VEN. Indeed, I'll tell him so.
    O, more uncivil, more unnatural,
    Than those base-titled creatures that look downward;
    Why does not Heaven turn black, or with a frown
    Undo the world? Why does not earth start up,
    And strike the sins that tread upon't? O,
    Were't not for gold and women, there would be no damnation.
    Hell would look like a lord's great kitchen without fire in't.
    But 'twas decreed, before the world began,
    That they should be the hooks to catch at man.

                                                           Exit

SCENE II

Enter Lussurioso, with Hippolito

LUS. I much applaud
    Thy judgment; thou art well-read in a fellow;
    And 'tis the deepest art to study man.
    I know this, which I never learnt in schools,
    The world's divided into knaves and fools.
HIP. [*Aside*] Knave in your face, my lord—behind your back—
LUS. And I much thank thee, that thou hast preferred
    A fellow of discourse, well-mingled,
    And whose brain time hath seasoned.
HIP. True, my lord,
    We shall find season[1] once, I hope. [*Aside*] O villain!
    To make such an unnatural slave of me—but—
LUS. Mass, here he comes.
HIP. [*Aside*] And now shall I have free leave to depart.

1. Opportunity.

LUS. Your absence, leave us.

HIP. [*Aside*] Are not my thoughts true?
    I must remove; but, brother, you may stay.
    Heart! we are both made bawds a new-found way!

                                              Exit

Enter Vendice, disguised

LUS. Now we're an even number, a third man's dangerous,
    Especially her brother;—say, be free,
    Have I a pleasure toward?

VEN. O my lord!

LUS. Ravish me in thine answer; art thou rare?
    Hast thou beguiled her of salvation,
    And rubbed hell o'er with honey? Is she a woman?

VEN. In all but in desire.

LUS. Then she's in nothing—I bate in courage[1] now.

VEN. The words I brought
    Might well have made indifferent honest naught.[2]
    A right good woman in these days is changed
    Into white money with less labor far;
    Many a maid has turned to Mahomet[3]
    With easier working: I durst undertake,
    Upon the pawn and forfeit of my life,
    With half those words to flat a Puritan's wife.
    But she is close and good; yet 'tis a doubt
    By this time.—O, the mother, the mother!

LUS. I never thought their sex had been a wonder,
    Until this minute. What fruit from the mother?

VEN. [*Aside*] How must I blister my soul, be forsworn,
    Or shame the woman that received me first!
    I will be true: thou liv'st not to proclaim.
    Spoke to a dying man, shame has no shame.
    My lord.

LUS. Who's that?

1. Desire.
2. Wicked.
3. i.e., Abandoned her religion.

VEN. Here's none but I, my lord.

LUS. What would thy haste utter?

VEN. Comfort.

LUS. Welcome.

VEN. The maid being dull, having no mind to travel
 Into unknown lands, what did I straight,
 But set spurs to the mother? golden spurs
 Will put her to a false gallop in a trice.

LUS. Is't possible that in this
 The mother should be damned before the daughter?

VEN. O, that's good manners, my lord; the mother for her age must go
 foremost, you know.

LUS. Thou'st spoke that true! but where comes mother in this comfort?

VEN. In a fine place, my lord,—the unnatural
 Did with her tongue so hard beset her honor,
 That the poor fool was struck to silent wonder;
 Yet still the maid, like an unlighted taper,
 Was cold and chaste, save that her mother's breath
 Did blow fire on her cheeks. The girl departed;
 But the good ancient madam, half mad, threw me
 These promising words, which I took deeply note of:
 "My lord shall be most welcome"—

LUS. Faith, I thank her.

VEN. "When his pleasure conducts him this way"—

LUS. That shall be soon, i'faith.

VEN. "I will sway mine own"—

LUS. She does the wiser: I commend her for't.

VEN. "Women with women can work best alone."

LUS. By this light, and so they can; give 'em their due, men are not
 comparable to 'em.

VEN. No, that's true; for you shall have one woman knit more in an
 hour, than any man can ravel again in seven-and-twenty years.

LUS. Now my desires are happy; I'll make 'em freemen now.
 Thou art a precious fellow; faith, I love thee;
 Be wise and make it thy revénue; beg, leg;[1]
 What office couldst thou be ambitious for?

---

1. Bow.

VEN. Office, my lord! marry, if I might have my wish, I would have one that was never begged yet.

LUS. Nay, then, thou canst have none.

VEN. Yes, my lord, I could pick out another office yet; nay, and keep a horse and drab[1] upon't.

LUS. Prythee, good bluntness, tell me.

VEN. Why, I would desire but this, my lord—to have all the fees behind the arras, and all the farthingales that fall plump about twelve o'clock at night upon the rushes.

LUS. Thou'rt a mad, apprehensive[2] knave; dost think to make any great purchase of that?

VEN. O, 'tis an unknown thing, my lord; I wonder't has been missed so long.

LUS. Well, this night I'll visit her, and 'tis till then
    A year in my desires—farewell, attend
    Trust me with thy preferment.

VEN. My loved lord!

                               Exit Lussurioso

    O, shall I kill him o' th' wrong side now? no!
    Sword, thou wast never a backbiter yet.
    I'll pierce him to his face; he shall die looking upon me.
    Thy veins are swelled with lust, this shall unfill 'em.
    Great men were gods, if beggars could not kill 'em.
    Forgive me, Heaven, to call my mother wicked!
    O, lessen not my days upon the earth,
    I cannot honor her. By this, I fear me,
    Her tongue has turned my sister unto use.
    I was a villain not to be forsworn
    To this our lecherous hope, the duke's son;
    For lawyers, merchants, some divines, and all,
    Count beneficial perjury a sin small.
    It shall go hard yet, but I'll guard her honor,
    And keep the ports sure.

                                        Exit

1. Whore.
2. Sharp-witted.

SCENE III

Enter Vendice, still disguised, and Hippolito

HIP. Brother, how goes the world? I would know news of you.
    But I have news to tell you.
VEN. What, in the name of knavery?
HIP. Knavery, faith;
    This vicious old duke's worthily abused;
    The pen of his bastard writes him cuckold?
VEN. His bastard?
HIP. Pray, believe it; he and the duchess
    By night meet in their linen; they have been seen
    By stair-foot panders.
VEN. O, sin foul and deep!
    Great faults are winked at when the duke's asleep.
    See, see, here comes the Spurio.
HIP. Monstrous luxur!
VEN. Unbraced! two of his valiant bawds with him!
    O, there's a wicked whisper; hell's in his ear.
    Stay, let's observe his passage—

Enter Spurio and Servants

SPU. O, but are you sure on't?
1ST SER. My lord, most sure on't; for 'twas spoke by one,
    That is most inward with the duke's son's lust,
    That he intends within this hour to steal
    Unto Hippolito's sister, whose chaste life
    The mother has corrupted for his use.
SPU. Sweet word! sweet occasion! faith, then, brother,
    I'll disinherit you in as short time
    As I was when I was begot in haste.
    I'll damn you at your pleasure: precious deed!
    After your lust, O, 'twill be fine to bleed.
    Come, let our passing out be soft and wary.

Exeunt Spurio and Servants

VEN. Mark! there; there; that step; now to the duchess!
    This their second meeting writes the duke cuckold

With new additions—his horns newly revived.
Night! thou that look'st like funeral heralds' fees,[1]
Torn down betimes i' the morning, thou hang'st fitly
To grace those sins that have no grace at all.
Now 'tis full sea abed over the world:
There's juggling of all sides; some that were maids
E'en at sunset, are now perhaps i' the toll-book.[2]
This woman in immodest thin apparel
Lets in her friend by water; here a dame
Cunning nails leather hinges to a door,
To avoid proclamation.
Now cuckolds are coining, apace, apace, apace, apace!
And careful sisters spin that thread i' the night,
That does maintain them and their bawds i' the day.

HIP. You flow well, brother.

VEN. Pooh! I'm shallow yet;
   Too sparing and too modest; shall I tell thee?
   If every trick were told that's dealt by night,
   There are few here that would not blush outright.

HIP. I am of that belief too. Who's this comes?

VEN. The duke's son up so late? Brother, fall back,
   And you shall learn some mischief. My good lord!

Enter Lussurioso

LUS. Piato! why, the man I wished for! Come,
   I do embrace this season for the fittest
   To taste of that young lady.

VEN. [*Aside*] Heart and hell!

HIP. [*Aside*] Damned villain!

VEN. [*Aside*] I have no way now to cross it, but to kill him.

LUS. Come, only thou and I.

VEN. My lord! my lord!

LUS. Why dost thou start us?

VEN. I'd almost forgot—the bastard!

LUS. What of him?

1. Hangings.
2. Register of prostitutes.

VEN. This night, this hour, this minute, now—
LUS. What? what?
VEN. Shadows[1] the duchess—
LUS. Horrible word!
VEN. And (like strong poison) eats
 Into the duke your father's forehead.
LUS. O!
VEN. He makes horn-royal.
LUS. Most ignoble slave!
VEN. This is the fruit of two beds.
LUS. I am mad.
VEN. That passage he trod warily.
LUS. He did?
VEN. And hushed his villains every step he took.
LUS. His villains! I'll confound them.
VEN. Take 'em finely—finely, now.
LUS. The duchess' chamber-door shall not control me.

Exeunt Lussurioso and Vendice

HIP. Good, happy, swift: there's gunpowder i' the court,
 Wildfire at midnight. In this heedless fury
 He may show violence to cross[2] himself.
 I'll follow the event.[3]

Exit

SCENE IV

Duke and Duchess screened within a bed
Enter Lussurioso and Vendice, disguised

LUS. Where is that villain?
VEN. Softly, my lord, and you may take 'em twisted.
LUS. I care not how.
VEN. O! 'twill be glorious
 To kill 'em doubled, when they're heaped. Be soft, my lord.

---

1. Covers.
2. Thwart.
3. See what happens next.

LUS. Away! my spleen is not so lazy: thus and thus
    I'll shake their eyelids ope, and with my sword
    Shut 'em again for ever. Villain! strumpet!
DUKE. You upper guard, defend us!
DUCH. Treason! treason!
DUKE. O, take me not in sleep!
    I have great sins; I must have days,
    Nay, months, dear son, with penitential heaves,
    To lift 'em out, and not to die unclear.
    O, thou wilt kill me both in Heaven and here.
LUS. I am amazed to death.
DUKE. Nay, villain, traitor,
    Worse than the foulest epithet; now I'll gripe thee
    E'en with the nerves of wrath, and throw thy head
    Amongst the lawyers!—guard!

Enter Ambitioso, Supervacuo, and Lords

1ST LORD. How comes the quiet of your grace disturbed?
DUKE. This boy, that should be myself after me,
    Would be myself before me; and in heat
    Of that ambition bloodily rushed in,
    Intending to depose me in my bed.
2ND LORD. Duty and natural loyalty forfend!
DUCH. He called his father villain, and me strumpet,
    A word that I abhor to file[1] my lips with.
AMB. That was not so well-done, brother.
LUS. [*Aside*] I am abused—I know there's no excuse can do me good.
VEN. [*Aside*] 'Tis now good policy to be from sight;
    His vicious purpose to our sister's honor
    I crossed beyond our thought.
HIP. You little dreamt his father slept here.
VEN. O, 'twas far beyond me:
    But since it fell so—without frightful words,
    Would he had killed him, 'twould have eased our swords.
DUKE. Be comforted, our duchess, he shall die.

Exeunt Vendice and Hippolito

---

1. Defile.

LUS. Where's this slave-pander now? out of mine eye,
    Guilty of this abuse.

Enter Spurio with Servants

SPU. Y' are villains, fablers![1]
    You have knaves' chins and harlots' tongues; you lie;
    And I will damn you with one meal a day.
1ST SER. O good my lord!
SPU. 'Sblood, you shall never sup.
2ND SER. O, I beseech you, sir!
SPU. To let my sword catch cold so long, and miss him!
1ST SER. Troth, my lord, 'twas his intent to meet there.
SPU. Heart! he's yonder.
    Ha, what news here? is the day out o' the socket,
    That it is noon at midnight? the court up?
    How comes the guard so saucy with his[2] elbows?
LUS. The bastard here?
    Nay, then the truth of my intent shall out;
    My lord and father, hear me.
DUKE. Bear him hence.
LUS. I can with loyalty excuse.
DUKE. Excuse? to prison with the villain!
    Death shall not long lag after him.
SPU. Good, i'faith: then 'tis not much amiss.
LUS. Brothers, my best release lies on your tongues;
    I pray, persuade for me.
AMB. It is our duties; make yourself sure of us.
SPU. We'll sweat in pleading.
LUS. And I may live to thank you.

                         Exit with Lords

AMB. No, thy death shall thank me better.
SPU. He's gone; I'll after him,
    And know his trespass; seem to bear a part
    In all his ills, but with a puritan[3] heart.

                        Exit with Servants

1. Liars.
2. Lussurioso's.
3. Hypocritical.

AMB. Now, brother, let our hate and love be woven
  So subtly together, that in speaking one word for his life,
  We may make three for his death:
  The craftiest pleader gets most gold for breath.
SUP. Set on, I'll not be far behind you, brother.
DUKE. Is't possible a son should be disobedient as far as the sword? It
  is the highest: he can go no farther.
AMB. My gracious lord, take pity—
DUKE. Pity, boys!
AMB. Nay, we'd be loath to move your grace too much;
  We know the trespass is unpardonable,
  Black, wicked, and unnatural.
SUP. In a son! O, monstrous!
AMB. Yet, my lord,
  A duke's soft hand strokes the rough head of law,
  And makes it lie smooth.
DUKE. But my hand shall ne'er do't.
AMB. That as you please, my lord.
SUP. We must needs confess,
  Some fathers would have entered into hate
  So deadly-pointed, that before his eyes
  He would ha' seen the execution sound
  Without corrupted favor.
AMB. But, my lord,
  Your grace may live the wonder of all times,
  In pardoning that offence, which never yet
  Had face to beg a pardon.
DUKE. Honey, how's this?
AMB. Forgive him, good my lord; he's your own son:
  And I must needs say, 'twas the vilier done.
SUP. He's the next heir: yet this true reason gathers,
  None can possess that dispossess their fathers.
  Be merciful!—
DUKE. [*Aside*] Here's no step-mother's wit;
  I'll try them both upon their love and hate.
AMB. Be merciful—although—
DUKE. You have prevailed.
  My wrath, like flaming wax, hath spent itself;

I know 'twas but some peevish moon[1] in him;
    Go, let him be released.
SUP. [*Aside*] 'Sfoot, how now, brother?
AMB. Your grace doth please to speak beside your spleen;[2]
    I would it were so happy.
DUKE. Why, go, release him.
SUP. O my good lord! I know the fault's too weighty,
    And full of general loathing: too inhuman,
    Rather by all men's voices worthy death.
DUKE. 'Tis true too; here, then, receive this signet.
    Doom shall pass;
    Direct it to the judges; he shall die
    Ere many days. Make haste.
AMB. All speed that may be.
    We could have wished his burden not so sore:
    We knew your grace did but delay before.
                   Exeunt Ambitioso and Supervacuo
DUKE. Here's envy with a poor thin cover o'er't;
    Like scarlet hid in lawn, easily spied through.
    This their ambition by the mother's side
    Is dangerous, and for safety must be purged.
    I will prevent[3] their envies; sure it was
    But some mistaken fury in our son,
    Which these aspiring boys would climb upon:
    He shall be released suddenly.

               Enter Nobles

1ST NOBLE. Good morning to your grace.
DUKE. Welcome, my lords.
2ND NOBLE. Our knees shall take
    Away the office of our feet for ever,
    Unless your grace bestow a father's eye
    Upon the clouded fortunes of your son,
    And in compassionate virtue grant him that,
    Which makes e'en mean men happy—liberty.

1. Fit of frenzy.
2. Leaving your anger aside.
3. Forestall.

DUKE. How seriously their loves and honors woo
    For that which I am about to pray them do!
    Arise, my lords; your knees sign his release.
    We freely pardon him.
1ST NOBLE. We owe your grace much thanks, and he much duty.

Exeunt Nobles

DUKE. It well becomes that judge to nod at crimes,
    That does commit greater himself, and lives.
    I may forgive a disobedient error,
    That expect pardon for adultery,
    And in my old days am a youth in lust.
    Many a beauty have I turned to poison
    In the denial, covetous of all.
    Age hot is like a monster to be seen;
    My hairs are white, and yet my sins are green.

ACT III, SCENE I

Enter Ambitioso and Supervacuo

SUP. Brother, let my opinion sway you once;
    I speak it for the best, to have him die
    Surest and soonest; if the signet come
    Unto the judge's hand, why then his doom
    Will be deferred till sittings and court-days,
    Juries, and further. Faiths are bought and sold;
    Oaths in these days are but the skin of gold.
AMB. In troth, 'tis true too.
SUP. Then let's set by the judges,
    And fall to the officers; 'tis but mistaking
    The duke our father's meaning; and where he named
    "Ere many days"—'tis but forgetting that,
    And have him die i' the morning.
AMB. Excellent!
    Then am I heir! duke in a minute!
SUP. [*Aside*] Nay,
    An he were once puffed out, here is a pin
    Should quickly prick your bladder.

AMB. Blessed occasion!
　He being packed, we'll have some trick and wile
　To wind our younger brother out of prison,
　That lies in for the rape. The lady's dead,
　And people's thoughts will soon be burièd.
SUP. We may with safety do't, and live and feed;
　The duchess' sons are too proud to bleed.
AMB. We are, i'faith, to say true—come, let's not linger:
　I'll to the officers; go you before,
　And set an edge upon the executioner.
SUP. Let me alone to grind.

Exit

AMB. Meet farewell!
　I am next now; I rise just in that place,
　Where thou'rt cut off; upon thy neck, kind brother;
　The falling of one head lifts up another.

Exit

SCENE II

Enter Lussurioso with Nobles

LUS. My lords, I am so much indebted to your loves
　For this, O, this delivery—
1ST NOBLE. But[1] our duties, my lord, unto the hopes that grow in
　you.
LUS. If e'er I live to be myself, I'll thank you.
　O liberty, thou sweet and heavenly dame!
　But hell for prison is too mild a name.

Exeunt

Enter Ambitioso and Supervacuo, with Officers

AMB. Officers, here's the duke's signet, your firm warrant,
　Brings the command of present death along with it
　Unto our brother, the duke's son; we are sorry
　That we are so unnaturally employed

---

1. Merely.

In such an unkind office, fitter far
For enemies than brothers.

SUP. But, you know,
The duke's command must be obeyed.

1ST OFF. It must and shall, my lord. This morning then—
So suddenly?

AMB. Ay, alas! poor, good soul!
He must breakfast betimes; the executioner
Stands ready to put forth his cowardly valor.

2ND OFF. Already?

SUP. Already, i'faith. O sir, destruction hies,
And that is least impudent,[1] soonest dies.

1ST OFF. Troth, you say true. My lord, we take our leaves:
Our office shall be sound; we'll not delay
The third part of a minute.

AMB. Therein you show
Yourselves good men and upright. Officers,
Pray, let him die as private as he may;
Do him that favor; for the gaping people
Will but trouble him at his prayers.
And make him curse and swear, and so die black.
Will you be so far kind?

1ST OFF. It shall be done, my lord.

AMB. Why, we do thank you; if we live to be—
You shall have a better office.

2ND OFF. Your good lordship—

SUP. Commend us to the scaffold in our tears.

1ST OFF. We'll weep, and do your commendations.

AMB. Fine fools in office!

Exeunt Officers

SUP. Things fall out so fit!

AMB. So happily! come, brother! ere next clock,
His head will be made serve a bigger block.[2]

Exeunt

1. Shameless.
2. i.e., Than a Hatter's.

Scene III

Enter the Duchess' Youngest Son and Keeper

Y. SON. Keeper!

KEEP. My lord.

Y. SON. No news lately from our brothers?
Are they unmindful of us?

KEEP. My lord, a messenger came newly in,
And brought this from 'em.

Y. SON. Nothing but paper-comforts?
I looked for my delivery before this,
Had they been worth their oaths.—Prythee, be from us.

Exit Keeper

Now what say you, forsooth? speak out, I pray.
[*Reads the letter*] "Brother, be of good cheer"; 'Slud, it begins like
a whore with good cheer. "Thou shalt not be long a prisoner."
Not six-and-thirty years, like a bankrupt—I think so. "We have
thought upon a device to get thee out by a trick." By a trick! pox
o' your trick, an' it be so long a playing. "And so rest comforted,
be merry, and expect it suddenly!" Be merry! hang merry, draw
and quarter merry; I'll be mad. Is't not strange that a man should
lie in a whole month for a woman? Well, we shall see how sudden
our brothers will be in their promise. I must expect still a trick:
I shall not be long a prisoner. How now, what news?

Re-enter Keeper

KEEP. Bad news, my lord; I am discharged of you.

Y. SON. Slave! call'st thou that bad news? I thank you, brothers.

KEEP. My lord, 'twill prove so. Here come the officers,
Into whose hands I must commit you.

Y. SON. Ha, officers! what? why?

Enter Officers

1ST OFF. You must pardon us, my lord:
Our office must be sound: here is our warrant,
The signet from the duke; you must straight suffer.

Y. SON. Suffer! I'll suffer you to begone; I'll suffer you
    To come no more; what would you have me suffer?
2ND OFF. My lord, those words were better changed to prayers.
    The time's but brief with you: prepare to die.
Y. SON. Sure, 'tis not so!
3RD OFF. It is too true, my lord.
Y. SON. I tell you 'tis not; for the duke my father
    Deferred me till next sitting; and I look,
    E'en every minute, threescore times an hour,
    For a release, a trick wrought by my brothers.
1ST OFF. A trick, my lord! if you expect such comfort,
    Your hope's as fruitless as a barren woman:
    Your brothers were the unhappy messengers
    That brought this powerful token for your death.
Y. SON. My brothers? no, no.
2ND OFF. 'Tis most true, my lord.
Y. SON. My brothers to bring a warrant for my death!
    How strange this shows!
3RD OFF. There's no delaying time.
Y. SON. Desire 'em hither: call 'em up—my brothers!
    They shall deny it to your faces.
1ST OFF. My lord,
    They're far enough by this; at least at court;
    And this most strict command they left behind 'em.
    When grief swam in their eyes, they showed like brothers,
    Brimful of heavy sorrow—but the duke
    "Must have his pleasure."
Y. SON. His pleasure!
1ST OFF. These were the last words, which my memory bears,
    "Commend us to the scaffold in our tears."
Y. SON. Pox dry their tears! what should I do with tears?
    I hate 'em worse than any citizen's son
    Can hate salt water. Here came a letter now,
    New-bleeding from their pens, scarce stinted[1] yet:
    Would I'd been torn in pieces when I tore it:

1. Staunched.

Look, you officious whoresons, words of comfort,
"Not long a prisoner."

1ST OFF. It says true in that, sir; for you must suffer presently.

Y. SON. A villainous Duns[1] upon the letter, knavish exposition!
Look you then here, sir: "we'll get thee out by a trick," says he.

2ND OFF. That may hold too, sir; for you know a trick is commonly
four cards,[2] which was meant by us four officers.

Y. SON. Worse and worse dealing.

1ST OFF. The hour beckons us.
The headsman waits: lift up your eyes to Heaven.

Y. SON. I thank you, faith; good pretty wholesome counsel!
I should look up to Heaven, as you said,
Whilst he behind me cosens me of my head.
Ay, that's the trick.

3RD OFF. You delay too long, my lord.

Y. SON. Stay, good authority's bastards; since I must,
Through brothers' perjury, die, O, let me venom
Their souls with curses.

3RD OFF. Come, 'tis no time to curse.

Y. SON. Must I bleed then without respect of sign?[3] well—
My fault was sweet sport which the world approves,
I die for that which every woman loves.

Exeunt

SCENE IV

Enter Vendice, disguised, and Hippolito

VEN. O, sweet, delectable, rare, happy, ravishing!

HIP. Why, what's the matter, brother?

VEN. O, 'tis able to make a man spring up and knock his forehead
Against yon silver ceiling.[4]

HIP. Prythee, tell me;

---

1. Sophistry.
2. In the card game primero.
3. Appropriate ceremony.
4. The spangled canopy over the stage.

Why may not I partake with you? you vowed once
To give me share to every tragic thought.

VEN. By the mass, I think I did too;
Then I'll divide it to thee. The old duke,
Thinking my outward shape and inward heart
Are cut out of one piece (for he that prates his secrets,
His heart stands o' the outside), hires me by price
To greet him with a lady
In some fit place, veiled from the eyes o' the court,
Some darkened, blushless angle, that is guilty
Of his forefather's lust and great folks' riots;
To which I easily (to maintain my shape)
Consented, and did wish his impudent grace
To meet her here in this unsunnèd lodge,
Wherein 'tis night at noon; and here the rather
Because, unto the torturing of his soul,
The bastard and the duchess have appointed
Their meeting too in this luxurious circle;
Which most afflicting sight will kill his eyes,
Before we kill the rest of him.

HIP. 'Twill, i'faith! Most dreadfully digested!¹
I see not how you could have missed me,² brother.

VEN. True; but the violence of my joy forgot it.

HIP. Ay, but where's that lady now?

VEN. O! at that word
I'm lost again; you cannot find me yet:
I'm in a throng of happy apprehensions.
He's suited for a lady; I have took care
For a delicious lip, a sparkling eye—
You shall be witness, brother:
Be ready; stand with your hat off.

Exit

HIP. Troth, I wonder what lady it should be!
Yet 'tis no wonder, now I think again,
To have a lady stoop to a duke, that stoops unto his men.

---

1. Worked out.
2. Left me out.

'Tis common to be common through the world:
And there's more private common shadowing vices,
Than those who are known both by their names and prices.
'Tis part of my allegiance to stand bare
To the duke's concubine; and here she comes.

Re-enter Vendice, with the skull of his Betrothed dressed up in tires[1]

VEN. Madam, his grace will not be absent long.[2]
   Secret! ne'er doubt us, madam; 'twill be worth
   Three velvet gowns to your ladyship. Known!
   Few ladies respect that disgrace: a poor thin shell!
   'Tis the best grace you have to do it well.
   I'll save your hand that labor: I'll unmask you!
HIP. Why, brother, brother!
VEN. Art thou beguiled now? tut, a lady can,
   As such all hid, beguile a wiser man.
   Have I not fitted the old surfeiter
   With a quaint piece of beauty? Age and bare bone
   Are e'er allied in action. Here's an eye,
   Able to tempt a great man—to serve God:
   A pretty hanging lip, that has forgot now to dissemble.
   Methinks this mouth should make a swearer tremble;
   A drunkard clasp his teeth, and not undo 'em.
   To suffer wet damnation to run through 'em.
   Here's a cheek keeps her color, let the wind go whistle:
   Spout, rain, we fear thee not: be hot or cold,
   All's one with us; and is not he absurd,
   Whose fortunes are upon their faces set,
   That fear no other god but wind and wet?
HIP. Brother, you've spoke that right:
   Is this the form that, living, shone so bright?
VEN. The very same.
   And now methinks I could e'en chide myself
   For doating on her beauty, though her death
   Shall be revenged after no common action.

---

1. Head-dress.
2. As if addressing the lady.

Does the silkworm expend her yellow labors
For thee? For thee does she undo herself?
Are lordships sold to maintain ladyships,
For the poor benefit of a bewitching minute?
Why does yon fellow falsify highways,
And put his life between the judge's lips,
To refine such a thing—keeps horse and men
To beat their valors for her?
Surely we are all mad people, and they
Whom we think are, are not: we mistake those;
'Tis we are mad in sense, they but in clothes.

HIP. Faith, and in clothes too we, give us our due.

VEN. Does every proud and self-affecting dame
Camphire[1] her face for this, and grieve her maker
In sinful baths of milk, when many an infant starves
For her superfluous outside—all for this?
Who now bids twenty pounds a night? prepares
Music, perfumes, and sweetmeats? All are hushed.
Thou may'st lie chaste now! it were fine, methinks,
To have thee seen at revels, forgetful feasts,
And unclean brothels! sure, 'twould fright the sinner,
And make him a good coward: put a reveller
Out of his antic amble,
And cloy an epicure with empty dishes.
Here might a scornful and ambitious woman
Look through and through herself. See, ladies, with false forms
You deceive men, but cannot deceive worms.—
Now to my tragic business. Look you, brother,
I have not fashioned this only for show
And useless property;[2] no, it shall bear a part
E'en in its own revenge. This very skull,
Whose mistress the duke poisoned, with this drug,
The mortal curse of the earth, shall be revenged
In the like strain, and kiss his lips to death.

1. Camphor.
2. Stage prop.

As much as the dumb thing can, he shall feel:
What fails in poison, we'll supply in steel.

HIP. Brother, I do applaud thy constant vengeance—
The quaintness[1] of thy malice—above thought.

VEN. So, 'tis laid on [*he poisons the lips of the skull*]: now come and
welcome, duke,
I have her for thee. I protest it, brother,
Methinks she makes almost as fair a fine,
As some old gentlewoman in a periwig.
Hide thy face now for shame; thou hadst need have a mask now:
'Tis vain when beauty flows; but when it fleets,[2]
This would become graves better than the streets.

HIP. You have my voice in that: hark, the duke's come.

VEN. Peace, let's observe what company he brings,
And how he does absent 'em; for you know
He'll wish all private. Brother, fall you back a little
With the bony lady.

HIP. That I will.

Retires

VEN. So, so; now nine years' vengeance crowd into a minute!

Enter Duke and Gentlemen

DUKE. You shall have leave to leave us, with this charge
Upon your lives, if we be missed by the duchess
Or any of the nobles, to give out,
We're privately rid forth.

VEN. O happiness!

DUKE. With some few honorable gentlemen, you may say—
You may name those that are away from court.

GEN. Your will and pleasure shall be done, my lord.

Exeunt Gentlemen

VEN. "Privately rid forth!"
He strives to make sure work on't. Your good grace!

[*Advances*]

---

1. Ingenuity.
2. Disappears.

DUKE. Piato, well done, hast brought her! what lady is't?

VEN. Faith, my lord, a country lady, a little bashful at first, as most of
them are; but after the first kiss, my lord, the worst is past with
them. Your grace knows now what you have to do; she has somewhat a grave look with her—but—

DUKE. I love that best; conduct her.

VEN. [*Aside*] Have at all.[1]

DUKE. In gravest looks the greatest faults seem less.
Give me that sin that's robed in holiness.

VEN. [*Aside*] Back with the torch! brother, raise the perfumes.

DUKE. How sweet can a duke breathe! Age has no fault.
Pleasure should meet in a perfumèd mist.
Lady, sweetly encountered: I came from court,
I must be bold with you. O, what's this? O!

VEN. Royal villain! white devil!

DUKE. O!

VEN. Brother, place the torch here, that his affrighted eyeballs
May start into those hollows. Duke, dost know
Yon dreadful vizard? View it well; 'tis the skull
Of Gloriana, whom thou poisonedst last.

DUKE. O! 't has poisoned me.

VEN. Didst not know that till now?

DUKE. What are you two?

VEN. Villains all three! the very ragged bone
Has been sufficiently revenged.

DUKE. O, Hippolito, call treason!

[*He sinks down*]

HIP. Yes, my lord; treason! treason! treason!

[*Stamping on him*]

DUKE. Then I'm betrayed.

VEN. Alas! poor lecher: in the hands of knaves,
A slavish duke is baser than his slaves.

DUKE. My teeth are eaten out.

VEN. Hadst any left?

---

1. Now for it!

HIP. I think but few.

VEN. Then those that did eat are eaten.

DUKE. O my tongue!

VEN. Your tongue? 'twill teach you to kiss closer,
Not like a slobbering Dutchman. You have eyes still:
Look, monster, what a lady hast thou made me
                                        [*Discovers himself*]
My once betrothèd wife.

DUKE. Is it thou, villain? nay, then—

VEN. 'Tis I, 'tis Vendice, 'tis I.

HIP. And let this comfort thee: our lord and father
Fell sick upon the infection of thy frowns,
And died in sadness: be that thy hope of life.

DUKE. O!

VEN. He had his tongue, yet grief made him die speechless.
Pooh! 'tis but early yet; now I'll begin
To stick thy soul with ulcers. I will make
Thy spirit grievous sore; it shall not rest,
But like some pestilent[1] man toss in thy breast.
Mark me, duke:
Thou art a renownèd, high and mighty cuckold.

DUKE. O!

VEN. Thy bastard, thy bastard rides a-hunting in thy brow.

DUKE. Millions of deaths!

VEN. Nay, to afflict thee more,
Here in this lodge they meet for damnèd clips.[2]
Those eyes shall see the incest of their lips.

DUKE. Is there a hell besides this, villains?

VEN. Villain!
Nay, Heaven is just; scorns are the hire[3] of scorns:
I ne'er knew yet adulterer without horns.

HIP. Once, ere they die, 'tis quitted.[4]

---

1. Plague-stricken.
2. Embraces.
3. Wages.
4. Requited.

VEN. Hark! the music;
    Their banquet is prepared, they're coming—
DUKE. O, kill me not with that sight!
VEN. Thou shalt not lose that sight for all thy dukedom.
DUKE. Traitors! murderers!
VEN. What! is not thy tongue eaten out yet?
    Then we'll invent a silence. Brother, stifle the torch.
DUKE. Treason! murder!
VEN. Nay, faith, we'll have you hushed. Now with thy dagger
    Nail down his tongue, and mine shall keep possession
    About his heart; if he but gasp, he dies;
    We dread not death to quittance[1] injuries.
    Brother, if he but wink, not brooking the foul object,
    Let our two other hands tear up his lids,
    And make his eyes like comets shine through blood.
    When the bad bleeds, then is the tragedy good.
HIP. Whist, brother! the music's at our ear; they come.

Enter Spurio, meeting the Duchess

SPU. Had not that kiss a taste of sin, 'twere sweet.
DUCH. Why, there's no pleasure sweet, but it is sinful.
SPU. True, such a bitter sweetness fate hath given;
    Best side to us is the worst side to Heaven.
DUCH. Pish! come: 'tis the old duke, thy doubtful father:
    The thought of him rubs Heaven in thy way.
    But I protest by yonder waxen fire,[2]
    Forget him, or I'll poison him.
SPU. Madam, you urge a thought which ne'er had life.
    So deadly do I loathe him for my birth,
    That if he took me hasped[3] within his bed,
    I would add murder to adultery,
    And with my sword give up his years to death.
DUCH. Why, now thou'rt sociable; let's in and feast:

1. Repay.
2. Candles.
3. Embracing.

Loud'st music sound; pleasure is banquet's guest.

Exeunt Duchess and Spurio

DUKE. I cannot brook—

Dies

VEN. The brook is turned to blood.

HIP. Thanks to loud music.

VEN. 'Twas our friend, indeed.
'Tis state in music for a duke to bleed.
The dukedom wants a head, though yet unknown;
As fast as they peep up, let's cut 'em down.

Exeunt

SCENE V

Enter Ambitioso and Supervacuo

AMB. Was not his execution rarely plotted?
We are the duke's sons now.

SUP. Ay, you may thank my policy[1] for that.

AMB. Your policy for what?

SUP. Why, was't not my invention, brother,
To slip the judges? and in lesser compass
Did I not draw the model of his death;
Advising you to sudden officers
And e'en extemporal execution?

AMB. Heart! 'twas a thing I thought on too.

SUP. You thought on't too! 'sfoot, slander not your thoughts
With glorious[2] untruth; I know 'twas from you.

AMB. Sir, I say, 'twas in my head.

SUP. Ay, like your brains then,
Ne'er to come out as long as you lived.

AMB. You'd have the honor on't, forsooth, that your wit
Led him to the scaffold.

SUP. Since it is my due,
I'll publish't, but I'll ha't in spite of you.

---

1. Skill in plotting.
2. Boastful.

AMB. Methinks, y'are much too bold; you should a little
 Remember us, brother, next to be honest[1] duke.
SUP. [*Aside*] Ay, it shall be as easy for you to be duke
 As to be honest; and that's never, i'faith.
AMB. Well, cold he is by this time; and because
 We're both ambitious, be it our amity,
 And let the glory be shared equally.
SUP. I am content to that.
AMB. This night our younger brother shall out of prison:
 I have a trick.
SUP. A trick! prithee, what is't?
AMB. We'll get him out by a wile.
SUP. Prythee, what wile?
AMB. No, sir; you shall not know it, till it be done;
 For then you'd swear 'twere yours.

Enter an Officer

SUP. How now, what's he?
AMB. One of the officers.
SUP. Desired news.
AMB. How now, my friend?
OFF. My lords, under your pardon, I am allotted
 To that desertless office, to present you
 With the yet bleeding head—
SUP. Ha, ha! excellent.
AMB. All's sure our own: brother, canst weep, think'st thou?
 'Twould grace our flattery much; think of some dame;
 'Twill teach thee to dissemble.
SUP. I have thought;—now for yourself.
AMB. Our sorrows are so fluent,
 Our eyes o'erflow our tongues; words spoke in tears
 Are like the murmurs of the waters—the sound
 Is loudly heard, but cannot be distinguished.
SUP. How died he, pray?
OFF. O, full of rage and spleen.

---

1. Rightful.

SUP. He died most valiantly, then; we're glad to hear it.

OFF. We could not woo him once to pray.

AMB. He showed himself a gentleman in that:
   Give him his due.

OFF. But, in the stead of prayer,
   He drew forth oaths.

SUP. Then did he pray, dear heart,
   Although you understood him not.

OFF. My lords,
   E'en at his last, with pardon be it spoke,
   He cursed you both.

SUP. He cursed us? 'las, good soul!

AMB. It was not in our powers, but the duke's pleasure.
   [*Aside*] Finely dissembled a both sides, sweet fate;
   O happy opportunity!

Enter Lussurioso

LUS. Now, my lords.

AMB. AND SUP. O!—

LUS. Why do you shun me, brothers?
   You may come nearer now:
   The savor of the prison has forsook me.
   I thank such kind lords as yourselves, I'm free.

AMB. Alive!

SUP. In health!

AMB. Released!
   We were both e'en amazed with joy to see it.

LUS. I am much to thank to you.

SUP. Faith, we spared no tongue unto my lord the duke.

AMB. I know your delivery, brother,
   Had not been half so sudden but for us.

SUP. O, how we pleaded!

LUS. Most deserving brothers!
   In my best studies I will think of it.

                                                    Exit

AMB. O death and vengeance!

SUP. Hell and torments!

AMB. Slave, cam'st thou to delude us?

Off. Delude you, my lords?

Sup. Ay, villain, where's his head now?

Off. Why here, my lord;
  Just after his delivery, you both came
  With warrant from the duke to behead your brother.

Amb. Ay, our brother, the duke's son.

Off. The duke's son, my lord, had his release before you came.

Amb. Whose head's that, then?

Off. His whom you left command for, your own brother's.

Amb. Our brother's? O furies.

Sup. Plagues!

Amb. Confusions!

Sup. Darkness!

Amb. Devils!

Sup. Fell it out so accursedly?

Amb. So damnedly?

Sup. Villain, I'll brain thee with it.

Off. O my good lord!

Sup. The devil overtake thee!

Amb. O fatal!

Sup. O prodigious[1] to our bloods!

Amb. Did we dissemble?

Sup. Did we make our tears women for thee?

Amb. Laugh and rejoice for thee?

Sup. Bring warrant for thy death?

Amb. Mock off thy head?

Sup. You had a trick: you had a wile, forsooth.

Amb. A murrain[2] meet 'em; there's none of these wiles that ever
    come to good: I see now, there's nothing sure in mortality, but
    mortality.
  Well, no more words: shalt be revenged, i'faith,
  Come, throw off clouds; now, brother, think of vengeance,
  And deeper-settled hate; sirrah,[3] sit fast,
  We'll pull down all, but thou shalt down at last.

Exeunt

---

1. Ominous.
2. Plague.
3. Lussurioso.

ACT IV, SCENE I

Enter Lussurioso with Hippolito

Lus. Hippolito!

Hip. My lord,
  Has your good lordship aught to command me in?

Lus. I prythee, leave us!

Hip. How's this? come and leave us!

Lus. Hippolito!

Hip. Your honor, I stand ready for any duteous employment.

Lus. Heart! what mak'st thou here?

Hip. A pretty lordly humor!
  He bids me be present to depart; something
  Has stung his honor.

Lus. Be nearer; draw nearer:
  Ye're not so good, methinks; I'm angry with you.

Hip. With me, my lord? I'm angry with myself for't.

Lus. You did prefer a goodly fellow to me:
  'Twas wittily elected; 'twas. I thought
  He had been a villain, and he proves a knave—
  To me a knave.

Hip. I chose him for the best, my lord:
  'Tis much my sorrow, if neglect in him
  Breed discontent in you.

Lus. Neglect! 'twas will. Judge of it.
  Firmly to tell of an incredible act,
  Not to be thought, less to be spoken of,
  'Twixt my step-mother and the bastard; oh!
  Incestuous sweets between 'em.

Hip. Fie, my lord!

Lus. I, in kind loyalty to my father's forehead,
  Made this a desperate arm; and in that fury
  Committed treason on the lawful bed,
  And with my sword e'en raced[1] my father's bosom,
  For which I was within a stroke of death.

---

1. Scratched.

HIP. Alack! I'm sorry. [*Aside*] 'Sfoot, just upon the stroke,
  Jars in my brother; 'twill be villainous music.

Enter Vendice, disguised

VEN. My honored lord.
LUS. Away! prithee, forsake us: hereafter we'll not know thee.
VEN. Not know me, my lord! your lordship cannot choose.
LUS. Begone, I say: thou art a false knave.
VEN. Why, the easier to be known, my lord.
LUS. Pish! I shall prove too bitter, with a word
  Make thee a perpetual prisoner,
  And lay this ironage¹ upon thee.
VEN. [*Aside*] Mum!
  For there's a doom would make a woman² dumb.
  Missing the bastard—next him—the wind's come about:
  Now 'tis my brother's turn to stay, mine to go out.

Exit

LUS. He has greatly moved me.
HIP. Much to blame, i'faith.
LUS. But I'll recover, to his ruin. 'Twas told me lately,
  I know not whether falsely, that you'd a brother.
HIP. Who, I? yes, my good lord, I have a brother.
LUS. How chance the court ne'er saw him? of what nature?
  How does he apply his hours?
HIP. Faith, to curse fates
  Who, as he thinks, ordained him to be poor—
  Keeps at home, full of want and discontent.
LUS. [*Aside*] There's hope in him; for discontent and want
  Is the best clay to mould a villain of.
  Hippolito, wish him repair to us:
  If there be ought in him to please our blood,
  For thy sake we'll advance him, and build fair
  His meanest fortunes; for it is in us
  To rear up towers from cottages.

---

1. Fetters.
2. Even a woman.

HIP. It is so, my lord: he will attend your honor;
    But he's a man in whom much melancholy dwells.
LUS. Why, the better; bring him to court.
HIP. With willingness and speed:
    Whom he cast off e'en now, must now succeed.
    [*Aside*] Brother, disguise must off;
    In thine own shape now I'll prefer thee to him:
    How strangely does himself work to undo him!

Exit

LUS. This fellow will come fitly; he shall kill
    That other slave, that did abuse my spleen,
    And made it swell to treason. I have put
    Much of my heart into him; he must die.
    He that knows great men's secrets, and proves slight,[1]
    That man ne'er lives to see his beard turn white.
    Ay, he shall speed him: I'll employ the brother;
    Slaves are but nails to drive out one another.
    He being of black condition, suitable
    To want and ill-content, hope of preferment
    Will grind him to an edge.

Enter Nobles

1ST NOBLE. Good days unto your honor.
LUS. My kind lords, I do return the like.
2ND NOBLE. Saw you my lord the duke?
LUS. My lord and father! is he from court?
1ST NOBLE. He's sure from court;
    But where—which way his pleasure took, we know not,
    Nor can we hear on't.
LUS. Here come those should tell.
    Saw you my lord and father?
3RD NOBLE. Not since two hours before noon, my lord,
    And then he privately rode forth.
LUS. O, he's rid forth.
1ST NOBLE. 'Twas wondrous privately.[2]

1. Unworthy.
2. Whim.

2ND NOBLE. There's none i' th' court had any knowledge on't.
LUS. His grace is old and sudden: 'tis no treason
　　To say the duke, my father, has a humor,
　　Or such a toy about him; what in us
　　Would appear light, in him seems virtuous.
3RD NOBLE. 'Tis oracle, my lord.

Exeunt

SCENE II

Enter Vendice, out of his disguise, and Hippolito

HIP. So, so, all's as it should be, y'are yourself.
VEN. How that great villain puts me to my shifts!
HIP. He that did lately in disguise reject thee,
　　Shall, now thou art thyself, as much respect thee.
VEN. 'Twill be the quainter fallacy.[1] But, brother,
　　'Sfoot, what use will he put me to now, think'st thou?
HIP. Nay, you must pardon me in that: I know not.
　　He has some employment for you: but what 'tis,
　　He and his secretary, the devil, know best.
VEN. Well, I must suit my tongue to his desires,
　　What color soe'er they be; hoping at last
　　To pile up all my wishes on his breast.
HIP. Faith, brother, he himself shows the way.
VEN. Now the duke is dead, the realm is clad in clay.
　　His death being not yet known, under his name
　　The people still are governed. Well, thou his son
　　Art not long-lived: thou shalt not joy his death.
　　To kill thee, then, I should most honor thee;
　　For 'twould stand firm in every man's belief,
　　Thou'st[2] a kind child, and only died'st with grief.
HIP. You fetch about well;[3] but let's talk in present.[4]
　　How will you appear in fashion different,

1. Craftier deception.
2. Thou wast.
3. Speculate.
4. Right now.

As well as in apparel, to make all things possible?
If you be but once tripped, we fall for ever.
It is not the least policy to be doubtful;[1]
You must change tongue: familiar was your first.

VEN. Why, I'll bear me in some strain of melancholy,
  And string myself with heavy-sounding wire,
  Like such an instrument, that speaks merry things sadly.

HIP. Then 'tis as I meant;
  I gave you out at first in discontent.

VEN. I'll tune myself, and then—

HIP. 'Sfoot, here he comes. Hast thought upon't?

VEN. Salute him; fear not me.[2]

Enter Lussurioso

LUS. Hippolito!

HIP. Your lordship—

LUS. What's he yonder?

HIP. 'Tis Vendice, my discontented brother,
  Whom, 'cording to your will, I've brought to court.

LUS. Is that thy brother? Beshrew me, a good presence;
  I wonder he has been from the court so long.
  Come nearer.

HIP. Brother! Lord Lussurioso, the duke's son.

LUS. Be more near to us; welcome; nearer yet.

VEN. How don you? gi' you good den.[3]

                 [Takes off his hat and bows]

LUS. We thank thee.
  How strangely such a coarse homely salute
  Shows in the palace, where we greet in fire,
  Nimble and desperate tongues! should we name
  God in a salutation, 'twould ne'er be stood on't;[4]—Heaven!
  Tell me, what has made thee so melancholy?

VEN. Why, going to law.

---

1. Not the worst plan to be suspicious.
2. Don't worry about me.
3. God give you good evening.
4. Understood.

LUS. Why, will that make a man melancholy?

VEN. Yes, to look long upon ink and black buckram. I went me to law in *anno quadragesimo secundo,* and I waded out of it in *anno sexagesimo tertio.*[1]

LUS. What, three-and-twenty years in law?

VEN. I have known those that have been five-and-fifty, and all about pullen[2] and pigs.

LUS. May it be possible such men should breathe,
To vex the terms[3] so much?

VEN. 'Tis food to some, my lord. There are old men at the present, that are so poisoned with the affectation of law-words (having had many suits canvassed), that their common talk is nothing but Barbary[4] Latin. They cannot so much as pray but in law, that their sins may be removed with a writ of error, and their souls fetched up to Heaven with a sasarara.[5]

LUS. It seems most strange to me;
Yet all the world meets round in the same bent:
Where the heart's set, there goes the tongue's consent.
How dost apply thy studies, fellow?

VEN. Study? why, to think how a great rich man lies a-dying, and a poor cobbler tolls the bell for him. How he cannot depart the world, and see the great chest stand before him; when he lies speechless, how he will point you readily to all the boxes; and when he is past all memory, as the gossips guess, then thinks he of forfeitures and obligations; nay, when to all men's hearings he whurls and rattles[6] in the throat, he's busy threatening his poor tenants. And this would last me now some seven years' thinking, or thereabouts. But I have a conceit a-coming in picture upon this; I draw it myself, which, i'faith, la, I'll present to your honor; you shall not choose but like it, for your honor shall give me nothing for it.

LUS. Nay, you mistake me, then,

---

1. 42nd and 63rd year of the reign.
2. Poultry.
3. Terms of the legal year.
4. Barbarian.
5. Writ of *a certiorari.* A complaint to a superior court.
6. Rumbles and rattles.

For I am published bountiful enough.

Let's taste of your conceit.

VEN. In picture, my Lord?

LUS. Ay, in picture.

VEN. Marry, this it is—"A usuring father to be boiling in hell, and his
son and heir with a whore dancing over him."

HIP. [*Aside*] He has pared him to the quick.

LUS. The conceit's pretty, i'faith;

But, take't upon my life, 'twill ne'er be liked.

VEN. No? why I'm sure the whore will be liked well enough.

HIP. [*Aside*] Aye, if she were out o' the picture, he'd like her then himself.

VEN. And as for the son and heir, he shall be an eyesore to no young
revellers, for he shall be drawn in cloth-of-gold breeches.

LUS. And thou hast put my meaning in the pockets,

And canst not draw that out? My thought was this:

To see the picture of a usuring father

Boiling in hell—our rich men would never like it.

VEN. O, true, I cry you heartily mercy,

I know the reason, for some of them had rather

Be damned in deed than damned in colors.

LUS. [*Aside*] A parlous melancholy! he was wit enough

To murder any man, and I'll give him means.

I think thou art ill-moneyed?

VEN. Money! ho, ho!

'T has been my want so long, 'tis now my scoff:

I've e'en forgot what color silver's of.

LUS. [*Aside*] It hits as I could wish.

VEN. I get good clothes

Of those that dread my humor; and for table-room

I feed on those that cannot be rid of me.

LUS. Somewhat to set thee up withal.

[*Gives him money*]

VEN. O mine eyes!

LUS. How now, man?

VEN. Almost struck blind;

This bright unusual shine to me seems proud;

I dare not look till the sun be in a cloud.

LUS. I think I shall affect[1] his melancholy,
    How are they now?

VEN. The better for your asking.

LUS. You shall be better yet, if you but fasten
    Truly on my intent. Now y'are both present,
    I will unbrace such a close private villain
    Unto your vengeful swords, the like ne'er heard of,
    Who hath disgraced you much, and injured us.

HIP. Disgraced us, my lord?

LUS. Ay, Hippolito.
    I kept it here till now, that both your angers
    Might meet him at once.

VEN. I'm covetous
    To know the villain.

LUS. You know him: that slave-pander,
    Piato, whom we threatened last
    With irons in perpetual 'prisonment.

VEN. [*Aside*] All this is I.

HIP. Is't he, my lord?

LUS. I'll tell you; you first preferred him to me.

VEN. Did you, brother?

HIP. I did indeed.

LUS. And the ungrateful villain,
    To quit[2] that kindness, strongly wrought with me—
    Being, as you see, a likely man for pleasure—
    With jewels to corrupt your virgin sister.

HIP. O villain!

VEN. He shall surely die that did it.

LUS. I, far from thinking any virgin harm,
    Especially knowing her to be as chaste
    As that part which scarce suffers to be touched—
    The eye—would not endure him.

VEN. Would you not, my lord?
    'Twas wondrous honorably done.

LUS. But with some fine frowns kept him out.

1. Like.
2. Requite.

VEN. Out, slave!

LUS. What did me he, but in revenge of that,
　Went of his own free will to make infirm
　Your sister's honor (whom I honor with my soul
　For chaste respect) and not prevailing there
　(As 'twas but desperate folly to attempt it),
　In mere spleen, by the way, waylays your mother,
　Whose honor being a coward as it seems,
　Yielded by little force.

VEN. Coward indeed!

LUS. He, proud of this advantage (as he thought),
　Brought me this news for happy. But I, Heaven forgive me for't—

VEN. What did your honor?

LUS. In rage pushed him from me,
　Trampled beneath his throat, spurned him, and bruised:
　Indeed I was too cruel, to say troth.

HIP. Most nobly managed!

VEN. [*Aside*] Has not Heaven an ear? is all the lightning wasted?

LUS. If I now were so impatient in a modest cause,
　What should you be?

VEN. Full mad: he shall not live
　To see the moon change.

LUS. He's about the palace;
　Hippolito, entice him this way, that thy brother
　May take full mark of him.

HIP. Heart! that shall not need, my lord:
　I can direct him so far.

LUS. Yet for my hate's sake,
　Go, wind him this way. I'll see him bleed myself.

HIP. [*Aside*] What now, brother?

VEN. [*Aside*] Nay, e'en what you will—y'are put to't, brother.

HIP. [*Aside*] An impossible task, I'll swear,
　To bring him hither, that's already here.

　　　　　　　　　　　　　　　　　　　　　Exit

LUS. Thy name? I have forgot it.

VEN. Vendice, my lord.

LUS. 'Tis a good name that.

VEN. Ay, a revenger.

LUS. It does betoken courage; thou shouldst be valiant,
And kill thine enemies.

VEN. That's my hope, my lord.

LUS. This slave is one.

VEN. I'll doom him.

LUS. Then I'll praise thee.
Do thou observe me best, and I'll best raise thee.

Re-enter Hippolito

VEN. Indeed, I thank you.

LUS. Now, Hippolito, where's the slave-pander?

HIP. Your good lordship
Would have a loathsome sight of him, much offensive.
He's not in case now to be seen, my lord.
The worst of all the deadly sins is in him—
That beggarly damnation, drunkenness.

LUS. Then he's a double slave.

VEN. [*Aside*] 'Twas well conveyed upon a sudden wit.

LUS. What, are you both
Firmly resolved? I'll see him dead myself.

VEN. Or else let not us live.

LUS. You may direct your brother to take note of him.

HIP. I shall.

LUS. Rise but in this, and you shall never fall.

VEN. Your honor's vassals.

LUS. [*Aside*] This was wisely carried.
Deep policy in use makes fools of such:
Then must a slave die, when he knows too much.

Exit

VEN. O thou almighty patience! 'tis my wonder
That such a fellow, impudent and wicked,
Should not be cloven as he stood;
Or with a secret wind burst open!
Is there no thunder left: or is't kept up
In stock for heavier vengeance? [*Thunder*] there it goes!

HIP. Brother, we lose ourselves.

VEN. But I have found it;
  'Twill hold, 'tis sure; thanks, thanks to any spirit,
  That mingled it 'mongst my inventions.
HIP. What is't?
VEN. 'Tis sound and good; thou shalt partake it;
  I'm hired to kill myself.
HIP. True.
VEN. Prithee, mark it;
  And the old duke being dead, but not conveyed,[1]
  For he's already missed too, and you know
  Murder will peep out of the closest husk—
HIP. Most true.
VEN. What say you then to this device?
  If we dressed up the body of the duke?
HIP. In that disguise of yours?
VEN. Y'are quick, y' have reached it.
HIP. I like it wondrously.
VEN. And being in drink, as you have published him.
  To lean him on his elbow, as if sleep had caught him
  Which claims most interest in such sluggy men?
HIP. Good yet; but here's a doubt;
  We, thought by the duke's son to kill that pander,
  Shall, when he is known, be thought to kill the duke.
VEN. Neither, O thanks! it is substantial:
  For that disguise being on him which I wore,
  It will be thought I, which he calls the pander, did kill the duke,
    and fled away in his apparel, leaving him so disguised to avoid
    swift pursuit.
HIP. Firmer and firmer.
VEN. Nay, doubt not, 'tis in grain: I warrant it holds color.
HIP. Let's about it.
VEN. By the way, too, now I think on't, brother,
  Let's conjure that base devil out of our mother.

                                                    Exeunt

---

1. Disposed of.

SCENE III

Enter the Duchess, arm in arm with Spurio, looking lasciviously
on her. After them, enter Supervacuo, with a rapier, running;
Ambitioso stops him

SPU. Madam, unlock yourself;
    Should it be seen, your arm would be suspected.
DUCH. Who is't that dares suspect or this or these?
    May not we deal our favors where we please?
SPU. I'm confident you may.

                                Exeunt Duchess and Spurio

AMB. 'Sfoot, brother, hold.
SUP. Wouldst let the bastard shame us?
AMB. Hold, hold, brother! there's fitter time than now.
SUP. Now, when I see it!
AMB. 'Tis too much seen already.
SUP. Seen and known;
    The nobler she's, the baser is she grown.
AMB. If she were bent lasciviously (the fault
    Of mighty women, that sleep soft)—O death!
    Must she needs choose such an unequal sinner,
    To make all worse?—
SUP. A bastard! the duke's bastard! shame heaped on shame!
AMB. O our disgrace!
    Most women have small waists the world throughout;
    But their desires are thousand miles about.
SUP. Come, stay not here, let's after, and prevent,
    Or else they'll sin faster than we'll repent.

                                         Exeunt

SCENE IV

Enter Vendice and Hippolito, bringing out Gratiana by
the shoulders, and with daggers in their hands

VEN. O thou, for whom no name is bad enough!
GRA. What mean my sons? what, will you murder me?
VEN. Wicked, unnatural parent!

HIP. Fiend of women!

GRA. O! are sons turned monsters? help!

VEN. In vain.

GRA. Are you so barbarous to set iron nipples
    Upon the breast that gave you suck?

VEN. That breast
    Is turned to quarled[1] poison.

GRA. Cut not your days for't! am not I your mother?

VEN. Thou dost usurp that title now by fraud,
    For in that shell of mother breeds a bawd.

GRA. A bawd! O name far loathsomer than hell!

HIP. It should be so, knew'st thou thy office well.

GRA. I hate it.

VEN. Ah! is't possible? thou only? Powers on high,
    That women should dissemble when they die!

GRA. Dissemble!

VEN. Did not the duke's son direct
    A fellow of the world's condition hither,
    That did corrupt all that was good in thee?
    Made thee uncivilly forget thyself,
    And work our sister to his lust?

GRA. Who, I?
    That had been monstrous. I defy that man
    For any such intent! none lives so pure,
    But shall be soiled with slander. Good son, believe it not.

VEN. [*Aside*] O, I'm in doubt,
    Whether I am myself, or no—
    Stay, let me look again upon this face.
    Who shall be saved, when mothers have no grace?

HIP. 'Twould make one half[2] despair.

VEN. I was the man.
    Defy me now; let's see, do't modestly.

GRA. O hell unto my soul!

VEN. In that disguise, I, sent from the duke's son,
    Tried you, and found you base metal,
    As any villain might have done.

1. Curdled(?).
2. i.e., Of the world.

GRA. O, no,

No tongue but yours could have bewitched me so.

VEN. O nimble in damnation, quick in tune!

There is no devil could strike fire so soon:

I am confuted in a word.

GRA. O sons, forgive me! to myself I'll prove more true;

You that should honor me, I kneel to you.

[*Kneels and weeps*]

VEN. A mother to give aim to[1] her own daughter!

HIP. True, brother; how far beyond nature 'tis.

VEN. Nay, an[2] you draw tears once, go you to bed;

We will make iron blush and change to red.

Brother, it rains. 'Twill spoil your dagger: house it.

HIP. 'Tis done.

VEN. I'faith, 'tis a sweet shower, it does much good.

The fruitful grounds and meadows of her soul

Have been long dry: pour down, thou blessèd dew!

Rise, mother; troth, this shower has made you higher!

GRA. O you Heavens! take this infectious spot out of my soul,

I'll rinse it in seven waters of mine eyes!

Make my tears salt enough to taste of grace.

To weep is to our sex naturally given:

But to weep truly, that's a gift from Heaven.

VEN. Nay, I'll kiss you now. Kiss her, brother:

Let's marry her to our souls, wherein's no lust,

And honorably love her.

HIP. Let it be.

VEN. For honest women are so seld and rare,

'Tis good to cherish those poor few that are.

O you of easy wax! do but imagine

Now the disease has left you, how leprously

That office would have clinged unto your forehead!

All mothers that had any graceful hue

Would have worn masks to hide their face at you:

It would have grown to this—at your foul name,

Green-colored maids would have turned red with shame.

1. Incite.
2. If.

HIP. And then our sister, full of hire and baseness—
VEN. There had been boiling lead again,
    The duke's son's great concubine!
    A drab of state, a cloth-o'-silver slut,
    To have her train borne up, and her soul trail i' the dirt!
HIP. Great, to be miserably great; rich, to be eternally wretched.
VEN. O common madness!
    Ask but the thrivingest harlot in cold blood,
    She'd give the world to make her honor good.
    Perhaps you'll say, but only to the duke's son
    In private; why she first begins with one,
    Who afterward to thousands prove a whore:
    "Break ice in one place, it will crack in more."
GRA. Most certainly applied!
HIP. O brother, you forget our business.
VEN. And well-remembered; joy's a subtle elf,
    I think man's happiest when he forgets himself.
    Farewell, once dry, now holy-watered mead;
    Our hearts wear feathers, that before wore lead.
GRA. I'll give you this—that one I never knew
    Plead better for and 'gainst the devil than you.
VEN. You make me proud on't.
HIP. Commend us in all virtue to our sister.
VEN. Ay, for the love of Heaven, to that true maid.
GRA. With my best words.
VEN. Why, that was motherly said.

                          Exeunt Vendice and Hippolito

GRA. I wonder now, what fury did transport me!
    I feel good thoughts begin to settle in me.
    O, with what forehead can I look on her,
    Whose honor I've so impiously beset?
    And here she comes—

                  Enter Castiza

CAS. Now, mother, you have wrought with me so strongly,
    That what for my advancement, as to calm
    The trouble of your tongue, I am content.

GRA. Content, to what?

CAS. To do as you have wished me;
    To prostitute my breast to the duke's son;
    And put myself to common usury.

GRA. I hope you will not so!

CAS. Hope you I will not?
    That's not the hope you look to be saved in.

GRA. Truth, but it is.

CAS. Do not deceive yourself;
    I am as you, e'en out of marble wrought.
    What would you now? are ye not pleased yet with me?
    You shall not wish me to be more lascivious
    Than I intend to be.

GRA. Strike not me cold.

CAS. How often have you charged me on your blessing
    To be a cursèd woman? When you knew
    Your blessing had no force to make me lewd,
    You laid your curse upon me; that did more,
    The mother's curse is heavy; where that fights,
    Suns set in storm, and daughters lose their lights.

GRA. Good child, dear maid, if there be any spark
    Of heavenly intellectual fire within thee,
    O, let my breath revive it to a flame!
    Put not all out with woman's wilful follies.
    I am recovered of that foul disease,
    That haunts too many mothers; kind, forgive me.
    Make me not sick in health! If then
    My words prevailed, when they were wickedness,
    How much more now, when they are just and good?

CAS. I wonder what you mean! are not you she,
    For whose infect persuasions I could scarce
    Kneel out my prayers, and had much ado
    In three hours' reading to untwist so much
    Of the black serpent as you wound about me?

GRA. 'Tis unfruitful, child, and tedious to repeat
    What's past; I'm now your present mother.

CAS. Tush! now 'tis too late.

GRA. Bethink again: thou know'st not what thou say'st.

CAS. No! deny advancement? treasure? the duke's son?

GRA. O, see! I spoke those words, and now they poison me!
    What will the deed do then?
    Advancement? true; as high as shame can pitch!
    For treasure; who e'er knew a harlot rich?
    Or could build by the purchase of her sin
    An hospital[1] to keep her bastards in?
    The duke's son! O, when women are young courtiers,
    They are sure to be old beggars;
    To know the miseries most harlots taste,
    Thou'dst wish thyself unborn, when thou art unchaste.

CAS. O mother, let me twine about your neck,
    And kiss you, till my soul melt on your lips!
    I did but this to try you.

GRA. O, speak truth!

CAS. Indeed I did but; for no tongue has force
    To alter me from honest.
    If maidens would, men's words could have no power;
    A virgin's honor is a crystal tower
    Which (being weak) is guarded with good spirits;
    Until she basely yields, no ill inherits.

GRA. O happy child! faith, and thy birth hath saved me.
    'Mong thousand daughters, happiest of all others:
    Be thou a glass for maids, and I for mothers.

                                          Exeunt

ACT V, SCENE I

The Duke's corpse, dressed in Vendice's disguise, lying on a couch
Enter Vendice and Hippolito

VEN. So, so, he leans well; take heed you wake him not, brother.

HIP. I warrant you my life for yours.

VEN. That's a good lay, for I must kill myself.

---

1. Orphanage.

Brother, that's I, that sits for me: do you mark it? And I must stand
ready here to make away myself yonder. I must sit to be killed,
and stand to kill myself. I could vary it not so little as thrice
over again; 't has some eight returns, like Michaelmas term.[1]

HIP. That's enow, o' conscience.

VEN. But, sirrah, does the duke's son come single?

HIP. No; there's the hell on't: his faith's too feeble to go alone. He
brings flesh-flies[2] after him, that will buzz against supper-time, and
hum for his coming out.

VEN. Ah, the fly-flap of vengeance beat 'em to pieces! Here was the
sweetest occasion, the fittest hour, to have made my revenge familiar with him; show him the body of the duke his father, and how
quaintly he died, like a politician, in hugger-mugger,[3] made no man
acquainted with it; and in catastrophe slay him over his father's
breast. O, I'm mad to lose such a sweet opportunity!

HIP. Nay, tush! prithee, be content! there's no remedy present; may
not hereafter times open in as fair faces as this?

VEN. They may, if they can paint so well.

HIP. Come now: to avoid all suspicion, let's forsake this room, and be
going to meet the duke's son.

VEN. Content: I'm for any weather. Heart! step close: here he comes.

Enter Lussurioso

HIP. My honored lord!

LUS. O me! you both present?

VEN. E'en newly, my lord, just as your lordship entered now: about
this place we had notice given he should be, but in some loathsome
plight or other.

HIP. Came your honor private?

LUS. Private enough for this; only a few
Attend my coming out.

HIP. [*Aside*] Death rot those few!

LUS. Stay, yonder's the slave.

---

1. i.e., He could kill himself over and over again. Eight days were allocated to the court
in Michaelmas term for reports.

2. His henchmen.

3. In secret.

VEN. Mass, there's the slave, indeed, my lord.

   [*Aside*] 'Tis a good child: he calls his father a slave!

LUS. Ay, that's the villain, the damned villain.

   Softly. Tread easy.

VEN. Pah! I warrant you, my lord, we'll stifle-in our breaths.

LUS. That will do well:

   Base rogue, thou sleepest thy last; 'tis policy

   To have him killed in's sleep; for if he waked,

   He would betray all to them.

VEN. But, my lord—

LUS. Ha, what say'st?

VEN. Shall we kill him now he's drunk?

LUS. Ay, best of all.

VEN. Why, then he will ne'er live to be sober.

LUS. No matter, let him reel to hell.

VEN. But being so full of liquor, I fear he will put out all the fire.

LUS. Thou art a mad beast.

VEN. And leave none to warm your lordship's golls[1] withal; for he that
   dies drunk falls into hell-fire like a bucket of water—qush, qush!

LUS. Come, be ready: nake[2] your swords: think of your wrongs; this
   slave has injured you.

VEN. Troth, so he has, and he has paid well for't.

LUS. Meet with him now.

VEN. You'll bear us out, my lord?

LUS. Pooh! am I a lord for nothing, think you? quickly now!

VEN. Sa, sa, sa,[3] thump [*stabs the Duke's corpse*]—there he lies.

LUS. Nimbly done.—Ha! O villains! murderers!

   'Tis the old duke, my father.

VEN. That's a jest.

LUS. What stiff and cold already!

   O, pardon me to call you from your names.[4]

   'Tis none of your deed. That villain Piato,

   Whom you thought now to kill, has murdered

   And left him thus disguised.

---

1. Hands.
2. Unsheathe.
3. A fencer's exclamation.
4. By other names than you deserve.

HIP. And not unlikely.

VEN. O rascal! was he not ashamed
    To put the duke into a greasy doublet?

LUS. He has been stiff and cold—who knows how long?

VEN. [*Aside*] Marry, that I do.

LUS. No words, I pray, of anything intended.

VEN. O my lord.

HIP. I would fain have your lordship think that we have small reason
    to prate.

LUS. Faith, thou say'st true; I'll forthwith send to court
    For all the nobles, bastard, duchess; tell,
    How here by miracle we found him dead,
    And in his raiment that foul villain fled.

VEN. That will be the best way, my lord,
    To clear us all; let's cast about to be clear.

LUS. Ho! Nencio, Sordido, and the rest!

Enter all of them

1ST SER. My lord.

2ND SER. My lord.

LUS. Be witnesses of a strange spectacle.
    Choosing for private conference that sad room,
    We found the duke my father gealed in blood.

1ST SER. My lord the duke! run, hie thee, Nencio.
    Startle the court by signifying so much.

VEN. [*Aside*] Thus much by wit a deep revenger can,
    When murder's known, to be the clearest man.
    We're farthest off, and with as bold an eye
    Survey his body as the standers-by.

LUS. My royal father, too basely let blood
    By a malevolent slave!

HIP. [*Aside*] Hark! he calls thee slave again.

VEN. [*Aside*] He has lost: he may.

LUS. O sight! look hither, see, his lips are gnawn
    With poison.

VEN. How! his lips? by the mass, they be.
    O villain! O rogue! O slave! O rascal!

HIP. [*Aside*] O good deceit! he quits him with like terms.

AMB. [*Within*] Where?

SUP. [*Within*] Which way?

Enter Ambitioso and Supervacuo, with Nobles and Gentlemen

AMB. Over what roof hangs this prodigious[1] comet
   In deadly fire?

LUS. Behold, behold, my lords, the duke my father's murdered by a
   vassal that owes[2] this habit, and here left disguised.

Enter Duchess and Spurio

DUCH. My lord and husband!

1ST NOBLE. Reverend majesty!

2ND NOBLE. I have seen these clothes often attending on him.

VEN. [*Aside*] That nobleman has been i' th' country, for he does not
   lie.

SUP. Learn of our mother; let's dissemble too:
   I am glad he's vanished; so, I hope, are you.

AMB. Ay, you may take my word for't.

SUP. Old dad dead!
   I, one of his cast sins, will send the Fates
   Most hearty commendations by his own son;
   I'll tug in the new stream, till strength be done.

LUS. Where be those two that did affirm to us,
   My lord the duke was privately rid forth?

1ST GENT. O, pardon us, my lords; he gave that charge—
   Upon our lives, if he were missed at court,
   To answer so; he rode not anywhere;
   We left him private with that fellow here.

VEN. [*Aside*] Confirmed.

LUS. O Heavens! that false charge was his death.
   Impudent beggars! durst you to our face
   Maintain such a false answer? Bear him straight
   To execution.

1ST GENT. My lord!

LUS. Urge me no more in this!
   The excuse may be called half the murder.

1. Ominous.
2. Owns.

VEN. [*Aside*] You've sentenced well.

LUS. Away; see it be done.

VEN. [*Aside*] Could you not stick? See what confession doth!
Who would not lie, when men are hanged for truth?

HIP. [*Aside*] Brother, how happy is our vengeance!

VEN. [*Aside*] Why, it hits past the apprehension of
Indifferent wits.

LUS. My lord, let post-horses be sent
Into all places to entrap the villain.

VEN. [*Aside*] Post-horses, ha, ha!

1ST NOBLE. My lord, we're something bold to know our duty.
Your father's accidentally departed;
The titles that were due to him meet you.

LUS. Meet me! I'm not at leisure, my good lord.
I've many griefs to despatch out o' the way.
[*Aside*] Welcome, sweet titles!—
Talk to me, my lords,
Of sepulchres and mighty emperors' bones;
That's thought for me.

VEN. [*Aside*] So one may see by this
How foreign markets go;[1]
Courtiers have feet o' the nines, and tongues o' the twelves;[2]
They flatter dukes, and dukes flatter themselves.

2ND NOBLE. My lord, it is your shine must comfort us.

LUS. Alas! I shine in tears, like the sun in April.

1ST NOBLE. You're now my lord's grace.

LUS. My lord's grace! I perceive you'll have it so.

2ND NOBLE. 'Tis but your own.

LUS. Then, Heavens, give me grace to be so!

VEN. [*Aside*] He prays well for himself.

1ST NOBLE. Madam, all sorrows
Must run their circles into joys. No doubt but time
Will make the murderer bring forth himself.

VEN. [*Aside*] He were an ass then, i'faith.

1ST NOBLE. In the mean season,

1. [Obscure].
2. [Obscure].

Let us bethink the latest funeral honors
Due to the duke's cold body. And withal,
Calling to memory our new happiness
Speed in his royal son: lords, gentlemen,
Prepare for revels.

VEN. [*Aside*] Revels!

1ST NOBLE. Time hath several falls.[1]
Grief lift up joys: feasts put down funerals.

LUS. Come then, my lords, my favor's to you all.
[*Aside*] The duchess is suspected foully bent;
I'll begin dukedom with her banishment.

Exeunt Lussurioso, Duchess, and Nobles

HIP. Revels!

VEN. Ay, that's the word: we are firm[2] yet;
Strike one strain more, and then we crown our wit.

Exeunt Vendice and Hippolito

SPU. Well, have at the fairest mark[3]—so said the duke when he begot
      me;
And if I miss his heart, or near about,
Then have at any; a bastard scorns to be out.[4]

                                                    Exit

SUP. Notest thou that Spurio, brother?

AMB. Yes, I note him to our shame.

SUP. He shall not live: his hair shall not grow much longer. In this time
     of revels, tricks may be set afoot. Seest thou yon new moon? it shall
     outlive the new duke by much; this hand shall dispossess him. Then
     we're mighty.
     A masque is treason's licence, that build upon:
     'Tis murder's best face, when a vizard's on.

                                                    Exit

1. [Like a wrestler].
2. Secure.
3. Target.
4. To fail.

AMB. Is't so? 'tis very good!
And do you think to be duke then, kind brother?
I'll see fair play; drop one, and there lies t'other.

Exit

SCENE II

Enter Vendice and Hippolito, with Piero and other Lords

VEN. My lords, be all of music, strike old griefs into other countries
That flow in too much milk,[1] and have faint livers,
Not daring to stab home their discontents.
Let our hid flames break out as fire, as lightning,
To blast this villainous dukedom, vexed with sin;
Wind up your souls to their full height again.
PIERO. How?
1ST LORD. Which way?
2ND LORD. Any way: our wrongs are such,
We cannot justly be revenged too much.
VEN. You shall have all enough. Revels are toward,
And those few nobles that have long suppressed you,
Are busied to the furnishing of a masque,
And do affect to make a pleasant tale on't:
The masquing suits are fashioning: now comes in
That which must glad us all. We too take pattern
Of all those suits, the color, trimming, fashion,
E'en to an undistinguished hair almost:
Then entering first, observing the true form,[2]
Within a strain or two we shall find leisure
To steal our swords out handsomely;
And when they think their pleasure sweet and good,
In midst of all their joys they shall sigh blood.
PIERO. Weightily, effectually!
3RD LORD. Before the t'other maskers come—
VEN. We're gone, all done and past.

1. Are not manly enough.
2. Of the dance.

PIERO. But how for the duke's guard?
VEN. Let that alone;
    By one and one their strengths shall be drunk down.[1]
HIP. There are five hundred gentlemen in the action,
    That will apply themselves, and not stand idle.
PIERO. O, let us hug your bosoms!
VEN. Come, my lords,
    Prepare for deeds: let other times have words.

Exeunt

SCENE III

In a dumb show, the possessing[2] of the Young Duke with all his Nobles;
sounding music. A furnished table is brought forth; then enter the
Duke and his Nobles to the banquet. A blazing star appeareth

1ST NOBLE. Many harmonious hours and choicest pleasures
    Fill up the royal number of your years!
LUS. My lords, we're pleased to thank you, though we know
    'Tis but your duty now to wish it so.
1ST NOBLE. That shine makes us all happy.
3RD NOBLE. His grace frowns.
2ND NOBLE. Yet we must say he smiles.
1ST NOBLE. I think we must.
LUS. [*Aside*] That foul incontinent duchess we have banished;
    The bastard shall not live. After these revels,
    I'll begin strange ones: he and the step-sons
    Shall pay their lives for the first subsidies;[3]
    We must not frown so soon, else't had been now.
1ST NOBLE. My gracious lord, please you prepare for pleasure.
    The masque is not far off.
LUS. We are for pleasure.
    Beshrew thee, what art thou? thou mad'st me start!
    Thou has committed treason. A blazing star![4]

---

1. Diminished by drink.
2. Installation.
3. Installments.
4. Comet.

1ST NOBLE. A blazing star! O, where, my lord?

LUS. Spy out.

2ND NOBLE. See, see, my lords, a wondrous dreadful one!

LUS. I am not pleased at that ill-knotted fire,
    That bushing, staring star. Am I not duke?
    It should not quake me now. Had it appeared
    Before, it I might then have justly feared;
    But yet they say, whom art and learning weds,
    When stars wear locks, they threaten great men's heads:
    Is it so? you are read, my lords.

1ST NOBLE. May it please your grace,
    It shows great anger.

LUS. That does not please our grace.

2ND NOBLE. Yet here's the comfort, my lord: many times,
    When it seems most near, it threatens farthest off.

LUS. Faith, and I think so too.

1ST NOBLE. Beside, my lord,
    You're gracefully established with the loves
    Of all your subjects; and for natural death,
    I hope it will be threescore years a-coming.

LUS. True? no more but threescore years?

1ST NOBLE. Fourscore, I hope, my lord.

2ND NOBLE. And fivescore, I.

3RD NOBLE. But 'tis my hope, my lord, you shall ne'er die.

LUS. Give me thy hand; these others I rebuke:
    He that hopes so is fittest for a duke:
    Thou shalt sit next me; take your places, lords;
    We're ready now for sports; let 'em set on:
    You thing!¹ we shall forget you quite anon!

3RD NOBLE. I hear 'em coming, my lord.

    Enter the Masque of revengers: Vendice and Hippolito,
        with two Lords

LUS. Ah, 'tis well!
    [*Aside*] Brothers and bastard, you dance next in hell!

---

1. The comet.

They dance; at the end they steal out their swords,
and kill the four seated at the table. Thunder

VEN. Mark, thunder!
  Dost know thy cue, thou big-voiced crier?
  Dukes' groans are thunder's watchwords.
HIP. So, my lords, you have enough.
VEN. Come, let's away, no lingering.
HIP. Follow! go!

Exeunt except Vendice

VEN. No power is angry when the lustful die;
  When thunder claps, heaven likes the tragedy.

Exit

LUS. O, O!

Enter the Masque of intended murderers: Ambitioso, Supervacuo,
Spurio, and a Lord, coming in dancing. Lussurioso recovers a little
in voice, groans, and calls, "A guard! treason!" at which the Dancers
start out of their measure,[1] and, turning towards the table, find them
all to be murdered

SPU. Whose groan was that?
LUS. Treason! a guard!
AMB. How now? all murdered!
SUP. Murdered!
3RD LORD. And those his nobles?
AMB. Here's a labor saved;
  I thought to have sped him. 'Sblood, how came this?
SPU. Then I proclaim myself; now I am duke.
AMB. Thou duke! brother, thou liest.
SPU. Slave! so dost thou.

[*Kills Ambitioso*]

3RD LORD. Base villain! hast thou slain my lord and master?

[*Stabs Spurio*]

Re-enter Vendice and Hippolito and the two Lords

VEN. Pistols! treason! murder! Help! guard my lord the duke!

---

1. Dance.

Enter Antonio and Guard

HIP. Lay hold upon this traitor.

LUS. O!

VEN. Alas! the duke is murdered.

HIP. And the nobles.

VEN. Surgeons! surgeons! [*Aside*] Heart! does he breathe so long?

ANT. A piteous tragedy! able to make
An old man's eyes bloodshot.

LUS. O!

VEN. Look to my lord the duke. [*Aside*] A vengeance throttle him!
Confess, thou murderous and unhallowed man,
Didst thou kill all these?

3RD LORD. None but the bastard, I.

VEN. How came the duke slain, then?

3RD LORD. We found him so.

LUS. O villain!

VEN. Hark!

LUS. Those in the masque did murder us.

VEN. La you now,[1] sir—
O marble impudence! will you confess now?

3RD LORD. 'Sblood, 'tis all false.

ANT. Away with that foul monster,
Dipped in a prince's blood.

3RD LORD. Heart! 'tis a lie.

ANT. Let him have bitter execution.

VEN. New marrow![2] no, I cannot be expressed.[3]
How fares my lord the duke?

LUS. Farewell to all;
He that climbs highest has the greatest fall.
My tongue is out of office.

VEN. Air, gentlemen, air.
[*Whispers in his ear*] Now thou'lt not prate on't, 'twas Vendice
murdered thee.

---

1. An exclamation.
2. i.e., Fine food.
3. Squeezed out.

LUS. O!

VEN. [*Whispers*] Murdered thy father.

LUS. O!

        Dies

VEN. [*Whispers*] And I am he—tell nobody: So, so, the duke's departed.

ANT. It was a deadly hand that wounded him.
    The rest, ambitious who should rule and sway
    After his death, were so made all away.

VEN. My lord was unlikely—

HIP. Now the hope
    Of Italy lies in your reverend years.

VEN. Your hair will make the silver age again,
    When there were fewer, but more honest men.

ANT. The burthen's weighty, and will press age down;
    May I so rule, that Heaven may keep the crown!

VEN. The rape of your good lady has been quitted
    With death on death.

ANT. Just is the law above.
    But of all things it put me most to wonder
    How the old duke came murdered!

VEN. O my lord!

ANT. It was the strangeliest carried: I've not heard of the like.

HIP. 'Twas all done for the best, my lord.

VEN. All for your grace's good. We may be bold to speak it now,
    'Twas somewhat witty carried, though we say it—
    'Twas we two murdered him.

ANT. You two?

VEN. None else, i'faith, my lord. Nay, 'twas well-managed.

ANT. Lay hands upon those villains!

VEN. How! on us?

ANT. Bear 'em to speedy execution.

VEN. Heart! was't not for your good, my lord?

ANT. My good! Away with 'em: such an old man as he!
    You, that would murder him, would murder me.

VEN. Is't come about?[1]

HIP. 'Sfoot, brother, you begun.

---

1. Turned round.

VEN. May not we set as well as the duke's son?
    Thou hast no conscience, are we not revenged?
    Is there one enemy left alive amongst those?
    'Tis time to die, when we're ourselves our foes:
    When murderers shut deeds close, this curse does seal 'em:
    If none disclose 'em, they themselves reveal 'em!
    This murder might have slept in tongueless brass[1]
    But for ourselves, and the world died an ass.
    Now I remember too, here was Piato
    Brought forth a knavish sentence once;
    No doubt (said he), but time
    Will make the murderer bring forth himself.
    'Tis well he died; he was a witch.
    And now, my lord, since we are in for ever,
    This work was ours, which else might have been slipped![2]
    And if we list, we could have nobles[3] clipped,
    And go for less than beggars; but we hate
    To bleed so cowardly: we have enough,
    I'faith, we're well, our mother turned, our sister true,
    We die after a nest of dukes. Adieu!

                                      Exeunt

ANT. How subtly was that murder closed!
    Bear up
    Those tragic bodies: 'tis a heavy season;
    Pray Heaven their blood may wash away all treason!

                                        Exit

---

1. On a memorial tablet.
2. Left undone.
3. With pun on "nobles" meaning gold coins.

THE MAID'S TRAGEDY

FRANCIS BEAUMONT
AND JOHN FLETCHER

DRAMATIS PERSONAE

KING
LYSIPPUS, *brother to the King*
AMINTOR, *a noble gentleman*

MELANTIUS
DIPHILUS } *brothers to* EVADNE

CALIANAX, *an old humorous lord*

CLEON
STRATO } *gentlemen*

DIAGORAS, *a servant to* CALIANAX
EVADNE, *sister to* MELANTIUS
ASPATIA, *troth-plight wife to Amintor*

ANTIPHILA
OLYMPIAS } *waiting-women to* ASPATIA

DULA, *waiting-woman to* EVADNE
LADIES
NIGHT, CYNTHIA, NEPTUNE, AEOLUS, *Proteus and Sea-Gods, Masquers, Favonius and Winds*
MESSENGER, GENTLEMEN, SERVANT, *Hautboys*

SCENE—THE CITY OF RHODES

THE MAID'S TRAGEDY

ACT I, SCENE I

Enter Cleon, Strato, Lysippus, Diphilus

CLE. The rest are making ready, sir.
LYS. So let them;
  There's time enough.
DIPH. You are the brother to the King, my lord;
  We'll take your word.
LYS. Strato, thou has some skill in poetry;
  What think'st thou of a masque? will it be well?
STRA. As well as masques can be.
LYS. As masques can be!
STRA. Yes; they must commend their king, and speak in praise
  Of the assembly, bless the bride and bridegroom
  In person of some god; they're tied to rules
  Of flattery.
CLE. See, good my lord, who is returned!

Enter Melantius

LYS. Noble Melantius!
  The land by me welcomes thy virtues home;
  Thou that with blood abroad buy'st us our peace!
  The breath of kings is like the breath of gods;
  My brother wished thee here, and thou art here:
  He will be too-too kind, and weary thee
  With often welcomes; but the time doth give thee
  A welcome above his or all the world's.
MEL. My lord, my thanks; but these scratched limbs of mine
  Have spoke my love and truth unto my friends,
  More than my tongue e'er could. My mind's the same

It ever was to you: where I find worth,
I love the keeper till he let it go,
And then I follow it.

DIPH. Hail, worthy brother!
He that rejoices not at your return
In safety is mine enemy for ever.

MEL. I thank thee, Diphilus. But thou art faulty:
I sent for thee to exercise thine arms
With me at Patria; thou cam'st not, Diphilus;
'Twas ill.

DIPH. My noble brother, my excuse
Is my King's strict command,—which you, my lord,
Can witness with me.

LYS. 'Tis most true, Melantius;
He might not come till the solemnities
Of this great match were past.

DIPH. Have you heard of it?

MEL. Yes, and have given cause to those that here
Envy my deeds abroad to call me gamesome;
I have no other business here at Rhodes.

LYS. We have a masque to-night, and you must tread
A soldier's measure.¹

MEL. Those soft and silken wars are not for me:
The music must be shrill and all confused
That stirs my blood; and then I dance with arms.
But is Amintor wed?

DIPH. This day.

MEL. All joys upon him! for he is my friend.
Wonder not that I call a man so young my friend:
His worth is great; valiant he is and temperate;
And one that never thinks his life his own,
If his friend need it. When he was a boy,
As oft as I returned (as, without boast,
I brought home conquest), he would gaze upon me
And view me round, to find in what one limb
The virtue lay to do those things he heard;

---

1. A stately dance.

Then would he wish to see my sword, and feel
The quickness of the edge, and in his hand
Weigh it: he oft would make me smile at this.
His youth did promise much, and his ripe years
Will see it all performed.—

Enter Aspatia, passing by

Hail, maid and wife!
Thou fair Aspatia, may the holy knot,
That thou hast tied to-day, last till the hand
Of age undo it! may'st thou bring a race
Unto Amintor, that may fill the world
Successively with soldiers!
ASP. My hard fortunes
Deserve not scorn, for I was never proud
When they were good.

Exit Aspatia

MEL. How's this?
LYS. You are mistaken, sir; she is not married.
MEL. You said Amintor was.
DIPH. 'Tis true; but—
MEL. Pardon me; I did receive
Letters at Patria from my Amintor,
That he should marry her.
DIPH. And so it stood
In all opinion long; but your arrival
Made me imagine you had heard the change.
MEL. Who hath he taken then?
LYS. A lady, sir,
That bears the light above her,[1] and strikes dead
With flashes of her eye; the fair Evadne,
Your virtuous sister.
MEL. Peace of heart betwixt them!
But this is strange.
LYS. The King, my brother, did it

1. Excels her.

To honor you; and these solemnities
Are at his charge.

MEL. 'Tis royal, like himself. But I am sad
My speech bears so unfortunate a sound
To beautiful Aspatia. There is rage
Hid in her father's breast, Calianax,
Bent long against me; and he should not think,
Could I but call it back, that I would take
So base revenges, as to scorn the state
Of his neglected daughter. Holds he still
His greatness with the King?

LYS. Yes. But this lady
Walks discontented, with her watery eyes
Bent on the earth. The unfrequented woods
Are her delight; where, when she sees a bank
Stuck full of flowers, she with a sigh will tell
Her servants what a pretty place it were
To bury lovers in; and make her maids
Pluck 'em, and strow her over like a corse.[1]
She carries with her an infectious grief,
That strikes all her beholders: she will sing
The mournful'st things that ever ear hath heard,
And sigh, and sing again; and when the rest
Of our young ladies, in their wanton blood,
Tell mirthful tales in course,[2] that fill the room
With laughter, she will, with so sad a look,
Bring forth a story of the silent death
Of some forsaken virgin, which her grief
Will put in such a phrase, that, ere she end,
She'll send them weeping one by one away.

MEL. She has a brother under my command,
Like her; a face as womanish as hers;
But with a spirit that hath much outgrown
The number of his years.

Enter Amintor

1. Corpse.
2. In turn.

CLE. My lord the bridegroom.

MEL. I might run fiercely, not more hastily,
Upon my foe. I love thee well, Amintor;
My mouth is much too narrow for my heart;
I joy to look upon those eyes of thine;
Thou art my friend, but my disordered speech
Cuts off my love.

AMIN. Thou art Melantius;
All love is spoke in that. A sacrifice,
To thank the gods Melantius is returned
In safety! Victory sits on his sword,
As she was wont: may she build there and dwell;
And may thy armor be, as it hath been,
Only thy valor and thine innocence!
What endless treasures would our enemies give,
That I might hold thee still thus!

MEL. I am poor
In words; but credit me, young man, thy mother
Could do no more but weep for joy to see thee
After long absence: all the wounds I gave
Fetched not so much away, nor all the cries
Of widowed mothers. But this is peace,
And that was war.

AMIN. Pardon, thou holy god
Of marriage-bed, and frown not, I am forced,
In answer of such noble tears as those,
To weep upon my wedding-day!

MEL. I fear thou art grown too fickle; for I hear
A lady mourns for thee; men say, to death;
Forsaken of thee; on what terms I know not.

AMIN. She had my promise; but the King forbade it,
And made me make this worthy change, thy sister,
Accompanied with graces [far] above her;
With whom I long to lose my lusty youth,
And grow old in her arms.

MEL. Be prosperous!

Enter Messenger

MESS. My lord, the masquers rage for you.
LYS. We are gone.—
   Cleon, Strato, Diphilus!
AMIN. We'll all attend you.—

Exeunt Lysippus, Cleon, Strato, Diphilus

   We shall trouble you
   With our solemnities.
MEL. Not so, Amintor:
   But if you laugh at my rude carriage
   In peace, I'll do as much for you in war,
   When you come thither. Yet I have a mistress
   To bring to your delights; rough though I am,
   I have a mistress, and she has a heart
   She says; but, trust me, it is stone, no better;
   There is no place that I can challenge in't.
   But you stand still, and here my way lies.

Exeunt

SCENE II

Enter Calianax with Diagoras

CAL. Diagoras, look to the doors better, for shame! you let in all the world, and anon the King will rail at me. Why, very well said. By Jove, the King will have the show i' th' court.

DIAG. Why do you swear so, my lord? you know he'll have it here.

CAL. By this light, if he be wise, he will not.

DIAG. And if he will not be wise, you are forsworn.

CAL. One must sweat his heart out with swearing, and get thanks on no side. I'll be gone, look to't who will.

DIAG. My lord, I shall never keep them out. Pray, stay; your looks will terrify them.

CAL. My looks terrify them, you coxcombly ass, you! I'll be judged by all the company whether thou hast not a worse face than I.

DIAG. I mean, because they know you and your office.

CAL. Office! I would I could put it off! I am sure I sweat quite through my office. I might have made room at my daughter's wedding: they ha' near killed her amongst them; and now I must do service for him that hath forsaken her. Serve that will!

Exit Calianax

DIAG. He's so humorous[1] since his daughter was forsaken! [*Knock within*] Hark, hark! there, there! so, so! codes, codes![2] What now?

MEL. [*Within*] Open the door.

DIAG. Who's there?

MEL. [*Within*] Melantius.

DIAG. I hope your lordship brings no troop with you; for, if you do, I must return them.[3]

[*Opens the door*]

Enter Melantius and a Lady

MEL. None but this lady, sir.

DIAG. The ladies are all placed above, save those that come in the King's troop: the best of Rhodes sit there, and there's room.

MEL. I thank you, sir.—When I have seen you placed, madam, I must attend the King; but, the masque done, I'll wait on you again.

DIAG. [*Opening another door*] Stand back there!—Room for my lord Melantius! [*Exeunt Melantius, Lady, other door*]—Pray, bear back— this is no place for such youths and their trulls—let the doors shut again.—No!—do your heads itch? I'll scratch them for you. [*Shuts the door*]—So, now thrust and hang. [*Knocking within*]—Again! who is't now?—I cannot blame my lord Calianax for going away: would he were here! he would run raging among them, and break a dozen wiser heads than his own in the twinkling of an eye.—What's the news now?

[*Within*] I pray you, can you help me to the speech of the master-cook?

DIAG. If I open the door, I'll cook some of your calves-heads. Peace, rogues! [*Knocking within*]—Again! who is't?

MEL. [*Within*] Melantius.

Enter Calianax to Melantius

1. Testy.
2. Euphemistic oath.
3. Turn them back.

CAL. Let him not in.

DIAG. O, my lord, a' must.—Make room there for my lord!
   Is your lady placed?

MEL. Yes, sir, I thank you.—
   My lord Calianax, well met:
   Your causeless hate to me I hope is burièd.

CAL. Yes, I do service for your sister here,
   That brings my own poor child to timeless death:
   She loves your friend Amintor; such another
   False-hearted lord as you.

MEL. You do me wrong,
   A most unmanly one, and I am slow
   In taking vengeance; but be well advised.

CAL. It may be so.—Who placed the lady there,
   So near the presence of the King?

MEL. I did.

CAL. My lord, she must not sit there.

MEL. Why?

CAL. The place
   Is kept for women of more worth.

MEL. More worth than she! It misbecomes your age
   And place to be thus womanish: forbear!
   What you have spoke, I am content to think
   The palsy shook your tongue to.

CAL. Why, 'tis well:
   If I stand here to place men's wenches—

MEL. I
   Shall quite forget this place, thy age, my safety,
   And, through all, cut that poor sickly week
   Thou hast to live away from thee!

CAL. Nay, I know you can fight for your whore.

MEL. Bate me the King,[1] and, be he flesh and blood,
   A' lies that says it! Thy mother at fifteen
   Was black and sinful to her.

DIAG. Good my lord—

MEL. Some god pluck threescore years from that fond[2] man,

---

1. Excepting the King.
2. Foolish.

That I may kill him, and not stain mine honor!
It is the curse of soldiers, that in peace
They shall be braved by such ignoble men,
As, if the land were troubled, would with tears
And knees beg succor from 'em. Would the blood,
That sea of blood, that I have lost in fight,
Were running in thy veins, that it might make thee
Apt to say less, or able to maintain,
Should'st thou say more! This Rhodes, I see, is nought
But a place privileged to do men wrong.

CAL. Ay, you may say your pleasure.

Enter Amintor

AMIN. What vile injury
Has stirred my worthy friend, who is as slow
To fight with words as he is quick of hand?

MEL. That heap of age, which I should reverence
If it were temperate; but testy years
Are most contemptible.

AMIN. Good sir, forbear.

CAL. There is just such another as yourself.

AMIN. He will wrong you, or me, or any man,
And talk as if he had no life to lose,
Since this our match. The King is coming in;
I would not for more wealth than I enjoy
He should perceive you raging: he did hear
You were at difference now, which hastened him.

CAL. Make room there!

[Hautboys play within]

Enter King, Evadne, Aspatia, Lords, and Ladies

KING. Melantius, thou art welcome, and my love
Is with thee still: but this is not a place
To brabble¹ in.—Calianax, join hands.

CAL. He shall not have mine hand.

KING. This is no time
To force you to't. I do love you both:—

1. Squabble.

Calianax, you look well to your office;—
And you, Melantius, are welcome home.—
Begin the masque.

MEL. Sister, I joy to see you and your choice;
You looked with my eyes when you took that man:
Be happy in him!

[Recorders' play]

EVAD. O, my dearest brother,
Your presence is more joyful than this day
Can be unto me!

THE MASQUE

Night rises in mists

NIGHT. Our reign is come; for in the quenching sea
The sun is drowned, and with him fell the Day.
Bright Cynthia, hear my voice! I am the Night,
For whom thou bear'st about thy borrowed light:
Appear! no longer thy pale visage shroud,
But strike thy silver horns quite through a cloud,
And send a beam upon my swarthy face,
By which I may discover all the place
And persons, and how many longing eyes
Are come to wait on our solemnities.

Enter Cynthia

How dull and black am I! I could not find
This beauty without thee, I am so blind:
Methinks they show like to those eastern streaks,
That warn us hence before the morning breaks.
Back, my pale servant! for these eyes know how
To shoot far more and quicker rays than thou.

CYNTH. Great queen, they be a troop for whom alone
One of my clearest moons I have put on;
A troop, that looks as if thyself and I

1. Flageolets.

Had plucked our reins in and our whips laid by,
To gaze upon these mortals, that appear
Brighter than we.
NIGHT. Then let us keep 'em here;
And never more our chariots drive away,
But hold our places and outshine the Day.
CYNTH. Great queen of shadows, you are pleased to speak
Of more than may be done: we may not break
The gods' decrees; but, when our time is come,
Must drive away, and give the Day our room.
Yet, whilst our reign lasts, let us stretch our power
To give our servants one contented hour,
With such unwonted solemn grace and state,
As may for ever after force them hate
Our brother's glorious beams, and wish the Night
Crowned with a thousand stars and our cold light:
For almost all the world their service bend
To Phœbus, and in vain my light I lend,
Gazed on unto my setting from my rise
Almost of none but of unquiet eyes.
NIGHT. Then shine at full, fair queen, and by thy power
Produce a birth, to crown this happy hour,
Of nymphs and shepherds; let their songs discover,
Easy and sweet, who is a happy lover;
Or, if thou woo't, thine own Endymion
From the sweet flowery bank he lies upon,
On Latmus' brow, thy pale beams drawn away,
And of his long night let him make this day.
CYNTH. Thou dream'st, dark queen; that fair boy was not mine,
Nor went I down to kiss him. Ease and wine
Have bred these bold tales: poets, when they rage,
Turn gods to men, and make an hour an age.
But I will give a greater state and glory,
And raise to time a nobler memory
Of what these lovers are.—Rise, rise, I say,
Thou power of deeps, thy surges laid away,
Neptune, great king of waters, and by me
Be proud to be commanded!

Neptune rises

NEPT. Cynthia, see,
　　Thy word hath fetched me hither: let me know
　　Why I ascend.
CYNTH. Doth this majestic show
　　Give thee no knowledge yet?
NEPT. Yes, now I see
　　Something intended, Cynthia, worthy thee.
　　Go on; I'll be a helper.
CYNTH. Hie thee, then,
　　And charge the Wind fly from his rocky den,
　　Let loose his subjects; only Boreas,
　　Too foul for our intention, as he was,
　　Still keep him fast chained: we must have none here
　　But vernal blasts and gentle winds appear,
　　Such as blow flowers, and through the glad boughs sing
　　Many soft welcomes to the lusty spring;
　　These are our music; next, thy watery race
　　Bring on in couples; we are pleased to grace
　　This noble night, each in their richest things
　　Your own deeps or the broken vessel brings:
　　Be prodigal, and I shall be as kind
　　And shine at full upon you.
NEPT. Ho, the wind
　　Commanding Æolus!

Enter Æolus out of a Rock

ÆOL. Great Neptune!
NEPT. He.
ÆOL. What is thy will?
NEPT. We do command thee free:
　　Favonius and thy milder winds, to wait
　　Upon our Cynthia; but tie Boreas strait,[1]
　　He's too rebellious.
ÆOL. I shall do it.
NEPT. Do.

1. Tightly.

Exit Æolus

ÆOL. [*Within*] Great master of the flood and all below,
    Thy full command has taken. Ho, the Main!
    Neptune!

      Re-enter Æolus, followed by Favonius and other Winds

NEPT. Here.
ÆOL. Boreas has broke his chain,
    And, struggling with the rest, has got away.
NEPT. Let him alone, I'll take him up at sea;
    I will not long be thence. Go once again,
    And call out of the bottoms of the main
    Blue Proteus and the rest; charge them put on
    Their greatest pearls, and the most sparkling stone
    The beaten rock breeds; tell this night is done
    By me a solemn honor to the Moon:
    Fly, like a full sail.
ÆOL. I am gone.

Exit

CYNTH. Dark Night,
    Strike a full silence, do a thorough right
    To this great chorus, that our music may
    Touch high as heaven, and make the east break day
    At midnight.

Music

FIRST SONG

During which Proteus and other Sea-deities enter

Cynthia, to thy power and thee
      We obey.
Joy to this great company!
      And no day
Come to steal this night away,
    Till the rites of love are ended,
And the lusty bridegroom say,
    Welcome, light, of all befriended!

Pace out, you watery powers below,
      Let your feet,

> Like the galleys when they row,
>> Even beat:
> Let your unknown measures, set
>> To the still winds, tell to all,
> That gods are come, immortal, great,
>> To honor this great nuptial.

The Measure

SECOND SONG

> Hold back thy hours, dark Night, till we have done;
>> The Day will come too soon:
> Young maids will curse thee, if thou steal'st away,
> And leav'st their losses open to the day:
>> Stay, stay, and hide
>> The blushes of the bride.
>
> Stay, gentle Night, and with thy darkness cover
>> The kisses of her lover;
> Stay, and confound her tears and her shrill cryings,
> Her weak denials, vows, and often-dyings;
>> Stay, and hide all:
>> But help not, though she call.

Another Measure

NEPT. Great queen of us and heaven, hear what I bring
> To make this hour a full one.
CYNTH. Speak, sea's king.
NEPT. The tunes my Amphitrite joys to have,
> When she will dance upon the rising wave,
> And court me as she sails. My Tritons, play
> Music to lay a storm! I'll lead the way.

Measure
[*The Masquers dance which Neptune leads*]

THIRD SONG

> To bed, to bed! Come, Hymen, lead the bride,
> And lay her by her husband's side;
>> Bring in the virgins every one,
>> That grieve to lie alone;

That they may kiss while they may say, a maid;
To-morrow 'twill be other kissed and said.
    Hesperus, be long a-shining,
    Whilst these lovers are a-twining.

ÆOL. [*Within*] Ho, Neptune!
NEPT. Æolus!

Re-enter Æolus

ÆOL. The sea goes high,
  Boreas hath raised a storm: go and apply
  Thy trident; else, I prophesy, ere day
  Many a tall ship will be cast away.
  Descend with all the gods and all their power,
  To strike a calm.

                                   Exit

CYNTH. We thank you for this hour:
  My favor to you all. To gratulate
  So great a service, done at my desire,
  Ye shall have many floods, fuller and higher
  Than you have wished for; and no ebb shall dare
  To let the Day see where your dwellings are.
  Now back unto your governments in haste,
  Lest your proud charge should swell above the waste,
  And win upon the island.
NEPT. We obey.

                    Neptune descends and the Sea-gods

CYNTH. Hold up thy head, dead Night; see'st thou not Day?
  The east begins to lighten: I must down,
  And give my brother place.
NIGHT. O, I could frown
  To see the Day, the Day that flings his light
  Upon my kingdom and contemns old Night!
  Let him go on and flame! I hope to see
  Another wild-fire in his axle-tree,[1]

---

1. The first occurred when Phaeton failed to control the horses of the sun.

And all fall drenched. But I forget; speak, queen:
    The Day grows on; I must no more be seen.
CYNTH. Heave up thy drowsy head again, and see
    A greater light, a greater majesty,
    Between our sect and us! whip up thy team:
    The Day breaks here, and yon sun-flaring stream
    Shot from the south.[1] Which way wilt thou go? say.
NIGHT. I'll vanish into mists.
CYNTH. I into Day.

                                            Exeunt

Finis Masque

KING. Take lights there!—Ladies, get the bride to bed.—
    We will not see you laid; good night, Amintor;
    We'll ease you of that tedious ceremony:
    Were it my case, I should think time run slow.
    If thou be'st noble, youth, get me a boy,
    That may defend my kingdom from my foes.
AMIN. All happiness to you!
KING. Good night, Melantius.

                                            Exeunt

ACT II, SCENE I

Enter Evadne, Aspatia, Dula, and other Ladies

DULA. Madam, shall we undress you for this fight?
    The wars are naked that you must make to-night.
EVAD. You are very merry, Dula.
DULA. I should be
    Far merrier, madam, if it were with me
    As it is with you.
EVAD. How's that?
DULA. That I might go
    To bed with him wi' th' credit that you do.
EVAD. Why, how now, wench?
DULA. Come, ladies, will you help?

---

1. The text is doubtful.

EVAD. I am soon undone.

DULA. And as soon done:
  Good store of clothes will trouble you at both.

EVAD. Art thou drunk, Dula?

DULA. Why, here's none but we.

EVAD. Thou think'st belike there is no modesty
  When we're alone.

DULA. Ay, by my troth, you hit my thoughts aright.

EVAD. You prick me, lady.

1 LADY. 'Tis against my will.

DULA. Anon you must endure more and lie still;
  You're best to practise.

EVAD. Sure, this wench is mad.

DULA. No, faith, this is a trick that I have had
  Since I was fourteen.

EVAD. 'Tis high time to leave it.

DULA. Nay, now I'll keep it till the trick leave me.
  A dozen wanton words, put in your head,
  Will make you livelier in your husband's bed.

EVAD. Nay, faith, then take it.[1]

DULA. Take it, madam! where?
  We all, I hope, will take it that are here.

EVAD. Nay, then, I'll give you o'er.

DULA. So I will make
  The ablest man in Rhodes, or his heart ache.

EVAD. Wilt take my place to-night?

DULA. I'll hold your cards against any two I know.

EVAD. What wilt thou do?

DULA. Madam, we'll do't, and make 'em leave play too.

EVAD. Aspatia, take her part.

DULA. I will refuse it:
  She will pluck down a side;[2] she does not use it.

EVAD. Why, do, I prithee.

DULA. You will find the play
  Quickly, because your head lies well that way.

---

1. This passage is made up of a series of plays upon words connected with games of cards.
2. Lose the game.

EVAD. I thank thee, Dula. Would thou couldst instil
    Some of thy mirth into Aspatia!
    Nothing but sad thoughts in her breast do dwell:
    Methinks, a mean betwixt you would do well.
DULA. She is in love: hang me, if I were so,
    But I could run my country. I love too
    To do those things that people in love do.
ASP. It was a timeless[1] smile should prove my cheek;
    It were a fitter hour for me to laugh,
    When at the altar the religious priest
    Were pacifying the offended powers
    With sacrifice, than now. This should have been
    My rite; and all your hands have been employed
    In giving me a spotless offering
    To young Amintor's bed, as we are now
    For you. Pardon, Evadne: would my worth
    Were great as yours, or that the King, or he,
    Or both, thought so! Perhaps he found me worthless:
    But till he did so, in these ears of mine,
    These credulous ears, he poured the sweetest words
    That art or love could frame. If he were false,
    Pardon it, heaven! and, if I did want
    Virtue, you safely may forgive that too;
    For I have lost none that I had from you.
EVAD. Nay, leave this sad talk, madam.
ASP. Would I could!
    Then should I leave the cause.
EVAD. See, if you have not spoiled all Dula's mirth!
ASP. Thou think'st thy heart hard; but, if thou be'st caught,
    Remember me; thou shalt perceive a fire
    Shot suddenly into thee.
DULA. That's not so good; let 'em shoot anything but fire,
    I fear 'em not.
ASP. Well, wench, thou may'st be taken.
EVAD. Ladies, good night: I'll do the rest myself.
DULA. Nay, let your lord do some.

1. Untimely.

ASP. [*Singing*] Lay a garland on my hearse
    Of the dismal yew—
EVAD. That's one of your sad songs, madam.
ASP. Believe me, 'tis a very pretty one.
EVAD. How is it, madam?
ASP. [*Singing*]

> Lay a garland on my hearse
>   Of the dismal yew;
> Maidens, willow-branches bear;
>   Say I died true.
> My love was false, but I was firm
>   From my hour of birth:
> Upon my buried body lie
>   Lightly, gentle earth!

EVAD. Fie on't, madam! the words are so strange, they are able to make
    one dream of hobgoblins.—
    I could never have the power—sing that, Dula.
DULA. [*Singing*]

> I could never have the power
> To love one above an hour,
> But my heart would prompt mine eye
> On some other man to fly.
>   Venus, fix mine eyes fast,
>   Or, if not, give me all that I shall see at last!

EVAD. So, leave me now.
DULA. Nay, we must see you laid.
ASP. Madam, good night. May all the marriage-joys
    That longing maids imagine in their beds
    Prove so unto you! May no discontent
    Grow 'twixt your love and you! but, if there do,
    Inquire of me, and I will guide your moan;
    Teach you an artificial[1] way to grieve,
    To keep your sorrow waking. Love your lord
    No worse than I: but, if you love so well,

---

1. Artful.

Alas, you may displease him! so did I.
This is the last time you shall look on me.—
Ladies, farewell. As soon as I am dead,
Come all and watch one night about my hearse;
Bring each a mournful story and a tear,
To offer at it when I go to earth;
With flattering ivy clasp my coffin round;
Write on my brow my fortune; let my bier
Be borne by virgins, that shall sing by course[1]
The truth of maids and perjuries of men.
EVAD. Alas, I pity thee.

Exit Evadne

ALL. Madam, good night.
1 LADY. Come, we'll let in the bridegroom.
DULA. Where's my lord?

Enter Amintor

1 LADY. Here, take this light:
DULA. You'll find her in the dark.
1 LADY. Your lady's scarce a-bed yet; you must help her.
ASP. Go, and be happy in your lady's love.
May all the wrongs that you have done to me
Be utterly forgotten in my death!
I'll trouble you no more; yet I will take
A parting kiss, and will not be denied.—

[*Kisses Amintor*]

You'll come, my lord, and see the virgins weep
When I am laid in earth, though you yourself
Can know no pity. Thus I wind myself
Into this willow-garland,[2] and am prouder
That I was once your love, though now refused,
Than to have had another true to me.
So with my prayers I leave you, and must try
Some yet unpractised way to grieve and die.

Exit Aspatia

DULA. Come, ladies, will you go?

1. In turn.
2. Emblem of the deserted lover.

ALL. Good night, my lord.
AMIN. Much happiness unto you all!

Ladies exeunt

I did that lady wrong. Methinks, I feel
A grief shoot suddenly through all my veins;
Mine eyes rain: this is strange at such a time.
It was the King first moved me to't; but he
Has not my will in keeping. Why do I
Perplex myself thus? Something whispers me,
Go not to bed. My guilt is not so great
As mine own conscience too sensible[1]
Would make me think; I only brake a promise,
And 'twas the King that forced me. Timorous flesh,
Why shak'st thou so? Away, my idle fears!

Enter Evadne

Yonder she is, the luster of whose eye
Can blot away the sad remembrance
Of all these things.—O, my Evadne, spare
That tender body; let it not take cold!
The vapors of the night shall not fall here.
To bed, my love: Hymen will punish us
For being slack performers of his rites.
Camest thou to call me?
EVAD. No.
AMIN. Come, come, my love,
And let us lose ourselves to one another.
Why art thou up so long?
EVAD. I am not well.
AMIN. To bed then; let me wind thee in these arms
Till I have banished sickness.
EVAD. Good my lord,
I cannot sleep.
AMIN. Evadne, we will watch;[2]
I mean no sleeping.

---

1. Sensitive.
2. Stay awake.

EVAD. I'll not go to bed.

AMIN. I prithee, do.

EVAD. I will not for the world.

AMIN. Why, my dear love?

EVAD. Why! I have sworn I will not.

AMIN. Sworn!

EVAD. Ay,

AMIN. How? sworn, Evadne!

EVAD. Yes, sworn, Amintor; and will swear again,
    If you will wish to hear me.

AMIN. To whom have you sworn this?

EVAD. If I should name him, the matter were not great.

AMIN. Come, this is but the coyness of a bride.

EVAD. The coyness of a bride!

AMIN. How prettily
    That frown becomes thee!

EVAD. Do you like it so?

AMIN. Thou canst not dress thy face in such a look
    But I shall like it.

EVAD. What look likes you best?

AMIN. Why do you ask?

EVAD. That I may show you one less pleasing to you.

AMIN. How's that?

EVAD. That I may show you one less pleasing to you.

AMIN. I prithee, put thy jests in milder looks;
    It shows as thou wert angry.

EVAD. So perhaps
    I am indeed.

AMIN. Why, who has done thee wrong?
    Name me the man, and by thyself I swear,
    Thy yet-unconquered self, I will revenge thee!

EVAD. Now I shall try thy truth. If thou dost love me,
    Thou weigh'st not any thing compared with me:
    Life, honor, joys eternal, all delights
    This world can yield, or hopeful people feign,
    Or in the life to come, are light as air
    To a true lover when his lady frowns,
    And bids him *do this*. Wilt thou kill this man?

Swear, my Amintor, and I'll kiss the sin
Off from thy lips.

AMIN. I wo' not swear, sweet love,
Till I do know the cause.

EVAD. I would thou wouldst.
Why, it is thou that wrong'st me; I hate thee;
Thou should'st have killed thyself.

AMIN. If I should know that, I should quickly kill
The man you hated.

EVAD. Know it, then, and do't.

AMIN. O, no! what look soe'er thou shalt put on
To try my faith, I shall not think thee false;
I cannot find one blemish in thy face,
Where falsehood should abide. Leave, and to bed.
If you have sworn to any of the virgins
That were your old companions to preserve
Your maidenhead a night, it may be done
Without this means.

EVAD. A maidenhead, Amintor,
At my years!

AMIN. Sure she raves; this cannot be
Her natural temper.—Shall I call thy maids?
Either thy healthful sleep hath left thee long,
Or else some fever rages in thy blood.

EVAD. Neither, Amintor: think you I am mad,
Because I speak the truth?

AMIN. Is this the truth?
Will you not lie with me to-night?

EVAD. To-night!
You talk as if you thought I would hereafter.

AMIN. Hereafter! yes, I do.

EVAD. You are deceived.
Put off amazement, and with patience mark
What I shall utter, for the oracle
Knows nothing truer: 'tis not for a night
Or two that I forbear thy bed, but ever.

AMIN. I dream. Awake, Amintor!

EVAD. You hear right:

I sooner will find out the beds of snakes,
And with my youthful blood warm their cold flesh,
Letting them curl themselves about my limbs,
Than sleep one night with thee. This is not feigned,
Nor sounds it like the coyness of a bride.

AMIN. Is flesh so earthly to endure all this?
Are these the joys of marriage?—Hymen, keep
This story (that will make succeeding youth
Neglect thy ceremonies) from all ears;
Let it not rise up, for thy shame and mine
To after-ages: we will scorn thy laws,
If thou no better bless them. Touch the heart
Of her that thou hast sent me, or the world
Shall know this: not an altar then will smoke
In praise of thee; we will adopt us sons;
Then virtue shall inherit, and not blood.
If we do lust, we'll take the next we meet,
Serving ourselves as other creatures do;
And never take note of the female more,
Nor of her issue. I do rage in vain;
She can but jest.—O, pardon me, my love!
So dear the thoughts are that I hold of thee,
That I must break forth. Satisfy my fear;
It is a pain, beyond the hand of death,
To be in doubt: confirm it with an oath,
If this be true.

EVAD. Do you invent the form:
Let there be in it all the binding words
Devils and conjurers can put together,
And I will take it. I have sworn before,
And here by all things holy do again,
Never to be acquainted with thy bed!
Is your doubt over now?

AMIN. I know too much; would I had doubted still!
Was ever such a marriage-night as this!
You powers above, if you did ever mean
Man should be used thus, you have thought a way
How he may bear himself, and save his honor:

Instruct me in it; for to my dull eyes
There is no mean, no moderate course to run;
I must live scorned, or be a murderer:
Is there a third? Why is this night so calm?
Why does not heaven speak in thunder to us,
And drown her voice?

EVAD. This rage will do no good.

AMIN. Evadne, hear me. Thou hast ta'en an oath,
But such a rash one, that to keep it were
Worse than to swear it: call it back to thee;
Such vows as that never ascend the heaven;
A tear or two will wash it quite away.
Have mercy on my youth, my hopeful youth,
If thou be pitiful! for, without boast,
This land was proud of me: what lady was there,
That men called fair and virtuous in this isle,
That would have shunned my love? It is in thee
To make me hold this worth.—O, we vain men,
That trust out all our reputation
To rest upon the weak and yielding hand
Of feeble woman! But thou art not stone;
Thy flesh is soft, and in thine eyes doth dwell
The spirit of love; thy heart cannot be hard.
Come, lead me from the bottom of despair
To all the joys thou hast; I know thou wilt;
And make me careful lest the sudden change
O'ercome my spirits.

EVAD. When I call back this oath,
The pains of hell environ me!

AMIN. I sleep, and am too temperate. Come to bed!
Or by those hairs, which, if thou hadst a soul
Like to thy locks, were threads for kings to wear
About their arms—

EVAD. Why, so perhaps they are.

AMIN. I'll drag thee to my bed, and make thy tongue
Undo this wicked oath, or on thy flesh
I'll print a thousand wounds to let out life!

EVAD. I fear thee not: do what thou darest to me!

Every ill-sounding word or threatening look
Thou showest to me will be revenged at full.
AMIN. It will not sure, Evadne?
EVAD. Do not you hazard that.
AMIN. Ha' ye your champions?
EVAD. Alas, Amintor, think'st thou I forbear
To sleep with thee, because I have put on
A maiden's strictness? Look upon these cheeks,
And thou shalt find the hot and rising blood
Unapt for such a vow. No; in this heart
There dwells as much desire and as much will
To put that wished act in practise as ever yet
Was known to woman; and they have been shown
Both. But it was the folly of thy youth
To think this beauty, to what hand soe'er
It shall be called, shall stoop[1] to any second.
I do enjoy the best, and in that height
Have sworn to stand or die: you guess the man.
AMIN. No; let me know the man that wrongs me so,
That I may cut his body into motes,
And scatter it before the northern wind.
EVAD. You dare not strike him.
AMIN. Do not wrong me so:
Yes, if his body were a poisonous plant
That it were death to touch, I have a soul
Will throw me on him.
EVAD. Why, 'tis the King.
AMIN. The King!
EVAD. What will you do now?
AMIN. It is not the King!
EVAD. What did he make this match for, dull Amintor?
AMIN. O, thou hast named a word that wipes away
All thoughts revengeful! In that sacred name,
"The King," there lies a terror: what frail man
Dares lift his hand against it? Let the gods

---

1. As a hawk.

Speak to him when they please: till when, let us
Suffer and wait.

EVAD. Why should you fill yourself so full of heat,
And haste so to my bed? I am no virgin.

AMIN. What devil put it in thy fancy, then,
To marry me?

EVAD. Alas, I must have one
To father children, and to bear the name
Of husband to me, that my sin may be
More honorable!

AMIN. What strange thing am I!

EVAD. A miserable one; one that myself
Am sorry for.

AMIN. Why, show it then in this:
If thou hast pity, though thy love be none,
Kill me; and all true lovers, that shall live
In after ages crossed in their desires,
Shall bless thy memory, and call thee good,
Because such mercy in thy heart was found,
To rid[1] a lingering wretch.

EVAD. I must have one
To fill thy room again, if thou wert dead;
Else, by this night, I would! I pity thee.

AMIN. These strange and sudden injuries have fallen
So thick upon me, that I lose all sense
Of what they are. Methinks, I am not wronged;
Nor is it aught, if from the censuring world
I can but hide it. Reputation,
Thou art a word, no more!—But thou hast shown
An impudence so high, that to the world
I fear thou wilt betray or shame thyself.

EVAD. To cover shame, I took thee; never fear
That I would blaze[2] myself.

AMIN. Nor let the King

1. Be rid of.
2. Declare.

Know I conceive he wrongs me; then mine honor
Will thrust me into action: that my flesh
Could bear with patience. And it is some ease
To me in these extremes, that I knew this
Before I touched thee; else, had all the sins
Of mankind stood betwixt me and the King,
I had gone through 'em to his heart and thine.
I have left one desire: 'tis not his crown
Shall buy me to thy bed, now I resolve
He has dishonored thee. Give me thy hand:
Be careful of thy credit, and sin close;[1]
'Tis all I wish. Upon thy chamber-floor
I'll rest to-night, that morning visitors
May think we did as married people use:
And, prithee, smile upon me when they come,
And seem to toy, as if thou hadst been pleased
With what we did.

EVAD. Fear not; I will do this.

AMIN. Come, let us practise; and, as wantonly
As ever longing bride and bridegroom met,
Let's laugh and enter here.

EVAD. I am content.

AMIN. Down all the swellings of my troubled heart!
When we walk thus intwined, let all eyes see
If ever lovers better did agree.

Exeunt

SCENE II

Enter Aspatia, Antiphila, and Olympias

ASP. Away, you are not sad! force it no further.
Good gods, how well you look! Such a full color
Young bashful brides put on: sure, you are new married!

ANT. Yes, madam, to your grief.

ASP. Alas, poor wenches!
Go learn to love first; learn to lose yourselves;

---

1. Secretly.

Learn to be flattered, and believe and bless
The double tongue that did it; make a faith
Out of the miracles of ancient lovers,
Such as spake truth, and died in't; and, like me,
Believe all faithful, and be miserable.
Did you ne'er love yet, wenches? Speak, Olympias;
Thou hast an easy temper, fit for stamp.

OLYM. Never.

ASP. Nor you, Antiphila?

ANT. Nor I.

ASP. Then, my good girls, be more than women, wise;
At least be more than I was; and be sure
You credit any thing the light gives life to,
Before a man. Rather believe the sea
Weeps for the ruined merchant, when he roars;
Rather, the wind courts but the pregnant sails,
When the strong cordage cracks; rather, the sun
Comes but to kiss the fruit in wealthy autumn,
When all falls blasted. If you needs must love,
(Forced by ill fate,) take to your maiden-bosoms
Two dead-cold aspics,[1] and of them make lovers:
They cannot flatter nor forswear; one kiss
Makes a long peace for all. But man.—
O, that beast man! Come, let's be sad, my girls:
That down-cast of thine eyes, Olympias,
Shows a fine sorrow.—Mark, Antiphila;
Just such another was the nymph Œnone's,
When Paris brought home Helen.—Now, a tear;
And then thou art a piece expressing fully
The Carthage-queen,[2] when from a cold sea-rock,
Full with her sorrow, she tied fast her eyes
To the fair Trojan ships; and, having lost them,
Just as thine eyes do, down stole a tear.—Antiphila,
What would this wench do, if she were Aspatia?
Here she would stand, till some more pitying god

1. Asps.
2. Dido, deserted by Aeneas.

Turned her to marble.—'Tis enough, my wench.—
Show me the piece of needlework you wrought.

ANT. Of Ariadne,[1] madam?

ASP. Yes, that piece.—
This should be Theseus; h'as a cozening[2] face.—
You meant him for a man?

ANT. He was so, madam.

ASP. Why, then, 'tis well enough.—Never look back;
You have a full wind and a false heart, Theseus.—
Does not the story say, his keel was split,
Or his masts spent, or some kind rock or other
Met with his vessel?

ANT. Not as I remember.

ASP. It should ha' been so. Could the gods know this,
And not, of all their number, raise a storm?
But they are all as evil. This false smile
Was well expressed; just such another caught me.—
You shall not go so.[3]—
Antiphila, in this place work a quicksand,
And over it a shallow smiling water,
And his ship ploughing it; and then a Fear;
Do that Fear to the life, wench.

ANT. 'Twill wrong the story.

ASP. 'Twill make the story, wronged by wanton poets,
Live long and be believed. But where's the lady?

ANT. There, madam.

ASP. Fie, you have missed it here, Antiphila;
You are much mistaken, wench:
These colors are not dull and pale enough
To show a soul so full of misery
As this sad lady's was. Do it by me,
Do it again by me, the lost Aspatia;
And you shall find all true but the wild island.[4]

1. Deserted by Theseus.
2. Deceiving.
3. Addressing the embroidered image of Theseus.
4. Ariadne was abandoned on the island of Naxos.

Suppose I stand upon the sea-beach now,
Mine arms thus, and mine hair blown with the wind,
Wild as that desert; and let all about me
Tell that I am forsaken. Do my face
(If thou hadst ever feeling of a sorrow)
Thus, thus, Antiphila: strive to make me look
Like Sorrow's monument; and the trees about me,
Let them be dry and leafless; let the rocks
Groan with continual surges; and behind me,
Make all a desolation. See, see, wenches,
A miserable life of this poor picture!

OLYM. Dear madam!

ASP. I have done. Sit down; and let us
Upon that point fix all our eyes, that point there.
Make a dull silence, till you feel a sudden sadness
Give us new souls.

Enter Calianax

CAL. The King may do this, and he may not do it:
My child is wronged, disgraced.—Well, how now, huswives?
What, at your ease! is this a time to sit still?
Up, you young lazy whores, up, or I'll swinge you!

OLYM. Nay, good my lord—

CAL. You'll lie down shortly. Get you in, and work!
What, are you grown so resty[1] you want heats?
We shall have some of the court-boys heat you shortly.

ANT. My lord, we do no more than we are charged:
It is the lady's pleasure we be thus;
In grief she is forsaken.

CAL. There's a rogue too.
A young dissembling slave!—Well, get you in.—
I'll have a bout with that boy. 'Tis high time
Now to be valiant: I confess my youth
Was never prone that way. What, made an ass!
A court-stale![2] Well, I will be valiant,

1. Indolent, idle.
2. A laughing-stock.

And beat some dozen of these whelps; I will!
And there's another of 'em, a trim cheating soldier,[1]
I'll maul that rascal; h'as out-braved me twice:
But now, I thank the gods, I am valiant.—
Go, get you in.—I'll take a course with all.

Exeunt omnes

ACT III, SCENE I

Enter Cleon, Strato, and Diphilus

CLE. Your sister is not up yet.

DIPH. O, brides must take their morning's rest; the night is troublesome.

STRA. But not tedious.

DIPH. What odds, he has not my sister's maidenhead tonight?

STRA. None; it's odds against any bridegroom living, he ne'er gets it while he lives.

DIPH. Y'are merry with my sister; you'll please to allow me the same freedom with your mother.

STRA. She's at your service.

DIPH. Then she's merry enough of herself; she needs no tickling. Knock at the door.

STRA. We shall interrupt them.

DIPH. No matter; they have the year before them.—Good morrow, sister. Spare yourself to-day; the night will come again.

Enter Amintor

AMIN. Who's there? my brother! I'm no readier yet.
Your sister is but now up.

DIPH. You look as you had lost your eyes to-night: I think you ha' not slept.

AMIN. I'faith I have not.

DIPH. You have done better, then.

AMIN. We ventured for a boy; when he is twelve,
'A shall command against the foes of Rhodes.
Shall we be merry?

---

1. Melantius.

STRA. You cannot; you want sleep.

AMIN. 'Tis true;—[*Aside*] but she,
  As if she had drunk Lethe, or had made
  Even with heaven, did fetch so still a sleep,
  So sweet and sound—

DIPH. What's that?

AMIN. Your sister frets
  This morning, and does turn her eyes upon me,
  As people on their headsman. She does chafe,
  And kiss, and chafe again, and clap my cheeks!
  She's in another world.

DIPH. Then I had lost: I was about to lay
  You had not got her maidenhead to-night.

AMIN. [*Aside*] Ha! does he not mock me?—Y'ad lost indeed;
  I do not use to bungle.

CLE. You do deserve her.

AMIN. [*Aside*] I laid my lips to hers, and that wild breath,
  That was so rude and rough to me last night,
  Was sweet as April. I'll be guilty too,
  If these be the effects.—

Enter Melantius

MEL. Good day, Amintor; for to me the name
  Of brother is too distant: we are friends,
  And that is nearer.

AMIN. Dear Melantius!
  Let me behold thee.—Is it possible?

MEL. What sudden gaze is this?

AMIN. 'Tis wondrous strange!

MEL. Why does thine eye desire so strict a view
  Of that it knows so well? There's nothing here
  That is not thine.

AMIN. I wonder much, Melantius,
  To see those noble looks, that make me think
  How virtuous thou art: and, on the sudden,
  'Tis strange to me thou shouldst have worth and honor;
  Or not be base, and false, and treacherous,
  And every ill. But—

MEL. Stay, stay, my friend;
  I fear this sound will not become our loves:
  No more; embrace me.
AMIN. O, mistake me not!
  I know thee to be full of all those deeds
  That we frail men call good; but by the course
  Of nature thou shouldst be as quickly changed
  As are the winds; dissembling as the sea,
  That now wears brows as smooth as virgins' be,
  Tempting the merchant to invade his face,
  And in an hour calls his billows up,
  And shoots 'em at the sun, destroying all
  'A carries on him.—[*Aside*] O, how near am I
  To utter my sick thoughts!—
MEL. But why, my friend, should I be so by nature?
AMIN. I have wed thy sister, who hath virtuous thoughts
  Enough for one whole family; and it is strange
  That you should feel no want.
MEL. Believe me, this is compliment too cunning for me.
DIPH. What should I be then by the course of nature,
  They having both robbed me of so much virtue?
STRA. O, call the bride, my lord Amintor,
  That we may see her blush, and turn her eyes down:
  It is the prettiest sport!
AMIN. Evadne!
EVAD. [*Within*] My lord?
AMIN. Come forth, my love:
  Your brothers do attend to wish you joy.
EVAD. I am not ready yet.
AMIN. Enough, enough.
EVAD. They'll mock me.
AMIN. Faith, thou shalt come in

Enter Evadne

MEL. Good morrow, sister. He that understands
  Whom you have wed, need not to wish you joy;
  You have enough: take heed you be not proud.
DIPH. O, sister, what have you done?

EVAD. I done! why, what have I done?

STRA. My lord Amintor swears you are no maid now.

EVAD. Pish!

STRA. I'faith, he does.

EVAD. I knew I should be mocked.

DIPH. With a truth.

EVAD. If 'twere to do again, in faith I would not marry.

AMIN. [*Aside*] Nor I, by heaven!—

DIPH. Sister, Dula swears she heard you cry two rooms off.

EVAD. Fie, how you talk!

DIPH. Let's see you walk, Evadne. By my troth y'are spoiled.

MEL. Amintor—

AMIN. Ha!

MEL. Thou art sad.

AMIN. Who, I? I thank you for that.
    Shall Diphilus, thou, and I, sing a catch?

MEL. How!

AMIN. Prithee, let's.

MEL. Nay, that's too much the other way.

AMIN. I'm so lightened with my happiness!—
    How dost thou, love? kiss me.

EVAD. I cannot love you, you tell tales of me.

AMIN. Nothing but what becomes us.—Gentlemen,
    Would you had all such wives, and all the world,
    That I might be no wonder! Y'are all sad:
    What, do you envy me? I walk, methinks,
    On water, and ne'er sink, I am so light.

MEL. 'Tis well you are so.

AMIN. Well! how can I be other, when she looks thus?
    Is there no music there? Let's dance.

MEL. Why, this is strange, Amintor!

AMIN. I do not know myself; yet I could wish
    My joy were less.

DIPH. I'll marry too, if it will make one thus.

EVAD. [*Aside*] Amintor, hark.

AMIN. What says my love? I must obey.—

EVAD. You do it scurvily, 'twill be perceived.

CLE. My lord, the King is here.

Enter King and Lysippus

AMIN. Where?

STRA. And his brother.

KING. Good morrow, all!—

    Amintor, joy on joy fall thick upon thee!—

    And, madam, you are altered since I saw you;

    (I must salute you) you are now another's.

    How liked you your night's rest?

EVAD. Ill, sir.

AMIN. Indeed she took but little.

LYS. You'll let her take more, and thank her too, shortly.

KING. Amintor, wert thou truly honest till thou wert married?

AMIN. Yes, sir.

KING. Tell me, then, how shows the sport unto thee?

AMIN. Why, well.

KING. What did you do?

AMIN. No more, nor less, than other couples use;

    You know what 'tis; it has but a coarse name.

KING. But prithee, I should think, by her black eye,

    And her red cheek, she would be quick[1] and stirring

    In this same business; ha?

AMIN. I cannot tell;

    I ne'er tried other, sir; but I perceive

    She is as quick as you delivered.

KING. Well, you'll trust me then, Amintor,

    To choose a wife for you again?

AMIN. No, never, sir.

KING. Why, like you this so ill?

AMIN. So well I like her.

    For this I bow my knee in thanks to you,

    And unto heaven will pay my grateful tribute

    Hourly; and do hope we shall draw out

    A long contented life together here,

    And die, both, full of grey hairs, in one day:

    For which the thanks is yours. But if the powers

    That rule us please to call her first away,

1. Lively.

Without pride spoke, this world holds not a wife
Worthy to take her room.

KING. [*Aside*] I do not like this.
All forbear the room, but you, Amintor,
And your lady. [*Exeunt all but the King, Amintor, and Evadne*]
I have some speech with you,
That may concern your after living well.

AMIN. [*Aside*] 'A will not tell me that he lies with her?
If he do, something heavenly stay my heart,
For I shall be apt to thrust this arm of mine
To acts unlawful!—

KING. You will suffer me
To talk with her, Amintor, and not have
A jealous pang?

AMIN. Sir, I dare trust my wife
With whom she dares to talk, and not be jealous.

Retires

KING. How do you like Amintor?

EVAD. As I did, sir.

KING. How's that?

EVAD. As one that, to fulfil your will and pleasure,
I have given leave to call me wife and love.

KING. I see there is no lasting faith in sin;
They that break word with heaven will break again
With all the world, and so dost thou with me.

EVAD. How, sir?

KING. This subtle woman's ignorance
Will not excuse you: thou hast taken oaths,
So great, methought they did not well become
A woman's mouth, that thou wouldst ne'er enjoy
A man but me.

EVAD. I never did swear so;
You do me wrong.

KING. Day and night have heard it.

EVAD. I swore indeed that I would never love
A man of lower place; but, if your fortune
Should throw you from this height, I bade you trust
I would forsake you, and would bend to him

That won your throne: I love with my ambition,
Not with my eyes. But, if I ever yet
Touched any other, leprosy light here
Upon my face! which for your royalty
I would not stain!

KING. Why, thou dissemblest, and it is in me
To punish thee.

EVAD. Why, it is in me, then,
Not to love you, which will more afflict
Your body than your punishment can mine.

KING. But thou hast let Amintor lie with thee.

EVAD. I ha' not.

KING. Impudence! he says himself so.

EVAD. 'A lies.

KING. 'A does not.

EVAD. By this light, he does,
Strangely and basely! and I'll prove it so:
I did not only shun him for a night,
But told him I would never close with him.

KING. Speak lower; 'tis false.

EVAD. I am no man
To answer with a blow; or, if I were,
You are the King. But urge me not; 'tis most true.

KING. Do not I know the uncontrollèd thoughts
That youth brings with him, when his blood is high
With expectation and desire of that
He long hath waited for? Is not his spirit,
Though he be temperate, of a valiant strain
As this our age hath known? What could he do,
If such a sudden speech had met his blood,
But ruin thee for ever, if he had not killed thee?
He could not bear it thus: he is as we,
Or any other wronged man.

EVAD. It is dissembling.

KING. Take him! farewell: henceforth I am thy foe;
And what disgraces I can blot thee with look for.

EVAD. Stay, sir!—Amintor!—You shall hear.—Amintor!

AMIN. What, my love?

EVAD. Amintor, thou hast an ingenious[1] look,
　　And shouldst be virtuous: it amazeth me
　　That thou canst make such base malicious lies!
AMIN. What, my dear wife?
EVAD. "Dear wife!" I do despise thee
　　Why, nothing can be baser than to sow
　　Dissension amongst lovers.
AMIN. Lovers! who?
EVAD. The King and me—
AMIN. O, God!
EVAD. Who should live long, and love without distaste,
　　Were it not for such pickthanks[2] as thyself.
　　Did you lie with me? swear now, and be punished
　　In hell for this!
AMIN. The faithless sin I made
　　To fair Aspatia is not yet revenged;
　　It follows me.—I will not lose a word
　　To this vile woman: but to you, my King,
　　The anguish of my soul thrusts out this truth,
　　Y' are a tyrant! and not so much to wrong
　　An honest man thus, as to take a pride
　　In talking with him of it.
EVAD. Now, sir, see
　　How loud this fellow lied!
AMIN. You that can know to wrong, should know how men
　　Must right themselves. What punishment is due
　　From me to him that shall abuse my bed?
　　Is it not death? nor can that satisfy,
　　Unless I show how nobly I have freed myself.
KING. Draw not thy sword; thou knowest I cannot fear
　　A subject's hand; but thou shalt feel the weight
　　Of this, if thou dost rage.
AMIN. The weight of that!
　　If you have any worth, for heaven's sake, think
　　I fear not swords; for, as you are mere man,

1. Ingenuous.
2. Flatterers.

I dare as easily kill you for this deed,
As you dare think to do it. But there is
Divinity about you, that strikes dead
My rising passions: as you are my king,
I fall before you, and present my sword
To cut mine own flesh, if it be your will.
Alas, I am nothing but a multitude
Of walking griefs! Yet, should I murder you,
I might before the world take the excuse
Of madness: for, compare my injuries,
And they will well appear too sad a weight
For reason to endure: but, fall I first
Amongst my sorrows, ere my treacherous hand
Touch holy things! But why (I know not what
I have to say), why did you choose out me
To make thus wretched? there were thousands, fools
Easy to work on, and of state enough,
Within the island.

EVAD. I would not have a fool;
It were no credit for me.

AMIN. Worse and worse!
Thou, that darest talk unto thy husband thus,
Profess thyself a whore, and, more than so,
Resolve to be so still!—It is my fate
To bear and bow beneath a thousand griefs,
To keep that little credit with the world.—
But there were wise ones too; you might have ta'en
Another.

KING. No: for I believed thee honest,
As thou wert valiant.

AMIN. All the happiness
Bestowed upon me turns into disgrace.
Gods, take your honesty again, for I
Am loaden with it!—Good my lord the King,
Be private in it.

KING. Thou mayst live, Amintor,
Free as thy king, if thou wilt wink at this,
And be a means that we may meet in secret.

AMIN. A bawd! Hold, hold, my breast! A bitter curse
    Seize me, if I forget not all respects
    That are religious, on another word
    Sounded like that; and through a sea of sins
    Will wade to my revenge, though I should call
    Pains here and after life upon my soul!
KING. Well, I am resolute you lay not with her;
    And so I leave you.

                                 Exit King

EVAD. You must needs be prating;
    And see what follows!
AMIN. Prithee, vex me not:
    Leave me; I am afraid some sudden start
    Will pull a murder on me.
EVAD. I am gone;
    I love my life well.

                                 Exit Evadne

AMIN. I hate mine as much.
    This 'tis to break a troth! I should be glad,
    If all this tide of grief would make me mad.

                                    Exit

SCENE II

Enter Melantius

MEL. I'll know the cause of all Amintor's griefs,
    Or friendship shall be idle.

Enter Calianax

CAL. O Melantius,
    My daughter will die.
MEL. Trust me, I am sorry:
    Would thou hadst ta'en her room![1]
CAL. Thou art a slave,
    A cut-throat slave, a bloody treacherous slave!

1. Place.

MEL. Take heed, old man; thou wilt be heard to rave,
   And lose thine offices.
CAL. I am valiant grown
   At all these years, and thou art but a slave!
MEL. Leave!
   Some company will come, and I respect
   Thy years, not thee, so much, that I could wish
   To laugh at thee alone.
CAL. I'll spoil your mirth:
   I mean to fight with thee. There lie, my cloak.
   This was my father's sword, and he durst fight.
   Are you prepared?
MEL. Why wilt thou dote thyself
   Out of thy life? Hence, get thee to bed;
   Have careful looking-to, and eat warm things,
   And trouble not me: my head is full of thoughts
   More weighty than thy life or death can be.
CAL. You have a name in war, where you stand safe
   Amongst a multitude; but I will try
   What you dare do unto a weak old man
   In single fight. You'll give ground, I fear.
   Come draw.
MEL. I will not draw, unless thou pull'st thy death
   Upon thee with a stroke. There's no one blow,
   That thou canst give hath strength enough to kill me.
   Tempt me not so far, then: the power of earth
   Shall not redeem thee.—
CAL. [*Aside*] I must let him alone;
   He's stout and able; and, to say the truth,
   However I may set a face and talk,
   I am not valiant. When I was a youth,
   I kept my credit with a testy trick[1]
   I had 'mongst cowards, but durst never fight.—
MEL. I will not promise to preserve your life,
   If you do stay.—

1. Trick of testiness.

CAL. [*Aside*] I would give half my land
    That I durst fight with that proud man a little:
    If I had men to hold him, I would beat him
    Till he asked me mercy.—
MEL. Sir, will you be gone?—
CAL. [*Aside*] I dare not stay; but I will go home, and beat
    My servants all over for this.

                                                          Exit

MEL. This old fellow haunts me.
    But the distracted carriage of mine Amintor
    Takes deeply on me. I will find the cause:
    I fear his conscience cries, he wronged Aspatia.

                      Enter Amintor

AMIN. [*Aside*] Men's eyes are not so subtle to perceive
    My inward misery: I bear my grief
    Hid from the world. How art thou wretched then?
    For aught I know, all husbands are like me;
    And every one I talk with of his wife
    Is but a well dissembler of his woes,
    As I am. Would I knew it! for the rareness
    Afflicts me now.
MEL. Amintor, we have not enjoyed our friendship of late; for we
    were wont to change our souls in talk.
AMIN. Melantius, I can tell thee a good jest of Strato and a lady the last
    day.
MEL. How was't?
AMIN. Why, such an odd one!
MEL. I have longed to speak with you; not of an idle jest, that's forced,
    but of matter you are bound to utter to me.
AMIN. What is that, my friend?
MEL. I have observed your words fall from your tongue
    Wildly; and all your carriage
    Like one that strove to show his merry mood,
    When he were ill-disposed: you were not wont
    To put such scorn into your speech, or wear
    Upon your face ridiculous jollity.

Some sadness sits here, which your cunning would
Cover o'er with smiles, and 'twill not be. What is it?
AMIN. A sadness here, Melantius! what cause
Can fate provide for me to make me so?
Am I not loved through all this isle? The King
Rains greatness on me. Have I not received
A lady to my bed, that in her eye
Keeps mounting fire, and on her tender cheeks
Inevitable color, in her heart
A prison for all virtue? Are not you,
Which is above all joys, my constant friend?
What sadness can I have? No; I am light,
And feel the courses of my blood more warm
And stirring than they were. Faith, marry too;
And you will feel so unexpressed a joy
In chaste embraces, that you will indeed
Appear another.
MEL. You may shape, Amintor,
Causes to cozen the whole world withal,
And yourself too; but 'tis not like a friend
To hide your soul from me. 'Tis not your nature
To be thus idle: I have seen you stand
As you were blasted 'midst of all your mirth;
Call thrice aloud, and then start, feigning joy
So coldly!—World, what do I here? a friend
Is nothing. Heaven, I would ha' told that man
My secret sins! I'll search an unknown land,
And there plant friendship; all is withered here.
Come with a compliment! I would have fought,
Or told my friend 'a lied, ere soothed[1] him so.
Out of my bosom!
AMIN. But there is nothing.
MEL. Worse and worse! farewell:
From this time have acquaintance, but no friend.
AMIN. Melantius, stay: you shall know what that is.

---

1. Deceived.

MEL. See, how you played with friendship! be advised
How you give cause unto yourself to say
You ha' lost a friend.

AMIN. Forgive what I ha' done;
For I am so o'ergone with injuries
Unheard of, that I lose consideration
Of what I ought to do,—O!—O!

MEL. Do not weep. What is't?
May I once but know the man
Hath turned my friend thus!

AMIN. I had spoke at first,
But that—

MEL. But what?

AMIN. I held it most unfit
For you to know. Faith, do not know it yet.

MEL. Thou see'st my love, that will keep company
With thee in tears; hide nothing, then, from me;
For when I know the cause of thy distemper,
With mine old armor I'll adorn myself,
My resolution, and cut through thy foes,
Unto thy quiet, till I place thy heart
As peaceable as spotless innocence.
What is it?

AMIN. Why, 'tis this—it is too big
To get out—let my tears make way awhile.

MEL. Punish me strangely, heaven, if he scape
Of life or fame, that brought this youth to this!

AMIN. Your sister—

MEL. Well said.

AMIN. You'll wish't unknown, when you have heard it.

MEL. No.

AMIN. Is much to blame,
And to the King has given her honor up,
And lives in whoredom with him.

MEL. How is this?
Thou art run mad with injury indeed;
Thou couldst not utter this else. Speak again;
For I forgive it freely; tell thy griefs.

AMIN. She's wanton: I am loath to say, a whore,
    Though it be true.
MEL. Speak yet again, before mine anger grow
    Up beyond throwing down: what are thy griefs?
AMIN. By all our friendship, these.
MEL. What, am I tame?
    After mine actions, shall the name of friend
    Blot all our family, and strike the brand
    Of whore upon my sister, unrevenged?
    My shaking flesh, be thou a witness for me,
    With what unwillingness I go to scourge
    This railer, whom my folly hath called friend!—
    I will not take thee basely: thy sword

                           [*Draws his sword*]

    Hangs near thy hand; draw it, that I may whip
    Thy rashness to repentance; draw thy sword!
AMIN. Not on thee, did thine anger swell as high
    As the wild surges. Thou shouldst do me ease
    Here and eternally, if thy noble hand
    Would cut me from my sorrows.
MEL. This is base
    And fearful. They that use to utter lies
    Provide not blows but words to qualify[1]
    The men they wronged. Thou hast a guilty cause.
AMIN. Thou pleasest me; for so much more like this
    Will raise my anger up above my griefs,
    (Which is a passion easier to be borne,)
    And I shall then be happy.
MEL. Take, then, more
    To raise thine anger: 'tis mere cowardice
    Makes thee not draw; and I will leave thee dead,
    However. But if thou art so much pressed
    With guilt and fear as not to dare to fight,
    I'll make thy memory loathed, and fix a scandal
    Upon thy name for ever.
AMIN. [*Drawing his sword*] Then I draw,

---

1. Mollify.

As justly as our magistrates their swords
To cut offenders off. I knew before
'Twould grate your ears; but it was base in you
To urge a weighty secret from your friend,
And then rage at it. I shall be at ease,
If I be killed; and, if you fall by me,
I shall not long outlive you.

MEL. Stay awhile.—
The name of friend is more than family,
Or all the world besides: I was a fool.
Thou searching human nature, that didst wake
To do me wrong, thou art inquisitive,
And thrust'st me upon questions that will take
My sleep away! Would I had died, ere known
This sad dishonor!—Pardon me, my friend.

[*Sheathes his sword*]

If thou wilt strike, here is a faithful heart;
Pierce it, for I will never heave my hand
To thine. Behold the power thou hast in me!
I do believe my sister is a whore,
A leprous one. Put up thy sword, young man.

AMIN. How should I bear it, then, she being so?
I fear, my friend, that you will lose me shortly;

[*Sheathes his sword*]

And I shall do a foul act on myself
Through these disgraces.

MEL. Better half the land
Were buried quick[1] together. No, Amintor;
Thou shalt have ease. O, this adulterous king,
That drew her to't; where got he the spirit
To wrong me so?

AMIN. What is it, then, to me,
If it be wrong to you?

MEL. Why, not so much:
The credit of our house is thrown away.
But from his iron den I'll waken Death,

---

1. Alive.

And hurl him on this king: my honesty
Shall steel my sword; and on its horrid point
I'll wear my cause, that shall amaze the eyes
Of this proud man, and be too glittering
For him to look on.

AMIN. I have quite undone my fame.

MEL. Dry up thy watery eyes,
And cast a manly look upon my face;
For nothing is so wild as I thy friend
Till I have freed thee: still this swelling breast.
I go thus from thee, and will never cease
My vengeance till I find thy heart at peace.

AMIN. It must not be so. Stay. Mine eyes would tell
How loath I am to this; but, love and tears,
Leave me awhile! for I have hazarded
All that this world calls happy.—Thou hast wrought
A secret from me, under name of friend,
Which art could ne'er have found, nor torture wrung
From out my bosom. Give it me again;
For I will find it, wheresoe'er it lies,
Hid in the mortal'st part: invent a way
To give it back.

MEL. Why would you have it back?
I will to death pursue him with revenge.

AMIN. Therefore I call it back from thee; for I know
Thy blood so high, that thou wilt stir in this,
And shame me to posterity. Take to thy weapon.

                                                [*Draws*]

MEL. Hear thy friend, that bears more years than thou.

AMIN. I will not hear: but draw, or I—

MEL. Amintor!

AMIN. Draw, then; for I am full as resolute
As fame and honor can enforce me be:
I cannot linger. Draw!

MEL. I do. [*Draws*] But is not
My share of credit equal with thine,
If I do stir?

AMIN. No; for it will be called

Honor in thee to spill thy sister's blood,
If she her birth abuse, and on the King
A brave revenge; but on me, that have walked
With patience in it, it will fix the name
Of fearful cuckold. O, that word! Be quick.

MEL. Then, join with me.

AMIN. I dare not do a sin, or else I would.
Be speedy.

MET. Then, dare not fight with me; for that's a sin.—
His grief distracts him.—Call thy thoughts again,
And to thy self pronounce the name of friend,
And see what that will work. I will not fight.

AMIN. You must.

MEL. [*Sheathing*] I will be killed first. Though my passions
Offered the like to you, 'tis not this earth
Shall buy my reason to it. Think awhile,
For you are (I must weep when I speak that)
Almost beside yourself.

AMIN. [*Sheathing*] O, my soft temper!
So many sweet words from thy sister's mouth,
I am afraid would make me take her to
Embrace, and pardon her. I am mad indeed,
And know not what I do. Yet have a care
Of me in what thou dost.

MEL. Why, thinks my friend
I will forget his honor? or, to save
The bravery of our house, will lose his fame,
And fear to touch the throne of majesty?

AMIN. A curse will follow that; but rather live
And suffer with me.

MEL. I will do what worth
Shall bid me, and no more.

AMIN. Faith, I am sick,
And desperately, I hope; yet, leaning thus,
I feel a kind of ease.

MEL. Come, take again
Your mirth about you.

AMIN. I shall never do't.

MEL. I warrant you; look up; we'll walk together;
    Put thine arm here; all shall be well again.
AMIN. Thy love (O, wretched!) ay, thy love, Melantius;
    Why, I have nothing else.
MEL. Be merry, then.

Exeunt

Enter Melantius again

MEL. This worthy young man may do violence
    Upon himself; but I have cherished him
    To my best power, and sent him smiling from me,
    To counterfeit again. Sword, hold thine edge;
    My heart will never fail me.—

Enter Diphilus

Diphilus!
Thou com'st as sent.
DIPH. Yonder has been such laughing.
MEL. Betwixt whom?
DIPH. Why, our sister and the King;
    I thought their spleens would break; they laughed us all
    Out of the room.
MEL. They must weep, Diphilus.
DIPH. Must they?
MEL. They must.
    Thou art my brother; and, if I did believe
    Thou hadst a base thought, I would rip it out,
    Lie where it durst.
DIPH. You should not; I would first
    Mangle myself and find it.
MEL. That was spoke
    According to our strain. Come, join thy hands,
    And swear a firmness to what project I
    Shall lay before thee.
DIPH. You do wrong us both;
    People hereafter shall not say, there passed
    A bond, more than our loves, to tie our lives
    And deaths together.

MEL. It is as nobly said as I would wish.
    Anon I'll tell you wonders: we are wronged.
DIPH. But I will tell you now, we'll right ourselves.
MEL. Stay not: prepare the armor in my house;
    And what friends you can draw unto our side,
    Not knowing of the cause, make ready too.
    Haste, Diphilus, the time requires it, haste!

Exit Diphilus

    I hope my cause is just; I know my blood
    Tells me it is; and I will credit it.
    To take revenge, and lose myself withal,
    Were idle; and to scape impossible,
    Without I had the fort, which (misery!)
    Remaining in the hands of my old enemy
    Calianax—but I must have it. See,

Enter Calianax

    Where he comes shaking by me!—Good my lord,
    Forget your spleen to me; I never wronged you,
    But would have peace with every man.
CAL. 'Tis well;
    If I durst fight, your tongue would lie at quiet.
MEL. Y'are touchy without all cause.
CAL. Do, mock me.
MEL. By mine honor, I speak truth.
CAL. Honor! where is't?
MEL. See, what starts you make
    Into your idle hatred to my love
    And freedom to you.
    I come with resolution to obtain
    A suit of you.
CAL. A suit of me!
    'Tis very like it should be granted, sir.
MEL. Nay, go not hence:
    'Tis this; you have the keeping of the fort,
    And I would wish you, by the love you ought
    To bear unto me, to deliver it
    Into my hands.

CAL. I am in hope thou art mad to talk to me thus.

MEL. But there is a reason to move you to it:
I would kill the King, that wronged you and your daughter.

CAL. Out, traitor!

MEL. Nay, but stay: I cannot scape,
The deed once done, without I have this fort.

CAL. And should I help thee?
Now thy treacherous mind betrays itself.

MEL. Come, delay me not;
Give me a sudden answer, or already
Thy last is spoke! refuse not offered love,
When it comes clad in secrets.

CAL. [*Aside*] If I say
I will not, he will kill me; I do see't
Writ in his looks; and should I say I will,
He'll run and tell the King.—I do not shun
Your friendship, dear Melantius; but this cause
Is weighty: give me but an hour to think.

MEL. Take it.—[*Aside*] I know this goes unto the King,
But I am armed.—

Exit Melantius

CAL. Methinks I feel myself
But twenty now again. This fighting fool
Wants policy: I shall revenge my girl,
And make her red again. I pray my legs
Will last that pace that I will carry them:
I shall want breath before I find the King.

Exit

ACT IV, SCENE I

Enter Melantius, Evadne, and Ladies

MEL. Save you!

EVAD. Save you, sweet brother!

MEL. In my blunt eye, methinks, you look, Evadne—

EVAD. Come, you would make me blush.

MEL. I would, Evadne;
I shall displease my ends else.

EVAD. You shall, if you command me; I am bashful.
    Come, sir, how do I look?

MEL. I would not have your women hear me
    Break into commendation of you; 'tis not seemly.

EVAD. Go wait me in the gallery.—

                             Exeunt Ladies

    Now speak.

MEL. I'll lock your doors first.

EVAD. Why?

MEL. I will not have your gilded things, that dance
    In visitation with their Milan skins,[1]
    Choke up my business.

EVAD. You are strangely disposed, sir.

MEL. Good madam, not to make you merry.

EVAD. No; if you praise me, 'twill make me sad.

MEL. Such a sad commendation I have for you.

EVAD. Brother, the court hath made you witty,
    And learn to riddle.

MEL. I praise the court for't: has it learned you nothing?

EVAD. Me!

MEL. Ay, Evadne; thou art young and handsome,
    A lady of a sweet complexion,
    And such a flowing carriage,[2] that it cannot
    Choose but inflame a kingdom.

EVAD. Gentle brother!

MEL. 'Tis yet in thy repentance, foolish woman,
    To make me gentle.

EVAD. How is this?

MEL. 'Tis base;
    And I could blush, at these years, thorough all
    My honored scars, to come to such a parley.

EVAD. I understand ye not.

MEL. Ye dare not, fool!
    They that commit thy faults fly the remembrance.

EVAD. My faults, sir! I would have you know, I care not
    If they were written here, here in my forehead.

---

1. Fine gloves made in Milan.
2. Graceful bearing.

MEL. Thy body is too little for the story,
 The lusts of which would fill another woman,
 Though she had twins within her.
EVAD. This is saucy:
 Look you intrude no more; there lies your way.
MEL. Thou art my way, and I will tread upon thee,
 Till I find truth out.
EVAD. What truth is that you look for?
MEL. Thy long-lost honor. Would the gods had set me
 Rather to grapple with the plague, or stand
 One of their loudest bolts! Come, tell me quickly,
 Do it without enforcement, and take heed
 You swell me not above my temper.
EVAD. How, sir!
 Where got you this report?
MEL. Where there was people,
 In every place.
EVAD. They and the seconds of it are base people:
 Believe them not, they lied.
MEL. Do not play with mine anger, do not, wretch!
 I come to know that desperate fool that drew thee
 From thy fair life: be wise, and lay him open.
EVAD. Unhand me, and learn manners! such another
 Forgetfulness forfeits your life.
MEL. Quench me this mighty humor, and then tell me
 Whose whore you are; for you are one, I know it.
 Let all mine honors perish but I'll find him,
 Though he lie locked up in thy blood! Be sudden;
 There is no facing it; and be not flattered;
 The burnt air, when the Dog reigns,[1] is not fouler
 Than thy contagious name, till thy repentance
 (If the gods grant thee any) purge thy sickness.
EVAD. Begone! you are my brother; that's your safety.
MEL. I'll be a wolf first: 'tis, to be thy brother,
 An infamy below the sin of coward.
 I am as far from being part of thee

---

1. The dog-star, Sirius.

    As thou art from thy virtue: seek a kindred
    'Mongst sensual beasts, and make a goat thy brother;
    A goat is cooler. Will you tell me yet?

EVAD. If you stay here and rail thus, I shall tell you
    I'll ha' you whipped. Get you to your command,
    And there preach to your sentinels, and tell them
    What a brave man you are: I shall laugh at you.

MEL. Y'are grown a glorious whore! Where be your fighters?
    What mortal fool durst raise thee to this daring,
    And I alive! By my just sword, h'ad safer
    Bestrid a billow when the angry north
    Ploughs up the sea, or made heaven's fire his foe!
    Work me no higher. Will you discover yet?

EVAD. The fellow's mad. Sleep, and speak sense.

MEL. Force my swoln heart no further: I would save thee.
    Your great maintainers are not here, they dare not:
    Would they were all, and armed! I would speak loud;
    Here's one should thunder to 'em! Will you tell me?—
    Thou hast no hope to scape: he that dares most,
    And damns away his soul to do thee service,
    Will sooner snatch meat from a hungry lion
    Than come to rescue thee; thou hast death about thee;—
    He has undone thine honor, poisoned thy virtue,
    And, of a lovely rose, left thee a canker.

EVAD. Let me consider.

MEL. Do, whose child thou wert,
    Whose honor thou hast murdered, whose grave opened
    And so pulled on the gods, that in their justice
    They must restore him flesh again and life,
    And raise his dry bones to revenge this scandal.

EVAD. The gods are not of my mind; they had better
    Let 'em lie sweet still in the earth; they'll stink here.

MEL. Do you raise mirth out of my easiness?
    Forsake me, then, all weaknesses of nature,

                     [Draws his sword]

    That make men women! Speak, you whore, speak truth,
    Or, by the dear soul of thy sleeping father,
    This sword shall be thy lover! tell, or I'll kill thee;

And, when thou hast told all, thou wilt deserve it.

EVAD. You will not murder me?

MEL. No; 'tis a justice, and a noble one,
To put the light out of such base offenders.

EVAD. Help!

MEL. By thy foul self, no human help shall help thee,
If thou criest! When I have killed thee, as I
Have vowed to do if thou confess not, naked,
As thou hast left thine honor, will I leave thee;
That on thy branded flesh the world may read
Thy black shame and my justice. Wilt thou bend yet?

EVAD. Yes.

MEL. Up, and begin your story.

EVAD. O, I
Am miserable!

MEL. 'Tis true, thou art. Speak truth still.

EVAD. I have offended: noble sir, forgive me!

MEL. With what secure slave?

EVAD. Do not ask me, sir;
Mine own remembrance is a misery
Too mighty for me.

MEL. Do not fall back again; my sword's unsheathed yet.

EVAD. What shall I do?

MEL. Be true, and make your fault less.

EVAD. I dare not tell.

MEL. Tell, or I'll be this day a-killing thee.

EVAD. Will you forgive me, then?

MEL. Stay; I must ask mine honor first.
I have too much foolish nature in me: speak.

EVAD. Is there none else here?

MEL. None but a fearful[1] conscience; that's too many.
Who is't?

EVAD. O, hear me gently! It was the King.

MEL. No more. My worthy father's and my services
Are liberally rewarded! King, I thank thee!
For all my dangers and my wounds thou hast paid me

---

1. Cowardly.

In my own metal: these are soldiers' thanks!—
How long have you lived thus, Evadne?

EVAD. Too long.

MEL. Too late you find it. Can you be sorry?

EVAD. Would I were half as blameless!

MEL. Evadne, thou wilt to thy trade again.

EVAD. First to my grave.

MEL. Would gods thou hadst been so blest!
Dost thou not hate this King now? prithee hate him:
Couldst thou not curse him? I command thee, curse him;
Curse till the gods hear, and deliver him
To thy just wishes. Yet I fear, Evadne,
You had rather play your game out.

EVAD. No; I feel
Too many sad confusions here, to let in
Any loose flame hereafter.

MEL. Dost thou not feel, amongst all those, one brave anger,
That breaks out nobly, and directs thine arm
To kill this base King?

EVAD. All the gods forbid it!

MEL. No, all the gods require it; they are
Dishonored in him.

EVAD. 'Tis too fearful.

MEL. Y'are valiant in his bed, and bold enough
To be a stale whore, and have your madam's name
Discourse for grooms and pages; and hereafter,
When his cool majesty hath laid you by,
To be at pension with some needy sir
For meat and coarser clothes: thus far you know
No fear. Come, you shall kill him.

EVAD. Good sir!

MEL. An 'twere to kiss him dead, thou'dst smother him:
Be wise, and kill him. Canst thou live, and know
What noble minds shall make thee, see thyself
Found out with every finger, made the shame
Of all successions, and in this great ruin
Thy brother and thy noble husband broken?
Thou shalt not live thus. Kneel, and swear to help me,

When I shall call thee to it; or, by all
Holy in heaven and earth, thou shalt not live
To breathe a full hour longer; not a thought!
Come, 'tis a righteous oath. Give me thy hands,
And, both to heaven held up, swear, by that wealth
This lustful thief stole from thee, when I say it,
To let his foul soul out.

EVAD. Here I swear it;

[Kneels]

And, all you spirits of abusèd ladies,
Help me in this performance!
MEL. [*Raising her*] Enough. This must be known to none
But you and I, Evadne; not to your lord,
Though he be wise and noble, and a fellow
Dares step as far into a worthy action
As the most daring, ay, as far as justice.
Ask me not why. Farewell.

Exit

EVAD. Would I could say so to my black disgrace!
O, where have I been all this time? how friended,
That I should lose myself thus desperately,
And none for pity show me how I wandered?
There is not in the compass of the light
A more unhappy creature: sure, I am monstrous;
For I have done those follies, those mad mischiefs,
Would dare[1] a woman. O, my loaded soul,
Be not so cruel to me; choke not up
The way to my repentance!

Enter Amintor

O, my lord!
AMIN. How now?
EVAD. My much-abusèd lord!

[Kneels]

AMIN. This cannot be!
EVAD. I do not kneel to live; I dare not hope it;

1. Daunt.

The wrongs I did are greater. Look upon me,
Though I appear with all my faults.

AMIN. Stand up.

This is a new way to beget more sorrow:
Heaven knows I have too many. Do not mock me:
Though I am tame, and bred up with my wrongs,
Which are my foster-brothers, I may leap,
Like a hand-wolf,[1] into my natural wildness,
And do an outrage: prithee, do not mock me.

EVAD. My whole life is so leprous, it infects
All my repentance. I would buy your pardon,
Though at the highest set,[2] even with my life:
That slight contrition, that's no sacrifice
For what I have committed.

AMIN. Sure, I dazzle:

There cannot be a faith in that foul woman,
That knows no god more mighty than her mischiefs.
Thou dost still worse, still number on thy faults,
To press my poor heart thus. Can I believe
There's any seed of virtue in that woman
Left to shoot up, that dares go on in sin
Known, and so known as thine is? O Evadne,
Would there were any safety in thy sex,
That I might put a thousand sorrows off,
And credit thy repentance! but I must not:
Thou hast brought me to that dull calamity,
To that strange misbelief of all the world
And all things that are in it, that I fear
I shall fall like a tree, and find my grave,
Only remembering that I grieve.

EVAD. My lord,

Give me your griefs: you are an innocent,
A soul as white as heaven; let not my sins
Perish your noble youth. I do not fall here
To shadow by dissembling with my tears,

---

1. Tame wolf.
2. Price.

(As all say women can,) or to make less
What my hot will hath done, which heaven and you
Know to be tougher than the hand of time
Can cut from man's remembrance; no, I do not;
I do appear the same, the same Evadne,
Dressed in the shames I lived in, the same monster.
But these are names of honor to what I am;
I do present myself the foulest creature,
Most poisonous, dangerous, and despised of men,
Lerna[1] e'er bred or Nilus. I am hell,
Till you, my dear lord, shoot your light into me,
The beams of your forgiveness; I am soulsick,
And wither with the fear of one condemned,
Till I have got your pardon.

AMIN. Rise, Evadne,
Those heavenly powers that put this good into thee
Grant a continuance of it! I forgive thee:
Make thyself worthy of it; and take heed,
Take heed, Evadne, this be serious.
Mock not the powers above, that can and dare
Give thee a great example of their justice
To all ensuing ages, if thou play'st
With thy repentance, the best sacrifice.

EVAD. I have done nothing good to win belief,
My life hath been so faithless. All the creatures,
Made for heaven's honors, have their ends, and good ones,
All but the cozening crocodiles, false women:
They reign here like those plagues, those killing sores,
Men pray against; and when they die, like tales
Ill told and unbelieved, they pass away,
And go to dust forgotten. But, my lord,
Those short days I shall number to my rest
(As many must not see me) shall, though too late,
Though in my evening, yet perceive a will,
Since I can do no good, because a woman,
Reach constantly at something that is near it:

1. A marsh, the haunt of Hydra, the monster slain by Hercules.

I will redeem one minute of my age,
Or, like another Niobe,[1] I'll weep,
Till I am water.

AMIN. I am now dissolved;
My frozen soul melts. May each sin thou hast,
Find a new mercy! Rise; I am at peace.
Hadst thou been thus, thus excellently good,
Before that devil-king tempted thy frailty,
Sure thou hadst made a star. Give me thy hand:
From this time I will know thee; and, as far
As honor gives me leave, by thy Amintor.
When we meet next, I will salute thee fairly,
And pray the gods to give thee happy days:
My charity shall go along with thee,
Though my embraces must be far from thee.
I should ha' killed thee, but this sweet repentance
Locks up my vengeance; for which thus I kiss thee—
The last kiss we must take: and would to heaven
The holy priest that gave our hands together
Had given us equal virtues! Go, Evadne;
The gods thus part our bodies. Have a care
My honor falls no farther: I am well, then.

EVAD. All the dear joys here, and above hereafter,
Crown thy fair soul! Thus I take leave, my lord;
And never shall you see the foul Evadne,
Till she have tried all honored means, that may
Set her in rest and wash her stains away.

Exeunt [severally]

SCENE II

Banquet. Enter King and Calianax. Hautboys play within

KING. I cannot tell how I should credit this
From you, that are his enemy.

---

1. Killed for boasting about the number of her children—a stock type of grieving, weeping woman.

CAL. I am sure
    He said it to me; and I'll justify it
    What way he dares oppose—but[1] with my sword.
KING. But did he break, without all circumstance,
    To you, his foe, that he would have the fort,
    To kill me, and then scape?
CAL. If he deny it,
    I'll make him blush.
KING. It sounds incredibly.
CAL. Ay, so does every thing I say of late.
KING. Not so, Calianax.
CAL. Yes, I should sit
    Mute whilst a rogue with strong arms cuts your throat.
KING. Well, I will try him; and, if this be true,
    I'll pawn my life I'll find it; if 't be false,
    And that you clothe your hate in such a lie,
    You shall hereafter dote in your own house,
    Not in the court.
CAL. Why, if it be a lie,
    Mine ears are false, for I'll be sworn I heard it.
    Old men are good for nothing: you were best
    Put me to death for hearing, and free him
    For meaning it. You would have trusted me
    Once, but the time is altered.
KING. And will still,
    Where I may do with justice to the world:
    You have no witness.
CAL. Yes, myself.
KING. No more,
    I mean, there were that heard it.
CAL. How? no more!
    Would you have more? why, am not I enough
    To hang a thousand rogues?
KING. But so you may
    Hang honest men too, if you please.
CAL. I may!

---

1. Except.

'Tis like I will do so: there are a hundred
Will swear it for a need too, if I say it—
KING. Such witnesses we need not.
CAL. And 'tis hard
If my word cannot hang a boisterous knave.
KING. Enough.—Where's Strato?

Enter Strato

STRA. Sir?
KING. Why, where's all the company? Call Amintor in;
Evadne. here's my brother, and Melantius?
Bid him come too; and Diphilus. Call all
That are without there.—

Exit Strato

If he should desire
The combat of you,[1] 'tis not in the power
Of all our laws to hinder it, unless
We mean to quit 'em.
CAL. Why, if you do think
'Tis fit an old man and a counselor
To fight for what he says, then you may grant it.

Enter Amintor, Evadne, Melantius, Diphilus, Lysippus, Cleon,
Strato, and Diagoras

KING. Come, sirs!—Amintor, thou art yet a bridegroom,
And I will use thee so; thou shalt sit down.—
Evadne, sit;—and you, Amintor, too;
This banquet is for you, sir.—Who has brought
A merry tale about him, to raise laughter
Amongst our wine? Why, Strato, where art thou?
Thou wilt chop out with them[2] unseasonably,
When I desire 'em not.
STRA. 'Tis my ill luck, sir, so to spend them, then.
KING. Reach me a bowl of wine.—Melantius, thou
Art sad.
MEL. I should be, sir, the merriest here,

1. Request trial by combat.
2. Pounce on them.

But I ha' ne'er a story of mine own
Worth telling at this time.
KING. Give me the wine.—
Melantius I am now considering
How easy 'twere for any man we trust
To poison one of us in such a bowl.
MEL. I think it were not hard, sir, for a knave.
CAL. [*Aside*] Such as you are.
KING. I'faith, 'twere easy. It becomes us well
To get plain-dealing men about ourselves,
Such as you all are here.—Amintor, to thee;
And to thy fair Evadne!

> [*Drinks*]

MEL. [*Apart to Calianax*] Have you thought
Of this, Calianax?
CAL. Yes, marry, have I.
MEL. And what's your resolution?
CAL. We shall have it,
Soundly, I warrant you.
KING. Reach to Amintor, Strato.
AMIN. Here, my love;

> [*Drinks, and then hands the cup to Evadne*]

This wine will do thee wrong, for it will set
Blushes upon thy cheeks; and, till thou dost
A fault, 'twere pity.
KING. Yet I wonder much
Of the strange desperation of these men,
That dare attempt such acts here in our state:
He could not scape that did it.
MEL. Were he known, unpossible.
KING. It would be known, Melantius.
MEL. It ought to be. If he got then away,
He must wear all our lives upon his sword:
He need not fly the island; he must leave
No one alive.
KING. No; I should think no man
Could kill me, and scape clear, but that old man.
CAL. But I! heaven bless me! I! should I, my liege?

KING. I do not think thou wouldst; but yet thou mightst,
  For thou hast in thy hands the means to scape,
  By keeping of the fort.—He has, Melantius,
  And he has kept it well.
MEL. From cobwebs, sir,
  'Tis clean swept: I can find no other art
  In keeping of it now: 'twas ne'er besieged
  Since he commanded.
CAL. I shall be sure
  Of your good word: but I have kept it safe
  From such as you.
MEL. Keep your ill temper in:
  I speak no malice; had my brother kept it,
  I should ha' said as much.
KING. You are not merry.
  Brother, drink wine. Sit you all still.—Calianax,
  [*Aside*] I cannot trust this: I have thrown out words,
  That would have fetched warm blood upon the cheeks
  Of guilty men, and he is never moved;
  He knows no such thing.
CAL. Impudence may scape,
  When feeble virtue is accused.
KING. 'A must,
  If he were guilty, feel an alteration
  At this our whisper, whilst we point at him:
  You see he does not.
CAL. Let him hang himself:
  What care I what he does? this he did say.
KING. Melantius, you can easily conceive
  What I have meant; for men that are in fault
  Can subtly apprehend when others aim
  At what they do amiss: but I forgive
  Freely before this man: heaven do so too!
  I will not touch thee, so much as with shame
  Of telling it. Let it be so no more.
CAL. Why, this is very fine!
MEL. I cannot tell
  What 'tis you mean; but I am apt enough

Rudely to thrust into an ignorant fault.
But let me know it: happily 'tis nought
But misconstruction; and, where I am clear,
I will not take forgiveness of the gods,
Much less of you.

KING. Nay, if you stand so stiff
I shall call back my mercy.

MEL. I want smoothness
To thank a man for pardoning of a crime
I never knew.

KING. Not to instruct your knowledge, but to show you
My ears are every where; you meant to kill me,
And get the fort to scape.

MEL. Pardon me, sir;
My bluntness will be pardoned. You preserve
A race of idle people here about you,
Facers[1] and talkers, to defame the worth
Of those that do things worthy. The man that uttered this
Had perished without food, be't who it will,
But for this arm, that fenced him from the foe:
And if I thought you gave a faith to this,
The plainness of my nature would speak more.
Give me a pardon (for you ought to do't)
To kill him that spake this.

CAL. [*Aside*] Ay, that will be
The end of all: then I am fairly paid
For all my care and service.—

MEL. That old man,
Who calls me enemy, and of whom I
(Though I will never match my hate so low)
Have no good thought, would yet, I think, excuse me,
And swear he thought me wronged in this.

CAL. Who, I?
Thou shameless fellow! didst thou not speak to me
Of it thyself?

MEL. O, then, it came from him!

---

1. Braggarts.

CAL. From me! who should it come from but from me?

MEL. Nay, I believe your malice is enough:
But I ha' lost my anger.—Sir, I hope
You are well satisfied.

KING. Lysippus, cheer
Amintor and his lady: there's no sound
Comes from you; I will come and do't myself.

AMIN. You have done already, sir, for me, I thank you.

KING. Melantius, I do credit this from him,
How slight soe'er you make't.

MEL. 'Tis strange you should.

CAL. 'Tis strange 'a should believe an old man's word,
That never lied in's life!

MEL. I talk not to thee.—
Shall the wild words of this distempered man,
Frantic with age and sorrow, make a breach
Betwixt your majesty and me? 'Twas wrong
To hearken to him; but to credit him,
As much at least as I have power to bear.
But pardon me—whilst I speak only truth,
I may commend myself—I have bestowed
My careless blood[1] with you, and should be loath
To think an action that would make me lose
That and my thanks too. When I was a boy,
I thrust myself into my country's cause,
And did a deed that plucked five years from time,
And styled me man then. And for you, my King,
Your subjects all have fed by virtue of
My arm: this sword of mine hath ploughed the ground,
And reaped the fruit in peace;
And you yourself have lived at home in ease.
So terrible I grew, that without swords
My name hath fetched you conquest: and my heart
And limbs are still the same; my will as great
To do you service. Let me not be paid
With such a strange distrust.

---

1. Blood in the shedding of which I have been careless.

KING. Melantius, I held it great injustice to believe
    Thine enemy, and did not; if I did,
    I do not; let that satisfy.—What, struck
    With sadness all? More wine!

CAL. A few fine words
    Have overthrown my truth. Ah, th'art a villain!

MEL. Why, thou wert better let me have the fort:
    [*Aside*] Dotard, I will disgrace thee thus for ever;
    There shall no credit lie upon thy words:
    Think better, and deliver it.

CAL. My liege,
    He's at me now again to do it.—Speak;
    Deny it, if thou canst.—Examine him
    Whilst he is hot, for, if he cool again,
    He will forswear it.

KING. This is lunacy,
    I hope, Melantius.

MEL. He hath lost himself
    Much, since his daughter missed the happiness
    My sister gained; and, though he call me foe,
    I pity him.

CAL. Pity! a pox upon you!

MEL. Mark his disordered words: and at the masque
    Diagoras knows he raged and railed at me,
    And called a lady "whore," so innocent
    She understood him not. But it becomes
    Both you and me too to forgive distraction:
    Pardon him, as I do.

CAL. I'll not speak for thee,
    For all thy cunning.—If you will be safe,
    Chop off his head; for there was never known
    So impudent a rascal.

KING. Some, that love him,
    Get him to bed. Why, pity should not let
    Age make itself contemptible; we must be
    All old. Have him away.

MEL. Calianax,
    The King believes you: come, you shall go home,

And rest; you ha' done well. [*Aside*]—You'll give it up,
When I have used you thus a month, I hope.—

CAL. Now, now, 'tis plain, sir: he does move me still:
He says, he knows I'll give him up the fort,
When he has used me thus a month. I am mad,
Am I not, still?

ALL. Ha, ha, ha!

CAL. I shall be mad indeed, if you do thus.
Why should you trust a sturdy fellow there,
That has no virtue in him, (all's in his sword)
Before me? Do but take his weapons from him,
And he's an ass; and I am a very fool,
Both with him and without him, as you use me.

ALL. Ha, ha, ha!

KING. 'Tis well, Calianax: but if you use
This once again, I shall entreat some other
To see your offices be well discharged.—
Be merry, gentlemen.—It grows somewhat late.—
Amintor, thou wouldst be a-bed again.

AMIN. Yes, sir.

KING. And you, Evadne.—Let me take
Thee in my arms, Melantius, and believe
Thou art, as thou deservest to be, my friend
Still and for ever.—Good Calianax,
Sleep soundly; it will bring thee to thyself.

Exeunt omnes. Manent Melantius and Calianax

CAL. Sleep soundly! I sleep soundly now, I hope;
I could not be thus else.—How darest thou stay
Alone with me, knowing how thou hast used me?

MEL. You cannot blast me with your tongue, and that's
The strongest part you have about you.

CAL. I
Do look for some great punishment for this;
For I begin to forget all my hate,
And take't unkindly that mine enemy
Should use me so extraordinarily scurvily.

MEL. I shall melt too, if you begin to take
    Unkindnesses: I never meant you hurt.
CAL. Thou'lt anger me again. Thou wretched rogue,
    Meant me no hurt! disgrace me with the King!
    Lose all my offices! This is no hurt,
    Is it? I prithee, what dost thou call hurt?
MEL. To poison men, because they love me not;
    To call the credit of men's wives in question;
    To murder children betwixt me and land;[1]
    This is all hurt.
CAL. All this thou think'st is sport;
    For mine is worse: but use thy will with me;
    For betwixt grief and anger I could cry.
MEL. Be wise, then, and be safe; thou may'st revenge.
CAL. Ay, o' the King: I would revenge of thee.
MEL. That you must plot yourself.
CAL. I am a fine plotter.
MEL. The short is, I will hold thee with the King
    In this perplexity, till peevishness
    And thy disgrace have laid thee in thy grave:
    But if thou wilt deliver up the fort,
    I'll take thy trembling body in my arms,
    And bear thee over dangers: thou shalt hold
    Thy wonted state.
CAL. If I should tell the King,
    Canst thou deny't again?
MEL. Try, and believe.
CAL. Nay, then, thou canst bring any thing about.
    Melantius, thou shalt have the fort.
MEL. Why, well.
    Here let our hate be buried; and this hand
    Shall right us both. Give me thy agèd breast
    To compass.
CAL. Nay, I do not love thee yet;
    I cannot well endure to look on thee;
    And if I thought it were a courtesy,

---

1. Heirs frustrating his succession.

Thou shouldst not have it. But I am disgraced;
My offices are to be ta'en away;
And, if I did but hold this fort a day,
I do believe the King would take it from me,
And give it thee, things are so strangely carried.
Ne'er thank me for't; but yet the King shall know
There was some such thing in't I told him of,
And that I was an honest man.

MEL. He'll buy
That knowledge very dearly.—

Enter Diphilus

Diphilus,
What news with thee?

DIPH. This were a night indeed
To do it in: the King hath sent for her.

MEL. She shall perform it, then.—Go, Diphilus,
And take from this good man, my worthy friend,
The fort, he'll give it thee.

DIPH. Ha' you got that?

CAL. Art thou of the same breed? canst thou deny
This to the King too?

DIPH. With a confidence
As great as his.

CAL. Faith, like enough.

MEL. Away, and use him kindly.

CAL. Touch not me;
I hate the whole strain.[1] If thou follow me
A great way off, I'll give thee up the fort;
And hang yourselves.

MEL. Begone.

DIPH. He's finely wrought.

Exeunt Calianax and Diphilus

MEL. This is a night, spite of astronomers,[2]
To do the deed in. I will wash the stain
That rests upon our house off with his blood.

1. Family.
2. Astrologers.

Enter Amintor

AMIN. Melantius, now assist me: if thou be'st
That which thou say'st, assist me. I have lost
All my distempers, and have found a rage
So pleasing! Help me.

MEL. [*Aside*] Who can see him thus,
And not swear vengeance?—What's the matter, friend?

AMIN. Out with thy sword; and, hand in hand with me,
Rush to the chamber of this hated King,
And sink him with the weight of all his sins
To hell for ever.

MEL. 'Twere a rash attempt,
Not to be done with safety. Let your reason
Plot your revenge, and not your passion.

AMIN. If thou refusest me in these extremes,
Thou art no friend. He sent for her to me;
By heaven, to me, myself! and I must tell ye,
I love her as a stranger: there is worth
In that vile woman, worthy things, Melantius;
And she repents. I'll do't myself alone,
Though I be slain. Farewell.

MEL. He'll overthrow
My whole design with madness.—Amintor,
Think what thou dost: I dare as much as valor;
But 'tis the King, the King, the King, Amintor,
With whom thou fightest!—[*Aside*] I know he's honest,
And this will work with him.—

AMIN. I cannot tell
What thou hast said; but thou hast charmed my sword
Out of my hand, and left me shaking here,
Defenceless.

MEL. I will take it up for thee.

AMIN. What wild beast is uncollected[1] man!
The thing that we call honor bears us all
Headlong unto sin, and yet itself is nothing.

MEL. Alas, how variable are thy thoughts!

1. Uncontrolled.

AMIN. Just like my fortunes. I was run to[1] that
    I purposed to have chid thee for. Some plot,
    I did distrust, thou hadst against the King,
    By that old fellow's carriage. But take heed;
    There's not the least limb growing to a king
    But carries thunder in it.
MEL.   I have none
    Against him.
AMIN. Why, come, then; and still remember
    We may not think revenge.
MEL. I will remember.

Exeunt

ACT V, SCENE I

Enter Evadne and a Gentleman

EVAD. Sir, is the King a-bed?
GENT. Madam, an hour ago.
EVAD. Give me the key, then; and let none be near;
    'Tis the King's pleasure.
GENT. I understand you, madam; would 'twere mine!
    I must not wish good rest unto your ladyship.
EVAD. You talk, you talk.
GENT. 'Tis all I dare do, madam; but the King
    Will wake, and then, methinks—
EVAD. Saving your imagination, pray, good night, sir.
GENT. A good night be it, then, and a long one, madam.
    I am gone.

Exit

EVAD. The night grows horrible; and all about me
    Like my black purpose. [*Draws a curtain disclosing the King abed*]
    O, the conscience
    Of a lost virtue, whither wilt thou pull me?
    To what things dismal as the depth of hell
    Wilt thou provoke me? Let no woman dare
    From this hour be disloyal, if her heart be flesh,
    If she have blood, and can fear. 'Tis a daring

---

1. Determined to do.

Above that desperate fool's that left his peace,
And went to sea to fight: 'tis so many sins
An age cannot repent 'em; and so great,
The gods want mercy for. Yet I must through 'em:
I have begun a slaughter on my honor,
And I must end it there.—'A sleeps. O God,
Why give you peace to this untemperate beast,
That hath so long transgressed you? I must kill him
And I will do it bravely: the mere joy
Tells me, I merit in it. Yet I must not
Thus tamely do it, as he sleeps—that were
To rock him to another world; my vengeance
Shall take him waking, and then lay before him
The number of his wrongs and punishments:
I'll shape his sins like Furies, till I waken
His evil angel, his sick conscience,
And then I'll strike him dead. King, by your leave;

           [*Ties his arms to the bed*]

I dare not trust your strength; your grace and I
Must grapple upon even terms no more.
So, if he rail me not from my resolution,
I shall be strong enough.—
My lord the King!—My lord!—'A sleeps,
As if he meant to wake no more.—My lord!—
Is he not dead already? Sir! my lord!

KING. Who's that?

EVAD. O, you sleep soundly, sir!

KING. My dear Evadne,
I have been dreaming of thee: come to bed.

EVAD. I am come at length, sir; but how welcome?

KING. What pretty new device is this, Evadne?
What, do you tie me to you? By my love,
This is a quaint one. Come, my dear, and kiss me;
I'll be thy Mars;[1] to bed, my queen of love:
Let us be caught together, that the gods may see
And envy our embraces.

---

1. Mars, making love to Venus, was caught in a net by her husband, Vulcan.

EVAD. Stay, sir, stay;
    You are too hot, and I have brought you physic
    To temper your high veins.
KING. Prithee, to bed, then; let me take it warm;
    There thou shalt know the state of my body better.
EVAD. I know you have a surfeited foul body;
    And you must bleed.

*   [Draws a dagger]*

KING. Bleed!
EVAD. Ay, you shall bleed. Lie still; and, if the devil,
    Your lust, will give you leave, repent. This steel
    Comes to redeem the honor that you stole,
    King, my fair name; which nothing but thy death
    Can answer to the world.
KING. How's this, Evadne?
EVAD. I am not she; nor bear I in this breast
    So much cold spirit to be called a woman:
    I am a tiger; I am any thing
    That knows not pity. Stir not: if thou dost,
    I'll take thee unprepared, thy fears upon thee,
    That make thy sins look double, and so send thee
    (By my revenge, I will!) to look those torments
    Prepared for such black souls.
KING. Thou dost not mean this; 'tis impossible;
    Thou art too sweet and gentle.
EVAD. No, I am not:
    I am as foul as thou art, and can number
    As many such hells here. I was once fair,
    Once I was lovely; not a blowing rose
    More chastely sweet, till thou, thou, thou, foul canker,
    (Stir not) didst poison me. I was a world of virtue,
    Till your cursed court and you (hell bless you for't)
    With your temptations on temptations
    Made me give up mine honor; for which, King,
    I am come to kill thee.
KING. No!
EVAD. I am.
KING. Thou art not!

    I prithee speak not these things: thou art gentle,
    And wert not meant thus rugged.
EVAD. Peace, and hear me.
    Stir nothing but your tongue, and that for mercy
    To those above us; by whose lights I vow
    Those blessèd fires[1] that shot to see our sin,
    If thy hot soul had substance with thy blood,[2]
    I would kill that too; which, being past my steel,
    My tongue shall reach. Thou art a shameless villain;
    A thing out of the overcharge of nature,
    Sent, like a thick cloud, to disperse a plague
    Upon weak catching[3] women; such a tyrant,
    That for his lust would sell away his subjects,
    Ay, all his heaven hereafter!
KING. Hear, Evadne,
    Thou soul of sweetness, hear! I am thy King.
EVAD. Thou art my shame! Lie still; there's none about you,
    Within your cries; all promises of safety
    Are but deluding dreams. Thus, thus, thou foul man,
    Thus I begin my vengeance!

                                  [*Stabs him*]

KING. Hold, Evadne!
    I do command thee hold!
EVAD. I do not mean, sir,
    To part so fairly with you; we must change
    More of these love-tricks yet.
KING. What bloody villain
    Provoked thee to this murder?
EVAD. Thou, thou monster!
KING. O!
EVAD. Thou kept'st me brave[4] at court, and whored me, King;
    Then married me to a young noble gentleman,
    And whored me still.

---

1. Shooting stars.
2. Were incorporated in your blood.
3. Susceptible.
4. Handsomely dressed and attended.

KING. Evadne, pity me!

EVAD. Hell take me, then! This for my lord Amintor.
This for my noble brother! and this stroke
For the most wronged of women!

[*Kills him*]

KING. O! I die.

EVAD. Die all our faults together! I forgive thee.

Exit

Enter two of the Bedchamber

1 GENT. Come, now she's gone, let's enter; the King expects it, and
will be angry.

2 GENT. 'Tis a fine wench; we'll have a snap at her one of these nights,
as she goes from him.

1 GENT. Content. How quickly he had done with her! I see kings can
do no more that way than other mortal people.

2 GENT. How fast he is! I cannot hear him breathe.

1 GENT. Either the tapers give a feeble light,
Or he looks very pale.

2 GENT. And so he does:
Pray heaven he be well! let's look.—Alas!
He's stiff, wounded, and dead! Treason, treason!

1 GENT. Run forth and call.

2 GENT. Treason, treason!

Exit

1 GENT. This will be laid on us: who can believe
A woman could do this?

Enter Cleon and Lysippus

CLE. How now! where's the traitor?

1 GENT. Fled, fled away; but there her woeful act
Lies still.

CLE. Her act! a woman!

LYS. Where's the body?

1 GENT. There.

LYS. Farewell, thou worthy man! There were two bonds
That tied our loves, a brother and a king,
The least of which might fetch a flood of tears;

But such the misery of greatness is,
They have no time to mourn; then, pardon me!

Enter Strato

Sirs, which way went she?
STRA. Never follow her;
  For she, alas! was but the instrument.
  News is now brought in, that Melantius
  Has got the fort, and stands upon the wall,
  And with a loud voice calls those few that pass
  At this dead time of night, delivering
  The innocence of this act.
LYS. Gentlemen, I am your King.
STRA. We do acknowledge it.
LYS. I would I were not! Follow, all; for this
  Must have a sudden stop.

Exeunt

SCENE II

Enter Melantius, Diphilus, and Calianax, on the wall

MEL. If the dull people can believe I am armed,
  (Be constant, Diphilus,) now we have time
  Either to bring our banished honors home,
  Or create new ones in our ends.[1]
DIPH. I fear not;
  My spirit lies not that way.—Courage, Calianax!
CAL. Would I had any! you should quickly know it.
MEL. Speak to the people; thou art eloquent.
CAL. 'Tis a fine eloquence to come to the gallows:
  You were born to be my end; the devil take you!
  Now must I hang for company. 'Tis strange,
  I should be old, and neither wise nor valiant.

Enter Lysippus, Diagoras, Cleon, Strato, and Guard

---

1. Deaths.

LYS. See where he stands, as boldly confident
　　As if he had his full command about him!
STRA. He looks as if he had the better cause, sir;
　　Under your gracious pardon, let me speak it.
　　Though he be mighty-spirited, and forward
　　To all great things, to all things of that danger
　　Worse men shake at the telling of, yet certainly
　　I do believe him noble, and this action
　　Rather pulled on than sought: his mind was ever
　　As worthy as his hand.
LYS. 'Tis my fear too.
　　Heaven forgive all!—Summon him, lord Cleon.
CLE. Ho, from the walls there!
MEL. Worthy Cleon, welcome:
　　We could a wished you here, lord: you are honest.
CAL. [*Aside*] Well, thou art as flattering a knave, though I dare not tell
　　thee so—
LYS. Melantius!
MEL. Sir?
LYS. I am sorry that we meet thus; our old love
　　Never required such distance. Pray to heaven,
　　You have not left yourself, and sought this safety
　　More out of fear than honor! You have lost
　　A noble master; which your faith, Melantius,
　　Some think might have preserved: yet you know best.
CAL. [*Aside*] When time was I was mad! Some that dares fight,
　　I hope will pay this rascal.
MEL. Royal young man, those tears look lovely on thee:
　　Had they been shed for a deserving one,
　　They had been lasting monuments. Thy brother,
　　Whilst he was good, I called him King, and served him
　　With that strong faith, that most unwearied valor,
　　Pulled people from the farthest sun to seek him,
　　And beg his friendship. I was then his soldier.
　　But since his hot pride drew him to disgrace me,
　　And brand my noble actions with his lust,
　　(That never-cured dishonor of my sister,
　　Base stain of whore, and, which is worse,

The joy to make it still so,) like myself,
Thus I have flung him off with my allegiance;
And stand here mine own justice, to revenge
What I have suffered in him, and this old man
Wronged almost to lunacy.

CAL. Who, I?
You would draw me in. I have had no wrong;
I do disclaim ye all.

MEL. The short is this.
'Tis no ambition to lift up myself
Urgeth me thus; I do desire again
To be a subject, so I may be free:
If not, I know my strength, and will unbuild
This goodly town. Be speedy, and be wise,
In a reply.

STRA. Be sudden, sir, to tie
All up again. What's done is past recall,
And past you to revenge; and there are thousands
That wait for such a troubled hour as this.
Throw him the blank.[1]

LYS. Melantius, write in that thy choice:
My seal is at it.

[Throws Melantius the paper]

MEL. It was our honors drew us to this act,
Not gain; and we will only work our pardons.

CAL. Put my name in too.

DIPH. You disclaimed us all, but now, Calianax.

CAL. That is all one;
I'll not be hanged hereafter by a trick:
I'll have it in.

MEL. You shall, you shall.—
Come to the back gate, and we'll call you King,
And give you up the fort.

LYS. Away, away!

Exeunt omnes

---

1. Paper to be filled in at his pleasure.

Scene III

Enter Aspatia, in nun's apparel and with artificial scars on her face

Asp. This is my fatal hour. Heaven may forgive
    My rash attempt, that causelessly hath laid
    Griefs on me that will never let me rest,
    And put a woman's heart into my breast.
    It is more honor for you that I die;
    For she that can endure the misery
    That I have on me, and be patient too,
    May live and laugh at all that you can do.

Enter Servant

    God save you, sir!
Ser. And you, sir! What's your business?
Asp. With you, sir, now; to do me the fair office
    To help me to your lord.
Ser. What, would you serve him?
Asp. I'll do him any service; but, to haste,
    For my affairs are earnest, I desire
    To speak with him.
Ser. Sir, because you are in such haste, I would be loath
    Delay you longer: you can not.
Asp. It shall become you, though, to tell your lord.
Ser. Sir, he will speak with nobody;
    But in particular, I have in charge,[1]
    About no weighty matters.
Asp. This is most strange.
    Art thou gold-proof? there's for thee; help me to him.

[Gives money]

Ser. Pray be not angry, sir: I'll do my best.

Exit

Asp. How stubbornly this fellow answered me!
    There is a vile dishonest trick in man,
    More than in woman. All the men I meet

---

1. I have been charged.

Appear thus to me, are harsh and rude,
And have a subtilty in every thing,
Which love could never know; but we fond[1] women
Harbor the easiest and the smoothest thoughts,
And think all shall go so. It is unjust
That men and women should be matched together.

Enter Amintor and his Man

AMIN. Where is he?
SER. There, my lord.
AMIN. What would you, sir?
ASP. Please it your lordship to command your man
    Out of the room, I shall deliver things
    Worthy your hearing.
AMIN. Leave us.

Exit Servant

ASP. [*Aside*] O, that that shape
    Should bury falsehood in it!—
AMIN. Now your will, sir.
ASP. When you know me, my lord, you needs must guess
    My business; and I am not hard to know;
    For, till the chance of war marked this smooth face
    With these few blemishes, people would call me
    My sister's picture, and her mine. In short,
    I am brother to the wronged Aspatia.
AMIN. The wronged Aspatia! would thou wert so too
    Unto the wronged Amintor! Let me kiss

[*Kisses her hand*]

    That hand of thine, in honor that I bear
    Unto the wronged Aspatia. Here I stand
    That did it. Would he could not! Gentle youth,
    Leave me; for there is something in thy looks
    That calls my sins in a most hideous form
    Into my mind; and I have grief enough
    Without thy help.
ASP. I would I could with credit!

---

1. Foolish.

Since I was twelve years old, I had not seen
My sister till this hour I now arrived:
She sent for me to see her marriage;
A woeful one! but they that are above
Have ends in every thing. She used few words,
But yet enough to make me understand
The baseness of the injuries you did her.
That little training I have had is war:
I may behave myself rudely in peace;
I would not, though. I shall not need to tell you,
I am but young, and would be loath to lose
Honor, that is not easily gained again.
Fairly I mean to deal: the age is strict
For[1] single combats; and we shall be stopped,
If it be published. If you like your sword,
Use it; if mine appear a better to you,
Change; for the ground is this, and this the time,
To end our difference.

                                           [Draws]

AMIN. Charitable youth,
   If thou be'st such, think not I will maintain
   So strange a wrong: and, for thy sister's sake,
   Know, that I could not think that desperate thing
   I durst not do; yet, to enjoy this world,
   I would not see her; for, beholding thee,
   I am I know not what. If I have aught
   That may content thee, take it, and begone,
   For death is not so terrible as thou;
   Thine eyes shoot guilt into me.
ASP. Thus, she swore,
   Thou wouldst behave thyself, and give me words
   That would fetch tears into mine eyes; and so
   Thou dost indeed. But yet she bade me watch,
   Lest I were cozened, and be sure to fight
   Ere I returned.
AMIN. That must not be with me.

---

1. In respect of.

For her I'll die directly; but against her
Will never hazard it.

ASP. You must be urged:
I do not deal uncivilly with those
That dare to fight; but such a one as you
Must be used thus.

[*She strikes him*]

AMIN. I prithee, youth, take heed.
Thy sister is a thing to me so much
Above mine honor, that I can endure
All this—Good gods! a blow I can endure;
But stay not, lest thou draw a timeless death
Upon thyself.

ASP. Thou art some prating fellow;
One that hath studied out a trick to talk,
And move soft-hearted people; to be kicked,

[*She kicks him*]

Thus to be kicked.—[*Aside*] Why should he be so slow
In giving me my death?

AMIN. A man can bear
No more, and keep his flesh. Forgive me, then?
I would endure yet, if I could. Now show

[*Draws*]

The spirit thou pretendest, and understand
Thou hast no hour to live.

[*They fight, Aspatia is wounded*]

What dost thou mean?
Thou canst not fight: the blows thou mak'st at me
Are quite besides; and those I offer at thee,
Thou spread'st thine arms, and tak'st upon thy breast,
Alas, defenceless!

ASP. I have got enough,
And my desire. There is no place so fit
For me to die as here.

[*Falls*]

Enter Evadne, her hands bloody, with a knife

EVAD. Amintor, I am loaden with events,

That fly to make thee happy; I have joys,
That in a moment can call back thy wrongs,
And settle thee in thy free state again.
It is Evadne still that follows thee,
But not her mischiefs.

AMIN. Thou canst not fool me to believe again;
But thou hast looks and things so full of news,
That I am stayed.

EVAD. Noble Amintor, put off thy amaze;
Let thine eyes loose, and speak. Am I not fair?
Looks not Evadne beauteous with these rites now?
Were those hours half so lovely in thine eyes
When our hands met before the holy man?
I was too foul within to look fair then:
Since I knew ill, I was not free till now.

AMIN. There is presage of some important thing
About thee, which, it seems, thy tongue hath lost:
Thy hands are bloody, and thou hast a knife.

EVAD. In this consists thy happiness and mine:
Joy to Amintor! for the King is dead.

AMIN. Those have most power to hurt us, that we love;
We lay our sleeping lives within their arms.
Why, thou hast raised up mischief to his height,
And found one to out-name[1] thy other faults;
Thou hast no intermission of thy sins
But all thy life is a continued ill:
Black is thy color now, disease thy nature.
"Joy to Amintor!" Thou hast touched a life,
The very name of which had power to chain
Up all my rage, and calm my wildest wrongs.

EVAD. 'Tis done; and, since I could not find a way
To meet thy love so clear as through this life,
I cannot now repent it.

AMIN. Couldst thou procure the gods to speak to me,
To bid me love this woman and forgive,
I think I should fall out with them. Behold,

---

1. Surpass.

Here lies a youth whose wounds bleed in my breast,
Sent by a violent fate to fetch his death
From my slow hand! And, to augment my woe,
You now are present, stained with a king's blood
Violently shed. This keeps night here,
And throws an unknown wilderness about me.

ASP. O, O, O!

AMIN. No more; pursue me not.

EVAD. Forgive me, then,
And take me to thy bed: we may not part.

AMIN. Forbear, be wise, and let my rage go this way.

EVAD. 'Tis you that I would stay, not it.

AMIN. Take heed;
It will return with me.

EVAD. If it must be,
I shall not fear to meet it: take me home.

AMIN. Thou monster of cruelty, forbear!

EVAD. For heaven's sake, look more calm: thine eyes are sharper
Than thou canst make thy sword.

                                                       [*Kneels*]

AMIN. Away, away!
Thy knees are more to me than violence;
I am worse than sick to see knees follow me
For that I must not grant. For heaven's sake, stand.

EVAD. Receive me, then.

AMIN. I dare not stay thy language:
In midst of all my anger and my grief,
Thou dost awake something that troubles me,
And says, I loved thee once. I dare not stay;
There is no end of woman's reasoning.

                                                [*Leaves her*]

EVAD. [*Rising*] Amintor, thou shalt love me now again:
Go; I am calm. Farewell, and peace for ever!
Evadne, whom thou hatest, will die for thee.

                                                [*Kills herself*]

AMIN. I have a little human nature yet,
That's left for thee, that bids me stay thy hand.

                                                [*Returns*]

EVAD. Thy hand was welcome, but it came too late.
  O, I am lost! the heavy sleep makes haste.

Dies

ASP. O, O, O!
AMIN. This earth of mine doth tremble, and I feel
  A stark affrighted motion in my blood;
  My soul grows weary of her house, and I
  All over am a trouble to myself.
  There is some hidden power in these dead things,
  That calls my flesh unto 'em; I am cold:
  Be resolute, and bear 'em company.
  There's something yet, which I am loath to leave:
  There's man enough in me to meet the fears
  That death can bring; and yet would it were done!
  I can find nothing in the whole discourse
  Of death, I durst not meet the boldest way;
  Yet still, betwixt the reason and the act,
  The wrong I to Aspatia did stands up;
  I have not such another fault to answer:
  Though she may justly arm herself with scorn
  And hate of me, my soul will part less troubled,
  When I have paid to her in tears my sorrow:
  I will not leave this act unsatisfied,
  If all that's left in me can answer it.
ASP. Was it a dream? there stands Amintor still;
  Or I dream still.
AMIN. How dost thou? speak; receive my love and help.
  Thy blood climbs up to his old place again;
  There's hope of thy recovery.
ASP. Did you not name Aspatia?
AMIN. I did
ASP. And talked of tears and sorrow unto her?
AMIN. 'Tis true; and, till these happy signs in thee
  Did stay my course, 'twas thither I was going.
ASP. Thou art there already, and these wounds are hers:
  Those threats I brought with me sought not revenge,
  But came to fetch this blessing from thy hand:
  I am Aspatia yet.

AMIN. Dare my soul ever look abroad again?

ASP. I shall sure live, Amintor; I am well;
  A kind of healthful joy wanders within me.

AMIN. The world wants lines to excuse thy loss;
  Come, let me bear thee to some place of help.

ASP. Amintor, thou must stay; I must rest here;
  My strength begins to disobey my will.
  How dost thou, my best soul? I would fain live
  Now, if I could: wouldst thou have loved me, then?

AMIN. Alas,
  All that I am's not worth a hair from thee!

ASP. Give me thine hand; mine hands grope up and down,
  And cannot find thee; I am wondrous sick:
  Have I thy hand, Amintor?

AMIN. Thou greatest blessing of the world, thou hast.

ASP. I do believe thee better than my sense.
  O, I must go! farewell!

                                                              Dies

AMIN. She swounds[1]—Aspatia!—Help! for God's sake, water,
  Such as may chain life ever to this frame!—
  Aspatia, speak!—What, no help yet? I fool;
  I'll chafe her temples. Yet there's nothing stirs:
  Some hidden power tell her, Amintor calls,
  And let her answer me!—Aspatia, speak!—
  I have heard, if there be any life, but bow
  The body thus, and it will show itself.
  O, she is gone! I will not leave her yet.
  Since out of justice we must challenge nothing,
  I'll call it mercy, if you'll pity me,
  You heavenly powers, and lend forth some few years
  The blessèd soul to this fair seat again!
  No comfort comes; the gods deny me too.
  I'll bow the body once again.—Aspatia!—
  The soul is fled for ever; and I wrong

---

1. Swoons.

Myself, so long to lose her company.
Must I talk now? Here's to be with thee, love!

[Wounds himself]

Enter Servant

SER. This is a great grace to my lord, to have the new king come to
him: I must tell him he is entering.—O God!—Help, help!

Enter Lysippus, Melantius, Calianax, Cleon, Diphilus, and Strato

LYS. Where's Amintor?
SER. O, there, there!
LYS. How strange is this!
CAL. What should we do here?
MEL. These deaths are such acquainted things with me,
That yet my heart dissolves not. May I stand
Stiff here for ever! Eyes, call up your tears!
This is Amintor: heart, he was my friend;
Melt! now it flows.—Amintor, give a word
To call me to thee.
AMIN. O!
MEL. Melantius calls his friend Amintor, O,
Thy arms are kinder to me than thy tongue!
Speak, speak!
AMIN. What?
MEL. That little word was worth all the sounds
That ever I shall hear again.
DIPH. O, brother,
Here lies your sister slain! you lose yourself
In sorrow there.
MEL. Why, Diphilus, it is
A thing to laugh at, in respect of this:
Here was my sister, father, brother, son;
All that I had.—Speak once again; what youth
Lies slain there by thee?
AMIN. 'Tis Aspatia.
My last is said. Let me give up my soul
Into thy bosom.

Dies

CAL. What's that? what's that? Aspatia!

MEL. I never did
Repent the greatness of my heart till now;
It will not burst at need.

CAL. My daughter dead here too! And you have all fine new tricks to
grieve; but I ne'er knew any but direct crying.

MEL. I am a prattler: but no more.

[Offers to stab himself]

DIPH. Hold, brother!

LYS. Stop him.

DIPH. Fie, how unmanly was this offer in you!
Does this become our strain?[1]

CAL. I know not what the matter is, but I am grown very kind, and am
friends with you all now. You have given me that among you will
kill me quickly; but I'll go home, and live as long as I can.

Exit

MEL. His spirit is but poor that can be kept
From death for want of weapons.
Is not my hands a weapon good enough
To stop my breath? or, if you tie down those,
I vow, Amintor, I will never eat,
Or drink, or sleep, or have to do with that
That may preserve life! This I swear to keep.

LYS. Look to him, though, and bear those bodies in.
May this a fair example be to me,
To rule with temper; for on lustful kings
Unlooked-for sudden deaths from God are sent;
But cursed is he that is their instrument.

Exeunt

1. Stock.

A Chaste Maid
in Cheapside

Thomas Middleton

DRAMATIS PERSONAE

SIR WALTER WHOREHOUND
SIR OLIVER KIX
TOUCHWOOD senior
TOUCHWOOD junior
ALLWIT
YELLOWHAMMER, *a goldsmith*
TIM, *his son*
Tutor to Tim
DAVY DAHANNA, *Sir Walter's poor kinsman and attendant*
Parson

WAT
NICK } *sons of Sir Walter by Mistress Allwit*

Two Promoters
Porter, Watermen, &c
LADY KIX
MISTRESS TOUCHWOOD, *wife of* TOUCHWOOD senior
MISTRESS ALLWIT
MAUDLIN, *wife of* YELLOWHAMMER
MOLL, *her daughter*
Welshwoman, mistress to SIR W. WHOREHOUND
Country Girl
SUSAN
Maid, Midwife, Nurses, Puritans, and other Gossips, &c

A Chaste Maid in Cheapside

Act I, Scene I

Enter Maudlin and Moll

MAUD. Have you played over all your old lessons o' the virginals?[1]

MOLL. Yes.

MAUD. Yes? you are a dull maid a' late; methinks you had need have somewhat to quicken your green sickness[2]—do you weep?—a husband: had not such a piece of flesh been ordained, what had us wives been good for? to make salads, or else cried up and down for samphire.[3] To see the difference of these seasons! when I was of your youth, I was lightsome and quick two years before I was married. You fit for a knight's bed! drowsy-browed, dull-eyed, drossy-spirited! I hold my life you have forgot your dancing: when was the dancer with you?

MOLL. The last week.

MAUD. Last week? when I was of your bord[4]
He missed me not a night; I was kept at it;
I took delight to learn, and he to teach me;
Pretty brown gentleman! he took pleasure in my company:
But you are dull, nothing comes nimbly from you;
You dance like a plumber's daughter, and deserve
Two thousand pound in lead to your marriage,
And not in goldsmith's ware.

---

1. Small keyboard instrument.
2. Adolescent melancholy in girls.
3. Aromatic herb used in salads.
4. Caliber.

Enter Yellowhammer

YEL. Now, what's the din
    Betwixt mother and daughter, ha?
MAUD. Faith, small;
    Telling your daughter, Mary, of her errors.
YEL. Errors? nay, the city cannot hold you, wife,
    But you must needs fetch words from Westminster:
    I ha' done, i'faith.
    Has no attorney's clerk been here a' late,
    And changed his half-crown-piece his mother sent him,
    Or rather cozened you with a gilded twopence,
    To bring the word in fashion for her faults
    Or cracks in duty and obedience?
    Term 'em even so, sweet wife,
    As there's no woman made without a flaw;
    Your purest lawns have frays, and cambrics bracks.[1]
MAUD. But 'tis a husband solders up all cracks.
MOLL. What, is he come, sir?
YEL. Sir Walter's come: he was met
    At Holborn Bridge, and in his company
    A proper fair young gentlewoman, which I guess,
    By her red hair and other rank[2] descriptions,
    To be his landed niece, brought out of Wales,
    Which Tim our son, the Cambridge boy, must marry:
    'Tis a match of Sir Walter's own making,
    To bind us to him and our heirs for ever.
MAUD. We're honored then, if this baggage would be humble,
    And kiss him with devotion when he enters.
    I cannot get her for my life
    To instruct her hand thus, before and after,—
    Which a knight will look for,—before and after:
    I've told her still 'tis the waving of a woman
    Does often move a man, and prevails strongly.
    But, sweet, ha' you sent to Cambridge? has Tim word on't?
YEL. Had word just the day after, when you sent him

---

1. Flaws.
2. Coarse.

The silver spoon to eat his broth in the hall
Amongst the gentlemen commoners.[1]
MAUD. O, 'twas timely.

Enter Porter

YEL. How now?
POR. A letter from a gentleman in Cambridge.
[Gives letter to Yellowhammer]
YEL. O, one of Hobson's[2] porters: thou art welcome.— I told thee,
Maud, we should hear from Tim. *[Reads] Amantissimis carissimisque*
ambobus parentibus, patri et matri.[3]
MAUD. What's the matter?
YEL. Nay, by my troth, I know not, ask not me:
He's grown too verbal; this learning's a great witch.
MAUD. Pray, let me see it; I was wont to understand him. *[Reads]*
Amantissimis carissimis, he has sent the carrier's man, he says; *ambobus*
parentibus, for a pair of boots; *patri et matri,* pay the porter, or it makes
no matter.
POR. Yes, by my faith, mistress; there's no true construction in that: I
have took a great deal of pains, and come from the Bell sweating.
Let me come to't, for I was a scholar forty years ago; 'tis thus, I warrant you: *[Reads] Matri,* it makes no matter; *ambobus parentibus,* for a
pair of boots; *patri,* pay the porter; *amantissimis carissimis,* he's the
carrier's man, and his name is Sims; and there he says true, forsooth,
my name is Sims indeed; I have not forgot all my learning: a money-
matter, I thought I should hit on't.
YEL. Go, thou'rt an old fox; there's a tester[4] for thee.
[Gives money]
POR. If I see your worship at Goose-fair, I have a dish of birds for you.
YEL. Why, dost dwell at Bow?
POR. All my lifetime, sir; I could ever say bo to a goose. Farewell to
your worship.

Exit

---

1. Rich students.
2. The Cambridge carrier, for whom Milton wrote an epitaph.
3. To both my dear, loving parents, my father and mother.
4. Sixpence.

YEL. A merry porter.

MAUD. How can he choose but be so,
Coming with Cambridge letters from our son Tim.

YEL. What's here? *maxime diligo*,[1] faith, I must to my learned counsel
with this gear,[2] 'twill ne'er be discerned else.

MAUD. Go to my cousin then, at Inns of Court.

YEL. Fie, they are all for French, they speak no Latin.

MAUD. The parson then will do it.

YEL. Nay, he disclaims it,
Calls Latin papistry, he will not deal with it.—

Enter a Gentleman

What is't you lack, gentleman?

GENT. Pray, weigh this chain.

[Gives chain, which Yellowhammer weighs]

Enter Sir Walter Whorehound, Welshwoman, and Davy

SIR WAL. Now, wench, thou art welcome
To the heart of the city of London.

WELSH. *Dugat a whee.*[3]

SIR WAL. You can thank me in English, if you list.

WELSH. I can, sir, simply.

SIR WAL. 'Twill serve to pass, wench;
'Twas strange that I should lie with thee so often.
To leave thee without English, that were unnatural.
I bring thee up to turn thee into gold, wench,
And make thy fortune shine like your bright trade;
A goldsmith's shop sets out a city maid.—
Davy Dahanna, not a word.

DAVY. Mum, mum, sir.

SIR WAL. Here you must pass for a pure virgin.

DAVY. Pure Welsh virgin!
[Aside] She lost her maidenhead in Brecknockshire.

---

1. I love greatly.
2. Business.
3. God keep you (Welsh).

SIR WAL. I hear you mumble, Davy.

DAVY. I have teeth, sir;
 I need not mumble yet this forty years.

SIR WAL. The knave bites plaguily!

YEL. What's your price, sir?

GENT. A hundred pound, sir.

YEL. A hundred marks[1] the utmost;
 'Tis not for me else.—What, Sir Walter Whorehound?

Exit Gentleman

MOLL. O death!

Exit

MAUD. Why, daughter—Faith, the baggage is
 A bashful girl, sir; these young things are shamefaced;
 Besides, you have a presence, sweet Sir Walter,
 Able to daunt a maid brought up i' the city:
 A brave court-spirit makes our virgins quiver,
 And kiss with trembling thighs; yet see, she comes, sir.

Re-enter Moll

SIR WAL. Why, how now, pretty mistress? now I've caught you:
 What, can you injure so your time to stray
 Thus from your faithful servant?

YEL. Pish, stop your words, good knight,—'twill make her blush else,—
 Which sound too high for the daughters of the freedom[2]
 Honor and faithful servant! they are compliments
 For the worthies of Whitehall or Greenwich;
 E'en plain, sufficient subsidy words[3] serves us, sir.
 And is this gentlewoman your worthy niece?

SIR WAL. You may be bold with her on these terms; 'tis she, sir,
 Heir to some nineteen mountains.

YEL. Bless us all!
 You overwhelm me, sir, with love and riches.

SIR WAL. And all as high as Paul's.

DAVY. [*Aside*] Here's work, i'faith!

---

1. The mark was worth 13s. 4d (two thirds of a pound).
2. i.e., Of the tradesman class.
3. Words of substantial bourgeois worth.

SIR WAL. How sayst thou, Davy?

DAVY. Higher, sir, by far;
  You cannot see the top of 'em.

YEL. What, man!—
  Maudlin, salute this gentlewoman, our daughter,
  If things hit right.

Enter Touchwood junior

TOUCH. JUN. My knight, with a brace of footmen,
  Is come, and brought up his ewe-mutton to find
  A ram at London; I must hasten it,
  Or else pick[1] a' famine; her blood is mine,
  And that's the surest. Well, knight, that choice spoil
  Is only kept for me.

MOLL. [*Aside*] Sir—

TOUCH. JUN. Turn not to me till thou mayst lawfully; it but whets my
  stomach, which is too sharp-set already. Read that note carefully
  [*giving letter to Moll*]; keep me from suspicion still, nor know my
  zeal but in thy heart:
  Read, and send but thy liking in three words;
  I'll be at hand to take it.

YEL. O turn, sir, turn.[2]
  A poor, plain boy, an university man;
  Proceeds next Lent to a bachelor of art;
  He will be called Sir Yellowhammer then
  Over all Cambridge, and that's half a knight.

MAUD. Please you, draw near
  And taste the welcome of the city, sir.

YEL. Come, good Sir Walter, and your virtuous niece here.

SIR WAL. 'Tis manners to take kindness.

YEL. Lead 'em in, wife.

SIR WAL. Your company, sir?

YEL. I'll give't you instantly.

---

1. Peak, grow meager.
2. Some lines referring to Tim seem to have been omitted. Perhaps the correct reading
is "O Tim, sir, Tim."

> *Exeunt Maudlin, Sir W. Whorehound, Welshwoman, and Davy*

TOUCH. JUN. [*Aside*] How strangely busy is the devil and riches!
  Poor soul! kept in too hard, her mother's eye
  Is cruel toward her, being kind[1] to him.
  'Twere a good mirth now to set him a-work
  To make her wedding-ring; I must about it:
  Rather than the gain should fall to a stranger,
  'Twas honesty in me t' enrich my father.

YEL. [*Aside*] The girl is wondrous peevish. I fear nothing
  But that she's taken with some other love,
  Then all's quite dashed: that must be narrowly looked to;
  We cannot be too wary in our children.—
  What is't you lack?

TOUCH. JUN. O, nothing now; all that I wish is present:
  I'd have a wedding-ring made for a gentlewoman
  With all speed that may be.

YEL. Of what weight, sir?

TOUCH. JUN. Of some half ounce, stand fair
  And comely, with the spark of a diamond;
  Sir, 'twere pity to lose the least grace.

YEL. Pray, let's see it.

> [*Takes stone from Touchwood junior*]

  Indeed, sir, 'tis a pure one.

TOUCH. JUN. So is the mistress.

YEL. Have you the wideness of her finger, sir?

TOUCH. JUN. Yes, sure, I think I have her measure about me:
  Good faith, 'tis down,[2] I cannot show it you;
  I must pull too many things out to be certain.
  Let me see—long and slender, and neatly jointed;
  Just such another gentlewoman—that's your daughter, sir?

YEL. And therefore, sir, no gentlewoman.

TOUCH. JUN. I protest
  I ne'er saw two maids handed more alike;
  I'll ne'er seek farther, if you'll give me leave, sir.

---

1. The original reads only "being."
2. Deep in my pocket (with an innuendo).

YEL. If you dare venture by her finger, sir.

TOUCH. JUN. Ay, and I'll bide all loss, sir.

YEL. Say you so, sir?
Let us see.—Hither, girl.

TOUCH. JUN. Shall I make bold
With your finger, gentlewoman?

MOLL. Your pleasure, sir.

TOUCH. JUN. That fits her to a hair, sir.

[*Trying ring on Moll's finger*]

YEL. What's your posy now, sir?

TOUCH. JUN. Mass, that's true: posy? i'faith, e'en thus, sir:

"Love that's wise
Blinds parents' eyes."

YEL. How, how? if I may speak without offence, sir,
I hold my life—

TOUCH. JUN. What, sir?

YEL. Go to,—you'll pardon me?

TOUCH. JUN. Pardon you? ay, sir.

YEL. Will you, i'faith?

TOUCH. JUN. Yes, faith, I will.

YEL. You'll steal away some man's daughter: am I near you?
Do you turn aside? you gentlemen are mad wags!
I wonder things can be so warily carried,
And parents blinded so: but they're served right,
That have two eyes and were so dull a' sight.

TOUCH. JUN. [*Aside*] Thy doom take hold of thee!

YEL. To-morrow noon
Shall show your ring well done.

TOUCH. JUN. Being so, 'tis soon.—
Thanks, and your leave, sweet gentlewoman.

MOLL. Sir, you're welcome.—

Exit Touchwood junior

[*Aside*] O were I made of wishes, I went with thee!

YEL. Come now, we'll see how the rules[1] go within.

1. Revels.

MOLL. [*Aside*] That robs my joy; there I lose all I win.

Exeunt

SCENE II

Enter Davy and Allwit severally

DAVY. [*Aside*] Honesty wash my eyes! I've spied a wittol.[1]

ALLWIT. What, Davy Dahanna? welcome from North Wales, i'faith!
And is Sir Walter come?

DAVY. New come to town, sir.

ALLWIT. In to the maids, sweet Davy, and give order
His chamber to be made ready instantly.
My wife's as great as she can wallow, Davy, and longs
For nothing but pickled cucumbers and his coming;
And now she shall ha't, boy.

DAVY. She's sure of them, sir.

ALLWIT. Thy very sight will hold my wife in pleasure
Till the knight come himself; go in, in, in, Davy.

Exit Davy

The founder's come to town: I'm like a man
Finding a table furnished to his hand,
As mine is still to me, prays for the founder,—
Bless the right worshipful the good founder's life!
I thank him, has maintained my house this ten years;
Not only keeps my wife, but 'a keeps me
And all my family; I'm at his table:
He gets me all my children, and pays the nurse
Monthly or weekly; puts me to nothing, rent,
Nor church-duties, not so much as the scavenger:
The happiest state that ever man was born to!
I walk out in a morning; come to breakfast,
Find excellent cheer; a good fire in winter;
Look in my coal-house about midsummer eve,
That's full, five or six chaldron new laid up;

1. Complaisant cuckold.

Look in my back-yard, I shall find a steeple
Made up with Kentish faggots, which o'erlooks
The water-house and the windmills: I say nothing,
But smile and pin the door. When she lies in,
As now she's even upon the point of grunting,
A lady lies not in like her; there's her embossings,
Embroiderings, spanglings, and I know not what,
As if she lay with all the gaudy-shops[1]
In Gresham's Burse[2] about her; then her restoratives,
Able to set up a young 'pothecary,
And richly stock the foreman of a drug-shop;
Her sugar by whole loaves, her wines by rundlets.[3]
I see these things, but, like a happy man,
I pay for none at all; yet fools think's mine;
I have the name, and in his gold I shine:
And where some merchants would in soul kiss hell
To buy a paradise for their wives, and dye
Their conscience in the bloods of prodigal heirs
To deck their night-piece, yet all this being done,
Eaten with jealousy to the inmost bone,—
As what affliction nature more constrains,
Than feed the wife plump for another's veins?—
These torments stand I freed of; I'm as clear
From jealousy of a wife as from the charge:[4]
O, two miraculous blessings! 'tis the knight
Hath took that labor all out of my hands:
I may sit still and play; he's jealous for me,
Watches her steps, sets spies; I live at ease,
He has both the cost and torment: when the string
Of his heart frets, I feed, laugh, or sing,

                                                    [*Sings*]

La dildo, dildo la dildo, la dildo dildo de dildo!

---

1. Where articles of finery were sold.
2. The Royal Exchange.
3. Casks.
4. Cost.

Enter two Servants

1ST SER. What, has he got a singing in his head now?

2ND SER. Now's out of work, he falls to making dildoes.

ALLWIT. Now, sirs, Sir Walter's come.

1ST SER. Is our master come?

ALLWIT. Your master! what am I?

1ST SER. Do not you know, sir?

ALLWIT. Pray, am not I your master?

1ST SER. O, you're but
Our mistress's husband.

ALLWIT. *Ergo,* knave, your master.

1ST SER. *Negatur argumentum.*[1]—Here comes Sir Walter:

Enter Sir Walter and Davy

Now 'a stands bare as well as we; make the most of him,
He's but one peep above a serving-man,
And so much his horns make him.

SIR WAL. How dost, Jack?

ALLWIT. Proud of your worship's health, sir.

SIR WAL. How does your wife?

ALLWIT. E'en after your own making, sir;
She's a tumbler, a' faith, the nose and belly meets.

SIR WAL. They'll part in time again.

ALLWIT. At the good hour they will, an't please your worship.

SIR WAL. Here, sirrah, pull off my boots.—Put on,[2] put on, Jack.

[Servant pulls off his boots]

ALLWIT. I thank your kind worship, sir.

SIR WAL. Slippers! heart, you are sleepy!

[Servant brings slippers]

ALLWIT. *[Aside]* The game begins already.

SIR WAL. Pish, put on, Jack.

ALLWIT. *[Aside]* Now I must do't, or he'll be as angry now,

---

1. The argument is denied.
2. i.e., Put on your hat.

As if I had put it on at first bidding;
'Tis but observing,
'Tis but observing a man's humor once,
And he may ha' him by the nose all his life.

SIR WAL. What entertainment has lain open here?
No strangers in my absence?

1ST SER. Sure, sir, not any.

ALLWIT. [*Aside*] His jealousy begins: am not I happy now,
That can laugh inward whilst his marrow melts?

SIR WAL. How do you satisfy me?

1ST SER. Good sir, be patient!

SIR WAL. For two months' absence I'll be satisfied.

1ST SER. No living creature entered—

SIR WAL. Entered? come, swear!

1ST SER. You will not hear me out, sir—

SIR WAL. Yes, I'll hear't out, sir.

1ST SER. Sir, he can tell himself—

SIR WAL. Heart, he can tell?
Do you think I'll trust him? as a usurer
With forfeited lordships:—him? O monstrous injury!
Believe him? can the devil speak ill of darkness?—
What can you say, sir?

ALLWIT. Of my soul and conscience, sir,
She's a wife as honest of her body to me
As any lord's proud lady e'er can be!

SIR WAL. Yet, by your leave, I heard you were once offering
To go to bed to her.

ALLWIT. No, I protest, sir!

SIR WAL. Heart, if you do, you shall take all! I'll marry.

ALLWIT. O, I beseech you, sir!

SIR WAL. [*Aside*] That wakes the slave,
And keeps his flesh in awe.

ALLWIT. [*Aside*] I'll stop that gap
Where'er I find it open: I have poisoned
His hopes in marriage already with
Some old rich widows, and some landed virgins;
And I'll fall to work still before I'll lose him;
He's yet too sweet to part from.

Enter Wat and Nick

WAT. God-den,[1] father.

ALLWIT. Ha, villain, peace!

NICK. God-den, father.

ALLWIT. Peace, bastard!
Should he hear 'em! [*Aside*]—These are two foolish children,
They do not know the gentleman that sits there.

SIR WAL. O, Wat—how dost, Nick? go to school, ply your books,
boys, ha!

ALLWIT. Where's your legs,[2] whoresons?—They should kneel indeed,
If they could say their prayers.

SIR WAL. [*Aside*] Let me see, stay,—
How shall I dispose of these two brats now
When I am married? for they must not mingle
Amongst my children that I get in wedlock;
'Twill make foul work that, and raise many storms.
I will bind Wat prentice to a goldsmith,
My father Yellowhammer, as fit as can be;
Nick with some vintner; good, goldsmith and vintner;
There will be wine in bowls, i'faith.

Enter Mistress Allwit

MIS. ALL. Sweet knight,
Welcome! I've all my longings now in town;
Now welcome the good hour!

SIR WAL. How cheers my mistress?

MIS. ALL. Made lightsome e'en by him that made me heavy.

SIR WAL. Methinks she shows gallantly, like a moon at full, sir.

ALLWIT. True, and if she bear a male child, there's the man in the
moon, sir.

SIR WAL. 'Tis but the boy in the moon yet, goodman calf.

ALLWIT. There was a man, the boy had ne'er been there else.

SIR WAL. It shall be yours, sir.

ALLWIT. [*Aside*] No, by my troth, I'll swear
It's none of mine; let him that got it keep it!—

1. A corruption of "good evening."
2. Bows.

Thus do I rid myself of fear,
Lie soft, sleep hard, drink wine, and eat good cheer.

Exeunt

ACT II, SCENE I

Enter Touchwood senior and Mistress Touchwood

MIS. TOUCH. 'Twill be so tedious, sir, to live from you,
    But that necessity must be obeyed.
TOUCH. SEN. I would it might not, wife! the tediousness
    Will be the most part mine, that understand
    The blessings I have in thee; so to part,
    That drives the torment to a knowing heart.
    But, as thou sayst, we must give way to need,
    And live awhile asunder; our desires
    Are both too fruitful for our barren fortunes.
    How adverse runs the destiny of some creatures!
    Some only can get riches and no children;
    We only can get children and no riches:
    Then 'tis the prudent'st part to check our wills,
    And, till our state rise, make our bloods lie still.
    'Life, every year a child, and some years two!
    Besides drinkings abroad, that's never reckoned;
    This gear will not hold out.[1]
MIS. TOUCH. Sir, for a time
    I'll take the courtesy of my uncle's house,
    If you be pleased to like on't, till prosperity
    Look with a friendly eye upon our states.
TOUCH. SEN. Honest wife, I thank thee! I never knew
    The perfect treasure thou brought'st with thee more
    Than at this instant minute: a man's happy
    When he's at poorest, that has matched his soul
    As rightly as his body: had I married
    A sensual fool now, as 'tis hard to 'scape it

---

1. We can't go on like this.

'Mongst gentlewomen of our time, she would ha' hanged
About my neck, and never left her hold
Till she had kissed me into wanton businesses,
Which at the waking of my better judgment
I should have cursed most bitterly,
And laid a thicker vengeance on my act
Than misery of the birth; which were enough
If it were born to greatness, whereas mine
Is sure of beggary, though 't were got in wine.
Fulness of joy showeth the goodness in thee;
Thou art a matchless wife: farewell, my joy!

MIS. TOUCH. I shall not want your sight?

TOUCH. SEN. I'll see thee often,
Talk in mirth, and play at kisses with thee;
Anything, wench, but what may beget beggars:
There I give o'er the set,[1] throw down the cards,
And dare not take them up.

MIS. TOUCH. Your will be mine, sir!

Exit

TOUCH. SEN. This does not only make her honesty perfect,
But her discretion, and approves her judgment.
Had her desires been wanton, they'd been blameless,
In being lawful ever; but of all creatures,
I hold that wife a most unmatchèd treasure,
That can unto her fortunes fix her pleasure,
And not unto her blood: this is like wedlock;
The feast of marriage is not lust, but love,
And care of the estate. When I please blood,
Merrily I sing and suck out others' then:
'Tis many a wise man's fault; but of all men
I am the most unfortunate in that game
That ever pleased both genders; I ne'er played yet
Under a bastard; the poor wenches curse me
To the pit where'er I come; they were ne'er served so,

---

1. The card game.

But used to have more words than one to a bargain:
I've such a fatal finger in such business,
I must forth with't; chiefly for country wenches,
For every harvest I shall hinder haymaking;
I had no less than seven lay in last progress,[1]
Within three weeks of one another's time.

Enter a Country Girl with a child

C. GIRL. O snaphance,[2] have I found you?
TOUCH. SEN. How snaphance?
C. GIRL. Do you see your workmanship? nay, turn not from't,
Nor offer to escape; for if you do,
I'll carry it through the streets, and follow you.
Your name may well be called Touchwood,—a pox on you!
You do but touch and take; thou hast undone me:
I was a maid before, I can bring a certificate
For it from both the churchwardens.
TOUCH. SEN. I'll have
The parson's hand too, or I'll not yield to't.
C. GIRL. Thou shalt have more, thou villain! Nothing grieves me
But Ellen my poor cousin in Derbyshire;
Thou'st cracked her marriage quite; she'll have a bout with thee.
TOUCH. SEN. Faith, when she will, I'll have a bout with her.
C. GIRL. A law bout, sir, I mean.
TOUCH. SEN. True, lawyers use
Such bouts as other men do; and if that
Be all thy grief, I'll tender her a husband;
I keep of purpose two or three gulls in pickle
To eat such mutton with, and she shall choose one.
Do but in courtesy, faith, wench, excuse me
Of this half yard of flesh, in which, I think,
It wants a nail or two.
C. GIRL. No; thou shalt find, villain,
It hath right shape, and all the nails it should have.

1. Royal journey.
2. A spring-lock to a gun.

TOUCH. SEN. Faith, I am poor; do a charitable deed, wench;
  I am a younger brother, and have nothing.
C. GIRL. Nothing? thou hast too much, thou lying villain,
  Unless thou wert more thankful!
TOUCH. SEN. I've no dwelling;
  I brake up house but this morning; pray thee, pity me;
  I'm a good fellow, faith; have been too kind
  To people of your gender; if I ha't
  Without¹ my belly, none of your sex shall want it;
  That word has been of force to move a woman.
  There's tricks enough to rid thy hand on't, wench;
  Some rich man's porch to-morrow before day,
  Or else anon i' the evening; twenty devices.
  Here's all I have, i'faith; take purse and all,
  And would I were rid of all the ware i' the shop so!

                                        [*Gives money*]

C. GIRL. Where I find manly dealings, I am pitiful:
  This shall not trouble you.
TOUCH. SEN. And I protest, wench,
  The next I'll keep myself.
C. GIRL. Soft, let it be got first.
  This is the fifth; if e'er I venture more,
  Where I now go for a maid, may I ride for a whore!²

                                              Exit

TOUCH. SEN. What shift she'll make now with this piece of flesh
  In this strict time of Lent, I cannot imagine;
  Flesh dare not peep abroad now: I have known
  This city now above this seven years,
  But, I protest, in better state of government
  I never knew it yet, nor ever heard of;
  There have been more religious wholesome laws
  In the half-circle of a year erected
  For common good than memory e'er knew of,

---

1. Outside.
2. An allusion to the carting of prostitutes.

Setting apart corruption of promoters,[1]
And other poisonous officers, that infect
And with a venomous breath taint every goodness.

Enter Sir Oliver Kix and Lady Kix

LADY KIX. O that e'er I was begot, or bred, or born!
SIR OL. Be content, sweet wife.
TOUCH. SEN. [*Aside*] What's here to do now?
  I hold my life she's in deep passion[2]
  For the imprisonment of veal and mutton,
  Now kept in garrets; weeps for some calf's head now:
  Methinks her husband's head might serve, with bacon.

Enter Touchwood junior

TOUCH. JUN. Hist!
SIR OL. Patience, sweet wife.
TOUCH. JUN. Brother, I've sought you strangely.
TOUCH. SEN. Why, what's the business?
TOUCH. JUN. With all speed thou canst
  Procure a license for me.
TOUCH. SEN. How, a license?
TOUCH. JUN. Cud's foot, she's lost else! I shall miss her ever.
TOUCH. SEN. Nay, sure thou shalt not miss so fair a mark
  For thirteen shillings fourpence.[3]
TOUCH. JUN. Thanks by hundreds!

                    Exeunt Touchwood senior and junior

SIR OL. Nay, pray thee, cease; I'll be at more cost yet,
  Thou know'st we're rich enough.
LADY KIX. All but in blessings,
  And there the beggar goes beyond us: O-o-o!
  To be seven years a wife, and not a child!
  O, not a child!
SIR OL. Sweet wife, have patience.

---

1. Common informers.
2. Sorrow.
3. The worth of a mark.

LADY KIX. Can any woman have a greater cut?
SIR OL. I know 'tis great, but what of that, sweet wife?
  I cannot do withal;[1] there's things making,
  By thine own doctor's advice, at pothecary's:
  I spare for nothing, wife; no, if the price
  Were forty marks a spoonful, I would give
  A thousand pound to purchase fruitfulness:
  It is but bating so many good works
  In the erecting of bridewells[2] and spittlehouses,[3]
  And so fetch it up again; for having none,
  I mean to make good deeds my children.
LADY KIX. Give me but those good deeds, and I'll find children.
SIR OL. Hang thee, thou'st had too many!
LADY KIX. Thou liest, brevity.
SIR OL. O horrible! dar'st thou call me brevity?
  Dar'st thou be so short with me?
LADY KIX. Thou deserv'st worse:
  Think but upon the goodly lands and livings
  That's kept back through want on't.
SIR OL. Talk not on't, pray thee;
  Thou'lt make me play the woman and weep too.
LADY KIX. 'Tis our dry barrenness puffs up Sir Walter;
  None gets by your not getting but that knight;[4]
  He's made by th' means, and fats his fortunes shortly
  In a great dowry with a goldsmith's daughter.
SIR OL. They may be all deceived; be but you patient, wife.
LADY KIX. I've suffered a long time.
SIR OL. Suffer thy heart out;
  A pox suffer thee!
LADY KIX. Nay, thee, thou desertless slave!
SIR OL. Come, come, I ha' done: you'll to the gossiping[5]
  Of Master Allwit's child?

---

1. i.e., I cannot help it.
2. Houses for the correction of prostitutes.
3. Hospitals treating venereal diseases.
4. For want of an heir the properties go to Sir Walter.
5. Christening.

LADY KIX. Yes, to my much joy!
  Every one gets before me; there's my sister
  Was married but at Bartholomew Eve[1] last,
  And she can have two children at a birth:
  O, one of them, one of them, would ha' served my turn!
SIR OL. Sorrow consume thee! thou'rt still crossing me,
  And know'st my nature.

Enter Maid

MAID. O mistress! [*Aside*] —weeping or railing,
  That's our house-harmony.
LADY KIX. What sayst, Jug?
MAID. The sweetest news!
LADY KIX. What is't, wench?
MAID. Throw down your doctor's drugs,
  They're all but heretics; I bring certain remedy,
  That has been taught and proved, and never failed.
SIR OL. O that, that, that, or nothing!
MAID. There's a gentleman,
  I haply have his name too, that has got
  Nine children by one water that he useth:
  It never misses; they come so fast upon him,
  He was fain to give it over.
LADY KIX. His name, sweet Jug?
MAID. One Master Touchwood, a fine gentleman.
  But run behind-hand much with getting children.
SIR OL. Is't possible!
MAID. Why, sir, he'll undertake,
  Using that water, within fifteen year,
  For all your wealth, to make you a poor man,
  You shall so swarm with children.
SIR OL. I'll venture that, i'faith.
LADY KIX. That shall you, husband.
MAID. But I must tell you first, he's very dear.
SIR OL. No matter, what serves wealth for?
LADY KIX. True, sweet husband;

1. August 23.

There's land to come; put case[1] his water stands me
In some five hundred pound a pint,
'Twill fetch a thousand, and a kersten[2] soul,
And that's worth all, sweet husband: I'll about it.

Exeunt

SCENE II

Enter Allwit

ALLWIT. I'll go bid gossips[3] presently myself,
    That's all the work I'll do; nor need I stir,
    But that it is my pleasure to walk forth,
    And air myself a little: I am tied
    To nothing in this business; what I do
    Is merely recreation, not constraint.
    Here's running to and fro! nurse upon nurse,
    Three charwomen, besides maids and neighbors' children.
    Fie, what a trouble have I rid my hands on!
    It makes me sweat to think on't.

Enter Sir Walter Whorehound

SIR WAL. How now, Jack?
ALLWIT. I'm going to bid gossips for your worship's child, sir;
    A goodly girl, i'faith! give you joy on her;
    She looks as if she had two thousand pound
    To her portion, and run away with a tailor;
    A fine plump black-eyed slut: under correction, sir,
    I take delight to see her.—Nurse!

Enter Dry Nurse

DRY N. Do you call, sir?
ALLWIT. I call not you, I call the wet nurse hither.

Exit Dry Nurse

Give me the wet nurse!—

1. i.e., Suppose.
2. A corruption of Christian.
3. Godparents.

Enter Wet Nurse carrying child

Ay, 'tis thou; come hither,
Come hither:
Let's see her once again; I cannot choose
But buss her thrice an hour.

WET N. You may be proud on't, sir;
'Tis the best piece of work that e'er you did.

ALLWIT. Think'st thou so, nurse? what sayst to Wat and Nick?

WET N. They're pretty children both, but here's a wench
Will be a knocker.

ALLWIT. Pup,—sayst thou me so?—pup, little countess!—
Faith, sir, I thank your worship for this girl
Ten thousand times and upward.

SIR WAL. I am glad
I have her for you, sir.

ALLWIT. Here, take her in, nurse;
Wipe her, and give her spoon-meat.

WET N. Wipe your mouth,[1] sir.

Exit with the child

ALLWIT. And now about these gossips.

SIR WAL. Get but two;
I'll stand for one myself.

ALLWIT. To your own child, sir?

SIR WAL. The better policy, it prevents suspicion;
'Tis good to play with rumor at all weapons.

ALLWIT. Troth, I commend your care, sir; 'tis a thing
That I should ne'er have thought on.

SIR WAL. The more slave:
When man turns base, out goes his soul's pure flame,
The fat of ease o'erthrows the eyes of shame.

ALLWIT. I'm studying who to get for godmother,
Suitable to your worship. Now I ha' thought on't.

SIR WAL. [*Aside*] I'll ease you of that care, and please myself in't—
My love the goldsmith's daughter, if I send,
Her father will command her.—Davy Dahanna!

---

1. Mind your own business (?).

Enter Davy

ALLWIT. I'll fit your worship then with a male partner.
SIR WAL. What is he?
ALLWIT. A kind, proper gentleman,
    Brother to Master Touchwood.
SIR WAL. I know Touchwood:
    Has he a brother living?
ALLWIT. A neat bachelor.
SIR WAL. Now we know him, we will make shift with him:
    Despatch, the time draws near.—Come hither, Davy.

Exit with Davy

ALLWIT. In troth, I pity him; he ne'er stands still:
    Poor knight, what pains he takes! sends this way one,
    That way another; has not an hour's leisure:
    I would not have thy toil for all thy pleasure.

Enter two Promoters

Ha, how now? what are these that stand so close
At the street-corner, pricking up their ears
And snuffing up their noses, like rich men's dogs
When the first course goes in? By the mass, promoters;[1]
'Tis so, I hold my life; and planted there
T' arrest the dead corps[2] of poor calves and sheep,
Like ravenous creditors, that will not suffer
The bodies of their poor departed debtors
To go to th' grave, but e'en in death to vex
And stay the corps with bills of Middlesex.
This Lent will fat the whoresons up with sweetbreads,
And lard their whores with lamb-stones:[3] what their golls[4]
Can clutch goes presently to their Molls and Dolls:
The bawds will be so fat with what they earn,
Their chins[5] will hang like udders by Easter-eve,

---

1. Informers.
2. Corpses.
3. Lamb's testicles.
4. A cant term for hands.
5. A double chin was regarded as the distinguishing mark of a bawd.

And, being stroked, will give the milk of witches.
How did the mongrels hear my wife lies in?
Well, I may baffle 'em gallantly. [*Aside*]—By your favour,
    gentlemen,
I am a stranger both unto the city
And to her carnal strictness.
1ST PRO. Good; your will, sir?
ALLWIT. Pray, tell me where one dwells that kills this Lent?
1ST PRO. How? kills?—Come hither, Dick; a bird, a bird!
2ND PRO. What is't that you would have?
ALLWIT. Faith, any flesh;
    But I long especially for veal and green-sauce.
1ST PRO. [*Aside*] Green goose, you shall be sauced.
ALLWIT. I've half a scornful stomach,
    No fish will be admitted.
1ST PRO. Not this Lent, sir?
ALLWIT. Lent? what cares colon[1] here for Lent?
1ST PRO. You say well, sir;
    Good reason that the colon of a gentleman,
    As you were lately pleased to term your worship's, sir,
    Should be fulfilled with answerable food,
    To sharpen blood, delight health, and tickle nature.
    Were you directed hither to this street, sir?
ALLWIT. That I was, ay, marry.
2ND PRO. And the butcher, belike,
    Should kill and sell close in some upper room?
ALLWIT. Some apple-loft, as I take it, or a coal-house;
    I know not which i'faith.
2ND PRO. Either will serve:
    [*Aside*] This butcher shall kiss Newgate, 'less he turn up
    The bottom of the pocket of his apron.—
    You go to seek him?
ALLWIT. Where you shall not find him:
    I'll buy, walk by your noses with my flesh,

---

1. A part of the intestines.

Sheep-biting mongrels, hand-basket freebooters!
My wife lies in—a foutra[1] for promoters!

Exit

1ST PRO. That shall not serve your turn.—What a rogue's this!
How cunningly he came over us!

Enter Man with a basket under his cloak

2ND PRO. Hush't, stand close!
MAN. I have 'scaped well thus far; they say the knaves
Are wondrous hot and busy.
1ST PRO. By your leave, sir,
We must see what you have under your cloak there.
MAN. Have? I have nothing.
1ST PRO. No? do you tell us that? what makes this lump
Stick out then? we must see, sir.
MAN. What will you see, sir?
A pair of sheets and two of my wife's foul smocks
Going to the washers.
2ND PRO. O, we love that sight well!
You cannot please us better. What, do you gull us?
Call you these shirts and smocks?

[*Seizes basket and takes out of it a piece of meat*]

MAN. Now, a pox choke you!
You've cozened me and five of my wife's kindred
Of a good dinner; we must make it up now
With herrings and milk-pottage

Exit

1ST PRO. 'Tis all veal.
2ND PRO. All veal?
Pox, the worse luck! I promised faithfully
To send this morning a fat quarter of lamb
To a kind gentlewoman in Turnbull Street[2]
That longs, and how I'm crost!

1. A term of contempt.
2. A street in Clerkenwell noted as the residence of thieves and prostitutes.

1ST PRO. Let us share this, and see what hap comes next then.
2ND PRO. Agreed. Stand close again, another booty:

Enter Man with a basket

What's he?
1ST PRO. Sir, by your favor.
MAN. Meaning me, sir?
1ST PRO. Good Master Oliver? cry thee mercy i'faith!
What hast thou there?
MAN. A rack of mutton, sir,
And half a lamb; you know my mistress' diet.
1ST PRO. Go, go, we see thee not; away, keep close!—
Heart, let him pass! thou'lt never have the wit
To know our benefactors.
2ND PRO. I have forgot him.
1ST PRO. 'Tis Master Beggarland's man, the wealthy merchant,
That is in fee with us.
2ND PRO. Now I've a feeling of him.

Exit Man

1ST PRO. You know he purchased the whole Lent together,
Gave us ten groats a-piece on Ash Wednesday.
2ND PRO. True, true.
1ST PRO. A wench!
2ND PRO. Why, then, stand close indeed.

Enter Country Girl with a basket

C. GIRL. [*Aside*] Women had need of wit, if they'll shift here,
And she that hath wit may shift anywhere.
1ST PRO. Look, look! poor fool, sh'as left the rump uncovered too,
More to betray her! this is like a murderer
That will outface the deed with a bloody band.[1]
2ND PRO. What time of the year is't, sister?
C. GIRL. O sweet gentlemen!
I'm a poor servant, let me go.

---

1. Blood-stained cuff.

1ST PRO. You shall, wench,
But this must stay with us.

C. GIRL. O you undo me, sir!
'Tis for a wealthy gentlewoman that takes physic, sir;
The doctor does allow my mistress mutton.
O, as you tender the dear life of a gentlewoman!
I'll bring my master to you; he shall show you
A true authority from the higher powers,
And I'll run every foot.

2ND PRO. Well, leave your basket then,
And run and spare not.

C. GIRL. Will you swear then to me
To keep it till I come?

1ST PRO. Now by this light I will.

C. GIRL. What say you, gentlemen?

2ND PRO. What a strange wench 'tis!—
Would we might perish else.

C. GIRL. Nay, then I run, sir.

Leaves the basket, and exit

1ST PRO. And ne'er return, I hope.

2ND PRO. A politic baggage! she makes us swear to keep it;
I prithee look what market she hath made.

1ST PRO. Imprimis, sir, a good fat loin of mutton.

[Taking out a loin of mutton]

What comes next under this cloth? now for a quarter
Of lamb.

2ND PRO. No, for a shoulder of mutton.

1ST PRO. Done!

2ND PRO. Why, done, sir!

1ST PRO. By the mass, I feel I've lost
'Tis of more weight, i'faith.

2ND PRO. Some loin of veal?

1ST PRO. No, faith, here's a lamb's head, I feel that plainly;
Why, I'll yet win my wager.

2ND PRO. Ha!

1ST PRO. 'Swounds, what's here!

[Taking out a child]

2ND PRO. A child!

1ST PRO. A pox of all dissembling cunning whores!

2ND PRO. Here's an unlucky breakfast!

1ST PRO. What shall's do?

2ND PRO. The quean made us swear to keep it too.

1ST PRO. We might leave it else.

2ND PRO. Villainous strange!
  Life, had she none to gull but poor promoters,
  That watch hard for a living?

1ST PRO. Half our gettings
  Must run in sugar-sops and nurses' wages now,
  Besides many a pound of soap and tallow;
  We've need to get loins of mutton still, to save
  Suet to change for candles.

2ND PRO. Nothing mads me
  But this was a lamb's head with you; you felt it:
  She has made calves' heads of us.

1ST PRO. Prithee, no more on't;
  There's time to get it up; it is not come
  To Mid-Lent Sunday yet.

2ND PRO. I am so angry,
  I'll watch no more to-day.

1ST PRO. Faith, nor I neither.

2ND PRO. Why, then, I'll make a motion.

1ST PRO. Well, what is't?

2ND PRO. Let's e'en go to the Checker at Queenhive,[1]
  And roast the loin of mutton till young flood,[2]
  Then send the child to Branford.[3]

                                        Exeunt

1. Inn at Queenhithe.
2. Beginning of flood tide.
3. Brentford.

Scene III

Enter Allwit in one of Sir Walter's suits, and Davy trussing[1] him

ALLWIT. 'Tis a busy day at our house, Davy.

DAVY. Always the kursning[2] day, sir.

ALLWIT. Truss, truss me, Davy.

DAVY. [*Aside*] No matter an you were hanged, sir.

ALLWIT. How does this suit fit me, Davy?

DAVY. Excellent neatly;

My master's things were ever fit for you, sir,

E'en to a hair, you know.

ALLWIT. Thou'st hit it right, Davy:

We ever jumped in one this ten years, Davy;

So, well said.—

Enter Man with a box

What art thou?

MAN. Your comfit-maker's man, sir.

ALLWIT. O sweet youth!

In to the nurse, quick, quick, 'tis time, i'faith.

Your mistress will be here?

MAN. She was setting forth, sir.

Exit

ALLWIT. Here comes our gossips now: O, I shall have

Such kissing work to-day.—

Enter two Puritans

Sweet Mistress Underman

Welcome, i'faith.

1ST PUR. Give you joy of your fine girl, sir:

Grant that her education may be pure,

And become one of the faithful!

ALLWIT. Thanks to your sisterly wishes, Mistress Underman.

2ND PUR. Are any of the brethren's wives yet come?

1. Tying the points of his trunk hose.
2. Christening.

ALLWIT. There are some wives within, and some at home.
1ST PUR. Verily, thanks, sir.

Exeunt Puritans

ALLWIT. Verily you're an ass, forsooth:
I must fit all these times, or there's no music.
Here comes a friendly and familiar pair:

Enter two Gossips

Now I like these wenches well.
1ST GOS. How dost, sirrah?
ALLWIT. Faith, well, I thank you, neighbor;—and how dost thou?
2ND GOS. Want nothing but such getting, sir, as thine.
ALLWIT. My gettings, wench? they're poor.
1ST GOS. Fie, that thou'lt say so;
Thou'st as fine children as a man can get.
DAVY. [*Aside*] Ay, as a man can get, and that's my master.
ALLWIT. They're pretty foolish things, put to making in minutes,
I ne'er stand long about 'em. Will you walk in, wenches?

Exeunt Gossips

Enter Touchwood junior and Moll

TOUCH. JUN. The happiest meeting that our souls could wish for!
Here is the ring ready; I'm beholden
Unto your father's haste, has kept his hour.
MOLL. He never kept it better.

Enter Sir Walter Whorehound

TOUCH. JUN. Back, be silent.
SIR WAL. Mistress and partner, I will put you both
Into one cup.
DAVY. [*Aside*] Into one cup? most proper;
A fitting compliment for a goldsmith's daughter.
ALLWIT. Yes, sir, that's he must be your worship's partner
In this day's business, Master Touchwood's brother.
SIR WAL. I embrace your acquaintance, sir.
TOUCH. JUN. It vows your service, sir.
SIR WAL. It's near high time; come, Master Allwit.
ALLWIT. Ready, sir.

Sir Wal. Wilt please you walk?

Touch. Jun. Sir, I obey your time.

Exeunt

Scene IV

Enter from the house Midwife with the child, Lady Kix and other Gossips, who exeunt; then Maudlin, Puritans, and other Gossips

1st Gos. Good Mistress Yellowhammer—

Maud. In faith, I will not.

1st Gos. Indeed it¹ shall be yours.

Maud. I have sworn, i'faith.

1st Gos. I'll stand still then.

Maud. So, will you let the child
  Go without company, and make me forsworn?

1st Gos. You are such another creature!

Exeunt 1st Gossip and Maudlin

2nd Gos. Before me?
  I pray come down a little.

3rd Gos. Not a whit;
  I hope I know my place.

2nd Gos. Your place? great wonder, sure!
  Are you any better than a comfit-maker's wife?

3rd Gos. And that's as good at all times as a pothecary's.

2nd Gos. Ye lie! yet I forbear you too.

Exeunt 2nd and 3rd Gossips

1st Pur. Come, sweet sister; we go
  In unity, and show the fruits of peace,
  Like children of the spirit.

2nd Pur. I love lowliness.

Exeunt Puritans

4th Gos. True, so say I, though they strive more;
  There comes as proud behind as goes before.

5th Gos. Every inch, i'faith.

Exeunt

---

1. The two are entreating each other to take precedence.

ACT III, SCENE I

Enter Touchwood junior and Parson

TOUCH. JUN. O sir, if e'er you felt the force of love,
    Pity it in me!
PAR. Yes, though I ne'er was married, sir,
    I've felt the force of love from good men's daughters,
    And some that will be maids yet three years hence.
    Have you got a license?
TOUCH. JUN. Here, 'tis ready, sir.
PAR. That's well.
TOUCH. JUN. The ring, and all things perfect; she'll steal hither.
PAR. She shall be welcome, sir; I'll not be long
    A clapping you together.
TOUCH. JUN. O, here she's come, sir!

Enter Moll and Touchwood senior

PAR. What's he?
TOUCH. JUN. My honest brother.
TOUCH. SEN. Quick, make haste, sirs!
MOLL. You must despatch with all the speed you can,
    For I shall be missed straight; I made hard shift
    For this small time I have.
PAR. Then I'll not linger,
    Place that ring upon her finger:
                    [Touchwood junior puts ring on Moll's finger]
    This the finger plays the part,
    Whose master-vein shoots from the heart:
    Now join hands—

Enter Yellowhammer and Sir W. Whorehound

YEL. Which I will sever,
    And so ne'er again meet, never!
MOLL. O, we're betrayed!
TOUCH. JUN. Hard fate!
SIR WAL. I'm struck with wonder!

YEL. Was this the politic fetch,[1] thou mystical[2] baggage,
   Thou disobedient strumpet!—And were you
   So wise to send for her to such an end?
SIR WAL. Now I disclaim the end; you'll make me mad.
YEL. And what are you, sir?
TOUCH. JUN. An you cannot see
   With those two glasses, put on a pair more.
YEL. I dreamed of anger still.—Here, take your ring, sir,—
                         [Taking ring off Moll's finger]
   Ha! this? life, 'tis the same! abominable!
   Did not I sell this ring?
TOUCH. JUN. I think you did;
   You received money for't.
YEL. Heart, hark you, knight;
   Here's no unconscionable villainy!
   Set me a-work to make the wedding-ring,
   And come with an intent to steal my daughter!
   Did ever runaway match it!
SIR WAL. This your brother, sir?
TOUCH. SEN. He can tell that as well as I.
YEL. The very posy mocks me to my face,—

        "Love that's wise
        Blinds parents' eyes."

I thank your wisdom, sir, for blinding of us;
We've good hope to recover our sight shortly:
In the meantime I will lock up this baggage
As carefully as my gold; she shall see
As little sun, if a close room or so
Can keep her from the light on't.
MOLL. O sweet father,
   For love's sake, pity me!
YEL. Away!
MOLL. Farewell, sir;

1. Trick.
2. Secretive.

All content bless thee! and take this for comfort,
Though violence keep me, thou canst lose me never,
I'm ever thine, although we part for ever.
YEL. Ay, we shall part you, minx.

Exit with Moll

SIR WAL. Your acquaintance, sir,
Came very lately, yet came too soon;
I must hereafter know you for no friend,
But one that I must shun like pestilence,
Or the disease of lust.
TOUCH. JUN. Like enough, sir;
You ha' ta'en me at the worst time for words
That e'er ye picked out: faith, do not wrong me, sir.

Exit with Parson

TOUCH. SEN. Look after him,[1] and spare not: there he walks
That ne'er yet received baffling:[2] you are blest
More than ever I knew; go, take your rest.

Exit

SIR WAL. I pardon you, you are both losers.

Exit

SCENE II

*Enter Midwife with the child, Lady Kix, Maudlin, Puritans,
and other Gossips*

1ST GOS. How is it, woman? we have brought you home
A kursen[3] soul.
MIS. ALL. Ay, I thank your pains.
1ST PUR. And, verily, well kursened, i' the right way,
Without idolatry or superstition,
After the pure manner of Amsterdam.[4]
MIS. ALL. Sit down, good neighbors.—Nurse.
NURSE. At hand, forsooth.

---

1. Watch him carefully.
2. Disgrace.
3. Christened.
4. Many Puritans took refuge at Amsterdam.

MIS. ALL. Look they have all low stools.

NURSE. They have, forsooth.

2ND GOS. Bring the child hither, nurse.—How say you now, gossip,
   Is't not a chopping[1] girl? so like the father.

3RD GOS. As if it had been spit out of his mouth!
   Eyed, nosed, and browed, as like as a girl can be,
   Only, indeed, it has the mother's mouth.

2ND GOS. The mother's mouth up and down, up and down.

3RD GOS. 'Tis a large child, she's but a little woman.

1ST PUR. No, believe me,
   A very spiny[2] creature, but all heart:
   Well mettled, like the faithful, to endure
   Her tribulation here, and raise up seed.

2ND GOS. She had a sore labor on't, I warrant you;
   You can tell, neighbor?

3RD GOS. O, she had great speed;
   We were afraid once, but she made us all
   Have joyful hearts again; 'tis a good soul, i'faith;
   The midwife found her a most cheerful daughter.

1ST PUR. 'Tis the spirit; the sisters are all like her.

*Enter Sir Walter Whorehound, carrying a silver standing-cup
and two spoons, and Allwit*

2ND GOS. O, here comes the chief gossip, neighbors!

Exit Nurse

SIR WAL. The fatness of your wishes to you all, ladies!

3RD GOS. O dear, sweet gentleman, what fine words he has!
   The fatness of our wishes!

2ND GOS. Calls us all ladies!

4TH GOS. I promise you, a fine gentleman and a courteous.

2ND GOS. Methinks her husband shows like a clown to him.

3RD GOS. I would not care what clown my husband were too,
   So I had such fine children.

2ND GOS. Sh'as all fine children, gossip.

3RD GOS. Ay, and see how fast they come!

1. Vigorous.
2. Lean.

1ST PUR. Children are blessings,
  If they be got with zeal by the brethren,
  As I have five at home.
SIR WAL. The worst is past,
  I hope, now, gossip.
MIS. ALL. So I hope too, good sir.
ALLWIT. What, then, so hope I too, for company;
  I've nothing to do else.
SIR WAL. A poor remembrance, lady,
  To the love of the babe; I pray, accept of it.
                        [*Giving cup and spoons*]
MIS. ALL. O, you are at too much charge, sir!
2ND GOS. Look, look, what has he given her? what is't, gossip?
3RD GOS. Now, by my faith, a fair high standing-cup
  And two great 'postle-spoons,[1] one of them gilt.
1ST PUR. Sure that was Judas then with the red beard.[2]
2ND PUR. I would not feed
  My daughter with that spoon for all the world,
  For fear of coloring her hair; red hair
  The brethren like not, it consumes them much;
  'Tis not the sisters' color.

Re-enter Nurse with comfits and wine

ALLWIT. Well said, nurse;
  About, about with them among the gossips!
                  [*Nurse hands about the comfits*]
  [*Aside*] Now out comes all the tasselled handkerchers,
  They're spread abroad between their knees already;
  Now in goes the long fingers that are washed
  Some thrice a day in urine; my wife uses it.
  Now we shall have such pocketing; see how
  They lurch[3] at the lower end!

---

1. Spoons with a little figure of an apostle on the handle; a common present at christenings.
2. Red is the traditional color of Judas's hair.
3. Cheat.

1st Pur. Come hither, nurse.

Allwit. [*Aside*] Again? she has taken twice already.

1st Pur. I had forgot a sister's child that's sick.

> [*Taking comfits*]

Allwit. [*Aside*] A pox! it seems your purity
Loves sweet things well that puts in thrice together.
Had this been all my cost now, I'd been beggared;
These women have no consciences at sweetmeats,
Where'er they come; see an they've not culled out
All the long plums too, they've left nothing here
But short wriggle-tail comfits, not worth mouthing:
No mar'l I heard a citizen complain once
That his wife's belly only broke his back;
Mine had been all in fitters[1] seven years since,
But for this worthy knight,
That with a prop upholds my wife and me,
And all my estate buried in Bucklersbury.[2]

Mis. All. Here, Mistress Yellowhammer, and neighbors,
To you all that have taken pains with me,
All the good wives at once!

> [*Drinks; after which Nurse hands round the wine*]

1st Pur. I'll answer for them;
They wish all health and strength, and that you may
Courageously go forward, to perform
The like and many such, like a true sister,
With motherly bearing.

> [*Drinks*]

Allwit. [*Aside*] Now the cups troll about
To wet the gossips' whistles; it pours down, i'faith;
They never think of payment.

1st Pur. Fill again, nurse.

> [*Drinks*]

---

1. Pieces.
2. Street of druggists who also sold sweetmeats.

ALLWIT. [*Aside*] Now bless thee, two at once! I'll stay no longer;
  It would kill me, an I paid for it.—
  Will't please you to walk down, and leave the women?
SIR WAL. With all my heart, Jack.
ALLWIT. Troth, I cannot blame you.
SIR WAL. Sit you all merry, ladies.
GOSSIPS. Thank your worship, sir.
1ST PUR. Thank your worship, sir.
ALLWIT. [*Aside*] A pox twice tipple¹ ye, you're last and lowest!

                          Exeunt Sir W. Whorehound and Allwit

1ST PUR. Bring hither that same cup, nurse; I would fain
  Drive away this—hup—antichristian grief.

                                              [*Drinks*]

3RD GOS. See, gossip, an she lies not in like a countess;
  Would I had such a husband for my daughter!
4TH GOS. Is not she toward marriage?
3RD GOS. O no, sweet gossip!
4TH GOS. Why, she's nineteen.
3RD GOS. Ay, that she was last Lammas;²
  But she has a fault, gossip, a secret fault.
4TH GOS. A fault? what is't?
3RD GOS. I'll tell you when I've drunk.

                                              [*Drinks*]

4TH GOS. [*Aside*] Wine can do that, I see, that friendship cannot.
3RD GOS. And now, I'll tell you, gossip; she's too free.

                                              Exit Nurse

4TH GOS. Too free?
3RD GOS. O ay, she cannot lie dry in her bed.
4TH GOS. What, and nineteen?
3RD GOS. 'Tis as I tell you, gossip.

              Re-enter Nurse, and whispers to Maudlin

MAUD. Speak with me, nurse? who is't?
NURSE. A gentleman.
  From Cambridge; I think it be your son, forsooth.

---

1. Topple.
2. August 1.

MAUD. 'Tis my son Tim, i'faith; prithee, call him up
   Among the women, 'twill embolden him well,—

Exit Nurse

[*Aside*] For he wants nothing but audacity.
   Would the Welsh gentlewoman at home were here now!
LADY KIX. Is your son come, forsooth?
MAUD. Yes, from the university, forsooth.
LADY KIX. 'Tis great joy on ye.
MAUD. There's a great marriage
   Towards[1] for him.
LADY KIX. A marriage?
MAUD. Yes, sure,
   A huge heir in Wales at least to nineteen mountains.
   Besides her goods and cattle.

Re-enter Nurse with Tim

TIM. O, I'm betrayed!

Exit

MAUD. What, gone again?—Run after him, good nurse;
   He is so bashful, that's the spoil of youth:

Exit Nurse

In the university they're kept still to men,
   And ne'er trained up to women's company.
LADY KIX. 'Tis a great spoil of youth indeed.

Re-enter Nurse and Tim

NURSE. Your mother will have it so.
MAUD. Why, son! why Tim!
   What, must I rise and fetch you? for shame, son!
TIM. Mother, you do intreat like a fresh-woman;
   'Tis against the laws of the university
   For any that has answered under[2] bachelor
   To thrust 'mongst married wives.
MAUD. Come, we'll excuse you here.
TIM. Call up my tutor, mother, and I care not.

---

1. In preparation.
2. Satisfied the university's requirements for.

MAUD. What, is your tutor come? have you brought him up?

TIM. I ha' not brought him up, he stands at door;
    Negatur, there's logic to begin with you, mother.

MAUD. Run, call the gentleman, nurse; he's my son's tutor.—

                                    Exit Nurse

    Here, eat some plums.

                                      [Offers comfits]

TIM. Come I from Cambridge,
    And offer me six plums?

MAUD. Why, how now, Tim?
    Will not your old tricks yet be left?

TIM. Served like a child,
    When I have answered under bachelor!

MAUD. You'll ne'er lin[1] till I make your tutor whip you;
    You know how I served you once at the free-school
    In Paul's Churchyard?

TIM. O monstrous absurdity!
    Ne'er was the like in Cambridge since my time;
    'Life, whip a bachelor! you'd be laughed at soundly;
    Let not my tutor hear you, 'twould be a jest
    Through the whole university. No more words, mother.

            Re-enter Nurse with Tutor

MAUD. Is this your tutor, Tim?

TUTOR. Yes, surely, lady,
    I am the man that brought him in league with logic,
    And read the Dunces[2] to him.

TIM. That did he, mother;
    But now I have 'em all in my own pate,
    And can as well read 'em to others.

TUTOR. That can he,
    Mistress, for they flow naturally from him.

MAUD. I am the more beholding to your pains, sir.

---

1. Cease.
2. The schoolmen, so named after Duns Scotus.

TUTOR. *Non ideo sane.*[1]

MAUD. True, he was an idiot indeed
  When he went out of London, but now he's well mended.
  Did you receive the two goose-pies I sent you?

TUTOR. And eat them heartily, thanks to your worship.

MAUD. 'Tis my son Tim; I pray bid him welcome, gentlewomen.

TIM. Tim? hark you, Timotheus, mother, Timotheus.

MAUD. How, shall I deny your name? Timotheus, quoth he!
  Faith, there's a name!—'Tis my son Tim, forsooth.

LADY KIX. You're welcome, master Tim.

                                                    [*Kisses Tim*]

TIM. [*Aside*] O this is horrible,
  She wets as she kisses! —Your handkercher, sweet tutor,
  To wipe them off as fast as they come on.

2ND GOS. Welcome from Cambridge.

                                                    [*Kisses Tim*]

TIM. [*Aside*] This is intolerable!
  This woman has a villainous sweet breath,
  Did she not stink of comfits. —Help me, sweet tutor,
  Or I shall rub my lips off!

TUTOR. I'll go kiss
  The lower end the whilst.

TIM. Perhaps that's the sweeter,
  And we shall despatch the sooner.

1ST PUR. Let me come next:
  Welcome from the wellspring of discipline,[2]
  That waters all the brethren.

                                                    [*Reels and falls*]

TIM. Hoist, I beseech thee!

3RD GOS. O bless the woman!—Mistress Underman—

                                                    [*They raise her up*]

1ST PUR. 'Tis but the common affliction of the faithful;
  We must embrace our falls.

---

1. Not for that reason.
2. Cambridge, favored by Puritans.

TIM. I'm glad I escaped it;
　　It was some rotten kiss sure, it dropt down
　　Before it came at me.

Re-enter Allwit with Davy

ALLWIT. [*Aside*] Here is a noise! not parted yet? heyday,
　　A looking-glass!¹—They've drunk so hard in plate,
　　That some of them had need of other vessels.—
　　Yonder the bravest show!
GOSSIPS. Where, where, sir?
ALLWIT. Come along presently by the Pissing-conduit,²
　　With two brave drums and a standard-bearer.
GOSSIPS. O brave!
TIM. Come, tutor.

Exit with Tutor

GOSSIPS. Farewell, sweet gossip!
MIS. ALL. I thank you all for your pains.
1ST PUR. Feed and grow strong.

Exeunt Lady Kix, Maudlin, and all the Gossips

ALLWIT. You had more need to sleep than eat;
　　Go take a nap with some of the brethren, go,
　　And rise up a well-edified, boldified sister.
　　O, here's a day of toil well passed over,
　　Able to make a citizen hare-mad!
　　How hot they've made the room with their thick bums!
　　Dost not feel it, Davy?
DAVY. Monstrous strong, sir.
ALLWIT. What's here under the stools?
DAVY. Nothing but wet, sir;
　　Some wine spilt here belike.
ALLWIT. Is't no worse, think'st thou?
　　Fair needlework stools cost nothing with them, Davy.

---

1. Chamberpot.
2. So-called from its running in a small stream.

DAVY. [*Aside*] Nor you neither, i'faith.

ALLWIT. Look how they have laid them,
    E'en as they lie themselves, with their heels up!
    How they have shuffled up the rushes[1] too, Davy,
    With their short figging little shittle-cock[2] heels!
    These women can let nothing stand as they find it.
    But what's the secret thou'st about to tell me,
    My honest Davy?

DAVY. If you should disclose it, sir—

ALLWIT. 'Life, rip my belly up to the throat then, Davy!

DAVY. My master's upon marriage.

ALLWIT. Marriage, Davy?
    Send me to hanging rather.

DAVY. [*Aside*] I have stung him!

ALLWIT. When? where? what is she, Davy?

DAVY. Even the same was gossip, and gave the spoon.

ALLWIT. I have no time to stay, nor scarce can speak;
    I'll stop those wheels, or all the work will break.

Exit

DAVY. I knew 'twould prick. Thus do I fashion still
    All mine own ends by him and his rank toil:
    Tis my desire to keep him still from marriage;
    Being his poor nearest kinsman, I may fare
    The better at his death; there my hopes build,
    Since my Lady Kix is dry,[3] and hath no child.

Exit

SCENE III

Enter Touchwood senior and Touchwood junior

TOUCH. JUN. You're in the happiest way t' enrich yourself
    And pleasure me, brother, as man's feet can tread in;

---

1. With which the floors were strewn.
2. The original form of shuttlecock.
3. Barren.

For though she be locked up, her vow is fixed
Only to me; then time shall never grieve me,
For by that vow e'en absent I enjoy her,
Assuredly confirmed that none else shall,
Which will make tedious years seem gameful to me:
In the mean space, lose you no time, sweet brother;
You have the means to strike at this knight's fortunes,
And lay him level with his bankrout[1] merit;
Get but his wife with child, perch at tree-top,
And shake the golden fruit into her lap;
About it before she weep herself to a dry ground,
And whine out all her goodness.

TOUCH. SEN. Prithee, cease;
I find a too much aptness in my blood
For such a business, without provocation;
You might well spared this banquet of eringoes,
Artichokes, potatoes, and your buttered crab;[2]
They were fitter kept for your wedding-dinner.

TOUCH. JUN. Nay, an you'll follow my suit, and save my purse too,
Fortune doats on me: he's in happy case
Finds such an honest friend i' the common-place.[3]

TOUCH. SEN. Life, what makes thee so merry? thou'st no cause
That I could hear of lately since thy crosses,[4]
Unless there be news come with new additions.

TOUCH. JUN. Why, there thou hast it right; I look for her
This evening, brother.

TOUCH. SEN. How's that? look for her?

TOUCH. JUN. I will deliver you of the wonder straight, brother:
By the firm secrecy and kind assistance
Of a good wench i' the house, who, made of pity,
Weighing the case her own, she's led through gutters,
Strange hidden ways, which none but love could find,
Or ha' the heart to venture: I expect her
Where you would little think.

1. Bankrupt.
2. All aphrodisiacs. Eringo is sea-holly.
3. i.e., A friend at court.
4. Adversities.

TOUCH. SEN. I care not where,
  So she be safe, and yours.
TOUCH. JUN. Hope tells me so;
  But from your love and time my peace must grow.
TOUCH. SEN. You know the worst then, brother.
  [*Exit Touchwood jun.*]—Now to my Kix,
  The barren he and she; they're i' the next room;
  But to say which of their two humors hold them
  Now at this instant, I cannot say truly.
SIR OL. [*Within*] Thou liest, barrenness!
TOUCH. SEN. O, is't that time of day? give you joy of your tongue,
  There's nothing else good in you: this their life
  The whole day, from eyes open to eyes shut,
  Kissing or scolding, and then must be made friends;
  Then rail the second part of the first fit out,
  And then be pleased again, no man knows which way:
  Fall out like giants, and fall in like children;
  Their fruit can witness as much.

Enter Sir Oliver Kix and Lady Kix

SIR OL. 'Tis thy fault.
LADY KIX. Mine, drouth and coldness?
SIR OL. Thine; 'tis thou art barren.
LADY KIX. I barren? O life, that I durst but speak now
  In mine own justice, in mine own right! I barren?
  'Twas otherwise with me when I was at court;
  I was ne'er called so till I was married.
SIR OL. I'll be divorced.
LADY KIX. Be hanged! I need not wish it,
  That will come too soon to thee: I may say
  Marriage and hanging goes by destiny,
  For all the goodness I can find in't yet.
SIR OL. I'll give up house, and keep some fruitful whore,
  Like an old bachelor, in a tradesman's chamber;
  She and her children shall have all.
LADY KIX. Where be they?
TOUCH. SEN. Pray, cease;
  When there are friendlier courses took for you,

To get and multiply within your house
At your own proper costs, in spite of censure,
Methinks an honest peace might be established.

SIR OL. What, with her? never.

TOUCH. SEN. Sweet sir—

SIR OL. You work all in vain.

LADY KIX. Then he doth all like thee.

TOUCH. SEN. Let me entreat, sir—

SIR OL. Singleness confound her!
I took her with one smock.

LADY KIX. But, indeed, you
Came not so single when you came from shipboard.[1]

SIR OL. [*Aside*] Heart, she bit sore there! —Prithee, make us friends.

TOUCH. SEN. [*Aside*] Is't come to that? the peal begins to cease.

SIR OL. I'll sell all at an out-cry.[2]

LADY KIX. Do thy worst, slave!—
Good, sweet sir, bring us into love again.

TOUCH. SEN. [*Aside*] Some would think this impossible to
compass.—
Pray, let this storm fly over.

SIR OL. Good sir, pardon me;
I'm master of this house, which I'll sell presently;
I'll clap up bills this evening.

TOUCH. SEN. Lady, friends, come!

LADY KIX. If ever ye loved woman, talk not on't, sir:
What, friends with him? good faith, do you think I'm mad?
With one that's scarce th' hinder quarter of a man?

SIR OL. Thou art nothing of a woman.

LADY KIX. Would I were less than nothing!

[*Weeps*]

SIR OL. Nay, prithee, what does mean?

LADY KIX. I cannot please you.

SIR OL. I'faith, thou'rt a good soul; he lies that says it;
Buss, buss, pretty rogue.

[*Kisses her*]

---

1. He brought more than one "smock" with him.
2. An auction announced by the common crier.

LADY KIX. You care not for me.

TOUCH. SEN. [*Aside*] Can any man tell now which way they
    came in?
  By this light, I'll be hanged then!

SIR OL. Is the drink come?

TOUCH. SEN. Here is a little vial of almond-milk—
  [*Aside*] That stood me in[1] some threepence.

SIR OL. I hope to see thee, wench, within these few years,
  Circled with children, pranking up a girl,
  And putting jewels in her little ears;
  Fine sport, i'faith!

LADY KIX. Ay, had you been aught, husband,
  It had been done ere this time.

SIR OL. Had I been aught?
  Hang thee, hadst thou been aught! but a cross thing
  I ever found thee.

LADY KIX. Thou'rt a grub, to say so.

SIR OL. A pox on thee!

TOUCH. SEN. [*Aside*] By this light, they're out again
  At the same door, and no man can tell which way!
  Come, here's your drink, sir.

SIR OL. I'll not take it now, sir,
  An I were sure to get three boys ere midnight.

LADY KIX. Why, there thou show'st now of what breed thou com'st
  To hinder generation: O thou villain,
  That knows how crookedly the world goes with us
  For want of heirs, yet put by[2] all good fortune!

SIR OL. Hang, strumpet! I will take it now in spite.

TOUCH. SEN. Then you must ride upon't five hours.

                  [*Gives vial to Sir Oliver*]

SIR OL. I mean so.—
  Within there!

---

1. Cost me.
2. Neglect.

Enter Servant

SER. Sir?

SIR OL. Saddle the white mare:

Exit Servant

I'll take a whore along, and ride to Ware.

LADY KIX. Ride to the devil!

SIR OL. I'll plague you every way:
Look ye, do you see? 'tis gone.

[*Drinks*]

LADY KIX. A pox go with it!

SIR OL. Ay, curse, and spare not now.

TOUCH. SEN. Stir up and down, sir;
You must not stand.

SIR OL. Nay, I'm not given to standing.

TOUCH. SEN. So much the better, sir, for the———[1]

SIR OL. I never could stand long in one place yet;
I learnt it of my father, ever figient.[2]
How if I crossed[3] this, sir?

[*Capers*]

TOUCH. SEN. O, passing good, sir,
And would show well 'a horseback: when you come to your inn,
If you leapt over a joint-stool or two,
'Twere not amiss [*Aside*] —although you brake your neck, sir.

SIR OL. What say you to a table thus high, sir?

TOUCH. SEN. Nothing better, sir, if't be furnished with good victuals.
You remember how the bargain runs 'bout this business?

SIR OL. Or else I had a bad head: you must receive, sir,
Four hundred pounds of me at four several payments;
One hundred pound now in hand.

TOUCH. SEN. Right, that I have, sir.

SIR OL. Another hundred when my wife is quick;
The third when she's brought a-bed; and the last hundred

1. Perhaps an obscenity followed and was deleted by the censor.
2. Fidgety.
3. Jumped over (a stool).

When the child cries, for if 't should be still-born,
It doth no good, sir.
TOUCH. SEN. All this is even[1] still:
A little faster, sir.
SIR OL. Not a whit, sir;
I'm in an excellent pace for any physic.

Re-enter Servant

SER. Your white mare's ready.
SIR OL. I shall up presently.—

Exit Servant

One kiss and farewell.   [*Kisses her*]
LADY KIX. Thou shalt have two, love.
SIR OL. Expect me about three.
LADY KIX. With all my heart, sweet.

Exit Sir Oliver Kix

TOUCH. SEN. [*Aside*] By this light, they've forgot their anger since,[2]
And are as far in again as e'er they were!
Which way the devil came they?[3] heart, I saw 'em not!
Their ways are beyond finding out. —Come, sweet lady.
LADY KIX. How must I take mine, sir?
TOUCH. SEN. Clean contrary;
Yours must be taken lying.
LADY KIX. A-bed, sir?
TOUCH. SEN. A-bed, or where you will, for your own ease;
Your coach will serve.
LADY KIX. The physic must needs please.

Exeunt

1. Fair.
2. Recent.
3. Into this new mood.

Act IV, Scene I

Enter Tim and Tutor

TIM. *Negatur argumentum,* tutor.[1]

TUTOR. *Probo tibi,* pupil, *stultus non est animal rationale.*

TIM. *Falleris sane.*

TUTOR. *Quæso ut taceas,—probo tibi—*

TIM. *Quomodo probas, domine?*

TUTOR. *Stultus non habet rationem, ergo non est animal rationale.*

TIM. *Sic argumentaris, domine; stultus non habet rationem, ergo non est animal rationale; negatur argumentum* again, tutor.

TUTOR. *Argumentum iterum probo tibi, domine; qui non participat de ratione, nullo modo potest vocari rationalis;* but *stultus non participat de ratione, ergo stultus nullo modo potest dici rationalis.*

TIM. *Participat.*

TUTOR. *Sic disputas: qui participat, quomodo participat?*

TIM. *Ut homo, probabo tibi in syllogismo.*

TUTOR. *Hunc proba.*

TIM. *Sic probo, domine; stultus est homo, sicut tu et ego sumus; homo est animal rationale, sicut stultus est animal rationale.*

Enter Maudlin

MAUD. Here's nothing but disputing all the day long with 'em!

TUTOR. *Sic disputas; stultus est homo, sicut tu et ego sumus; homo est animal rationale, sicut stultus est animal rationale.*

MAUD. Your reasons are both good, whate'er they be.
Pray, give them over; faith, you'll tire yourselves;
What's the matter between you?

TIM. Nothing but reasoning
About a fool, mother.

MAUD. About a fool, son?
Alas, what need you trouble your heads 'bout that!
None of us all but knows what a fool is.

TIM. Why, what's a fool, mother? I come to you now.

MAUD. Why, one that's married before he has wit.

---

1. For a translation of this passage, see Appendix to *A Chaste Maid in Cheapside,* p. 462.

TIM. 'Tis pretty, i'faith, and well guessed of a woman never brought
up at the university; but bring forth what fool you will, mother, I'll
prove him to be as reasonable a creature as myself or my tutor here.

MAUD. Fie, 'tis impossible!

TUTOR. Nay, he shall do't, forsooth.

TIM. 'Tis the easiest thing to prove a fool by logic;
By logic I'll prove anything.

MAUD. What, thou wilt not?

TIM. I'll prove a whore to be an honest woman.

MAUD. Nay, by my faith, she must prove that herself,
Or logic will ne'er do't.

TIM. 'Twill do't, I tell you.

MAUD. Some in this street would give a thousand pounds
That you could prove their wives so.

TIM. Faith, I can,
And all their daughters too, though they had three bastards.
When comes your tailor hither?

MAUD. Why, what of him?

TIM. By logic I'll prove him to be a man,
Let him come when he will.

MAUD. How hard at first
Was learning to him! truly, sir, I thought
He would never 'a took the Latin tongue:
How many accidences do you think he wore out
Ere he came to his grammar?

TUTOR. Some three or four.

MAUD. Believe me, sir, some four and thirty.

TIM. Pish, I made haberdines[1] of 'em in church-porches.

MAUD. He was eight years in his grammar, and stuck horribly
At a foolish place there, called *as in præsenti*.[2]

TIM. Pox, I have it here now.

MAUD. He so shamed me once,
Before an honest gentleman that knew me
When I was a maid.

TIM. These women must have all out!

---

1. This has not been explained.
2. Signifying the first conjugation in the standard Latin grammar.

MAUD. *Quid est grammatica?*[1] says the gentleman to him,—
   I shall remember by a sweet, sweet token,—
   But nothing could he answer.

TUTOR. How now, pupil, ha?
   Quid est grammatica?

TIM. *Grammatica?* ha, ha, ha!

MAUD. Nay, do not laugh, son, but let me hear you say't now:
   There was one word went so prettily off
   The gentleman's tongue, I shall remember it
   The longest day of my life.

TUTOR. Come, *quid est grammatica?*

TIM. Are you not ashamed, tutor, *grammatica?*
   Why, *recte scribendi atque loquendi ars,*[2]
   Sir-reverence[3] of my mother.

MAUD. That was it, i'faith: why now, son,
   I see you're a deep scholar:—and, master tutor,
   A word, I pray; let us withdraw a little
   Into my husband's chamber; I'll send in
   The North Wales gentlewoman to him, she looks for wooing:
   I'll put together both, and lock the door.

TUTOR. I give great approbation to your conclusion.

                              Exeunt Maudlin and Tutor

TIM. I mar'l[4] what this gentlewoman should be
   That I should have in marriage; she's a stranger to me;
   I wonder what my parents mean, i'faith,
   To match me with a stranger so,
   A maid that's neither kiff[5] nor kin to me:
   'Life, do they think I've no more care of my body
   Than to lie with one that I ne'er knew, a mere stranger,
   One that ne'er went to school with me neither,
   Nor ever play-fellows together?

---

1. What is grammar?
2. The art of correct writing and speaking.
3. A common form of apology, usually for an indecency.
4. Marvel.
5. Kith.

They're mightily o'erseen¹ in it, methinks.
They say she has mountains to her marriage,
She's full of cattle, some two thousand runts:
Now, what the meaning of these runts² should be,
My tutor cannot tell me; I have looked
In Rider's Dictionary³ for the letter R,
And there I can hear no tidings of these runts neither;
Unless they should be Romford hogs,⁴ I know them not.

Enter Welshwoman

And here she comes. If I know what to say to her now
In the way of marriage, I'm no graduate:
Methinks, i'faith, 'tis boldly done of her
To come into my chamber, being but a stranger;
She shall not say I am so proud yet but
I'll speak to her; marry, as I will order it,
She shall take no hold of my words, I'll warrant her.

[*Welshwoman curtsies*]

She looks and makes a curtsy.—
Salve tu quoque, puella pulcherrima; quid vis nescio nec sane curo,—⁵
Tully's⁶ own phrase to a heart.

WELSH. [*Aside*] I know not what he means: a suitor, quoth'a?
I hold my life he understands no English.

TIM. *Fertur, mehercule, tu virgo, Walliâ ut opibus abundas maximis.*⁷

WELSH. What's this *fertur* and *abundundis?*
He mocks me sure, and calls me a bundle of farts.

TIM. [*Aside*] I have no Latin word now for their runts;
I'll make some shift or other:

---

1. Mistaken.
2. Oxen of small size.
3. The familiar Latin dictionary of the period.
4. Romford, near London, was famous for its hog market.
5. Save thee, also, most beautiful maiden: I don't know what you want, and don't care.
6. Cicero.
7. By heaven, it's said, young lady, that in Wales you rejoice in great riches.

Iterum dico, opibus abundas maximis, montibus, et fontibus et ut ita dicam rontibus; attamen vero homunculus ego sum natura, simul et arte baccalaureus, lecto profecto non parato.[1]

WELSH. This is most strange: may be he can speak Welsh.
Avedera whee comrage, der due cog foginis.[2]

TIM. *Cog foggin?* I scorn to cog[3] with her; I'll tell her so too in a word near her own language,—*Ego non cogo.*[4]

WELSH. *Rhegosin a whiggin harle ron corid ambro.*[5]

TIM. By my faith, she's a good scholar, I see that already;
She has the tongues plain; I hold my life sh'as travelled:
What will folks say? there goes the learned couple!
Faith, if the truth were known, she hath proceeded.[6]

Re-enter Maudlin

MAUD. How now? how speeds your business?

TIM. [*Aside*] I'm glad
My mother's come to part us.

MAUD. How do you agree, forsooth?

WELSH. As well as e'er we did before we met.

MAUD. How's that?

WELSH. You put me to a man I understand not:
Your son's no Englishman, methinks.

MAUD. No Englishman?
Bless my boy, and born i' the heart of London!

WELSH. I ha' been long enough in the chamber with him,
And I find neither Welsh nor English in him.

MAUD. Why, Tim, how have you used the gentlewoman?

TIM. As well as a man might do, mother, in modest Latin.

MAUD. Latin, fool?

TIM. And she recoiled in Hebrew.

MAUD. In Hebrew, fool? 'tis Welsh.

1. I say again, your rejoice in great riches, in mountains and fountains and, so to speak, runts; however, I am a small man by nature and by art a bachelor, not really ready for bed.

2. Can you speak Welsh? (partly unintelligible).

3. Cheat, lie (with sexual sense).

4. I won't lie with you.

5. Some cheese and whey after a walk.

6. Taken a degree.

TIM. All comes to one, mother.

MAUD. She can speak English too.

TIM. Who told me so much?
   Heart, an she can speak English, I'll clap to her;
   I thought you'd marry me to a stranger.

MAUD. You must forgive him; he's so inured to Latin,
   He and his tutor, that he hath quite forgot
   To use the Protestant tongue.

WELSH. 'Tis quickly pardoned, forsooth.

MAUD. Tim, make amends and kiss her.—
   He makes towards you, forsooth.

                                                    [*They kiss*]

TIM. O delicious!
   One may discover her country by her kissing:
   'Tis a true saying, there's nothing tastes so sweet
   As your Welsh mutton.—'Twas reported you could sing.

MAUD. O, rarely, Tim, the sweetest British[1] songs!

TIM. And 'tis my mind, I swear, before I marry,
   I would see all my wife's good parts at once,
   To view how rich I were.

MAUD. Thou shalt hear sweet music, Tim.—
   Pray, forsooth.

WELSH. [*Sings*]

> Cupid is Venus' only joy,
> But he is a wanton boy,
> A very, very wanton boy;
> He shoots at ladies' naked breasts,
> He is the cause of most men's crests
> I mean upon the forehead,
> Invisible but horrid;
> 'Twas he first thought upon the way
> To keep a lady's lips in play.
>
> Why should not Venus chide her son
> For the pranks that he hath done,
> The wanton pranks that he hath done?
> He shoots his fiery darts so thick,

---

1. i.e., Welsh.

They hurt poor ladies to the quick,
Ah me, with cruel wounding!
His darts are so confounding,
That life and sense would soon decay,
But that he keeps their lips in play.

Can there be any part of bliss
In a quickly fleeting kiss,
A quickly fleeting kiss?
To one's pleasure leisures are but waste,
The slowest kiss makes too much haste,
And lose it ere we find it:
The pleasing sport they only know
That close above and close below.

TIM. I would not change my wife for a kingdom:
I can do somewhat too in my own lodging.

Enter Yellowhammer and Allwit

YEL. Why, well said, Tim! the bells go merrily;
I love such peals a' life.[1]—Wife, lead them in awhile;
Here's a strange gentleman desires private conference.—
Exeunt Maudlin, Welshwoman, and Tim
You're welcome, sir, the more for your name's sake,
Good Master Yellowhammer: I love my name well:
And which o' the Yellowhammers take you descent from,
If I may be so bold with you? which, I pray?
ALLWIT. The Yellowhammers in Oxfordshire, near Abingdon.
YEL. And those are the best Yellowhammers, and truest bred;
I came from thence myself, though now a citizen:
I will be bold with you; you are most welcome.
ALLWIT. I hope the zeal I bring with me shall deserve it.
YEL. I hope no less: what is your will, sir?
ALLWIT. I understand, by rumors, you've a daughter,
Which my bold love shall henceforth title cousin.
YEL. I thank you for her, sir.
ALLWIT. I heard of her virtues
And other confirmed graces.

---

1. As my life; i.e., extremely.

YEL. A plaguy girl, sir!

ALLWIT. Fame sets her out with richer ornaments
   Than you are pleased to boast of; 'tis done modestly:
   I hear she's towards marriage.

YEL. You hear truth, sir.

ALLWIT. And with a knight in town, Sir Walter Whorehound.

YEL. The very same, sir.

ALLWIT. I'm the sorrier for't.

YEL. The sorrier? why, cousin?

ALLWIT. 'Tis not too far past, is't?
   It may be yet recalled?

YEL. Recalled! why, good sir?

ALLWIT. Resolve[1] me in that point, ye shall hear from me.

YEL. There's no contract past.

ALLWIT. I'm very joyful, sir.

YEL. But he's the man must bed her.

ALLWIT. By no means, coz;
   She's quite undone then, and you'll curse the time
   That e'er you made the match; he's an arrant whoremaster,
   Consumes his time and state———[2]
   Whom in my knowledge he hath kept this seven years;
   Nay, coz, another man's wife too.

YEL. O, abominable!

ALLWIT. Maintains the whole house, apparels the husband,
   Pays servant's wages, not so much but———[3]

YEL. Worse and worse; and doth the husband know this?

ALLWIT. Knows? ay, and glad he may too, 'tis his living:
   As other trades thrive, butchers by selling flesh,
   Poulters by vending conies, or the like, coz.

YEL. What an incomparable wittol's[4] this!

ALLWIT. Tush, what cares he for that? believe me, coz,
   No more than I do.

YEL. What a base slave's that!

ALLWIT. All's one to him; he feeds and takes his ease,

1. Satisfy.
2. Perhaps censored.
3. Perhaps censored.
4. A complaisant cuckold.

Was ne'er the man that ever broke his sleep
To get a child yet, by his own confession,
And yet his wife has seven.

YEL. What, by Sir Walter?

ALLWIT. Sir Walter's like to keep 'em and maintain 'em
In excellent fashion; he dares do no less, sir.

YEL. 'Life, has he children too?

ALLWIT. Children! boys thus high,
In their Cato and Corderius.[1]

YEL. What? you jest, sir?

ALLWIT. Why, one can make a verse, and now's at Eton College.

YEL. O, this news has cut into my heart, coz!

ALLWIT. 'Thad eaten nearer, if it had not been prevented:
One Allwit's wife.

YEL. Allwit! 'foot, I have heard of him;
He had a girl kursened lately?

ALLWIT. Ay, that work
Did cost the knight above a hundred mark.

YEL. I'll mark him for a knave and villain for't;
A thousand thanks and blessings! I have done with him.

ALLWIT. [*Aside*] Ha, ha, ha! this knight will stick by my ribs still;
I shall not lose him yet; no wife will come;
Where'er he woos, I find him still at home:
Ha, ha!

Exit

YEL. Well, grant all this, say now his deeds are black,
Pray, what serves marriage but to call him back;[2]
I've kept a whore myself, and had a bastard
By Mistress Anne, in *anno*—
I care not who knows it; he's now a jolly fellow,
Has been twice warden;[3] so may his fruit be,
They were but base begot, and so was he.
The knight is rich, he shall be my son-in-law;
No matter, so the whore he keeps be wholesome,

1. Puritan schoolbooks.
2. Reform him.
3. An officer of a city company; also a pear.

My daughter takes no hurt then; so let them wed:
I'll have him sweat well[1] ere they go to bed.

Re-enter Maudlin

MAUD. O husband, husband!
YEL. How now, Maudlin?
MAUD. We are all undone; she's gone, she's gone!
YEL. Again? death, which way?
MAUD. Over the houses: lay[2] the water-side,
    She's gone for ever else.
YEL. O venturous baggage!

Exeunt

SCENE II

Enter Tim and Tutor severally

TIM. Thieves, thieves! my sister's stolen: some thief hath got her:
    O how miraculously did my father's plate 'scape!
    'Twas all left out, tutor.
TUTOR. Is't possible?
TIM. Besides three chains of pearl and a box of coral.
    My sister's gone; let's look at Trig-stairs[3] for her;
    My mother's gone to lay the common stairs
    At Puddle-wharf; and at the dock below
    Stands my poor silly father; run, sweet tutor, run!

Exeunt

SCENE III

Enter Touchwood senior and Touchwood junior

TOUCH. SEN. I had been taken, brother, by eight sergeants,
    But for the honest watermen; I'm bound to them;
    They are the most requitefull'st[4] people living,

1. Take the cure for venereal disease.
2. Scour.
3. Landing-place on the Thames.
4. Willing to return favors.

For as they get their means by gentlemen,
They're still the forwardest to help gentlemen:
You heard how one 'scaped out of the Blackfriars,
But a while since, from two or three varlets came
Into the house with all their rapiers drawn,
As if they'd dance the sword-dance on the stage,
With candles in their hands, like chandlers' ghosts;
Whilst the poor gentleman so pursued and banded,
Was by an honest pair of oars safely landed.

TOUCH. JUN. I love them with my heart for't!

Enter several Watermen

1ST W. Your first man, sir.

2ND W. Shall I carry you, gentlemen, with a pair of oars?

TOUCH. SEN. These be the honest fellows: take one pair,
And leave the rest for her.

TOUCH. JUN. Barn Elms.

TOUCH. SEN. No more, brother.

Exit

1ST W. Your first man.

2ND W. Shall I carry your worship?

TOUCH. JUN. Go; and you honest watermen that stay,
Here's a French crown for you [*gives money*]: there comes a maid
With all speed to take water, row her lustily
To Barn Elms after me.

2ND W. To Barn Elms,[1] good sir.—
Make ready the boat, Sam; we'll wait below.

Exeunt Watermen

Enter Moll

TOUCH. JUN. What made you stay so long?

MOLL. I found the way more dangerous than I looked for.

TOUCH. JUN. Away, quick; there's a boat waits for you; and I'll
Take water at Paul's wharf, and overtake you.

MOLL. Good sir, do; we cannot be too safe.

Exeunt

---

1. On the Thames, upstream to the west.

Enter Sir Walter Whorehound, Yellowhammer, Tim, and Tutor

SIR WAL. Life, call you this close keeping?

YEL. She was kept
Under a double lock.

SIR WAL. A double devil!

TIM. That's a buff sergeant, tutor; he'll ne'er wear out.

YEL. How would you have women locked?

TIM. With padlocks, father;
The Venetian uses it;[1] my tutor reads it.

SIR WAL. Heart, if she were so locked up, how got she out?

YEL. There was a little hole looked into the gutter;
But who would have dreamt of that?

SIR WAL. A wiser man would.

TIM. He says true, father; a wise man for love
Will seek every hole; my tutor knows it.

TUTOR. *Verum poeta dicit.*

TIM. *Dicit Virgilius,* father.[2]

YEL. Prithee, talk of thy gills[3] somewhere else; sh'as played
The gill with me: where's your wise mother now?

TIM. Run mad, I think; I thought she would have drowned herself;
She would not stay for oars, but took a smelt-boat;
Sure I think she be gone a-fishing for her.

YEL. She'll catch a goodly dish of gudgeons now,
Will serve us all to supper.

Enter Maudlin, drawing in Moll by the hair, and Watermen

MAUD. I'll tug thee home by the hair.

1ST W. Good mistress, spare her!

MAUD. Tend your own business.

1ST W. You're a cruel mother.

Exeunt Watermen

MOLL. O, my heart dies!

MAUD. I'll make thee an example
For all the neighbors' daughters.

1. Chastity belt.
2. The poet speaks truth; Virgil says it.
3. Wanton girls.

MOLL. Farewell, life!

MAUD. You that have tricks can counterfeit.

YEL. Hold, hold, Maudlin!

MAUD. I've brought your jewel by the hair.

YEL. She's here, knight.

SIR WAL. Forbear, or I'll grow worse.

TIM. Look on her, tutor;
    She hath brought her from the water like a mermaid;
    She's but half my sister now, as far as the flesh goes,
    The rest may be sold to fishwives.

MAUD. Dissembling, cunning baggage!

YEL. Impudent strumpet!

SIR WAL. Either give over, both, or I'll give over.—
    Why have you used me thus unkindly, mistress?
    Wherein have I deserved?

YEL. You talk too fondly,[1] sir:
    We'll take another course and prevent all:
    We might have done't long since; we'll lose no time now,
    Nor trust to't any longer: to-morrow morn,
    As early as sunrise, we'll have you joined.

MOLL. O, bring me death to-night, love-pitying fates;
    Let me not see to-morrow up on the world!

YEL. Are you content, sir? till then she shall be watched.

MAUD. Baggage, you shall.

TIM. Why, father, my tutor and I
    Will both watch in armor.

          Exeunt Maudlin, Moll, and Yellowhammer

TUTOR. How shall we do for weapons?

TIM. Take you
    No care for that; if need be, I can send
    For conquering metal, tutor, ne'er lost day yet.
    'Tis but at Westminster; I am acquainted
    With him that keeps the monuments; I can borrow
    Harry the Fifth's sword; it will serve us both
    To watch with.

          Exeunt Tim and Tutor

---

1. Indulgently.

SIR WAL. I never was so near my wish
  As this chance makes me: ere to-morrow noon
  I shall receive two thousand pound in gold,
  And a sweet maidenhead worth forty.

Re-enter Touchwood junior and Waterman

TOUCH. JUN. O, thy news splits me!
WATER. Half-drowned, she cruelly tugged her by the hair,
  Forced her disgracefully, not like a mother.
TOUCH. JUN. Enough; leave me, like my joys.—

Exit Waterman

  Sir, saw you not a wretched maid pass this way?
  Heart, villain, is it thou?
SIR WAL. Yes, slave, 'tis I.
TOUCH. JUN. I must break through thee then: there is no stop
  That checks my tongue[1] and all my hopeful fortunes,
  That breast excepted, and I must have way.
SIR WAL. Sir, I believe 'twill hold your life in play.
TOUCH. JUN. Sir, you will gain the heart in my breast first.
SIR WAL. There is no dealing then; think on the dowry
  For two thousand pounds.

[They fight]

TOUCH. JUN. O, now 'tis quit, sir.
SIR WAL. And being of even hand, I'll play no longer.
TOUCH. JUN. No longer, slave?
SIR WAL. I've certain things to think on,
  Before I dare go further.
TOUCH. JUN. But one bout!
  I'll follow thee to death, but ha' it out.

Exeunt

ACT V, SCENE I

Enter Allwit, Mistress Allwit, and Davy

MIS. ALL. A misery of a house!
ALLWIT. What shall become of us!

1. Perhaps meaning "suit" or "purpose."

DAVY. I think his wound be mortal.

ALLWIT. Think'st thou so, Davy?
  Then am I mortal too, but a dead man, Davy;
  This is no world for me, whene'er he goes;
  I must e'en truss up all, and after him, Davy;
  A sheet with two knots, and away.

DAVY. O see, sir!

> *Enter Sir Walter Whorehound led in by two Servants,*
> *who place him in a chair*

  How faint he goes! two of my fellows lead him.

MIS. ALL. O me!

　　　　　　　　　　　　　　　　　　　　　　　　　　[Swoons]

ALLWIT. Heyday, my wife's laid down too; here's like to be
  A good house kept, when we're all together down:
  Take pains with her, good Davy, cheer her up there;
  Let me come to his worship, let me come.

SIR WAL. Touch me not, villain; my wound aches at thee,
  Thou poison to my heart!

ALLWIT. He raves already;
  His senses are quite gone, he knows me not.—
  Look up, an't like your worship; heave those eyes,
  Call me to mind; is your remembrance left?
  Look in my face; who am I, an't like your worship?

SIR WAL. If anything be worse than slave or villain,
  Thou art the man!

ALLWIT. Alas, his poor worship's weakness!
  He will begin to know me by little and little.

SIR WAL. No devil can be like thee!

ALLWIT. Ah, poor gentleman.
  Methinks the pain that thou endurest mads thee.

SIR WAL. Thou know'st me to be wicked; for thy baseness
  Kept the eyes open still on all my sins;
  None knew the dear account my soul stood charged with
  So well as thou, yet, like hell's flattering angel,
  Wouldst never tell me on't, lett'st me go on,
  And join with death in sleep; that if I had not

Waked now by chance, even by a stranger's pity,
I had everlasting slept out all hope
Of grace and mercy.

ALLWIT. Now he's worse and worse.
Wife, to him, wife; thou wast wont to do good on him.

MIS. ALL. How is it with you, sir?

SIR WAL. Not as with you,
Thou loathsome strumpet! Some good, pitying man
Remove my sins out of my sight a little;
I tremble to behold her, she keeps back
All comfort while she stays. Is this a time,
Unconscionable woman, to see thee?
Art thou so cruel to the peace of man,
Not to give liberty now? the devil himself
Shows a far fairer reverence and respect
To goodness than thyself; he dares not do this,
But parts in time of penitence, hides his face;
When man withdraws from him, he leaves the place:
Hast thou less manners and more impudence
Than thy instructor? prithee, show thy modesty,
If the least grain be left, and get thee from me:
Thou shouldst be rather locked many rooms hence
From the poor miserable sight of me,
If either love or grace had part in thee.

MIS. ALL. [*Aside*] He's lost for ever!

ALLWIT. Run, sweet Davy, quickly,
And fetch the children hither; sight of them
Will make him cheerful straight.

Exit Davy

SIR WAL. O death! is this
A place for you to weep? what tears are those!
Get you away with them, I shall fare the worse
As long as they're a-weeping, they work against me;
There's nothing but thy appetite in that sorrow,
Thou weep'st for lust; I feel it in the slackness
Of comforts coming towards me; I was well
Till thou began'st t' undo me: this shows like

The fruitless sorrow of a careless mother,
That brings her son with dalliance to the gallows,
And then stands by and weeps to see him suffer.

Re-enter Davy with Nick, Wat, and other children

DAVY. There are the children, sir, an' like your worship,
    Your last fine girl; in troth, she smiles;
    Look, look, in faith, sir.
SIR WAL. O my vengeance!
    Let me for ever hide my cursèd face
    From sight of those that darken all my hopes,
    And stand between me and the sight of Heaven!
    Who sees me now—O, and those so near me,
    May rightly say I am o'ergrown with sin.
    O, how my offences wrestle with my repentance!
    It hath scarce breath;
    Still my adulterous guilt hovers aloft,
    And with her black wings beats down all my prayers
    Ere they be half-way up. What's he knows now
    How long I have to live? O, what comes then?
    My taste grows bitter; the round world all gall now;
    Her pleasing pleasures now hath poisoned me,
    Which I exchanged my soul for!
    Make way a hundred sighs at once for me!
ALLWIT. Speak to him, Nick.
NICK. I dare not, I'm afraid.
ALLWIT. Tell him he hurts his wounds, Wat, with making moan.
SIR WAL. Wretched, death of seven![1]
ALLWIT. Come let's be talking
    Somewhat to keep him alive. Ah, sirrah Wat,
    And did my lord bestow that jewel on thee
    For an epistle thou mad'st in Latin? thou
    Art a good forward boy, there's great joy on thee.
SIR WAL. O sorrow!
ALLWIT. [*Aside*] Heart, will nothing comfort him?
    If he be so far gone, 'tis time to moan.

---

1. His seven children by Allwit's wife.

Here's pen and ink, and paper, and all things ready;
Will't please your worship for to make your will?
SIR WAL. My will! yes, yes, what else? who writes apace now?
ALLWIT. That can your man Davy, an't like your worship;
A fair, fast, legible hand.
SIR WAL. Set it down then.

[Davy writes]

Imprimis, I bequeath to yonder wittol
Three times his weight in curses.
ALLWIT. How!
SIR WAL. All plagues
Of body and of mind.
ALLWIT. Write them not down, Davy.
DAVY. It is his will; I must.
SIR WAL. Together also
With such a sickness ten days ere his death.
ALLWIT. *[Aside]* There's a sweet legacy! I'm almost choked with't.
SIR WAL. Next, I bequeath to that foul whore his wife
All barrenness of joy, a drouth of virtue,
And dearth of all repentance: for her end,
The common misery of an English strumpet,
In French and Dutch; beholding, ere she dies,
Confusion[1] of her brats before her eyes,
And never shed a tear for't.

Enter 3rd Servant

3RD SER. Where's the knight—
O sir, the gentleman you wounded is
Newly departed!
SIR WAL. Dead, lift, lift, who helps me?
ALLWIT. Let the law lift you now, that must have all;
I have done lifting on you, and my wife too.
3RD SER. You were best lock yourself close.
ALLWIT. Not in my house, sir;
I'll harbor no such persons as men-slayers;
Lock yourself where you will.

1. Ruin.

SIR WAL. What's this?

MIS. ALL. Why, husband!

ALLWIT. I know what I do, wife.

MIS. ALL. You cannot tell yet;

 For having killed the man in his defence,

 Neither his life nor estate will be touched, husband.

ALLWIT. Away, wife! hear a fool! his lands will hang him.

SIR WAL. Am I denied a chamber?—What say you, forsooth?

MIS. ALL. Alas, sir, I am one that would have all well,

 But must obey my husband.—Prithee, love,

 Let the poor gentleman stay, being so sore wounded:

 There's a close chamber at one end of the garret

 We never use; let him have that, I prithee.

ALLWIT. We never use? you forgot sickness then,

 And physic-times; is't not a place for easement?

SIR WAL. O, death! do I hear this with part

 Of former life in me?—

Enter 4th Servant

 What's the news now?

4TH SER. Troth, worse and worse; you're like to lose your land,

 If the law save your life, sir, or the surgeon.

ALLWIT. Hark you there, wife.

SIR WAL. Why, how, sir?

4TH SER. Sir Oliver Kix's wife is new quickened;

 That child undoes you, sir.

SIR WAL. All ill at once!

ALLWIT. I wonder what he makes here with his consorts?

 Cannot our house be private to ourselves,

 But we must have such guests? I pray, depart, sirs,

 And take your murderer along with you;

 Good he were apprehended ere he go,

 Has killed some honest gentleman; send for officers.

SIR WAL. I'll soon save you that labor.

ALLWIT. I must tell you, sir,

 You have been somewhat bolder in my house

 Than I could well like of; I suffered you

Till it stuck here at my heart; I tell you truly
  I thought y'had been familiar with my wife once.
MIS. ALL. With me! I'll see him hanged first; I defy him,
  And all such gentlemen in the like extremity.
SIR WAL. If ever eyes were open, these are they:
  Gamesters, farewell, I've nothing left to play.
ALLWIT. And therefore get you gone, sir.

Exit Sir Walter, led off by Servants

DAVY. Of all wittols
  Be thou the head—thou the grand whore of spittles!

Exit

ALLWIT. So, since he's like now to be rid of all,
  I am right glad I'm so well rid of him.
MIS. ALL. I knew he durst not stay when you named officers.
ALLWIT. That stopped his spirits straight. What shall we do now, wife?
MIS. ALL. As we were wont to do.
ALLWIT. We're richly furnished, wife,
  With household stuff.
MIS. ALL. Let's let out lodgings then,
  And take a house in the Strand.
ALLWIT. In troth, a match, wench!
  We're simply stocked with cloth-of-tissue cushions
  To furnish out bay-windows; pish, what not
  That's quaint and costly, from the top to the bottom;
  Life, for furniture we may lodge a countess:
  There's a close-stool of tawny velvet too,
  Now I think on it, wife.
MIS. ALL. There's that should be, sir;
  Your nose must be in everything.
ALLWIT. I've done, wench.
  And let this stand in every gallant's chamber,—
  There is no gamester like a politic sinner,
  For whoe'er games, the box is sure a winner.

Exeunt

SCENE II

Enter Yellowhammer and Maudlin

MAUD. O husband, husband, she will die, she will die!
　There is no sign but death.

YEL. 'Twill be our shame then.

MAUD. O, how she's changed in compass of an hour!

YEL. Ah, my poor girl! good faith, thou wert too cruel
　To drag her by the hair.

MAUD. You'd have done as much, sir.
　To curb her of her humor.

YEL. 'Tis curbèd sweetly;
　She catched her bane o' th' water.

Enter Tim

MAUD. How now, Tim?

TIM. Faith, busy, mother, about an epitaph
　Upon my sister's death.

MAUD. Death? she's not dead, I hope?

TIM. No, but she means to be, and that's as good,
　And when a thing's done, 'tis done; you taught me that, mother.

YEL. What is your tutor doing?

TIM. Making one too, in principal[1] pure Latin,
　Culled out of Ovid *de Tristibus.*

YEL. How does your sister look? is she not changed?

TIM. Changed? gold into white money was ne'er so changed
　As is my sister's color into paleness.

Enter Moll, led in by Servants, who place her in a chair

YEL. O, here she's brought; see how she looks like death!

TIM. Looks she like death, and ne'er a word made yet?
　I must go beat my brains against a bed-post,
　And get before my tutor.

Exit

YEL. Speak, how dost thou?

---

1. Excellent.

MOLL. I hope I shall be well, for I'm as sick
    At heart as I can be.

YEL. 'Las, my poor girl!
    The doctor's making a most sovereign drink for thee,
    The worst ingredience dissolved pearl and amber;
    We spare no cost, girl.

MOLL. Your love comes too late,
    Yet timely thanks reward it. What is comfort,
    When the poor patient's heart is past relief?
    It is no doctor's art can cure my grief.

YEL. All is cast away, then;
    Prithee, look upon me cheerfully.

MAUD. Sing but a strain or two; thou wilt not think
    How 'twill revive thy spirits; strive with thy fit,
    Prithee, sweet Moll.

MOLL. You shall have my good will, mother.

MAUD. Why, well said, wench.

MOLL. [*Sings*]

> Weep eyes, break heart!
> My love and I must part.
> Cruel fates true love do soonest sever:
> O, I shall see thee never, never, never!
> O, happy is the maid whose life takes end
> Ere it knows parent's frown or loss of friend!
> Weep eyes, break heart!
> My love and I must part.

MAUD. O, I could die with music!—Well sung, girl.

MOLL. If you call't so, it was.

YEL. She plays the swan,
    And sings herself to death.

           Enter Touchwood senior

TOUCH. SEN. By your leave, sir.

YEL. What are you, sir? or what's your business, pray?

TOUCH. SEN. I may be now admitted, though the brother
    Of him your hate pursued: it spreads no further.
    Your malice sets in death, does it not, sir?

YEL. In death?

TOUCH. SEN. He's dead: 'twas a dear love to him,
  It cost him but his life, that was all, sir;
  He paid enough, poor gentleman, for his love.
YEL. [*Aside*] There's all our ill removed, if she were well now.—
  Impute not, sir, his end to any hate
  That sprung from us; he had a fair wound brought that.
TOUCH. SEN. That helped him forward, I must needs confess;
  But the restraint of love, and your unkindness,
  Those were the wounds that from his heart drew blood;
  But being past help, let words forget it too:
  Scarcely three minutes ere his eyelids closed,
  And took eternal leave of this world's light,
  He wrote this letter, which by oath he bound me
  To give to her own hands; that's all my business.
YEL. You may perform it then; there she sits.
TOUCH. SEN. O, with a following look!
YEL. Ay, trust me, sir,
  I think she'll follow him quickly.
TOUCH. SEN. Here's some gold
  He willed me to distribute faithfully
  Amongst your servants.

                              [*Gives gold to Servants*]

YEL. 'Las, what doth he mean, sir?
TOUCH. SEN. How cheer you, mistress?
MOLL. I must learn of you, sir.
TOUCH. SEN. Here is a letter from a friend of yours,

                              [*Giving letter to Moll*]

  And where that fails in satisfaction,
  I have a sad tongue ready to supply.
MOLL. How does he, ere I look on't?
TOUCH. SEN. Seldom better;
  Has a contented health now.
MOLL. I'm most glad on't.
MAUD. Dead, sir?
YEL. He is: now, wife, let's but get the girl
  Upon her legs again, and to church roundly with her.
MOLL. O, sick to death, he tells me: how does he after this?
TOUCH. SEN. Faith, feels no pain at all; he's dead, sweet mistress.

MOLL. Peace close mine eyes!

[*Swoons*]

YEL. The girl! look to the girl, wife!

MAUD. Moll, daughter, sweet girl, speak! look but once up,
   Thou shalt have all the wishes of thy heart
   That wealth can purchase!

YEL. O, she's gone for ever!
   That letter broke her heart.

TOUCH. SEN. As good now then
   As let her lie in torment, and then break it.

Enter Susan

MAUD. O Susan, she thou lovedst so dear is gone!

SUSAN. O sweet maid!

TOUCH. SEN. This is she that helped her still.—
   I've a reward here for thee.

YEL. Take her in,
   Remove her from my sight, our shame and sorrow.

TOUCH. SEN. Stay, let me help thee, 'tis the last cold kindness
   I can perform for my sweet brother's sake.
       Exeunt Touchwood senior, Susan, and Servants, carrying out Moll

YEL. All the whole street will hate us, and the world
   Point me out cruel: it's our best course, wife,
   After we've given order for the funeral,
   T' absent ourselves till she be laid in ground.

MAUD. Where shall we spend that time!

YEL. I'll tell thee where, wench:
   Go to some private church, and marry Tim
   To the rich Brecknock gentlewoman.

MAUD. Mass, a match;
   We'll not lose all at once, somewhat we'll catch.

Exeunt

SCENE III

Enter Sir Oliver Kix and Servants

SIR OL. Ho, my wife's quickened; I'm a man for ever!
   I think I have bestirred my stumps, i'faith.

Run, get your fellows all together instantly,
Then to the parish church and ring the bells.
1ST SER. It shall be done, sir.

Exit

SIR OL. Upon my love
I charge you, villain, that you make a bonfire
Before the door at night.
2ND SER. A bonfire, sir?
SIR OL. A thwacking one, I charge you.
2ND SER. [*Aside*] This is monstrous.

Exit

SIR OL. Run, tell[1] a hundred pound out for the gentleman
That gave my wife the drink, the first thing you do.
3RD SER. A hundred pounds, sir?
SIR OL. A bargain: as our joy grows,
We must remember still from whence it flows,
Or else we prove ungrateful multipliers:

Exit 3rd Servant

The child is coming, and the land comes after;
The news of this will make a poor Sir Walter:
I've struck it home, i'faith.
4TH SER. That you have, marry, sir;
But will not your worship go to the funeral
Of both these lovers?
SIR OL. Both? go both together?
4TH SER. Ay, sir, the gentleman's brother will have it so:
'Twill be the pitifull'st sight! there is such running,
Such rumors, and such throngs, a pair of lovers
Had never more spectators, more men's pities,
Or women's wet eyes.
SIR OL. My wife helps the number then.
4TH SER. There is such drawing out of handkerchers;
And those that have no handkerchers lift up aprons.
SIR OL. Her parents may have joyful hearts at this:
I would not have my cruelty so talked on
To any child of mine for a monopoly.

---

1. Count out.

4TH SER. I believe you, sir.
'Tis cast[1] so, too, that both their coffins meet,
   Which will be lamentable.
SIR OL. Come, we'll see't.

Exeunt

SCENE IV

Recorder dolefully playing, enter at one door the coffin of Touchwood junior, solemnly decked, his sword upon it, attended by many gentlemen in black, among whom are Sir Oliver Kix, Allwit, and Parson, Touchwood senior being the chief mourner: at the other door the coffin of Moll, adorned with a garland of flowers, and epitaphs pinned on it, attended by many matrons and maids, among whom are Lady Kix, Mistress Allwit, and Susan; the coffins are set down, one right over against the other; and while all the company seem to weep and mourn, there is a sad song in the music-room

TOUCH. SEN. Never could death boast of a richer prize
   From the first parent;[2] let the world bring forth
   A pair of truer hearts. To speak but truth
   Of this departed gentleman, in a brother
   Might, by hard censure, be called flattery,
   Which makes me rather silent in his right
   Than so to be delivered to the thoughts
   Of any envious hearer, starved in virtue,
   And therefore pining to hear others thrive;
   But for this maid, whom envy cannot hurt
   With all her poisons, having left to ages
   The true, chaste monument of her living name,
   Which no time can deface, I say of her
   The full truth freely, without fear of censure:
   What nature could there shrine, that might redeem
   Perfection home to woman, but in her
   Was fully glorious? beauty set in goodness

1. Contrived.
2. Since Adam.

Speaks what she was; that jewel so infixed,
There was no want of anything of life
To make these virtuous precedents[1] man and wife,
ALLWIT. Great pity of their deaths!
1ST MOUR. Never more pity!
LADY KIX. It makes a hundred weeping eyes, sweet gossip.
TOUCH. SEN. I cannot think there's any one amongst you
    In this full fair assembly, maid, man, or wife,
    Whose heart would not have sprung with joy and gladness
    To have seen their marriage-day.
2ND MOUR. It would have made
    A thousand joyful hearts.
TOUCH. SEN. Up then apace,
    And take your fortunes, make these joyful hearts;
    Here's none but friends.

  Moll and Touchwood junior rise out of their coffins

ALL. Alive, sir? O sweet, dear couple!
TOUCH. SEN. Nay, do not hinder 'em now, stand from about 'em;
    If she be caught again, and have this time,
    I'll ne'er plot further for 'em, nor this honest chambermaid,
    That helped all at a push.[2]
TOUCH. JUN. Good sir, apace.
PAR. Hands join now, but hearts for ever,
      [*Moll and Touchwood junior join hands*]
    Which no parent's mood shall sever.
    You shall forsake all widows, wives, and maids—
    You lords, knights, gentlemen, and men of trades;—
    And if in haste any article misses,
    Go interline it with a brace of kisses.
TOUCH. SEN. Here's a thing trolled nimbly.—Give you joy, brother;
    Were't not better thou shouldst have her than the maid should die?
MIS. ALL. To you, sweet mistress bride.
ALL. Joy, joy to you both.

---

1. Examples.
2. In an emergency.

TOUCH. SEN. Here be your wedding-sheets you brought along with
    you;
    You may both go to bed when you please too.
TOUCH. JUN. My joy wants utterance.
TOUCH. SEN. Utter all at night
    Then, brother.
MOLL. I am silent with delight.
TOUCH. SEN. Sister, delight will silence any woman;
    But you'll find your tongue again 'mong maid servants,
    Now you keep house, sister.
2ND MOUR. Never was hour so filled with joy and wonder.
TOUCH. SEN. To tell you the full story of this chambermaid,
    And of her kindness in this business to us,
    'Twould ask an hour's discourse; in brief, 'twas she
    That wrought it to this purpose cunningly.
3RD MOUR. We shall all love her for't.
4TH MOUR. See, who comes here now

Enter Yellowhammer and Maudlin

TOUCH. SEN. A storm, a storm! but we are sheltered for it.
YEL. I will prevent[1] you all, and mock you thus,
    You and your expectations; I stand happy,
    Both in your lives, and your hearts' combination.
TOUCH. SEN. Here's a strange day again!
YEL. The knight's proved villain;
    All's come out now, his niece an arrant baggage;
    My poor boy Tim is cast away this morning,
    Even before breakfast, married a whore
    Next to his heart.
MOURNERS. A whore!
YEL. His niece, forsooth.
ALLWIT. I think we rid our hands in good time of him.
MIS. ALL. I knew he was past the best when I gave him over,—
    What is become of him, pray, sir?
YEL. Who, the knight?
    He lies i' th' Knight's ward;[2]—now your belly, lady,

1. Anticipate.
2. A ward in the prison.

[*To Lady Kix*]

Begins to blossom, there's no peace for him,
His creditors are so greedy.

SIR OL. Master Touchwood,
Hear'st thou this news? I'm so endeared to thee
For my wife's fruitfulness, that I charge you both,
Your wife and thee, to live no more asunder
For the world's frowns; I've purse, and bed, and board for you:
Be not afraid to go to your business roundly;
Get children, and I'll keep them.

TOUCH. SEN. Say you so, sir?

SIR OL. Prove me with three at a birth, an thou dar'st now.

TOUCH. SEN. Take heed how you dare a man, while you live, sir,
That has good skill at his weapon.

SIR OL. 'Foot, I dare you, sir!

Enter Tim, Welshwoman, and Tutor

YEL. Look, gentlemen, if e'er you saw the picture
Of the unfortunate marriage, yonder 'tis.

WELSH. Nay, good sweet Tim—

TIM. Come from the university
To marry a whore in London, with my tutor too!
O tempora! O mores![1]

TUTOR. Prithee, Tim, be patient.

TIM. I bought a jade[2] at Cambridge;
I'll let her out to execution,[3] tutor,
For eighteenpence a-day, or Brainford horse-races;
She'll serve to carry seven miles out of town well.
Where be these mountains? I was promised mountains
But there's such a mist, I can see none of 'em.
What are become of those two thousand runts?
Let's have a bout with them in the meantime;
A vengeance runt thee!

MAUD. Good sweet Tim, have patience.

---

1. "O times, O manners!"

2. i.e., He already had a "jade" (broken-down) horse.

3. Now he has another "jade" (loose woman) and will recoup his expenses by hiring her out.

TIM. *Flectere si nequeo superos, Acheronta movebo,* mother.[1]

MAUD. I think you have married her in logic, Tim.
    You told me once by logic you would prove
    A whore an honest woman; prove her so, Tim,
    And take her for thy labor.

TIM. Troth, I thank you:
    I grant you, I may prove another man's wife so,
    But not mine own.

MAUD. There's no remedy now, Tim;
    You must prove her so as well as you may.

TIM. Why then
    My tutor and I will about her as well as we can:
    Uxor non est meretrix ergo falleris.[2]

WELSH. Sir, if your logic cannot prove me honest,
    There's a thing called marriage, and that makes me honest.

MAUD. O, there's a trick beyond your logic, Tim!

TIM. I perceive then a woman may be honest
    According to the English print, when she's
    A whore in the Latin; so much for marriage and logic:
    I'll love her for her wit, I'll pick out my runts there;
    And for my mountains, I'll mount upon——[3]

YEL. So fortune seldom deals two marriages
    With one hand, and both lucky; the best is,
    One feast will serve them both: marry, for room,
    I'll have the dinner kept in Goldsmith's Hall,
    To which, kind gallants, I invite you all.

                                    Exeunt

1. If I cannot move the gods I will move the lower world.
2. A wife is not a whore, therefore you lie.
3. Word missing: obscene?

Appendix to
A Chaste Maid in Cheapside

ACT IV; OPENING

TIM. Your proof is denied, tutor.

TUTOR. I prove to you, pupil, that a fool is not a rational animal.

TIM. You will certainly fail.

TUTOR. Please be silent. I show you—

TIM. How do you prove it, master?

TUTOR. A fool does not have reason, therefore is not a rational animal.

TIM. So you argue, master; a fool does not have reason and is therefore not a rational animal. Your proof is denied again, tutor.

TUTOR. Once more I prove it to you, sir: he who does not share in reason can in no way be called rational; but a fool does not share in reason, therefore the fool can in no way be termed rational.

TIM. He does share in reason.

TUTOR. So you maintain. Who shares in it, and how?

TIM. As a man. I will prove this to you by a syllogism.

TUTOR. Prove it.

TIM. I prove it thus, master. A fool is a man, just as you and I are; a man is a rational animal; so a fool is a rational animal.

TUTOR. Thus you argue: a fool is a man, just as you and I are; a man is a rational animal; so a fool is a rational animal.

The Duchess
of Malfi

John Webster

DRAMATIS PERSONAE

FERDINAND, *Duke of Calabria*
THE CARDINAL, *his Brother*
ANTONIO BOLOGNA, *Steward of the household to the Duchess*
DELIO, *his Friend*
DANIEL DE BOSOLA, *Gentleman of the horse to the Duchess*
CASTRUCHIO
MARQUIS OF PESCARA
COUNT MALATESTE

SILVIO, *a Lord, of Milan* ⎫
RODERIGO ⎬ *Gentlemen attending on the Duchess*
⎭

GRISOLAN
DOCTOR
Several Madmen, Pilgrims, Executioners, Officers, Attendants, &c.
DUCHESS OF MALFI, *sister of Ferdinand and the Cardinal*
CARIOLA, *her Woman*
JULIA, *Castruchio's Wife, and the Cardinal's Mistress*
Old Lady, *Ladies and Children*

The Duchess of Malfi

Act I, Scene I

Enter Antonio and Delio

DEL. You are welcome to your country, dear Antonio;
    You have been long in France, and you return
    A very formal Frenchman in your habit:
    How do you like the French court?
ANT. I admire it:
    In seeking to reduce both state and people
    To a fixed order, their judicious king
    Begins at home; quits[1] first his royal palace
    Of flattering sycophants, of dissolute
    And infamous persons,—which he sweetly terms
    His master's masterpiece, the work of Heaven;
    Considering duly that a prince's court
    Is like a common fountain, whence should flow
    Pure silver drops in general, but if 't chance
    Some cursed example poison 't near the head,
    Death and diseases through the whole land spread.
    And what is 't makes this blessed government
    But a most provident council, who dare freely
    Inform him the corruption of the times?
    Though some o' th' court hold it presumption
    To instruct princes what they ought to do,
    It is a noble duty to inform them
    What they ought to foresee.—Here comes Bosola,
    The only court-gall; yet I observe his railing
    Is not for simple love of piety:

1. Frees.

Indeed, he rails at those things which he wants;
Would be as lecherous, covetous, or proud,
Bloody, or envious, as any man,
If he had means to be so.—Here's the Cardinal.

Enter the Cardinal and Bosola

BOS. I do haunt you still.

CARD. So.

BOS. I have done you better service than to be slighted thus. Miserable age, where only the reward of doing well is the doing of it!

CARD. You enforce your merit too much.

BOS. I fell into the galleys in your service; where, for two years together, I wore two towels instead of a shirt, with a knot on the shoulder, after the fashion of a Roman mantle. Slighted thus? I will thrive some way: blackbirds fatten best in hard weather; why not I in these dog-days?

CARD. Would you could become honest!

BOS. With all your divinity do but direct me the way to it. I have known many travel far for it, and yet return as arrant knaves as they went forth, because they carried themselves always along with them. [*Exit Cardinal*] Are you gone? Some fellows, they say, are possessed with the devil, but this great fellow were able to possess the greatest devil, and make him worse.

ANT. He hath denied thee some suit?

BOS. He and his brother are like plum-trees that grow crooked over standing-pools; they are rich and o'er-laden with fruit, but none but crows, pies, and caterpillars feed on them. Could I be one of their flattering panders, I would hang on their ears like a horseleech, till I were full, and then drop off. I pray, leave me. Who would rely upon these miserable dependencies, in expectation to be advanced to-morrow what creature ever fed worse than hoping Tantalus?[1] nor ever died any man more fearfully than he that hoped for a pardon. There are rewards for hawks and dogs when they have done us service; but for a soldier that hazards his limbs in a battle, nothing but a kind of geometry in his last supportation.

---

1. His punishment in hell was to be hungry and thirsty with food and water just out of his reach.

DEL. Geometry?

BOS. Aye, to hang in a fair pair of slings, take his latter swing in the world upon an honorable pair of crutches, from hospital to hospital. Fare ye well, sir: and yet do not you scorn us; for places in the court are but like beds in the hospital, where this man's head lies at that man's foot, and so lower and lower.

Exit

DEL. I knew this fellow seven years in the galleys
For a notorious murder; and 'twas thought
The Cardinal suborned it: he was released
By the French general, Gaston de Foix,[1]
When he recovered Naples.

ANT. 'Tis great pity
He should be thus neglected: I have heard
He's very valiant. This foul melancholy
Will poison all his goodness; for, I'll tell you,
If too immoderate sleep be truly said
To be an inward rust unto the soul,
It then doth follow want of action
Breeds all black malcontents; and their close rearing,
Like moths in cloth, do hurt for want of wearing.

DEL. The presence 'gins to fill: you promised me
To make me the partaker of the natures
Of some of your great courtiers.

ANT. The lord Cardinal's,
And other strangers' that are now in court?
I shall.—Here comes the great Calabrian duke.

*Enter Ferdinand, Castruchio, Silvio, Roderigo, Grisolan,
and Attendants*

FERD. Who took the ring oftenest?[2]

SILV. Antonio Bologna, my lord.

FERD. Our sister duchess's great-master of her household? give him the jewel.—When shall we leave this sportive action, and fall to action indeed?

---

1. He failed to recover Naples.
2. In tilting at the ring.

CAS. Methinks, my lord, you should not desire to go to war in person.

FERD. Now for some gravity:—why, my lord?

CAS. It is fitting a soldier arise to be a prince, but not necessary a prince descend to be a captain.

FERD. No?

CAS. No, my lord; he were far better do it by a deputy.

FERD. Why should he not as well sleep or eat by a deputy? this might take idle, offensive, and base office from him, where as the other deprives him of honor.

CAS. Believe my experience, that realm is never long in quiet where the ruler is a soldier.

FERD. Thou told'st me thy wife could not endure fighting.

CAS. True, my lord.

FERD. And of a jest she broke of a captain she met full of wounds: I have forgot it.

CAS. She told him, my lord, he was a pitiful fellow, to lie, like the children of Ismael, all in tents.[1]

FERD. Why, there's a wit were able to undo all the chirurgeons o' the city; for although gallants should quarrel, and had drawn their weapons, and were ready to go to it, yet her persuasions would make them put up.

CAS. That she would, my lord.

FERD. How do you like my Spanish gennet?

ROD. He is all fire.

FERD. I am of Pliny's opinion, I think he was begot by the wind; he runs as if he were ballasted with quick-silver.

SILV. True, my lord, he reels from the tilt often.

ROD. AND GRIS. Ha, ha, ha!

FERD. Why do you laugh? methinks you that are courtiers should be my touchwood, take fire when I give fire; that is, laugh but when I laugh, were the subject never so witty.

CAS. True, my lord: I myself have heard a very good jest, and have scorned to seem to have so silly a wit as to understand it.

FERD. But I can laugh at your fool, my lord.

---

1. In surgery, *tent* is a roll of lint or other material placed in a wound. The joke lies in the reference to 2 Kings 13:5—"the children of Israel *dwelt* in their tents."

CAS. He cannot speak, you know, but he makes faces: my lady cannot abide him.

FERD. No?

CAS. Nor endure to be in merry company; for she says too much laughing, and too much company, fills her too full of the wrinkle.

FERD. I would, then, have a mathematical instrument made for her face, that she might not laugh out of compass.—I shall shortly visit you at Milan, Lord Silvio.

SILV. Your grace shall arrive most welcome.

FERD. You are a good horseman, Antonio: you have excellent riders in France: what do you think of good horsemanship?

ANT. Nobly, my lord: as out of the Grecian horse issued many famous princes, so out of brave horsemanship arise the first sparks of growing resolution, that raise the mind to noble action.

FERD. You have bespoke it worthily.

SILV. Your brother, the lord Cardinal, and sister duchess.

Re-enter Cardinal, with Duchess, Cariola, and Julia

CARD. Are the galleys come about?

GRIS. They are, my lord.

FERD. Here's the Lord Silvio is come to take his leave.

DEL. [*Aside to Antonio*] Now, sir, your promise; what's that Cardinal?
I mean his temper? they say he's a brave fellow,
Will play his five thousand crowns at tennis, dance,
Court ladies, and one that hath fought single combats.

ANT. Some such flashes superficially hang on him for form; but observe his inward character: he is a melancholy churchman; the spring in his face is nothing but the engendering of toads; where he is jealous of any man, he lays worse plots for them than ever was imposed on Hercules, for he strews in his way flatterers, panders, intelligencers,[1] atheists, and a thousand such political monsters. He should have been Pope; but instead of coming to it by the primitive decency[2] of the Church, he did bestow bribes so largely and so impudently as if he would have carried it away without Heaven's knowledge. Some good he hath done—

---

1. Informers.
2. Uncorrupted manners.

DEL. You have given too much of him. What's his brother?
ANT. The duke there? a most perverse and turbulent nature:
    What appears in him mirth is merely outside;
    If he laughs heartily, it is to laugh
    All honesty out of fashion.
DEL. Twins?
ANT. In quality.
    He speaks with others' tongues, and hears men's suits
    With others' ears; will seem to sleep o' th' bench
    Only to entrap offenders in their answers;
    Dooms men to death by information;
    Rewards by hearsay.
DEL. Then the law to him
    Is like a foul black cobweb to a spider,—
    He makes of it his dwelling and a prison
    To entangle those shall feed him.
ANT. Most true:
    He never pays debts unless they be shrewd turns,
    And those he will confess that he doth owe.
    Last, for his brother there, the Cardinal,
    They that do flatter him most say oracles
    Hang at his lips; and verily I believe them,
    For the devil speaks in them.
    But for their sister, the right noble duchess,
    You never fixed your eye on three fair medals
    Cast in one figure, of so different temper.
    For her discourse, it is so full of rapture,
    You only will begin then to be sorry
    When she doth end her speech, and wish, in wonder,
    She held it less vain-glory to talk much,
    Than your penance to hear her: whilst she speaks,
    She throws upon a man so sweet a look,
    That it were able to raise one to a galliard[1]
    That lay in a dead palsy, and to dote
    On that sweet countenance; but in that look
    There speaketh so divine a continence

---

1. A lively dance in triple time.

As cuts off all lascivious and vain hope.
Her days are practised in such noble virtue,
That sure her nights, nay, more, her very sleeps,
Are more in heaven than other ladies' shrifts.[1]
Let all sweet ladies break their flattering glasses,
And dress themselves in her.

DEL. Fie, Antonio,
You play the wire-drawer[2] with her commendations.

ANT. I'll case the picture up: only thus much;
All her particular worth grows to this sum—
She stains the time past, lights the time to come.

CAR. You must attend my lady in the gallery,
Some half an hour hence.

ANT. I shall.

Exeunt Antonio and Delio

FERD. Sister, I have a suit to you.

DUCH. To me, sir?

FERD. A gentleman here, Daniel de Bosola,
One that was in the galleys—

DUCH. Yes, I know him.

FERD. A worthy fellow he is: pray, let me entreat for
The provisorship of your horse.

DUCH. Your knowledge of him
Commends him and prefers him.

FERD. Call him hither.

Exit Attendant

We are now upon parting. Good Lord Silvio,
Do us commend to all our noble friends
At the leaguer.[3]

SILV. Sir, I shall.

DUCH. You are for Milan?

SILV. I am.

DUCH. Bring the caroches.[4] We'll bring you down
To the haven.

1. Absolutions.
2. i.e., Spin out at tedious length.
3. Military camp.
4. Coaches.

Exeunt all but Ferdinand and the Cardinal

CARD. Be sure you entertain¹ that Bosola
    For your intelligence: I would not be seen in't;
    And therefore many times I have slighted him
    When he did court our furtherance, as this morning.
FERD. Antonio, the great-master of her household,
    Had been far fitter.
CARD. You are deceived in him:
    His nature is too honest for such business.—
    He comes: I'll leave you.

Exit

Re-enter Bosola

BOS. I was lured to you.
FERD. My brother, here, the Cardinal could never
    Abide you.
BOS. Never since he was in my debt.
FERD. Maybe some oblique character in your face
    Made him suspect you.
BOS. Doth he study physiognomy?
    There's no more credit to be given to th' face
    Than to a sick man's urine, which some call
    The physician's whore because she cozens him.
    He did suspect me wrongfully.
FERD. For that
    You must give great men leave to take their times.
    Distrust doth cause us seldom be deceived:
    You see the oft shaking of the cedar-tree
    Fastens it more at root.
BOS. Yet, take heed;
    For to suspect a friend unworthily
    Instructs him the next way to suspect you,
    And prompts him to deceive you.
FERD. [*Giving him money*] There's gold.

---

1. Employ.

BOS. So:

What follows? never rained such showers as these

Without thunderbolts i' th' tail of them: whose throat must
I cut?

FERD. Your inclination to shed blood rides post

Before my occasion to use you. I give you that

To live i' th' court here, and observe the duchess;

To note all the particulars of her havior,

What suitors do solicit her for marriage,

And whom she best affects. She's a young widow:

I would not have her marry again.

BOS. No, sir?

FERD. Do not you ask the reason; but be satisfied

I say I would not.

BOS. It seems you would create me

One of your familiars.

FERD. Familiar? what's that?

BOS. Why, a very quaint invisible devil in flesh,

An intelligencer.

FERD. Such a kind of thriving thing

I would wish thee; and ere long thou may'st arrive

At a higher place by 't.

BOS. Take your devils,

Which hell calls angels; these cursed gifts would make

You a corrupter, me an impudent traitor;

And should I take these, they'd take me to hell.

FERD. Sir, I'll take nothing from you that I have given:

There is a place that I procured for you

This morning, the provisorship o' th' horse;

Have you heard on't?

BOS. No.

FERD. 'Tis yours: is't not worth thanks?

BOS. I would have you curse yourself now, that your bounty,

Which makes men truly noble, e'er should make me

A villain. Oh, that to avoid ingratitude

For the good deed you have done me, I must do

All the ill man can invent! Thus the devil

Candies all sins o'er; and what heaven terms vile,
That names he complimental.[1]

FERD. Be yourself;
 Keep your old garb of melancholy; 'twill express
 You envy those that stand above your reach,
 Yet strive not to come near 'em: this will gain
 Access to private lodgings, where yourself
 May, like a politic dormouse—

BOS. As I have seen some
 Feed in a lord's dish, half asleep, not seeming
 To listen to any talk; and yet these rogues
 Have cut his throat in a dream. What's my place?
 The provisorship o' th' horse? say, then, my corruption
 Grew out of horse-dung: I am your creature.

FERD. Away!

               Exit

BOS. Let good men, for good deeds, covet good fame,
 Since place and riches oft are bribes of shame:
 Sometimes the devil doth preach.

               Exit

SCENE II

Enter Ferdinand, Duchess, Cardinal, and Cariola

CARD. We are to part from you; and your own discretion
 Must now be your director.

FERD. You are a widow:
 You know already what man is; and therefore
 Let not youth, high promotion, eloquence—

CARD. No,
 Nor any thing without the addition, honor,
 Sway your high blood.

FERD. Marry! they are most luxurious[2]
 Will wed twice.

CARD. Oh, fie!

---

1. Required by courtesy.
2. Lascivious.

FERD. Their livers are more spotted
Than Laban's sheep.[1]
DUCHESS. Diamonds are of most value,
They say, that have passed through most jewellers' hands.
FERD. Whores by that rule are precious.
DUCH. Will you hear me?
I'll never marry.
CARD. So most widows say;
But commonly that motion lasts no longer
Than the turning of an hour-glass: the funeral sermon
And it end both together.
FERD. Now hear me:
You live in a rank pasture, here, i' th' court;
There is a kind of honey-dew that's deadly;
'Twill poison your fame; look to't: be not cunning;
For they whose faces do belie their hearts
Are witches ere they arrive at twenty years,
Aye, and give the devil suck.
DUCH. This is terrible good counsel.
FERD. Hypocrisy is woven of a fine small thread,
Subtler than Vulcan's engine:[2] yet, believe't,
Your darkest actions, nay, your privat'st thoughts,
Will come to light.
CARD. You may flatter yourself,
And take your own choice; privately be married
Under the eaves of night—
FERD. Think'st the best voyage
That e'er you made; like the irregular crab,
Which, though't goes backward, thinks that it goes right
Because it goes its own way; but observe,
Such weddings may more properly be said
To be executed than celebrated.
CARD. The marriage night
Is the entrance into some prison.
FERD. And those joys,

1. Genesis 30.
2. The net in which he caught Mars and Venus.

Those lustful pleasures, are like heavy sleeps
Which do forerun man's mischief.
CARD. Fare you well.
Wisdom begins at the end: remember it.

Exit

DUCHESS. I think this speech between you both was studied,
It came so roundly off.
FERD. You are my sister;
This was my father's poniard, do you see?
I'd be loath to see't look rusty, 'cause 'twas his.
I would have you to give o'er these chargeable revels:
A visor and a mask are whispering-rooms
That were never built for goodness;—fare ye well;—
And women like that part which, like the lamprey,
Hath never a bone in't.
DUCH. Fie, sir!
FERD. Nay,
I mean the tongue; variety of courtship:
What cannot a neat knave with a smooth tale
Make a woman believe? Farewell, lusty widow.

Exit

DUCH. Shall this move me? If all my royal kindred
Lay in my way unto this marriage,
I'd make them my low footsteps: and even now,
Even in this hate, as men in some great battles,
By apprehending danger, have achieved
Almost impossible actions (I have heard soldiers say so),
So I through frights and threatenings will assay
This dangerous venture. Let old wives report
I winked[1] and chose a husband.—Cariola,
To thy known secrecy I have given up
More than my life—my fame.
CAR. Both shall be safe;
For I'll conceal this secret from the world
As warily as those that trade in poison
Keep poison from their children.

1. Closed my eyes.

DUCH. Thy protestation
   Is ingenious[1] and hearty: I believe it.
   Is Antonio come?
CAR. He attends you.
DUCH. Good dear soul,
   Leave me; but place thyself behind the arras,
   Where thou mayst overhear us. Wish me good speed;
   For I am going into a wilderness
   Where I shall find nor path nor friendly clue
   To be my guide.

Cariola goes behind the arras

Enter Antonio

   I sent for you: sit down;
   Take pen and ink, and write: are you ready?
ANT. Yes.
DUCH. What did I say?
ANT. That I should write somewhat.
DUCH. Oh, I remember.
   After these triumphs and this large expense,
   It's fit, like thrifty husbands, we inquire
   What's laid up for to-morrow.
ANT. So please your beauteous excellence.
DUCH. Beauteous?
   Indeed, I thank you: I look young for your sake;
   You have ta'en my cares upon you.
ANT. I'll fetch your grace
   The particulars of your revenue and expense.
DUCH. Oh, you are an upright treasurer: but you mistook;
   For when I said I meant to make inquiry
   What's laid up for to-morrow, I did mean
   What's laid up yonder for me.
ANT. Where?
DUCH. In heaven.
   I am making my will (as 'tis fit princes should,
   In perfect memory), and, I pray, sir, tell me,
   Were not one better make it smiling, thus,

1. Ingenuous.

> Than in deep groans and terrible ghastly looks,
> As if the gifts we parted with procured
> That violent distraction?

ANT. Oh, much better.

DUCH. If I had a husband now, this care were quit:
> But I intend to make you overseer.
> What good deed shall we first remember? say.

ANT. Begin with that first good deed began i' th' world
> After man's creation, the sacrament of marriage:
> I'd have you first provide for a good husband;
> Give him all.

DUCH. All?

ANT. Yes, your excellent self.

DUCH. In a winding-sheet?

ANT. In a couple.

DUCH. Saint Winfred,[1]
> That were a strange will!

ANT. 'Twere stranger if there were no will in you
> To marry again.

DUCH. What do you think of marriage?

ANT. I take't, as those that deny purgatory;
> It locally contains or Heaven or hell;
> There's no third place in't.

DUCH. How do you affect it?

ANT. My banishment, feeling my melancholy,
> Would often reason thus.

DUCH. Pray, let's hear it.

ANT. Say a man never marry, nor have children,
> What takes that from him? only the bare name
> Of being a father, or the weak delight
> To see the little wanton ride a-cock-horse
> Upon a painted stick, or hear him chatter
> Like a taught starling.

DUCH. Fie, fie, what's all this?
> One of your eyes is blood-shot; use my ring to't,
> They say 'tis very sovereign: 'twas my wedding-ring,

---

1. Martyred because of her refusal to marry.

And I did vow never to part with it
But to my second husband.

ANT. You have parted with it now.

DUCH. Yes, to help your eyesight.

ANT. You have made me stark blind.

DUCH. How?

ANT. There is a saucy and ambitious devil
Is dancing in this circle.

DUCH. Remove him.

ANT. How?

DUCH. There needs small conjuration, when your finger
May do it: this; is it fit?

          [She puts the ring upon his finger: he kneels]

ANT. What said you?

DUCH. Sir,
This goodly roof of yours is too low built;
I cannot stand upright in't nor discourse,
Without I raise it higher: raise yourself;
Or, if you please, my hand to help you: so.

                 [Raises him]

ANT. Ambition, madam, is a great man's madness,
That is not kept in chains and close-pent rooms,
But in fair lightsome lodgings, and is girt
With the wild noise of prattling visitants,
Which makes it lunatic beyond all cure.
Conceive not I am so stupid but I aim[1]
Whereto your favors tend: but he's a fool
That, being a-cold, would thrust his hands i' th' fire
To warm them.

DUCH. So, now the ground's broke,
You may discover what a wealthy mine
I make you lord of.

ANT. O my unworthiness!

DUCH. You were ill to sell yourself:
This darkening of your worth is not like that
Which tradesmen use i' th' city, their false lights

1. Guess.

Are to rid bad wares off: and I must tell you,
If you will know where breathes a complete man
(I speak it without flattery), turn your eyes,
And progress through yourself.

ANT. Were there nor heaven
Nor hell, I should be honest: I have long served virtue,
And ne'er ta'en wages of her.

DUCH. Now she pays it.
The misery of us that are born great!
We are forced to woo, because none dare woo us;
And as a tyrant doubles with his words,
And fearfully equivocates, so we
Are forced to express our violent passions
In riddles and in dreams, and leave the path
Of simple virtue, which was never made
To seem the thing it is not. Go, go brag
You have left me heartless; mine is in your bosom:
I hope 'twill multiply love there. You do tremble:
Make not your heart so dead a piece of flesh,
To fear more than to love me. Sir, be confident:
What is't distracts you? This is flesh and blood, sir;
'Tis not the figure cut in alabaster
Kneels at my husband's tomb. Awake, awake, man!
I do here put off all vain ceremony,
And only do appear to you a young widow
That claims you for her husband, and, like a widow,
I use but half a blush in't.

ANT. Truth speak for me,
I will remain the constant sanctuary
Of your good name.

DUCH. I thank you, gentle love:
And 'cause you shall not come to me in debt,
Being now my steward, here upon your lips
I sign your *Quietus est.*[1] This you should have begged now:
I have seen children oft eat sweetmeats thus,
As fearful to devour them too soon.

---

1. Acquittance, clearance of debt.

ANT. But for your brothers?

DUCH. Do not think of them:
All discord without this circumference
Is only to be pitied, and not feared:
Yet, should they know it, time will easily
Scatter the tempest.

ANT. These words should be mine,
And all the parts you have spoke, if some part of it
Would not have savored flattery.

DUCH. Kneel.

> [*Cariola comes from behind the arras*]

ANT. Ha!

DUCH. Be not amazed; this woman's of my counsel:
I have heard lawyers say, a contract in a chamber
Per *verba* [*de*] *presenti* is absolute marriage.

> [*She and Antonio kneel*]

Bless, heaven, this sacred gordian,[1] which let violence
Never untwine!

ANT. And may our sweet affections, like the spheres,
Be still[2] in motion!

DUCH. Quickening, and make
The like soft music!

ANT. That we may imitate the loving palms,
Best emblem of a peaceful marriage, that ne'er
Bore fruit, divided!

DUCH. What can the Church force more?

ANT. That fortune may not know an accident,
Either of joy or sorrow, to divide
Our fixèd wishes!

DUCH. How can the Church build faster?
We now are man and wife, and 'tis the Church
That must but echo this.—Maid, stand apart:
I now am blind.

ANT. What's your conceit[3] in this?

---

1. Knot that cannot be untied.
2. Always.
3. Witty notion.

DUCH. I would have you lead your fortune by the hand
  Unto your marriage bed:
  (You speak in me this, for we now are one:)
  We'll only lie, and talk together, and plot
  To appease my humorous[1] kindred; and if you please,
  Like the old tale in "Alexander and Lodowick,"[2]
  Lay a naked sword between us, keep us chaste.
  Oh, let me shroud my blushes in your bosom,
  Since 'tis the treasury of all my secrets!

                                    Exeunt Duchess and Antonio

CAR. Whether the spirit of greatness or of woman
  Reign most in her, I know not; but it shows
  A fearful madness: I owe her much of pity.

                                                            Exit

ACT II, SCENE I

Enter Bosola and Castruchio

BOS. You say you would fain be taken for an eminent courtier?

CAS. 'Tis the very main of my ambition.

BOS. Let me see: you have a reasonable good face for't already, and
  your nightcap expresses your ears sufficient largely. I would have
  you learn to twirl the strings of your band[3] with a good grace, and in
  a set speech, at th' end of every sentence, to hum three or four
  times, or blow your nose till it smart again, to recover your memory.
  When you come to be a president in criminal causes, if you smile
  upon a prisoner, hang him, but if you frown upon him and threaten
  him, let him be sure to scape the gallows.

CAS. I would be a very merry president.

BOS. Do not sup o' night; 'twill beget you an admirable wit.

CAS. Rather it would make me have a good stomach to quarrel; for
  they say, your roaring boys eat meat seldom, and that makes them so
  valiant. But how shall I know whether the people take me for an
  eminent fellow?

---

1. Ill-tempered.
2. *The Two Faithful Friends, the Pleasant History of Alexander and Lodwicke,* a popular romance.
3. A collar.

BOS. I will teach a trick to know it: give out you lie a-dying, and if you hear the common people curse you, be sure you are taken for one of the prime nightcaps.[1]

Enter an Old Lady

You come from painting now.

OLD L. From what?

BOS. Why, from your scurvy face-physic. To behold thee not painted inclines somewhat near a miracle; these in thy face here were deep ruts and foul sloughs the last progress.[2] There was a lady in France that, having had the small-pox, flayed the skin off her face to make it more level; and whereas before she looked like a nutmeg-grater, after she resembled an abortive hedgehog.

OLD L. Do you call this painting?

BOS. No, no, but you call it careening of an old morphewed[3] lady, to make her disembogue[4] again: there's rough-cast phrase to your plastic.[5]

OLD L. It seems you are well acquainted with my closet.

BOS. One would suspect it for a shop of witchcraft, to find in it the fat of serpents, spawn of snakes, Jews' spittle, and their young children's ordure; and all these for the face. I would sooner eat a dead pigeon taken from the soles of the feet of one sick of the plague than kiss one of you fasting. Here are two of you, whose sin of your youth is the very patrimony of the physician; makes him renew his foot-cloth[6] with the spring, and change his high-priced courtezan with the fall of the leaf. I do wonder you do not loathe yourselves. Observe my meditation now.

What thing is in this outward form of man
To be beloved? We account it ominous,
If nature do produce a colt, or lamb,
A fawn, or goat, in any limb resembling

---

1. A cant name for the Mohocks or "roaring boys" of the time.
2. State procession.
3. Leprous.
4. Discharge herself.
5. i.e., Plain language instead of your fine phrases.
6. Ornamental covering for a horse.

A man, and fly from 't as a prodigy:
Man stands amazed to see his deformity
In any other creature but himself.
But in our own flesh, though we bear diseases
Which have their true name only ta'en from beasts,
As the most ulcerous wolf[1] and swinish measle,[2]
Though we are eaten up of lice and worms,
And though continually we bear about us
A rotten and dead body, we delight
To hide it in rich tissue:[3] all our fear,
Nay, all our terror, is lest our physician
Should put us in the ground to be made sweet—
Your wife's gone to Rome: you two couple,[4] and get you
To the wells at Lucca[5] to recover your aches.
I have other work on foot.

      Exeunt Castruchio and Old Lady

I observe our duchess
Is sick a-days, she pukes, her stomach seethes,
The fins of her eye-lids look most teeming blue,
She wanes i' th' cheek, and waxes fat i' th' flank,
And, contrary to our Italian fashion,
Wears a loose-bodied gown: there's somewhat in't.
I have a trick may chance discover it,
A pretty one; I have brought some apricocks,
The first our spring yields.

   Enter Antonio and Delio, talking together apart

DEL. And so long since married?
 You amaze me.
ANT. Let me seal your lips for ever:
 For, did I think that anything but th' air
 Could carry these words from you, I should wish

---

1. Lupus.
2. A disease to which swine are subject, not the same as the human ailment.
3. Cloth.
4. Get together.
5. Tuscan city, famous for its therapeutic baths.

You had no breath at all.—Now, sir, in your contemplation?
You are studying to become a great wise fellow?

BOS. Oh, sir, the opinion of wisdom is a foul tetter[1] that runs all over a man's body: if simplicity direct us to have no evil, it directs us to a happy being; for the subtlest folly proceeds from the subtlest wisdom: let me be simply honest.

ANT. I do understand your inside.

BOS. Do you so?

ANT. Because you would not seem to appear to th' world
Puffed up with your preferment, you continue
This out-of-fashion melancholy: leave it, leave it.

BOS. Give me leave to be honest in any phrase, in any compliment whatsoever. Shall I confess myself to you? I look no higher than I can reach: they are the gods that must ride on winged horses. A lawyer's mule of a slow pace will both suit my disposition and business; for, mark me, when a man's mind rides faster than his horse can gallop, they quickly both tire.

ANT. You would look up to heaven, but I think
The devil, that rules i' th' air, stands in your light.

BOS. Oh, sir, you are lord of the ascendant, chief man with the duchess; a duke was your cousin-german removed. Say you were lineally descended from King Pepin, or he himself, what of this? search the heads of the greatest rivers in the world, you shall find them but bubbles of water. Some would think the souls of princes were brought forth by some more weighty cause than those of meaner persons: they are deceived; there's the same hand to them; the like passions sway them; the same reason that makes a vicar go to law for a tithe-pig, and undo his neighbors, makes them spoil a whole province, and batter down goodly cities with the cannon.

Enter Duchess and Ladies

DUCH. Your arm, Antonio: do I not grow fat?
I am exceeding short-winded.—Bosola,
I would have you, sir, provide for me a litter;
Such a one as the Duchess of Florence rode in.

BOS. The duchess used one when she was great with child.

1. Skin disease.

DUCH. I think she did.——Come hither, mend my ruff;
    Here, when?[1]
    Thou art such a tedious lady; and thy breath smells
    Of lemon-peels; would thou hadst done! Shall I swoon
    Under thy fingers! I am so troubled
    With the mother![2]

BOS. [*Aside*] I fear too much.

DUCH. I have heard you say
    That the French courtiers wear their hats on 'fore
    The king.

ANT. I have seen it.

DUCH. In the presence?

ANT. Yes.

DUCH. Why should not we bring up that fashion? 'Tis
    Ceremony more than duty that consists
    In the removing of a piece of felt:
    Be you the example to the rest o' th' court;
    Put on your hat first.

ANT. You must pardon me:
    I have seen, in colder countries than in France,
    Nobles stand bare to th' prince; and the distinction
    Methought showed reverently.

BOS. I have a present for your grace.

DUCH. For me, sir?

BOS. Apricocks, madam.

DUCH. O, sir, where are they?
    I have heard of none to-year.[3]

BOS. [*Aside*] Good; her color rises.

DUCH. Indeed, I thank you: they are wondrous fair ones.
    What an unskilful fellow is our gardener!
    We shall have none this month.

BOS. Will not your grace pare them?

DUCH. No: they taste of musk, methinks; indeed they do.

BOS. I know not: yet I wish your grace had pared 'em.

---

1. A common exclamation of impatience.
2. Hysteria.
3. This year.

DUCH. Why?

BOS. I forgot to tell you, the knave gardener,
   Only to raise his profit by them the sooner,
   Did ripen them in horse-dung.

DUCH. O, you jest.—
   You shall judge: pray taste one.

ANT. Indeed, madam, I do not love the fruit.

DUCH. Sir, you are loath
   To rob us of our dainties: 'tis a delicate fruit;
   They say they are restorative.

BOS. 'Tis a pretty art,
   This grafting.

DUCH. 'Tis so; a bettering of nature.

BOS. To make a pippin grow upon a crab,
   A damson on a blackthorn.—[*Aside*] How greedily she eats them!
   A whirlwind strike off these bawd farthingales!¹
   For, but for that and the loose-bodied gown,
   I should have discovered apparently
   The young springal² cutting a caper in her belly.

DUCH. I thank you, Bosola: they were right good ones,
   If they do not make me sick.

ANT. How now, madam?

DUCH. This green fruit and my stomach are not friends:
   How they swell me!

BOS. [*Aside*] Nay, you are too much swelled already.

DUCH. Oh, I am in an extreme cold sweat!

BOS. I am very sorry.

DUCH. Lights to my chamber!—O good Antonio,
   I fear I am undone!

DEL. Lights there, lights!

   Exeunt Duchess and Ladies.—Exit, on the other side, Bosola

ANT. O my most trusty Delio, we are lost!
   I fear she's fall'n in labor; and there's left
   No time for her remove.

DEL. Have you prepared

---

1. Hoops of whalebone.
2. Stripling.

Those ladies to attend her? and procured
That politic safe conveyance for the midwife
Your duchess plotted?

ANT. I have.

DEL. Make use, then, of this forced occasion:
Give out that Bosola hath poisoned her
With these apricocks; that will give some color
For her keeping close.

ANT. Fie, fie, the physicians
Will then flock to her.

DEL. For that you may pretend
She'll use some prepared antidote of her own,
Lest the physicians should re-poison her.

ANT. I am lost in amazement: I know not what to think on't.

Exeunt

SCENE II

Enter Bosola

BOS. So, so, there's no question but her tetchiness and most vulturous
eating of the apricocks are apparent signs of breeding.

Enter an Old Lady

Now?

OLD L. I am in haste, sir.

BOS. There was a young waiting-woman had a monstrous desire to
see the glass-house—

OLD L. Nay, pray let me go.

BOS. And it was only to know what strange instrument it was should
swell up a glass to the fashion of a woman's belly.

OLD L. I will hear no more of the glass-house. You are still abusing
women?

BOS. Who, I? no; only, by the way now and then, mention your frail-
ties. The orange-tree bears ripe and green fruit and blossoms all together; and some of you give entertainment for pure love, but more
for more precious reward. The lusty spring smells well; but droop-
ing autumn tastes well. If we have the same golden showers that
rained in the time of Jupiter the thunderer, you have the same

Danaës still, to hold up their laps to receive them. Didst thou never study the mathematics?

OLD L. What's that, sir?

BOS. Why, to know the trick how to make a many lines meet in one center. Go, go, give your foster-daughters good counsel: tell them, that the devil takes delight to hang at a woman's girdle, like a false rusty watch, that she cannot discern how the time passes.

Exit Old Lady

Enter Antonio, Delio, Roderigo, and Grisolan

ANT. Shut up the court-gates.

ROD. Why, sir? what's the danger?

ANT. Shut up the posterns presently, and call
All the officers o' th' court.

GRIS. I shall instantly.

Exit

ANT. Who keeps the key o' th' park gate?

ROD. Forobosco.

ANT. Let him bring 't presently.

Re-enter Grisolan with Servants

1 SERV. O, gentlemen o' the court, the foulest treason!

BOS. [*Aside*] If that these apricocks should be poisoned now,
Without my knowledge!

1 SERV. There was taken even now
A Switzer in the duchess' bed chamber—

2 SERV. A Switzer?

1 SERV. With a pistol in his great cod-piece.

BOS. Ha, ha, ha!

1 SERV. The cod-piece was the case for't.

2 SERV. There was
A cunning traitor: who would have searched his cod-piece?

1 SERV. True, if he had kept out of the ladies' chambers:
And all the moulds of his buttons were leaden bullets.

2 SERV. O wicked cannibal!
A fire-lock in 's cod-piece!

1 SERV. 'Twas a French plot,
Upon my life.

2 SERV. To see what the devil can do!

ANT. Are all the officers here?

SERVANTS. We are.

ANT. Gentlemen,
We have lost much plate you know; and but this evening
Jewels, to the value of four thousand ducats,
Are missing in the duchess' cabinet.
Are the gates shut?

SERV. Yes.

ANT. 'Tis the duchess' pleasure
Each officer be locked into his chamber
Till the sun-rising; and to send the keys
Of all their chests and of their outward doors
Into her bed-chamber. She is very sick.

ROD. At her pleasure.

ANT. She entreats you take't not ill:
The innocent shall be the more approved[1] by it.

BOS. Gentleman o' th' wood-yard, where's your Switzer now?

1 SERV. By this hand, 'twas credibly reported by one o' th' black guard.[2]

Exeunt all except Antonio and Delio

DEL. How fares it with the duchess?

ANT. She's exposed
Unto the worst of torture, pain and fear.

DEL. Speak to her all happy comfort.

ANT. How I do play the fool with mine own danger!
You are this night, dear friend, to post to Rome:
My life lies in your service.

DEL. Do not doubt me.

ANT. Oh, 'tis far from me: and yet fear presents me
Somewhat that looks like danger.

DEL. Believe it,
'Tis but the shadow of your fear, no more;
How superstitiously we mind our evils!
The throwing down salt, or crossing of a hare,
Bleeding at nose, the stumbling of a horse,

1. Found worthy.
2. Menials.

Or singing of a cricket, are of power
To daunt whole man in us. Sir, fare you well:
I wish you all the joys of a blessed father:
And, for my faith, lay this unto your breast,—
Old friends, like old swords, still are trusted best.

Exit

Enter Cariola

CAR. Sir, you are the happy father of a son:
Your wife commends him to you.
ANT. Blessèd comfort!—
For Heaven's sake tend her well: I'll presently
Go set a figure for 's nativity.[1]

Exeunt

SCENE III

Enter Bosola, with a dark lantern

BOS. Sure I did hear a woman shriek: list, ha!
And the sound came, if I received it right,
From the duchess' lodgings. There's some stratagem
In the confining all our courtiers
To their several wards: I must have part of it;
My intelligence will freeze else. List, again!
It may be 'twas the melancholy bird,
Best friend of silence and of solitariness,
The owl, that screamed so.—Ha! Antonio?

Enter Antonio with a Candle, his Sword drawn

ANT. I heard some noise.—Who's there? what art thou? speak.
BOS. Antonio? put not your face nor body
To such a forced expression of fear:
I am Bosola, your friend.
ANT. Bosola!—
[*Aside*] This mole does undermine me.—Heard you not
A noise even now?

1. Cast his horoscope.

BOS. From whence?

ANT. From the duchess' lodging.

BOS. Not I: did you?

ANT. I did, or else I dreamed.

BOS. Let's walk towards it.

ANT. No: it may be 'twas
But the rising of the wind.

BOS. Very likely.
Methinks 'tis very cold, and yet you sweat:
You look wildly.

ANT. I have been setting a figure
For the duchess' jewels.

BOS. Ah, and how falls your question?
Do you find it radical?[1]

ANT. What's that to you?
'Tis rather to be questioned what design,
When all men were commanded to their lodgings,
Makes you a night-walker.

BOS. In sooth, I'll tell you:
Now all the court's asleep, I thought the devil
Had least to do here; I came to say my prayers;
And if it do offend you I do so,
You are a fine courtier.

ANT. [*Aside*] This fellow will undo me.—
You gave the duchess apricocks to-day:
Pray Heaven they were not poisoned!

BOS. Poisoned? A Spanish fig
For the imputation!

ANT. Traitors are ever confident
Till they are discovered. There were jewels stolen too:
In my conceit, none are to be suspected
More than yourself.

BOS. You are a false steward.

ANT. Saucy slave, I'll pull thee up by the roots.

BOS. Maybe the ruin will crush you to pieces.

ANT. You are an impudent snake indeed, sir:

1. i.e., Capable of solution.

Are you scarce warm, and do you show your sting?
You libel well, sir.
BOS. No, sir: copy it out,
    And I will set my hand to't.
ANT. [*Aside*] My nose bleeds.
    One that were superstitious would count
    This ominous, when it merely comes by chance:
    Two letters, that are wrought here for my name,
    Are drowned in blood!
    Mere accident.—For you, sir, I'll take order
    I' th' morn you shall be safe:—[*Aside*] 'tis that must color
    Her lying-in:—sir, this door you pass not:
    I do not hold it fit that you come near
    The duchess' lodgings, till you have quit yourself.[1]—
    [*Aside*] The great are like the base, nay, they are the same,
    When they seek shameful ways to avoid shame.

                                                    Exit

BOS. Antonio hereabout did drop a paper:—
    Some of your help, false friend: [*Opening his lantern*]—Oh, here it is.
    What's here? a child's nativity calculated?

                                                    [*Reads*]

"The duchess was delivered of a son, 'tween the hours twelve and
one in the night, Anno Dom. 1504,"—that's this year—"decimo
nono Decembris,"[2]—that's this night,—"taken according to the
meridian of Malfi,"—that's our duchess: happy discovery!—"The
lord of the first house being combust in the ascendant, signifies short
life; and Mars being in a human sign, joined to the tail of the Dragon,
in the eighth house, doth threaten a violent death. *Caetera non scru-
tantur.*"[3]
    Why, now 'tis most apparent: this precise fellow
    Is the duchess' bawd:—I have it to my wish!
    This is a parcel of intelligency
    Our courtiers were cased up for: it needs must follow
    That I must be committed on pretence
    Of poisoning her; which I'll endure, and laugh at.

1. i.e., Of blame.
2. December 19.
3. The remainder is not readable.

If one could find the father now! but that
Time will discover. Old Castruchio
I' th' morning posts to Rome: by him I'll send
A letter that shall make her brothers' galls
O'erflow their livers. This was a thrifty way.
Though lust do mask in ne'er so strange disguise,
She's oft found witty, but is never wise.

Exit

SCENE IV

Enter Cardinal and Julia

CARD. Sit: thou art my best of wishes. Prithee, tell me
What trick didst thou invent to come to Rome
Without thy husband.
JUL. Why, my lord, I told him
I came to visit an old anchorite
Here for devotion.
CARD. Thou art a witty false one,—
I mean, to him.
JUL. You have prevailed with me
Beyond my strongest thoughts! I would not now
Find you inconstant.
CARD. Do not put thyself
To such a voluntary torture, which proceeds
Out of your own guilt.
JUL. How, my lord?
CARD. You fear
My constancy, because you have approved
Those giddy and wild turnings in yourself.
JUL. Did you e'er find them?
CARD. Sooth, generally for women;
A man might strive to make glass malleable,
Ere he should make them fixed.
JUL. So, my lord.
CARD. We had need go borrow that fantastic glass
Invented by Galileo the Florentine

To view another spacious world i' th' moon,
And look to find a constant woman there.
JUL. This is very well, my lord.
CARD. Why do you weep?
Are tears your justification? the self-same tears
Will fall into your husband's bosom, lady,
With a loud protestation that you love him
Above the world. Come, I'll love you wisely,
That's jealously; since I am very certain
You cannot make me cuckold.
JUL. I'll go home
To my husband.
CARD. You may thank me, lady,
I have taken you off your melancholy perch,
Bore you upon my fist, and showed you game,
And let you fly at it.—I pray thee, kiss me.—
When thou wast with thy husband, thou wast watched
Like a tame elephant:—still you are to thank me:—
Thou hadst only kisses from him and high feeding;
But what delight was that? 'twas just like one
That hath a little fingering on the lute,
Yet cannot tune it:—still you are to thank me.
JUL. You told me of a piteous wound i' th' heart
And a sick liver, when you wooed me first,
And spake like one in physic.
CARD. Who's that?—

Enter Servant

Rest firm, for my affection to thee,
Lightning moves slow to't.
SERV. Madam, a gentleman,
That's come post from Malfi, desires to see you.
CARD. Let him enter: I'll withdraw.

Exit

SERV. He says
Your husband, old Castruchio, is come to Rome,
Most pitifully tired with riding post.

Exit

Enter Delio

JUL. Signior Delio! [*Aside*] 'tis one of my old suitors.
DEL. I was bold to come and see you.
JUL. Sir, you are welcome.
DEL. Do you lie here?
JUL. Sure, your own experience
　　Will satisfy you no: our Roman prelates
　　Do not keep lodging for ladies.
DEL. Very well:
　　I have brought you no commendations from your husband,
　　For I know none by him.
JUL. I hear he's come to Rome.
DEL. I never knew man and beast, of a horse and a knight,
　　So weary of each other: if he had had a good back,
　　He would have undertook to have borne his horse,
　　His breech was so pitifully sore.
JUL. Your laughter
　　Is my pity.
DEL. Lady, I know not whether
　　You want money, but I have brought you some.
JUL. From my husband?
DEL. No, from mine own allowance.
JUL. I must hear the condition, ere I be bound to take it.
DEL. Look on't, 'tis gold: hath it not a fine color?
JUL. I have a bird more beautiful.
DEL. Try the sound on't.
JUL. A lute-string far exceeds it:
　　It hath no smell, like cassia or civet;
　　Nor is it physical,[1] though some fond doctors
　　Persuade us seethe 't in cullises.[2] I'll tell you,
　　This is a creature bred by—

Re-enter Servant

SERV. Your husband's come,

1. Good for the health.
2. Broths.

Hath delivered a letter to the Duke of Calabria
That, to my thinking, hath put him out of his wits.

Exit

JUL. Sir, you hear:
Pray, let me know your business and your suit
As briefly as can be.
DEL. With good speed: I would wish you,
At such time as you are non-resident
With your husband, my mistress.
JUL. Sir, I'll go ask my husband if I shall,
And straight return your answer.

Exit

DEL. Very fine!
Is this her wit, or honesty, that speaks thus?
I heard one say the duke was highly moved
With a letter sent from Malfi. I do fear
Antonio is betrayed: how fearfully
Shows his ambition now! unfortunate fortune!
They pass through whirlpools, and deep woes do shun,
Who the event weigh ere the action's done.

Exit

SCENE V

Enter Cardinal, and Ferdinand with a letter

FERD. I have this night digged up a mandrake.
CARD. Say you?
FERD. And I am grown mad with't.
CARD. What's the prodigy?
FERD. Read there,—a sister damned: she's loose i' th' hilts;
Grown a notorious strumpet.
CARD. Speak lower.
FERD. Lower?
Rogues do not whisper't now, but seek to publish't
(As servants do the bounty of their lords)
Aloud; and with a covetous searching eye,
To mark who note them. O, confusion seize her!
She hath had most cunning bawds to serve her turn,

And more secure conveyances[1] for lust
Than towns of garrison for service.

CARD. Is't possible?
Can this be certain?

FERD. Rhubarb, oh, for rhubarb
To purge this choler! here's the cursèd day
To prompt my memory; and here't shall stick
Till of her bleeding heart I make a sponge
To wipe it out.

CARD. Why do you make yourself
So wild a tempest?

FERD. Would I could be one,
That I might toss her palace 'bout her ears,
Root up her goodly forests, blast her meads,
And lay her general territory as waste
As she hath done her honors.

CARD. Shall our blood,
The royal blood of Arragon and Castile,
Be thus attainted?

FERD. Apply desperate physic:
We must not now use balsamum, but fire.
The smarting cupping-glass, for that's the mean
To purge infected blood, such blood as hers.
There is a kind of pity in mine eye,—
I'll give it to my handkercher; and now 'tis here,
I'll bequeath this to her bastard.

CARD. What to do?

FERD. Why, to make soft lint for his mother's wounds,
When I have hewed her to pieces.

CARD. Cursed creature!
Unequal nature, to place women's hearts
So far upon the left side!

FERD. Foolish men,
That e'er will trust their honor in a bark
Made of so slight weak bulrush as is woman.
Apt every minute to sink it!

1. Means of communication.

CARD. Thus ignorance, when it hath purchased honor,
    It cannot wield it.
FERD. Methinks I see her laughing—
    Excellent hyena! Talk to me somewhat, quickly,
    Or my imagination will carry me
    To see her in the shameful act of sin.
CARD. With whom?
FERD. Happily[1] with some strong-thighed bargeman,
    Or one o' the woodyard that can quoit the sledge[2]
    Or toss the bar, or else some lovely squire
    That carries coals up to her privy lodgings.
CARD. You fly beyond your reason.
FERD. Go to, mistress!
    'Tis not your whore's milk that shall quench my wild fire,
    But your whore's blood.
CARD. How idly shows this rage, which carries you,
    As men conveyed by witches through the air,
    On violent whirlwinds! this intemperate noise
    Fitly resembles deaf men's shrill discourse,
    Who talk aloud, thinking all other men
    To have their imperfection.
FERD. Have not you
    My palsy?
CARD. Yes, I can be angry, but
    Without this rupture:[3] there is not in nature
    A thing that makes man so deformed, so beastly,
    As doth intemperate anger. Chide yourself.
    You have divers men who never yet expressed
    Their strong desire of rest but by unrest,
    By vexing of themselves. Come, put yourself
    In tune.
FERD. So; I will only study to seem
    The thing I am not. I could kill her now,
    In you, or in myself; for I do think

---

1. Often used for "haply"; "perhaps."
2. Throw the hammer.
3. Outburst.

It is some sin in us heaven doth revenge
By her.

CARD. Are you stark mad?

FERD. I would have their bodies
Burnt in a coal-pit with the ventage stopped,
That their cursed smoke might not ascend to heaven;
Or dip the sheets they lie in in pitch or sulphur,
Wrap them in't, and then light them like a match;
Or else to boil their bastard to a cullis,
And give't his lecherous father to renew
The sin of his back.

CARD. I'll leave you.

FERD. Nay, I have done.
I am confident, had I been damned in hell,
And should have heard of this, it would have put me
Into a cold sweat. In, in; I'll go sleep.
Till I know who leaps my sister, I'll not stir:
That known, I'll find scorpions to string my whips,
And fix her in a general eclipse.

Exeunt

ACT III, SCENE I

Enter Antonio and Delio

ANT. Our noble friend, my most beloved Delio!
Oh, you have been a stranger long at court;
Came you along with the Lord Ferdinand?

DEL. I did, sir: and how fares your noble duchess?

ANT. Right fortunately well: she's an excellent
Feeder of pedigrees; since you last saw her,
She hath had two children more, a son and daughter.

DEL. Methinks 'twas yesterday: let me but wink,
And not behold your face, which to mine eye
Is somewhat leaner, verily I should dream
It were within this half-hour.

ANT. You have not been in law, friend Delio,
Nor in prison, nor a suitor at the court,
Nor begged the reversion of some great man's place,

Nor troubled with an old wife, which doth make
Your time so insensibly hasten.

DEL. Pray, sir, tell me,
Hath not this news arrived yet to the ear
Of the lord cardinal?

ANT. I fear it hath:
The Lord Ferdinand, that's newly come to court,
Doth bear himself right dangerously.

DEL. Pray, why?

ANT. He is so quiet that he seems to sleep
The tempest out, as dormice do in winter:
Those houses that are haunted are most still
Till the devil be up.

DEL. What say the common people?

ANT. The common rabble do directly say
She is a strumpet.

DEL. And your graver heads
Which would be politic, what censure they?[1]

ANT. They do observe I grow to infinite purchase,[2]
The left hand way, and all suppose the duchess
Would amend it, if she could; for, say they,
Great princes, though they grudge their officers
Should have such large and unconfinèd means
To get wealth under them, will not complain,
Lest thereby they should make them odious
Unto the people; for other obligation
Of love or marriage between her and me
They never dream of.

DEL. The Lord Ferdinand
Is going to bed.

Enter Duchess, Ferdinand, and Bosola

FERD. I'll instantly to bed,
For I am weary.—I am to bespeak
A husband for you.

---

1. What is their judgment?
2. Acquired property, wealth.

DUCH. For me, sir? pray, who is't?

FERD. The great Count Malateste.

DUCH. Fie upon him!
  A count? he's a mere stick of sugar-candy;
  You may look quite thorough him. When I choose
  A husband, I will marry for your honor.

FERD. You shall do well in't.—How is't, worthy Antonio?

DUCH. But, sir, I am to have private conference with you
  About a scandalous report is spread
  Touching mine honor.

FERD. Let me be ever deaf to't:
  One of Pasquil's paper bullets,[1] court-calumny,
  A pestilent air, which princes' palaces
  Are seldom purged of. Yet, say that it were true,
  I pour it in your bosom, my fixed love
  Would strongly excuse, extenuate, nay, deny
  Faults, were they apparent in you. Go, be safe
  In your own innocency.

DUCH. [*Aside*] O blessed comfort!
  This deadly air is purged.

                    Exeunt Duchess, Antonio, and Delio

FERD. Her guilt treads on
  Hot-burning coulters.—Now, Bosola,
  How thrives our intelligence?

BOS. Sir, uncertainly
  'Tis rumored she hath had three bastards, but
  By whom we may go read i' th' stars.

FERD. Why, some
  Hold opinion all things are written there.

BOS. Yes, if we could find spectacles to read them.
  I do suspect there hath been some sorcery
  Used on the duchess.

FERD. Sorcery? to what purpose?

BOS. To make her dote on some desertless fellow
  She shames to acknowledge.

FERD. Can your faith give way

---

1. Lampoons, satires.

    To think there's power in potions or in charms,
    To make us love whether we will or no?
Bos. Most certainly.
Ferd. Away! these are mere gulleries, horrid things,
    Invented by some cheating mountebanks
    To abuse us. Do you think that herbs or charms
    Can force the will? Some trials have been made
    In this foolish practice, but the ingredients
    Were lenitive[1] poisons, such as are of force
    To make the patient mad; and straight the witch
    Swears by equivocation they are in love.
    The witchcraft lies in her rank blood. This night
    I will force confession from her. You told me
    You had got, within these two days, a false key
    Into her bed-chamber.
Bos. I have.
Ferd. As I would wish.
Bos. What do you intend to do?
Ferd. Can you guess?
Bos. No.
Ferd. Do not ask, then:
    He that can compass me, and know my drifts,
    May say he hath put a girdle 'bout the world,
    And sounded all her quicksands.
Bos. I do not
    Think so.
Ferd. What do you think, then, pray?
Bos. That you
    Are your own chronicle too much, and grossly
    Flatter yourself.
Ferd. Give me thy hand; I thank thee:
    I never gave pension but to flatterers,
    Till I entertained thee. Farewell.
    That friend a great man's ruin strongly checks,
    Who rails into his belief all his defects.[2]

Exeunt

---

1. Soothing.
2. Who forces him to believe in his own faults.

SCENE II

Enter Duchess, Antonio, and Cariola

DUCH. Bring me the casket hither, and the glass.—
    You get no lodging here to-night, my lord.
ANT. Indeed, I must persuade one.
DUCH. Very good:
    I hope in time 'twill grow into a custom,
    That noblemen shall come with cap and knee
    To purchase a night's lodging of their wives.
ANT. I must lie here.
DUCH. Must! you are a lord of misrule.
ANT. Indeed, my rule is only in the night.
DUCH. To what use will you put me?
ANT. We'll sleep together.
DUCH. Alas,
    What pleasure can two lovers find in sleep!
CAR. My lord, I lie with her often; and I know
    She'll much disquiet you.
ANT. See, you are complained of.
CAR. For she's the sprawling'st bedfellow.
ANT. I shall like her
    The better for that.
CAR. Sir, shall I ask you a question?
ANT. Oh, I pray thee, Cariola.
CAR. Wherefore still, when you lie
    With my lady, do you rise so early?
ANT. Laboring men
    Count the clock oftenest, Cariola, are glad
    When their task's ended.
DUCH. I'll stop your mouth.

                         [Kisses him]

ANT. Nay, that's but one; Venus had two soft doves
    To draw her chariot; I must have another—

                      [She kisses him again]

    When wilt thou marry, Cariola?
CAR. Never, my lord.

ANT. Oh, fie upon this single life! forgo it.
    We read how Daphne, for her peevish[1] flight,
    Became a fruitless bay-tree; Syrinx turned
    To the pale empty reed; Anaxarete
    Was frozen into marble: whereas those
    Which married, or proved kind unto their friends,
    Were by a gracious influence transhaped
    Into the olive, pomegranate, mulberry,
    Became flowers, precious stones, or eminent stars.

CAR. This is a vain poetry: but I pray you tell me,
    If there were proposed me, wisdom, riches, and beauty,
    In three several young men, which should I choose?

ANT. 'Tis a hard question: this was Paris' case,
    And he was blind in't, and there was great cause;
    For how was't possible he could judge right,
    Having three amorous goddesses in view,
    And they stark naked? 'twas a motion
    Were able to benight the apprehension
    Of the severest counsellor of Europe.
    Now I look on both your faces so well formed,
    It puts me in mind of a question I would ask.

CAR. What is't?

ANT. I do wonder why hard-favored ladies,
    For the most part, keep worse-favored waiting-women
    To attend them, and cannot endure fair ones.

DUCH. Oh, that's soon answered.
    Did you ever in your life know an ill painter
    Desire to have his dwelling next door to the shop
    Of an excellent picture-maker? 'twould disgrace
    His face-making, and undo him. I prithee,
    When were we so merry?—My hair tangles.

ANT. Pray thee, Cariola, let's steal forth the room,
    And let her talk to herself: I have divers times
    Served her the like, when she hath chafed extremely.
    I love to see her angry. Softly, Cariola.

Exeunt Antonio and Cariola

1. Foolish.

DUCH. Doth not the color of my hair 'gin to change?
　　When I wax grey, I shall have all the court
　　Powder their hair with arras,[1] to be like me.
　　You have cause to love me; I entered you into my heart
　　Before you would vouchsafe to call for the keys.

Enter Ferdinand behind

　　We shall one day have my brothers take you napping;
　　Methinks his presence, being now in court,
　　Should make you keep your own bed; but you'll say
　　Love mixed with fear is sweetest. I'll assure you,
　　You shall get no more children till my brothers
　　Consent to be your gossips. Have you lost your tongue?
　　'Tis welcome:
　　For know, whether I am doomed to live or die,
　　I can do both like a prince.
FERD. Die, then, quickly!

　　　　　　　　　　　　　　　　[*Giving her a poniard*]

　　Virtue, where art thou hid? what hideous thing
　　Is it that doth eclipse thee?
DUCH. Pray, sir, hear me.
FERD. Or is it true thou art but a bare name,
　　And no essential thing?
DUCH. Sir,—
FERD. Do not speak.
DUCH. No, sir: I will plant my soul in mine ears, to hear you.
FERD. O most imperfect light of human reason,
　　That mak'st us so unhappy to foresee
　　What we can least prevent! Pursue thy wishes,
　　And glory in them: there's in shame no comfort
　　But to be past all bounds and sense of shame.
DUCH. I pray, sir, hear me: I am married.
FERD. So!
DUCH. Happily, not to your liking: but for that,
　　Alas, your shears do come untimely now
　　To clip the bird's wings that's already flown!

---

1. Orris powder, which was the color of flour.

Will you see my husband?

FERD. Yes, if I could change
Eyes with a basilisk.[1]

DUCH. Sure, you came hither
By his confederacy.

FERD. The howling of a wolf
Is music to thee, screech-owl: prithee, peace.—
Whate'er thou art that hast enjoyed my sister,
For I am sure thou hear'st me, for thine own sake
Let me not know thee. I came hither prepared
To work thy discovery; yet am now persuaded
It would beget such violent effects
As would damn us both. I would not for ten millions
I had beheld thee: therefore use all means
I never may have knowledge of thy name;
Enjoy thy lust still, and a wretched life,
On that condition.—And for thee, vile woman,
If thou do wish thy lecher may grow old
In thy embracements, I would have thee build
Such a room for him as our anchorites
To holier use inhabit. Let not the sun
Shine on him till he's dead; let dogs and monkeys
Only converse with him, and such dumb things
To whom nature denies use to sound his name;
Do not keep a paraquito, lest she learn it;
If thou do love him, cut out thine own tongue,
Lest it bewray him.

DUCH. Why might not I marry?
I have not gone about in this to create
Any new world or custom.

FERD. Thou art undone;
And thou hast ta'en that massy sheet of lead
That hid thy husband's bones, and folded it
About my heart.

DUCH. Mine bleeds for't.

FERD. Thine? thy heart?

---

1. Reptile that kills by sight.

What should I name 't unless a hollow bullet
Filled with unquenchable wild-fire?
DUCH. You are in this
    Too strict; and were you not my princely brother,
    I would say, too wilful: my reputation
    Is safe.
FERD. Dost thou know what reputation is?
    I'll tell thee,—to small purpose, since the instruction
    Comes now too late.
    Upon a time Reputation, Love, and Death,
    Would travel o'er the world; and it was concluded
    That they should part, and take three several ways.
    Death told them, they should find him in great battles,
    Or cities plagued with plagues: Love gives them counsel
    To inquire for him 'mongst unambitious shepherds,
    Where dowries were not talked of, and sometimes
    'Mongst quiet kindred that had nothing left
    By their dead parents: "Stay," quoth Reputation,
    "Do not forsake me; for it is my nature,
    If once I part from any man I meet,
    I am never found again." And so for you:
    You have shook hands with Reputation,
    And made him invisible. So, fare you well:
    I will never see you more.
DUCH. Why should only I,
    Of all the other princes of the world,
    Be cased up, like a holy relic? I have youth
    And a little beauty.
FERD. So you have some virgins
    That are witches. I will never see thee more.

                                    Exit

        Re-enter Antonio with a Pistol, and Cariola

DUCH. You saw this apparition?
ANT. Yes: we are
    Betrayed. How came he hither?—I should turn
    This to thee, for that.

                    [*Pointing the pistol at Cariola*]

CAR. Pray, sir, do; and when
That you have cleft my heart, you shall read there
Mine innocence.

DUCH. That gallery gave him entrance.

ANT. I would this terrible thing would come again,
That, standing on my guard, I might relate
My warrantable love.—

[She shows the poniard]

Ha! what means this?

DUCH. He left this with me.

ANT. And it seems did wish
You would use it on yourself.

DUCH. His action seemed
To intend so much.

ANT. This hath a handle to't.
As well as a point: turn it towards him, and
So fasten the keen edge in his rank gall.

[Knocking within]

How now! who knocks? more earthquakes?

DUCH. I stand
As if a mine beneath my feet were ready
To be blown up.

CAR. 'Tis Bosola.

DUCH. Away!
O Misery! methinks unjust actions
Should wear these masks and curtains, and not we.
You must instantly part hence: I have fashioned it
Already.

Exit Antonio

Enter Bosola

BOS. The duke your brother is ta'en up in a whirlwind,
Hath took horse, and 's rid post to Rome.

DUCH. So late?

BOS. He told me, as he mounted into th' saddle,
You were undone.

DUCH. Indeed, I am very near it.

BOS. What's the matter?

DUCH. Antonio, the master of our household,
    Hath dealt so falsely with me in 's accounts:
    My brother stood engaged with me for money
    Ta'en up of certain Neapolitan Jews,
    And Antonio lets the bonds be forfeit.
BOS. Strange!—[*Aside*] This is cunning.
DUCH. And hereupon
    My brother's bills at Naples are protested
    Against.—Call up our officers.
BOS. I shall.

                                                     Exit

                Re-enter Antonio

DUCH. The place that you must fly to is Ancona:
    Hire a house there; I'll send after you
    My treasure and my jewels. Our weak safety
    Runs upon enginous wheels:[1] short syllables
    Must stand for periods. I must now accuse you
    Of such a feignèd crime as Tasso calls
    Magnanima menzogna, a noble lie,
    'Cause it must shield our honors.—Hark! they are coming,

      Re-enter Bosola and Officers

ANT. Will your grace hear me?
DUCH. I have got well by you; you have yielded me
    A million of loss: I am like to inherit
    The people's curses for your stewardship.
    You had the trick in audit-time to be sick,
    Till I had signed your quietus; and that cured you
    Without help of a doctor.—Gentlemen,
    I would have this man be an example to you all;
    So shall you hold my favor; I pray, let him;
    For h'as done that, alas, you would not think of,
    And, because I intend to be rid of him,
    I mean not to publish.—Use your fortune elsewhere.
ANT. I am strongly armed to brook my overthrow;

---

1. i.e., Is rapidly leaving us.

As commonly men bear with a hard year,
I will not blame the cause on't; but do think
The necessity of my malevolent star
Procures this, not her humor. Oh, the inconstant
And rotten ground of service! you may see,
'Tis even like him, that in a winter night,
Takes a long slumber o'er a dying fire,
A-loth to part from't; yet parts thence as cold
As when he first sat down.

DUCH. We do confiscate,
Towards the satisfying of your accounts,
All that you have.

ANT. I am all yours; and 'tis very fit
All mine should be so.

DUCH. So, sir, you have your pass.

ANT. You may see, gentlemen, what 'tis to serve
A prince with body and soul.

Exit

BOS. Here's an example for extortion: what moisture is drawn out of the sea, when foul weather comes, pours down, and runs into the sea again.

DUCH. I would know what are your opinions of this Antonio.

2 OFF. He could not abide to see a pig's head gaping: I thought your grace would find him a Jew.

3 OFF. I would you had been his officer, for your own sake.

4 OFF. You would have had more money.

1 OFF. He stopped his ears with black wool, and to those came to him for money said he was thick of hearing.

2 OFF. Some said he was an hermaphrodite, for he could not abide a woman.

4 OFF. How scurvy proud he would look when the treasury was full! Well, let him go!

1 OFF. Yes, and the chippings of the buttery fly after him, to scour his gold chain!

DUCH. Leave us. [*Exeunt officers*] What do you think of these?

BOS. That these are rogues that in 's prosperity, but to have waited on his fortune, could have wished his dirty stirrup riveted through their noses, and followed after 's mule, like a bear in a ring; would have prostituted their daughters to his lust; made their first-born intelligencers; thought none happy but such as were born under his blest planet, and wore his livery: and do these lice drop off now? Well, never look to have the like again: he hath left a sort of flattering rogues behind him; their doom must follow. Princes pay flatterers in their own money: flatterers dissemble their vices, and they dissemble their lies;[1] that's justice. Alas, poor gentleman!

DUCH. Poor? he hath amply filled his coffers.

BOS. Sure, he was too honest. Pluto,[2] the god of riches, when he's sent by Jupiter to any man, he goes limping, to signify that wealth that comes on God's name comes slowly; but when he's sent on the devil's errand, he rides post and comes in by scuttles.[3] Let me show you what a most unvalued jewel you have in a wanton humor thrown away, to bless the man shall find him. He was an excellent courtier and most faithful; a soldier that thought it as beastly to know his own value too little as devilish to acknowledge it too much. Both his virtue and form deserved a far better fortune: his discourse rather delighted to judge itself than show itself: his breast was filled with all perfection, and yet it seemed a private whispering-room, it made so little noise of 't.

DUCH. But he was basely descended.

BOS. Will you make yourself a mercenary herald, rather to examine men's pedigrees than virtues? You shall want him: for know, an honest statesman to a prince is like a cedar planted by a spring; the spring bathes the tree's root, the grateful tree rewards it with his shadow: you have not done so. I would sooner swim to the Bermoothes on two politicians' rotten bladders, tied together with an intelligencer's heart-string, than depend on so changeable a prince's favor. Fare thee well, Antonio! since the malice of the world would needs down with thee, it cannot be said yet that any ill happened unto thee, considering thy fall was accompanied with virtue.

DUCH. Oh, you render me excellent music!

BOS. Say you?

---

1. i.e., Flatterers pretend that kings have no vices, and kings pretend that flatterers tell no lies.

2. Put for Plutus.

3. Short, hurried runs.

DUCH. This good one that you speak of is my husband.
BOS. Do I not dream? can this ambitious age
    Have so much goodness in't as to prefer
    A man merely for worth, without these shadows
    Of wealth and painted honors? possible?
DUCH. I have had three children by him.
BOS. Fortunate lady!
    For you have made your private nuptial bed
    The humble and fair seminary of peace.
    No question but many an unbeneficed scholar
    Shall pray for you for this deed, and rejoice
    That some preferment in the world can yet
    Arise from merit. The virgins of your land
    That have no dowries shall hope your example
    Will raise them to rich husbands. Should you want
    Soldiers, 'twould make the very Turks and Moors
    Turn Christians, and serve you for this act.
    Last, the neglected poets of your time,
    In honor of this trophy of a man,
    Raised by that curious engine, your white hand,
    Shall thank you, in your grave, for't; and make that
    More reverend than all the cabinets
    Of living princes. For Antonio,
    His fame shall likewise flow from many a pen,
    When heralds shall want coats[1] to sell to men.
DUCH. As I taste comfort in this friendly speech,
    So would I find concealment.
BOS. Oh, the secret of my prince,
    Which I will wear on th' inside of my heart!
DUCH. You shall take charge of all my coin and jewels,
    And follow him; for he retires himself
    To Ancona.
BOS. So.
DUCH. Whither, within few days,
    I mean to follow thee.
BOS. Let me think:

1. Coats of arms.

I would wish your grace to feign a pilgrimage
To our Lady of Loretto, scarce seven leagues
From fair Ancona; so may you depart
Your country with more honor, and your flight
Will seem a princely progress, retaining
Your usual train about you.

DUCH. Sir, your direction
Shall lead me by the hand.

CAR. In my opinion,
She were better progress to the baths at Lucca,
Or go visit the Spa in Germany;
For, if you will believe me, I do not like
This jesting with religion, this feigned
Pilgrimage.

DUCH. Thou art a superstitious fool:
Prepare us instantly for our departure.
Past sorrows, let us moderately lament them;
For those to come, seek wisely to prevent them.

Exeunt Duchess and Cariola

BOS. A politician is the devil's quilted[1] anvil;
He fashions all sins on him, and the blows
Are never heard: he may work in a lady's chamber,
As here for proof. What rests but I reveal
All to my lord? Oh, this base quality
Of intelligencer! why, every quality i' th' world
Prefers[2] but gain or commendation:
Now for this act I am certain to be raised,
And men that paint weeds to the life are praised.

Exit

SCENE III

Enter Cardinal, Ferdinand, Malateste, Pescara, Silvio, and Delio

CARD. Must we turn soldier, then?

MAL. The emperor

---

1. i.e., Muffled.
2. Produces.

Hearing your worth that way, ere you attained
This reverend garment, joins you in commission
With the right fortunate soldier the Marquis of Pescara,
And the famous Lannoy.

CARD. He that had the honor
Of taking the French king prisoner?

MAL. The same.
Here's a plot¹ drawn for a new fortification
At Naples.

[*They talk apart*]

FERD. This great Count Malateste, I perceive,
Hath got employment?

DEL. No employment, my lord;
A marginal note in the muster-book, that he is
A voluntary lord.

FERD. He's no soldier?

DEL. He has worn gunpowder in 's hollow tooth for the toothache.

SIL. He comes to the leaguer² with a full intent
To eat fresh beef and garlic, means to stay
Till the scent be gone, and straight return to court.

DEL. He hath read all the late service as the city chronicle relates it;
and keeps two pewterers going, only to express battles in model.

SIL. Then he'll fight by the book.

DEL. By the almanac, I think, to choose good days and shun the critical; that's his mistress's scarf.

SIL. Yes, he protests he would do much for that taffeta.

DEL. I think he would run away from a battle, to save it from taking³
prisoner.

SIL. He is horribly afraid gunpowder will spoil the perfume on't.

DEL. I saw a Dutchman break his pate once for calling him pot-gun;
he made his head have a bore in't like a musket.

SIL. I would he had made a touchhole to't. He is indeed a guarded
sumpter-cloth,⁴ only for the remove of the court.

---

1. Plan.
2. Camp.
3. i.e., Being taken.
4. An ornamental horse-cloth.

Enter Bosola and speaks to Ferdinand and the Cardinal

PES. Bosola arrived? what should be the business?
　Some falling-out amongst the cardinals.
　These factions amongst great men, they are like
　Foxes; when their heads are divided,
　They carry fire in their tails, and all the country
　About them goes to wrack for't.

SIL. What's that Bosola?

DEL. I knew him in Padua—a fantastical scholar, like such who study
　to know how many knots was in Hercules' club, of what color
　Achilles' beard was, or whether Hector were not troubled with the
　toothache. He hath studied himself half blear-ey'd to know the true
　symmetry of Caesar's nose by a shoeing-horn; and this he did to
　gain the name of a speculative man.[1]

PES. Mark Prince Ferdinand:
　A very salamander lives in 's eye,
　To mock the eager violence of fire.

SIL. That Cardinal hath made more bad faces with his oppression than
　ever Michael Angelo made good ones: he lifts up 's nose, like a foul
　porpoise before a storm.

PES. The Lord Ferdinand laughs.

DEL. Like a deadly cannon that lightens
　Ere it smokes.

PES. These are your true pangs of death,
　The pangs of life, that struggle with great statesmen.

DEL. In such a deformed silence witches whisper
　Their charms.

CARD. Doth she make religion her riding-hood
　To keep her from the sun and tempest?

FERD. That,
　That damns her. Methinks her fault and beauty,
　Blended together, show like leprosy,
　The whiter, the fouler. I make it a question
　Whether her beggarly brats were ever christened.

---

1. i.e., A student.

CARD. I will instantly solicit the state of Ancona
    To have them banished.
FERD. You are for Loretto?
    I shall not be at your ceremony; fare you well.—
    Write to the Duke of Malfi, my young nephew
    She had by her first husband, and acquaint him
    With 's mother's honesty.
BOS. I will.
FERD. Antonio!
    A slave that only smelled of ink and counters,
    And never in 's life looked like a gentleman,
    But in the audit-time.—Go, go presently,
    Draw me out an hundred and fifty of our horse,
    And meet me at the fort-bridge.

Exeunt

SCENE IV

Enter Two Pilgrims

1 PIL. I have not seen a goodlier shrine than this;
    Yet I have visited many.
2 PIL. The Cardinal of Arragon
    Is this day to resign his cardinal's hat:
    His sister duchess likewise is arrived
    To pay her vow of pilgrimage. I expect
    A noble ceremony.
1 PIL. No question.
    —They come.
    Here the ceremony of the Cardinal's instalment, in the habit of a
    soldier, is performed in delivering up his cross, hat, robes, and ring,
at the shrine, and investing him with sword, helmet, shield, and spurs;
    then Antonio, the Duchess, and their children, having presented
    themselves at the shrine, are, by a form of banishment in dumb-show
    expressed towards them by the Cardinal and the state of Ancona,
    banished: during all which ceremony, this ditty is sung,
    to very solemn music, by divers churchmen

Arms and honors deck thy story,
To thy fame's eternal glory!
Adverse fortune ever fly thee;
No disastrous fate come nigh thee!

I alone will sing thy praises,
Whom to honor virtue raises;
And thy study, that divine is,
Bent to martial discipline is.
Lay aside all those robes lie by thee;
Crown thy arts with arms, they'll beautify thee.

O worthy of worthiest name, adorned in this manner,
Lead bravely thy forces on under war's warlike banner!
Oh, mayst thou prove fortunate in all martial courses!
Guide thou still by skill in arts and forces!
Victory attend thee nigh, whilst fame sings loud thy
    powers;
Triumphant conquest crown thy head, and blessings
    pour down showers![1]

Exeunt all except the Two Pilgrims

1 PIL. Here's a strange turn of state! who would have thought
So great a lady would have matched herself
Unto so mean a person? yet the Cardinal
Bears himself much too cruel.

2 PIL. They are banished.

1 PIL. But I would ask what power hath this state
Of Ancona to determine of[2] a free prince?

2 PIL. They are a free state, sir, and her brother showed
How that the Pope, fore-hearing of her looseness,
Hath seized into th' protection of the Church
The dukedom which she held as dowager.

1 PIL. But by what justice?

2 PIL. Sure, I think by none,
Only her brother's instigation.

1 PIL. What was it with such violence he took
Off from her finger?

---

1. The Author disclaims this Ditty to be his. (Note in the 1623 quarto.)
2. Judge.

2 PIL. 'Twas her wedding-ring;
    Which he vowed shortly he would sacrifice
    To his revenge.
1 PIL. Alas, Antonio!
    If that a man be thrust into a well,
    No matter who sets hands to't, his own weight
    Will bring him sooner to th' bottom. Come, let's hence.
    Fortune makes this conclusion general,
    All things do help th' unhappy man to fall.

Exeunt

SCENE V

Enter Duchess, Antonio, Children, Cariola, and Servants

DUCH. Banished Ancona?
ANT. Yes, you see what power
    Lightens in great men's breath.
DUCH. Is all our train
    Shrunk to this poor remainder?
ANT. These poor men,
    Which have got little in your service, vow
    To take your fortune: but your wiser buntings,
    Now they are fledged, are gone.
DUCH. They have done wisely.
    This puts me in mind of death: physicians thus,
    With their hands full of money, use to give o'er
    Their patients.
ANT. Right the fashion of the world:
    From decayed fortunes every flatterer shrinks;
    Men cease to build where the foundation sinks.
DUCH. I had a very strange dream to-night.
ANT. What was't?
DUCH. Methought I wore my coronet of state,
    And on a sudden all the diamonds
    Were changed to pearls.
ANT. My interpretation
    Is, you'll weep shortly; for to me the pearls
    Do signify your tears.

DUCH. The birds that live
    I' th' field on the wild benefit of nature
    Live happier than we; for they may choose their mates,
    And carol their sweet pleasures to the spring.

Enter Bosola with a letter

BOS. You are happily o'erta'en.
DUCH. From my brother?
BOS. Yes, from the Lord Ferdinand your brother
    All love and safety.
DUCH. Thou dost blanch mischief,
    Wouldst make it white. See, see, like to calm weather
    At sea before a tempest, false hearts speak fair
    To those they intend most mischief.

                                                     [Reads]

"Send Antonio to me; I want his head in a business."
A politic equivocation!
He doth not want your counsel, but your head;
That is, he cannot sleep till you be dead.
And here's another pitfall that's strewed o'er
With roses: mark it, 'tis a cunning one:

                                                     [Reads]

"I stand engaged for your husband for several debts at Naples: let
not that trouble him; I had rather have his heart than his money:"—
And I believe so too.
BOS. What do you believe?
DUCH. That he so much distrusts my husband's love,
    He will by no means believe his heart is with him
    Until he see it: the devil is not cunning
    Enough to circumvent us in riddles.
BOS. Will you reject that noble and free league
    Of amity and love which I present you?
DUCH. Their league is like that of some politic kings,
    Only to make themselves of strength and power
    To be our after-ruin: tell them so.
BOS. And what from you?
ANT. Thus tell him; I will not come.

BOS. And what of this?

[*Pointing to the letter*]

ANT. My brothers[1] have dispersed
    Blood-hounds abroad; which till I hear are muzzled,
    No truce, though hatched with ne'er such politic skill,
    Is safe, that hangs upon our enemies' will.
    I'll not come at them.

BOS. This proclaims your breeding:
    Every small thing draws a base mind to fear,
    As the adamant[2] draws iron. Fare you well, sir
    You shall shortly hear from 's.

Exit

DUCH. I suspect some ambush:
    Therefore by all my love I do conjure you
    To take your eldest son, and fly towards Milan.
    Let us not venture all this poor remainder
    In one unlucky bottom.

ANT. You counsel safely.
    Best of my life, farewell. Since we must part,
    Heaven hath a hand in't; but no otherwise
    Than as some curious artist takes in sunder
    A clock or watch, when it is out of frame,
    To bring't in better order.

DUCH. I know not
    Which is best, to see you dead, or part with you.
    —Farewell, boy:
    Thou art happy that thou hast not understanding
    To know thy misery; for all our wit
    And reading brings us to a truer sense
    Of sorrow.—In the eternal church, sir,
    I do hope we shall not part thus.

ANT. Oh, be of comfort!
    Make patience a noble fortitude,

---

1. Brothers-in-law.
2. Magnetic stone.

And think not how unkindly we are used:
Man, like to cassia, is proved best being bruised.

DUCH. Must I, like to a slave-born Russian,
Account it praise to suffer tyranny?
And yet, O heaven, thy heavy hand is in't!
I have seen my little boy oft scourge his top,
And compared myself to't: naught made me e'er
Go right but heaven's scourge-stick.

ANT. Do not weep:
Heaven fashioned us of nothing, and we strive
To bring ourselves to nothing.—Farewell, Cariola,
And thy sweet armful.—If I do never see thee more,
Be a good mother to your little ones,
And save them from the tiger: fare you well.

DUCH. Let me look upon you once more; for that speech
Came from a dying father.—Your kiss is colder
Than that I have seen an holy anchorite
Give to a dead man's skull.

ANT. My heart is turned to a heavy lump of lead,
With which I sound[1] my danger: fare you well.

Exeunt Antonio and his Son

DUCH. My laurel is all withered.

CAR. Look, madam, what a troop of armèd men
Make toward us.

DUCH. Oh, they are very welcome:
When Fortune's wheel is over-charged with princes,
The weight makes it move swift: I would have my ruin
Be sudden.

Re-enter Bosola visarded, with a Guard

I am your adventure,[2] am I not?

BOS. You are: you must see your husband no more.

DUCH. What devil art thou that counterfeits heaven's thunder?

BOS. Is that terrible? I would have you tell me whether
Is that note worse that frights the silly birds

1. Determine the depth of.
2. The object of your mission.

    Out of the corn, or that which doth allure them
    To the nets? you have hearkened to the last too much.
DUCH. Oh, misery! like to a rusty o'ercharged cannon,
    Shall I never fly in pieces?—Come, to what prison?
BOS. To none.
DUCH. Whither, then?
BOS. To your palace.
DUCH. I have heard
    That Charon's boat serves to convey all o'er
    The dismal lake, but brings none back again.
BOS. Your brothers mean you safety and pity.
DUCH. Pity!
    With such a pity men preserve alive
    Pheasants and quails, when they are not fat enough
    To be eaten.
BOS. These are your children?
DUCH. Yes.
BOS. Can they prattle?
DUCH. No;
    But I intend, since they were born accursed,
    Curses shall be their first language.
BOS. Fie, madam!
    Forget this base, low fellow,—
DUCH. Were I a man,
    I'd beat that counterfeit face into thy other.[1]
BOS. One of no birth.
DUCH. Say that he was born mean,
    Man is most happy when 's own actions
    Be arguments and examples of his virtue.
BOS. A barren, beggarly virtue!
DUCH. I prithee, who is greatest? can you tell?
    Sad tales befit my woe: I'll tell you one.
    A salmon, as she swam unto the sea,
    Met with a dog-fish, who encounters her
    With this rough language: "Why art thou so bold
    To mix thyself with our high state of floods,

1. i.e., The vizard into his real face.

Being no eminent courtier, but one
That for the calmest and fresh time o' the year
Dost live in shallow rivers, rankest thyself
With silly smelts and shrimps? and darest thou
Pass by our dog-ship without reverence?"
"Oh!" quoth the salmon, "sister, be at peace:
Thank Jupiter we both have passed the net!
Our value never can be truly known,
Till in the fisher's basket we be shown:
I' th' market then my price may be the higher,
Even when I am nearest to the cook and fire."
So to great men the moral may be stretchèd;
Men oft are valued high, when they're most wretched.—
But come, whither you please. I am armed 'gainst misery;
Bent to all sways of the oppressor's will:
There's no deep valley but near some great hill.

Exeunt

ACT IV, SCENE I

Enter Ferdinand and Bosola

FERD. How doth our sister duchess bear herself
    In her imprisonment?
BOSOLA. Nobly: I'll describe her.
    She's sad as one long used to't, and she seems
    Rather to welcome the end of misery
    Than shun it; a behavior so noble
    As gives a majesty to adversity:
    You may discern the shape of loveliness
    More perfect in her tears than in her smiles:
    She will muse four hours together; and her silence,
    Methinks, expresseth more than if she spake.
FERD. Her melancholy seems to be fortified
    With a strange disdain.
BOS. 'Tis so; and this restraint,
    Like English mastiffs that grow fierce with tying,
    Makes her too passionately apprehend
    Those pleasures she's kept from.

FERD. Curse upon her!
    I will no longer study in the book
    Of another's heart. Inform her what I told you.

                                             Exit

Enter Duchess

BOS. All comfort to your grace!
DUCH. I will have none.
    Pray thee, why dost thou wrap thy poisoned pills
    In gold and sugar?
BOS. Your elder brother, the Lord Ferdinand,
    Is come to visit you, and sends you word,
    'Cause once he rashly made a solemn vow
    Never to see you more, he comes i' th' night;
    And prays you gently neither torch nor taper
    Shine in your chamber: he will kiss your hand.
    And reconcile himself; but for his vow
    He dares not see you.
DUCH. At his pleasure.—Take hence the lights.—
    He's come.

Enter Ferdinand

FERD. Where are you?
DUCH. Here, sir.
FERD. This darkness suits you well.
DUCH. I would ask you pardon.
FERD. You have it; for I account it
    The honorabl'st revenge, where I may kill
    To pardon.—Where are your cubs?
DUCH. Whom?
FERD. Call them your children;
    For though our national law distinguish bastards
    From true legitimate issue, compassionate nature
    Makes them all equal.
DUCH. Do you visit me for this?
    You violate a sacrament o' th' Church
    Shall make you howl in hell for't.
FERD. It had been well

Could you have lived thus always; for, indeed,
You were too much i' th' light:—but no more;
I come to seal my peace with you. Here's a hand

                        [Gives her a dead man's hand]

To which you have vowed much love; the ring upon't
You gave.

DUCH. I affectionately kiss it.

FERD. Pray, do, and bury the print of it in your heart.
I will leave this ring with you for a love-token;
And the hand as sure as the ring; and do not doubt
But you shall have the heart too: when you need a friend,
Send it to him that owned it; you shall see
Whether he can aid you.

DUCH. You are very cold:
I fear you are not well after your travel.—
Ha! lights!—Oh, horrible!

FERD. Let her have lights enough.

                                                 Exit

DUCH. What witchcraft doth he practise, that he hath left
A dead man's hand here?

    *[Here is discovered, behind a traverse,[1] the artificial figures of
    Antonio and his Children, appearing as if they were dead]*

BOS. Look you, here's the piece from which 'twas ta'en.
He doth present you this sad spectacle,
That, now you know directly they are dead,
Hereafter you may wisely cease to grieve
For that which cannot be recovered.

DUCH. There is not between heaven and earth one wish
I stay for after this: it wastes me more
Than were't my picture, fashioned out of wax,
Stuck with a magical needle, and then buried
In some foul dunghill; and yond's an excellent property
For a tyrant, which I would account mercy.

BOS. What's that?

---

1. Curtain.

DUCH. If they would bind me to that lifeless trunk,
    And let me freeze to death.
BOS. Come, you must live.
DUCH. That's the greatest torture souls feel in hell,
    In hell, that they must live, and cannot die.
    Portia, I'll new kindle thy coals again,
    And revive the rare and almost dead example
    Of a loving wife.[1]
BOS. Oh, fie! despair? remember
    You are a Christian.
DUCH. The Church enjoins fasting:
    I'll starve myself to death.
BOS. Leave this vain sorrow.
    Things being at the worst begin to mend: the bee
    When he hath shot his sting into your hand, may then
    Play with your eyelid.
DUCH. Good comfortable fellow,
    Persuade a wretch that's broke upon the wheel
    To have all his bones new set; entreat him live
    To be executed again. Who must dispatch me?
    I account this world a tedious theater,
    For I do play a part in't 'gainst my will.
BOS. Come, be of comfort; I will save your life.
DUCH. Indeed,
    I have not leisure to tend so small a business.
BOS. Now, by my life, I pity you.
DUCH. Thou art a fool, then.
    To waste thy pity on a thing so wretched
    As cannot pity itself. I am full of daggers.
    Puff, let me blow these vipers from me.

Enter Servant

    What are you?
SERV. One that wishes you long life.
DUCH. I would thou wert hanged for the horrible curse

---

1. Portia, wife of Brutus, killed herself by swallowing burning coals.

Thou hast given me: I shall shortly grow one
Of the miracles of pity. I'll go pray;—
No, I'll go curse.

BOS. Oh, fie!

DUCH. I could curse the stars—

BOS. Oh, fearful!

DUCH. And those three smiling seasons of the year
Into a Russian winter: nay, the world
To its first chaos.

BOS. Look you, the stars shine still.

DUCH. Oh, but you must
Remember, my curse hath a great way to go.—
Plagues, that make lanes through largest families
Consume them!—

BOS. Fie, lady!

DUCH. Let them, like tyrants,
Never be remembered but for the ill they have done;
Let all the zealous prayers of mortified
Churchmen forget them!—

BOS. Oh, uncharitable!

DUCH. Let Heaven a little while cease crowning martyrs
To punish them!—
Go, howl them this, and say, I long to bleed:
It is some mercy when men kill with speed.

Exeunt Duchess and Servant

Re-enter Ferdinand

FERD. Excellent, as I would wish; she's plagued in art:
These presentations are but framed in wax
By the curious master in that quality,
Vincentio Lauriola, and she takes them
For true substantial bodies.

BOS. Why do you do this?

FERD. To bring her to despair.

BOS. 'Faith, end here,
And go no farther in your cruelty:
Send her a penitential garment to put on

Next to her delicate skin, and furnish her
With beads and prayer-books.
FERD. Damn her! that body of hers,
    While that my blood ran pure in't, was more worth
    Than that which thou wouldst comfort, called a soul.
    I will send her masks of common courtezans,
    Have her meat served up by bawds and ruffians,
    And, 'cause she'll needs be mad, I am resolved
    To remove forth the common hospital
    All the mad-folk, and place them near her lodging;
    There let them practise together, sing and dance,
    And act their gambols to the full o' th' moon:
    If she can sleep the better for it, let her.
    Your work is almost ended.
BOS. Must I see her again?
FERD. Yes.
BOS. Never.
FERD. You must.
BOS. Never in mine own shape;
    That's forfeited by my intelligence
    And this last cruel lie: when you send me next,
    The business shall be comfort.
FERD. Very likely;
    Thy pity is nothing of kin to thee. Antonio
    Lurks about Milan: thou shalt shortly thither
    To feed a fire as great as my revenge,
    Which ne'er will slack till it have spent his fuel:
    Intemperate agues make physicians cruel.

Exeunt

SCENE II

Enter Duchess and Cariola

DUCH. What hideous noise was that?
CAR. 'Tis the wild consort[1]

---

1. Band.

Of madmen, lady, which your tyrant brother
Hath placed about your lodging: this tyranny,
I think, was never practised till this hour.

DUCH. Indeed, I thank him: nothing but noise and folly
Can keep me in my right wits; whereas reason
And silence make me stark mad. Sit down;
Discourse to me some dismal tragedy.

CAR. Oh, 'twill increase your melancholy.

DUCH. Thou art deceived:
To hear of greater grief would lessen mine.
This is a prison?

CAR. Yes, but you shall live
To shake this durance off.

DUCH. Thou art a fool:
The robin-redbreast and the nightingale
Never live long in cages.

CAR. Pray, dry your eyes.
What think you of, madam?

DUCH. Of nothing; when I muse thus,
I sleep.

CAR. Like a madman, with your eyes open?

DUCH. Dost thou think we shall know one another in th' other world?

CAR. Yes, out of question.

DUCH. Oh, that it were possible
We might but hold some two days' conference
With the dead! From them I should learn somewhat, I am sure,
I never shall know here. I'll tell thee a miracle;
I am not mad yet, to my cause of sorrow:
Th' heaven o'er my head seems made of molten brass,
The earth of flaming sulphur, yet I am not mad.
I am acquainted with sad misery
As the tanned galley-slave is with his oar;
Necessity makes me suffer constantly,
And custom makes it easy. Who do I look like now?

CAR. Like to your picture in the gallery,
A deal of life in show, but none in practice;
Or rather like some reverend monument
Whose ruins are even pitied.

DUCH. Very proper;
　And Fortune seems only to have her eyesight
　To behold my tragedy.—
　How now! what noise is that?

Enter Servant

SERV. I am come to tell you
　Your brother hath intended you some sport.
　A great physician, when the Pope was sick
　Of a deep melancholy, presented him
　With several sorts of madmen, which wild object
　Being full of change and sport, forced him to laugh,
　And so the imposthume broke: the self-same cure
　The duke intends on you.
DUCH. Let them come in.
SERV. There's a mad lawyer; and a secular priest;
　A doctor that hath forfeited his wits
　By jealousy; an astrologian
　That in his works said such a day o' th' month
　Should be the day of doom, and, failing of 't,
　Ran mad; an English tailor crazed i' th' brain
　With the study of new fashions; a gentleman-usher
　Quite beside himself with care to keep in mind
　The number of his lady's salutations
　Or "How do you['s]" she employed him in each morning;
　A farmer, too, an excellent knave in grain,
　Mad 'cause he was hindered transportation:
　And let one broker that's mad loose to these,
　You'd think the devil were among them.
DUCH. Sit, Cariola.—Let them loose when you please,
　For I am chained to endure all your tyranny.

Enter Madmen

Here this Song is sung by a Madman to a dismal kind of music

　　　Oh, let us howl some heavy note,
　　　　Some deadly dogged howl,
　　　Sounding as from the threatening throat
　　　　Of beasts and fatal fowl!

As ravens, screech-owls, bulls, and bears,
   We'll bell,[1] and bawl our parts,
Till irksome noise have cloyed your ears
   And corrosived your hearts.
At last, whenas our quire wants breath,
   Our bodies being blest,
We'll sing, like swans, to welcome death,
   And die in love and rest.

1 MADMAN. Doom's-day not come yet? I'll draw it nearer by a per-spective, or make a glass that shall set all the world on fire upon an in-stant. I cannot sleep; my pillow is stuffed with a litter of porcupines.

2 MADMAN. Hell is a mere glass-house, where the devils are continu-ally blowing up women's souls on hollow irons, and the fire never goes out.

3 MADMAN. I will lie with every woman in my parish the tenth night; I will tithe them over like haycocks.

4 MADMAN. Shall my pothecary out-go me because I am a cuckold? I have found out his roguery; he makes alum of his wife's urine, and sells it to Puritans that have sore throats with overstraining.

1 MADMAN. I have skill in heraldry.

2 MADMAN. Hast?

1 MADMAN. You do give for your crest a woodcock's head with the brains picked out on't; you are a very ancient gentleman.

3 MADMAN. Greek is turned Turk: we are only to be saved by the Helvetian translation.[2]

1 MADMAN. Come on, sir, I will lay the law to you.

2 MADMAN. Oh, rather lay a corrosive: the law will eat to the bone.

3 MADMAN. He that drinks but to satisfy nature is damned.

4 MADMAN. If I had my glass here, I would show a sight should make all the women here call me mad doctor.

1 MADMAN. What's he? a rope-maker?

2 MADMAN. No, no, no, a snuffling knave that, while he shows the tombs, will have his hand in a wench's placket.

1. Bellow.
2. Sc. of the Bible, made by English refugees at Geneva and published in 1560 ("the Geneva Bible").

3 MADMAN. Woe to the caroche[1] that brought home my wife from the masque at three o'clock in the morning! it had a large feather-bed in it.

4 MADMAN. I have pared the devil's nails forty times, roasted them in raven's eggs, and cured agues with them.

3 MADMAN. Get me three hundred milchbats, to make possets to procure sleep.

4 MADMAN. All the college may throw their caps at me: I have made a soap-boiler costive; it was my masterpiece.

Here the dance, consisting of Eight Madmen, with music answerable thereunto; after which Bosola, like an Old Man, enters

DUCH. Is he mad too?

SERV. Pray, question him. I'll leave you.

Exeunt Servant and Madmen

BOS. I am come to make thy tomb.

DUCH. Ha! my tomb?

Thou speak'st as if I lay upon my death-bed,
Gasping for breath: dost thou perceive me sick?

BOS. Yes, and the more dangerously, since thy sickness
Is insensible.

DUCH. Thou art not mad, sure: dost know me?

BOS. Yes.

DUCH. Who am I?

BOS. Thou art a box of worm-seed, at best but a salvatory[2] of green mummy. What's this flesh? a little crudded[3] milk, fantastical puff-paste. Our bodies are weaker than those paper-prisons boys use to keep flies in; more contemptible, since ours is to preserve earth-worms. Didst thou ever see a lark in a cage? Such is the soul in the body: this world is like her little turf of grass, and the heaven o'er our heads, like her looking-glass, only gives us a miserable knowledge of the small compass of our prison.

DUCH. Am not I thy duchess?

1. Coach.
2. Ointment box.
2. Curdled.

Bos. Thou art some great woman, sure, for riot begins to sit on thy
forehead (clad in grey hairs) twenty years sooner than on a merry
milk-maid's. Thou sleep'st worse than if a mouse should be forced
to take up her lodging in a cat's ear: a little infant that breeds its
teeth, should it lie with thee, would cry out, as if thou wert the more
unquiet bedfellow.

Duch. I am Duchess of Malfi still.

Bos. That makes thy sleeps so broken:
Glories, like glow-worms, afar off shine bright,
But looked to near, have neither heat nor light.

Duch. Thou art very plain.

Bos. My trade is to flatter the dead, not the living; I am a tomb-maker.

Duch. And thou com'st to make my tomb?

Bos. Yes.

Duch. Let me be a little merry:—of what stuff wilt thou make it?

Bos. Nay, resolve me first, of what fashion?

Duch. Why, do we grow fantastical in our death-bed? do we affect
fashion in the grave?

Bos. Most ambitiously. Princes' images on their tombs do not lie, as
they were wont, seeming to pray up to heaven; but with their hands
under their cheeks, as if they died of the toothache: they are not
carved with their eyes fixed upon the stars; but as their minds were
wholly bent upon the world, the self-same way they seem to turn
their faces.

Duch. Let me know fully therefore the effect
Of this thy dismal preparation,
This talk fit for a charnel.

Bos. Now I shall:—

Enter Executioners, with a coffin, cords, and a bell

Here is a present from your princely brothers;
And may it arrive welcome, for it brings
Last benefit, last sorrow.

Duch. Let me see it:
I have so much obedience in my blood,
I wish it in their veins to do them good.

Bos. This is your last presence-chamber.

Car. O my sweet lady!

DUCH. Peace; it affrights not me.

BOS. I am the common bellman,
  That usually is sent to condemned persons
  The night before they suffer.

DUCH. Even now
  Thou said'st thou wast a tomb-maker.

BOS. 'Twas to bring you
  By degrees to mortification. Listen.

>   Hark, now every thing is still
>   The screech-owl and the whistler shrill
>   Call upon our dame aloud,
>   And bid her quickly don her shroud!
>   Much you had of land and rent:
>   Your length in clay's now competent:[1]
>   A long war disturbed your mind;
>   Here your perfect peace is signed.
>   Of what is't fools make such vain keeping?
>   Sin their conception, their birth weeping,
>   Their life a general mist of error,
>   Their death a hideous storm of terror.
>   Strew your hair with powders sweet,
>   Don clean linen, bathe your feet,
>   And (the foul fiend more to check)
>   A crucifix let bless your neck:
>   'Tis now full tide 'tween night and day;
>   End your groan, and come away.

CAR. Hence, villains, tyrants, murderers! alas!
  What will you do with my lady?—Call for help.

DUCH. To whom? to our next neighbors? they are madfolks.

BOS. Remove that noise.

DUCH. Farewell, Cariola.
  In my last will I have not much to give:
  A many hungry guests have fed upon me;
  Thine will be a poor reversion.

CAR. I will die with her.

DUCH. I pray thee, look thou giv'st my little boy

---

1. i.e., All you require.

Some syrup for his cold, and let the girl
Say her prayers ere she sleep.

                            Cariola is forced out by the Executioners

Now what you please:
What death?
BOS. Strangling;
    Here are your executioners.
DUCH. I forgive them:
    The apoplexy, catarrh, or cough o' th' lungs,
    Would do as much as they do.
BOS. Doth not death fright you?
DUCH. Who would be afraid on't,
    Knowing to meet such excellent company
    In th' other world?
BOS. Yet, methinks,
    The manner of your death should much afflict you:
    This cord should terrify you.
DUCH. Not a whit:
    What would it pleasure me to have my throat cut
    With diamonds? or to be smothered
    With cassia? or to be shot to death with pearls?
    I know death hath ten thousand several doors
    For men to take their exits; and 'tis found
    They go on such strange geometrical hinges,
    You may open them both ways.—Any way, for heaven sake,
    So I were out of your whispering. Tell my brothers
    That I perceive death, now I am well awake,
    Best gift is they can give or I can take.
    I would fain put off my last woman's fault,
    I'd not be tedious to you.
FIRST EXECUTIONER. We are ready.
DUCH. Dispose my breath how please you; but my body
    Bestow upon my women, will you?
FIRST EXECUTIONER. Yes.
DUCH. Pull, and pull strongly, for your able strength
    Must pull down heaven upon me:—
    Yet stay; heaven-gates are not so highly arched
    As princes' palaces; they that enter there

Must go upon their knees [*kneels*].—Come, violent death.
Serve for mandragora to make me sleep!—
Go tell my brothers, when I am laid out,
They then may feed in quiet.

[They strangle her]

BOS. Where's the waiting-woman? Fetch her: some other
Strangle the children.

Exeunt Executioners, some of whom return with Cariola

Look you, there sleeps your mistress.
CAR. Oh, you are damned
Perpetually for this! My turn is next,
Is't not so ordered?
BOS. Yes, and I am glad
You are so well prepared for't.
CAR. You are deceived, sir,
I am not prepared for't, I will not die;
I will first come to my answer, and know
How I have offended.
BOS. Come, dispatch her.—
You kept her counsel; now you shall keep ours.
CAR. I will not die, I must not; I am contracted
To a young gentleman.
FIRST EXECUTIONER. Here's your wedding-ring.
CAR. Let me but speak with the duke; I'll discover
Treason to his person.
BOS. Delays:—throttle her.
FIRST EXECUTIONER. She bites and scratches.
CAR. If you kill me now,
I am damned: I have not been at confession
This two years.
BOS. [*To Executioners*] When?[1]
CAR. I am quick with child.
BOS. Why, then,
Your credit's saved.

[They strangle Cariola]

---

1. A common exclamation of impatience.

Bear her into th' next room;
Let this lie still.

Exeunt the Executioners with the body of Cariola

Enter Ferdinand

FERD. Is she dead?
BOS. She is what
You'd have her. But here begin your pity:
[*Shows the Children strangled*[1]]
Alas, how have these offended?
FERD. The death
Of young wolves is never to be pitied.
BOS. Fix
Your eye here.
FERD. Constantly.
BOS. Do you not weep?
Other sins only speak; murder shrieks out:
The element of water moistens the earth,
But blood flies upwards and bedews the heavens.
FERD. Cover her face; mine eyes dazzle: she died young.
BOS. I think not so; her infelicity
Seemed to have years too many.
FERD. She and I were twins;
And should I die this instant, I had lived
Her time to a minute.
BOS. It seems she was born first:
You have bloodily approved the ancient truth,
That kindred commonly do worse agree
Than remote strangers.
FERD. Let me see her face
Again. Why didst not thou pity her? what
An excellent honest man mightst thou have been,
If thou hadst borne her to some sanctuary!
Or, bold in a good cause, opposed thyself,
With thy advancèd sword above thy head,

1. Probably by drawing a curtain.

Between her innocence and my revenge!
I bade thee, when I was distracted of my wits,
Go kill my dearest friend, and thou hast done't.
For let me but examine well the cause:
What was the meanness of her match to me?
Only I must confess I had a hope,
Had she continued widow, to have gained
An infinite mass of treasure by her death:
And that was the main cause; her marriage,
That drew a stream of gall quite through my heart.
For thee, as we observe in tragedies
That a good actor many times is cursed
For playing a villain's part, I hate thee for't,
And, for my sake, say thou hast done much ill well.

BOS. Let me quicken your memory, for I perceive
    You are falling into ingratitude: I challenge
    The reward due to my service.

FERD. I'll tell thee
    What I'll give thee.

BOS. Do.

FERD. I'll give thee a pardon
    For this murder.

BOS. Ha!

FERD. Yes, and 'tis
    The largest bounty I can study to do thee.
    By what authority didst thou execute
    This bloody sentence?

BOS. By yours.

FERD. Mine? was I her judge?
    Did any ceremonial form of law
    Doom her to not-being? did a complete jury
    Deliver her conviction up i' th' court?
    Where shalt thou find this judgment registered,
    Unless in hell? See, like a bloody fool,
    Thou'st forfeited thy life, and thou shalt die for't.

BOS. The office of justice is perverted quite
    When one thief hangs another. Who shalt dare
    To reveal this?

FERD. Oh, I'll tell thee;
    The wolf shall find her grave, and scrape it up,
    Not to devour the corpse, but to discover
    The horrid murder.
BOS. You, not I, shall quake for't.
FERD. Leave me.
BOS. I will first receive my pension.
FERD. You are a villain.
BOS.   When your ingratitude
    Is judge, I am so.
FERD. Oh, horror, that not the fear
    Of him which binds the devils can prescribe man
    Obedience!—Never look upon me more.
BOS. Why, fare thee well.
    Your brother and yourself are worthy men:
    You have a pair of hearts are hollow graves,
    Rotten, and rotting others; and your vengeance,
    Like two chained bullets, still goes arm in arm:
    You may be brothers; for treason, like the plague,
    Doth take much in a blood. I stand like one
    That long hath ta'en a sweet and golden dream:
    I am angry with myself, now that I wake.
FERD. Get thee into some unknown part o' th' world,
    That I may never see thee.
BOS. Let me know
    Wherefore I should be thus neglected. Sir,
    I served your tyranny, and rather strove
    To satisfy yourself than all the world:
    And though I loathed the evil, yet I loved
    You that did counsel it; and rather sought
    To appear a true servant than an honest man.
FERD. I'll go hunt the badger by owl-light:
    'Tis a deed of darkness.

                        Exit

BOS. He's much distracted. Off, my painted honor!
    While with vain hopes our faculties we tire,
    We seem to sweat in ice and freeze in fire.
    What would I do, were this to do again?

I would not change my peace of conscience
For all the wealth of Europe.—She stirs; here's life:—
Return, fair soul, from darkness, and lead mine
Out of this sensible hell:—she's warm, she breathes:—
Upon thy pale lips I will melt my heart,
To store them with fresh color.—Who's there!
Some cordial drink!—Alas! I dare not call:
So pity would destroy pity.—Her eye opes,
And heaven in it seems to ope, that late was shut,
To take me up to mercy.

DUCH. Antonio!

BOS. Yes, madam, he is living;
The dead bodies you saw were but feigned statues:
He's reconciled to your brothers: the Pope hath wrought
The atonement.

DUCH. Mercy!

Dies

BOS. Oh, she's gone again! there the cords of life broke.
Oh, sacred innocence, that sweetly sleeps
On turtles' feathers, whilst a guilty conscience
Is a black register wherein is writ
All our good deeds and bad, a perspective
That shows us hell! That we cannot be suffered
To do good when we have a mind to it!
This is manly sorrow; these tears, I am very certain,
Never grew in my mother's milk: my estate
Is sunk below the degree of fear: where were
These penitent fountains while she was living?
Oh, they were frozen up! Here is a sight
As direful to my soul as is the sword
Unto a wretch hath slain his father. Come, I'll bear thee
Hence, and execute thy last will; that's deliver
Thy body to the reverend dispose
Of some good women: that the cruel tyrant
Shall not deny me. Then I'll post to Milan,
Where somewhat I will speedily enact
Worth my dejection.

Exit with the body

ACT V, SCENE I

Enter Antonio and Delio

ANT. What think you of my hope of reconcilement
　　To the Arragonian brethren?
DEL. I misdoubt it;
　　For though they have sent their letters of safe-conduct
　　For your repair to Milan, they appear
　　But nets to entrap you. The Marquis of Pescara,
　　Under whom you hold certain land in cheat,[1]
　　Much 'gainst his noble nature hath been moved
　　To seize those lands; and some of his dependants
　　Are at this instant making it their suit
　　To be invested in your revenues.
　　I cannot think they mean well to your life
　　That do deprive you of your means of life,
　　Your living.
ANT. You are still an heretic
　　To any safety I can shape myself.
DEL. Here comes the marquis: I will make myself
　　Petitioner for some part of your land,
　　To know whither it is flying.
ANT. I pray do.

　　　　　　　　　　　　　　[Withdraws to back]

Enter Pescara

DEL. Sir, I have a suit to you.
PESC. To me?
DEL. An easy one:
　　There is the citadel of Saint Bennet,
　　With some demesnes, of late in the possession
　　Of Antonio Bologna,—please you bestow them on me.
PESC. You are my friend; but this is such a suit,
　　Nor fit for me to give, nor you to take.
DEL. No, sir?

---

1. Escheat, subject to forfeiture on the outlawry of the tenant.

PESC. I will give you ample reason for't
Soon in private:—here's the Cardinal's mistress.

Enter Julia

JUL. My lord, I am grown your poor petitioner,
    And should be an ill beggar, had I not
    A great man's letter here, the Cardinal's,
    To court you in my favor.

                                            [*Gives a letter*]

PESC. He entreats for you
    The citadel of Saint Bennet, that belonged
    To the banished Bologna.
JUL. Yes.
PESC. I could not
    Have thought of a friend I could rather pleasure with it:
    'Tis yours.
JUL. Sir, I thank you; and he shall know
    How doubly I am engaged both in your gift,
    And speediness of giving, which makes your grant
    The greater.

                                                    Exit

ANT. [*Aside*] How they fortify themselves
    With my ruin!
DEL. Sir, I am little bound to you.
PESC. Why?
DEL. Because you denied this suit to me, and gave't
    To such a creature.
PESC. Do you know what it was?
    It was Antonio's land; not forfeited
    By course of law, but ravished from his throat
    By the Cardinal's entreaty: it were not fit
    I should bestow so main a piece of wrong
    Upon my friend; 'tis a gratification
    Only due to a strumpet, for it is injustice.
    Shall I sprinkle the pure blood of innocents
    To make those followers I call my friends
    Look ruddier upon me? I am glad
    This land, ta'en from the owner by such wrong,

Returns again unto so foul an use
As salary for his lust. Learn, good Delio,
To ask noble things of me, and you shall find
I'll be a noble giver.

DEL. You instruct me well.

ANT. [*Aside*] Why, here's a man who would fright impudence
From sauciest beggars.

PESC. Prince Ferdinand's come to Milan,
Sick, as they give out, of an apoplexy;
But some say 'tis a frenzy: I am going
To visit him.

Exit

ANT. 'Tis a noble old fellow.

DEL. What course do you mean to take, Antonio?

ANT. This night I mean to venture all my fortune,
Which is no more than a poor lingering life,
To the Cardinal's worst of malice: I have got
Private access to his chamber; and intend
To visit him about the mid of night,
As once his brother did our noble duchess.
It may be that the sudden apprehension
Of danger,—for I'll go in mine own shape,—
When he shall see it fraight¹ with love and duty,
May draw the poison out of him, and work
A friendly reconcilement: if it fail,
Yet it shall rid me of this infamous calling;
For better fall once than be ever falling.

DEL. I'll second you in all danger; and, howe'er,
My life keeps rank with yours.

ANT. You are still my loved
And best friend.

Exeunt

1. Fraught.

SCENE II

Enter Pescara and Doctor

PESC. Now, doctor, may I visit your patient?
DOC. If 't please your lordship: but he's instantly
   To take the air here in the gallery
   By my direction.
PESC. Pray thee, what's his disease?
DOC. A very pestilent disease, my lord,
   They call it lycanthropia.
PESC. What's that?
   I need a dictionary to 't.
DOC. I'll tell you.
   In those that are possessed with 't there o'erflows
   Such melancholy humor they imagine
   Themselves to be transformed into wolves;
   Steal forth to churchyards in the dead of night,
   And dig dead bodies up: as two nights since
   One met the duke 'bout midnight in a lane
   Behind Saint Mark's Church, with the leg of a man
   Upon his shoulder; and he howled fearfully;
   Said he was a wolf, only the difference
   Was, a wolf's skin was hairy on the outside,
   His on the inside; bade them take their swords,
   Rip up his flesh, and try: straight I was sent for,
   And, having ministered to him, found his grace
   Very well recovered.
PESC. I am glad on 't.
DOC. Yet not without some fear
   Of a relapse. If he grow to his fit again,
   I'll go a nearer way to work with him
   Than ever Paracelsus[1] dreamed of; if
   They'll give me leave, I'll buffet his madness
   Out of him. Stand aside; he comes.

---

1. Swiss physician and alchemist.

Enter Ferdinand, Cardinal, Malateste, and Bosola

FERD. Leave me.

MAL. Why doth your lordship love this solitariness?

FERD. Eagles commonly fly alone: they are crows, daws, and starlings
that flock together. Look, what's that follows me?

MAL. Nothing, my lord.

FERD. Yes.

MAL. 'Tis your shadow.

FERD. Stay it; let it not haunt me.

MAL. Impossible, if you move, and the sun shine.

FERD. I will throttle it.

[Throws himself on the ground]

MAL. O, my lord, you are angry with nothing.

FERD. You are a fool: how is't possible I should catch my shadow, unless I fall upon't? When I go to hell, I mean to carry a bribe; for, look
you, good gifts evermore make way for the worst persons.

PESC. Rise, good my lord.

FERD. I am studying the art of patience.

PESC. 'Tis a noble virtue.

FERD. To drive six snails before me from this town to Moscow; neither use goad nor whip to them, but let them take their own time;—
the patient'st man i' th' world match me for an experiment;—and
I'll crawl after like a sheep-biter.[1]

CARD. Force him up.

[They raise him]

FERD. Use me well, you were best. What I have done, I have done: I'll
confess nothing.

DOC. Now let me come to him.—Are you mad, my lord? are you out
of your princely wits?

FERD. What's he?

PESC. Your doctor.

FERD. Let me have his beard sawed off, and his eyebrows filed more
civil.

DOC. I must do mad tricks with him, for that's the only way on't.—I

---

1. Censorious fellow.

have brought your grace a salamander's skin to keep you from sun-
burning.

FERD. I have cruel sore eyes.

DOC. The white of a cockatrix's egg[1] is present remedy.

FERD. Let it be a new laid one, you were best.—Hide me from him:
physicians are like kings,—they brook no contradiction.

DOC. Now he begins to fear me: now let me alone with him.

CARD. How now? put off your gown?

DOC. Let me have some forty urinals filled with rosewater: he and I'll
go pelt one another with them.—Now he begins to fear me.—Can
you fetch a frisk,[2] sir?—Let him go, let him go, upon my peril: I find
by his eye he stands in awe of me; I'll make him as tame as a dormouse.

FERD. Can you fetch your frisks, sir?—I will stamp him into a cullis,
flay off his skin, to cover one of the anatomies[3] this rogue hath set i'
th' cold yonder in Barber-Chirurgeon's-hall.—Hence, hence! you
are all of you like beasts for sacrifice: there's nothing left of you but
tongue and belly, flattery and lechery.

Exit

PESC. Doctor, he did not fear you throughly.

DOC. True;
I was somewhat too forward.

BOS. Mercy upon me,
What a fatal judgment hath fallen upon this Ferdinand!

PESC. Knows your grace what accident hath brought
Unto the prince this strange distraction?

CARD. [*Aside*] I must feign somewhat.—Thus they say it grew.
You have heard it rumored, for these many years
None of our family dies but there is seen
The shape of an old woman, which is given
By tradition to us to have been murdered
By her nephews for her riches. Such a figure
One night, as the prince sat up late at 's book,

---

1. Cockatrix = basilisk.
2. Cut a caper.
3. Skeletons.

Appeared to him; when crying out for help,
The gentlemen of 's chamber found his grace
All on a cold sweat, altered much in face
And language: since which apparition,
He hath grown worse and worse, and I much fear
He cannot live.

BOS. Sir, I would speak with you.

PESC. We'll leave your grace,
Wishing to the sick prince, our noble lord,
All health of mind and body.

CARD. You are most welcome.

Exeunt Pescara, Malateste, and Doctor

Are you come? so.—[*Aside*] This fellow must not know
By any means I had intelligence
In our duchess' death; for, though I counselled it,
The full of all th' engagement seemed to grow
From Ferdinand.—Now, sir, how fares our sister?
I do not think but sorrow makes her look
Like to an oft-dyed garment: she shall now
Taste comfort from me. Why do you look so wildly?
Oh, the fortune of your master here the prince
Dejects you; but be you of happy comfort:
If you'll do one thing for me I'll entreat,
Though he had a cold tombstone o'er his bones,
I'd make you what you would be.

BOS. Anything;
Give it me in a breath, and let me fly to't:
They that think long small expedition win,
For musing much o' th' end cannot begin.

Enter Julia

JUL. Sir, will you come in to supper?

CARD. I am busy;
Leave me.

JUL. [*Aside*] What an excellent shape hath that fellow!

Exit

CARD. 'Tis thus. Antonio lurks here in Milan:
Inquire him out, and kill him. While he lives,

Our sister cannot marry; and I have thought
Of an excellent match for her. Do this, and style me
Thy advancement.

BOS. But by what means shall I find him out?

CARD. There is a gentleman called Delio
Here in the camp, that hath been long approved
His loyal friend. Set eye upon that fellow;
Follow him to mass; maybe Antonio,
Although he do account religion
But a school-name, for fashion of the world
May accompany him; or else go inquire out
Delio's confessor, and see if you can bribe
Him to reveal it. There are a thousand ways
A man might find to trace him; as to know
What fellows haunt the Jews for taking up
Great sums of money, for sure he's in want;
Or else to go to th' picture-makers, and learn
Who bought her picture lately: some of these
Happily may take.

BOS. Well, I'll not freeze i' th' business:
I would see that wretched thing, Antonio,
Above all sights i' th' world.

CARD. Do, and be happy.

Exit

BOS. This fellow doth breed basilisks in 's eyes,
He's nothing else but murder; yet he seems
Not to have notice of the duchess' death.
'Tis his cunning: I must follow his example;
There cannot be a surer way to trace
Than that of an old fox.

Re-enter Julia, with a pistol

JUL. So, sir, you are well met.

BOS. How now?

JUL. Nay, the doors are fast enough: Now, sir,
I will make you confess your treachery.

BOS. Treachery?

JUL. Yes,

Confess to me which of my women 'twas
You hired to put love-powder into my drink?

Bos. Love-powder?

Jul. Yes, when I was at Malfi.
Why should I fall in love with such a face else?
I have already suffered for thee so much pain,
The only remedy to do me good
Is to kill my longing.

Bos. Sure, your pistol holds
Nothing but perfumes or kissing-comfits.[1]
Excellent lady! You have a pretty way on't
To discover your longing. Come, come, I'll disarm you,
And arm you thus: yet this is wondrous strange.

Jul. Compare thy form and my eyes together, you'll find
My love no such great miracle. Now you'll say
I am wanton: this nice modesty in ladies
Is but a troublesome familiar that haunts them.

Bos. Know you me, I am a blunt soldier.

Jul. The better:
Sure, there wants fire where there are no lively sparks
Of roughness.

Bos. And I want compliment.[2]

Jul. Why, ignorance
In courtship cannot make you do amiss,
If you have a heart to do well.

Bos. You are very fair.

Jul. Nay, if you lay beauty to my charge,
I must plead unguilty.

Bos. Your bright eyes carry
A quiver of darts in them sharper than sunbeams.

Jul. You will mar me with commendation,
Put yourself to the charge of courting me,
Whereas now I woo you.

Bos. [*Aside*] I have it, I will work upon this creature.—
Let us grow most amorously familiar:

---

1. Perfumed sugarplums, to sweeten the breath.
2. I don't understand courtly manners.

    If the great Cardinal now should see me thus,
    Would he not count me a villain?

JUL. No; he might
    Count me a wanton, not lay a scruple
    Of offence on you; for if I see and steal
    A diamond, the fault is not i' th' stone,
    But in me the thief that purloins it. I am sudden
    With you: we that are great women of pleasure
    Use to cut off these uncertain wishes
    And unquiet longings, and in an instant join
    The sweet delight and the pretty excuse together.
    Had you been i' th' street, under my chamber-window,
    Even there I should have courted you.

BOS. Oh, you are
    An excellent lady!

JUL. Bid me do somewhat for you
    Presently to express I love you.

BOS. I will;
    And if you love me, fail not to effect it.
    The Cardinal is grown wondrous melancholy;
    Demand the cause, let him not put you off
    With feigned excuse; discover the main ground on't.

JUL. Why would you know this?

BOS. I have depended on him,
    And I hear that he is fallen in some disgrace
    With the emperor: if he be, like the mice
    That forsake falling houses, I would shift
    To other dependence.

JUL. You shall not need
    Follow the wars: I'll be your maintenance.

BOS. And I your loyal servant: but I cannot
    Leave my calling.

JUL. Not leave an ungrateful
    General for the love of a sweet lady?
    You are like some cannot sleep in feather-beds,
    But must have blocks for their pillows.

BOS. Will you do this?

JUL. Cunningly.

BOS. To-morrow I'll expect th' intelligence.

JUL. To-morrow? get you into my cabinet;
You shall have it with you. Do not delay me,
No more than I do you: I am like one
That is condemned; I have my pardon promised,
But I would see it sealed. Go, get you in:
You shall see me wind my tongue about his heart
Like a skein of silk.

Exit Bosola

Re-enter Cardinal

CARD. Where are you?

Enter Servants

SERVANTS. Here.

CARD. Let none, upon your lives, have conference
With the Prince Ferdinand, unless I know it.—
[*Aside*] In this distraction he may reveal
The murder.

Exeunt Servants

Yond's my lingering consumption:
I am weary of her, and by any means
Would be quit of.

JUL. How now, my lord? what ails you?

CARD. Nothing.

JUL. Oh, you are much altered: come, I must be
Your secretary,[1] and remove this lead
From off your bosom: what's the matter?

CORD. I may not
Tell you.

JUL. Are you so far in love with sorrow
You cannot part with part of it? or think you
I cannot love your grace when you are sad
As well as merry? or do you suspect
I, that have been a secret to your heart
These many winters, cannot be the same
Unto your tongue?

1. Confidant.

CARD. Satisfy thy longing,—
    The only way to make thee keep my counsel
    Is, not to tell thee.
JUL. Tell your echo this,
    Or flatterers, that like echoes still report
    What they hear though most imperfect, and not me;
    For if that you be true unto yourself,
    I'll know.
CARD. Will you rack me?
JUL. No, judgment shall
    Draw it from you: it is an equal fault,
    To tell one's secrets unto all or none.
CARD. The first argues folly.
JUL. But the last tyranny.
CARD. Very well: why, imagine I have committed
    Some secret deed which I desire the world
    May never hear of.
JUL. Therefore may not I know it?
    You have concealed for me as great a sin
    As adultery. Sir, never was occasion
    For perfect trial of my constancy
    Till now: sir, I beseech you—
CARD. You'll repent it.
JUL. Never.
CARD. It hurries thee to ruin: I'll not tell thee.
    Be well advised, and think what danger 'tis
    To receive a prince's secrets: they that do,
    Had need have their breasts hooped with adamant
    To contain them. I pray thee, yet be satisfied;
    Examine thine own frailty; 'tis more easy
    To tie knots than unloose them: 'tis a secret
    That, like a lingering poison, may chance lie
    Spread in thy veins, and kill thee seven year hence.
JUL. Now you dally with me.
CARD. No more; thou shalt know it.
    By my appointment the great Duchess of Malfi
    And two of her young children, four nights since,
    Were strangled.

JUL. O Heaven! sir, what have you done!

CARD. How now? how settles this? think you your bosom
Will be a grave dark and obscure enough
For such a secret?

JUL. You have undone yourself, sir.

CARD. Why?

JUL. It lies not in me to conceal it.

CARD. No?
Come, I will swear you to't upon this book.

JUL. Most religiously.

CARD. Kiss it.

> [*She kisses the book*]

Now you shall
Never utter it; thy curiosity
Hath undone thee: thou'rt poisoned with that book;
Because I knew thou couldst not keep my counsel,
I have bound thee to't by death.

Re-enter Bosola

BOS. For pity sake,
Hold!

CARD. Ha! Bosola?

JUL. I forgive you
This equal piece of justice you have done;
For I betrayed your counsel to that fellow:
He overheard it; that was the cause I said
It lay not in me to conceal it.

BOS. O foolish woman,
Couldst not thou have poisoned him?

JUL. 'Tis weakness,
Too much to think what should have been done. I go,
I know not whither.

> *Dies*

CARD. Wherefore com'st thou hither?

BOS. That I might find a great man like yourself,
Not out of his wits as the Lord Ferdinand,
To remember my service.

CARD. I'll have thee hewed in pieces.

BOS. Make not yourself such a promise of that life
   Which is not yours to dispose of.

CARD. Who placed thee here?

BOS. Her lust, as she intended.

CARD. Very well:
   Now you know me for your fellow-murderer.

BOS. And wherefore should you lay fair marble colors
   Upon your rotten purposes to me?
   Unless you imitate some that do plot great treasons,
   And when they have done, go bide themselves i' th' graves
   Of those were actors in't?

CARD. No more; there is
   A fortune attends thee.

BOS. Shall I go sue
   To Fortune any longer? 'Tis the fool's
   Pilgrimage.

CARD. I have honors in store for thee.

BOS. There are a many ways that conduct to seeming
   Honor, and some of them very dirty ones.

CARD. Throw
   To the devil thy melancholy. The fire burns well:
   What need we keep a stirring of 't, and make
   A greater smother? Thou wilt kill Antonio?

BOS. Yes.

CARD. Take up that body.

BOS. I think I shall
   Shortly grow the common bearer for churchyards.

CARD. I will allow thee some dozen of attendants
   To aid thee in the murder.

BOS. Oh, by no means. Physicians that apply horseleeches to any rank
   swelling use to cut off their tails, that the blood may run through
   them the faster: let me have no train[1] when I go to shed blood, lest
   it make me have a greater when I ride to the gallows.

CARD. Come to me after midnight, to help to remove
   That body to her own lodging: I'll give out
   She died o' th' plague; 'twill breed the less inquiry

---

1. Attendants.

After her death.

BOS. Where's Castruchio her husband?

CARD. He's rode to Naples, to take possession
    Of Antonio's citadel.

BOS. Believe me, you have done
    A very happy turn.

CARD. Fail not to come:
    There is the master-key of our lodgings; and by that
    You may conceive what trust I plant in you.

BOS. You shall find me ready.

                                    Exit Cardinal

O poor Antonio,
Though nothing be so needful to thy estate
As pity, yet I find nothing so dangerous;
I must look to my footing:
In such slippery ice-pavements men had need
To be frost-nailed well, they may break their necks else;
The precedent's here afore me. How this man
Bears up in blood! seems fearless! Why, 'tis well:
Security some men call the suburbs of hell,
Only a dead wall between. Well, good Antonio,
I'll seek thee out; and all my care shall be
To put thee into safety from the reach
Of these most cruel biters that have got
Some of thy blood already. It may be,
I'll join with thee in a most just revenge:
The weakest arm is strong enough that strikes
With the sword of justice. Still methinks the duchess
Haunts me.—There, there, 'tis nothing but my melancholy.
O Penitence, let me truly taste thy cup,
That throws men down only to raise them up!

                                               Exit

SCENE III

Enter Antonio and Delio

DEL. Yond's the Cardinal's window. This fortification
    Grew from the ruins of an ancient abbey;

And to yond side o' th' river lies a wall,
Piece of a cloister, which in my opinion
Gives the best echo that you ever heard,
So hollow and so dismal, and withal
So plain in the distinction of our words,
That many have supposed it is a spirit
That answers.

ANT. I do love these ancient ruins.
We never tread upon them but we set
Our foot upon some reverend history:
And, questionless, here in this open court,
Which now lies naked to the injuries
Of stormy weather, some men lie interred
Loved the church so well, and gave so largely to't,
They thought it should have canopied their bones
Till doomsday; but all things have their end:
Churches and cities, which have diseases
Like to men, must have like death that we have.

ECHO. "Like death that we have."

DEL. Now the echo hath caught you.

ANT. It groaned, methought, and gave
A very deadly accent.

ECHO. "Deadly accent."

DEL. I told you 'twas a pretty one: you may make it
A huntsman, or a falconer, a musician,
Or a thing of sorrow.

ECHO. "A thing of sorrow."

ANT. Aye, sure, that suits it best.

ECHO. "That suits it best."

ANT. 'Tis very like my wife's voice.

ECHO. "Aye, wife's voice."

DEL. Come, let's walk further from't. I would not have you
Go to th' Cardinal's to-night: do not.

ECHO. "Do not."

DEL. Wisdom doth not more moderate wasting sorrow
Than time: take time for't; be mindful of thy safety.

ECHO. "Be mindful of thy safety."

ANT. Necessity compels me:

Make scrutiny throughout the passes of
Your own life, you'll find it impossible
To fly your fate.

ECHO. "Oh, fly your fate."

DEL. Hark!
The dead stones seem to have pity on you, and give you
Good counsel.

ANT. Echo, I will not talk with thee,
For thou art a dead thing.

ECHO. "Thou art a dead thing."

ANT. My duchess is asleep now,
And her little ones, I hope sweetly: O Heaven,
Shall I never see her more?

ECHO. "Never see her more."

ANT. I marked not one repetition of the echo
But that; and on the sudden a clear light
Presented me a face folded in sorrow.

DEL. Your fancy merely.

ANT. Come, I'll be out of this ague,
For to live thus is not indeed to live;
It is a mockery and abuse of life:
I will not henceforth save myself by halves;
Lose all, or nothing.

DEL. Your own virtue save you!
I'll fetch your eldest son, and second you:
It may be that the sight of his own blood
Spread in so sweet a figure may beget
The more compassion. However, fare you well.
Though in our miseries Fortune have a part,
Yet in our noble sufferings she hath none:
Contempt of pain, that we may call our own.

Exeunt

SCENE IV

Enter Cardinal, Pescara, Malateste, Roderigo, and Grisolan

CARD. You shall not watch to-night by the sick prince;
His grace is very well recovered.

MAL. Good my lord, suffer us.

CARD. Oh, by no means;
  The noise, and change of object in his eye,
  Doth more distract him: I pray, all to bed;
  And though you hear him in his violent fit,
  Do not rise, I entreat you.

PESC. So, sir; we shall not.

CARD. Nay, I must have you promise upon your honors,
  For I was enjoined to't by himself; and he seemed
  To urge it sensibly.

PESC. Let our honors bind
  This trifle.

CARD. Nor any of your followers.

MAL. Neither.

CARD. It may be, to make trial of your promise,
  When he's asleep, myself will rise and feign
  Some of his mad tricks, and cry out for help,
  And feign myself in danger.

MAL. If your throat were cutting,
  I'd not come at you, now I have protested against it.

CARD. Why, I thank you.

GRIS. 'Twas a foul storm to-night.

ROD. The Lord Ferdinand's chamber shook like an osier.

MAL. 'Twas nothing but pure kindness in the devil,
  To rock his own child.

Exeunt all except the Cardinal

CARD. The reason why I would not suffer these
  About my brother, is, because at midnight
  I may with better privacy convey
  Julia's body to her own lodging. Oh, my conscience!
  I would pray now; but the devil takes away my heart
  For having any confidence in prayer.
  About this hour I appointed Bosola
  To fetch the body: when he hath served my turn,
  He dies.

Exit

Enter Bosola

BOS. Ha! 'twas the Cardinal's voice; I heard him name
    Bosola and my death. Listen; I hear
    One's footing.

Enter Ferdinand

FERD. Strangling is a very quiet death.
BOS. [*Aside*] Nay, then, I see I must stand upon my guard.
FERD. What say to that? whisper softly; do you agree to't? So; it must
    be done i' th' dark: the Cardinal would not for a thousand pounds
    the doctor should see it.
BOS. My death is plotted; here's the consequence of murder.
    We value not desert nor Christian breath,
    When we know black deeds must be cured with death.

Enter Antonio and Servant

SERV. Here stay, sir, and be confident, I pray:
    I'll fetch you a dark lantern.

Exit

ANT. Could I take him
    At his prayers, there were hope of pardon.
BOS. Fall right, my sword!—

[*Stabs him*]

I'll not give thee so much leisure as to pray.
ANT. Oh, I am gone! Thou hast ended a long suit
    In a minute.
BOS. What art thou?
ANT. A most wretched thing,
    That only have thy benefit in death,
    To appear myself.

Re-enter Servant with a lantern

SERV. Where are you, sir?
ANT. Very near my home.—Bosola?
SERV. Oh, misfortune!
BOS. Smother thy pity, thou art dead else.—Antonio?
    The man I would have saved 'bove mine own life!
    We are merely the stars' tennis-balls, struck and bandied
    Which way please them.—O good Antonio,

I'll whisper one thing in thy dying ear
Shall make thy heart break quickly! thy fair duchess
And two sweet children—

ANT. Their very names
Kindle a little life in me.

BOS. Are murdered.

ANT. Some men have wished to die
At the hearing of sad tidings; I am glad
That I shall do't in sadness:¹ I would not now
Wish my wounds balmed nor healed, for I have no use
To put my life to. In all our quest of greatness,
Like wanton boys, whose pastime is their care,
We follow after bubbles blown in th' air.
Pleasure of life, what is't? only the good
Hours of an ague; merely a preparative
To rest, to endure vexation. I do not ask
The process of my death; only commend me
To Delio.

BOS. Break, heart!

ANT. And let my son
Fly the courts of princes.

Dies

BOS. Thou seem'st
To have loved Antonio?

SERV. I brought him hither,
To have reconciled him to the Cardinal.

BOS. I do not ask thee that.
Take him up, if thou tender thine own life,
And bear him where the lady Julia
Was wont to lodge.—Oh, my fate moves swift;
I have this Cardinal in the forge already;
Now I'll bring him to th' hammer. O direful misprision!²
I will not imitate things glorious,
No more than base; I'll be mine own example.—

1. i.e., In earnest.
2. Mistake.

On, on, and look thou represent, for silence,
The thing thou bear'st.

Exeunt

Scene V

Enter Cardinal, with a book

CARD. I am puzzled in a question about hell:
　　He says, in hell there's one material fire,
　　And yet it shall not burn all men alike.
　　Lay him by. How tedious is a guilty conscience!
　　When I look into the fish-ponds in my garden,
　　Methinks I see a thing armed with a rake,
　　That seems to strike at me.

Enter Bosola, and Servant bearing Antonio's body

　　Now, art thou come?
　　Thou lookest ghastly:
　　There sits in thy face some great determination
　　Mixed with some fear.
BOS. Thus it lightens into action:
　　I am come to kill thee.
CARD. Ha!—Help! our guard!
BOS. Thou art deceived; they are out of thy howling.
CARD. Hold; and I will faithfully divide
　　Revenues with thee.
BOS. Thy prayers and proffers
　　Are both unseasonable.
CARD. Raise the watch!
　　We are betrayed!
BOS. I have confined your flight:
　　I'll suffer your retreat to Julia's chamber,
　　But no further.
CARD. Help! we are betrayed!

Enter, above, Pescara, Malateste, Roderigo, and Grisolan

MAL. Listen.
CARD. My dukedom for rescue!

ROD. Fie upon
  His counterfeiting!
MAL. Why, 'tis not the Cardinal.
ROD. Yes, yes, 'tis he: but I'll see him hanged
  Ere I'll go down to him.
CARD. Here's a plot upon me;
  I am assaulted! I am lost, unless some rescue.
GRIS. He doth this pretty well; but it will not serve
  To laugh me out of mine honor.
CARD. The sword's at my throat!
ROD. You would not bawl so loud then.
MAL. Come, come,
  Let's go to bed: he told us thus much aforehand.
PESC. He wished you should not come at him; but, believe't,
  The accent of the voice sounds not in jest:
  I'll down to him, howsoever, and with engines
  Force ope the doors.

                                Exit above

ROD. Let's follow him aloof,
  And note how the Cardinal will laugh at him.

    Exeunt, above, Malateste, Roderigo, and Grisolan

BOS. There's for first,

                        [Kills the Servant]
  'Cause you shall not unbarricade the door
  To let in rescue.
CARD. What cause hast thou to pursue my life?
BOS. Look there.
CARD. Antonio?
BOS. Slain by my hand unwittingly.
  Pray, and be sudden: when thou killed'st thy sister,
  Thou took'st from Justice her most equal balance,
  And left her naught but her sword.
CARD. Oh, mercy!
BOS. Now, it seems thy greatness was only outward;
  For thou fall'st faster of thyself than calamity
  Can drive thee. I'll not waste longer time; there!

                                  [Stabs him]

CARD. Thou hast hurt me.

BOS. Again!

> [*Stabs him again*]

CARD. Shall I die like a leveret,
   Without any resistance?—Help, help, help!
   I am slain!

Enter Ferdinand

FERD. Th' alarum? give me a fresh horse;
   Rally the vaunt-guard, or the day is lost.
   Yield, yield! I give you the honor of arms,
   Shake my sword over you; will you yield?

CARD. Help me;
   I am your brother!

FERD. The devil! My brother fight
   Upon the adverse party?

> [*He wounds the Cardinal, and, in the scuffle,*
> *gives Bosola his death-wound*]

There flies your ransom.

CARD. O justice!
   I suffer now for what hath former been:
   Sorrow is held the eldest child of sin.

FERD. Now you 're brave fellows. Caesar's fortune was harder than
Pompey's; Caesar died in the arms of prosperity, Pompey at the feet
of disgrace. You both died in the field. The pain's nothing: pain
many times is taken away with the apprehension of greater, as the
toothache with the sight of a barber that comes to pull it out: there's
philosophy for you.

BOS. Now my revenge is perfect.—Sink, thou main cause

> [*Kills Ferdinand*]

Of my undoing!—The last part of my life
Hath done me best service.

FERD. Give me some wet hay; I am broken-winded. I do account this
world but a dog-kennel: I will vault credit[1] and affect high pleasures
beyond death.

---

1. Do incredible deeds.

BOS. He seems to come to himself, now he's so near
    The bottom.
FERD. My sister, O my sister! there's the cause on't.
    Whether we fall by ambition, blood, or lust,
    Like diamonds we are cut with our own dust.

                                                        Dies

CARD. Thou hast thy payment too.
BOS. Yes, I hold my weary soul in my teeth.
    'Tis ready to part from me. I do glory
    That thou, which stood'st like a huge pyramid
    Begun upon a large and ample base,
    Shalt end in a little point, a kind of nothing.

    Enter, below, Pescara, Malateste, Roderigo, and Grisolan

PESC. How now, my lord?
MAL. O sad disaster!
ROD. How
    Comes this?
BOS. Revenge for the Duchess of Malfi murdered
    By th' Arragonian brethren; for Antonio
    Slain by this hand; for lustful Julia
    Poisoned by this man; and lastly for myself,
    That was an actor in the main of all,
    Much 'gainst mine own good nature, yet i' th' end
    Neglected.
PESC. How now, my lord?
CARD. Look to my brother: he gave us these large wounds
    As we were struggling here i' the rushes. And now,
    I pray, let me be laid by and never thought of.

                                                        Dies

PESC. How fatally, it seems, he did withstand
    His own rescue!
MAL. Thou wretched thing of blood,
    How came Antonio by his death?
BOS. In a mist;
    I know not how: such a mistake as I
    Have often seen in a play. Oh, I am gone!
    We are only like dead walls or vaulted graves,

That, ruined, yield no echo. Fare you well.
It may be pain, but no harm, to me to die
In so good a quarrel. Oh, this gloomy world!
In what a shadow, or deep pit of darkness,
Doth, womanish and fearful, mankind live!
Let worthy minds ne'er stagger in distrust
To suffer death or shame for what is just:
Mine is another voyage.

Dies

PESC. The noble Delio, as I came to the palace,
Told me of Antonio's being here, and showed me
A pretty gentleman, his son and heir.

Enter Delio and Antonio's Son

MAL. O sir,
You come too late!
DEL. I heard so, and was armed for't,
Ere I came. Let us make noble use
Of this great ruin; and join all our force
To establish this young hopeful gentleman
In 's mother's right. These wretched eminent things
Leave no more fame behind 'em, than should one
Fall in a frost, and leave his print in snow;
As soon as the sun shines, it ever melts,
Both form and matter. I have ever thought
Nature doth nothing so great for great men
As when she's pleased to make them lords of truth:
Integrity of life is fame's best friend,
Which nobly, beyond death, shall crown the end.

Exeunt

The Changeling

Thomas Middleton
with William Rowley

DRAMATIS PERSONAE

VERMANDERO, *father to* BEATRICE
TOMASO DE PIRACQUO, *a noble lord*
ALONZO DE PIRACQUO, *his brother, suitor to* BEATRICE
ALSEMERO, *a nobleman, afterward married to* BEATRICE
JASPERINO, *his friend*
ALIBIUS, *a jealous doctor*
LOLLIO, *his man*
PEDRO, *friend to Antonio*
ANTONIO, *the Changeling*
FRANCISCUS, *the counterfeit madman*
DE FLORES, *servant to* VERMANDERO
MADMEN
SERVANTS
BEATRICE-JOANNA, *daughter to* VERMANDERO
DIAPHANTA, *her waiting-woman*
ISABELLA, *wife to Alibius*

The Changeling

Act I, Scene I

Enter Alsemero

ALS. 'Twas in the temple where I first beheld her,
    And now again the same: what omen yet
    Follows of that? none but imaginary;
    Why should my hopes or fate be timorous?
    The place is holy, so is my intent:
    I love her beauties to the holy purpose;
    And that, methinks, admits comparison
    With man's first creation, the place blessèd,
    And is his right home back,[1] if he achieve it.
    The church hath first begun our interview,[2]
    And that's the place must join us into one;
    So there's beginning and perfection[3] too.

Enter Jasperino

JAS. O sir, are you here? come, the wind's fair with you;
    You're like to have a swift and pleasant passage.
ALS. Sure, you're deceived, friend, it is contrary,
    In my best judgment.
JAS. What, for Malta?
    If you could buy a gale amongst the witches,
    They could not serve you such a lucky pennyworth
    As comes a' God's name.
ALS. Even now I observed

---

1. Paradise regained.
2. Meeting.
3. Ending, completion.

The temple's vane to turn full in my face;
I know it is against me.

JAS. Against you?
Then you know not where you are.

ALS. Not well, indeed.

JAS. Are you not well, sir?

ALS. Yes, Jasperino,
Unless there be some hidden malady
Within me, that I understand not.

JAS. And that
I begin to doubt,[1] sir: I never knew
Your inclination to travel at a pause,
With any cause to hinder it, till now.
Ashore you were wont to call your servants up,
And help to trap[2] your horses for the speed;
At sea I've seen you weigh the anchor with 'em,
Hoist sails for fear to lose the foremost breath,
Be in continual prayers for fair winds;
And have you changed your orisons?

ALS. No, friend;
I keep the same church, same devotion.

JAS. Lover I'm sure you're none; the stoic was
Found in you long ago; your mother nor
Best friends, who have set snares of beauty, ay,
And choice ones too, could never trap you that way:
What might be the cause?

ALS. Lord, how violent
Thou art! I was but meditating of
Somewhat I heard within the temple.

JAS. Is this
Violence? 'tis but idleness compared
With your haste yesterday.

ALS. I'm all this while
A-going, man.

JAS. Backwards, I think, sir. Look, your servants.

---

1. Suspect.
2. Harness.

Enter Servants

1ST SER. The seamen call; shall we board your trunks?
ALS. No, not to-day.
JAS. 'Tis the critical day, it seems, and the sign in Aquarius.[1]
2ND SER. We must not to sea to-day; this smoke will bring forth fire.
ALS. Keep all on shore; I do not know the end,
    Which needs I must do, of an affair in hand
    Ere I can go to sea.
1ST SER. Well, your pleasure.
2ND SER. Let him e'en take his leisure too; we are safer on land.

Exeunt Servants

Enter Beatrice, Diaphanta, and Servants; Alsemero accosts
Beatrice and then kisses her

JAS. [*Aside*] How now? the laws of the Medes[2] are changed sure;
    salute a woman! he kisses too; wonderful! where learnt he this? and
    does it perfectly too; in my conscience, he ne'er rehearsed it before.
    Nay, go on; this will be stranger and better news at Valencia than if
    he had ransomed half Greece from the Turk.
BEAT. You are a scholar, sir?
ALS. A weak one, lady.
BEAT. Which of the sciences is this love you speak of?
ALS. From your tongue I take it to be music.
BEAT. You're skilful in it, can sing at first sight.
ALS. And I have showed you all my skill at once;
    I want more words to express me further,
    And must be forced to repetition;
    I love you dearly.
BEAT. Be better advised, sir:
    Our eyes are sentinels unto our judgments,
    And should give certain judgment what they see;
    But they are rash sometimes, and tell us wonders
    Of common things, which when our judgments find,
    They can then check the eyes, and call them blind.

---

1. Promising good conditions for travel by water.
2. Rigorous laws.

ALS. But I am further, lady; yesterday
　　Was mine eyes' employment, and hither now
　　They brought my judgment, where are both agreed:
　　Both houses then consenting, 'tis agreed;
　　Only there wants the confirmation
　　By the hand royal, that is your part, lady.
BEAT. There's one above me, sir. [*Aside*] —O, for five days past
　　To be recalled! sure mine eyes were mistaken;
　　This was the man was meant me: that he should come
　　So near his time, and miss it!
JAS. We might have come by the carriers from Valencia,
　　I see, and saved all our sea-provision; we are at farthest[1] sure:
　　methinks I should do something too;
　　I mean to be a venturer[2] in this voyage:
　　Yonder's another vessel, I'll board her;
　　If she be lawful prize, down goes her topsail.

　　　　　　　　　　　　　　　　[*Accosts Diaphanta*]

Enter De Flores

DE F. Lady, your father—
BEAT. Is in health, I hope.
DE F. Your eye shall instantly instruct you, lady;
　　He's coming hitherward.
BEAT. What needed then
　　Your duteous preface? I had rather
　　He had come unexpected; you must stale
　　A good presence with unnecessary blabbing;
　　And how welcome for your part you are,
　　I'm sure you know.
DE F. [*Aside*] Will't never mend, this scorn,
　　One side nor other? must I be enjoined
　　To follow still whilst she flies from me? well,
　　Fates, do your worst, I'll please myself with sight
　　Of her at all opportunities,

1. From success.
2. Investor.

If but to spite her anger: I know she had
Rather see me dead than living; and yet
She knows no cause for't but a peevish will.

ALS. You seem displeasèd, lady, on the sudden.

BEAT. Your pardon, sir, 'tis my infirmity;
Nor can I other reason render you,
Than his or hers, of some particular thing
They must abandon as a deadly poison,
Which to a thousand other tastes were wholesome;
Such to mine eyes is that same fellow there,
The same that report speaks of the basilisk.[1]

ALS. This is a frequently frailty in our nature;
There's scarce a man amongst a thousand found
But hath his imperfection: one distastes
The scent of roses, which to infinites
Most pleasing is and odoriferous;
One oil, the enemy of poison;
Another wine, the cheerer of the heart
And lively refresher of the countenance:
Indeed this fault, if so it be, is general;
There's scarce a thing but is both loved and loathed:
Myself, I must confess, have the same frailty.

BEAT. And what may be your poison, sir? I'm bold with you.

ALS. What might be your desire, perhaps; a cherry.

BEAT. I am no enemy to any creature
My memory has, but yon gentleman.

ALS. He does ill to tempt your sight, if he knew it.

BEAT. He cannot be ignorant of that, sir,
I have not spared to tell him so; and I want[2]
To help myself, since he's a gentleman
In good respect with my father, and follows him.

ALS. He's out of his place then now.

[*They talk apart*]

---

1. Which kills with a glance.
2. Lack means.

JAS. I am a mad wag, wench.

DIA. So methinks; but for your comfort, I can tell you, we have a doctor in the city that undertakes the cure of such.

JAS. Tush, I know what physic is best for the state of mine own body.

DIA. 'Tis scarce a well-governed state, I believe.

JAS. I could show thee such a thing with an ingredience that we two would compound together, and if it did not tame the maddest blood i' th' town for two hours after, I'll ne'er profess physic again.

DIA. A little poppy, sir, were good to cause you sleep.

JAS. Poppy? I'll give thee a pop i' th' lips for that first, and begin there: poppy is one simple[1] indeed, and cuckoo-what-you-call't another: I'll discover[2] no more now; another time I'll show thee all.

Exit

BEAT. My father, sir.

Enter Vermandero and Servants

VER. O Joanna, I came to meet thee;
Your devotion's ended?

BEAT. For this time, sir.—
[*Aside*] I shall change my saint, I fear me; I find
A giddy turning in me.—Sir, this while
I am beholden to this gentleman, who
Left his own way to keep me company,
And in discourse I find him much desirous
To see your castle; he hath deserved it, sir,
If ye please to grant it.

VER. With all my heart, sir:
Yet there's an article between; I must know
Your country; we use not to give survey
Of our chief strengths to strangers; our citadels
Are placed conspicuous to outward view,
On promonts'[3] tops, but within our secrets.

ALS. A Valencian, sir.

---

1. Herb.
2. Reveal.
3. Promontories.

VER. A Valencian?
 That's native, sir: of what name, I beseech you?
ALS. Alsemero, sir.
VER. Alsemero? not the son
 Of John de Alsemero?
ALS. The same, sir.
VER. My best love bids you welcome.
BEAT. He was wont
 To call me so, and then he speaks a most
 Unfeignèd truth.
VER. O sir, I knew your father;
 We two were in acquaintance long ago,
 Before our chins were worth iulan[1] down,
 And so continued till the stamp of time
 Had coined us into silver: well, he's gone;
 A good soldier went with him.
ALS. You went together in that, sir.
VER. No, by Saint Jacques,[2] I came behind him;
 Yet I've done somewhat too: an unhappy day
 Swallowed him at last at Gibraltar,
 In fight with those rebellious Hollanders;
 Was it not so?
ALS. Whose death I had revenged,
 Or followed him in fate, had not the late league[3]
 Prevented me.
VER. Ay, ay, 'twas time to breathe.—
 O Joanna, I should ha' told thee news;
 I saw Piracquo lately.
BEAT. [*Aside*] That's ill news.
VER. He's hot preparing for this day of triumph:
 Thou must be a bride within this sevennight.
ALS. [*Aside*] Ha!
BEAT. Nay, good sir, be not so violent; with speed
 I cannot render satisfaction

1. From the Greek, meaning the first tender down.
2. Patron saint of Spain.
3. Treaty.

Unto the dear companion of my soul,
Virginity, whom I thus long have lived with,
And part with it so rude and suddenly;
Can such friends divide, never to meet again,
Without a solemn farewell?

VER. Tush, tush! there's a toy.[1]

ALS. [*Aside*] I must now part, and never meet again
With any joy on earth. —Sir, your pardon;
My affairs call on me.

VER. How, sir? by no means:
Not changed so soon, I hope? you must see my castle,
And her best entertainment, e'er we part,
I shall think myself unkindly used else.
Come, come, let's on; I had good hope your stay
Had been a while with us in Alicant;
I might have bid you to my daughter's wedding.

ALS. [*Aside*] He means to feast me, and poisons me beforehand.—
I should be dearly glad to be there, sir,
Did my occasions suit as I could wish.

BEAT. I shall be sorry if you be not there
When it is done, sir; but not so suddenly.

VER. I tell you, sir, the gentleman's complete,
A courtier and a gallant, enriched
With many fair and noble ornaments;
I would not change him for a son-in-law
For any he in Spain, the proudest he,
And we have great ones, that you know.

ALS. He's much
Bound to you, sir.

VER. He shall be bound to me
As fast as this tie can hold him; I'll want
My will else.

BEAT. [*Aside*] I shall want mine, if you do it.

VER. But come, by the way I'll tell you more of him.

ALS. [*Aside*] How shall I dare to venture in his castle,

---

1. Whim, fancy.

When he discharges murderers[1] at the gate?
But I must on, for back I cannot go.

BEAT. [*Aside*] Not this serpent gone yet?

[*Drops a glove*]

VER. Look, girl, thy glove's fallen.
Stay, stay; De Flores, help a little.

Exeunt Vermandero, Alsemero, and Servants

DE F. Here, lady.

[*Offers her the glove*]

BEAT. Mischief on your officious forwardness;
Who bade you stoop? they touch my hand no more:
There! for the other's sake I part with this;

[*Takes off and throws down the other glove*]

Take 'em, and draw thine own skin off with 'em!

Exit with Diaphanta and Servants

DE F. Here's a favor come with a mischief now! I know
She had rather wear my pelt[2] tanned in a pair
Of dancing pumps, than I should thrust my fingers
Into her sockets here. I know she hates me,
Yet cannot choose but love her: no matter,
If but to vex her, I will haunt her still;
Though I get nothing else, I'll have my will.

Exit

SCENE II

Enter Alibius and Lollio

ALIB. Lollio, I must trust thee with a secret,
But thou must keep it.

LOL. I was ever close to a secret, sir.

ALIB. The diligence that I have found in thee,
The care and industry already past,
Assures me of thy good continuance.
Lollio, I have a wife.

---

1. Pieces of ordnance; also styled *murdering-pieces.*
2. Skin.

LOL. Fie, sir, 'tis too late to keep her secret; she's known to be married
  all the town and country over.

ALIB. Thou goest too fast, my Lollio; that knowledge
  I allow no man can be barred it;
  But there is a knowledge which is nearer,
  Deeper, and sweeter, Lollio.

LOL. Well, sir, let us handle that between you and I.

ALIB. 'Tis that I go about, man: Lollio,
  My wife is young.

LOL. So much the worse to be kept secret, sir.

ALIB. Why, now thou meet'st the substance of the point;
  I am old, Lollio.

LOL. No, sir, 'tis I am old Lollio.

ALIB. Yet why may not these concord and sympathise?
  Old trees and young plants often grow together,
  Well enough agreeing.

LOL. Ay, sir, but the old trees raise themselves higher and broader than
  the young plants.

ALIB. Shrewd application![1] there's the fear, man;
  I would wear my ring on my own finger;
  Whilst it is borrowed, it is none of mine,
  But his that useth it.

LOL. You must keep it on still then; if it but lie by, one or other will be
  thrusting into't.

ALIB. Thou conceiv'st me, Lollio; here thy watchful eye
  Must have employment; I cannot always be
  At home.

LOL. I dare swear you cannot.

ALIB. I must look out.

LOL. I know't, you must look out, 'tis every man's case.

ALIB. Here, I do say, must thy employment be;
  To watch her treadings, and in my absence
  Supply my place.

LOL. I'll do my best, sir; yet surely I cannot see who you should have
  cause to be jealous of.

---

1. Taking L's point that the older man may wear a cuckold's horns.

ALIB. Thy reason for that, Lollio? it is
    A comfortable question.

LOL. We have but two sorts of people in the house, and both under
    the whip, that's fools[1] and madmen; the one has not wit enough to
    be knaves, and the other not knavery enough to be fools.

ALIB. Ay, those are all my patients, Lollio;
    I do profess the cure of either sort,
    My trade, my living 'tis, I thrive by it;
    But here's the care that mixes with my thrift;
    The daily visitants, that come to see
    My brain-sick patients, I would not have
    To see my wife: gallants I do observe
    Of quick enticing eyes, rich in habits,
    Of stature and proportion very comely:
    These are most shrewd temptations, Lollio.

LOL. They may be easily answered, sir; if they come to see the fools
    and madmen, you and I may serve the turn, and let my mistress
    alone, she's of neither sort.

ALS. 'Tis a good ward;[2] indeed, come they to see
    Our madmen or our fools, let 'em see no more
    Than what they come for; but that consequent
    They must not see her, I'm sure she's no fool.

LOL. And I'm sure she's no madman.

ALIB. Hold that buckler fast, Lollio, my trust
    Is on thee, and I account it firm and strong.
    What hour is't, Lollio?

LOL. Towards belly-hour, sir.

ALIB. Dinner-time? thou mean'st twelve o'clock?

LOL. Yes, sir, for every part has his hour: we wake at six and look about
    us, that's eye-hour; at seven we should pray, that's knee-hour; at
    eight walk, that's leg-hour; at nine gather flowers and pluck a rose,[3]
    that's nose-hour; at ten we drink, that's mouth-hour; at eleven lay
    about us for victuals, that's hand-hour; at twelve go to dinner, that's
    belly-hour.

---

1. Idiots.
2. i.e., Guard (in fencing).
3. Slang for "urinate."

ALIB. Profoundly, Lollio! it will be long
   Ere all thy scholars learn this lesson, and
   I did look to have a new one entered;—stay,
   I think my expectation is come home.

Enter Pedro, and Antonio disguised as an idiot

PED. Save you, sir; my business speaks itself,
   This sight takes off the labor of my tongue.
ALIB. Ay, ay, sir, it is plain enough, you mean
   Him for my patient.
PED. And if your pains prove but commodious, to give but some little
strength to the sick and weak part of nature in him, these are [*gives
him money*] but patterns to show you of the whole pieces that will
follow to you, beside the charge of diet, washing, and other neces-
saries, fully defrayed.
ALIB. Believe it, sir, there shall no care be wanting.
LOL. Sir, an officer in this place may deserve something, the trouble
will pass through my hands.
PED. 'Tis fit something should come to your hands then, sir.
                                         [*Gives him money*]
LOL. Yes, sir, 'tis I must keep him sweet, and read to him: what is his
name?
PED. His name is Antonio; marry, we use but half to him, only Tony.
LOL. Tony, Tony, 'tis enough, and a very good name for a fool.—
What's your name, Tony?
ANT. He, he, he! well, I thank you, cousin; he, he, he!
LOL. Good boy! hold up your head.—He can laugh; I perceive by that
he is no beast.
PED. Well, sir,
   If you can raise him but to any height,
   Any degree of wit, might he attain,
   As I might say, to creep but on all four
   Towards the chair of wit, or walk on crutches,
   'Twould add an honor to your worthy pains,
   And a great family might pray for you,
   To which he should be heir, had he discretion
   To claim and guide his own: assure you, sir,
   He is a gentleman.

LOL. Nay, there's nobody doubted that; at first sight I knew him for a gentleman, he looks no other yet.

PED. Let him have good attendance and sweet lodging.

LOL. As good as my mistress lies in, sir; and as you allow us time and means, we can raise him to the higher degree of discretion.

PED. Nay, there shall no cost want, sir.

LOL. He will hardly be stretched up to the wit of a magnifico.

PED. O no, that's not to be expected; far shorter will be enough.

LOL. I'll warrant you I'll make him fit to bear office in five weeks; I'll undertake to wind him up to the wit of constable.

PED. If it be lower than that, it might serve turn.

LOL. No, fie; to level him with a headborough,[1] beadle, or watchman, were but little better than he is: constable I'll able[2] him; if he do come to be a justice afterwards, let him thank the keeper: or I'll go further with you; say I do bring him up to my own pitch, say I make him as wise as myself.

PED. Why, there I would have it.

LOL. Well, go to; either I'll be as arrant a fool as he, or he shall be as wise as I, and then I think 'twill serve his turn.

PED. Nay, I do like thy wit passing well.

LOL. Yes, you may; yet if I had not been a fool, I had had more wit than I have too; remember what state you find me in.

PED. I will, and so leave you: your best cares, I beseech you.

ALIB. Take you none with you, leave 'em all with us.

Exit Pedro

ANT. O, my cousin's gone! cousin, cousin, O!

LOL. Peace, peace, Tony; you must not cry, child, you must be whipped if you do; your cousin is here still; I am your cousin, Tony.

ANT. He, he! then I'll not cry, if thou be'st my cousin; he, he, he!

LOL. I were best try his wit a little, that I may know what form[3] to place him in.

ALIB. Ay, do, Lollio, do.

LOL. I must ask him easy questions at first.—Tony, how many true fingers has a tailor on his right hand?

---

1. Parish officer.
2. Fit him for.
3. Class in school.

ANT. As many as on his left, cousin.

LOL. Good: and how many on both?

ANT. Two less than a deuce,[1] cousin.

LOL. Very well answered: I come to you again, cousin Tony; how many fools goes to a wise man?

ANT. Forty in a day sometimes, cousin.

LOL. Forty in a day? how prove you that?

ANT. All that fall out amongst themselves, and go to a lawyer to be made friends.

LOL. A parlous fool! he must sit in the fourth form at least, I perceive that—I come again, Tony; how many knaves make an honest man?

ANT. I know not that, cousin.

LOL. No, the question is too hard for you: I'll tell you, cousin; there's three knaves may make an honest man, a sergeant, a jailor, and a beadle; the sergeant catches him, the jailor holds him, and the beadle lashes him; and if he be not honest then, the hangman must cure him.

ANT. Ha, ha, ha! that's fine sport, cousin.

ALIB. This was too deep a question for the fool, Lollio.

LOL. Yes, this might have served yourself, though I say't.—Once more and you shall go play, Tony.

ANT. Ay, play at push-pin,[2] cousin; ha, he!

LOL. So thou shalt: say how many fools are here—

ANT. Two, cousin; thou and I.

LOL. Nay, you're too forward there, Tony: mark my question; how many fools and knaves are here; a fool before a knave, a fool behind a knave, between every two fools a knave; how many fools, how many knaves?

ANT. I never learnt so far, cousin.

ALIB. Thou puttest too hard questions to him, Lollio.

LOL. I'll make him understand it easily.—Cousin, stand there.

ANT. Ay, cousin.

LOL. Master, stand you next the fool.

ALIB. Well, Lollio.

LOL. Here's my place: mark now, Tony, there's a fool before a knave.

---

1. i.e., None.

2. Children's game played with pins.

ANT. That's I, cousin.

LOL. Here's a fool behind a knave, that's I; and between us two fools there is a knave, that's my master; 'tis but we three, that's all.

ANT. We three, we three, cousin.

1ST MAD. [*Within*] Put's head i' th' pillory, the bread's too little.

2ND MAD. [*Within*] Fly, fly, and he catches the swallow.

3RD MAD. [*Within*] Give her more onion, or the devil put the rope about her crag.[1]

LOL. You may hear what time of day it is, the chimes of Bedlam goes.

ALIB. Peace, peace, or the wire[2] comes!

3RD MAD. [*Within*] Cat whore, cat whore! her parmasant, her parmasant![3]

ALIB. Peace, I say!—Their hour's come, they must be fed, Lollio.

LOL. There's no hope of recovery of that Welsh madman; was undone by a mouse that spoiled him a parmasant; lost his wits for't.

ALIB. Go to your charge, Lollio; I'll to mine.

LOL. Go you to your madman's ward, let me alone with your fools.

ALIB. And remember my last charge, Lollio.

Exit

LOL. Of which your patients do you think I am?—Come, Tony, you must amongst your school-fellows now; there's pretty scholars amongst 'em, I can tell you; there's some of 'em at *stultus, stulta, stultum.*

ANT. I would see the madmen, cousin, if they would not bite me.

LOL. No, they shall not bite thee, Tony.

ANT. They bite when they are at dinner, do they not, coz?

LOL. They bite at dinner indeed, Tony. Well, I hope to get credit by thee; I like thee the best of all the scholars that ever I brought up, and thou shalt prove a wise man, or I'll prove a fool myself.

Exeunt

1. Neck.
2. Whip.
3. Parmesan cheese.

ACT II, SCENE I

Enter Beatrice and Jasperino severally

BEAT. O sir, I'm ready now for that fair service
    Which makes the name of friend sit glorious on you!
    Good angels and this conduct be your guide!
                             [Giving a paper]
    Fitness of time and place is there set down, sir.
JAS. The joy I shall return rewards my service.
                                 Exit

BEAT. How wise is Alsemero in his friend!
    It is a sign he makes his choice with judgment;
    Then I appear in nothing more approved
    Than making choice of him; for 'tis a principle,
    He that can choose
    That bosom well who of his thoughts partakes,
    Proves most discreet in every choice he makes.
    Methinks I love now with the eyes of judgment,
    And see the way to merit, clearly see it.
    A true deserver like a diamond sparkles;
    In darkness you may see him, that's in absence,
    Which is the greatest darkness falls on love;
    Yet is he best discernèd then
    With intellectual eyesight. What's Piracquo,
    My father spends his breath for? and his blessing
    Is only mine as I regard his name,
    Else it goes from me, and turns head against me,
    Transformed into a curse: some speedy way
    Must be remembered; he's so forward too,
    So urgent that way, scarce allows me breath
    To speak to my new comforts.

Enter De Flores

DE F. *[Aside]* Yonder's she;
    Whatever ails me, now a-late especially,
    I can as well be hanged as refrain seeing her;

Some twenty times a day, nay, not so little,
Do I force errands, frame ways and excuses,
To come into her sight; and I've small reason for't,
And less encouragement, for she baits me still
Every time worse than other; does profess herself
The cruellest enemy to my face in town;
At no hand can abide the sight of me,
As if danger or ill-luck hung in my looks.
I must confess my face is bad enough,
But I know far worse has better fortune,
And not endured alone, but doted on;
And yet such pick-haired[1] faces, chins like witches',
Here and there five hairs whispering in a corner,
As if they grew in fear one of another,
Wrinkles like troughs, where swine-deformity swills
The tears of perjury, that lie there like wash
Fallen from the slimy and dishonest eye;
Yet such a one plucks sweets without restraint,
And has the grace of beauty to his sweet.[2]
Though my hard fate has thrust me out to servitude,
I tumbled into th' world a gentleman.
She turns her blessèd eye upon me now,
And I'll endure all storms before I part with't.

BEAT. Again?
    [*Aside*] This ominous ill-faced fellow more disturbs me
    Than all my other passions.

DE F. [*Aside*] Now 't begins again;
    I'll stand this storm of hail, though the stones pelt me.

BEAT. Thy business? what's thy business?

DE F. [*Aside*] Soft and fair!
    I cannot part so soon now.

BEAT. The villain's fixed.—
    Thou standing toad-pool—

---

1. Bristly.
2. Sweetheart.

DE F. [*Aside*] The shower falls amain now.

BEAT. Who sent thee? what's thy errand? leave my sight!

DE F. My lord, your father, charged me to deliver
    A message to you.

BEAT. What, another since?
    Do't, and be hanged then; let me be rid of thee.

DE F. True service merits mercy.

BEAT. What's thy message?

DE F. Let beauty settle but in patience,
    You shall hear all.

BEAT. A dallying, trifling torment!

DE F. Signor Alonzo de Piracquo, lady,
    Sole brother to Tomaso de Piracquo—

BEAT. Slave, when wilt make an end?

DE F. Too soon I shall.

BEAT. What all this while of him?

DE F. The said Alonzo,
    With the foresaid Tomaso—

BEAT. Yet again?

DE F. Is new alighted.

BEAT. Vengeance strike the news!
    Thou thing most loathed, what cause was there in this
    To bring thee to my sight?

DE F. My lord, your father,
    Charged me to seek you out.

BEAT. Is there no other
    To send his errand by?

DE F. It seems 'tis my luck
    To be i' th' way still.

BEAT. Get thee from me!

DE F. So:
    [*Aside*] Why, am not I an ass to devise ways
    Thus to be railed at? I must see her still!
    I shall have a mad qualm within this hour again,
    I know't; and, like a common Garden-bull,[1]

---

1. Paris Garden, where bulls were baited.

I do but take breath to be lugged[1] again.
What this may bode I know not; I'll despair the less,
Because there's daily precedents of bad faces
Beloved beyond all reason; these foul chops
May come into favor one day 'mongst their fellows:
Wrangling has proved the mistress of good pastime;
As children cry themselves asleep, I ha' seen
Women have chid themselves a-bed to men.

Exit

BEAT. I never see this fellow but I think
Of some harm towards me, danger's in my mind still;
I scarce leave trembling of[2] an hour after:
The next good mood I find my father in,
I'll get him quite discarded. O, I was
Lost in this small disturbance, and forgot
Affliction's fiercer torment that now comes
To bear down all my comforts!

Enter Vermandero, Alonzo, and Tomaso

VER. You're both welcome,
But an especial one belongs to you, sir,
To whose most noble name our love presents
Th' addition[3] of a son, our son Alonzo.
ALON. The treasury of honor cannot bring forth
A title I should more rejoice in, sir.
VER. You have improved it well.—Daughter, prepare;
The day will steal upon thee suddenly.
BEAT. [*Aside*] Howe'er I will be sure to keep the night,
If it should come so near me.

[*Beatrice and Vermandero talk apart*]

TOM. Alonzo.
ALON. Brother?
TOM. In troth I see small welcome in her eye.

---

1. Dragged by the ear.
2. For.
3. Title.

ALON. Fie, you are too severe a censurer
    Of love in all points, there's no bringing on you:[1]
    If lovers should mark everything a fault,
    Affection would be like an ill-set book,
    Whose faults might prove as big as half the volume.
BEAT. That's all I do entreat.
VER. It is but reasonable;
    I'll see what my son says to't.—Son Alonzo,
    Here is a motion made but to reprieve
    A maidenhead three days longer; the request
    Is not far out of reason, for indeed
    The former time is pinching.[2]
ALON. Though my joys
    Be set back so much time as I could wish
    They had been forward, yet since she desires it,
    The time is set as pleasing as before,
    I find no gladness wanting.
VER. May I ever
    Meet it in that point still! you're nobly welcome, sirs.

Exit with Beatrice

TOM. So; did you mark the dulness of her parting now?
ALON. What dulness? thou art so exceptious[3] still!
TOM. Why, let it go then; I am but a fool
    To mark your harms so heedfully.
ALON. Where's the oversight?
TOM. Come, your faith's cozened in her, strongly cozened:
    Unsettle your affections with all speed
    Wisdom can bring it to; your peace is ruined else.
    Think what a torment 'tis to marry one
    Whose heart is leaped into another's bosom:
    If ever pleasure she receive from thee,
    It comes not in thy name, or of thy gift;

1. Persuading you.
2. Too constricting.
3. Quick to see objections.

She lies but with another in thine arms,
He the half-father unto all thy children
In the conception; if he get 'em not,
She helps to get 'em for him; and how dangerous
And shameful her restraint may go in time to,
It is not to be thought on without sufferings.

ALON. You speak as if she loved some other, then.

TOM. Do you apprehend so slowly?

ALON. Nay, an that
Be your fear only, I am safe enough:
Preserve your friendship and your counsel, brother,
For times of more distress; I should depart
An enemy, a dangerous, deadly one,
To any but thyself, that should but think
She knew the meaning of inconstancy,
Much less the use and practice: yet we're friends;
Pray, let no more be urged; I can endure
Much, till I meet an injury to her,
Then I am not myself. Farewell, sweet brother;
How much we're bound to Heaven to depart lovingly.

Exit

TOM. Why, here is love's tame madness; thus a man
Quickly steals into his vexation.

Exit

SCENE II

Enter Diaphanta and Alsemero

DIA. The place is my charge; you have kept your hour,
And the reward of a just meeting bless you!
I hear my lady coming: complete gentleman,
I dare not be too busy with my praises,
They're dangerous things to deal with.

Exit

ALS. This goes well;
These women are the ladies' cabinets,
Things of most precious trust are locked into 'em.

Enter Beatrice

BEAT. I have within mine eye all my desires:
    Requests that holy prayers ascend Heaven for,
    And brings 'em down to furnish our defects,
    Come not more sweet to our necessities
    Than thou unto my wishes.
ALS. We're so like
    In our expressions, lady, that unless I borrow
    The same words, I shall never find their equals.
BEAT. How happy were this meeting, this embrace,
    If it were free from envy! this poor kiss
    It has an enemy, a hateful one,
    That wishes poison to't: how well were I now,
    If there were none such name known as Piracquo,
    Nor no such tie as the command of parents!
    I should be but too much blessed.
ALS. One good service
    Would strike off both your fears, and I'll go near't too,
    Since you are so distressed; remove the cause,
    The command ceases; so there's two fears blown out
    With one and the same blast.
BEAT. Pray, let me find you, sir:
    What might that service be, so strangely happy?
ALS. The honorablest piece about man, valor:
    I'll send a challenge to Piracquo instantly.
BEAT. How? call you that extinguishing of fear,
    When 'tis the only way to keep it flaming?
    Are not you ventured[1] in the action,
    That's all my joys and comforts? pray, no more, sir:
    Say you prevailed, you're danger's and not mine[2] then:
    The law would claim you from me, or obscurity
    Be made the grave to bury you alive.
    I'm glad these thoughts come forth; O, keep not one
    Of this condition, sir! here was a course
    Found to bring sorrow on her way to death;

1. Risked.
2. You belong to danger, not to me.

The tears would ne'er ha' dried, till dust had choked 'em.
Blood-guiltiness becomes a fouler visage;—
[*Aside*] And now I think on one;[1] I was to blame,
I ha' marred so good a market with my scorn;
'Thad been done questionless: the ugliest creature
Creation framed for some use: yet to see
I could not mark[2] so much where it should be!

ALS. Lady—

BEAT. [*Aside*] Why, men of art make much of poison,
Keep one to expel another; where was my art?

ALS. Lady, you hear not me.

BEAT. I do especially, sir:
The present times are not so sure of our side
As those hereafter may be; we must use 'em then
As thrifty folks their wealth, sparingly now,
Till the time opens.

ALS. You teach wisdom, lady.

BEAT. Within there! Diaphanta!

Re-enter Diaphanta

DIA. Did you call, madam?

BEAT. Perfect your service, and conduct this gentleman
The private way you brought him.

DIA. I shall, madam.

ALS. My love's as firm as love e'er built upon.

Exit with Diaphanta

Enter De Flores

DE F. [*Aside*] I've watched this meeting, and do wonder much
What shall become of t'other; I'm sure both
Cannot be served unless she transgresses; haply
Then I'll put in for one; for if a woman
Fly from one point, from him she makes a husband,
She spreads and mounts then like arithmetic;
One, ten, a hundred, a thousand, ten thousand.

1. De Flores.
2. Perceive.

Proves in time sutler[1] to an army royal.
Now do I look to be most richly railed at,
Yet I must see her.

BEAT. [*Aside*] Why, put case I loathed him
As much as youth and beauty hates a sepulchre,
Must I needs show it? cannot I keep that secret,
And serve my turn upon him? See, he's here.—
De Flores.

DE F. [*Aside*] Ha, I shall run mad with joy!
She called me fairly by my name De Flores,
And neither rogue nor rascal.

BEAT. What ha' you done
To your face a' late? you've met with some good physician;
You've pruned yourself, methinks: you were not wont
To look so amorously.

DE F. Not I;—
[*Aside*] 'Tis the same physnomy, to a hair and pimple,
Which she called scurvy scarce an hour ago:
How is this?

BEAT. Come hither; nearer, man.

DE F. [*Aside*] I'm up to the chin in Heaven!

BEAT. Turn, let me see;
Faugh, 'tis but the heat of the liver, I perceive't;
I thought it had been worse.

DE F. [*Aside*] Her fingers touched me!
She smells all amber.[2]

BEAT. I'll make a water for you shall cleanse this
Within a fortnight.

DE F. With your own hands, lady?

BEAT. Yes, mine own, sir; in a work of cure
I'll trust no other.

DE F. [*Aside*] 'Tis half an act of pleasure
To hear her talk thus to me.

---

1. Camp-follower; whore.
2. Ambergris.

BEAT. When we're used
    To a hard face, it is not so unpleasing;
    It mends still in opinion, hourly mends;
    I see it by experience.
DE F. [*Aside*] I was blessed
    To light upon this minute; I'll make use on't.
BEAT. Hardness becomes the visage of a man well;
    It argues service, resolution, manhood,
    If cause were of employment.
DE F. 'Twould be soon seen
    If e'er your ladyship had cause to use it;
    I would but wish the honor of a service
    So happy as that mounts to.
BEAT. We shall try you:
    O my De Flores!
DE F. [*Aside*] How's that? she calls me hers!
    Already, *my* De Flores! —You were about
    To sigh out somewhat, madam?
BEAT. No, was I?
    I forgot,—O!—
DE F. There 'tis again, the very fellow on't.
BEAT. You are too quick, sir.
DE F. There's no excuse for't now; I heard it twice, madam;
    That sigh would fain have utterance: take pity on't,
    And lend it a free word; 'las, how it labors
    For liberty! I hear the murmur yet
    Beat at your bosom.
BEAT. Would creation—
DE F. Ay, well said, that is it.
BEAT. Had formed me man!
DE F. Nay, that's not it.
BEAT. O, 'tis the soul of freedom!
    I should not then be forced to marry one
    I hate beyond all depths; I should have power
    Then to oppose my loathings, nay, remove 'em
    For ever from my sight.
DE F. [*Aside*] O blessed occasion!

Without change to your sex you have your wishes;
Claim so much man in me.

BEAT. In thee, De Flores?
There is small cause for that.

DE F. Put it not from me,
It is a service that I kneel for to you.

[*Kneels*]

BEAT. You are too violent to mean faithfully:
There's horror in my service, blood and danger;
Can those be things to sue for?

DE F. If you knew
How sweet it were to me to be employed
In any act of yours, you would say then
I failed, and used not reverence enough
When I received the charge on't.

BEAT. [*Aside*] This is much, methinks;
Belike his wants are greedy; and to such
Gold tastes like angel's food. —De Flores, rise.

DE F. I'll have the work first.

BEAT. [*Aside*] Possible his need
Is strong upon him. —There's to encourage thee;

[*Gives money*]

As thou art forward, and thy service dangerous,
Thy reward shall be precious.

DE F. That I've thought on;
I have assured myself of that beforehand,
And know it will be precious; the thought ravishes!

BEAT. Then take him to thy fury!

DE F. I thirst for him.

BEAT. Alonzo de Piracquo.

DE F. [*Rising*] His end's upon him;
He shall be seen no more.

BEAT. How lovely now
Dost thou appear to me! never was man
Dearlier rewarded.

DE F. I do think of that.

BEAT. Be wondrous careful in the execution.

DE F. Why, are not both our lives upon the cast?

BEAT. Then I throw all my fears upon thy service.

DE F. They ne'er shall rise to hurt you.

BEAT. When the deed's done,
  I'll furnish thee with all things for thy flight;
  Thou may'st live bravely in another country.

DE F. Ay, ay;
  We'll talk of that hereafter.

BEAT. [*Aside*] I shall rid myself
  Of two inveterate loathings at one time,
  Piracquo, and his dog-face.

Exit

DE F. O my blood!
  Methinks I feel her in mine arms already;
  Her wanton fingers combing out this beard,
  And, being pleasèd, praising this bad face.
  Hunger and pleasure, they'll commend sometimes
  Slovenly dishes, and feed heartily on 'em.
  Nay, which is stranger, refuse daintier for 'em:
  Some women are odd feeders.—I am too loud.
  Here comes the man goes supperless to bed,
  Yet shall not rise to-morrow to his dinner.

Enter Alonzo

ALON. De Flores.

DE F. My kind, honorable lord?

ALON. I'm glad I ha' met with thee.

DE F. Sir?

ALON. Thou canst show me
  The full strength of the castle?

DE F. That I can, sir.

ALON. I much desire it.

DE F. And if the ways and straits
  Of some of the passages be not too tedious for you,
  I'll assure you, worth your time and sight, my lord.

ALON. Pooh, that shall be no hindrance.

DE F. I'm your servant, then:

'Tis now near dinner-time; 'gainst your lordship's rising
I'll have the keys about me.
ALON. Thanks, kind De Flores.
DE F. [*Aside*] He's safely thrust upon me beyond hopes.

Exeunt severally

ACT III, SCENE I

*Enter Alonzo and De Flores. (In the act-time[1] De Flores hides a
naked rapier behind a door)*

DE FLORES. Yes, here are all the keys;
 I was afraid, my lord,
 I'd wanted for the postern, this is it:
 I've all, I've all, my lord: this for the sconce.[2]
ALON. 'Tis a most spacious and impregnable fort.
DE F. You will tell me more, my lord: this descent
 Is somewhat narrow, we shall never pass
 Well with our weapons, they'll but trouble us.
ALON. Thou sayest true.
DE F. Pray, let me help your lordship.
ALON. 'Tis done: thanks, kind De Flores.
DE F. Here are hooks, my lord,
 To hang such things on purpose.
        [*Hanging up his own sword and that of Alonzo*]
ALON. Lead, I'll follow thee.

Exeunt

1. i.e., Between the acts.
2. Small fort.

SCENE II

Enter Alonzo and De Flores

DE F. All this is nothing; you shall see anon
    A place you little dream on.
ALON. I am glad
    I have this leisure; all your master's house
    Imagine I ha' taken a gondola.
DE F. All but myself, sir, [*Aside*] —which makes up my safety.
    My lord, I'll place you at a casement here
    Will show you the full strength of all the castle.
    Look, spend your eye awhile upon that object.
ALON. Here's rich variety, De Flores.
DE F. Yes, sir.
ALON. Goodly munition.
DE F. Ay, there's ordnance, sir,
    No bastard metal, will ring you a peal like bells
    At great men's funerals: keep your eye straight, my lord;
    Take special notice of that sconce before you,
    There you may dwell awhile.
                [*Takes the rapier which he had hid behind the door*]
ALON. I am upon't.
DE F. And so am I.
                                 [*Stabs him*]
ALON. De Flores! O De Flores!
    Whose malice hast thou put on?
DE F. Do you question
    A work of secrecy? I must silence you.
                                 [*Stabs him*]
ALON. O, O, O!
DE F. I must silence you.
                                 [*Stabs him*]
    So here's an undertaking well accomplished:
    This vault serves to good use now: ha, what's that
    Threw sparkles in my eye? O, 'tis a diamond
    He wears upon his finger; 'twas well found,

This will approve the work.[1] What, so fast on?
Not part in death? I'll take a speedy course then.
Finger and all shall off. [*Cuts off the finger*] So, now I'll clear
The passages from all suspect or fear.

Exit with body

SCENE III

Enter Isabella and Lollio

ISA. Why, sirrah, whence have you commission
      To fetter the doors against me?
      If you keep me in a cage, pray, whistle to me,[2]
      Let me be doing something.
LOL. You shall be doing, if it please you; I'll whistle to you, if you'll
      pipe after.
ISA. Is it your master's pleasure, or your own,
      To keep me in this pinfold?[3]
LOL. 'Tis for my master's pleasure, lest being taken in another man's
      corn, you might be pounded in another place.
ISA. 'Tis very well, and he'll prove very wise.
LOL. He says you have company enough in the house, if you please to
      be sociable, of all sorts of people.
ISA. Of all sorts? why, here's none but fools and madmen.
LOL. Very well: and where will you find any other, if you should go
      abroad? there's my master, and I to boot too.
ISA. Of either sort one, a madman and a fool.
LOL. I would even participate of both then if I were as you; I know
      you're half mad already, be half foolish too.
ISA. You're a brave saucy rascal! come on, sir,
      Afford me then the pleasure of your bedlam;
      You were commending once to-day to me
      Your last-come lunatic; what a proper[4]
      Body there was without brains to guide it,

1. i.e., Prove it has been done.
2. As to a caged bird.
3. Pound for strayed cattle.
4. Handsome.

And what a pitiful delight appeared
In that defect, as if your wisdom had found
A mirth in madness; pray, sir, let me partake,
If there be such a pleasure.

LOL. If I do not show you the handsomest, discreetest madman, one that I may call the understanding madman, then say I am a fool.

ISA. Well, a match, I will say so.

LOL. When you have had a taste of the madman, you shall, if you please, see Fool's College, o' th' other side. I seldom lock there; 'tis but shooting a bolt or two, and you are amongst 'em. [*Exit, and brings in Franciscus*]—Come on, sir; let me see how handsomely you'll behave yourself now.

FRAN. How sweetly she looks! O, but there's a wrinkle in her brow as deep as philosophy. Anacreon,[1] drink to my mistress' health, I'll pledge it; stay, stay, there's a spider in the cup! no, 'tis but a grapestone; swallow it, fear nothing, poet; so, so, lift higher.

ISA. Alack, alack, it is too full of pity
To be laughed at! How fell he mad? canst thou tell?

LOL. For love, mistress: he was a pretty poet too, and that set him forwards first: the muses then forsook him; he ran mad for a chambermaid, yet she was but a dwarf neither.

FRAN. Hail, bright Titania!
Why stand'st thou idle on these flowery banks?
Oberon is dancing with his Dryades;
I'll gather daisies, primrose, violets,
And bind them in a verse of poesy.

LOL. [*Holding up a whip*] Not too near! you see your danger.

FRAN. O, hold thy hand, great Diomede![2]
Thou feed'st thy horses well, they shall obey thee:
Get up, Bucephalus[3] kneels.

[*Kneels*]

LOL. You see how I awe my flock; a shepherd has not his dog at more obedience.

---

1. The Greek poet said to have choked on a grape pip.
2. He fed his horses on human flesh.
3. Alexander's horse, which only he could ride.

ISA. His conscience is unquiet; sure that was
    The cause of this: a proper gentleman!
FRAN. Come hither, Æsculapius;[1] hide the poison.
LOL. Well, 'tis hid.

                                       [Hides the whip]

FRAN. Didst thou ne'er hear of one Tiresias,[2]
    A famous poet?
LOL. Yes, that kept tame wild geese.
FRAN. Tha's he; I am the man.
LOL. No?
FRAN. Yes; but make no words on't: I was a man
    Seven years ago.
LOL. A stripling, I think, you might.
FRAN. Now I'm a woman, all feminine.
LOL. I would I might see that!
FRAN. Juno struck me blind.
LOL. I'll never believe that: for a woman, they say, has an eye more
    than a man.
FRAN. I say she struck me blind.
LOL. And Luna made you mad: you have two trades to beg with.
FRAN. Luna is now big-bellied, and there's room
    For both of us to ride with Hecate;
    I'll drag thee up into her silver sphere,
    And there we'll kick the dog—and beat the bush—
    That barks against the witches of the night;
    The swift lycanthropi[3] that walks the round,
    We'll tear their wolvish skins, and save the sheep.

                                  [Attempts to seize Lollio]

LOL. Is't come to this? nay, then, my poison comes forth again *[show-*
    ing the whip]: mad slave, indeed, abuse your keeper!
ISA. I prithee, hence with him, now he grows dangerous.
FRAN. *[Sings]* Sweet love, pity me,
    Give me leave to lie with thee.
LOL. No, I'll see you wiser first: to your own kennel!

---

1. Greek god of medicine.
2. The seer who changed his sex.
3. Persons suffering from *lycanthropia*, or wolf-madness, at one time believed to be
common.

FRAN. No noise, she sleeps; draw all the curtains round,
Let no soft sound molest the pretty soul,
But love, and love creeps in at a mouse-hole.

LOL. I would you would get into your hole! [*Exit Franciscus*]—Now,
mistress, I will bring you another sort; you shall be fooled another
while. [*Exit, and brings in Antonio*]—Tony, come hither, Tony: look
who's yonder, Tony.

ANT. Cousin, is it not my aunt?[1]

LOL. Yes, 'tis one of 'em, Tony.

ANT. He, he! how do you, uncle?

LOL. Fear him not, mistress, 'tis a gentle nigget;[2] you may play with
him, as safely with him as with his bauble.

ISA. How long hast thou been a fool?

ANT. Ever since I came hither, cousin.

ISA. Cousin? I'm none of thy cousins, fool.

LOL. O, mistress, fools have always so much wit as to claim their kindred.

MADMAN [*Within*] Bounce, bounce! he falls, he falls!

ISA. Hark you, your scholars in the upper room
Are out of order.

LOL. Must I come amongst you there?—Keep you the fool, mistress;
I'll go up and play left-handed Orlando amongst the madmen.

Exit

ISA. Well, sir.

ANT. 'Tis opportuneful now, sweet lady! nay,
Cast no amazing eye upon this change.

ISA. Ha!

ANT. This shape of folly shrouds your dearest love,
The truest servant to your powerful beauties,
Whose magic had this force thus to transform me.

ISA. You're a fine fool indeed!

ANT. O, 'tis not strange!
Love has an intellect that runs through all
The scrutinous sciences, and, like a cunning poet,
Catches a quantity of every knowledge,

---

1. Cant term for procuress or bawd.
2. Nidget, i.e., idiot.

Yet brings all home into one mystery,
Into one secret, that he proceeds in.

ISA. You're a parlous fool.

ANT. No danger in me; I bring nought but love
And his soft-wounding shafts to strive you with:
Try but one arrow; if it hurt you, I
Will stand you twenty back in recompense.

ISA. A forward fool too!

ANT. This was love's teaching:
A thousand ways he fashioned out my way,
And this I found the safest and the nearest,
To tread the galaxia to my star.

ISA. Profound withal! certain you dreamed of this,
Love never taught it waking.

ANT. Take no acquaintance
Of these outward follies, there's within
A gentleman that loves you.

ISA. When I see him,
I'll speak with him; so, in the meantime, keep
Your habit, it becomes you well enough:
As you're a gentleman, I'll not discover you;
That's all the favor that you must expect:
When you are weary, you may leave the school,
For all this while you have but played the fool.

Re-enter Lollio

ANT. And must again.—He, he! I thank you, cousin;
I'll be your valentine to-morrow morning.

LOL. How do you like the fool, mistress?

ISA. Passing well, sir.

LOL. Is he not witty, pretty well, for a fool?

ISA. If he holds on as he begins, he's like
To come to something.

LOL. Ay, thank a good tutor: you may put him to't; he begins to answer
pretty hard questions.—Tony, how many is five times six?

ANT. Five times six is six times five.

LOL. What arithmetician could have answered better?
How many is one hundred and seven?

ANT. One hundred and seven is seven hundred and one, cousin.

LOL. This is no wit to speak on!—Will you be rid of the fool now?

ISA. By no means; let him stay a little.

MADMAN [*Within*] Catch there, catch the last couple in hell![1]

LOL. Again! must I come amongst you? Would my master were come
    home! I am not able to govern both these wards together.

                                       Exit

ANT. Why should a minute of love's hour be lost?

ISA. Fie, out[2] again! I had rather you kept
    Your other posture; you become not your tongue
    When you speak from your clothes.

ANT. How can he freeze
    Lives near so sweet a warmth? shall I alone
    Walk through the orchard of th' Hesperides,[3]
    And, cowardly, not dare to pull an apple?

             Enter Lollio above

This with the red cheeks I must venture for.

                     [*Attempts to kiss her*]

ISA. Take heed, there's giants keep 'em.

LOL. How now, fool, are you good at that? have you read Lipsius?[4]
    [*Aside*] he's past *Ars Amandi*;[5] I believe I must put harder questions to
    him, I perceive that.

ISA. You're bold without fear too.

ANT. What should I fear,
    Having all joys about me? Do you but smile,
    And love shall play the wanton on your lip,
    Meet and retire, retire and meet again;
    Look you but cheerfully, and in your eyes
    I shall behold mine own deformity,
    And dress myself up fairer: I know this shape

---

1. An allusion to the game of barley-break, the ground for which was divided into three
compartments, of which the middle one was termed "hell."

2. Forgetting your part.

3. Mythical garden in which the trees bore golden apples, guarded by a dragon.

4. Famous scholar (here mentioned to provide a pun on "lips").

5. Ovid's *Art of Love*.

Becomes me not, but in those bright mirrors
I shall array me handsomely.

[*Cries of madmen are heard within, like those of birds and beasts*]

LOL. Cuckoo, cuckoo!

Exit above

ANT. What are these?

ISA. Of fear enough to part us;
Yet are they but our schools of lunatics,
That act their fantasies in any shapes,
Suiting their present thoughts: if sad, they cry;
If mirth be their conceit, they laugh again:
Sometimes they imitate the beasts and birds,
Singing or howling, braying, barking; all
As their wild fancies prompt 'em.

ANT. These are no fears.

ISA. But here's a large one, my man.

Re-enter Lollio

ANT. Ha, he! that's fine sport indeed, cousin.

LOL. I would my master were come home! 'tis too much for one shepherd to govern two of these flocks; nor can I believe that one churchman can instruct two benefices at once; there will be some incurable
mad of the one side, and very fools on the other.—Come, Tony.

ANT. Prithee, cousin, let me stay here still.

LOL. No, you must to your book now; you have played sufficiently.

ISA. Your fool has grown wondrous witty.

LOL. Well, I'll say nothing: but I do not think but he will put you down
one of these days.

Exit with Antonio

ISA. Here the restrainèd current might make breach,
Spite of the watchful bankers: would a woman stray,
She need not gad abroad to seek her sin,
It would be brought home one way or other:
The needle's point will to the fixèd north;
Such drawing arctics[1] women's beauties are.

___

1. North poles.

Re-enter Lollio

LOL. How dost thou, sweet rogue?

ISA. How now?

LOL. Come, there are degrees; one fool may be better than another.

ISA. What's the matter?

LOL. Nay, if thou givest thy mind to fool's flesh, have at thee!

[*Tries to kiss her*]

ISA. You bold slave, you!

LOL. I could follow now as t'other fool did:
  "What should I fear,
  Having all joys about me? Do you but smile,
  And love shall play the wanton on your lip,
  Meet and retire, retire and meet again;
  Look you but cheerfully, and in your eyes
  I shall behold my own deformity,
  And dress myself up fairer: I know this shape
  Becomes me not—"
  And so as it follows: but is not this the more foolish way? Come,
  sweet rogue; kiss me, my little Lacedæmonian;[1] let me feel how thy
  pulses beat; thou hast a thing about thee would do a man pleasure,
  I'll lay my hand on't.

ISA. Sirrah, no more! I see you have discovered
  This love's knight errant, who hath made adventure
  For purchase of my love: be silent, mute,
  Mute as a statue, or his injunction
  For me enjoying, shall be to cut thy throat;
  I'll do it, though for no other purpose; and
  Be sure he'll not refuse it.

LOL. My share, that's all;
  I'll have my fool's part with you.

ISA. No more! your master.

Enter Alibius

ALIB. Sweet, how dost thou?

ISA. Your bounden servant, sir.

---

1. Perhaps slang for "prostitute."

ALIB. Fie, fie, sweetheart,
  No more of that.
ISA. You were best lock me up.
ALIB. In my arms and bosom, my sweet Isabella,
  I'll lock thee up most nearly.—Lollio,
  We have employment, we have task in hand:
  At noble Vermandero's, our castle's captain,
  There is a nuptial to be solemnised—
  Beatrice-Joanna, his fair daughter, bride—
  For which the gentleman hath bespoke our pains,
  A mixture of our madmen and our fools,
  To finish, as it were, and make the fag[1]
  Of all the revels, the third night from the first;
  Only an unexpected passage over,
  To make a frightful pleasure,[2] that is all,
  But not the all I aim at; could we so act it,
  To teach it in a wild distracted measure,
  Though out of form and figure, breaking time's head,[3]
  It were no matter, 'twould be healed again
  In one age or other, if not in this:
  This, this, Lollio, there's a good reward begun,
  And will beget a bounty, be it known.
LOL. This is easy, sir, I'll warrant you: you have about you fools and
  madmen that can dance very well; and 'tis no wonder, your best
  dancers are not the wisest men; the reason is, with often jumping
  they jolt their brains down into their feet, that their wits lie more in
  their heels than in their heads.
ALIB. Honest Lollio, thou giv'st me a good reason,
  And a comfort in it.
ISA. You've a fine trade on't;
  Madmen and fools are a staple commodity.
ALIB. O wife, we must eat, wear clothes, and live:
  Just at the lawyer's haven we arrive,
  By madmen and by fools we both do thrive.

                                                    Exeunt

1. Fag end.
2. To scare the audience.
3. Not keeping time.

SCENE IV

Enter Vermandero, Beatrice, Alsemero, and Jasperino

VER. Valencia speaks so nobly of you, sir,
  I wish I had a daughter now for you.
ALS. The fellow of this creature were a partner
  For a king's love.
VER. I had her fellow once, sir,
  But Heaven has married her to joys eternal;
  'Twere sin to wish her in this vale again.
  Come, sir, your friend and you shall see the pleasures
  Which my health¹ chiefly joys in.
ALS. I hear
  The beauty of this seat largely commended.
VER. It falls much short of that.

Exit with Alsemero and Jasperino

BEAT. So, here's one step
  Into my father's favor; time will fix him;
  I've got him now the liberty of the house;
  So wisdom, by degrees, works out her freedom:
  And if that eye be darkened that offends me,—
  I wait but that eclipse,—this gentleman
  Shall soon shine glorious in my father's liking,
  Through the refulgent virtue of my love.

Enter De Flores

DE F. [*Aside*] My thoughts are at a banquet; for the deed,
  I feel no weight in't; 'tis but light and cheap
  For the sweet recompense that I set down for't.
BEAT. De Flores?
DE F. Lady?
BEAT. Thy looks promise cheerfully.
DE F. All things are answerable, time, circumstance,
  Your wishes, and my service.
BEAT. It is done, then?

---

1. i.e., Such health as I have.

DE F. Piracquo is no more.

BEAT. My joys start at mine eyes; our sweet'st delights
Are evermore born weeping.

DE F. I've a token for you.

BEAT. For me?

DE F. But it was sent somewhat unwillingly;
I could not get the ring without the finger.

[*Producing the finger and ring*]

BEAT. Bless me, what hast thou done?

DE F. Why, is that more
Than killing the whole man? I cut his heart-strings;
A greedy hand thrust in a dish at court,
In a mistake hath had as much as this.

BEAT. 'Tis the first token my father made me send him.

DE F. And I have made him send it back again
For his last token; I was loath to leave it,
And I'm sure dead men have no use of jewels;
He was as loath to part with't, for it stuck
As if the flesh and it were both one substance.

BEAT. At the stag's fall, the keeper has his fees;
'Tis soon applied, all dead men's fees are yours, sir:
I pray, bury the finger, but the stone
You may make use on shortly; the true value,
Tak't of my truth, is near three hundred ducats.

DE F. 'Twill hardly buy a capcase[1] for one's conscience though,
To keep it from the worm, as fine as 'tis:
Well, being my fees, I'll take it;
Great men have taught me that, or else my merit
Would scorn the way on't.

BEAT. It might justly, sir;
Why, thou mistak'st, De Flores, 'tis not given
In state of recompense.

DE F. No, I hope so, lady;
You should soon witness my contempt to't then.

BEAT. Prithee,—thou look'st as if thou wert offended.

1. Small case.

DE F. That were strange, lady; 'tis not possible
    My service should draw such a cause[1] from you:
    Offended! could you think so? that were much
    For one of my performance, and so warm
    Yet in my service.
BEAT. 'Twere misery in me to give you cause, sir.
DE F. I know so much, it were so: misery
    In her most sharp condition.
BEAT. 'Tis resolved then;
    Look you, sir, here's three thousand golden florins;
    I have not meanly thought upon thy merit.
DE F. What! salary? now you move me.
BEAT. How, De Flores?
DE F. Do you place me in the rank of verminous fellows,
    To destroy things for wages? offer gold
    For the life-blood of man? is anything
    Valued too precious for my recompense?
BEAT. I understand thee not.
DE F. I could ha' hired
    A journeyman in murder at this rate,
    And mine own conscience might have slept at ease,
    And have had the work brought home.
BEAT. [*Aside*] I'm in a labyrinth;
    What will content him? I'd fain be rid of him.
    I'll double the sum, sir.
DE F. You take a course
    To double my vexation, that's the good you do.
BEAT. [*Aside*] Bless me, I'm now in worse plight than I was;
    I know not what will please him.—For my fear's sake,
    I prithee, make away with all speed possible;
    And if thou be'st so modest not to name
    The sum that will content thee, paper blushes not,
    Send thy demand in writing, it shall follow thee;
    But, prithee, take thy flight.
DE F. You must fly too then.

---

1. Accusation.

BEAT. I?

DE F. I'll not stir a foot else.

BEAT. What's your meaning?

DE F. Why, are not you as guilty? in, I'm sure,
    As deep as I; and we should stick together:
    Come, your fears counsel you but ill; my absence
    Would draw suspect upon you instantly;
    There were no rescue for you.

BEAT. [*Aside*] He speaks home!

DE F. Nor is it fit we two, engaged so jointly,
    Should part and live asunder.

BEAT. How now, sir?
    This shows not well.

DE F. What makes your lip so strange?
    This must not be betwixt us.

BEAT. The man talks wildly!

DE F. Come, kiss me with a zeal now.

BEAT. [*Aside*] Heaven, I doubt[1] him!

DE F. I will not stand so long to beg 'em shortly.

BEAT. Take heed, De Flores, of forgetfulness,
    'Twill soon betray us.

DE F. Take you heed first;
    Faith, you're grown much forgetful, you're to blame in't.

BEAT. [*Aside*] He's bold, and I am blamed for't.

DE F. I have eased you
    Of your trouble, think on it; I am in pain,
    And must be eased of you; 'tis a charity,
    Justice invites your blood to understand me.

BEAT. I dare not.

DE F. Quickly!

BEAT. O, I never shall!
    Speak it yet further off, that I may lose
    What has been spoken, and no sound remain on't;
    I would not hear so much offence again
    For such another deed.

---

1. Mistrust.

DE F. Soft, lady, soft!
 The last is not yet paid for: O, this act
 Has put me into spirit; I was as greedy on't
 As the parched earth of moisture, when the clouds weep:
 Did you not mark, I wrought myself into't,
 Nay, sued and kneeled for't? why was all that pains took?
 You see I've thrown contempt upon your gold;
 Not that I want it not, for I do piteously,
 In order I'll come unto't, and make use on't,
 But 'twas not held so precious to begin with,
 For I place wealth after the heels of pleasure;
 And were not I resolved in my belief
 That thy virginity were perfect in thee,
 I should but take my recompense with grudging,
 As if I had but half my hopes I agreed for.
BEAT. Why, 'tis impossible thou canst be so wicked,
 Or shelter such a cunning cruelty,
 To make his death the murderer of my honor!
 Thy language is so bold and vicious,
 I cannot see which way I can forgive it
 With any modesty.
DE F. Pish! you forget yourself;
 A woman dipped in blood, and talk of modesty!
BEAT. O misery of sin! would I'd been bound
 Perpetually unto my living hate
 In that Piracquo, than to hear these words!
 Think but upon the distance that creation
 Set 'twixt thy blood and mine, and keep thee there.
DE F. Look but into your conscience, read me there;
 'Tis a true book, you'll find me there your equal:
 Pish! fly not to your birth, but settle you
 In what the act has made you; you're no more now.
 You must forget your parentage to me;[1]
 You are the deed's creature; by that name
 You lost your first condition, and I challenge[2] you,

1. In my favor.
2. Claim.

As peace and innocency has turned you out,
And made you one with me.

BEAT. With thee, foul villain!

DE F. Yes, my fair murderess; do you urge me,
    Though thou writ'st maid, thou whore in thy affection?
    'Twas changed from thy first love, and that's a kind
    Of whoredom in the heart; and he's changed now
    To bring thy second on, thy Alsemero,
    Whom by all sweets that ever darkness tasted,
    If I enjoy thee not, thou ne'er enjoyest!
    I'll blast the hopes and joys of marriage,
    I'll confess all; my life I rate at nothing.

BEAT. De Flores!

DE F. I shall rest from all plagues then;
    I live in pain now; that shooting eye
    Will burn my heart to cinders.

BEAT. O sir, hear me!

DE F. She that in life and love refuses me,
    In death and shame my partner she shall be.

BEAT. [*Kneeling*] Stay, hear me once for all; I make thee master
    Of all the wealth I have in gold and jewels;
    Let me go poor unto my bed with honor,
    And I am rich in all things!

DE F. Let this silence thee:
    The wealth of all Valencia shall not buy
    My pleasure from me;
    Can you weep Fate from its determined purpose?
    So soon may you weep me.

BEAT. Vengeance begins;
    Murder, I see, is followed by more sins:
    Was my creation in the womb so curst,
    It must engender with a viper first?

DE F. [*Raising her*] Come, rise and shroud your blushes in my bosom;
    Silence is one of pleasure's best receipts:[1]
    Thy peace is wrought for ever in this yielding.

---

1. Recipes.

'Las! how the turtle pants! thou'lt love anon
What thou so fear'st and faint'st to venture on.

Exeunt

Act IV

Dumb Show

*Enter Gentlemen, Vermandero meeting them with action of
wonderment at the flight of Piracquo. Enter Alsemero with
Jasperino and gallants: Vermandero points to him, the gentlemen
seeming to applaud the choice. Exeunt in procession Alsemero,
Jasperino, and Gentlemen, Beatrice as a bride following in great
state, accompanied by Diaphanta, Isabella, and other gentlewomen;
De Flores after all, smiling at the accident:*[1] *Alonzo's ghost appears to
him in the midst of his smile, and startles him, showing the hand
whose finger he had cut off. They pass over in great solemnity*

Scene I

Enter Beatrice

BEAT. This fellow has undone me endlessly;
   Never was bride so fearfully distressed:
   The more I think upon th' ensuing night,
   And whom I am to cope with in embraces,
   One who's ennobled both in blood and mind,
   So clear in understanding,—that's my plague now—
   Before whose judgment will my fault appear
   Like malefactors' crimes before tribunals
   There is no hiding on't, the more I dive
   Into my own distress: how a wise man
   Stands for a great calamity! there's no venturing
   Into his bed, what course soe'er I light upon,
   Without my shame, which may grow up to danger;

---

1. The way things have fallen out.

He cannot but in justice strangle me
As I lie by him, as a cheater use me;
'Tis a precious craft to play with a false die
Before a cunning gamester. Here's his closet;
The key left in't, and he abroad i' th' park!
Sure 'twas forgot; I'll be so bold as look in't.

[*Opens closet*]

Bless me! a right physician's closet 'tis,
Set round with vials; every one her mark too:
Sure he does practice physic for his own use,
Which may be safely called your great man's wisdom.
What manuscript lies here?
[*Reads*] "The Book of Experiment, called Secrets in Nature:"
So 'tis so:
[*Reads*] "How to know whether a woman be with child or no:"
I hope I am not yet; if he should try though!
Let me see [*reads*] "folio forty-five," here 'tis,
The leaf tucked down upon't, the place suspicious:
[*Reads*] "If you would know whether a woman be with child or not,
give her two spoonfuls of the white water in glass C—"
Where's that glass C? O yonder, I see 't now—
[*reads*] "and if she be with child, she sleeps full twelve hours after;
   if not, not:"
None of that water comes into my belly;
I'll know you from a hundred; I could break you now,
Or turn you into milk, and so beguile
The master of the mystery; but I'll look to you.
Ha! that which is next is ten times worse:
[*Reads*] "How to know whether a woman be a maid or not."
If that should be applied, what would become of me?
Belike he has a strong faith of my purity,
That never yet made proof; but this he calls
[*reads*] "A merry sleight,[1] but true experiment; the author Antonius
Mizaldus. Give the party you suspect the quantity of a spoonful of
the water in the glass M, which, upon her that is a maid, makes three

---

1. Trick.

several effects; 'twill make her incontinently[1] gape, then fall into a
sudden sneezing, last into a violent laughing; else, dull, heavy, and
lumpish."
Where had I been?
I fear it, yet 'tis seven hours to bed-time.

Enter Diaphanta

DIA. Cuds, madam, are you here?
BEAT. [*Aside*] Seeing that wench now,
    A trick comes in my mind; 'tis a nice piece[2]
    Gold cannot purchase. —I come hither, wench,
    To look[3] my lord.
DIA. [*Aside*] Would I had such a cause
    Too look him to! —Why, he's i' th' park, madam.
BEAT. There let him be.
DIA. Ay, madam, let him compass
    Whole parks and forests, as great rangers do,
    At roosting-time a little lodge can hold 'em:
    Earth-conquering Alexander, that thought the world
    To narrow for him, in th' end had but his pit-hole.
BEAT. I fear thou art not modest, Diaphanta.
DIA. Your thoughts are so unwilling to be known, madam.
    'Tis ever the bride's fashion, towards bed-time,
    To set light by her joys, as if she owned 'em not.
BEAT. Her joys? her fears thou wouldst say.
DIA. Fear of what?
BEAT. Art thou a maid, and talk'st so to a maid?
    You leave a blushing business beind;
    Beshrew your heart for't!
DIA. Do you mean good sooth,[4] madam?
BEAT. Well, if I'd thought upon the fear at first,
    Man should have been unknown.

---

1. Immediately.
2. Unusually moral girl.
3. Look for.
4. Are you serious?

DIA. Is't possible?

BEAT. I'd give a thousand ducats to that woman
　　Would try what my fear were, and tell me true
　　To-morrow, when she gets from't; as she likes,
　　I might perhaps be drawn to't.

DIA. Are you in earnest?

BEAT. Do you get the woman, then challenge me,
　　And see if I'll fly from't; but I must tell you
　　This by the way, she must be a true maid,
　　Else there's no trial, my fears are not hers else.

DIA. Nay, she that I would put into your hands, madam.
　　Shall be a maid.

BEAT. You know I should be shamed else,
　　Because she lies for me.

DIA. 'Tis a strange humor!
　　But are you serious still? would you resign
　　Your first night's pleasure, and give money too?

BEAT. As willingly as live. [*Aside*] —Alas, the gold
　　Is but a by-bet to wedge in the honor!

DIA. I do not know how the world goes abroad
　　For faith or honesty; there's both required in this.
　　Madam, what say you to me, and stray no further?
　　I've a good mind, in troth, to earn your money.

BEAT. You are too quick,[1] I fear, to be a maid.

DIA. How? not a maid? nay, then you urge[2] me, madam;
　　Your honorable self is not a truer,
　　With all your fears upon you—

BEAT. [*Aside*] Bad enough then.

DIA. Than I with all my lightsome joys about me.

BEAT. I'm glad to hear't: then you dare put your honesty
　　Upon an easy trial.

DIA. Easy? anything.

BEAT. I'll come to you straight.

　　　　　　　　　　　　　　　　　[*Goes to the closet*]

1. Lively.
2. Provoke.

DIA. She will not search me, will she,
　　Like the forewoman of a female jury?[1]
BEAT. Glass M: ay, this is it. [*Brings vial*]—Look, Diaphanta,
　　You take no worse than I do.

　　　　　　　　　　　　　　　　　　　[*Drinks*]

DIA. And in so doing,
　　I will not question what it is, but take it.

　　　　　　　　　　　　　　　　　　　[*Drinks*]

BEAT. [*Aside*] Now if th' experiment be true, 'twill praise itself,[2]
　　And give me noble ease: begins already;

　　　　　　　　　　　　　　　[*Diaphanta gapes*]

　　There's the first symptom; and what haste it makes
　　To fall into the second, there by this time!

　　　　　　　　　　　　　　　[*Diaphanta sneezes*]

　　Most admirable secret! on the contrary,
　　It stirs not me a whit, which most concerns it.
DIA. Ha, ha, ha!
BEAT. [*Aside*] Just in all things, and in order
　　As if 'twere circumscribed; one accident
　　Gives way unto another.
DIA. Ha, ha, ha!
BEAT. How now, wench?
DIA. Ha, ha, ha! I'm so, so light
　　At heart—ha, ha, ha!—so pleasurable!
　　But one swig more, sweet madam.
BEAT. Ay, to-morrow,
　　We shall have time to sit by't.[3]
DIA. Now I'm sad again.
BEAT. [*Aside*] It lays itself[4] so gently too! —Come, wench.
　　Most honest Diaphanta I dare call thee now.
DIA. Pray, tell me, madam, what trick call you this?

1. In a scandalous contemporary case the Countess of Essex was so examined.
2. Show its worth.
3. Enjoy it at leisure.
4. Ends.

BEAT. I'll tell thee all hereafter; we must study
    The carriage of this business.

DIA. I shall carry't well,
    Because I love the burthen.

BEAT. About midnight
    You must not fail to steal forth gently,
    That I may use the place.[1]

DIA. O, fear not, madam,
    I shall be cool by that time: the bride's place,
    And with a thousand ducats! I'm for a justice[2] now,
    I bring a portion with me; I scorn small fools.

Exeunt

SCENE II

Enter Vermandero and Servant

VER. I tell thee, knave, mine honor is in question,
    A thing till now free from suspicion,
    Nor ever was there cause. Who of my gentlemen
    Are absent?
    Tell me, and truly, how many, and who?

SER. Antonio, sir, and Franciscus.

VER. When did they leave the castle?

SER. Some ten days since, sir; the one intending to Briamata, th' other
    for Valencia.

VER. The time accuses 'em; a charge of murder
    Is brought within my castle-gate, Piracquo's murder;
    I dare not answer faithfully their absence:
    A strict command of apprehension
    Shall pursue 'em suddenly, and either wipe
    The stain off clear, or openly discover it.
    Provide me wingèd warrants for the purpose.

Exit Servant

See, I am set on[3] again.

1. i.e., In bed.
2. Justice of the Peace.
3. Assaulted.

Enter Tomaso

TOM. I claim a brother of you.

VER. You're too hot;
Seek him not here.

TOM. Yes, 'mongst your dearest bloods,[1]
If my peace find no fairer satisfaction:
This is the place must yield account for him,
For here I left him; and the hasty tie
Of this snatched marriage gives strong testimony
Of his most certain ruin.

VER. Certain falsehood!
This is the place indeed; his breach of faith
Has too much marred both my abusèd love,
The honorable love I reserved for him,
And mocked my daughter's joy; the prepared morning
Blushed at his infidelity; he left
Contempt and scorn to throw upon those friends
Whose belief hurt 'em: O, twas most ignoble
To take his flight so unexpectedly,
And throw such public wrongs on those that loved him!

TOM. Then this is all your answer?

VER. 'Tis too fair
For one of his alliance; and I warn you
That this place no more see you.

Exit

Enter De Flores

TOM. The best is,
There is more ground to meet a man's revenge on.—
Honest De Flores?

DE F. That's my name indeed.
Saw you the bride? good sweet sir, which way took she?

TOM. I've blessed mine eyes from seeing such a false one.

DE F. [*Aside*] I'd fain get off, this man's not for my company;
I smell his brother's blood when I come near him.

---

1. Relations.

TOM. Come hither, kind and true one; I remember
My brother loved thee well.

DE F. O, purely, dear sir!—
[*Aside*] Methinks I'm now again a-killing on him,
He brings it so fresh to me.

TOM. Thou canst guess, sirrah—
An honest friend has an instinct of jealousy[1]—
At some foul guilty person.

DE F. Alas! sir,
I am so charitable, I think none
Worse than myself! you did not see the bride then?

TOM. I prithee, name her not: is she not wicked?

DE F. No, no; a pretty, easy, round-packed sinner,
As your most ladies are, else you might think
I flattered her; but, sir, at no hand[2] wicked,
Till they're so old their chins and noses meet,
And they salute witches. I'm called, I think, sir.—
[*Aside*] His company even overlays my conscience.

Exit

TOM. That De Flores has a wondrous honest heart;
He'll bring it[3] out in time, I'm assured on't.
O, here's the glorious master of the day's joy!
'Twill not be long till he and I do reckon.

Enter Alsemero

Sir.

ALS. You're most welcome.

TOM. You may call that word back;
I do not think I am, nor wish to be.

ALS. 'Tis strange you found the way to this house, then.

TOM. Would I'd ne'er known the cause! I'm none of those, sir,
That come to give you joy, and swill your wine;
'Tis a more precious liquor that must lay
The fiery thirst I bring.

---

1. Suspicion.
2. Not at all.
3. The truth about Alonzo.

ALS. Your words and you
    Appear to me great strangers.
TOM. Time and our swords
    May make us more acquainted; this the business:
    I should have had a brother in your place;
    How treachery and malice have disposed of him,
    I'm bound to inquire of him which holds his right,[1]
    Which never could come fairly.
ALS. You must look
    To answer for that word, sir.
TOM. Fear you not,
    I'll have it ready drawn at our next meeting.
    Keep your day solemn; farewell, I disturb it not;
    I'll bear the smart with patience for a time.

                                                  Exit

ALS. 'Tis somewhat ominous this; a quarrel entered
    Upon this day; my innocence relieves me,

              Enter Jasperino

    I should be wondrous sad else.—Jasperino,
    I've news to tell thee, strange news.
JAS. I ha' some too,
    I think as strange as yours: would I might keep
    Mine, so my faith and friendship might be kept in't!
    Faith, sir, dispense a little with my zeal,
    And let it cool in this.
ALS. This puts me on,
    And blames me for thy slowness.
JAS. All may prove nothing,
    Only a friendly fear that leapt from me, sir.
ALS. No question, 't may prove nothing; let's partake it though.
JAS. 'Twas Diaphanta's chance—for to that wench
    I pretend[2] honest love, and she deserves it—
    To leave me in a back part of the house,

---

1. i.e., Alonzo's bride.
2. Offer.

A place we chose for private conference;
She was no sooner gone, but instantly
I heard your bride's voice in the next room to me;
And lending more attention, found De Flores
Louder than she.

ALS. De Flores! thou art out now.

JAS. You'll tell me more anon.

ALS. Still I'll prevent[1] thee,
The very sight of him is poison to her.

JAS. That made me stagger too; but Diaphanta
At her return confirmed it.

ALS. Diaphanta!

JAS. Then fell we both to listen, and words passed
Like those that challenge interest in a woman.[2]

ALS. Peace; quench thy zeal, 'tis dangerous to thy bosom.

JAS. Then truth is full of peril.

ALS. Such truths are.
O, were she the sole glory of the earth,
Had eyes that could shoot fire into king's breasts,
And touched,[3] she sleeps not here! yet I have time,
Though night be near, to be resolved hereof;
And, prithee, do not weigh me by my passions.

JAS. I never weighed friend so.

ALS. Done charitably!
That key will lead thee to a pretty secret,

[*Giving key*]

By a Chaldean[4] taught me, and I have
My study upon some: bring from my closet
A glass inscribed there with the letter M,
And question not my purpose.

JAS. It shall be done, sir.

Exit

1. Anticipate.
2. Claim a right in a woman.
3. Tainted.
4. Magician.

ALS. How can this hang together? not an hour since
    Her woman came pleading her lady's fears,
    Delivered her for the most timorous virgin
    That ever shrunk at man's name, and so modest,
    She charged her weep out her request to me,
    That she might come obscurely to my bosom.

Enter Beatrice

BEAT. [*Aside*] All things go well; my woman's preparing yonder
    For her sweet voyage, which grieves me to lose;
    Necessity compels it; I lose all else.
ALS. [*Aside*] Tush! modesty's shrine is set in yonder forehead:
    I cannot be too sure though.—My Joanna!
BEAT. Sir, I was bold to weep a message to you;
    Pardon my modest fears.
ALS. [*Aside*] The dove's not meeker;
    She's abused, questionless.

Re-enter Jasperino with vial

    O, are you come, sir?
BEAT. [*Aside*] The glass, upon my life! I see the letter.
JAS. Sir, this is M.

                           [*Giving vial*]

ALS. 'Tis it.
BEAT. [*Aside*] I am suspected.
ALS. How fitly our bride comes to partake with us!
BEAT. What is't, my lord?
ALS. No hurt.
BEAT. Sir, pardon me,
    I seldom taste of any composition.
ALS. But this, upon my warrant, you shall venture on.
BEAT. I fear 'twill make me ill.
ALS. Heaven forbid that.
BEAT. [*Aside*] I'm put now to my cunning: th' effects I know,
    If I can now but feign 'em handsomely.

                                [*Drinks*]

ALS. It has that secret virtue, it ne'er missed, sir.
    Upon a virgin.

JAS. Treble-qualitied?

[Beatrice gapes and sneezes]

ALS. By all that's virtuous it takes there! proceeds!

JAS. This is the strangest trick to know a maid by.

BEAT. Ha, ha, ha!
   You have given me joy of heart to drink, my lord.

ALS. No, thou hast given me such joy of heart,
   That never can be blasted.

BEAT. What's the matter, sir?

ALS. *[Aside]* See now 'tis settled in a melancholy;
   Keeps both the time and method.—My Joanna,
   Chaste as the breath of Heaven, or morning's womb,
   That brings the day forth! thus my love encloses thee.

Exeunt

SCENE III

Enter Isabella and Lollio

ISA. O Heaven! is this the waxing moon?
   Does love turn fool, run mad, and all at once?
   Sirrah, here's a madman, akin to the fool too,
   A lunatic lover.

LOL. No, no, not he I brought the letter from.

ISA. Compare his inside with his out, and tell me.

LOL. That out's mad, I'm sure of that; I had a taste on't.

ISA. *[Reads letter]* "To the bright Andromeda, chief chambermaid to
   the Knight of the Sun, at the sign of Scorpio, in the middle region,
   sent by the bellows-mender of Æolus. Pay the post."

LOL. This is stark madness!

ISA. Now mark the inside. *[Reads]* "Sweet lady, having now cast off
   this counterfeit cover of a madman, I appear to your best judgment
   a true and faithful lover of your beauty."

LOL. He is mad still.

ISA. *[Reads]* "If any fault you find, chide those perfections in you
   which have made me imperfect; 'tis the same sun that causeth to
   grow and enforceth to wither—"

LOL. O rogue!

ISA. [*Reads*] "Shapes and transhapes, destroys and builds again: I come in winter to you, dismantled of my proper ornaments; by the sweet splendor of your cheerful smiles, I spring and live a lover."

LOL. Mad rascal still!

ISA. [*Reads*] "Tread him not under foot, that shall appear an honor to your bounties. I remain—mad till I speak with you, from whom I expect my cure, yours all, or one beside himself, Franciscus."

LOL. You are like to have a fine time on't; my master and I may give over our professions; I do not think but you can cure fools and madmen faster than we, with little pains too.

ISA. Very likely.

LOL. One thing I must tell you, mistress; you perceive that I am privy to your skill; if I find you minister once, and set up the trade, I put in for my thirds; I shall be mad or fool else.

ISA. The first place is thine, believe it, Lollio,
　　If I do fall.

LOL. I fall upon you.

ISA. So.

LOL. Well, I stand to my venture.

ISA. By thy counsel now; how shall I deal with 'em?

LOL. Why, do you mean to deal with 'em?

ISA. Nay, the fair understanding, how to use 'em.

LOL. Abuse 'em! that's the way to mad the fool, and make a fool of the madman, and then you use 'em kindly.

ISA. 'Tis easy, I'll practice; do thou observe it;
　　The key of thy wardrobe.

LOL. There [*gives key*]; fit yourself for 'em, and I'll fit 'em both for you.

ISA. Take thou no further notice than the outside.

LOL. Not an inch [*exit Isabella*]; I'll put you to the inside.

Enter Alibius

ALIB. Lollio, art there? will all be perfect, think'st thou?
　　To-morrow night, as if to close up the
　　Solemnity,[1] Vermandero expects us.

1. Festivity.

LOL. I mistrust the madmen most; the fools will do well enough; I
have taken pains with them.

ALIB. Tush! they cannot miss; the more absurdity,
The more commends it, so no rough behaviors
Affright the ladies; they're nice things, thou knowest.

LOL. You need not fear, sir; so long as we are there with our commanding pizzles,[1] they'll be as tame as the ladies themselves.

ALIB. I'll see them once more rehearse before they go.

LOL. I was about it, sir: look you to the madmen's morris, and let me
alone with the other: there is one or two that I mistrust their footing; I'll instruct them, and then they shall rehearse the whole measure.

ALIB. Do so; I'll see the music prepared: but, Lollio,
By the way, how does my wife brook her restraint?
Does she not grudge at it?

LOL. So, so; she takes some pleasure in the house, she would abroad
else; you must allow her a little more length, she's kept too short.

ALIB. She shall along to Vermandero's with us,
That will serve her for a month's liberty.

LOL. What's that on your face, sir?

ALIB. Where, Lollio? I see nothing.

LOL. Cry you mercy, sir, 'tis your nose; it showed like the trunk of a
young elephant.

ALIB. Away, rascal! I'll prepare the music, Lollio.

LOL. Do, sir, and I'll dance the whilst.

Exit Alibius

—Tony, where art thou, Tony?

Enter Antonio

ANT. Here, cousin; where art thou?

LOL. Come, Tony, the footmanship I taught you.

ANT. I had rather ride, cousin.

LOL. Ay, a whip take you! but I'll keep you out; vault: look you, Tony;
fa, la, la, la, la.

[Dances]

---

1. Whips.

ANT. [*Sings and dances*] Fa, la, la, la, la.

LOL. There, an honor.[1]

ANT. Is this an honor, coz?

LOL. Yes, an it please your worship.

ANT. Does honor bend in the hams, coz?

LOL. Marry does it, as low as worship, squireship, nay, yeomanry itself sometimes, from whence it first stiffened: there rise, a caper.

ANT. Caper after an honor, coz?

LOL. Very proper, for honor is but a caper, rises as fast and high, has a knee or two, and falls to th' ground again: you can remember your figure, Tony?

ANT. Yes, cousin; when I see thy figure, I can remember mine.

Exit Lollio

Re-enter Isabella, dressed as a madwoman

ISA. Hey, how he treads the air! shough, shough, t'other way! he burns his wings else: here's wax enough below, Icarus, more than will be cancelled[2] these eighteen moons: he's down, he's down! what a terrible fall he had!
Stand up, thou son of Cretan Dædalus,
And let us tread the lower labyrinth;
I'll bring thee to the clue.[3]

ANT. Prithee, coz, let me alone.

ISA. Art thou not drowned?
About thy head I saw a heap of clouds
Wrapt like a Turkish turban; on thy back
A crooked chamelon-colored rainbow hung
Like a tiara down unto thy hams:
Let me suck out those billows in thy belly;
Hark, how they roar and rumble in the straits!
Bless thee from the pirates!

ANT. Pox upon you, let me alone!

ISA. Why shouldst thou mount so high as Mercury,
Unless thou hadst reversion of his place?

---

1. Bow.

2. The wax that melted from the wings of Icarus becomes the wax used for seals.

3. The thread that guided Theseus out of the labyrinth.

Stay in the moon with me, Endymion,[1]
And we will rule these wild rebellious waves,
That would have drowned my love.

ANT. I'll kick thee, if
Again thou thouch me, thou wild unshapen antic;[2]
I am no fool, you bedlam!

ISA. But you are, as sure as I am mad:
Have I put on this habit of a frantic,
With love as full of fury, to beguile
The nimble eyes of watchful jealousy,
And am I thus rewarded?

ANT. Ha! dearest beauty!

ISA. No, I have no beauty now,
Nor never had but what was in my garments:
You a quick-sighted lover! come not near me:
Keep your caparisons, you're aptly clad;
I come a feigner, to return stark mad.

ANT. Stay, or I shall change condition,
And become as you are.

Exit Isabella

Re-enter Lollio

LOL. Why, Tony, whither now? why, fool—

ANT. Whose fool, usher[3] of idiots? you coxcomb!
I have fooled too much.

LOL. You were best be mad another while then.

ANT. So I am, stark mad; I have cause enough;
And I could throw the full effects on thee,
And beat thee like a fury.

LOL. Do not, do not; I shall not forbear the gentleman under the fool,
if you do: alas! I saw through your fox-skin before now! Come, I can
give you comfort; my mistress loves you; and there is as arrant a
madman i' th' house as you are a fool, your rival, whom she loves

---

1. With whom the moon fell in love.
2. Freak.
3. Teacher.

not: if after the masque we can rid her of him, you earn her love, she says, and the fool shall ride her.

ANT. May I believe thee?

LOL. Yes, or you may choose whether you will or no.

ANT. She's eased of him; I've a good quarrel on't.

LOL. Well, keep your old station yet, and be quiet.

ANT. Tell her I will deserve her love.

Exit

LOL. And you are like to have your desert.

Enter Franciscus

FRAN. [*Sings*] "Down, down, down a-down a-down,"—and then with a horse-trick
To kick Latona's forehead, and break her bowstring.

LOL. This is t'other counterfeit; I'll put him out of his humor. [*Aside. Takes out a letter and reads*] "Sweet lady, having now cast this counterfeit cover of a madman, I appear to your best judgment a true and faithful lover of your beauty." This is pretty well for a madman.

FRAN. Ha! what's that?

LOL. [*Reads*] "Chide those perfections in you which have made me imperfect."

FRAN. I am discovered to the fool.

LOL. I hope to discover the fool in you ere I have done with you. [*Reads*] "Yours all, or one beside himself, *Franciscus*." This madman will mend sure.

FRAN. What do you read, sirrah?

LOL. Your destiny, sir; you'll be hanged for this trick, and another that I know.

FRAN. Art thou of counsel with thy mistress?

LOL. Next her apron-strings.

FRAN. Give me thy hand.

LOL. Stay, let me put yours in my pocket first [*putting letter into his pocket*]: your hand is true,[1] is it not? it will not pick? I partly fear it, because I think it does lie.

FRAN. Not in a syllable.

1. Honest.

LOL. So if you love my mistress so well as you have handled the matter here, you are like to be cured of your madness.

FRAN. And none but she can cure it.

LOL. Well, I'll give you over then, and she shall cast your water next.

FRAN. Take for thy pains past.

[*Gives him money*]

LOL. I shall deserve more, sir, I hope: my mistress loves you, but must
have some proof of your love to her.

FRAN. There I meet my wishes.

LOL. That will not serve, you must meet her enemy and yours.

FRAN. He's dead already.

LOL. Will you tell me that, and I parted but now with him?

FRAN. Show me the man.

LOL. Ay, that's a right course now; see him before you kill him, in any
case; and yet it needs not go so far neither, 'tis but a fool that haunts
the house and my mistrss in the shape of an idiot; bang but his fool's
coat well-favoredly, and 'tis well.

FRAN. Soundly, soundly!

LOL. Only reserve him till the masque be past; and if you find him not
now in the dance yourself, I'll show you. In, in! my master!

[*Dancing*]

FRAN. He handles him like a feather. Hey!

Exit

Enter Alibius

ALIB. Well said: in a readiness, Lollio?

LOL. Yes, sir.

ALIB. Away then, and guide them in, Lollio:
Entreat your mistress to see this sight.
Hark, is there not one incurable fool
That might be begged?[1] I have friends.

LOL. I have him for you,
One that shall deserve it too.

Exit

---

1. Begging a person for a fool meant applying to be his guardian, to whom the profits of
his lands and the custody of his person were granted by the king.

Re-enter Isabella: then re-enter Lollio with the madmen and fools,
who dance

ALIB. Good boy, Lollio!
'Tis perfect: well, fit but once these strains,
We shall have coin and credit for our pains.

Exeunt

ACT V, SCENE I

Enter Beatrice: a clock strikes one

BEAT. One struck, and yet she lies by't! O my fears!
This strumpet serves her own ends, 'tis apparent now,
Devours the pleasure with a greedy appetite,
And never minds my honor or my peace,
Makes havoc of my right; but she pays dearly for't;
No trusting of her life with such a secret,
That cannot rule her blood to keep her promise;
Beside, I've some suspicion of her faith to me,
Because I was suspected of my lord,
And it must come from her [*clock strikes two*]: hark! by my horrors,
Another clock strikes two!

Enter De Flores

DE F. Hist! where are you?
BEAT. De Flores?
DE F. Ay: is she not come from him yet?
BEAT. As I'm a living soul, not!
DE F. Sure the devil
Hath sowed his itch within her; who would trust
A waiting-woman?
BEAT. I must trust somebody.
DE F. Tush! they're termagants;
Especially when they fall upon their masters
And have their ladies' first-fruits; they're mad whelps,
You cannot stave 'em off from game royal:[1] then

1. Game reserved for the king.

You are so rash and hardy, ask no counsel;
And I could have helped you to a 'pothecary's daughter
Would have fall'n off before eleven, and thanked you too.

BEAT. O me, not yet! this whore forgets herself.

DE F. The rascal fares so well: look, you're undone;
The day-star, by this hand! see Phosphorus[1] plain yonder.

BEAT. Advise me now to fall upon some ruin;
There is no counsel safe else.

DE F. Peace! I ha't now,
For we must force a rising, there's no remedy.

BEAT. How? take heed of that.

DE F. Tush! be you quiet, or else give over all.

BEAT. Prithee, I ha' done then.

DE F. This is my reach:[2] I'll set
Some part a-fire of Diaphanta's chamber.

BEAT. How? fire, sir? that may endanger the whole house.

DE F. You talk of danger when your fame's on fire?

BEAT. That's true; do what thou wilt now.

DE F. Tush! I aim
At a most rich success strikes all dead sure:
The chimney being a-fire, and some light parcels
Of the least danger in her chamber only,
If Diaphanta should be met by chance then
Far from her lodging, which is now suspicious,
It would be thought her fears and affrights then
Drove her to seek for succor; if not seen
Or met at all, as that's the likeliest,
For her own shame she'll hasten towards her lodging;
I will be ready with a piece high-charged,[3]
As 'twere to cleanse the chimney, there 'tis proper now
But she shall be the mark.

BEAT. I'm forced to love thee now,
'Cause thou provid'st so carefully for my honor.

DE F. 'Slid, it concerns the safety of us both,
Our pleasure and continuance.

1. Venus.
2. Plan.
3. Loaded gun.

BEAT. One word now, prithee;
    How for the servants?
DE F. I will despatch them,
    Some one way, some another in the hurry,
    For buckets, hooks, ladders; fear not you,
    The deed shall find its time; and I've thought since
    Upon a safe conveyance for the body too:
    How this fire purifies wit! watch you your minute.
BEAT. Fear keeps my soul upon't, I cannot stray from't.

Enter Ghost of Alonzo

DE F. Ha! what art thou that tak'st away the light
    Betwixt that star and me? I dread thee not:
    'Twas but a mist of conscience; all's clear again.

Exit

BEAT. Who's that, De Flores? bless me, it slides by!

Exit Ghost

    Some ill thing haunts the house; 't has left behind it
    A shivering sweat upon me; I'm afraid now:
    This night hath been so tedious! O this strumpet!
    Had she a thousand lives, he should not leave her
    Till he had destroyed the last. List! O my terrors!

[*Clock strikes three*]

    Three struck by Sebastian's!
VOICES. [*Within*] Fire, fire, fire!
BEAT. Already? how rare is that man's speed!
    How heartily he serves me! his face loathes one;
    But look upon his care, who would not love him?
    The east is not more beauteous than his service.
VOICES. [*Within*] Fire, fire, fire!

Re-enter De Flores: Servants pass over the stage, ring a bell

DE F. Away, despatch! hooks, buckets, ladders! that's well said.
    The fire-bell rings; the chimney works, my charge;[1]
    The piece[2] is ready.

1. Task.
2. Gun.

Exit

BEAT. Here's a man worth loving!

Enter Diaphanta

O you're a jewel!

DIA. Pardon frailty, madam;
In troth, I was so well, I even forgot myself.

BEAT. You've made trim work!

DIA. What?

BEAT. Hie quickly to your chamber;
Your reward follows you.

DIA. I never made
So sweet a bargain.

Exit

Enter Alsemero

ALS. O, my dear Joanna,
Alas! art thou risen too? I was coming,
My absolute treasure!

BEAT. When I missed you,
I could not choose but follow.

ALS. Thou'rt all sweetness:
The fire is not so dangerous.

BEAT. Think you so, sir?

ALS. I prithee, tremble not; believe me, 'tis not.

Enter Vermandero and Jasperino

VER. O bless my house and me!

ALS. My lord your father.

Re-enter De Flores with a gun

VER. Knave, whither goes that piece?

DE F. To scour the chimney.

VER. O, well said, well said!

Exit De Flores

That fellow's good on all occasions.

BEAT. A wondrous necessary man, my lord.

VER. He hath a ready wit; he's worth 'em all, sir;

Dog at[1] a house of fire; I ha' seen him singed ere now.——

[*Gun fired off within*]

Ha, there he goes!

BEAT. [*Aside*] 'Tis done!

ALS. Come, sweet, to bed now;
　　Alas! thou wilt get cold.

BEAT. Alas! the fear keeps that out!
　　My heart will find no quiet till I hear
　　How Diaphanta, my poor woman, fares;
　　It is her chamber, sir, her lodging chamber.

VER. How should the fire come there?

BEAT. As good a soul as every lady countenanced,
　　But in her chamber negligent and heavy:
　　She 'scaped a mine[2] twice.

VER. Twice?

BEAT. Strangely twice, sir.

VER. Those sleepy sluts are dangerous in a house,
　　An they be ne'er so good.

Re-enter De Flores

DE F. O poor virginity,
　　Thou hast paid dearly for't!

VER. Bless us, what's that?

DE F. A thing you all knew once, Diaphanta's burnt.

BEAT. My woman! O my woman!

DE F. Now the flames
　　Are greedy of her; burnt, burnt, burnt to death, sir!

BEAT. O my presaging soul!

ALS. Not a tear more!
　　I charge you by the last embrace I gave you
　　In bed, before this raised us.

BEAT. Now you tie me;
　　Were it my sister, now she gets no more.

---

1. Skilled in dealing with.
2. Disaster.

Enter Servant

VER. How now?

SER. All danger's past; you may now take
  Your rests, my lords; the fire is thoroughly quenched:
  Ah, poor gentlewoman, how soon was she stifled!

BEAT. De Flores, what is left of her inter,
  And we as mourners all will follow her:
  I will entreat that honor to my servant
  Even of my lord himself.

ALS. Command it, sweetness.

BEAT. Which of you spied the fire first?

DE F. 'Twas I, madam.

BEAT. And took such pains in't too? a double goodness!
  'Twere well he were rewarded.

VER. He shall be.—
  De Flores, call upon me.

ALS. And upon me, sir.

Exeunt all except De Flores

DE F. Rewarded? precious! here's a trick beyond me:
  I see in all bouts, both of sport and wit,
  Always a woman strives for the last hit.

Exit

SCENE II

Enter Tomaso

TOM. I cannot taste the benefits of life
  With the same relish I was wont to do:
  Man I grow weary of, and hold his fellowship
  A treacherous bloody friendship; and because
  I'm ignorant in whom my wrath should settle,
  I must think all men villains, and the next
  I meet, whoe'er he be, the murderer
  Of my most worthy brother. Ha! what's he?

De Flores passes across the stage

O, the fellow that some call honest De Flores;
But methinks honesty was hard bested
To come here for a lodging; as if a queen
Should make her palace of a pest-house:
I find a contrariety in nature
Betwixt that face and me; the least occasion
Would give me game upon[1] him; yet he's so foul
One would scarce touch him with a sword he loved
And made account of; so most deadly venomous,
He would go near to poison any weapon
That should draw blood on him; one must resolve
Never to use that sword again in fight
In way of honest manhood that strikes him;
Some river must devour it; 'twere not fit
That any man should find it. What, again?

Re-enter De Flores

He walks a' purpose by, sure, to choke me up,
T' infect my blood.
DE F. My worthy noble lord!
TOM. Dost offer to come near and breathe upon me?

[*Strikes him*]

DE F. A blow!

[*Draws*]

TOM. Yea, are you so prepared?
I'll rather like a soldier die by the sword,
Than like a politician by thy poison.

[*Draws*]

DE F. Hold, my lord, as you are honorable!
TOM. All slaves that kill by poison are still cowards.
DE F. [*Aside*] I cannot strike; I see his brother's wounds
Fresh bleeding in his eye, as in a crystal.—
I will not question this, I know you're noble;
I take my injury with thanks given, sir,

1. Occasion to fight.

Like a wise lawyer, and as a favor
Will wear it for the worthy hand that gave it.—
[*Aside*] Why this from him that yesterday appeared
So strangely loving to me?
O, but instinct is of a subtler strain!
Guilt must not walk so near his lodge again;
He came near me now.

Exit

TOM. All league with mankind I renounce for ever,
    Till I find this murderer; not so much
    As common courtesy but I'll lock up;
    For in the state of ignorance I live in,
    A brother may salute his brother's murderer,
    And wish good speed to the villain in a greeting.

Enter Vermandero, Alibius, and Isabella

VER. Noble Piracquo!
TOM. Pray, keep on your way, sir;
    I've nothing to say to you.
VER. Comforts bless you, sir!
TOM. I've forsworn compliment, in troth I have, sir;
    As you are merely man, I have not left
    A good wish for you, nor for any here.
VER. Unless you be so far in love with grief,
    You will not part from't upon any terms,
    We bring that news will make a welcome for us.
TOM. What news can that be?
VER. Throw no scornful smile
    Upon the zeal I bring you, 'tis worth more, sir;
    Two of the chiefest men I kept about me
    I hide not from the law of your just vengeance.
TOM. Ha!
VER. To give your peace more ample satisfaction,
    Thank these discoverers.
TOM. If you bring that calm,
    Name but the manner I shall ask forgiveness in
    For that contemptuous smile I threw upon you,

I'll perfect it with reverence that belongs
Unto a sacred altar.

[Kneels]

VER. [*Raising him*] Good sir, rise;
    Why, now you overdo as much 'a this hand
    As you fell short 'a t'other.—Speak, Alibius.
ALIB. 'Twas my wife's fortune, as she is most lucky
    At a discovery, to find out lately,
    Within our hospital of fools and madmen,
    Two counterfeits slipped into these disguises,
    Their names Franciscus and Antonio.
VER. Both mine, sir, and I ask no favor for 'em.
ALIB. Now that which draws suspicion to their habits,
    The time of their disguisings agrees justly
    With the day of the murder.
TOM. O blest revelation!
VER. Nay, more, nay, more, sir—I'll not spare mine own
    In way of justice—they both feigned a journey
    To Briamata, and so wrought out their leaves;
    My love was so abused in it.
TOM. Time's too precious
    To run in waste now; you have brought a peace
    The riches of five kingdoms could not purchase:
    Be my most happy conduct; I thirst for 'em:
    Like subtle lightning will I find about 'em,
    And melt their marrow in 'em.

Exeunt

Scene III

Enter Alsemero and Jasperino

JAS. Your confidence, I'm sure, is now of proof;[1]
    The prospect from the garden has showed
    Enough for deep suspicion.

---

1. Fully tested.

ALS. The black mask
    That so continually was worn upon't
    Condemns the face for ugly ere't be seen,
    Her despite to him, and so seeming bottomless.
JAS. Touch it home then; 'tis not a shallow probe
    Can search this ulcer soundly; I fear you'll find it
    Full of corruption: 'tis fit I leave you,
    She meets you opportunely from that walk;
    She took the back door at his parting with her.

Exit

ALS. Did my fate wait for this unhappy stroke
    At my first sight of woman? She is here.

Enter Beatrice

BEAT. Alsemero!
ALS. How do you?
BEAT. How do I?
    Alas, sir! how do you? you look not well.
ALS. You read me well enough, I am not well.
BEAT. Not well, sir? is't in my power to better you?
ALS. Yes.
BEAT. Nay, then you're cured again.
ALS. Pray, resolve me one question, lady.
BEAT. If I can.
ALS. None can so sure: are you honest?
BEAT. Ha, ha, ha! that's a broad question, my lord.
ALS. But that's not a modest answer, my lady:
    Do you laugh? my doubts are strong upon me.
BEAT. 'Tis innocence that smiles, and no rough brow
    Can take away the dimple in her cheek:
    Say I should strain a tear to fill the vault,
    Which would you give the better faith to?
ALS. 'Twere but hypocrisy of a sadder color,
    But the same stuff; neither your smiles nor tears
    Shall move or flatter me from my belief:
    You are a whore!
BEAT. What a horrid sound it hath!
    It blasts a beauty to deformity;

Upon what face soever that breath falls,
It strikes it ugly: O, you have ruined
What you can ne'er repair again!

ALS. I'll all
Demolish, and seek out truth within you,
If there be any left; let your sweet tongue
Prevent your heart's rifling;[1] there I'll ransack
And tear out my suspicion.

BEAT. You may, sir;
It is an easy passage; yet, if you please,
Show me the ground whereon you lost your love;
My spotless virtue may but tread on that
Before I perish.

ALS. Unanswerable;
A ground you cannot stand on; you fall down
Beneath all grace and goodness when you set
Your ticklish[2] heel on it: there was a visor
Over that cunning face, and that became you;
Now impudence in triumph rides upon't;
How comes this tender reconcilement else
'Twixt you and your despite, your rancorous loathing,
De Flores? he that your eye was sore at sight of,
He's now become your arm's supporter, your
Lip's saint!

BEAT. Is there the cause?

ALS. Worse, your lust's devil,
Your adultery!

BEAT. Would any but yourself say that,
'Twould turn him to a villain!

ALS. It was witnessed
By the counsel of your bosom, Diaphanta.

BEAT. Is your witness dead then?

ALS. 'Tis to be feared
It was the wages of her knowledge; poor soul,
She lived not long after the discovery.

1. The tearing out of your heart.
2. Unsteady.

BEAT. Then hear a story of not much less horror
    Than this your false suspicion is beguiled with;
    To your bed's scandal I stand up innocence,
    Which even the guilt of one black other deed
    Will stand for proof of; your love has made me
    A cruel murderess.
ALS. Ha!
BEAT. A bloody one;
    I have kissed poison for it, stroked a serpent:
    The thing of hate, worthy in my esteem
    Of no better employment, and him most worthy
    To be so employed, I caused to murder
    That innocent Piracquo, having no
    Better means than that worst to assure
    Yourself to me.
ALS. O, the place itself e'er since
    Has crying been for vengeance! the temple,
    Where blood and beauty first unlawfully
    Fired their devotion and quenched the right one;[1]
    'Twas in my fears at first, 'twill have it now:
    O, thou art all deformed!
BEAT. Forget not, sir,
    It for your sake was done: shall greater dangers
    Make the less welcome?
ALS. O, thou should'st have gone
    A thousand leagues about to have avoided
    This dangerous bridge of blood! here we are lost.
BEAT. Remember, I am true unto your bed.
ALS. The bed itself's a charnel, the sheets shrouds
    For murdered carcasses. It must ask pause
    What I must do in this; meantime you shall
    Be my prisoner only: enter my closet;

                                Exit Beatrice into closet

    I'll be your keeper yet. O, in what part

---

1. i.e., Devotion to God.

Of this sad story shall I first begin? Ha!
This same fellow has put me in.[1]—

Enter De Flores

De Flores!

DE F. Noble Alsemero!

ALS. I can tell you
News, sir; my wife has her commended to you.

DE F. That's news indeed, my lord; I think she would
Commend me to the gallows if she could,
She ever loved me so well; I thank her.

ALS. What's this blood upon your band, De Flores?

DE F. Blood! no, sure 'twas washed since.

ALS. Since when, man?

DE F. Since t'other day I got a knock
In a sword-and-dagger school; I think 'tis out.

ALS. Yes, 'tis almost out, but 'tis perceived though.
I had forgot my message; this it is,
What price goes murder?

DE F. How, sir?

ALS. I ask you, sir;
My wife's behindhand with you, she tells me,
For a brave bloody blow you gave for her sake
Upon Piracquo.

DE F. Upon? 'twas quite through him sure:
Has she confessed it?

ALS. As sure as death to both of you;
And much more than that.

DE F. It could not be much more;
'Twas but one thing, and that—she is a whore.

ALS. It could not choose but follow: O cunning devils!
How should blind men know you from fair-faced saints?

BEAT. [*Within*] He lies! the villain does belie me!

DE F. Let me go to her, sir.

---

1. Shown me where to begin.

ALS. Nay, you shall to her.—

    Peace, crying crocodile, your sounds are heard;
    Take your prey to you;—get you in to her, sir:

                         Exit De Flores into closet

    I'll be your pander now; rehearse again
    Your scene of lust, that you may be perfect[1]
    When you shall come to act it to the black audience,
    Where howls and gnashings shall be music to you:
    Clip[2] your adulteress freely, 'tis the pilot
    Will guide you to the *mare mortuum*,[3]
    Where you shall sink to fathoms bottomless.

      Enter Vermandero, Tomaso, Alibius, Isabella, Franciscus,
                      and Antonio

VER. O Alsemero! I've a wonder for you.

ALS. No, sir, 'tis I, I have a wonder for you.

VER. I have suspicion near as proof itself
    For Piracquo's murder.

ALS.   Sir, I have proof
    Beyond suspicion for Piracquo's murder.

VER. Beseech you, hear me: these who have been disguised
    E'er since the deed was done.

ALS.   I have two other
    That were more close disguised than your two could be
    E'er since the deed were done.

VER. You'll hear me—these mine own servants—

ALS. Hear me—those nearer than your servants
    That shall acquit them, and prove them guiltless.

FRAN. That may be done with easy truth, sir.

TOM. How is my cause bandied through your delays!
    'Tis urgent in my blood and calls for haste;
    Give me a brother or alive or dead;
    Alive, a wife with him; if dead, for both
    A recompense, for murder and adultery.

---

1. i.e., In your parts.
2. Embrace.
3. Dead Sea.

BEAT. [*Within*] O, O, O!

ALS. Hark! 'tis coming to you.

DE F. [*Within*] Nay, I'll along for company.

BEAT. [*Within*] O, O!

VER. What horrid sounds are these?

ALS. Come forth, you twins
   Of mischief!

Re-enter De Flores, dragging in Beatrice wounded

DE F. Here we are; if you have any more
   To say to us, speak quickly, I shall not
   Give you the hearing else; I am so stout yet,
   And so, I think, that broken rib of mankind.

VER. An host of enemies entered my citadel
   Could not amaze like this: Joanna! Beatrice! Joanna!

BEAT. O, come not near me, sir, I shall defile you!
   I am that of your blood was taken from you
   For your better health; look no more upon't,
   But cast it to the ground regardlessly,
   Let the common sewer take it from distinction:
   Beneath the stars, upon yon meteor

                          [*Pointing to De Flores*]

   Ever hung my fate, 'mongst things corruptible;
   I ne'er could pluck it from him; my loathing
   Was prophet to the rest, but ne'er believed:
   Mine honor fell with him, and now my life.—
   Alsemero, I'm a stranger to your bed;
   Your bed was cozened on the nuptial night,
   For which your false bride died.

ALS. Diaphanta?

DE F. Yes, and the while I coupled with your mate
   At barley-break; now we are left in hell.[1]

VER. We are all there, it circumscribes us here.

DE F. I loved this woman in spite of her heart:
   Her love I earned out of Piracquo's murder.

---

1. Barley-break was a game in which one of three couples was left in "hell." "Hell" was
the name for the area occupied by the third and last couple.

TOM. Ha! my brother's murderer?

DE F. Yes, and her honor's prize
    Was my reward; I thank life for nothing
    But that pleasure; it was so sweet to me,
    That I have drunk up all, left none behind
    For any man to pledge me.

VER. Horrid villain!
    Keep life in him for further tortures.

DE F. No!
    I can prevent you; here's my pen-knife still;
    It is but one thread more [*stabbing himself*], and now 'tis cut.—
    Make haste, Joanna, by that token to thee,
    Canst not forget, so lately put in mind;
    I would not go to leave thee far behind.

Dies

BEAT. Forgive me, Alsemero, all forgive!
    'Tis time to die when 'tis a shame to live.

Dies

VER. O, my name's entered now in that record
    Where till this fatal hour 'twas never read.

ALS. Let it be blotted out; let your heart lose it,
    And it can never look you in the face,
    Nor tell a tale behind the back of life
    To your dishonor; justice hath so right
    The guilty hit, that innocence is quit
    By proclamation, and may joy again.—
    Sir, you are sensible of what truth hath done;
    'Tis the best comfort that your grief can find.

TOM. Sir, I am satisfied; my injuries
    Lie dead before me; I can exact no more,
    Unless my soul were loose, and could o'ertake
    Those black fugitives that are fled from hence,
    To take a second vengeance; but there are wraths
    Deeper than mine, 'tis to be feared, about 'em.

ALS. What an opacous body had that moon
    That last changed on us! here is beauty changed
    To ugly whoredom; here servant-obedience
    To a master-sin, imperious murder;

I, a supposed husband, changed embraces
With wantonness,—but that was paid before.—
Your change is come too, from an ignorant wrath
To knowing friendship.—Are there any more on's?

ANT. Yes, sir, I was changed too from a little ass as I was to a great fool
as I am; and had like to ha' been changed to the gallows, but that you
know my innocence[1] always excuses me.

FRAN. I was changed from a little wit to be stark mad,
Almost for the same purpose.

ISA. Your change is still behind,[2]
But deserve best your transformation:
You are a jealous coxcomb, keep schools of folly,
And teach your scholars how to break your own head.

ALIB. I see all apparent, wife, and will change now
Into a better husband, and ne'er keep
Scholars that shall be wiser than myself.

ALS. Sir, you have yet a son's duty living,
Please you, accept it; let that your sorrow,
As it goes from your eye, go from your heart,
Man and his sorrow at the grave must part.

EPILOGUE

ALS. All we can do to comfort one another,
To stay[3] a brother's sorrow for a brother,
To dry a child from the kind father's eyes,
Is to no purpose, it rather multiplies:
Your only smiles[4] have power to cause re-live
The dead again, or in their rooms to give
Brother a new brother, father a child;
If these appear, all griefs are reconciled.

Exeunt

1. Idiocy.
2. To come.
3. Halt.
4. Only your smiles (the audience).

ABOUT THE EDITOR

FRANK KERMODE is Britain's most distinguished scholar of sixteenth- and seventeenth-century literature. He has written and edited numerous works, including *Shakespeare's Language, Forms of Attention, Not Entitled, The Genesis of Secrecy, The Sense of an Ending,* and *The Age of Shakespeare.* He has taught at many universities, including University College, London, and Cambridge University, and has been a visiting professor at Columbia, Harvard, Yale, and several other American colleges. He lives in Cambridge, England.

A Note on the Type

The principal text of this Modern Library edition
was set in a digitized version of Janson, a typeface that
dates from about 1690 and was cut by Nicholas Kis,
a Hungarian working in Amsterdam. The original matrices have
survived and are held by the Stempel foundry in Germany.
Hermann Zapf redesigned some of the weights and sizes for
Stempel, basing his revisions on the original design.